Company Law

The International Library of Essays in Law and Legal Theory
Series Editor: Tom D. Campbell

Schools

Natural Law, Vols I & II *John Finnis*
Justice *Thomas Morawetz*
Law and Economics, Vols I & II *Jules Coleman and Jeffrey Lange*
Critical Legal Studies *James Boyle*
Marxian Legal Theory *Csaba Varga*
Legal Reasoning, Vols I & II *Aulis Aarnio and D. Neil MacCormick*
Legal Positivism *Mario Jori*
American Legal Theory *Robert Samuel Summers*
Postmodernism and Law *Dennis Patterson*
Law and History *David Sugarman*
Law and Language *Fred Schauer*
Sociological Theories of Law *Kahei Rokumoto*
Rights *Carlos Nino*
Law and Psychology *Martin Lyon Levine*
Feminist Legal Theory, Vols I & II *Frances Olsen*
Law and Society *Roger Cotterell*
Contemporary Criminological Theory *Francis T. Cullen and Velmer S. Burton Jr.*

Areas

Criminal Law *Thomas Morawetz*
Tort Law *Ernest J. Weinrib*
Contract Law, Vols I & II *Larry Alexander*
Anti-Discrimination Law *Christopher McCrudden*
Consumer Law *Iain Ramsay*
International Law *Martti Koskenniemi*
Property Law, Vols I & II *Elizabeth Mensch and Alan Freeman*
Constitutional Law *Mark V. Tushnet*
Procedure *D.J. Galligan*
Evidence and Proof *William Twining and Alex Stein*
Company Law *Sally Wheeler*
Privacy, Vols I & II *Raymond Wacks*
Lawyers' Ethics *David J. Luban*
Administrative Law *D.J. Galligan*
Child Law *Harry D. Krause*
Family Law, Vols I & II *Harry D. Krause*
Welfare Law *Peter Robson*
Medicine and the Law *Bernard M. Dickens*
Commercial Law *Ross Cranston*
Environmental Law *Michael C. Blumm*
Conflict of Laws *Richard Fentiman*
Law and Religion *Wojciech Sadurski*
Human Rights Law *Philip Alston*
European Community Law, Vols I & II *Francis Snyder*
Tax Law, Vols I & II *Patricia D. White*
Media Law *Eric Barendt*
Labour Law *David L. Gregory*
Alternative Dispute Resolution *Michael D.A. Freeman*

Legal Cultures

Comparative Legal Cultures *Csaba Varga*
Law and Anthropology *Peter Sack*
Hindu Law and Legal Theory *Ved Nanda*
Islamic Law and Legal Theory *Ian Edge*
Chinese Law and Legal Theory *Michael Palmer*
Socialist Law *W. Butler*
Common Law *Michael Arnheim*
Japanese Law and Legal Theory *Koichiro Fujikura*
Law and Development *Anthony Carty*
Jewish Law and Legal Theory *Martin P. Golding*
Legal Education *Martin Lyon Levine*
Civil Law *Ralf Rogowski*

Future Volumes

African Law and Legal Theory and Cumulative index.

Company Law

Edited by

Sally Wheeler

University of Nottingham

NEW YORK UNIVERSITY PRESS
REFERENCE COLLECTION

First published in the U.S.A. in 1993 by
NEW YORK UNIVERSITY PRESS
Washington Square
New York NY 10003

Library of Congress Cataloging-in-Publication Data
Company law / edited by Sally Wheeler.
p. cm. – (International library of essays in law and legal theory. Areas ; 23)
Includes bibliographical references.
ISBN 0-8147-9274-X
1. Corporation law. I. Wheeler, Sally. II. Series.
K1315.6.C66 1993
346'.066—dc20
[342.666] 93-27761
CIP

Contents

PART IV THE END OF CORPORATE LIFE

Acknowledgements

The editor and publishers wish to thank the following for permission to use copyright material.

American Association for the Comparative Study of Law for the essay: Gunther Teubner (1988), 'Enterprise Corporatism: New Industrial Policy and the "Essence" of the Legal Person', *The American Journal of Comparative Law*, **36**, pp. 130–55.

Columbia University in the City of New York for the essays: Melvin Aron Eisenberg (1989), 'The Structure of Corporation Law', *Columbia Law Review*, **89**, pp. 1461–525; Mark J. Roe (1991), 'A Political Theory of American Corporate Finance', *Columbia Law Review*, **91**, pp. 10–67.

Harvard Law Review Association for the essay: Lucian Arye Bebchuk (1992), 'Federalism and the Corporation: The Desirable Limits on State Competition in Corporate Law', *Harvard Law Review*, **105**, pp. 1437–510.

The Michigan Law Review Association for the essay: Klaus J. Hopt (1984), 'New Ways in Corporate Governance: European Experiments with Labor Representation on Corporate Boards', *Michigan Law Review*, **82**, pp. 1338–363.

University of Chicago Law Review for the essays: Frank H. Easterbrook and Daniel R. Fischel (1985), 'Limited Liability and the Corporation', *The University of Chicago Law Review*, **52**, pp. 89–117; Elizabeth Warren (1987), 'Bankruptcy Policy', *The University of Chicago Law Review*, **54**, pp. 775–814.

University of Chicago Press for the essays: Eugene F. Fama and Michael C. Jensen (1983), 'Separation of Ownership and Control', *The Journal of Law and Economics*, **XXVI**, pp. 301–25; Neil Fligstein and Peter Brantley (1992), 'Bank Control, Owner Control, or Organizational Dynamics: Who Controls the Large Modern Corporation?', *American Journal of Sociology*, **98**, pp. 280–307.

The Yale Law Journal and Fred B. Rothman & Co. for the essay: Thomas H. Jackson (1982), 'Bankruptcy, Non-Bankruptcy Entitlements, and the Creditors' Bargain', *The Yale Law Journal*, **91**, pp. 857–907. Reprinted by permission of The Yale Law Journal Company and Fred B. Rothman & Company from The Yale Law Journal, Vol. **91**, pp. 857–907.

Every effort has been made to trace all the copyright holders, but if any have been inadvertently overlooked the publishers will be pleased to make the necessary arrangement at the first opportunity.

Series Preface

The International Library of Law and Legal Theory is designed to provide important research materials in an accessible form. Each volume contains essays of central theoretical importance in its subject area. The series as a whole makes available an extensive range of valuable material which will be of considerable interest to those involved in the research, teaching and study of law.

The series has been divided into three sections. The Schools section is intended to represent the main distinctive approaches and topics of special concern to groups of scholars. The Areas section takes in the main branches of law with an emphasis on essays which present analytical and theoretical insights of broad application. The section on Legal Cultures makes available the distinctive legal theories of different legal traditions and takes up topics of general comparative and developmental concern.

I have been delighted and impressed by the way in which the editors of the individual volumes have set about the difficult task of selecting, ordering and presenting essays from the immense quantity of academic legal writing published in journals throughout the world. Editors were asked to pick out those essays from law, philosophy and social science journals which they consider to be fundamental for the understanding of law, as seen from the perspective of a particular approach or sphere of legal interest. This is not an easy task and many difficult decisions have had to be made in order to ensure that a representative sample of the best journal essays available takes account of the scope of each topic or school.

I should like to express my thanks to all the volume editors for their willing participation and scholarly judgement. The interest and enthusiasm which the project has generated is well illustrated by the fact that an original projection of 12 volumes drawn up in 1989 has now become a list of some 60 volumes. I must also acknowledge the vision, persistence and constant cheerfulness of John Irwin and the marvellous work done by Mrs Margaret O'Reilly and Sonia Hubbard.

TOM D. CAMPBELL
Series Editor
The Faculty of Law
The Australian National University

Introduction

The wealth of literature available on corporate law necessarily makes any selection such as this open to criticism on the grounds of what it has omitted. In order to deal in some small way with that criticism, I feel it is appropriate to explain the criteria employed for selection. First of all, only complete essays and not book extracts can be included in these volumes. Second, I tried to select essays which I felt situated their argument in the context of debate in that particular field. Third, my preference has been for recent essays which, while including and referencing previous theories, seek to advance and build on them; this seemed to be the most efficient way of covering a large amount of material in a confined space. There was also the consideration that older pieces will have already been selected for materials collections and so are familiar and readily accessible.

Part I The Birth of the Company

The collection begins with an essay by Teubner. It is his contention that the essence of the legal person as a field of inquiry has been largely abandoned in current debates on the theoretical basis of legal personality. His suggestion for reopening the debate is to look at the overall social function and performance of the legal person in the context of an expansion of organizational autonomy. Teubner's discussion of the legal person is situated in autopoetic theory – a theory which analyses concepts as issues of self-referentiality. For Teubner, an analysis of the legal person in this way centres on 'collectivity' defined as the 'socially binding self-description of an organised action system as a cyclical linkage of identity and action' (p. 6). The result of this analysis is a model of enterprise corporatism based on systems theory, which sees a differential between those involved internally and externally with the corporate actor, leading into an autonomous economic actor.

This application of autopoetic theory to the question of the legal person is indicative of the interest shown in the concept of separate personality and the corporation by disciplines other than law and those closely related to it. For an interesting analysis from a linguistics standpoint see Schane, 'The Corporation is a Person: The Language of Legal Fiction'. A comprehensive overview of the various theories is provided by Hagar, 'Bodies Politic: The Progressive History of Organizational "Real Entity" Theory', and Horowitz, 'Santa Clara Revisited'. Recent contributions from the UK to this debate have centred on the issue of the capacity of the corporation to commit manslaughter; on this, see Moran, 'Corporate Criminal Capacity: Nostalgia for Representation'.

Side by side with legal personality is the issue of limited liability for members of the corporation which is the subject of Chapter 2 by Easterbrook and Fischel. They seek to build on the work of Manne, 'Our Two Corporation Systems: Law and Economics', who concluded that limited liability was essential if corporations were to continue to have a large number of small shareholders. If limited liability were not a feature of corporate law and the whole of an investor's personal wealth was at risk, then there would be a disincentive to hold anything other than large stakes in a few corporations. Easterbrook and Fischel's concern is to use economic analysis to explain why creditors are prepared to accept the transfer of some of the risk to themselves, which is a consequence of limited liability. They compare the cost of capital to a firm with limited liability and to a firm without. They conclude that it cannot be shown that the cost is any higher in instances of limited liability.

The authors focus on the costs of monitoring, which they believe will be as high for investors who lose their stake first as for secured creditors who will rank as superior creditors and in any event need to monitor only the value of their security and not that of the whole firm. The acquisition of information is of central importance to their analysis of cost. Institutional investors are likely to have detailed knowledge about some industries through extensive investment or involvement as investors through debt. This last case may give an institutional investor certain rights of control and veto over the management of the firm. Finally an investor through debt rather than equity is not obliged to share the fruit of his information with anyone else other than perhaps those creditors who rank in priority to himself; an investor through equity, in contrast, will have to share his information with all other equity investors.

Employees, insurers, trade creditors and lenders are classed as voluntary creditors by Easterbrook and Fischel. Their protection against the firm undertaking activities which may jeopardize their position is in their ability to charge higher prices or higher interest rates. If these prices exceed the benefits to the firm of undertaking the activity, then the firm will cease to undertake that activity. The availability of insurance does not, according to Easterbrook and Fischel, encourage a firm to undertake risky activities. The argument is that by insuring and so in effect passing the risk to a third party, those within the firm can remove even the small incentive provided by limited liability to take care. This is rejected on the grounds that risk results in a higher premium cost for the firm, so encouraging it to undertake a cost-benefit analysis of its activities. However if potential losses are high, insurance may not be available and, even where it is, a firm may prefer to pay managers more and decrease its capital base.

Easterbrook and Fischel examine judicial pronouncements on the piercing of the corporate veil and conclude that what the courts are trying to achieve is a cost-benefit exposition of limited liability; the courts will allow the corporate veil to be pierced so that creditors can reach the personal assets of shareholders where limited liability has provided little advantage for investors and also a high probablity that the firm is engaging in risky activities. To support this contention, they point out that piercing the veil usually takes place in closely-held corporations where there is less separation between ownership and control; those who invest in the corporation make its decisions; there is little monitoring by the capital market and the transfer of shares is entrusted to those with the same philosophy as existing investors. The instances where the court has allowed piercing of the veil are identified as situations involving creditors seeking to make parent companies liable for the debts of their subsidiaries, cases involving fraud, and cases where the firm is severely undercapitalized. Easterbrook and Fischel conclude by offering four alternatives to piercing the veil which they feel would have some part to play in preventing limited liability being used as a vehicle for the carrying on of risky business ventures: minimum capital requirements, mandatory insurances, managerial liability and the regulation of inputs.

In the UK the policing of limited liability to prevent possible abuses has gone down the road of imposing personal managerial liability with two pieces of recent statutory intervention. Wrongful trading is a concept created by the 1986 insolvency legislation; it imposes personal liability on the directors of a company for debts incurred after a date at which a reasonable director would have concluded that there was no future for the company other than insolvent liquidation. Under other legislation also enacted in 1986, a director can be disqualified from holding office as such for a period assessed by the court of not less than two but not more than 15 years. The trigger for this is corporate insolvency and a finding that the conduct of the director has been unfit in relation to that company. Unfitness is judged by criteria such as compliance with corporate accounting requirements, deposits taken from the public for goods, and non-payment of statutory liabilities to the proper authorities, such as tax deductions from employees.

Part II Conceptions of the Company

The essays in Part II look at the debates surrounding the structure of the corporation and the consequences of the separation between ownership and control identified by Berle and Means in *The Modern Corporation and Private Property*. An overview of the various (mainly economic) theories is found in several of the essays in this section, but see also Hart, 'An Economist's Perspective on the Theory of the Firm'. Also very relevant in this context is the work of Oliver Williamson (see, for example, *The Economic Institutions of Capitalism*).

Williamson expounds the transaction cost theory of the firm by building on the work of Coase, 'The Nature of the Firm'. Coase identified the firm as a mechanism for minimizing the transaction costs of planning an exchange, through maximizing within one organization, knowledge of the market and through placing authority in one party to conduct transactions. The rationale for the firm's existence ceases if the inefficiency of this authority is such that it incurs costs exceeding the cost saving of transacting within the firm. A good exposition of Coase's work is provided by Cheung, 'The Contractual Nature of the Firm'.

Williamson's contribution has been to identify more specifically the transaction costs that Coase relied upon. His theory rests on three planks: bounded rationality, opportunism and asset specificity. Bounded rationality refers to the situation where actors behave rationally but on the basis of imperfect information. In the context of the firm, this means that parties to a transaction are locked together and unable to access the excuses of the other for only partial or even non-performance. There will be costs associated with locating another supplier or customer. The lack of perfect information also leads to opportunism as there may be no way of identifying in advance situations where this could occur. Asset specificity is used by Williamson in the sense of worker versus employer within the organization: the employee acquires, while working for the firm, specific skills which cannot easily be found elsewhere in the labour market; this gives the employee considerable bargaining power.

The solution to these problems, according to transaction cost theorists, is for firms to engage in vertical integration and acquire distribution outlets or, in reverse, to acquire a source of supply; this results in control and reduces costs. A useful critique of Williamson and transaction cost theories of the firm is provided by Perrow, 'Economic Theories of Organisation'.

An exposition of another leading theory of the firm is provided by Easterbrook and Fischel in 'The Corporate Contract'. This has been omitted for editorial reasons, but a brief summary is in order. Easterbrook and Fischel explain the firm as a series of contracts. A contract is defined as any voluntary arrangement entered into in connection with the running of the firm. They point out that no particular governance structure can be dictated as different firms have different needs and actors within the firm need to be able to set up the arrangements that best suit them. Elsewhere, in 'The Corporate Governance Movement', they have described corporate law as providing 'a set of standard-form terms [which] firms are generally free to alter ... in their charter or by-laws'. This need for flexibility exists alongside the fact that certain terms of certain contracts within the firm are dictated by judicial decisions and legislative rules.

Chapter 4 by Eisenberg in Part II picks up on this coexistence of contracts by voluntary arrangement and mandatory rules and uses it to dismiss the nexus of contracts theory of the firm as inaccurate and a misdescription. For Eisenberg the structure of the corporate law is a set of rules divided into three categories: enabling, suppletory and mandatory. Enabling rules give legal effect to positions that those in the firm adopt; suppletory rules assist a particular position unless actors in the corporation operate in a different way, and mandatory rules dictate the manner in which actors in the company must behave. The nature of particular rules depends on the organizational context in which they occur. The organizational contexts identified by Eisenberg are closely-held corporations and publicly-held corporations. Within a specific organizational context, the rules governing corporate law are separated according to their function: structural rules which deal with such areas as the allocation of decision-making powers, distributional rules which govern the sharing of corporate assets, and fiduciary rules which focus on the duties of shareholders and managers.

According to Eisenberg, in closely-held corporations, structural and distributional rules will be largely enabling and suppletory to reflect the closeness between managers and investors. There will be a mandatory provision only to ensure that privately agreed bargains concerning the constitution and asset distribution structure of the company do not impinge on the fair expectations of parties involved. Fiduciary rules, on the other hand, are with, only a few exceptions, mandatory because, according to Eisenberg, few shareholders will realize the significance of bargaining out of the protection that is necessary and that fiduciary rules offer.

In publicly-held corporations the situation is rather different. The divergence of ownership and management points to an internally generated bureaucratic structure for the constitution and management of the company. This divergence of interests results in a certain amount of 'positional conflict', defined by Eisenberg as self-interest by corporate managers seeking to increase their power, prestige and salary within the corporation at the expense of shareholders. Thus (for Eisenberg) fiduciary, structural and distributional rules which control this positional conflict should be mandatory and will also be supported by moral principles created by social pressure, whereas rules which corporate managers use to control those beneath them in the company should be enabling or suppletory. Those who wish to know more about Eisenberg's debate with the contractarians should read McChesney's critical comment, 'Economics, Law and Science in the Corporate Field: A Critique of Eisenberg'.

The contribution from Fama and Jensen in Chapter 3 is in the tradition of a principal and agent theory. This seeks to explain the separation of ownership and control in terms of principal and agent relationship and focuses on how the principal controls the agent, in this instance the employee. The problem of control is how to prevent the agent from acting in his own self-interest. Fama and Jensen analyse the decision-making process within firms as being divided into four separate parts: initiation, ratification, implementation and monitoring. They then place the elements of initiation and implementation together (called decision management) because they assert that these functions are usually devolved to the same agents. The heads of ratification and monitoring are then termed decision control. It is the authors' contention that organizations with a separation of ownership and control can only deal with the resulting agency problems if they also undertake the above divisions of responsibility. They then posit this theory against different forms of business organizations such as open corporations, non-profit organizations, etc. Like much of this type of work, it lacks any direct empirical input, hence the criticisms of Perrow (supra) and others.

Chapter 5 by Fligstein and Brantley seeks to provide an empirical input to this debate by examining the 100 largest corporations in the US in 1969 and the corporations which entered that list between 1969 and 1979. They looked at whether different forms of control of the corporations affected their performance. The forms of control they were concerned with were owner control, managerial control and bank control. The hypothesis against which they tested their data (and which they ultimately found to be proved) was one drawn from previous work by Fligstein, *The Transformation of Corporate Control*. They asserted that what affects both decision-making in corporations and the performance of corporations is not the presence of different groups with different interests – for example the positional conflict suggested by Eisenberg between managers and investors or the desire of managers to reinvest profits in the firm rather than distribute them to shareholders – but the organizational context in which the firm exists. They call their standpoint political/cultural and identify three factors which are central to it: the behaviour of other competitor firms, existing strategies within the firm, and the identity of the group within the firm which is in control. This third factor, however, appears to feed back into the models of different interest groups that Fligstein and Brantley reject.

In the next essay Roe explores yet another facet of the debate triggered by Berle and Means in an attempt to explain why fragmented ownership, and not control by institutional investors, has survived as the means for holding property in public corporations. His answer is on two levels. First he argues that the legal rules governing financial institutions acquiring shares and dealing in them are such that they are prevented from acquiring a controlling holding. Roe seeks to show this by analysing the rules which affect different forms of institutional finance. He then moves to a second level by situating these rules in a context of concerted political agenda-making and ideology supported by various groups within American society which have pushed for the preservation of the archetypal Berle and Means style of corporation.

This political context is explained by references to three principal strands: (1) ideology created by a populist distrust of large institutions, the impact of scandals involving financial institutions, and the stances of some political leaders; (2) interest groups, mainly small financial institutions and small businesses, which wished to remain small and independent: on a local level, wealth and influence were concentrated in their hands and gave them the ear of Congress; and (3) the political structure of the US, with its federal character, further allowed those whose interests were served by curbing the power of the financial institutions to entrench their own positions. The banking system, for example, was fragmented by federalism, and those who wished it to remain that way were able to use their influence at state level.

Roe also considers the benefits and costs of fragmentation in terms of the efficiency of management, the monitoring of management and the advancement of the shareholders' position. His conclusion is that benefits can be seen in the way that fragmentation is maintained, but equally that these benefits could be achieved by other methods. For example, the supposed benefit of preventing cartellization of markets through fragmentation of ownership could be achieved by a more modern mechanism, such as the creation of a single market. This type of approach, which looks behind the Berle and Means conception of the corporation at the broader political factors which helped to create and sustain it, adds a powerful background dimension to the economic and organizational perspective presented by the other essays.

Part III Corporate Law and the Role of the State

The two essays in Part III focus on the role that legislative structures and intervention can play in corporate governance in situations where there is a plurality of jurisdictions. When this is the case, there would appear to be a number of choices: competition between jurisdictions can be allowed so that each has free rein to attract as many first-time corporations and reincorporations as possible; a programme of harmonization can be conducted between the laws of the competing jurisdictions, or a unitary law can be created for whole or part of the corporate law field. In the US the positions taken in the debate on the desirability of jurisdictions competing for corporate charters are described as 'the race to the bottom' and 'the race to the top'. Those who take the view that competition for incorporation involves a race to the bottom believe that the result of competition is the production of a set of corporate rules that benefit the interests of managers over the interests of shareholders, since in practice the decision on where to incorporate will be taken by managers who will choose the jurisdiction that is most favourable to them. See, for example, the views of Cary, 'Federalism and Corporate Law: Reflections upon Delaware'.

The supporters of the race to the top theory agree with their opponents that the most attractive form of corporate charter is one which maximizes the interests of shareholders, but that the form of charter offered has to be attractive to managers who will make the decision on place of incorporation. However, this is where the similarity ends. The race to the top theorists assert that the market prevents managers from choosing to incorporate in jurisdictions where they will be the recipients of benefits at the expense of shareholders, as in those circumstances there will be few investors willing to invest, the corporation will be vulnerable to takeover bids and the result will be lower returns to managers in the form of bonuses and wages. Consequently, jurisdictions where incorporation is popular must be those which offer the best maximization of value to shareholders and are therefore efficient.

Some of the most interesting work that has been done on competing jurisdictions is that of Romano (see 'Law as a Product: Some Pieces of the Incorporation Puzzle'). She seeks to explain why it is that for 50 years Delaware has remained the most popular state for incorporation and reincorporation in a supposedly competitive market. On the basis of an empirical investigation questioning firms which had reincorporated in Delaware and firms that had located elsewhere, she concluded that Delaware had certain self-perpetuating characteristics that helped it to maintain its position. First, the large number of previous incorporations meant that many corporate law issues had been litigated in Delaware, giving it a very comprehensive corporate law attractive to corporations. Second, its history of incorporations ensured a small and highly competent judiciary and legal profession; this led to predictable decisions on litigated issues and to experienced counsel to advise corporations. As Romano points out, it is virtually impossible for any other state to replicate the position of Delaware.

Chapter 7 is that of Lucian Bebchuk. His starting point is that competition between jurisdictions is more desirable than harmonization because competition itself is socially desirable where it appears to reward those who produce the best product and because law-makers at state level are more likely to be attune to the needs of incorporators.

What prevents Bebchuk from unreservedly joining the race to the top theorists is his contention that in some areas a divergence of interests between managers and shareholders leads competing jurisdictions to produce undesirable corporate laws in that they do not prevent management opportunism. He also points out that, in situations where the key interests are those of parties external to the corporations, competition between jurisdictions may lead to rules which favour the interests of shareholders and managers over what is socially the most desirable rule. The specific occasions on which Bebchuk feels corporate managers may opt for value-decreasing rather than value-maximizing rules (when encouraged to do so by the results of competition) are set out in the second part of his essay. Broadly they concern the fiduciary duties of directors, the parts of takeover regulation that are not already controlled at federal level, and the allocation of opportunities between parent and subsidiary.

On the issue of external interests, Bebchuk identifies the problem for law at state level as being one of these interests extinguished by competition: if regulation were at federal level, then the rules produced could take these interests into account free from the concern that competition would penalize their inclusion by allowing resort to another jurisdiction. The external interests identified by Bebchuk are the benefits to bidders in takeover scenarios, which at state level are ignored or subordinated to the interests of shareholders; the protection of creditors, particularly trade creditors and tort victims who are often not in a position to protect themselves contractually in their dealings with the company; also the disclosure of corporate information where Bebchuk himself recognizes that there is already substantial federal involvement. His point here is similar to that which he makes in relation to his final externality – corporate social responsibility in circumstances where that is considered desirable. He argues that it is impossible for the optimal level of protection to be achieved while other jurisdictions are able to intervene and bargain down the requirements through competition.

Bebchuk's answer to this problem in relation to both managerial opportunism and third-party interests is for federal law to take over this part of corporate law-making. He concludes that federal law would be better in these contexts, as federal law-makers are no more susceptible to lobbying than state law-makers (it is interesting to compare this point with Roe's about the impact of lobbying on the federal system in connection with institutional investors). Also, any lack of feedback on laws from incorporators will be balanced by the fact that socially desirable rules would be adopted with the correct sentiments in mind, which may not be the case at state level.

As Bebchuk points out, the European Community is currently experiencing similar problems in its desire to create a single market. The EC is concerned to prevent national law boundaries from forming an obstacle to economic growth, but at the same time it wishes to retain control over multinational enterprises. It has tried to solve the problem by means of two solutions: first by creating supranational vehicles for incorporation and cooperation, and second by embarking on a programme of harmonization to make national laws sufficiently similar to enable easier and less costly cross-border cooperation. The subject of Chapter 8 by Klaus Hopt – worker participation – now fits into the second category but began life as part of the first. It was included as a mandatory element of the draft Statute of a European Company or Societas Europaea (OJ 1970 C124/35). This proposal foundered almost immediately, criticized on the grounds that it was too rigid, demanding, for example, two-tier boards and compulsory worker participation on the supervisory board. Subsequent drafts in 1989 and 1991 hived off the worker participation provisions into a separate directive which would allow member-states greater flexibility; worker participation could be brought about by other mechanisms such as collective bargaining.

From 1989, corporations within member-states have been able to set up European Economic Interest Groupings (EEIG) designed to allow transnational cooperation. EEIGs enjoy limited liability and legal personality, but have to be non-profit-making and are not considered incorporated bodies. The legal basis is a contract between the members which must come from at least two member-states. The group has to be registered in the state of its establishment. Its non-profit-making status was designed to overcome the problems of taxation since this is levied on a state basis. However, this has sparked a debate about how profits resulting from the group will be taxed in the hands of its members. To overcome the requirements of worker participation that exist in some states but not in others, EEIGs are allowed to have only 500 workers. The limitations placed on EEIGs illustrate the difficulties of trying to create a supranational system over and above the highly developed systems of the states themselves. The difficulties inherent in the political process itself are explained more fully in Buxbaum and Hopt, *Legal Harmonization and the Business Enterprise*.

The harmonization process tends to be characterized by technical directives which, unlike Regulations, require implementation at national level. Directives have been successfully adopted in relation to corporate formation requirements, disclosure requirements and accounting standards. For a detailed list of enacted and proposed directives see Dine, 'Harmonization of Company Law'.

Further difficulties are experienced in the EC when the harmonization process attempts to harmonize laws on a functional level. An example of this, the draft Fifth Directive (OJ 1972 C131/49), which proposed a corporate structure of two-tier boards and worker participation, is the subject of Hopt's essay. The Directive was modelled on existing German legislation but, as Hopt points out, displayed all the signs of political compromise. The Directive only applied to stock corporations where transnational activities were paramount, leaving untouched other corporate forms. It permitted firms to continue with a unitary board but with some elements of separation between management and supervision, so enabling compliance with a minimum amount of real change. Two further drafts of this directive which have appeared since the Hopt essay have maintained this position. Firms are now offered four different mechanisms of worker participation and will be able to retain a unitary board structure. While making a neat compromise, this does not really fulfil the harmonization objective of giving workers a meaningful input into corporate governance.

One of the problems with this type of functional harmonization is that there are no detailed empirical studies on how the proposed changes will affect the running of the corporation. In the third section of his essay, Hopt tries to identify what these changes might be by looking at the German model. As far as the intra-enterprise situation is concerned, Hopt cannot predict whether the enterprise will be more efficient, but it does seem that the character of corporate decision-making will change: worker representatives will insist that the social impact of management decisions in areas such as employment prospects and working conditions be taken into account. Hopt adjudges the effect on the market and the economy in general to be a bilateral one: worker representatives will insist on more worker benefits and less revenue distributed to shareholders; also, the decision-making process may be slower. This may have a detrimental effect on share values but, for all that, decision-making should be better informed leading, arguably, to greater efficiency in production. As far as the effects on society are concerned, assessment is made more difficult by the fact that divergent political and economic cultures will evaluate this differently. However worker participation does lead to the corporation being run on a consensus basis with free dialogue between different groups, which is seen by some as the most effective way for society to conduct its affairs (see the work of Luhmann, for example *A Sociological Theory of Law*).

A further reason why worker participation has not been welcomed by some member-states is that it is seen as part of EC social policy rather than as an aspect of corporate law harmonization. For example, in 1974 the EC launched its first major social policy initiative, the Social Action Programme (Supp Bull EC 2/74). One of the limbs of this programme was increased democratization and participation within the workplace from the two sides of industry. A similar development can be seen in the Works Council directive of 1991 which comes out of the most recent EC social policy initiative – the Community Charter of Fundamental Social Rights for Workers. Some member-states, in particular the UK, are implacably opposed to any form of social policy development by the EC. It is regarded as an issue of national sovereignty that social policy should be a matter of national competence regardless of whether or not EC harmonization might have beneficial effects for the economy. As long as there is a two-fold thrust in EC policy-making towards the corporation – between wanting to encourage European firms to evolve and compete with the American and Japanese markets and at the same time wanting to maintain 'social regulation' over the activities of these firms – harmonization rules will be affected by the results of political compromise to overcome national sensitivities.

Part IV The End of Corporate Life

Part IV of this collection deals with corporate bankruptcy and offers two contrasting perspectives on the purpose of bankruptcy law and policy. In Chapter 9, Jackson puts forward the theory that bankruptcy rules should mirror the system of rights that creditors themselves would settle upon if they negotiated *inter se* about the corporate assets that were available to satisfy the various debts owed to them prior to the bankruptcy of the corporation. According to Jackson, the system that best reflects the content of this agreement is a collective procedure, as it (1) reduces the strategic costs involved in executing individual recovery, (2) increases the pool of assets available for creditors by preventing piecemeal break-up and disposal and, (3) as a variation upon the reduction of strategic costs, increases administrative efficiency by requiring, for example, only one inquiry into the affairs of the bankrupt corporation.

As Jackson recognizes, there is nothing to prevent moves by creditors for the early realization of debts; thus the bankruptcy rules themselves have to present a model which is sufficiently attractive to all classes of creditors to prevent this. He examines the position of secured creditors in a collective regime and concludes that there is no reason why they should object to such a mandatory regime if they were left as well off as under individual pursuit. However the application of the rule of indubitable equivalence in the bankruptcy process is not carried out with reference to market values; this is attacked by Jackson as being a leading example of why a secured creditor might seek to realize that security rather than participate in a collective regime.

Warren's position in Chapter 10 is that the rationale for bankruptcy law and also the yardstick by which policy is formulated cannot be condensed into a single construct; namely, that the sole concern of bankruptcy rules is to enhance the creditors' collective position. Warren's view is that bankruptcy law has much wider concerns in its efforts to conserve and divide corporate assets which, by definition, are not sufficient to meet all the liabilities claimed. She draws an analogy between the debtor-against-creditor situation that is likely to occur in state law and the Federal Bankruptcy Code's concern with creditor-versus-creditor battles and establishing a priority system. She points to the preservation of the rights of future claimants, for example tort victims, as evidence of the Federal Code's wider distributive concern.

For Warren, bankruptcy law and policy are and should remain a combination of empirical and normative conclusions. The distributional issues of bankruptcy cannot be hived off into a sealed category that ignores such questions as which groups will be hurt by the corporate bankruptcy and in what way, whether injuries can be avoided and at what cost, and whether the cost of helping those hurt will exceed the benefits to those helped by corporate failure. It is Warren's contention that, while the current bankruptcy system may not be flawless, its function can only be ascertained by seeking both empirical and normative answers to questions such as those identified above.

The reader interested in pursuing the topics covered in this collection in greater depth has a great deal of material from which to choose. In addition to the references already mentioned, the following may be of some assistance: Easterbrook and Fischel, *The Economic Structure of Corporate Law*; Jackson, *The Logic and Limits of Bankruptcy Law*; Jensen and Meckling, 'Theory of the Firm: Managerial Behaviour, Agency Costs, and Ownership Structure'; Fama, 'Agency Problems and the Theory of the Firm', and Hopt and Teubner, *Corporate Governance and Directors' Liabilities.*

Bibliography

Books

Berle, A. and Means, G. (1932), *The Modern Corporation and Private Property*, New York: Commerce Clearing House.

Buxbaum, R. and Hopt, K. (1988), *Legal Harmonization and the Business Enterprise*, Berlin: Walter de Gruyter.

Easterbrook, F. and Fischel, D. (1991), *The Economic Structure of Corporate Law*, Cambridge, Mass: Harvard University Press.

Fligstein, N. (1990), *The Transformation of Corporate Control*, Cambridge, Mass: Harvard University Press.

Hopt, K. and Teubner, G. (eds) (1985), *Corporate Governance and Directors' Liabilities*, Berlin: Walter de Gruyter.

Jackson, T. (1989), *The Logic and Limits of Bankruptcy Law*, Cambridge, Mass: Harvard University Press.

Luhmann, N. (1985), *A Sociological Theory of Law*, London: Routledge Kegan Paul.
Williamson, O. (1985), *The Economic Institutions of Capitalism*, New York: The Free Press.

Articles

Cary, W. (1974), 'Federalism and Corporate Law: Reflections upon Delaware', *Yale Law Journal*, **83**, 663.
Cheung, S. (1983), 'The Contractual Nature of the Firm', *Journal of Law and Economics*, **26**, 1.
Coase, R. (1937), 'The Nature of the Firm', *Economica NS*, 386.
Dine, J. (1989), 'Harmonization of Company Law', *Yearbook of European Law*, **9**, 93.
Easterbrook, F. and Fischel, D. (1982), 'The Corporate Governance Movement', *Vanderbilt Law Review*, **35**, 1255.
Easterbrook, F. and Fischel, D. (1989), 'The Corporate Contract', *Columbia Law Review*, **89**, 1416.
Fama, E. (1980), 'Agency Problems and the Theory of the Firm', *Journal of Political Economy*, **88**, 288.
Hagar, M. (1989), 'Bodies Politic: The Progressive History of Organizational "Real Entity" Theory', *University of Pittsburgh Law Review*, **50**, 575.
Hart, O. (1989), 'An Economist's Perspective on the Theory of the Firm', *Columbia Law Review*, **89**, 1757.
Horowitz, M. (1985), 'Santa Clara Revisited', *West Virginia Law Review*, **88**, 173.
Jensen, M. and Meckling, W. (1976), 'Theory of the Firm: Managerial Behaviour, Agency Costs, and Ownership Structure', *Journal of Financial Economics*, **3**, 305.
Manne, H. (1976), 'Our Two Corporation Systems: Law and Economics', *Virginia Law Review*, **53**, 259.
McChesney, F. (1989), 'Economics, Law and Science in the Corporate Field: A Critique of Eisenberg', *Columbia Law Review*, **89**, 1530.
Moran, L. (1992), 'Corporate Criminal Capacity: Nostalgia for Representation', *Social and Legal Studies*, **1**, 371.
Perrow, C. (1986), 'Economic Theories of Organisation', *Theory and Society*, **15**, 11.
Romano, R. (1985), 'Law as a Product: Some Pieces of the Incorporation Puzzle', *Journal of Law, Economics and Organisation*, **1**, 225.
Schane, S. (1987), 'The Corporation is a Person: The Language of Legal Fiction', *Tulane Law Review*, **61**, 563.

Part I
The Birth of the Company

[1]

GUNTHER TEUBNER

Enterprise Corporatism: New Industrial Policy and the "Essence" of the Legal Person

I. PERSONA MYSTICA REVISITED

The legal person has become an inert person indeed. While in the 19th century it was a fiery fighter for political and economic freedoms against government regulation, today it is no longer trusted with any role in major economic policy controversies. What can the legal person, of all persons, possibly contribute to current issues such as the "new industrial divide," the European choice between "Americanization" and "Japanization" of industrial organization, the strategies of new flexibility, and the "management of uncertainty"?[1] The search for the "essence" of the legal person, which has fascinated whole generations of lawyers, has now been tacitly abandoned due to an everyday familiarity with this legal entity. Today the legal person is having to pay the price of success: nobody is interested in its essence any longer, and, despite warnings to the contrary, it is no longer taken seriously, not even when the issue involved is the famous "piercing of the corporate veil" that so inflames the legal imagination.[2]

To be sure, there have been some recent attempts to rediscover the political dimensions of the legal person.[3] In an impressive rein-

---

GUNTHER TEUBNER is Professor of Law, University of Bremen and European University Institute, Florence.

1. Piore & Sabel, *The New Industrial Divide* (1984); Kern & Schumann, *Das Ende der Arbeitsteilung? Rationalisierung in der Industriellen Produktion* (1984); Streeck, "The Management of Uncertainty and the Uncertainty of Management" (manuscript 1985).

2. Wilhelm calls for the legal person to be taken seriously: *Rechtsform and Haftung bei der juristischen Person* (1981).

3. Joerges, "Juristische Person," in Goerlitz, *Handlexikon zur Rechtswissenschaft*, 222 ff. (1972); Ott, *Recht und Realität der Unternehmenskorporation* 43 ff., 85ff. (1977); Dan-Cohen, *Rights, Persons and Organizations* 26ff., 163ff. (1986). From a political science viewpoint, Mayntz, "Corporate Actors in Public Policy: Changing Perspectives in Political Analysis" (manuscript 1986). From an economic viewpoint, see Hutter, *Die Produktion von Recht*, ch. 4D (1986). From a sociological view, see Simmanck, "Der mangelnde Akteursbezug systemtheoretischer Erklärungen gesellschaftlicher Differenzierung," 6 *Zeitschrift für Soziologie* 421, 430 (1986); Japp, "Kollektive Akteure als soziale Systeme," in Unverferth, *System und Selbstproduktion* 166 (1986).

terpretation, for instance, Claus Ott has described the old dispute over the "essence" of the legal person as a political conflict over the function and legitimation of intermediary forces in society, raising the question of its political legitimation under present-day conditions.[4] But while a pluralist concept of corporate governance did emerge from Ott's analysis, it made no contribution to the theory of the legal person. And no wonder, for if Ott proposes to solve the corporate person's legitimation problems by establishing links to interest groups and regional parliaments, then the real achievement of the legal person—namely to increase organizational autonomy—has to take second place.

In order to rediscover the social dimension of the legal person, it would seem advisable to invert completely the approach adopted. It is not a reduction of organizational autonomy that is needed, but its expansion. If the legitimation of the first is sought primarily not in the consent of those involved, but in its overall social function and performance,[5] then the heightening of organizational autonomy vis-à-vis the persons and interest groups involved is not only compatible with this legitimation, but indeed its precondition. We can then start to see what the concept of the legal person might be able to contribute to industrial policy. Industrial policy might be able to find a viable alternative to the current strategies of contractual flexibility in the expanded autonomy of an action system which is independent vis-à-vis the groups involved and which is capable of reacting sensitively, in autonomous goal-seeking, to the demands of, threats to, and changes in the environment.[6] To achieve such flexibility through organization,[7] however, it is necessary, in the interest of society as a whole to strengthen the "corporate actor"—a newfangled term for the legal person—and its autonomy vis-à-vis the internal interest groups involved. This turns the current logic of legitimation entirely on its head. It is not pluralism within the firm that justifies the actions of the corporate actor, but the contrary: internal pluralism is legitimate only insofar as it is oriented towards the corporate actor's goals, which in turn must be legitimized by the firm's function and performance in society.

To give such preeminence to the collective identity of organizations is certainly problematic today.[8] With the spread of economic

4. Ott, supra n. 3 at 283 ff.; for the discussion in the U.S., see Horwitz, supra n.3.

5. Buxbaum, "Corporate Legitimacy, Economic Theory, and Legal Doctrine," 45 *Ohio State L.J.* 515ff., 520 (1984); Teubner, "Corporate Responsibility als Problem der Unternehmensverfassung," 1983 *ZGR* 34ff.

6. Strauss, "Industrial Relations: Times of Change," 23 *Industrial Relations* 1ff. (1984).

7. Streeck, supra n. 1 at 21ff.

8. On the individualism/collectivism debate, decisively influenced by Popper and Hayek, cf. Phillips, *Holistic Thought in Social Science* (1976); Vanberg, *Die zwei*

models adhering strictly to methodological individualism, collective actors have fallen into disrepute. The firm is dissolved into a network of contracts among the individuals involved, or into a "transactional network" in which, while a "central agent" does appear as a natural person, the legal person either does not feature at all, or does so only as a bizarre fiction of jurists.[9] Even sociologists, who by the nature of their discipline ought to develop a feeling for the reality of the collectivity, analyze the corporate actor out of existence by conceptualizing it as resource pooling by individuals.[10] Those who assert the social reality of collective units are liable to be suspected of a methodologically and politically doubtful holism/collectivism.

If instead a systems theory approach is chosen, the very distinction between individualism and collectivism becomes questionable.[11] This theory neither reduces collective action to individual action nor vice versa, but interprets both as different forms of social attribution of action. The theory of self-referential systems allows the legal person and its social reality to be understood without collectivist or organicist metaphors, without "invoking some mystic entity, the social group, and endowing it with superorganic, self-sustaining powers."[12] The thesis to be developed below is that the legal person is neither a fiction à la Savigny, nor has it as its substratum the "physico-spiritual unity" of Gierke's *reale Verbands-persoenlichkeit*

Soziologien: Individualismus und Kollektivismus in der Sozialtheorie (1975); Bohnen, *Individualismus und Gesellschaftstheorie* (1975). Elster, *Making Sense of Marx* 34 ff. (1985); Teubner, "Corporate Responsibility as a Problem of Company Constitution," EUI-Working Paper.

9. Alchian & Demsetz, "Production, Information Costs and Economic Organization," 62 *Am. Econ. Rev.* 777 (1972); Jensen & Meckling, "Theory of the Firm: Managerial Behavior, Agency Costs and Ownership Structures," 3 *Financial Econ.* 305 (1976); Fama, "Agency Problems and the Theory of the Firm," 88 *J. Polit. Econ.* 288 (1980); Cheung, "The Contractual Nature of the Firm," 26 *J.L. Econ.* 1ff. (1983); for the transactional approach, see Williamson, *The Economic Institutions of Capitalism* (1985). For an interesting expansion of the network model, see Schanze, "Potential and Limits of Economic Analysis," in Daintith & Teubner, *Contract and Organization* 204, 212 ff. (1986).

10. Coleman, *Power and Structure in Society* (1974); idem., *The Asymmetric Society* (1982); idem. "Responsibility in Corporate Action: A Sociologist's View," in Hopt & Teubner, *Corporate Governance and Directors' Liabilities* 69 ff. (1985); Swanson, "An Organizational Analysis of Collectivities," in Genevie, *Collective Behavior* 270 ff. (1978); Vanberg, *Markt und Organisation* 8ff., 37ff. (1982); idem., "Das Unternehmen als Sozialverband," 1 *Jahrbuch für Neue Politische Oekonomie* 276ff. (1982); also Krause, "Corporate Social Responsibility: Interests and Goals," in Hopt & Teubner, *Corporate Governance* 99ff., 102f. (1985).

11. This must be explicitly stressed because systems theory has the reputation of taking the stance of holism/collectivism. However, collectivism and individualism are "over-hasty options" for system theory; cf. Luhmann, "Wie ist soziale Ordnung möglich?," ibid., 2 *Gesellschaftsstruktur und Semantik* 245ff. (1981).

12. This is a critique of the old Philadelphian Social epistemology; cf. Douglas, *How Institutions Think* 10 (1986). On the connection between self-reference and personification of the organization, see Teubner, *"Hypercycle in Law and Organization"* in *European Yearbook in the Sociology of Law* (1988).

(real corporate personality), nor is it merely an autonomized pool of resources. Nor has a convincing social basis for the legal person yet been found in the social action system, not even with formal organization. Instead, I would suggest that the *social reality* of a legal person is to be found in the "*collectivity*": the socially binding self-description of an organized action system as a cyclical linkage of identity and action.

The compactness of this thesis admittedly makes it obscure and therefore in need of considerable amplification (given in Part II). This approach also has far-reaching implications for legal theory, legal doctrine, and legal policy, which certainly cannot be worked out fully in this article. Some of the legal theory implications will be touched upon in a discussion of the relationship between the social reality and the legal regulation of the legal person (in Part III): What degree of freedom does the legal person have vis-à-vis the corporate actor? What is the function of legal personification of collectivities? Some consequences of our thesis for legal doctrine (Part IV) will be treated, especially how the relationship between legal person and economic organization is to be conceptualized in law. Finally, some legal policy implications (Part V) will be discussed under the heading of "enterprise corporatism": if a strategy of neo-corporatist producers' coalitions is developed as an industrial policy alternative to contractual flexibilization, how does this strategy relate to the impersonal order that the corporate actor represents?

II. Social Substration of the Legal Person

The contemporary debate on the legal person seems content to accept its purely technically legal character,[13] but there are nevertheless views that stress its dynamic social reality.[14] The most advanced proponents of this position are prepared to "award Gierke the palm," as long as his *reale Verbandspersoenlichkeit* is cleansed of collectivist and organicist metaphors. But a peculiar embarrassment makes itself felt when it comes to defining how thorough the cleansing should be. What is left, after this purge, of the "physico-spiritual life-unit" of Gierke's "real corporate personality?"[15] After

13. For the older debate on the legal person, see in detail Wolff, I *Organschaft und juristische Person* 1-87 (1933); Hallis, *Corporate Personality* (1930). Kantorowicz, *The King's Two Bodies* (1957); Stein, "Nineteenth Century English Company Law and Theories of Legal Personality," 12 *Quaderni Fiorentini* 502 (1983).

14. For the recent debate in the U.S.A., see Dan-Cohen, supra n. 3. A survey of the recent German debate is in, for instance, Reuter, *MK* paras. 21, 1ff.; Staudinger-Coing, Einleitung zu, paras. 21-89, 1ff. Schmidt, *Verbandszweck und Rechtsfähigkeit im Vereinsrecht* 4 (1984); idem, *Gesellschaftsrecht* 142 ff. (1986).

15. Gierke, *Das Wesen der menschlichen Verbaende* 12 (1902). On the problems of the organism analogy, see Rottleuthner, "Biological Metaphors in Legal

Rittner's treatment, we still have the objective spirit: a "special spiritual action center of objectivity," which makes possible "the supra-individual continuity of (in the broadest sense) cultural substances."[16] Taking a suitable distance from neo-idealistic formulations, Wieacker in his turn has a go at social psychology. Then all that is left is the empirical reality of the legal person in "group consciousness."[17] Ott allows the legal person more of a political reality: as the power and action center of "private government."[18] In a particularly thorough cleansing, finally, Flume reduces the hard reality of "social entities" to Savigny's *ideale Ganze* (ideal whole), the more detailed definition of which, however, with wise self-restraint, he leaves open.[19] By contrast with the burgeoning fullness of Gierke's real corporate personality, such a cleansed and filleted legal entity looks rather thin. Considering the original grandiose concept, this present state of debate seems rather petty-minded. Is Jellinek's call to make the pre-legal reality of associations independent of organism theory[20] unfulfillable even today?

Gierke's cardinal error was to conceive of the components of the association as flesh and blood people.[21] When he called associations "organisms whose parts are human beings,"[22] he programmed the errors of organicist collectivism. Not only does this entail difficulties for the treatment of institutions, foundations, and one-man companies, but by taking actual human beings as the essential elements of an association, it bars access to the social reality of associations, for then collectivities can be seen only as "supermen." Methodological individualism is quite right to attack such mystifications of collective units as supra-individual entities linking separate individuals into new wholes. It is, however, quite wrong to reduce the specific dynamics of social processes to individuals' actions, and correspondingly to see collectivities such as the legal person only as mere abbreviations, shorthand expressions, or "verbal symbols" for the

Thought," in Teubner, *Autopoietic Law* (1988) and more generally, Dachler, "Some Explanatory Boundaries of Organismic Analogies for the Understanding of Social Systems," in Probst & Ulrich, *Self-Organization and Management of Social Systems* 132ff. (1984).

16. Rittner, *Die werdende juristische Person* 211, 214 et passim (1973). For a skeptical review, see Ulmer, "Zu einer neuen Theorie der juristischen Person," 1976 *ZHR* 61 ff; Reich, *Markt und Recht* 297ff. (1977).

17. Wieacker, "Zur Theorie der juristischen Person des Privatrechts," in *Festschrift für Huber* 339ff., 367 (1973).

18. Ott, supra n. 3 at 85ff.

19. Flume, *Die Juristische Person* 25ff. (1983).

20. Jellinek, *Allgemeine Staatslehre* 170 (1920).

21. Gierke, III *Deutsches Genossenschaftsrecht* (1881); IV (1913) (English translation by Maitland, 1913, and Heiman, 1977) idem., supra n. 15; idem., I *Deutsches Privatrecht* 466 ff. (1895).

22. Gierke, supra n. 15 at 13.

complex aggregates of individual actions that are really involved.[23] The internal dynamics of the legal person's substratum can be better understood by viewing the substratum as an autonomous communicative process, with actual people simply being treated as part of this process' environment. If this step is not taken and yet the social reality of the legal person is nevertheless maintained, one falls into the trap of organicist collectivism—or else one escapes into neo-idealism, social psychology, or politics.

If, then, the substratum of the legal person does not consist of an assemblage of individuals, what is it? Is it a social relation, an aggregate of roles, a decision-making sequence, a chain of transactions or a resource pool? All these solutions have their advocates: Max Weber saw the associational reality as a "relation"[24]; Talcott Parsons conceived of "actions" or "roles" as the reality of social systems[25]; Chester Barnard dissolved the organization into "activities,"[26] Herbert Simon into "decision premises,"[27] Oliver E. Williamson into "transactions"[28]; James Coleman sees the reality of the corporate actor in "pooled resources."[29] These are just a few of the authorities that have done without actual individuals as the units of the prelegal reality of legal persons. But which of these elements ought to take the place of actual people?

With unerring intuition, Gierke found the criterion by insisting on the "livingness" of the association, on its internal dynamics and continual self-reproduction, concomitantly ridiculing the theories of *Zweckvermögen* (resource pools, special-purpose funds) because only "organized associations of individuals with unitary associative will could have the animated body to which a genuine legal personality can be attributed, such as a mere purpose or a dead fund could never acquire."[30]

This argument of course reveals the second major error of organicist collectivism. Social systems are in fact not constituted on a basis of life as "real physico-spiritual units." This does not mean, however, that they need necessarily be taken, as does Rittner, as

23. For an extreme formulation, see, e.g., Radin, "The Endless Problem of Corporate Personality," 32 *Colum. L. Rev.* 643 (1932).

24. Weber, *Economy and Society* 48 ff. (1978).

25. Parsons, *The System of Modern Societies* 4ff. (1971); Parsons & Shils, *Toward a General Theory of Social Action* 190 (1981).

26. Barnard, *The Functions of the Executive* 73 ff. (1938).

27. Simon, *Administrative Behavior* XVIIf. (3rd ed. 1976).

28. Williamson, supra n. 9 passim.

29. Coleman, supra n. 10.

30. Gierke, *Die Genossenschaftstheorie und die deutsche Rechtsprechung*, 11ff. (1887). See also idem., I *Deutsches Privatrecht*, supra n. 21 at 472: ". . . a living being that wills and acts as such." Today it is notably Selznick, *Law Society and Industrial Justice* 43ff. (1969), who stresses the living, dynamic character of the "corporate entity."

substances of the objective spirit. One size smaller will still do. It is enough for social systems to be constituted as communicative units on the basis of social meaning, which in principle excludes both biologism and idealism. Nevertheless, if one abstracts from "life" and "meaning" in the direction of a theory of "self-reproducing systems," then one has found the criterion, with Gierke. The social substratum to be personified is not simply a (static) social structure. Instead, it is an internal dynamics system, with selections of its own, and with a capacity for self-organization and self-reproduction. All that Gierke had available to express this dynamism was the misleading metaphor of "life." Today for this we have the cooler, remoter concept of an autopoietic social system: a system of actions/communications that reproduces itself by constantly producing from the network of its elements new communications/actions as elements.[31] Therein lies the dynamic social reality of the substratum: the legal person is based not on a mere social relation (Weber) or social structure (Parsons), but on a "pulsating" sequence of meaningfully interrelated communicative events, that constantly reproduce themselves.[32]

From this position we can see that the purpose and pool theories of the legal person,[33] in their more recent versions of the *organisiertes Zweckvermögen* (organized special-purpose fund, or resource pooling)[34] are incomplete, applicable to only a partial aspect of the whole. Even if we ignore the less advanced purpose theories, which disqualify themselves by trivially defining the *Vermögen* as things or assemblages of things, and consider only the more ambitious definition of *Vermögen* as a bundle of property rights, such theories are of only limited scope. For they apply only to a (relatively static) substructure of a whole dynamic system of action—Gierke's "dead fund." For this reason, the more recent legal

31. Luhmann, *Soziale Systeme* (1984), is basic. On the autopoietic nature of social systems, see the lively discussion in the collective volumes: Benseler, Hejl & Koeck, *Autopoiesis, Communication and Society* (1980); Dumouchel & Dupuy, *L'auto-organisation. De la physique au politique* (1983); Ulrich & Probst, *Self-Organization and Management of Social Systems* (1984); Baecker, et al., *Theorie als Passion* (1987); Haferkamp & Schmid. supra n. 12; Teubner, supra n. 15. For an assessment of the theory of self referential systems in its implications for law by a "fascinated sceptic," see Wiethölter, "Sanierungskonkurs der Juristenausbildung"? 1 *Kritische Vierteljahresschrift für Gesetzgebung und Rechtswissenschaft* 21ff. (1986).

32. In this sense, Hutter, supra n. 3 at 112, defines persons as "social systems to which communications are ascribed." See also Ladeur, *Alternativkommentar Grundgesetz*, art. 19 III, 28 ("organized collectivities").

33. The founders are Brinz, I *Lehrbuch der Pandekten* ss 60f., III, ss 432 ff. (3rd ed. 1884); Bekker, *System des heutigen Pandektenrechts* 1886, ss 42ff. (1886).

34. Wiedemann, "Juristische Person and Gesamthand als Sondervermögen," 1975 *Wertpapiermitteilungen* Sonderbeilage Nr. 4; ibid., *Gesellschaftsrecht* I 195ff. (1980); Coleman, supra n. 10; Vanberg, supra n. 10.

theories which argue on a corporate actor basis are superior in principle to those which argue on a basis of a resource pool,[35] since they at least aim at the personification of the whole action system, and not merely of the partial aspect of the property rights structure.

Ought we, then, to take a self-reproducing action system as the social substratum of the legal person? No, for this, too, is accurate only in a very provisional, not to say misleading, sense. The term "social action system" covers a multitude of social phenomena, from simple conversation and the group via law, the economy and politics, right up to the world society, far from all of which have any entitlement to legal personification. A qualifying characteristic must be added that justifies giving a social system the honorary title of "collectivity" or "corporate actor."

The criterion which is frequently chosen for this today is formal organization.[36] The substratum of the legal person is said to be a formally organized social action system.[37] This certainly provides a plausible criterion, and at the same time covers the majority of empirical phenomena, namely formal organizations.

But however formal organization is defined, whether as a goal-oriented social system,[38] a relation of bureaucratic domination,[39] or a governance structure,[40] none of these definitions catches the reality of the corporate actor or the collectivity. An organization does not become capable of action (in a pre-legal sense) by merely constituting itself as a goal-oriented system.[41] Indeed, the social reality of the corporate actor is not located at all at the level of actual system operations (communications, actions, decisions). *The emergent quality of a "corporate actor" arises from self-description in the action system itself.* It is reflexive communication in the action system, com-

35. Rittner, supra n. 3 at 210 ff.; idem, "Juristische Person," in *Staatslexikon* 267ff. (1987); Ott, supra n. 18 at 85ff.; Flume, supra n. 19; Schmidt supra n.14.

36. For organization in a specifically legal sense, see John, *Die organisierte Rechtsperson* passim (1977). The more recent "technical legal" definitions of the legal person also like to use the metaphor of "organization"; see, e.g., 25 BGHZ 134, 144; Enneccerus & Nipperdey, *Lehrbuch des Bürgerlichen Rechts* 1959, paras. 103; Soergel & Schulze-von Lasaulx, BGB, vor s 21, 3; Reuter, *MK*, vor s 21, 3; Staudinger-Coing, Einleitung zu ss 21-89, 5ff.

37. For organization in a sociological sense, see Rotter, *Zur Funktion der juristischen Person in der Bundesrepublik und in der DDR* 30 ff. (1967); Raiser, *Das Unternehmen als Organisation* 93ff., 166ff. (1969); Ott, supra n. 3 at 85ff.; Dan-Cohen, supra n. 3 at 26ff.

38. Parsons, *Structure and Process in Modern Society* 17, 63 (1960); Mayntz, *Soziologie der Organisation* 40 (9th ed. 1977). Etzioni, *Complex Organizations* 1 (1961). Blau & Scott, *Formal Organizations* 5 (1962).

39. Weber, supra n. 24 at 48 ff., 720 ff. and the literature on "private government."

40. Williamson, supra n. 9 at 298 ff.

41. Luhmann, "Einfache Sozialsysteme," in idem., 2 *Soziologische Aufklärung* 21ff. 32ff. (1975); idem., supra n. 31 at 270ff. For Giddens, *The Constitution of Society* 200 (1986), it is reflexive monitoring of action "which masks the decisive difference."

munication on its own identity and its capacity for action, that constitutes the corporate actor or the collectivity as a mere semantic artifact, as a linguistically condensed perception of group identity.[42] It is only to the extent that such a corporate actor becomes institutionalized, i.e., that organizational actions are actually oriented round this self-description, that the corporate actor takes on social reality.

Looking back from here once again at the old dispute on the nature of corporate personality, the ambivalence of the corporate actor, its remarkably fluctuating reality becomes clear. It is neither Savigny's pure fiction nor Gierke's real corporate personality—or else it is both at the same time. The corporate actor is "fictional" because it is not identical with the real organization but only with the semantics of its self-description. It is "real" because this fiction takes on structural effect and orients social actions by binding them collectively. Max Weber came closest to capturing this ambivalence by treating collectivities only as "ideas" in the heads of judges, officials and the public, while at the same time assigning them "a powerful, often a decisive, causal influence on the course of action of real individuals."[43] Another who came close is Franz Wieacker, for whom "the socio-empirical reality of the social group types 'association, corporation' . . . lies in the group consciousness of the members and their partners and in the specific nature of the group's behavior."[44]

To be sure, both formulated only the psychic but not the social reality of the collectivity. It is not unexpressed ideas in the heads of those involved, but communicative self-descriptions in the organization as an action system that constitute the hard reality of the collectivity, the collective bond: "collective action is adopted as a premise in the meaning of other system actions, thereby limiting possibilities."[45]

42. On this, see Teubner, supra n. 12, which also gives more details on the connection between interaction, group and organization, seen as a cumulative rise in self-referentiality to the point of hypercyclical linkage. The view of the corporate actor as a semantic artifact of social communication is supported by the linguistic analysis; Schane, "The Corporation is a Person: The Language of a Legal Fiction," 61 *Tulane L.R.* 563 ff., 609 (1987): "The Law has been able to exploit to its advantage and to maximize for its needs conceptualizations that are deeply embedded within the structure of language."

43. Weber, supra n. 24 at 13 ff.

44. Wieacker, supra n. 17 at 367. Dworkin, *Law's Empire* 168 ff. (1986) develops a concept of "working personification": "The personification is deep: it consists in taking the corporation seriously as a moral agent. But it is still a personification, not a discovery, because we recognize that the community has no independent metaphysical existence, that it is itself a creature of the practices of thought and language in which it figures." (at 171).

45. Luhmann, supra n. 31 at 273 f. The fact that this is supposed to be a merely psychological reality is seen by Wieacker, supra n. 17 at 369, as a problem, since the

An additional step further beyond Max Weber, who explicitly denied collective entities the capacity for action, is necessary in order to throw full light on the substratum of the legal person. For the social self-description of collective identity—"corporate identity"—only succeeds in conveying a half impression of the corporate actor. Only a first approximation of the collectivization of a group can be obtained from representing it as the institutionalization of collective identity, be it on the model of a human person or of an organism. To gain a full understanding, the collectivity must instead be seen as a dyadic relationship. This is, say, what Parsons does in construing it as a relationship between "solidarity" and capacity for "action in concert."[46]

The key to understanding lies in the cyclical linkage of action and collective identity via mechanisms of attribution. Even in the case of simple interaction or of the group, the everyday understanding of acting individuals must be redirected so that events become system actions only once the communication network regards its participants or members as "persons," i.e., only once individuals are constituted as social constructs, and particular events are then assigned to these self-created communicative realities.[47] Even at the level of interactions and groups, then, it is mechanisms of attribution that constitute system actions as actions of people *within* the system. It is only by taking this construction seriously that one can understand the process of collectivization. Collectivization means a shift in the attribution of an action from one social construct to another, from a "natural" to a "legal" person. *A self-description of the system as a whole is produced and to this construct actions are attributed as actions of the system.* This is a self-supporting construction: collective actions are the product of the corporate actor to which events are attributed, and the corporate actor is nothing but the product of these actions.

A first interim result might then be as follows: the social substratum of the legal person is neither an assemblage of people nor a pool of resources nor a mere organizational structure. Nor is it adequately characterized as an action system or as a formal organization. The substratum is conceived properly as a "collectivity" or

---

legal order has only an external (i.e., social) approach to the object. It is, then, all the more important to be able to analyze the social reality of the collective and the collective bond by comparison with the merely psychic one. On the emergent quality of collective vis-à-vis individual constructions of reality, see Dachler, supra n. 15 at 132ff., 140.

46. Parsons, *The Social System* 41, 96 (1951); idem, *Societies* 187 (1966); idem, supra n.25 at 6 ff., 23 ff. (1971); Parsons & Shils, supra n. 25 at 61, 192; Parsons & Smelser, *Economy and Society* 15ff. (1956).

47. Luhmann, supra n. 31 at 155, 225 ff. The issue of "personifying" human individuals and institutions is also stressed by Vining, *Legal Identity* (1978) 156f.

"corporate actor," i.e., the self-description of a (usually formally) organized social action system that brings about a cyclical linkage of self-referentially constituted system identity and system elements.

III. Freedoms vis-à-vis the Corporate Actor

If we now know everything about the "substratum" of the legal person, we still know nothing about its "essence." For the question of "essence" changes the system reference from the organization to the law, bringing up the question of what room the legal system has for maneuver in its external description of the self-description of an organized social system. What freedoms can the legal person assume vis-à-vis the corporate actor? All freedoms and every freedom, is the answer in good positivist language. Even if we no longer see the substratum merely diffusely as a "social phenomenon," an "action center," an "acting unit" and the like, but more precisely as a "collectivity" in the sense defined above, there still remains a difference in principle between the social structures and the legal structure of corporate personality. There are no fixed objective relationships between pre-legal structures and legal construction. There is no sociological natural law of the legal person. If legal positivity is to be taken seriously here, too, then one would on the contrary have to expect a high degree of variability between law and social substratum. As Selznick says: ". . . the institutional perspective is quite compatible with a more selective policy-oriented concept of the corporation."[48]

From the standpoint of the theory of self-referential systems, too, the autonomy of the law in the construction of its own environment and in the choice of its distinctions must be stressed. This is external observation of a self-observation: the legal system observes, using its own conceptualizations, how the organized social system observes itself as a "collectivity," or else how it is observed as such by its environment. The legal system is in no way "bound" by the self-observation, nor by other (e.g., psychological, sociological or "life world") external observations of this self-observation.[49] There

48. Selznick, supra n. 30 at 48. On the parallel question of the "Gesamthand," cf. Teubner, in *Alternativkommentar BGB* ss 705 ff., 21 ff. Herein lies the relative justification for the present "technical legal" understanding of the legal person, in, e.g., Staudinger-Coing, Einleitung zu ss 21ff., 4ff., in *Münchner Kommentar* vor s 21, 2; John, supra n. 36 at 66 ff. Its problem is, however, to derive from the variability between legal concept and social phenomenon to the irrelevance of the social phenomenon for the legal concept. The legal system, as the debate on the legal concept of the firm decisively shows (see IV below), needs not only a legal concept of the legal person but also a legal concept of the substrate.

49. From this point of view one may sympathize with Hart, "Definition and Theory in Jurisprudence," 70 *L.Q. Rev.* 37 (1954), when he calls for abandonment of the "ever baffling question" of "what is any association or organized group?" and its re-

is therefore no contradiction between on the one hand stressing the social reality of the substratum and on the other defending a positivist or constructivist concept of the legal person. The most decisive advocate of this position was perhaps Kelsen: the legal person is a partial legal suborder, a complex of norms relating to a particular legally defined entity (contract, corporation, association, federation, municipality, state). In the personification, the norm complex is nothing but a point of attribution.[50] Kelsen's problem, however, lies in his rigid separation of the social and the legal spheres, the interaction of which is set aside by erecting a conceptual barrier between them.

Accordingly, nothing prevents the legal system from taking any object whatever—divinities, saints, temples, plots of land, art objects—as points of attribution and giving them legal capacity.[51] Trees particularly are prominent candidates. In legal theory and legal policy discussion they are continually raised as potential legal subjects—quite rightly today. ("Should trees have standing?")[52]

It is amazing that, despite an extremely high degree of freedom and choice, there are nevertheless such great structural similarities between "collectivity" and "legal person."[53] It is not only that the social and legal mechanisms of action attribution to constructs produced within the system (individual/collectivity in the social world, natural person/legal person in the legal world) are in principle structured in a parallel fashion. It is more striking that the law today makes practically no use of its positivist freedom and exclusively promotes "collectivities" to the status of legal persons. (In the sense defined above, even a one-man-company is a "collectivity"!) Flume has argued forcefully that it makes no sense to subsume the complex reality of the legal person under a "unitary concept": "What meaning is it supposed to have if one covers the reality of the state, of municipalities, of churches, of a corporation, of a foundation, of a

---

placement by the question "Under what conditions do we refer to numbers and sequences of men as aggregates of individuals and under what conditions do we adopt instead unifying phrases extended by analogy from individuals?"

50. Kelsen, *Allgemeine Staatslehre* 66ff. (1925) (English translation, *General Theory of Law and State* 96 ff. (1954)); similarly Wolff, supra n. 13 at 170 ff.

51. Wieacker, supra n. 17 at 359.

52. Kohler, *Lehrbuch des buergerlichen Rechts* I 230 (1906); Wolff, supra n. 13 at 62; Stone, *Should Trees Have Standing? Toward Legal Rights for Natural Objects* (1974).

53. In the prevailing technical legal understanding, too, a "regular linkage" between legal person and particular types of association is admitted, without, however, this putting the technical legal conception in question; e.g., Westermann, *Vertragsfreiheit und Typengesetzlichkeit im Recht der Personengesellschaften* 7ff. (1970); Staudinger-Coing, Einleitung zu ss 21ff., 6. By contrast, e.g., Wieacker, supra n. 17 at 359ff. and Ott, supra n. 3 at 50ff., 69ff. take this "regular linkage" as a basis for more precise treatment of the connection between social structure and legal structure.

sporting association, etc., in a unitary concept?"[54] But the concept of "collectivity" or "corporate actor" developed above (i.e., self-description of an organized social system as the link between identity and capacity for action) shows instead that it certainly does make sense to subsume these social phenomena under a unitary concept.

What are the objections to the unitary concept? Certainly not the fact of acting in different spheres (e.g., politics, economy, culture, religion, leisure). More problematic are the important differences that exist between associations, institutions and foundations. Because of these differences it is often believed that there can be no unitary concept of the substratum. For in the case of associations it can only consist of human beings, whereas for foundations and institutions it is only the resource pools that could be the real substratum.[55] But this is precisely the point at which collectivity and the corporate actor step in, supplying a more precise unitary concept of the substratum than, say, Rittner's and Flume's vague concepts of "action unit" and "social phenomenon" could do.

The thesis is that, without being normatively compelled to do so, the law regularly binds up legal capacity with a large set of prerequisites of a particular social reality, which can be described by a "unitary concept." These prerequisites are: (1) (formally) organized action system; (2) a self-description of a collective identity; and (3) a cyclical linkage of identity and action via mechanisms of attribution. And thus we return to the social system's unitary concept of the collectivity.

The reasons for this close correspondence between law and society, astonishing from the viewpoint of positivist freedoms, are neither of natural law nor of legal logic, but merely of legal policy. Giving legal capacity to social formations makes policy sense only when they have a highly developed internal order.[56] Social capacity

54. Flume, supra n. 19 at 25. Similarly, also Wolff, "On the Nature of Legal Persons," 54 *L.Q. Rev.* 494ff., 506 (1938), "lawyers as a rule have no concern with the structural differences underlying the various kinds of legal persons, as that is a question of sociology." Cf. also Staudinger-Coing, Einleitung zu ss 21-89, 17.

55. The difficulties that authors that argue in "*Personal law*" terms have with institution and foundation make the advantages of thinking in systemic categories (system of action, collectivity) clear. Gierke's difficulties with institution and foundation are notorious: cf. Gierke, supra n. 30 at 9ff.; see also Nobel, *Anstalt und Unternehmen* 174ff. (1975). But Rittner and Flume have their problems too: Rittner, supra n.16 at 232 ff., with the personal element so highly rated by him, without which the "spirit freezes;" Flume, supra n. 19 at 29 ff., with the limits of the legal person, since because of his over-concrete understanding of "social phenomena" he is forced to define individuals and special assets of the legal person as "belonging" to it. On the relationship between the firm and institution, see the penetrating analyses in Nobel, supra.

56. This observation and the following ones are oversimplified to the extent that they take it that the legal system is "building upon" particular social structures. For the moment, they leave socio-legal interactions out of account. In reality, of course,

for action, i.e., the capacity for attributing external effects to the social system as such, implies that actions of certain individuals are attributed to all participants, socially entitling and obligating them. This calls for an order that has many social prerequisites: "the development of leadership structures, the formation of media for transferring selections in the system, mainly of power, the legitimation of representation rules and distributive processes with external or internal effect, and, not least, a certain alleviation of personal attribution, plus provision, despite this, for motivation and responsibility."[57]

These requirements can be summarized in the formula "social capacity for collective action." As a rule, it makes legal policy sense to grant legal capacity to social systems that already have social capacity for collective action. As the German example of the *nichtrechtsfähiger Verein* (association without legal capacity) or the Italian example of the *Mafia* shows, there may be powerful legal policy reasons which militate against the granting of legal capacity to certain social systems even though they are effectively capable of collective action. At the same time, the examples of political parties and trade unions show that once social capacity for collective action has been developed, the legal system is exposed to massive pressure to complete the social personification by legal personification.

The second reason supporting a correspondence between the social and legal structure lies deeper. It concerns the social function of legal personification. This is understood quite inadequately if only the advantages of limited liability are taken into consideration and if the disadvantages are partially compensated for by "piercing the corporate veil."[58] Much more important aspects are, for example, the saving in transaction costs and the coordination advantages of "resource pooling"[59]; efficiency gains deriving from the legal support of the capacity for action of the system as such[60]; the positional advan-

---

social capacity for action is regularly partly constituted through legal norms, indeed sometimes "artificially" created by the law alone.

57. Luhmann, supra n. 41 at 33; idem., supra n. 31 at 271; cf. Parsons & Smelser, supra n. 46 at 15; Popitz, *Prozesse der Machtbildung* (1968); Moore, "Legal Liability and Evolutionary Interpretation: Some Aspects of Strict Liability, Self-help and Collective Responsibility," in Gluckman, *The Allocation of Responsibility* 51ff. (1972); Coleman, "Loss of Power," 38 *Am. Sociol. Rev.* 1ff. (1973); idem, supra n. 10; Vanberg, supra n. 10.; French, *Collective and Corporate Responsibility* 48 ff. (1984).

58. This seems to be the prevailing trend, and not only in Germany: see the collective volume by Bastid, David & Luchaire, *La personnalité morale et ses limites* (1960), with country by country reports; Fletcher, *Cyclopedia Corporations*, I, 92ff. 1974; for the U.S.A., see Blumberg, *The Law of Corporate Groups* Vol. 3, Substantive Law (1987); Fabritius, "Parent and Subsidiary Corporations under U.S. Law—A Functional Analysis of Disregard-Criteria," EUI Working Paper (1986). A critique of this trend can be found in Flume, supra n. 19 at 24f.

59. Williamson, supra n. 9; Coleman, supra n. 10; Vanberg, supra n. 10.

60. Raiser, supra n. 37 at 166 ff.

tages for the organization in contacts with the environment[61]; or, last but not least, the well known "legal immortality."[62] The really interesting "emergent property" lies, however, in the building up of a (second order) autopoietic system.[63] By the cyclical linkage of identity and action perfected in the legal person, the organization acquires a hitherto unachieved autonomy vis-à-vis its environment, both the external environment of market and politics and the internal environment of members and others involved in the organization. The legally supported personification is a decisive step towards complete operational closure, which at the same time means a new type of environmental openness, i.e., a step towards that linkage between closure and openness which is typical of autopoietic systems and is the basis of their evolutionary success.[64]

This clears the way for transferring the profit motive from shareholders to the *Unternehmen an sich* (enterprise in and of itself), and would make the criteria of social responsibility apply not only to the personal actors, but also to the organization in terms of "corporate" social responsibility.[65] The development of autopoietic autonomy thereby also opens up far-reaching perspectives of economic and political control. As Mayntz recently rightly stressed, although autopoietic closure of formal organizations produces opaqueness and therefore control problems, it nevertheless at the same time also creates new opportunities for political and legal control.[66] On the whole, then, the self-description as "collectivity" contributes to producing the "unity" of the system. It allows for "operational closure" of the self-referential information process and

61. Luhmann, supra n. 31 at 270ff.

62. Blackstone, *Commentaries on the Law of England* 467 ff. (1771).

63. On this, using the construction of the hypercycle, see Teubner, supra n. 12. On second-order autopoiesis, cf. Maturana & Varela, *Autopoiesis and Cognition* 107ff. (1980) Mossakowski & Nettmann, "Is There a Linear Hierarchy of Biological Systems?," in Roth & Schwegler, *Self-Organizing Systems* 39ff. (1981); Jessop, "Relative Autonomy and Autopoiesis in Economy, Law and State," in Teubner, *State, Law, Economy as Autopoietic Systems* (1988).

64. On the symmetry of closure and openness in autopoietic systems, see in particular, Varela, "Autonomy and Autopoiesis," in Roth & Schwegler, supra n.63 at 14 ff.; ibid., "L'auto-organisation: de l'apparence au mechanisme," in Dumouchel & Dupuy, *L'auto-organisation* 147ff. (1983); Luhmann, supra n. 31 passim; Gomez & Probst, "Organisationelle Geschlossenheit im Management sozialer Institutionen," 5 *Delfin* 22ff. 1985; Teubner, "Social Order from Legislative Noise," in Teubner, supra n.63; Dupuy, "On the Supposed Closure of Normative Systems," in Teubner, supra n.15. Zolo, "The Epistemological Status of the Theory of Autopoiesis and its Application to the Social Sciences," in Teubner, supra n.63.

65. Cf. Kübler, "Verrechtlichung von Unternehmensstrukturen," in idem., *Verrechtlichung von Wirtschaft, Arbeit und sozialer Solidarität* 214ff. (1984); Teubner, supra n. 5; idem., "Unternehmensinteresse—das gesellschaftliche Interesse des Unternehmens an sich?," 149 *ZHR* 470 (1985).

66. Mayntz, "Steuerung, Steuerungsakteure und Steuerungsinstrumente," 70 *HIMON*, Universitaet Siegen (1986).

for "structural coupling" to the needs and interests of the environment.

The second interim result could be formulated as follows: in the sense of positivist or constructivist theories of the legal person, the law has great freedom as to what social phenomena are to be given legal capacity. Nevertheless, in practice there exists a great correspondence between social structures and legal structures of corporate personality, which justifies a unitary concept of the substratum as collectivity or corporate actor. The basis for this is the linking of legal capacity to the social capacity for collective action. Its function is the building up of a second-order autopoietic system which allows a new combination of operational closure and environmental openness.

IV. Legal Capacity of the Enterprise?

Of what concern is all this to the practicing lawyer? A great deal, for apart from consequences in legal theory, this view of the "essence" of the corporate personality also has implications for legal doctrine. If its "essence" lies not in resources nor in people but in the legal reconstruction of a collectivized action system, this has immediately foreseeable consequences for such exotic legal phenomena as the one-man company, and the "personless corporation." The "personless corporation" not only becomes conceivable, but is always presupposed.[67] But consequences then also have to be drawn for the legal conceptualization of corporate membership and of corporate bodies (*Organe*), since in the glaring light of systems theory corporate members and corporate bodies evaporate into mere bundles of roles.[68] When the issue of the disregard of the corporate entity is raised, the legal person is to be "taken seriously" in a different sense than that recently proposed.[69] And the relationship between "unity and multiplicity in the group enterprise" should be re-thought in relation to the legal capacity for action of the group enterprise as a whole.[70] Obviously the new "group theory" of German partnership

67. Kreutz, "Von der Einmann-zur Keinmann-GmbH?," *Festschrift für Walter Stimpel* 379 ff. (1985); for a comparative view, see Ziebe, *Der Erwerb eigener Aktien und eigener GmbH-Geschäftsanteile in den Staaten der europäischen Gemeinschaft* (1981). On the debate in the U.S., cf. Dan-Cohen, supra n. 3 at 41ff.

68. For a recent systematic approach to membership, see Lutter, "Theorie der Mitgliedschaft," 1980 *AcP* 84 (1980); on the concept of 'corporate body' (*Organ*), the absence of a theory is generally bewailed; see, e.g., Coing, 65ff. (1979); Wiedemann, supra n. 34 at 212 ff. (1980). For the present situation, see, e.g., Ulmer, "Zur Haftung der abordnenden Körperschaft nach ss 31 BGB für Sorgfaltsverstösse des von ihr benannten Aufsichtsratsmitglieds," in *Festschrift für Stimpel* 705 ff. (1985).

69. Wilhelm, supra 2; for interesting suggestions, see Schanze, *Einmanngesellschaft und Durchgriffshaftung* 102 ff. (1975); Schmidt, supra n.14 at 170 ff., 177 ff. (1986).

70. Ambitious formulations can be found in Baelz, "Einheit und Vielheit im

law (*Personengesellschaft*) developed by Flume would require critical examination specifically as to whether the distinctions still affirmed in the concept of "group" between an association of persons and the person of the association can in fact be maintained.[71] Here, however, we shall consider only one legal problem in more detail, specifically because it lies at the crossing point of questions of legal theory, legal doctrine and legal policy: the "legal nature" of the business enterprise, in particular the relationship between the enterprise and the legal person.[72]

On this issue Thomas Raiser's bold sortie has assured prolonged controversy, fuelled still further by its legal policy implications in the codermination debate. Raiser argued that *de lege lata* the enterprise as such (as opposed to the association of shareholders) was increasingly developing into the real point of attribution for legal rules, that it was "pressing" for legal capacity, and that *de lege ferenda* the enterprise as such should be assigned legal capacity.[73]

This thesis has been challenged on many grounds, the most interesting of which for our purposes here are the legal theory arguments which purport to refute the "suitable ideology"[74] from a seemingly higher standpoint. Rittner teaches that "for logical reasons alone it is out of the question to declare that the enterprise itself is the 'subject' (*Traeger*) of the enterprise."[75] Flume caps this

Konzern," in *Festschrift für L. Raiser* 287ff. (1974); "Groups of Companies—the German Approach: "Unternehmen" versus "Konzern," EUI Working Paper (1985).

71. Flume, *Die Personengesellschaft* 1ff. (1977); Ulmer, "Die Lehre von der fehlerhaften Gesellschaft," in *Festschrift für Flume* 301 ff. (1978); for a (constructive) criticism, see Teubner, *Alternativkommentar BGB*, vor ss 705ff., 16ff.; a tempting systematization in Baelz, "Treuhandkommanditist, Treuhänder der Kommanditisten und Anlegerschutz," 1980 *ZGR* 1ff., 37ff.

72. The economic aspects of a legal concept of the firm are stressed by Koehler, "Rechtsform und Unternehmensverfassung," 115 *ZgStw* 721ff. (1959); Ballerstedt, "GmbH-Reform, Mitbestimmung und Unternehmensrecht," 135 *ZHR* 184 (1971); Rittner, supra n. 16 at 282ff.; Wiedemann, supra n. 34 at 307ff. (1980); Flume, supra n. 19, at 48ff.

The aspect of a social association is stressed by Fechner, *Die Treubindungen des Aktionärs* 64ff. (1943); Duden, "Zur Methode der Entwicklung des Gesellschaftsrechts zum Unternehmensrecht," in *Festschrift für Schilling* 309 (1973); Kunze, "Unternehmen und Gesellschaft," 147 *ZHR* 16ff. (1983); Steinmann & Gerum, *Reform der Unternehmensverfassung* (1978); Steimann, "The Enterprise as a Political System," in Hopt & Teubner, *Corporate Governance* 401ff. (1985).

The organization-theory perspective is stressed by Raiser, supra n. 37 at 166ff. Baelz, supra n. 70 at 293ff. (1974); Ott, supra n. 3; Brinkmann, *Unternehmensinteresse und Unternehmensrechtsstruktur* (1983); Teubner, supra n. 5; parallel approaches in the U.S. are in Seeznick, *Law, Society and Industrial Justice* (1969); Stone, *Where the Law Ends* (1975); Dan-Cohen, supra n. 3.

73. Raiser, supra n. 37 at 166 ff.; idem., "Die Zukunft des Unternehmensrechts," in *Festschrift für Robert Fischer*, 561ff., 572ff. (1979); Rittner, supra n. 16 at 306 f.; Wiedemann, supra n. 34 at 308ff. (1980).

74. Wiedemann, "Grundfragen der Unternehmensverfassung," 1975 *ZGR* 402.

75. Rittner, supra n. 16 at 283ff., 288.

with: "Muenchhausen jurisprudence!"[76] That is intended to discourage pursuit of the idea. Yet one's ears prick up when both scholars thereupon themselves start operating in the immediate vicinity of Muenchhausen. In the case of the stock corporation (*Aktiengesellschaft*), Flume "identifies" (!) the enterprise with the legal person "because it belongs (!) to it."[77] Can something belong to itself? Rittner, too, builds a self-referential construction whose compatibility with the presupposed logic would require some checking, when he maintains that the "enterprise in the broader sense" is the representative of the "enterprise in the narrower sense." Furthermore, in the area of overlap between the "narrower" and "broader" enterprise he does just what he previously said was out of the question, namely, he declares "the enterprise to be the representative of the enterprise."

It is striking how many arguments for and against Muenchhausen accumulate around the topic of the legal person. There is the time-honored argument that the fiction theory is false because the State itself, as a legal person, would then have to be a fiction, whereas the State could not, like Muenchhausen, have erected itself by mere motion into a legal fiction.[78] Then, by contrast with Flume, who angrily rejects this argument as speculation, Hofstadter of Goedel-Escher-Bach would joyfully welcome it: "Reflexivity of law!"[79] We also find that Kelsen's concept of legal person as legal suborder and point of attribution has been objected to on the grounds that the statement that the legal suborder is itself a bearer of norms is a tautology: the construction would have to support itself "like the late Baron Muenchhausen."[80] And in this same context we are confronted with the attempt of German corporation law to circumvent Muenchhausen by making the enterprise have a "subject" (*Traeger*) different from itself, namely, the legal person, which in turn is supposed to have a substratum different from itself, namely, the association of persons or the resource pool.[81] Obviously this is an attempt to avoid such tautologies and circular arguments as that the firm "represents" itself or that the legal person is "based" on itself.

76. Flume, supra n. 19, at 48.

77. Id.

78. 1 Beseler, *System des gemeinen deutschen Privatrechts* 236 (1847). Saleilles, *De la personnalité juridique* 354 (1922); Wolff, supra n. 13 at 63ff.; Flume, supra n.19 at 13.

79. Hofstadter, *Goedel, Escher, Bach: An Eternal Golden Braid*, esp. 692 ff. (1979). About the connections between self-reference and paradox in law, see Suber, *The Paradox of Self-Amendment, Law, Omnipotence and Change* (1982); Fletcher, "Paradoxes in Legal Thought," 85 *Colum. L. Rev.* 1263 ff. (1985).

80. Wolff, supra n. 13 at 69, with other references.

81. Rittner, supra n. 16 at 232ff., 283ff.

But perhaps the mendacious Baron was not so wrong after all? Perhaps there really are, in the area of the legal person, circular relationships. May not the legal person's function indeed consist in making self-reference possible and in increasing self-reference still further in the interest of organizational autonomy? This, at any rate, is what the theory of self-referential systems, which has been successfully applied in such varied fields as logic, computer science, neurophysiology, sociology, business organization and legal theory[82] would suggest.

This prompts the following two theses: (1) the traditional demarcations between the enterprise, the legal person, and its substratum are to be interpreted as attempts to avoid self-referentiality in corporation law. Under this smokescreen, however, self-referentiality was actually able to make its way into the reality of the enterprise: (2) If the taboo of self-referential circularity is broken, the view opens up on to a self-supporting construction: the "subject" (*Träger*) of the enterprise is the collectivity, constituted as legal person; the "substratum" of the legal person is the enterprise personified as collectivity.[83]

This formulation of a strictly circular relationship between the enterprise and the legal person seems tautological, incompatible with existing law and unconstitutional as expropriation.[84] But before condemning it out of hand, one ought to examine the formulation very closely, bearing in mind that in a systems-theory formulation both concepts—enterprise and legal person—are related to a third, that of the collectivity. They thus go through a change in meaning, able to transform the tautology into impure self-reference, the illegality into a defensible alternative interpretation and the expropriation into a legitimate state interference (*Sozialbindung*).

Let us clarify this against the two most advanced positions (Raiser and Flume). Raiser's definition of both terms—enterprise and legal person—is still too person-related and insufficiently sys-

82. For example, see supra, n. 31 and 64. Scepticism about the whole trend comes from Lüderssen, "Wär' der Gedank' nicht so verwünscht gescheit, man wär' versucht, ihn herzlich dumm zu nennen," 5 *Rechtshistorisches J.* 344 (1986); see also Teubner's reply, "Münchhausen-Jurisprudenz," loc. cit. at 350 and Hejl, "Autopoiesis-muss es das sein?," loc. cit. at 357.

83. This can be read as the attempt to clarify the (confusing) definition of Ott, supra n. 3 at 52: "legal person and corporate structure, legal person, and corporation, coincide," which has frequently been criticized, e.g., Staudinger-Coing, Einleitung zu, ss 21 ff., 18; Reuter in *Münchner Kommentar*, vor s 21, 5ff. Of course the expression "corporate" is misleading here, and "coincide" should be replaced by the formulation "are in self-referential relationship to the self-description as collectivity"—another example of the difficulty of choosing between precision and comprehensibility in the formulation!

84. This anticipated criticism is based on Flume, supra n. 19 at 47ff.

temic. While he does manage, as he himself rightly comments,[85] to reach a higher stage of academic reflection using the organization sociology approach (mainly Parsons and Mayntz) to expose the enterprise as an organized system of actions, he nevertheless frequently falls back on the current stage of formulations in the course of analysis. Thus, for instance, he argues that "as the aggregate of its members," the enterprise is also a "stock of material and personal resources."[86] He thereby plays away the advantages of the systems-theory conception of the firm, according to which members and material resources constitute environment. When he goes on to see the workers as members of the organization in the legal sense, then he is, admittedly, forced to postulate the legal personification of the enterprise only *de lege ferenda*.

On the other hand, Raiser also conceives of the legal person too personalistically. He stresses its associational character and thereby "internalizes" the shareholders into the legal person. The association of shareholders thereby implicitly becomes the legal person, while the other sub-associations, that of the workers and that of the managers, as well as the enterprise as the overall association that incorporates these sub-associations, are (still) denied the privilege of legal personification. This corresponds to current conceptions whereby the company of shareholders as a legal person is the subject of the enterprise[87]; but it nevertheless leads to group-specific asymmetries which do not at all originate in the legal person—even, indeed, in Savigny's classical conception. If the legal person is bound up to that extent with the group of shareholders, and no clear division of spheres is made between legal person and members,[88] then here too all one can do is call for changes *de lege ferenda*.

With two bold conceptual steps, Flume has overtaken Raiser and managed in the outcome to identify the enterprise, already *de lege lata*, with the legal person, at any rate for the case of the stock corporation. In all rigor, he brings about the separation, already begun in Savigny, between the sphere of the legal person and the sphere of the members.[89] He thereby disqualifies the identification of the shareholders' association with the legal person as the famous major error that "identifies the totality of current members with the

85. Raiser, supra n. 73 at 565 (1979).

86. Raiser, supra n. 37 at 168; idem. n. 73 at 565 (1979); idem., "Unternehmensziele und Unternehmensbegriff," 1980 *ZHR* 231.

87. Raiser, supra n. 36 at 138ff.

88. This is Savigny's great achievement, which, however, is constantly negated by attempts to "internalize" the membership structure in the legal person: Savigny, *System des heutigen roemischen Rechts* II, 283ff., 332 (1840).

89. On the other hand, he modifies it again later; Flume, supra n.19 at 28 ff., when he stresses the "involvement" of the members.

corporation itself."[90] The sphere of the "ideal whole," as if it were hovering free, can then be linked with the enterprise whereby "both the enterprise with everything belonging to it, those working in it, the assets and liabilities and the members of the legal person"[91] are brought together as integral components of the "ideal whole" of the legal person. Flume thereby goes a considerable step beyond Raiser. The latter, in strict obedience to *lex lata*, declares the firm to have legal capacity only insofar as rules of law in force positivize the enterprise explicitly as a point of attribution and sees the enterprise's full legal capacity as a task *de lege ferenda*. Flume, by contrast, takes a cavalier attitude towards the law and already identifies the enterprise with the legal person under the prevailing state of the law.

Yet for all the boldness of the construction, even Flume has still not gone far enough. He limits the identification explicitly to the stock corporation, remaining remarkably ambivalent as regards the limited liability company (*Gesellschaft mit beschränkter Haftung*).[92] He understands it substantively as a kind of partnership (*Personengesellschaft*) which is, however, autonomized as a legal person by virtue of its limited liability limitation alone. But he sees at the same time that this is untenable for the "big" limited company. He takes refuge in the legal policy recommendation of making the legal form of the stock corporation compulsory in these cases.[93] There is a similar ambivalence about Flume's sharp distinction between corporations (*Kapitalgesellschaften*), where legal person and enterprise are supposed to be identical, and partnerships (*Personengesellschaften*), where the old notion that the partners are the "subjects" of the firm is supposed to remain. Whether, without internal splits, it is possible on the one hand to transform the partnership into a quasi-collectivity, with the "group" as the "action center," and on the other to make a fundamental distinction between "group" and legal person in their relationship to the enterprise, seems at least questionable.

The second objection is that Flume, although he consistently separates the sphere of the "ideal whole" from that of the members, ultimately is not consistent enough to define the human individuals as the environment of the spheres of enterprise and legal person, but instead includes both the members (i.e., shareholders) and those

90. Savigny, supra n. 88 at 347.

91. Flume, supra n. 19 at 48ff.; idem, "Körperschaftliche juristische Person und Personenverband," in *Festschrift für Gerhard Kegel* 154 (1987).

92. Cf. also the criticism by John, "Personrecht und Verbandsrecht im Allgemeinen Teil des Bürgerlichen Rechts," 1985 *AcP* 209ff., 220ff.; Raiser, 1981 *AcP* 245 ff.

93. Flume, *Um ein neues Unternehmensrecht* (1980).

working in the firm (i.e., management and employees) in the concept of the enterprise and that of the legal person.[94] This means that he inevitably gets bogged down again in a misconceived debate that links the relationship between legal person and enterprise with the membership question, i.e., the question whether only shareholders are members of the enterprise, or also managers and workers, or even major customers, consumers, etc.

That this debate is misconceived can be demonstrated on the basis of the third objection to Flume's theory. Flume falls for the current conceptual model which allows as the reference point for the legal person only the alternative between the shareholders' association or the enterprise. What has legal capacity, according to this model, is either the association comprising only the shareholders, or else the whole enterprise, including shareholders, management and others involved. *Tertium non datur*? Here the circuit to the systems-theory concepts developed above is closed, and at the same time it becomes clear that for all the "technical" legal understanding, the question of the substratum cannot be foisted off on to sociology. Neither the shareholders' association nor the enterprise as a whole are identifiable with the legal person, but only the above defined corporate actor or the collectivity.

The point that, due to the clear separation of spheres, the association of shareholders and the legal person are not identical has been made adequately clear by Flume. Their spheres of action overlap only as regards the actions of corporate bodies. But to make the *whole* enterprise into the legal person instead, as Flume does, is to go far too far. For what acts as the "center of action" is not the whole action system of the enterprise, but only the subcomplex which above we called "collectivity." Legal capacity is given only to the extent that collective action is involved. All that is affected is the subset of action in the whole enterprise which is to be attributed to the system as a whole in the collective bond. The legal person covers not the whole action system of the enterprise, but only the subset of action called collectivity, i.e., only those actions covered by the attribution mechanisms of corporation law, agency law, and labor law. It may sound unusual to name these phenomena in one breath, but they have one function in common: they transform individual action (of "members" or "workers") *in* the system into collective action *by* the system.

This makes clear why the problem of the legal person vis-à-vis the enterprise is not to be bound up with the membership question, as keeps on happening. Put rather crudely, not the scope of the membership but the scope of the corporate organs (*Organe*) decides

94. Flume, supra n. 19 at 49.

what actions belong to the legal person. Or, as Rittner puts it, the corporate organs (*Organe*) are "parts of the legal person itself, through which alone the latter can come to life."[95] It is important, however, not to forget the other two attribution mechanisms (agency law and labor law). The transformation processes that are decisive for the action area of the legal person accordingly take place not in the area of membership (expropriation!), but within the attribution mechanisms for collective action.

Both factual and legal transformations play a part here, as do private law-making and governmental regulation. The action area of the legal person expands through the private installation of new corporate bodies in the firm, particularly newly established consultative councils, committees, etc., through which environments of the firm are co-opted.[96] It likewise changes through the creation or alteration of corporate bodies by governmental regulation (corporate governance and codetermination). But factual transformation processes within the firm, notably decentralization, divisionalization, and functional democratization also change the action area of the legal person. The attribution mechanisms are changed: hierarchical attribution to the top of the organization gives place to an attribution to the action of autonomous decisionmaking centers within the firm based on its executive bodies (divisions, profit centers, autonomous working groups, and quality circles).

A further interim result might, thus, be added to the differentiation between enterprise and collectivity: it is an error to identify the legal person with the association of shareholders. Even *de lege lata*—Raiser would have to be reformulated—the enterprise personified as collectivity has legal capacity, and for all enterprises with legal capacity—Flume would have to be re-formulated—the legal person is identical with the collectivity, as the personification of the enterprise.

V. *Enterprise Corporation as a Legal Policy*

A new "suitable ideology?" It has already been claimed about theories of the enterprise as a "social association" (*Sozialverbandstorien*) that they were created in order to provide ideological support for codetermination.[97] The "*Unternehmen an sich*", enterprise in and of itself, too, is supposed to have been only an ideology aimed at helping managerial capitalism over the hurdles against financial

95. Rittner, supra n. 16 at 255.

96. See Teubner, "Der Beirat zwischen Verbandssouveränität und Mitbestimmung," 1986 *ZGR* 565.

97. Wiedemann, supra n. 74 at 402; idem., supra n. 34 at 309 (1980); Flume, supra n. 19 at 45.

capitalism.[98] This obviously prompts the search for political interests being pursued in a theory of the firm as a self-referential system. The systemic approach formally takes its distance from the models of financial, managerial, labor and state capitalism. At most it could be said that it is pursuing the interests of an organizational capitalism. Or rather more seriously, a theory of the firm as a self-reproducing social system may suggest a legal policy of "enterprise corporatism."

This cautious formulation should ward off too much 'dietrologia' in advance. It would be rather unreasonable to maintain that neo-corporatism is the political consequence of the theory of self-referential systems.[99] For there are many versions of systems theory—"emancipatory," "technocratic," and "evolutionary." And the systems theory analyses of enterprise, collectivity and legal person attempted above still claim to be correct even if enterprise corporatism should prove to be a legal policy failure.

All the same, there is a link between systems theory analyses and legal policy recommendations, albeit a much looser one than the suspicion of a "suitable ideology" supposes. On the one hand a theoretical apparatus always perceives reality only selectively (for instance, a systems theoretician sees only elements, structures and processes, where other observers see flesh-and-blood people acting) and correspondingly makes legal policy recommendations directed only to this selected reality. Secondly, systems theory asserts quite specific evolutionary trends which only when formulated can be influenced through legal policy intervention. In economic enterprises a trend can be observed to the autonomization of an impersonal economic complex of action, consisting of the differentiation of the corporate actor with a sharp demarcation between those involved internally and externally. This trend is perceived as collectivization of an autopoietic social system. One may seek to combat this trend in legal policy through such concepts as shareholders' democracy, codetermination or government participation, or else one may see the autonomization of the organization as a promising development in the interest of society as a whole in guaranteeing need satisfaction for the future, following a direction that the law can to some extent help to influence.[100] The name for that direction is enterprise corporatism.

Neo-corporatist strategies are not in vogue at present. On the

98. Flume, supra n. 19 at 37ff.; Horwitz, supra n.3 at 183.

99. Or—to exhaust the whole of the political spectrum—neo-Liberalism or neo-Conservatism, see, e.g., Bercusson, "Juridification and Disorder," in Teubner, *Juridification of Social Spheres* 55ff. (1987); Nahamowitz, "Difficulties with Economic Law," in Teubner, supra n. 63.

100. Teubner, supra n. 5.

contrary, in a period of extremely rapid market changes, increased pressure of competition and weakening or collapse of governmental regulatory systems, industrial strategies are being pursued for which neo-corporatist arrangements appear rigid, centralist and immobile.[101] The new slogan is decentralization and flexibility through contractual arrangements, and this applies also to methods of finance, technologies, product range, customer relations, and labor relations.[102] The aim of recent industrial policy is flexibility as a value in itself: "a general capacity of enterprises to reorganize in close response to fluctuations in their environment."[103]

While flexibility through contract is the prevailing demand at the moment, there is also an alternative put forward in the heated debate on "Americanization" or "Japanization" of the European economy: flexibility through organization.[104] Its defenders can point out that flexibility can be brought about not only through contractual arrangements but also through decentralization of organization, and that a policy based on organization can additionally use the productivity advantages of a "producers' coalition" (capital, management, labor, state), which in the conditions of the new industrial divide are becoming increasingly necessary.

This industrial policy position is close to the ideas developed here. In fact, to privilege one group, whether shareholders or management, that acquires flexibility through contractual arrangements would be bound to be sub-optimal in the interest of the corporate actor. Certainly, the advantage of contractual arrangements lies in the speed of reactions with which action systems can be built up and demolished in the short term, in accordance with the fluctuations of environmental pressures. The drawback, however, is that contractual solutions cannot exhaust the "organizational surplus value."[105] "Organizational surplus value" arises (1) through the building up of long-term cooperative arrangements which would be continually destroyed by contractual flexibility; (2) through the diffuseness of "commitments" in the organization which by comparison with rigid, sharply defined contractual obligations produce more situational flexibility; and finally (3) in the orientation towards the organiza-

101. A realistic assessment can be found in Simitis, "Jusification of Labor Relations," in Teubner, *Juridification of Social Spheres* 113ff. 134ff. (1987); see Dittrich, *Mitbestimmung—eine korporatistische Strategie*? (1975).

102. Cf. Piore & Sabel, supra n. 1; Strauss, supra n. 6; Willman, *The Implications of Process and Product Innovations for Labor Relations* (1985).

103. Streeck, supra n. 1, at 11.

104. Gutchess, *Employment Security in Action: Strategies that Work* (1985); Streeck, supra n. 1 at 18ff., 27ff.

105. A stimulating comparison between contractual and organizational solutions to the flexibility problem can be found in Streeck, supra n. 1 at 14ff. On this, cf. the "classical" formulation in Selznick, supra n. 30 at 54 ff.

tion's interest, which provides stronger orientation than mere linkage to a contractual purpose.

This suggests a law of corporate governance based on a microcorporatist producers' coalition. According to this, none of the resource providers, neither the factor of capital, nor that of labor, nor that of management, nor indeed the factor of state control, has any natural claim to "sovereignty over the association." In principle, the connection between resource provision and control rights is loosened, and all control rights over all resources are assigned to the corporate actor as such. The idea of "organizationally bound property rights"[106] is diametrically opposed to the idea that the firm constitutes a mere "contractual network." The distribution of control rights within the firm is then made neither according to the primacy of one resource interest nor according to exchange logic in a contractual network, but according to efficiency considerations oriented towards the interest of the "corporate actor," which is different from all of the participating interests.

Even if the external integration effects and internal motivation effects of microcorporatist arrangements are recognized, still the external disadvantages of producers' coalitions have to be pointed out, especially the fact that they may arrive at their agreements at the expense of third parties and even of the public interest.[107] Here is the real weak point of enterprise corporatism in the sense of a producers' coalition. However, the "corporate actor," the existence of which is asserted against all methodological individualism, steps in to set the legal policy direction. Efforts should concentrate on the institutional strengthening of the corporate actor and the autonomization of an impersonal complex of action which imposes effective constraints on action upon the individual interests involved in the interest of the organization defined in terms of society as a whole.

106. Krause, "From Old to New Monism: An Approach to an Economic Theory of the Constitution of the Firm," in Daintith & Teubner, *Contract and Organisation* 219ff., 225 (1986).

107. Cf. the interpretation of the empirical material in Hopt, "New Ways of Corporate Governance," 82 *Mich. L. Rev.* 1338 (1984); Streeck, "Co-determination: The Fourth Decade," *International Yearbook of Organizational Democracy* (1984); Krause, "Mitbestimmung und Effizienz," 23 *Sociologica Internationalis* 148 ff. (1985); Teubner, "Industrial Democracy Through Law?," in Daintith & Teubner, *Contract and Organisation*, supra n. 106 at 261 ff., 268 ff.

[2]

Limited Liability and the Corporation

Frank H. Easterbrook†
Daniel R. Fischel††

Limited liability is a fundamental principle of corporate law. Yet liability has never been absolutely limited. Courts occasionally allow creditors to "pierce the corporate veil," which means that shareholders must satisfy creditors' claims. "Piercing" seems to happen freakishly. Like lightning, it is rare, severe, and unprincipled. There is a consensus that the whole area of limited liability, and conversely of piercing the corporate veil, is among the most confusing in corporate law.[1]

We argue to the contrary that economic analysis—in particular the theory of the firm and the economics of insurance—explains the legal treatment of limited liability. Both the rules and the exceptions serve valuable functions.

I. Introduction

It may be helpful to recall what limited liability is. The liability of "the corporation" is limited by the fact that the corporation is not real. It is no more than a name for a complex set of contracts among managers, workers, and contributors of capital. It has no existence independent of these relations. The rule of limited liabil-

† Judge, United States Court of Appeals for the Seventh Circuit; Lee and Brena Freeman Professor of Law, University of Chicago.

†† Professor of Law, University of Chicago. We thank Douglas G. Baird, Walter J. Blum, William M. Landes, Bernard D. Meltzer, A. Mitchell Polinsky, Richard A. Posner, Steven Shavell, and George J. Stigler for helpful comments on earlier drafts. The Law and Economics Program of the University of Chicago Law School provided support for the research and writing of this paper. The paper is part of an ongoing project that should appear under the title The Economic Structure of Corporate Law.

[1] One commentator described the legal analysis as

> jurisprudence by metaphor or epithet. It does not contribute to legal understanding because it is an intellectual construct, divorced from business realities. The metaphors are no more than conclusory terms, affording little understanding of the considerations and policies underlying the court's actions and little help in predicting results in future cases . . . . As a result, we are faced with hundreds of decisions that are irreconcilable and not entirely comprehensible. Few areas of the law have been so sharply criticized by commentators.

Phillip Blumberg, The Law of Corporate Groups: Procedural Problems in the Law of Parent and Subsidiary Corporations 8 (1983) (footnote omitted).

ity means that the investors in the corporation are not liable for more than the amount they invest. A person who pays $100 for stock risks that $100, but no more. A person why buys a bond for $100 or sells goods to the firm for $100 on credit risks $100, but no more. The managers and the other workers are not vicariously liable for the firm's deeds. No one risks more than he invests.

Limited liability is not unique to corporations. Indeed it is the rule. Suppose a bank lends $100 to a partnership, and the partnership's liabilities later greatly exceed its assets. (Perhaps the partnership buries toxic waste and incurs stupendous costs of cleaning up the mess.) The bank may lose the $100, but it will not be required to contribute any additional capital. Its liability is limited to its investment, exactly as the shareholder's liability is limited in a corporation.

The instances of "unlimited" liability are few. The general partners of a partnership may be required to contribute additional capital to satisfy the association's debts. Even here, though, a discharge in bankruptcy enables the partner to limit his liability to the assets he possesses at the time the partnership requires more capital. Limitations on liability turn out to be pervasive.

In order to understand these limitations on further contributions of capital, it is necessary to ask two questions. First, why are the contributions of investors *ever* limited? Why do equity and debt investors risk no more than the amount of their investments? Second, why is risk sometimes shifted among the investors? The equity investors in a corporation lose their investments before the debt investors do. Debt consequently is less risky. Why is this beneficial? And if the reallocation of some risk is beneficial, why aren't there gains from greater reallocations, such as requiring equity investors to chip in additional capital, thus reducing the debt investors' risk even further?

In addressing these questions, we do not write on a clean slate. Henry Manne, in an important contribution, argues that the modern publicly held corporation with many small shareholders could not exist without limited liability.[2] If investors could be required to supply unlimited amounts of additional capital, wealthy people would be reluctant to make small investments. Every share of stock would place all of their personal assets at risk. To guard against this risk, the investor would reduce the number of different firms he holds and monitor each more closely.

---

[2] Manne, *Our Two Corporation Systems: Law and Economics*, 53 VA. L. REV. 259 (1967).

Manne's insight is powerful but incomplete. Limited liability does not eliminate the risk of business failure but rather shifts some of the risk to creditors. The creditors can invest in T-bills and other riskless securities, and they will not make risky investments in firms unless offered more interest, which comes out of the shareholders' returns. Why are the increased returns demanded by creditors not exactly offset by the lower returns paid to shareholders? Manne's analysis does not explain why creditors bear as much risk as they do.

There are several reasons why the value of the firm might be maximized if creditors bear a substantial portion of the risk of business failure. Richard Posner maintains that creditors might be appropriate risk bearers because they are less risk averse than stockholders or have superior information.[3] We find this implausible. Creditors are generally more risk averse than stockholders; why else do creditors arrange for the equity claimants to bear the most risk? Creditors accept a lower rate of return on investment precisely because the stockholders are wiped out first. The variance of stockholders' returns is greater; they take the most risk and reap the gains if the firms do well.

The possibility that creditors might be the superior risk bearers because of superior information has considerably more appeal, but it cannot completely explain limited liability. It does not explain, for example, why investors need not contribute more capital to satisfy the claims of involuntary (tort) creditors. Moreover, though creditors may sometimes possess superior information, this will not always be true. To the contrary, we expect creditors to know less. The equity investors have the residual claim. They stand to gain or lose almost the whole value of modest fluctuations in the fortunes of the firm. The residual claimants therefore have incentives to invest in the amount of monitoring likely to produce these gains (or avoid the losses), net of the costs of monitoring.[4] Debt claimants, protected by the "equity cushion," are more likely to be ignorant. They might do more monitoring if debt claims were more concentrated than equity claims, so that there would be less free riding on information, but no data show dramatic differences in the concentration of holdings.

---

[3] Posner, *The Rights of Creditors of Affiliated Corporations*, 43 U. CHI. L. REV. 499 (1976).

[4] *See* Easterbrook & Fischel, *Voting in Corporate Law*, 26 J.L. & ECON. 395, 402-06 (1983); Fama & Jensen, *Agency Problems and Residual Claims*, 26 J.L. & ECON. 327, 331-32 (1983).

Halpern, Trebilcock, and Turnbull have advanced a different explanation for limited liability.[5] Their stimulating article argues that limited liability is necessary for the existence of an organized securities market. If equity investors could be required to contribute additional capital, the value of shares would not be the same to every investor. The greater a particular investor's wealth in relation to that of other investors in the same firm, the higher the probability that the investor's personal wealth would be reached in the event of corporate default. The greater the anticipated cost of this additional capital contribution, the less this investor would be willing to pay for shares. Because different investors would attach different values to shares, depending on the investors' wealth, it would be impossible to conduct an organized liquid market. Limited liability makes markets possible.

The relation between limited liability and organized securities markets is fundamental to an understanding of the rule of limited liability, but it is not a complete explanation. Indeed in one sense it merely restates the question. Why is it important for the residual claimants of one kind of firm (publicly held corporations) to have access to organized securities markets while residual claimants of other firms (partnerships, close corporations, cooperatives, and so forth) do not? A complete explanation of limited liability must answer this question. A related point is that organized securities markets provide benefits that cannot be completely appropriated by the participants. Unless investors in a firm can capture private benefits exceeding the private costs, they will not incur these costs. An understanding of why some firms but not others incur the costs of participation in an organized securities market sheds much light on the rationale of limited liability.

Finally, why could markets with unlimited liability not be organized in ways that would prevent wealth from making a difference? Firms could obtain insurance for the investors, or the actual investments could be made by clearing houses or other intermediaries with constant wealth. Investors in futures markets regularly put at risk more than their initial investments, but guarantees issued by brokers and clearing houses permit the operation of liquid markets. An explanation of limited liability must establish why we do not see risk shifting or guarantees of this sort among investors in corporations.

We provide an explanation for why limited liability facilitates

---

[5] Halpern, Trebilcock & Turnbull, *An Economic Analysis of Limited Liability in Corporation Law*, 30 U. TORONTO L.J. 117 (1980).

the corporate form of organization. We show in Part II that the distinctive aspects of the publicly held corporation—delegation of management to a diverse group of agents and risk bearing by those who contribute capital—depend on an institution like limited liability. We also argue that (voluntary) creditors as well as stockholders benefit from a rule of limited liability. If limited liability were not provided by law, firms would attempt to create it by contract. The legal rule enables firms to obtain the benefits of limited liability at lower cost.

In Part III we discuss the perennial question whether limited liability allows stockholders to transfer the risk of business failure to creditors. Although the existence of involuntary creditors ensures the existence of uncompensated risk, its magnitude is minimized by firms' incentives to insure. We discuss why firms might choose to insure and why it is not worthwhile for them to insure completely. We analyze in Part IV the rules for piercing the corporate veil. We argue that the various formulations that have been advanced by courts can be understood, at least roughly, as attempts to balance the benefits of limited liability against the costs associated with excessive risk taking. Finally, we consider in Part V a variety of other legal doctrines that are or could be used to reduce the probability of uncompensated risk transfers.

II. The Rationale of Limited Liability

We begin this section with a discussion of the relation between the theory of the firm and limited liability. We then analyze the effect of limited liability on firms' cost of capital.

A. Limited Liability and the Theory of the Firm

People can conduct economic activity in many forms. Those who perceive entrepreneurial opportunities must decide whether to organize a sole proprietorship, general or limited partnership, business trust, close or publicly held corporation. Debt investors in all of these ventures possess limited liability. Equity investors in publicly held corporations, limited partnerships, and business trusts do too. Limited liability for equity investors has long been explained as a benefit bestowed on investors by the state. It is much more accurately analyzed as a logical consequence of the differences among the forms for conducting economic activity.

Publicly held corporations typically dominate other organizational forms when the technology of production requires firms to combine both the specialized skills of multiple agents and large amounts of capital.[6] The publicly held corporation facilitates the division of labor. The distinct functions of managerial skills and the provision of capital (and the bearing of risk) may be separated and assigned to different people—workers who lack capital, and owners of funds who lack specialized production skills. Those who invest capital can bear additional risk, because each investor is free to participate in many ventures. The holder of a diversified portfolio of investments is more willing to bear the risk that a small fraction of his investments will not pan out.

Of course this separation of functions is not costless. The separation of investment and management requires firms to create devices by which these participants monitor each other and guarantee their own performance. Neither group will be perfectly trustworthy. Moreover, managers who do not obtain the full benefits of their own performance do not have the best incentives to work efficiently. The costs of the separation of investment and management (agency costs) may be substantial. Nonetheless, we know from the survival of large corporations that the costs generated by agency relations are outweighed by the gains from separation and specialization of function. Limited liability reduces the costs of this separation and specialization.[7]

First, limited liability decreases the need to monitor. All investors risk losing wealth because of the actions of agents. They could monitor these agents more closely. The more risk they bear, the more they will monitor. But beyond a point more monitoring is not worth the cost. Moreover, specialized risk bearing implies that many investors will have diversified holdings. Only a small portion of their wealth will be invested in any one firm. These diversified investors have neither the expertise nor the incentive to monitor the actions of specialized agents. Limited liability makes diversification and passivity a more rational strategy and so potentially reduces the cost of operating the corporation.

Of course, rational shareholders understand the risk that the managers' acts will cause them loss. They do not meekly accept it. The price they are willing to pay for shares will reflect the risk. Managers therefore find ways to offer assurances to investors with-

[6] For a fuller analysis, see Fama, *Agency Problems and the Theory of the Firm*, 88 J. Pol. Econ. 288 (1980); Fama & Jensen, *supra* note 4; Fama & Jensen, *Separation of Ownership and Control*, 26 J.L. & Econ. 301 (1983).

[7] Firms develop a large number of other devices that reduce the costs of the agency relation. *See generally* Agency: The Structure of Business (J. Pratt & R. Zeckhauser eds. forthcoming); Easterbrook, *Managers' Discretion and Investors' Welfare: Theories and Evidence*, Del. J. Corp. L. (forthcoming).

out the need for direct monitoring; those who do this best will attract the most capital from investors. Managers who do not implement effective controls increase the discount. As it grows, so does the investors' incentive to incur costs to reduce the divergence of interest between specialized managers and risk bearers.[8] Limited liability reduces these costs. Because investors' potential losses are "limited" to the amount of their investment as opposed to their entire wealth, they spend less to protect their positions.

Second, limited liability reduces the costs of monitoring other shareholders.[9] Under a rule exposing equity investors to additional liability, the greater the wealth of other shareholders, the lower the probability that any one shareholder's assets will be needed to pay a judgment. Thus existing shareholders would have incentives to engage in costly monitoring of other shareholders to ensure that they do not transfer assets to others or sell to others with less wealth. Limited liability makes the identity of other shareholders irrelevant and thus avoids these costs.

Third, by promoting free transfer of shares, limited liability gives managers incentives to act efficiently. We have emphasized that individual shareholders lack the expertise and incentive to monitor the actions of specialized agents. Investors individually respond to excessive agency costs by disinvesting. Of course, the price at which shareholders are able to sell reflects the value of the firm as affected by decisions of specialized agents. But the ability of individual investors to sell creates new opportunities for investors as a group and thus constrains agents' actions. So long as shares are tied to votes, poorly run firms will attract new investors who can assemble large blocs at a discount and install new managerial teams.[10] This potential for displacement gives existing managers incentives to operate efficiently in order to keep share prices high.

Although this effect of the takeover mechanism is well known, the relation between takeovers and limited liability is not. Limited liability reduces the costs of purchasing shares. Under a rule of limited liability, the value of shares is determined by the present value of the income stream generated by a firm's assets. The iden-

---

[8] *See* Jensen & Meckling, *Theory of the Firm: Managerial Behavior, Agency Costs and Ownership Structure*, 3 J. FIN. ECON. 305, 313 (1976).

[9] *See* Halpern, Trebilcock & Turnbull, *supra* note 5.

[10] *See* Easterbrook & Fischel, *supra* note 4; Easterbrook & Fischel, *Corporate Control Transactions*, 91 YALE L.J. 698 (1982); Manne, *Mergers and the Market for Corporate Control*, 73 J. POL. ECON. 110 (1965).

tity and wealth of other investors is irrelevant. Shares are fungible; they trade at one price in liquid markets. Under a rule of unlimited liability, as Halpern, Trebilcock, and Turnbull emphasized, shares would not be fungible. Their value would be a function of the present value of future cash flows *and* of the wealth of shareholders. The lack of fungibility would impede their acquisition. An acquiror who wanted to purchase a control bloc of shares under a rule of unlimited liability might have to negotiate separately with individual shareholders, paying different prices to each. Worse, the acquiror in corporate control transactions typically is much wealthier than the investors from which it acquires the shares. The anticipated cost of additional capital contributions would be higher to the new holder than the old ones. This may be quite important to a buyer considering the acquisition of a firm in financial trouble, for there would be a decent chance of being required to contribute to satisfy debts if the plan for revitalization of the firm should go awry. Limited liability allows a person to buy a large bloc without taking any risk of being surcharged, and thus it facilitates beneficial control transactions. A rule that facilitates transfers of control also induces managers to work more effectively to stave off such transfers, and so it reduces the costs of specialization whether or not a firm is acquired.

Fourth, limited liability makes it possible for market prices to impound additional information about the value of firms. With unlimited liability, shares would not be homogeneous commodities, so they would no longer have one market price. Investors would therefore be required to expend greater resources analyzing the prospects of the firm in order to know whether "the price is right." When all can trade on the same terms, though, investors trade until the price of shares reflects the available information about a firm's prospects. Most investors need not expend resources on search; they can accept the market price as given and purchase at a "fair" price.[11]

Fifth, as Henry Manne emphasized, limited liability allows more efficient diversification. Investors can minimize risk by owning a diversified portfolio of assets. Firms can raise capital at lower costs because investors need not bear the special risk associated with nondiversified holdings. This is true, though, only under a

---

[11] *See* J. Lorie & M. Hamilton, The Stock Market: Theories and Evidence (1973); Fischel, *Use of Modern Finance Theory in Securities Fraud Cases Involving Actively Traded Securities*, 38 Bus. Law. 1 (1982); Gilson & Kraakman, *The Mechanisms of Market Efficiency*, 70 Va. L. Rev. 549 (1984).

rule of limited liability or some good substitute. Diversification would increase rather than reduce risk under a rule of unlimited liability. If any one firm went bankrupt, an investor could lose his entire wealth. The rational strategy under unlimited liability, therefore, would be to minimize the number of securities held. As a result, investors would be forced to bear risk that could have been avoided by diversification, and the cost to firms of raising capital would rise.

Sixth, limited liability facilitates optimal investment decisions. When investors hold diversified portfolios, managers maximize investors' welfare by investing in any project with a positive net present value. They can accept high-variance ventures (such as the development of new products) without exposing the investors to ruin. Each investor can hedge against the failure of one project by holding stock in other firms. In a world of unlimited liability, though, managers would behave differently. They would reject as "too risky" some projects with positive net present values. Investors would want them to do this because it would be the best way to reduce risks.[12] By definition this would be a social loss, because projects with a positive net present value are beneficial uses of capital.

Both those who want to raise capital for entrepreneurial ventures, and society as a whole, receive benefits from limited liability. The equity investors will do about as well under one rule of liability as another. Every investor must choose between riskless T-bills and riskier investments. The more risk comes with an equity investment, the less the investor will pay. Investors bid down the price of equity until, at the margin, the risk-adjusted returns of stock and T-bills are the same. So long as the rule of liability is known, investors will price shares accordingly.[13] The choice of an inefficient rule, however, will shrink the pool of funds available for investment in projects that would subject investors to risk. The increased availability of funds for projects with positive net values is the real benefit of limited liability.

[12] In the jargon of portfolio theory, when investors are or can be diversified, managers should consider only systematic risk in making decisions. When investors cannot diversify their holdings, managers should consider both systematic and unsystematic risk. The consideration of unsystematic risk may lead them to forgo profitable investments.

[13] This is an implication of the Coase Theorem. Coase, *The Problem of Social Cost*, 3 J.L. & ECON. 1 (1960).

B. Limited Liability and Firms' Cost of Capital

Limited liability does not eliminate the risk of business failure. Someone must bear that loss. Limited liability is an arrangement under which the loss largely lies where it falls. Loss is swallowed rather than shifted. Each investor has a guaranteed maximum on the loss he will bear. In a firm with debt, that guaranteed maximum is combined with a preference for the debtholder. The shareholder is wiped out first. To this extent risk is "shifted" from debt investor to equity investor. In a regime of unlimited liability still more risk would be shifted.

Because someone must bear the entire risk of business failure under any rule, some have argued that the importance of limited liability has been exaggerated.[14] The benefit to stockholders from limited liability, the argument runs, is exactly offset by the detriment to creditors. Stockholders are more secure and so demand a lower rate of return under limited liability, but creditors demand a higher rate; the opposite is true under unlimited liability. The firm's cost of capital, the argument continues, is the same under either rule. (We postpone to Part III the question of tort creditors, who are not compensated for bearing risks.)

The validity of this argument depends on whether the risk that the value of the firm will be less than the value of the creditors' claims can be borne equally well by creditors and stockholders. Several factors are pertinent to this question: the extent of common interests, relative monitoring costs, relative information and coordination costs, and attitudes toward risk.

1. *The Extent of Common Interests.* The argument that firms' cost of capital does not vary with the liability rule depends on the assumption that the benefit to stockholders from limited liability is exactly offset by the detriment to creditors. This assumption is false, for the reasons developed in Part II-A.

Consider the relation between limited liability and takeover bids. Takeovers are beneficial for shareholders—takeovers are a mechanism for transferring assets to higher-valued uses, and even the threat of takeover provides managers with an incentive to operate efficiently and keep share prices high. The effect of takeovers on creditors is less clear. Managers who pursue an overly conservative investment strategy that benefits creditors but does not maxi-

---

[14] Ekelund & Tollison, *Mercantilist Origins of the Corporation*, 11 Bell J. Econ. 715 (1980); Meiners, Mofsky & Tollison, *Piercing the Veil of Limited Liability*, 4 Del. J. Corp. L. 351 (1979).

mize the value of the firm, for example, may be ousted in a takeover. Thus some takeovers may cause creditors to be worse off ex post. But so long as takeovers increase the probability that the value of firms' assets will be maximized, shareholders and creditors, joint claimants on a bigger pie, will be better off. Thus a regime including takeovers benefits creditors as well as shareholders.[15] The other effects are straightforward, too. The capital market is more likely to be efficient under a rule of limited liability. An efficient capital market generates price signals that are useful to all investors in a firm, including creditors. Limited liability decreases the cost of searching for good investments for creditors as well as stockholders.

2. *Relative Monitoring Costs.* Shareholders have less reason to incur costs in monitoring managers and other shareholders under limited than under unlimited liability. The decreased incentive to monitor managers is arguably offset by the increased incentive of creditors to monitor managers' actions. But this will not happen because of the preference among the investors. Because equity investors lose their investments first, they will have a greater interest in monitoring the firm. Indeed, this intra-investor preference is an important ingredient in a system of optimal monitoring. Concentrating the entire marginal gain and loss on one group of investors induces them to make the appropriate expenditures on monitoring (or to sell to someone who will), while enabling the more secure investors to avoid making redundant expenditures. The secured creditor has the safest claim of all and may elect to monitor only the state of its security rather than the state of the whole firm. Secured debt thus may be a way of reducing monitoring costs still further.[16]

So debt claimants do not increase their monitoring of managers to offset shareholders' reductions exactly. Moreover, debt investors do not incur costs that offset the reduction of intra-shareholder monitoring under limited liability. The wealth of other creditors is irrelevant whether or not shareholders possess limited liability, because creditors possess limited liability under either rule. Thus monitoring costs are lower when both shareholders and

---

[15] The available evidence suggests that shareholders gain and creditors do not lose in control transactions. Asquith & Kim, *The Impact of Merger Bids on the Participating Firms' Security Holders*, 37 J. FIN. 1209 (1982).

[16] This argument avoids the critique Alan Schwartz offers of previous efforts to explain secured debt. *Compare* Schwartz, *The Continuing Puzzle of Secured Debt*, 37 VAND. L. REV. 1051, 1055-59 (1984), *with* Levmore, *Monitors and Freeriders in Commercial and Corporate Settings*, 92 YALE L.J. 49, 55-59 (1982).

creditors possess limited liability than when only creditors do.

3. *Relative Information and Coordination Costs.* Another reason why shareholders pay creditors to assume more of the risk of business failure might be that the creditors possess a comparative advantage in monitoring particular managerial actions. As we have stressed, individual shareholders, specialized suppliers of capital, do not actively monitor managers' actions. They rely on third parties (such as large institutional holders or prospective contestants for control) to do so and buy shares at appropriate moments. Though the debt investors do not have the residual claim, and thus do not have optimal incentives to monitor day-to-day activities, they may be especially well suited to watch certain kinds of conduct.

Banks and other institutional investors tend to have specialized knowledge about particular industries and may be good monitors of major decisions such as building new plants. The lender may provide financing to several firms in an industry and thus augment its knowledge. These debt investors commonly negotiate detailed contracts giving them the right to disapprove managers' decisions that are important enough to create significant new risk for the firm, though perhaps not important enough to spark a contest for control.

An investor's possession of particular information does not, however, explain why an investment takes the form of debt rather than equity. Lower coordination costs might explain debt financing. Compare the situation of a sophisticated shareholder with a sophisticated creditor (or the indenture trustee for a group of creditors). Even if the sophisticated shareholder has the ability to monitor, he has little incentive to do so. He bears all the costs, but the benefits accrue to all other shareholders according to the size of their holdings. The creditor, by contrast, captures more of the benefits of his monitoring activity, because there are fewer other members of the same class of investor. When there are many creditors of the same class, the indenture trustee is the response to the free-rider problem. Because the costs of monitoring by the trustee are shared by all the bondholders of a particular class, the trustee is not plagued by the same coordination problems facing any individual investor.[17] When creditors have lower coordination and infor-

[17] For a discussion of the role of secured creditors and indenture trustees in overcoming the free-rider problem, see Levmore, *supra* note 16, at 68-73. The introduction of multiple classes of investors creates problems of its own, but we do not address them here. *See* Jackson, *Bankruptcy, Non-Bankruptcy Entitlements, and the Creditors' Bargain*, 91 YALE L.J.

mation costs than shareholders, limited liability has a clear advantage. Because creditors bear more of the risk of business failure under a rule of limited liability, they have more incentive to employ their knowledge.

4. *Attitudes Toward Risk.* Both equity and debt investors can diversify their holdings, thus minimizing the risk of investing in any one firm. Economy-wide (systematic) risk, however, cannot be eliminated by diversification. Where two parties are risk averse, the optimal contractual arrangement is one in which each bears some risk.[18] Limited liability is such a risk-sharing arrangement. Under limited liability, both shareholders and creditors risk the loss of their investments; under unlimited liability, shareholders would bear almost all risk. Risk sharing therefore might be a good explanation of limited liability.

C. Insurance as an Alternative to Limited Liability

The advantages of limited liability suggest that, if it did not exist, firms would attempt to invent it. One close substitute is insurance. If firms could purchase insurance to cover their liabilities to debt investors, the firms' structure would be much the same as now.[19] Shareholders' liability would be limited to the amount of their investment; creditors would receive a lower rate of return because of their greater security.

The firm could purchase insurance for investors as a group. (The transaction costs of shareholders individually purchasing insurance would be prohibitive. Each shareholder would have to negotiate with the insurer. The insurer would have to monitor the wealth of the insured and all other shareholders to assess the riskiness of its own position.) The firm could buy its insurance from existing creditors, a separate insurer, or both. It would make a decision based on factors including relative information and coordination costs.

In some circumstances creditors might have a comparative ad-

857 (1982).

[18] For applications of this point, see Marcus, *Risk Sharing and the Theory of the Firm*, 13 Bell J. Econ. 369 (1982); Polinsky, *Risk Sharing through Breach of Contract Remedies*, 12 J. Legal Stud. 427, 433 (1983); Shavell, *Risk Sharing and Incentives in the Principal-Agent Relationship*, 10 Bell J. Econ. 55, 65 (1979).

[19] Halpern, Trebilcock & Turnbull, *supra* note 5, at 138-45, also analyze the combination of unlimited liability and insurance as an alternative to limited liability. Their perspective is somewhat different from ours. We are more optimistic than they that insurance markets could exist in a world of unlimited liability. Indeed, as we discuss below, corporations obtain insurance despite the existence of limited liability.

vantage in assessing the riskiness of a transaction initially and superior ability to monitor the conduct of the firm for the duration of the agreement. In that event, the firm would buy its insurance from the creditors. This is essentially what we observe. The creditors assume some risks of business failure, just as they would if they were "insurers" as well as creditors. The legal rule of limited liability is a shortcut to this position, avoiding the costs of separate transactions.[20]

One advantage of purchasing insurance from separate insurers is that some of the free-rider problems that face groups of creditors are avoided. Third-party insurers might have superior ability to monitor. Firms obtain insurance from the cheapest insurer regardless of the legal rule. Corporations commonly purchase insurance despite the existence of limited liability.[21] But if third-party insurers frequently had a comparative advantage in bearing risk, we would expect to see corporate "debt insurance" commonly used. The debt investors would pay the firm to secure such insurance, receiving lower risk in return. We do not see such transactions.

In light of the ability of firms to duplicate or at least approximate either limited or unlimited liability by contract, does the legal rule of limited liability matter? The answer is yes, but probably not much.[22] Under the plausible assumption that creditors often are the most efficient risk bearers, a rule of limited liability economizes on transaction costs by eliminating the need for individual negotiations with every creditor. By contrast, limited liability will not cause a corresponding increase in the number of transactions with third-party insurers. Such transactions will occur whenever third parties are the cheapest insurers, no matter what the legal rule.

Limited liability also makes a difference if the firm would purchase inadequate insurance or insurance would not be available in a competitive market. It is hard to imagine, for example, a market for insurance against all bankruptcy. Bankruptcies may be

---

[20] Sometimes it would be too costly to strike such separate deals. Involuntary creditors who are victims of torts can hardly negotiate with the firm in advance. Even here, however, the benefits of limited liability could be retained if firms insured against expected liabilities from tort claims. (We discuss in Part III whether tort creditors should stand in a different position from voluntary creditors.)

[21] *See* Mayers & Smith, *On the Corporate Demand for Insurance*, 55 J. Bus. 281 (1982) (discussing a variety of incentives for corporations to purchase insurance).

[22] This conclusion depends on the existence of well-developed insurance markets. We do not doubt that limited liability played a crucial role in the growth of the publicly held corporation in the nineteenth century when insurance markets were much less well developed.

caused by economy-wide events against which the insurer cannot diversify. Moreover, complete bankruptcy insurance creates a moral hazard: it invites managers to take excessive risks. Both equity and debt investors would stop monitoring the managers, and insurers are not likely to provide optimal monitoring in the face of this moral hazard.

Without complete bankruptcy insurance, some group must bear the risk of business failure. If shareholders bear all the risk, the problems of unlimited liability reappear; if creditors share some of this risk, the situation is identical to the rule of limited liability.

The bankruptcy example illustrates a more general problem with insurance as an alternative to limited liability—who will insure the insurer? If insurers assume the risk of business failure, unpaid claims of the insured firms could exceed the capital of the insurer. This risk must be borne by someone. Shareholders of insurance companies might have unlimited liability, but this could inhibit the formation of large insurers, thus exacerbating the problem. Alternatively, both shareholders and creditors of the insured firm could bear the risk, and the same analysis would govern whether limited or unlimited liability is the superior institutional arrangement.

In sum, the problem all along has been: is it better to allow losses to lie where they fall, or to try to shift those losses to some other risk bearer? This is an empirical question. The market's answer is partial risk shifting. The equity investors bear more risk than the debt investors, but debt investors continue to bear substantial risk, and the risk of all investors is limited to the amount they sink at the start. This arrangement appears to have substantial survival value, for reasons we have discussed. If greater risk shifting were beneficial, we should have seen it evolve in the market. It is no answer to say that transaction costs are high, so the evidence from survival is ambiguous. It is easy to make contracts governing stockholders' liability. Lenders to close corporations commonly require personal guarantees by investors or other modifications of limited liability. We discuss in Part IV why they do so. For now the point is that if people frequently contract around limited liability for the smallest firms, it is impossible to attribute the failure to do likewise for larger firms to transaction costs. The survival of limited liability is indeed highly informative.

III. Limited Liability and the Externalization of Risk

Because limited liability increases the probability that there will be insufficient assets to pay creditors' claims, shareholders of a firm reap all of the benefits of risky activities but do not bear all of the costs. These are borne in part by creditors. Critics of limited liability have focused on this moral hazard—the incentive created by limited liability to transfer the cost of risky activities to creditors—as a justification for substantial modification of the doctrine.[23]

Externalization of risk imposes social costs and thus is undesirable. The implications of this point, however, are unclear, both because modifying limited liability has its costs and because moral hazard would exist without limited liability. The social loss from reducing investment in certain types of projects—a consequence of seriously modifying limited liability—might far exceed the gains from reducing moral hazard. Too, even the abolition of limited liability would not eliminate the moral-hazard problem. The incentive to engage in overly risky activities is a general phenomenon that exists whenever a person or firm has insufficient assets to cover its expected liabilities.[24] Although the problem of moral hazard may be more severe under limited liability, it will exist under any rule. As we have stressed, the magnitude of these gains and losses is an empirical matter on which the dominance of limited liability—when it is simple to pass greater risks to equity investors by contract—speaks eloquently.

At all events, the magnitude of the externality under limited liability has been exaggerated. As Richard Posner has demonstrated, there is no externality with respect to voluntary creditors.[25] In addition, firms have incentives to insure for amounts greater than their existing capital. The insurance company becomes a contract creditor, reducing the externality. We discuss these points below.

A. Limited Liability and Voluntary Creditors

Employees, consumers, trade creditors, and lenders are voluntary creditors. The compensation they demand will be a function of the risk they face. One risk is the possibility of nonpayment be-

---

[23] *See, e.g.*, Landers, *A Unified Approach to Parent, Subsidiary, and Affiliate Questions in Bankruptcy*, 42 U. CHI. L. REV. 589 (1975); Stone, *The Place of Enterprise Liability in the Control of Corporate Conduct*, 90 YALE L.J. 1, 65-76 (1980).

[24] *See* Keeton & Kwerel, *Externalities in Automobile Insurance and the Uninsured Driver Problem*, 27 J.L. & ECON. 149 (1984); Shavell, *Liability for Harm versus Regulation of Safety*, 13 J. LEGAL STUD. 357 (1984); Steven Shavell, The Judgment Proof Problem (1984) (unpublished manuscript on file with *The University of Chicago Law Review*).

[25] Posner, *supra* note 3, at 503.

cause of limited liability. Another is the prospect, common to all debtor-creditor relations, that after the terms of the transaction are set the debtor will take increased risk, to the detriment of the lender.

So long as these risks are known, the firm pays for the freedom to engage in risky activities. Any creditor can get the risk-free rate by investing in T-bills or some low-risk substitute. The firm must offer a better risk-return combination to attract investment. If it cannot make credible promises to refrain from taking excessive risks, it must pay higher interest rates (or, when the creditors are employees and trade creditors, higher prices for the work or goods delivered on credit). There is no "externality." Voluntary creditors receive compensation in advance for the risk that the firm will be unable to meet its obligations.

Equity investors and managers have incentives to make arrangements that reduce risk and thus reduce the premium they must pay to debt claimants. Bond indentures, which commonly contain detailed provisions limiting the ability of the firm to engage in conduct to the detriment of creditors, are one method of reducing this premium.[26] If the compensation that must be paid to third parties for engaging in a particular activity exceeds the benefits to the firm, the activity will not be undertaken under a rule of either limited or unlimited liability.[27] This is a simple application of the Coase Theorem. The optimal amount of risk is not zero, though. Managers will take steps to reduce risk only so long as the gains from risk reduction exceed the costs.

The incentive to take optimal precautions against increases in risk does not depend on all voluntary creditors having perfect information. In certain cases, the actions of informed actors will result in the appropriate risk premium being charged. For example, risks created by a firm's activities may be understood by an indenture trustee or a union even if not by individual bondholders or workers. If the risk premium is correctly set, it is irrelevant whether each voluntary creditor is informed. Each is protected by the market price.[28] And so long as the firm must pay the correct

[26] *See* Smith & Warner, *On Financial Contracting: An Analysis of Bond Covenants*, 7 J. Fin. Econ. 117 (1979). Legal rules also reduce the premium that is paid to debt claimants. The legal capital rules, for example, limit the ability of equity holders to withdraw capital from the firm and thereby decrease the pool of assets that creditors can reach. These rules are beneficial because they decrease the cost of writing contracts.

[27] A. Mitchell Polinsky, An Introduction to Law and Economics 95-102 (1983).

[28] For various applications of this point, see Easterbrook & Fischel, *Mandatory Disclosure and the Protection of Investors*, 70 Va. L. Rev. 669, 693-94 (1984) (discussing securities

risk premium, it has no incentive to engage in excessively risky conduct.

Sometimes, though, no voluntary creditor will have sufficient information or incentive to assess risk correctly or monitor the actions of the debtor. This might lead voluntary creditors to charge a risk premium that is prohibitively high, because they will equate their inability to monitor with a belief that firms will take much too much risk. It is in precisely these situations, however, that firms have incentives to insure. By contracting with a superior monitor (a more efficient insurer), the firm reduces the risk premium it must pay.[29] The insurer, in turn, may use its superior monitoring ability to induce the firm to internalize the costs of its risky activities.

Our point is not that limited liability will never result in a socially excessive amount of risk taking in situations involving voluntary creditors. Rather, we argue that it is unlikely that any rule will lead to systematically excessive risk taking; indeed, it is unlikely that the legal rule will matter much.

Limited liability's greatest effect is on the probability that any given creditor will be fully paid ex post. Even if firms pay for engaging in risky activities, and thus take the correct precautions, creditors of failed businesses are less likely to receive full compensation under a rule of limited liability. This is not an "argument" against limited liability, however, unless distributional concerns dominate. There is little role for distributional arguments when all of the parties are in privity, for they can strike their own bargains and are apt to contract around any unwelcome rule purportedly designed for their benefit.[30] They can readjust the risk. More to the point, they can simply choose to hold, under any rule, a different proportion of debt and equity, which rearranges the risk. Tax and welfare policies are likely to be better ways to redistribute wealth than the modification of terms of private contracts. Moreover, the existence of first-party insurance makes distributional concerns much less serious than they might at first appear. The ability of potential victims to protect themselves against loss

---

markets); Fischel, *supra* note 11 (same); Schwartz & Wilde, *Intervening in Markets on the Basis of Imperfect Information: A Legal and Economic Analysis*, 127 U. PA. L. REV. 630 (1979) (discussing markets for consumer goods).

[29] *See* Mayers & Smith, *supra* note 21, at 286.

[30] *See, e.g.*, Baird & Jackson, *Corporate Reorganizations and the Treatment of Diverse Ownership Interests: A Comment on Adequate Protection of Secured Interests in Bankruptcy*, 51 U. CHI. L. REV. 97 (1984); Epstein, *The Social Consequences of Common Law Rules*, 95 HARV. L. REV. 1717 (1982).

through insurance is a strong reason for disregarding distributional concerns in choosing among liability rules.

B. Involuntary Creditors and Corporations' Incentives to Insure

When corporations must pay for the right to engage in risky activities, they will tend to undertake projects only where social benefits equal social costs at the margin. Where high transactions costs prohibit those affected by risky activities from charging an appropriate risk premium, however, the probability that firms with limited liability will undertake projects with an inefficiently high level of risk increases. Firms capture the benefits from such activities while bearing only some of the costs; other costs are shifted to involuntary creditors. This is a real cost of limited liability, but its magnitude is reduced by corporations' incentives to insure.

The common explanation for insurance is risk aversion. A risk-averse person may be willing to pay a known insurance premium to eliminate the possibility of a large, uncertain loss, even though the premium exceeds the expected value of the loss. By pooling unrelated risks, the insurer can diversify. A completely diversified insurer is risk neutral. Insurance enables those who are risk averse to pay risk-neutral parties to bear risk.

Corporate purchase of insurance seems inconsistent with this explanation. Investors can diversify, and this is a cheap way to reduce risk. Limited liability facilitates this diversification. Thus investors should not be willing to pay insurers to reduce risk. Why buy something you already have for free?

But not all who enter into contracts with a firm have the same ability to minimize risk by diversification. Human capital, for example, is notoriously difficult to diversify. Managers who have firm-specific investments of human capital cannot diversify the risk of business failure. To the contrary, investors want managers' fortunes tied to the fate of the firms under their control, and so they induce managers to bear extra costs if these firms fail, and they offer disproportionate rewards for success.[31] The possibility of bankruptcy also represents a real cost to those with firm-specific investments of human capital, and firms must compensate those who bear this risk. The purchase of insurance in amounts greater than the amount of the firm's capital is one method of reducing

[31] *See* Carlton & Fischel, *The Regulation of Insider Trading*, 35 STAN. L. REV. 857, 869-72 (1983); Easterbrook, *supra* note 7.

the amount that the firm must pay.[32] A firm with insurance against tort claims is less likely to become bankrupt, and thus less likely to impose costs on managers and other employees. Insurance thus induces people to make firm-specific investments of human capital.[33]

Whether the purchase of insurance in amounts greater than the size of the firm's capital will reduce the incentive to engage in overly risky activities is a complex question.[34] Before purchasing insurance, the firm's investors have the full amount of their investment at risk. After the purchase, the investors have much less at risk—in the limit, nothing at risk. The insurance company now bears the risk of business failure caused by tortious conduct. Thus the purchase of insurance might be thought to reduce the managers' incentives to take care, incentives already too low because of the existence of limited liability. The purchase of insurance has the effect, however, of creating a contract creditor where none may have existed before. The insured corporation must pay (through higher premiums) for engaging in risky activities. Because the firm will now bear the costs of engaging in risky projects, it will tend to equate social benefits and costs when making investment decisions.

Our argument is not that firms' incentive to purchase insurance eliminates the possibility that firms will engage in excessively risky activities. There may well be situations where firms will decide not to insure even if insurance is available. If potential losses are extremely large, the premium paid to risk-averse managers with firm-specific investments of human capital to compensate them for bearing the risk of bankruptcy might be less than the premium that would have to be paid to the insurance company. In other words, the limited liability of the manager (particularly in a world where discharge in bankruptcy is available) coupled with the limited liability of the firm may cause firms faced with large expected liabilities to involuntary creditors to pay managers a premium and simultaneously decrease their capitalization. Moreover, there is no guarantee that insurance will be offered if risks are

[32] This conclusion would be qualified in a world of perfect information. Corporate bankruptcy is not equivalent to the liquidation of all assets. The bankrupt firm could be reorganized, and the manager with a firm-specific investment rehired. In a world of uncertainty, however, the manager could not be confident that he would be rehired and would thus demand a premium. Even a rehired manager would suffer a loss of reputational capital because of the possibility that his shortcomings caused the failure.

[33] Alan Schwartz has argued that corporate insurance also enables investors in risky industries to ensure that firms will be in existence long enough to enable them to earn a positive return on investment. *See* Schwartz, *Products Liability, Corporate Structure and Bankruptcy: Toxic Substances and the Remote Risk Relationship*, YALE L.J. (forthcoming).

[34] *See* Steven Shavell, *supra* note 24.

highly correlated. Even when offered, the insurance will exclude very large losses. On the other hand, our discussion of firms' incentives to insure suggests that firms will insure in some situations where people and partnerships would not. A corporation with a fleet of trucks might insure for an amount in excess of its capital, for example, while an individual owner with few assets might insure for a small amount or not insure at all.[35]

IV. Piercing the Corporate Veil

Courts have allowed creditors in some situations to reach the assets of shareholders. The justification for this is obscure. State law typically says that limited liability is absolute.[36] Moreover, the nominal tests used by courts—whether a corporation has a "separate mind of its own," whether it is a "mere instrumentality," and so forth—are singularly unhelpful. The arbitrariness of these nominal tests casts further doubt on the utility of the doctrine.

We conclude, however, that the doctrine of piercing the corporate veil, and the distinctions drawn by courts, may make more sense than at first appears. The cases may be understood, at least roughly, as attempts to balance the benefits of limited liability against its costs. Courts are more likely to allow creditors to reach the assets of shareholders where limited liability provides minimal gains from improved liquidity and diversification, while creating a high probability that a firm will engage in a socially excessive level of risk taking. We discuss below the more important aspects of the doctrine.

A. Close Versus Public Corporations

Almost every case in which a court has allowed creditors to reach the assets of shareholders has involved a close corporation.[37] The distinction between close and public corporations is supported

---

[35] *See* Keeton & Kwerel, *supra* note 24, at 154-56.

[36] *See, e.g.*, Del. Code Ann. tit. 8, § 152 (1983) (stock is "fully paid and nonassessable" once paid for in cash); *id.* § 162 (investor's liability on partially paid-for shares is limited to the balance of the agreed-upon consideration); *see also* Model Business Corp. Act § 6.22 (1984) (a stockholder "is not liable to the corporation or its creditors with respect to the shares except to pay the consideration for which such shares were authorized to be issued (section 6.21) or specified in the subscription agreement (section 6.20)").

[37] We say "almost every" only because we have not examined them all. The most famous cases where piercing was an issue all involve close corporations. *See, e.g.*, Minton v. Cavaney, 56 Cal. 2d 576, 364 P.2d 473, 15 Cal. Rptr. 641 (1961); Walkovszky v. Carlton, 18 N.Y.2d 414, 223 N.E.2d 6, 276 N.Y.S.2d 585 (1966); Bartle v. Home Owners Cooperative, Inc., 309 N.Y. 103, 127 N.E.2d 832 (1955).

by economic logic. In close corporations, there is much less separation between management and risk bearing. This has profound implications for the role of limited liability. Because those who supply capital in close corporations typically are also involved in decisionmaking, limited liability does not reduce monitoring costs. Other benefits of limited liability in public corporations—facilitating efficient risk bearing and monitoring by the capital market—also are absent for close corporations. Because those who contribute capital often manage, diversification is much less important in close corporations. Similarly, close corporations restrict the transfer of their shares to ensure that those who invest will be compatible with existing decisionmakers. Takeover bids are impossible; they are not needed because of the lack of separation of the management and risk-bearing functions.

Moreover, the incentive created by limited liability for managers to undertake overly risky projects is much more severe in close corporations. Whatever the liability rule, managers of publicly held corporations do not bear all of the costs of their actions. There are many of them, and each owns but a small fraction of the firm's shares. This is not necessarily true in close corporations. Under a rule of unlimited liability, investor-managers bear all of the costs of their actions. Under a rule of absolutely limited liability, by contrast, investor-managers can limit their risk to the amount of capital in the corporate treasury and transfer more of the risk to third parties.[38] Piercing the veil—especially in favor of trade and tort creditors who cannot negotiate with the firm—reduces the extent to which third parties bear these costs.[39]

B. Corporate Versus Personal Shareholders

The other major category of piercing cases involves parent-subsidiary combinations, where creditors of the subsidiary attempt to reach assets of the parent.[40] Courts' greater willingness to allow

[38] Sometimes the appropriate response to this is a statute requiring the firm to insure. *See* New Jersey v. Ventron Corp., 94 N.J. 473, 468 A.2d 150 (1983) (limited liability protects the shareholders from paying the cost of cleaning up toxic waste, but the investors are directly liable nonetheless under a special antipollution statute); *see also* Ohio v. Kovacs, 105 S. Ct. 705 (1985) (obligation to clean up toxic wastes may be discharged in bankruptcy); Baird & Jackson, Kovacs *and Toxic Wastes in Bankruptcy*, 36 STAN. L. REV. 1199 (1984).

[39] On the other hand, there is no reason to pierce the veil of even a "shell" corporation in favor of a creditor that can negotiate for such protection as it desires. Courts routinely enforce limited liability in such cases. *See, e.g.*, Brunswick Corp. v. Waxman, 599 F.2d 34 (2d Cir. 1979).

[40] *See* Hackney & Bensen, *Shareholder Liability for Inadequate Capital*, 43 U. PITT. L.

creditors to reach the assets of corporate as opposed to personal shareholders is again consistent with economic principles.

Allowing creditors to reach the assets of parent corporations does not create unlimited liability for any people. Thus the benefits of diversification, liquidity, and monitoring by the capital market are unaffected. Moreover, the moral-hazard problem is probably greater in parent-subsidiary situations because subsidiaries have less incentive to insure. In publicly held corporations, the inability of managers to diversify their firm-specific investments in human capital creates incentives to insure. The same is not true for managers of subsidiaries if, as often will be the case, these people are also managers of the parent. Bankruptcy of the subsidiary will not cause them to lose their positions in the parent or suffer any other loss of firm-specific human capital (though it might impose a reputational loss on them). If limited liability is absolute, a parent can form a subsidiary with minimal capitalization for the purpose of engaging in risky activities. If things go well, the parent captures the benefits. If things go poorly, the subsidiary declares bankruptcy, and the parent creates another with the same managers to engage in the same activities. This asymmetry between benefits and costs, if limited liability were absolute, would create incentives to engage in a socially excessive amount of risky activities.

It does not follow that parent and affiliate corporations always should be liable for the debts of those in which they hold stock. Far from it. Such general liability would give unaffiliated firms a competitive advantage. Think of the taxicab business. Taxi firms may incorporate each cab or put just a few cabs in a firm. If courts routinely pierced this arrangement and put the assets of the full venture at risk for the accidents of each cab, then "true" single-cab firms would have lower costs of operation because they alone could cut off liability. That would create a perverse incentive because, as we have emphasized, larger firms are apt to carry more insurance. Potential victims of torts would not gain from a legal rule that promoted corporate dis-integration. As a result, courts properly disregard the corporate form only when the corporate arrangement has increased risks over what they would be if firms generally were organized as separate ventures.

REV. 837, 873 (1982) (citing cases for the proposition that courts are more willing to disregard the entity of a subsidiary corporation than one owned by one or more individuals); *see also* Hamilton, *The Corporate Entity*, 49 TEX. L. REV. 979, 992 (1971).

C. Contracts Versus Torts, and the Fraud or Misrepresentation Exception

Courts are more willing to disregard the corporate veil in tort than in contract cases.[41] The rationale for this distinction follows directly from the economics of moral hazard—where corporations must pay for the risk faced by creditors as a result of limited liability, they are less likely to engage in activities with social costs that exceed their social benefits. Contract creditors, in other words, are compensated ex ante for the increased risk of default ex post. Tort creditors, by contrast, are not compensated.

This distinction between contract and tort creditors breaks down when the debtor engages in fraud or misrepresentation.[42] For the costs of excessive risk taking to be fully internalized, creditors must be able to assess the risk of default accurately. If the creditor is misled into believing that the risk of default is lower than it actually is, the creditor will not demand adequate compensation. This will lead to an excessive amount of risk taking by firms, because some of the costs are now shifted to creditors.

Courts have responded to this problem by allowing creditors to go beyond the assets of the corporation in cases of fraud or misrepresentation.[43] The problem can arise in a variety of ways. The most obvious occurs when a corporation misrepresents the nature of its activities, its ability to perform, or its financial condition. Less obvious situations crop up when a firm misleads a creditor into believing that it would have recourse to the assets of other corporations in the event of nonperformance. This could occur if managers make express statements that a parent corporation will stand behind the debts of a subsidiary or if the parent and the subsidiary have confusingly similar names, so that the creditor believes it is dealing with the parent. In all these situations, creditors are unable to assess the risk of default accurately and thus the probability that the firm will engage in excessively risky activities is increased.

---

[41] The difference in judicial treatment of contracts and torts cases was noticed at least as early as Douglas & Shanks, *Insulation from Liability Through Subsidiary Corporations*, 39 YALE L.J. 193, 210-11 (1929). For a recent case emphasizing the distinction, see Edwards v. Monogram Indus., 730 F.2d 977, 980-84 (5th Cir. 1984) (en banc).

[42] For a fuller discussion of the misrepresentation exception, see Posner, *supra* note 3, at 520-24.

[43] *See, e.g.*, Edwards v. Monogram Indus., 730 F.2d 977, 980-84 (5th Cir. 1984) (en banc); *see also* Krendl & Krendl, *Piercing the Corporate Veil: Focusing the Inquiry*, 55 DEN. L.J. 1, 31-34 (1978) (citing cases).

D. Undercapitalization

A final factor commonly emphasized by courts in deciding whether to allow creditors to go beyond the corporation's assets is the extent of the firm's capitalization.[44] Again the reason is clear: the lower the amount of the firm's capital, the greater the incentive to engage in excessively risky activities.

The extent of a firm's capitalization is most important in situations involving involuntary creditors, where high transactions costs preclude negotiation. But undercapitalization can also be relevant in situations involving voluntary creditors. Many credit transactions are too small to warrant a full investigation of the debtor's finances by the creditor. Someone who sells the firm a chair on thirty-days' credit is not going to engage in detailed negotiations about risk and security. In these situations, it is desirable that creditors be able to assume that the debtor is adequately capitalized. The firm should have a duty to notify the creditor of any unusual capitalization. It is cheaper for the firm (which has the best information about its capital structure) to notify creditors in the unusual case than for creditors to investigate in all cases. (By "adequately" capitalized we mean an amount of equity that is within the ordinary range for the business in question. Both the absolute level of equity investment and the debt-equity ratio will depend on the kind of business on which the firm is embarked.)

Allowing creditors to look beyond the assets of the undercapitalized corporate debtor provides the debtor with the incentive to disclose its situation at the time of the transaction.[45] The creditor then can decide not to transact or charge increased compensation for the increased risk. Alternatively, the creditor could ask for prepayment, personal guarantees, or other security. Under any of these alternatives, the debtor will have to pay for engaging in risky activities and thus will have better incentives to balance social benefits and costs.[46]

---

[44] Douglas & Shanks, *supra* note 41, at 218, for example, state that "the adequacy or inadequacy of the capital and financial arrangements of the subsidiary weigh heavily in the determination of liability or non-liability of the parent, greatly overshadowing the other so-called indicia of identity between the companies such as common officers, directors, office and lack of separate books."

[45] There is an analogy in contract law. The foreseeability doctrine of Hadley v. Baxendale, 9 Ex. 341, 156 Eng. Rep. 145 (1854), denies recovery for nonforeseeable losses, which gives plaintiffs an incentive to disclose any unusual conditions and risks at the time of the transaction. Disclosure, in turn, allows the other party to take extra precautions or to charge appropriate compensation for bearing increased risk.

[46] Though our discussion is addressed to "piercing," the same considerations apply to

V. Alternative Methods for Reducing the Problem of Moral Hazard

Piercing the corporate veil is one of several methods for decreasing the incentive created by limited liability to engage in overly risky activities. We briefly analyze in this section the costs and benefits of four other methods of decreasing this risk: minimum-capital requirements, mandatory insurance, managerial liability, and regulation of inputs. Our discussion is general and descriptive. A normative analysis would require data, not currently available, on the size of the externality created by limited liability and the net effects of regulatory attempts to reduce it.

The lower a firm's capitalization, the higher the probability that it will engage in excessively risky activities. Legislatively imposed minimum-capitalization requirements are one method of internalizing the costs of risk taking. But such regulations have problems of their own. One is the obvious administrative cost associated with determining what amount of capital firms should raise.[47] Another is the cost of error. If capital requirements are set too high, this will impede new entry and permit the existing firms to charge monopoly prices. Still another is the question of how firms must satisfy their capitalization requirements. For such requirements to be effective, the corporation must post a bond equal to its highest expected liability[48] or hold sufficient funds in the corporate treasury and invest them in risk-free assets. The total held in this way will far exceed the expected risk created by firms as a group (because not all firms go bankrupt or incur the maximum possible loss). Under either alternative, the rate of return on equity investments will decrease. Thus at the margin people will shift

equitable subordination, a doctrine under which insiders' debt paper may be subordinated to the debt claims of trade creditors and others who did not have actual knowledge of the nature of the insiders' claims. A thinly capitalized firm exposes trade creditors to unsuspected risks, and the doctrine of equitable subordination induces the insiders to make unusual patterns of equity and debt claims known. *See* Costello v. Fazio, 256 F.2d 903 (9th Cir. 1958); Clark, *The Duties of the Corporate Debtor to Its Creditors*, 90 Harv. L. Rev. 505 (1977). Subordination should be handled as an implied term in the debt contract, not as a special rule of bankruptcy. *See* Jackson, *Translating Assets and Liabilities to the Bankruptcy Forum*, 14 J. Legal Stud. 73, 86-87 (1985); *cf.* Taylor v. Standard Gas & Elec. Co., 306 U.S. 307 (1939) (holding that bankruptcy statute compelled subordination of parent company's claims against subsidiary, but suggesting that such a result would also follow from broader equitable principles).

[47] This problem also arises in piercing cases when undercapitalization is involved. The problem is less severe in piercing cases, however, because administrative costs are incurred only when there is a bankruptcy, not in every case.

[48] As Posner proposes. Posner, *supra* note 3, at 520.

capital away from equity investment in risky industries. This too represents a social cost.

Mandatory-insurance requirements are similar in some respects to minimum-capitalization requirements. Both involve administrative costs and may act as barriers to entry. Whether mandatory insurance poses a greater barrier to entry is difficult to determine. New firms, with less experience than existing ones, have higher risks, as insurers see things, and must therefore pay higher premiums. If these premiums are less than the cost of self-insurance, then mandatory insurance facilitates new entry (compared with minimum-capitalization rules). On the other hand, some firms, particularly new firms, might find it difficult to obtain insurance at all. The effect of mandatory insurance on new firms, therefore, might be greater than minimum-capitalization requirements.

One important difference between the two regimes is the effect each has on firms' incentives to engage in excessively risky activities. Minimum-capitalization requirements decrease this incentive. Mandatory insurance requirements, by contrast, may increase or decrease the level of risky activities, depending on insurers' ability to monitor. Where the insurer is unable to monitor, the level of risky activities will increase because of the existence of the insurance. This is a problem, for example, in the market for automobile insurance. State laws frequently require insurance companies to issue insurance to poor drivers (the assigned risk pool) and forbid the setting of rates that would price these drivers out of the market. Mandatory insurance of other activities may have the same sorts of problems.

One method of minimizing the incentive to engage in overly risky activities while avoiding the administrative costs of minimum-capitalization requirements or mandatory insurance is to impose liability on managers as well as enterprises. Managerial liability is an additional risk for which firms must compensate the managers. From the firm's perspective, however, there are problems with paying managers for bearing risk. Because of their inability to diversify their human capital, managers are inefficient risk bearers. Thus firms have incentives to undo managerial liability by providing managers with indemnification or insurance.[49]

This risk shifting does not, however, defeat the purpose of managerial liability. If only the firm may be held liable, the value-maximizing strategy for a firm with few firm-specific investments

[49] For a fuller discussion of risk shifting, see Kraakman, *Corporate Liability Strategies and the Costs of Legal Controls*, 93 YALE L.J. 857 (1984).

of human capital may well be to maintain assets less than expected liabilities. If managers may also be held liable, they have incentives to monitor the firm's capitalization and insurance, because they bear the costs if risk shifting is not complete. Thus the value-maximizing strategy under managerial liability is for firms to self-insure by increasing their capitalization or purchase insurance, whichever is cheaper.[50] In either case, the incentive to engage in overly risky activities is reduced.

The problem with managerial liability is that risk shifting may not work perfectly. It is unlikely, for example, that managers who are liable for mass torts, with huge but uncertain expected liabilities, could shift all of this risk. Because of the huge amounts involved and the difficulty of monitoring, insurers are unwilling to assume the highest possible expected liability. To the extent that risk is not completely shifted, a legal rule of managerial liability creates risk for a group with a comparative disadvantage in bearing that risk. This inefficiency leads to both an increase in the competitive wage for managers and a shift away from risky activities. And there is no guarantee that the social costs of this shift away from risky activities will not exceed the social costs of the excessively risky activities in the absence of managerial liability.

A final method of reducing the incentive to engage in overly risky activities created by limited liability is the regulation of inputs. The regulation of nuclear power plants, for example, could be justified as a response to the perverse incentives created by limited liability. Again, however, there are costs associated with direct regulation of risk taking. Regulators have no better incentives than market participants to balance the social costs and benefits of engaging in certain activities. Indeed the economic theory of regulation suggests that many regulatory schemes arise in order to create, rather than eliminate, "defects" in markets.[51] Thus the regulation of nuclear power plants may have the purpose and effect of shielding other types of energy producers from competition rather than eliminating perverse incentives created by limited liability. Whether the social costs of regulation exceed the social costs of excessively risky activities is an empirical question. The desirability of regulation cannot be established simply by identifying the potential incentive to engage in overly risky activities created by

---

[50] Provided, as we discussed above, that the costs of insurance are less than the premium that would otherwise have to be paid to managers.

[51] *See* George Stigler, The Citizen and the State 105-88 (1975); Becker, *A Theory of Competition Among Pressure Groups for Political Influence*, 98 Q.J. Econ. 371 (1983).

limited liability.

Conclusion

Limited liability facilitates the efficient specialization of function in publicly held corporations. It also allows corporations in some circumstances to externalize the costs of engaging in risky activities. To reduce this social cost of limited liability, courts have pierced the corporate veil in situations where the incentive to engage in excessively risky activities is the greatest. Other legal rules, such as managerial liability, minimum-capitalization requirements, and mandatory insurance, can also be understood as attempts to reduce the social costs of limited liability.

Part II
Conceptions of the Company

[3]

SEPARATION OF OWNERSHIP AND CONTROL*

EUGENE F. FAMA and *MICHAEL C. JENSEN*
University of Chicago *University of Rochester*

I. Introduction

ABSENT fiat, the form of organization that survives in an activity is the one that delivers the product demanded by customers at the lowest price while covering costs.[1] Our goal is to explain the survival of organizations characterized by separation of "ownership" and "control"—a problem that has bothered students of corporations from Adam Smith to Berle and Means and Jensen and Meckling.[2] In more precise language, we are concerned with the survival of organizations in which important decision agents do not bear a substantial share of the wealth effects of their decisions.

We argue that the separation of decision and risk-bearing functions observed in large corporations is common to other organizations such as large professional partnerships, financial mutuals, and nonprofits. We contend that separation of decision and risk-bearing functions survives in these organizations in part because of the benefits of specialization of

* This paper is a revision of parts of our earlier paper, The Survival of Organizations (September 1980). In the course of this work we have profited from the comments of R. Antle, R. Benne, F. Black, F. Easterbrook, A. Farber, W. Gavett, P. Hirsch, R. Hogarth, C. Holderness, R. Holthausen, C. Horne, J. Jeuck, R. Leftwich, S. McCormick, D. Mayers, P. Pashigian, M. Scholes, C. Smith, G. Stigler, R. Watts, T. Whisler, R. Yeaple, J. Zimmerman, and especially A. Alchian, W. Meckling, and C. Plosser. Financial support for Fama's participation is from the National Science Foundation. Jensen is supported by the Managerial Economics Research Center of the University of Rochester.

[1] Armen A. Alchian, Uncertainty, Evolution and Economic Theory, 58 J. Pol. Econ. 211 (1950), is an early proponent of the use of natural selection in economic analysis. For a survey of general issues in the analysis of organizations, see Michael C. Jensen, Organization Theory and Methodology, 50 Accounting Rev. (1983).

[2] Adam Smith, The Wealth of Nations (Cannan ed. 1904) (1st ed. London 1776); Adolf A. Berle & Gardiner C. Means, The Modern Corporation and Private Property (1932); Michael C. Jensen & William H. Meckling, Theory of the Firm: Managerial Behavior, Agency Costs and Ownership Structure, 3 J. Financial Econ. 305 (1976).

[*Journal of Law & Economics*, vol. XXVI (June 1983)]

management and risk bearing but also because of an effective common approach to controlling the agency problems caused by separation of decision and risk-bearing functions. In particular, our hypothesis is that the contract structures of all of these organizations separate the ratification and monitoring of decisions from initiation and implementation of the decisions.

II. Residual Claims and Decision Processes

An organization is the nexus of contracts, written and unwritten, among owners of factors of production and customers.[3] These contracts or internal "rules of the game" specify the rights of each agent in the organization, performance criteria on which agents are evaluated, and the payoff functions they face. The contract structure combines with available production technologies and external legal constraints to determine the cost function for delivering an output with a particular form of organization.[4] The form of organization that delivers the output demanded by customers at the lowest price, while covering costs, survives.

The central contracts in any organization specify (1) the nature of residual claims and (2) the allocation of the steps of the decision process among agents. These contracts distinguish organizations from one another and explain why specific organizational forms survive. We first discuss the general characteristics of residual claims and decision processes. We then present the major hypotheses about the relations between efficient allocations of residual claims and decision functions. The analysis focuses on two broad types of organizations—those in which risk-bearing and decision functions are separated and those in which they are combined in the same agents. We analyze only private organizations that depend on voluntary contracting and exchange.

A. *Residual Claims*

The contract structures of most organizational forms limit the risks undertaken by most agents by specifying either fixed promised payoffs or incentive payoffs tied to specific measures of performance. The residual risk—the risk of the difference between stochastic inflows of resources and promised payments to agents—is borne by those who contract for the rights to net cash flows. We call these agents the residual claimants or residual risk bearers. Moreover, the contracts of most agents contain the

[3] See Jensen & Meckling, *supra* note 2.

[4] See Michael C. Jensen & William H. Meckling, Rights and Production Functions: An Application to Labor-managed Firms and Codetermination, 52 J. Bus. 469 (1979).

implicit or explicit provision that, in exchange for the specified payoff, the agent agrees that the resources he provides can be used to satisfy the interests of residual claimants.

Having most uncertainty borne by one group of agents, residual claimants, has survival value because it reduces the costs incurred to monitor contracts with other groups of agents and to adjust contracts for the changing risks borne by other agents. Contracts that direct decisions toward the interests of residual claimants also add to the survival value of organizations. Producing outputs at lower cost is in the interests of residual claimants because it increases net cash flows, but lower costs also contribute to survival by allowing products to be delivered at lower prices.

The residual claims of different organizational forms contain different restrictions. For example, the least restricted residual claims in common use are the common stocks of large corporations. Stockholders are not required to have any other role in the organization; their residual claims are alienable without restriction; and, because of these provisions, the residual claims allow unrestricted risk sharing among stockholders. We call these organizations *open* corporations to distinguish them from *closed* corporations that are generally smaller and have residual claims that are largely restricted to internal decision agents.[5]

B. The Decision Process

By focusing on entrepreneurial firms in which all decision rights are concentrated in the entrepreneur, economists tend to ignore analysis of the steps of the decision process. However, the way organizations allocate the steps of the decision process across agents is important in explaining the survival of organizations.

In broad terms, the decision process has four steps:

1. *initiation*—generation of proposals for resource utilization and structuring of contracts;
2. *ratification*—choice of the decision initiatives to be implemented;
3. *implementation*—execution of ratified decisions; and
4. *monitoring*—measurement of the performance of decision agents and implementation of rewards.

Because the initiation and implementation of decisions typically are

[5] The terms "public corporation" and "close corporation," which are common in the legal literature, are not used here. "Closed corporation" seems more descriptive than "close corporation." The term "public corporation" best describes government-owned corporations such as Amtrak and the TVA. In contrast, what we call "open corporations" are private organizations.

allocated to the same agents, it is convenient to combine these two functions under the term *decision management*. Likewise, the term *decision control* includes the ratification and monitoring of decisions. Decision management and decision control are the components of the organization's decision process or decision system.

III. Fundamental Relations between Risk-bearing and Decision Processes

We first state and then elaborate the central complementary hypotheses about the relations between the risk-bearing and decision processes of organizations.

1. Separation of residual risk bearing from decision management leads to decision systems that separate decision management from decision control.
2. Combination of decision management and decision control in a few agents leads to residual claims that are largely restricted to these agents.

A. *The Problem*

Agency problems arise because contracts are not costlessly written and enforced. Agency costs include the costs of structuring, monitoring, and bonding a set of contracts among agents with conflicting interests. Agency costs also include the value of output lost because the costs of full enforcement of contracts exceed the benefits.[6]

Control of agency problems in the decision process is important when the decision managers who initiate and implement important decisions are not the major residual claimants and therefore do not bear a major share of the wealth effects of their decisions. Without effective control procedures, such decision managers are more likely to take actions that deviate from the interests of residual claimants. An effective system for decision control implies, almost by definition, that the control (ratification and monitoring) of decisions is to some extent separate from the management (initiation and implementation) of decisions. Individual decision agents can be involved in the management of some decisions and the control of others, but separation means that an individual agent does not exercise exclusive management and control rights over the same decisions.

The interesting problem is to determine when separation of decision management, decision control, and residual risk bearing is more efficient

[6] This definition of agency costs comes from Jensen & Meckling, *supra* note 2.

than combining these three functions in the same agents. We first analyze the factors that make combination of decision management, decision control, and residual risk bearing efficient. We then analyze the factors that make separation of these three functions efficient.

B. Combination of Decision Management, Decision Control, and Residual Risk Bearing

Suppose the balance of cost conditions, including both technology and the control of agency problems, implies that in a particular activity the optimal organization is noncomplex. For our purposes, *noncomplex* means that specific information relevant to decisions is concentrated in one or a few agents. (Specific information is detailed information that is costly to transfer among agents.)[7] Most small organizations tend to be noncomplex, and most large organizations tend to be complex, but the correspondence is not perfect. For example, research oriented universities, though often small in terms of assets or faculty size, are nevertheless complex in the sense that specific knowledge, which is costly to transfer, is diffused among both faculty and administrators. On the other hand, mutual funds are often large in terms of assets but noncomplex in the sense that information relevant to decisions is concentrated in one or a few agents. We take it as given that optimal organizations in some activities are noncomplex. Our more limited goal is to explain the implications of noncomplexity for control of agency problems in the decision process.

If we ignore agency problems between decision managers and residual claimants, the theory of optimal risk bearing tells us that residual claims that allow unrestricted risk sharing have advantages in small as well as in large organizations.[8] However, in a small noncomplex organization, specific knowledge important for decision management and control is concentrated in one or a few agents. As a consequence, it is efficient to allocate decision control as well as decision management to these agents. Without separation of decision management from decision control, resid-

[7] Specific information is closely related to the notions of "information impactedness" and "bounded rationality" discussed in Oliver E. Williamson, Markets and Hierarchies: Analysis and Antitrust Implications (1975) and The Modern Corporation: Origins, Evolution, Attributes, 19 J. Econ. Literature 1537 (1981). Friedrich A. von Hayek, The Use of Knowledge in Society, 35 Am. Econ. Rev. 519 (1945) uses specific information to discuss the role of markets in complex economies. See also Thomas Sowell, Knowledge and Decisions 13–14 (1980). Our analysis of the relations between specific information and efficient decision processes owes much to ongoing work with William Meckling.

[8] See, for example, Kenneth J. Arrow, The Role of Securities in the Optimal Allocation of Risk Bearing, 31 Rev. Econ. Stud. 91 (1964); or Eugene F. Fama, Foundations of Finance chs. 6 & 7 (1976).

ual claimants have little protection against opportunistic actions of decision agents, and this lowers the value of unrestricted residual claims.

A feasible solution to the agency problem that arises when the same agents manage and control important decisions is to restrict residual claims to the important decision agents. In effect, restriction of residual claims to decision agents substitutes for costly control devices to limit the discretion of decision agents. The common stocks of closed corporations are this type of restricted residual claim, as are the residual claims in proprietorships and partnerships. The residual claims of these organizations (especially closed corporations) are also held by other agents whose special relations with decision agents allow agency problems to be controlled without separation of the management and control of decisions. For example, family members have many dimensions of exchange with one another over a long horizon and therefore have advantages in monitoring and disciplining related decision agents. Business associates whose goodwill and advice are important to the organization are also potential candidates for holding minority residual claims of organizations that do not separate the management and control of decisions.[9]

Restricting residual claims to decision makers controls agency problems between residual claimants and decision agents, but it sacrifices the benefits of unrestricted risk sharing and specialization of decision functions. The decision process suffers efficiency losses because decision agents must be chosen on the basis of wealth and willingness to bear risk as well as for decision skills. The residual claimants forgo optimal risk reduction through portfolio diversification so that residual claims and decision making can be combined in a small number of agents. Forgone diversification lowers the value of the residual claims and raises the cost of risk-bearing services.

Moreover, when residual claims are restricted to decision agents, it is generally rational for the residual claimant–decision makers to assign lower values to uncertain cash flows than residual claimants would in organizations where residual claims are unrestricted and risk bearing can be freely diversified across organizations. As a consequence, restricting residual claims to agents in the decision process leads to decisions (for example, less investment in risky projects that lower the costs of outputs) that tend to penalize the organization in the competition for survival.[10]

[9] In contrast, the analysis predicts that when venture equity capital is put into a small entrepreneurial organization by outsiders, mechanisms for separating the management and control of important decisions are instituted.

[10] These propositions are developed in Eugene F. Fama & Michael C. Jensen, Organizational Forms and Investment Decisions (Working Paper No. MERC 83-03, Univ. Rochester, Managerial Economics Research Center 1983).

However, because contracts are not costlessly written and enforced, all decision systems and systems for allocating residual claims involve costs. Organizational survival involves a balance of the costs of alternative decision systems and systems for allocating residual risk against the benefits. Small noncomplex organizations do not have demands for a wide range of specialized decision agents; on the contrary, concentration of specific information relevant to decisions implies that there are efficiency gains when the rights to manage and control decisions are combined in one or a few agents. Moreover, the risk-sharing benefits forgone when residual claims are restricted to one or a few decision agents are less serious in a small noncomplex organization than in a large organization, because the total risk of net cash flows to be shared is generally smaller in small organizations. In addition, small organizations do not often have large demands for wealth from residual claimants to bond the payoffs promised to other agents and to purchase risky assets. As a consequence, small noncomplex organizations can efficiently control the agency problems caused by the combination of decision management and control in one or a few agents by restricting residual claims to these agents. Such a combining of decision and risk-bearing functions is efficient in small noncomplex organizations because the benefits of unrestricted risk sharing and specialization of decision functions are less than the costs that would be incurred to control the resulting agency problems.

The proprietorships, partnerships, and closed corporations observed in small scale production and service activities are the best examples of classical entrepreneurial firms in which the major decision makers are also the major residual risk bearers. These organizations are evidence in favor of the hypothesis that combination of decision management and decision control in one or a few agents leads to residual claims that are largely restricted to these agents.

We analyze next the forces that make separation of decision management, decision control, and residual risk bearing efficient—in effect, the forces that cause the classical entrepreneurial firm to be dominated by organizational forms in which there are no decision makers in the classical entrepreneurial sense.

C. Separation of Decision Management, Decision Control, and Residual Risk Bearing

Our concern in this section is with the organizational forms characterized by separation of decision management from residual risk bearing—what the literature on open corporations calls, somewhat imprecisely, separation of ownership and control. Our hypothesis is that all such organizations, including large open corporations, large professional partnerships, financial mutuals, and nonprofits, control the agency problems that result from separation of decision management from residual risk bearing by separating the management (initiation and implementation) and control (ratification and monitoring) of decisions. Documentation of this hypothesis takes up much of the rest of the paper.

1. *Specific Knowledge and Diffusion of Decision Functions.* Most organizations characterized by separation of decision management from residual risk bearing are *complex* in the sense that specific knowledge relevant to different decisions—knowledge which is costly to transfer across agents—is diffused among agents at all levels of the organization. Again, we take it as given that the optimal organizations in some activities are complex. Our theory attempts to explain the implications of complexity for the nature of efficient decision processes and for control of agency problems in the decision process.

Since specific knowledge in complex organizations is diffused among agents, diffusion of decision management can reduce costs by delegating the initiation and implementation of decisions to the agents with valuable relevant knowledge. The agency problems of diffuse decision management can then be reduced by separating the management (initiation and implementation) and control (ratification and monitoring) of decisions.

In the unusual cases where residual claims are not held by important decision managers but are nevertheless concentrated in one or a few residual claimants, control of decision managers can in principle be direct and simple, with the residual claimants ratifying and monitoring important decisions and setting rewards.[11] Such organizations conform to our hypothesis, because top-level decision control is separated from top-level decision managers and exercised directly by residual claimants.

However, in complex organizations valuable specific knowledge relevant to decision control is diffused among many internal agents. This generally means that efficient decision control, like efficient decision management, involves delegation and diffusion of decision control as well as separation of decision management and control at different levels of the organization. We expect to observe such delegation, diffusion, and separation of decision management and control below the top level of complex organizations, even in those unusual complex organizations where residual claims are held primarily by top-level decision agents.

2. *Diffuse Residual Claims and Delegation of Decision Control.* In the more common complex organizations, residual claims are diffused

[11] See Armen A. Alchian & Harold Demsetz, Production, Information Costs, and Economic Organization, 62 Am. Econ. Rev. 777 (1972).

among many agents. Having many residual claimants has advantages in large complex organizations because the total risk of net cash flows to be shared is generally large and there are large demands for wealth from residual claimants to bond the payoffs promised to a wide range of agents and to purchase risky assets. When there are many residual claimants, it is costly for all of them to be involved in decision control and it is efficient for them to delegate decision control. For example, some delegation of decision control is observed even in the large professional partnerships in public accounting and law, where the residual claimants are expert internal decision agents. When there are many partners it is inefficient for each to participate in ratification and monitoring of all decisions.

Nearly complete separation and specialization of decision control and residual risk bearing is common in large open corporations and financial mutuals where most of the diffuse residual claimants are not qualified for roles in the decision process and thus delegate their decision control rights to other agents. When residual claimants have no role in decision control, we expect to observe separation of the management and control of important decisions at all levels of the organization.

Separation and diffusion of decision management and decision control—in effect, the absence of a classical entrepreneurial decision maker—limit the power of individual decision agents to expropriate the interests of residual claimants. The checks and balances of such decision systems have costs, but they also have important benefits. Diffusion and separation of decision management and control have benefits because they allow valuable knowledge to be used at the points in the decision process where it is most relevant and they help control the agency problems of diffuse residual claims. In complex organizations, the benefits of diffuse residual claims and the benefits of separation of decision functions from residual risk bearing are generally greater than the agency costs they generate, including the costs of mechanisms to separate the management and control of decisions.

3. *Decision Control in Nonprofits and Financial Mutuals.* Most organizations characterized by separation of decision management from residual risk bearing are complex. However, separation of the management and control of decisions contributes to the survival of any organization where the important decision managers do not bear a substantial share of the wealth effects of their decisions—that is, any organization where there are serious agency problems in the decision process. We argue below that separation of decision management and residual risk bearing is a characteristic of nonprofit organizations and financial mutuals, large and small, complex and noncomplex. Thus, we expect to observe separation of the management and control of important decisions

even in small noncomplex nonprofits and financial mutuals where, ignoring agency problems in the decision process, concentrated and combined decision management and control would be more efficient.

4. *Common General Features of Decision Control Systems*. Our hypothesis about the decision systems of organizations characterized by separation of decision management and residual risk bearing gets support from the fact that the major mechanisms for diffusing and separating the management and control of decisions are much the same across different organizations.

Decision hierarchies. A common feature of the diffuse decision management and control systems of complex organizations (for example, large nonprofit universities as well as large open corporations) is a formal decision hierarchy with higher level agents ratifying and monitoring the decision initiatives of lower level agents and evaluating their performance.[12] Such hierarchical partitioning of the decision process makes it more difficult for decision agents at all levels of the organization to take actions that benefit themselves at the expense of residual claimants. Decision hierarchies are buttressed by organizational rules of the game, for example, accounting and budgeting systems, that monitor and constrain the decision behavior of agents and specify the performance criteria that determine rewards.[13]

Mutual monitoring systems. The formal hierarchies of complex organizations are also buttressed by information from less formal mutual monitoring among agents. When agents interact to produce outputs, they acquire low-cost information about colleagues, information not directly available to higher level agents. Mutual monitoring systems tap this information for use in the control process. Mutual monitoring systems derive their energy from the interests of agents to use the internal agent markets of organizations to enhance the value of human capital.[14] Agents choose

[12] See Max Weber, The Theory of Social and Economic Organization (1947); Peter M. Blau, Bureaucracy in Modern Society (1956); Herbert A. Simon, The Architecture of Complexity, 106 Proc. Am. Philosophical Soc'y 467 (1962); and the titles by Williamson, *supra* note 7. The historical development of hierarchies in open corporations is analyzed in Alfred D. Chandler, The Visible Hand (1977); and Alfred D. Chandler & Herman Daems, Managerial Hierarchies (1980).

[13] The separation of decision management from decision control that we emphasize is reflected in the auditing profession's concern with allocating operating and accounting responsibility to different agents. For instance, it is recommended that an agent with responsibility for billing should not have a role in receiving or recording customer payments. See, for example, Charles Horngren, Cost Accounting: A Managerial Emphasis ch. 27 (1982); or Howard P. Stettler, Auditing Principles chs. 4 & 8 (1977).

[14] See Eugene F. Fama, Agency Problems and the Theory of the Firm, 88 J. Pol. Econ. 288 (1980).

among organizations on the basis of rewards offered and potential for development of human capital. Agents value the competitive interaction that takes place within an organization's internal agent market because it enhances current marginal products and contributes to human capital development. Moreover, if agents perceive that evaluation of their performance is unbiased (that is, if they cannot systematically fool their evaluators) then they value the fine tuning of the reward system that results from mutual monitoring information, because it lowers the uncertainty of payoffs from effort and skill. Since the incentive structures and diffuse decision control systems that result from the interplay of formal hierarchies and less formal mutual monitoring systems are also in the interests of residual claimants, their survival value is evident.

Boards of directors. The common apex of the decision control systems of organizations, large and small, in which decision agents do not bear a major share of the wealth effects of their decisions is some form of board of directors. Such boards always have the power to hire, fire, and compensate the top-level decision managers and to ratify and monitor important decisions. Exercise of these top-level decision control rights by a group (the board) helps to ensure separation of decision management and control (that is, the absence of an entrepreneurial decision maker) even at the top of the organization.[15]

IV. The Spectrum of Organizations

A. *Introduction*

Organizations in which important decision agents do not bear a major share of the wealth effects of their decisions include open corporations, large professional partnerships, financial mutuals, and nonprofits. We are concerned now with analyzing the data each of these organizations provides to test the hypothesis that separation of decision management functions from residual risk bearing leads to decision systems that separate the management and control of decisions.

To motivate the discussion of specific organizational forms, we also outline a set of more specialized propositions to explain the survival value of the special features of their residual claims. These more specialized hypotheses about the survival of specific organizational forms in specific

[15] Decision functions can be delegated in two general ways: (1) joint delegation to several agents (as in a committee), or (2) partitioning and delegation of the parts to different agents. Boards of directors are examples of the former approach; decision hierarchies are examples of the latter.

activities are developed in our paper "Agency Problems and Residual Claims."[16]

B. *Open Corporations*

1. *Unrestricted Common Stock Residual Claims.* Most large nonfinancial organizations are open corporations. The common stock residual claims of such organizations are unrestricted in the sense that stockholders are not required to have any other role in the organization, and their residual claims are freely alienable. As a result of the unrestricted nature of the residual claims of open corporations, there is almost complete specialization of decision management and residual risk bearing. Even managers who own substantial blocs of stock, and thus are residual risk bearers, may elect to sell these shares.

Unrestricted common stock is attractive in complicated risky activities where substantial wealth provided by residual claimants is needed to bond the large aggregate payoffs promised to many other agents. Unrestricted common stock, with its capacity for generating large amounts of wealth from residual claimants on a permanent basis, is also attractive in activities more efficiently carried out with large amounts of risky assets owned within the organization rather than rented. Moreover, since decision skills are not a necessary consequence of wealth or willingness to bear risk, the specialization of decision management and residual risk bearing allowed by unrestricted common stock enhances the adaptability of a complex organization to changes in the economic environment. The unrestricted risk sharing and diversification allowed by common stock also contributes to survival by lowering the cost of risk-bearing services.

2. *Control of the Agency Problems of Common Stock.* Separation and specialization of decision management and residual risk bearing leads to agency problems between decision agents and residual claimants. This is the problem of separation of ownership and control that has long troubled students of corporations. For example, potential exploitation of residual claimants by opportunistic decision agents is reflected in the arguments leading to the establishment of the Securities and Exchange Commission and in the concerns of the modern corporate governance movement. Less well appreciated, however, is the fact that the unrestricted nature of common stock residual claims also allows special market and organizational mechanisms for controlling the agency problems of specialized risk bearing.

[16] Eugene F. Fama & Michael C. Jensen, Agency Problems and Residual Claims, in this issue.

The stock market. The unrestricted alienability of the residual claims of open corporations gives rise to an external monitoring device unique to these organizations—a stock market that specializes in pricing common stocks and transferring them at low cost. Stock prices are visible signals that summarize the implications of internal decisions for current and future net cash flows. This external monitoring exerts pressure to orient a corporation's decision process toward the interests of residual claimants.

The market for takeovers. External monitoring from a takeover market is also unique to the open corporation and is attributable to the unrestricted nature of its residual claims.[17] Because the residual claims are freely alienable and separable from roles in the decision process, attacking managers can circumvent existing managers and the current board to gain control of the decision process, either by a direct offer to purchase stock (a tender offer) or by an appeal for stockholder votes for directors (a proxy fight).

Expert boards. Internal control in the open corporation is delegated by residual claimants to a board of directors. Residual claimants generally retain approval rights (by vote) on such matters as board membership, auditor choice, mergers, and new stock issues. Other management and control functions are delegated by the residual claimants to the board. The board then delegates most decision management functions and many decision control functions to internal agents, but it retains ultimate control over internal agents—including the rights to ratify and monitor major policy initiatives and to hire, fire, and set the compensation of top level decision managers. Similar delegation of decision management and control functions, at the first step to a board and then from the board to internal decision agents, is common to other organizations, such as financial mutuals, nonprofits, and large professional partnerships, in which important decision agents do not bear a major share of the wealth effects of their decisions.

However, the existence of the stock market and the market for takeovers, both special to open corporations, explains some of the special features of corporate boards, in particular: (1) why inside manager board members are generally more influential than outside members, and (2) why outside board members are often decision agents in other complex organizations.[18]

Since the takeover market provides an external court of last resort for

[17] Monitoring from the takeover market is emphasized in Henry Manne, Mergers and the Market for Corporate Control, 73 J. Pol. Econ. 110 (1965).

[18] See Edward S. Herman, Corporate Control, Corporate Power ch. 2 (1981), for data on the characteristics of corporate boards.

protection of residual claimants, a corporate board can be in the hands of agents who are decision experts. Given that the board is to be composed of experts, it is natural that its most influential members are internal managers since they have valuable specific information about the organization's activities. It is also natural that when the internal decision control system works well, the outside members of the board are nominated by internal managers. Internal managers can use their knowledge of the organization to nominate outside board members with relevant complementary knowledge: for example, outsiders with expertise in capital markets, corporate law, or relevant technology who provide an important support function to the top managers in dealing with specialized decision problems.

However, the board is not an effective device for decision control unless it limits the decision discretion of individual top managers. The board is the top-level court of appeals of the internal agent market,[19] and as such it must be able to use information from the internal mutual monitoring system. To accomplish this and to achieve effective separation of top-level decision management and control, we expect the board of a large open corporation to include several of the organization's top managers. The board uses information from each of the top managers about his decision initiatives and the decision initiatives and performance of other managers. The board also seeks information from lower level managers about the decision initiatives and performance of top managers.[20] This information is used to set the rewards of the top managers, to rank them, and to choose among their decision initiatives. To protect information flows to the board, we expect that top managers, especially those who are members of the board, can effectively be fired only with consent of the board and thus are protected from reprisals from other top managers.

The decision processes of some open corporations seem to be dominated by an individual manager, generally the chief executive officer. In some cases, this signals the absence of separation of decision management and decision control, and, in our theory, the organization suffers in the competition for survival. We expect, however, that the apparent

[19] See Fama, *supra* note 14.

[20] For example, Horngren, *supra* note 13, at 911, describes the role of the audit committee of the board (generally composed of outside board members) as a collector and conduit of information from the internal mutual monitoring system: "The objective of the audit committee is to oversee the accounting controls, financial statements, and financial affairs of the corporation. The committee represents the full board and provides personal contact and communication among the board, the external auditors, the internal auditors, the financial executives, and the operating executives."

dominance of some top managers is more often due to their ability to work with the decision control systems of their organizations than to their ability to suppress diffuse and separate decision control. In any case, the financial press regularly reports instances where apparently dominant executives are removed by their boards.

Corporate boards generally include outside members, that is, members who are not internal managers, and they often hold a majority of seats.[21] The outside board members act as arbiters in disagreements among internal managers and carry out tasks that involve serious agency problems between internal managers and residual claimants, for example, setting executive compensation or searching for replacements for top managers.

Effective separation of top-level decision management and control means that outside directors have incentives to carry out their tasks and do not collude with managers to expropriate residual claimants. Our hypothesis is that outside directors have incentives to develop reputations as experts in decision control. Most outside directors of open corporations are either managers of other corporations or important decision agents in other complex organizations.[22] The value of their human capital depends primarily on their performance as internal decision managers in other organizations. They use their directorships to signal to internal and external markets for decision agents that (1) they are decision experts, (2) they understand the importance of diffuse and separate decision control, and (3) they can work with such decision control systems. The signals are credible when the direct payments to outside directors are small, but there is substantial devaluation of human capital when internal decision control breaks down and the costly last resort process of an outside takeover is activated.

C. Professional Partnerships

1. *Mutual Monitoring, Specific Knowledge, and Restricted Residual Claims.* The residual claims of professional partnerships in activities such as law, public accounting, medicine, and business consulting are restricted to the major professional agents who produce the organization's services. This restriction increases the incentives of agents to monitor each other's actions and to consult with each other to improve the quality of services provided to customers. Such mutual monitoring and consulting are attractive to the professional agents in service activities where responsibility for variation in the quality of services is easily as-

[21] See Herman, *supra* note 18, at ch. 2.

[22] *Id.*

signed and the value of professional human capital is sensitive to performance. The monitoring and consulting are likely to be effective when professional agents with similar specialized skills agree to share liability for the actions of colleagues.

In both large and small partnerships, individuals or small teams work on cases, audits, and so forth. Because of the importance of specific knowledge about particular clients and circumstances, it is efficient for the teams to make most decisions locally. At this level, however, decision management and decision control are not separate. To control the resulting agency problems, the residual claims in professional partnerships, large and small, are restricted to the professional agents who have the major decision-making roles. This is consistent with our hypothesis that combination of decision management and control functions leads to restriction of residual claims to the agents who both manage and control important decisions.

2. *Large Professional Partnerships.* The partners in large professional partnerships are diffuse residual claimants whose welfare depends on the acts of agents they do not directly control. Thus, these organizations provide a test of our hypothesis that separation of residual risk bearing and decision management induces decision systems that separate the management and control of important decisions. The major decision control devices of large professional partnerships are similar to those of other organizations with diffuse residual claims. For example, residual claimants in large partnerships delegate to boards the ratification and monitoring of important decisions above the level of individual cases and audits. Moreover, the sharing of liability and residual cash flows among important decision agents (the partners) ensures that large partnerships have strong versions of the mutual monitoring systems that we contend are common to the decision control systems of complex organizations.

The boards of large partnerships have special features that relate to the restriction of the residual claims to important internal agents. The residual claimants are experts in the organization's activities, and they observe directly the effects of actions taken by the board of managing partners. Thus, unlike the stockholders of open corporations, the residual claimants in large partnerships have little demand for outside experts to protect their interests, and their boards are composed entirely of partners.

The board is involved in decisions with respect to the management of the partnership, for example, where new offices should be opened, who should be admitted to the partnership, and who should be dismissed. The board is also involved in renegotiating the shares of the partners. Here, as in other decisions, the boards of large partnerships combine the valuable specific knowledge available at the top level with information from partner–residual claimants. The role of the board is to develop acceptable consensus decisions from this information. Thus, the boards of large professional partnerships are generally called committees of managing partners rather than boards of directors. The idea is that such committees exist to manage agency problems among partners and to study and determine major policy issues in a manner that is less costly than when performed jointly by all partners.

Since the residual claims in a large professional partnership are not alienable, unfriendly outside takeovers are not possible. Inside takeovers by dissident partners are possible, however, because the managing boards of these organizations are elected by the partner–residual claimants.

D. *Financial Mutuals*

A common form of organization in financial activities is the mutual. An unusual characteristic of mutuals is that the residual claimants are customers, for example, the policyholders of mutual insurance companies, the depositors of mutual savings banks, and the shareholders of mutual funds. Like the diffuse stockholders of large nonfinancial corporations, most of the diffuse depositors, policyholders, and mutual fund shareholders of financial mutuals do not participate in the internal decision process. Thus, financial mutuals provide another test of our hypothesis that substantial separation of decision management and residual risk bearing leads to decision systems that separate the management and control of decisions.

1. *The Control Function of Redeemable Claims.* For the purpose of decision control, the unique characteristic of the residual claims of mutuals is that they are redeemable on demand. The policyholder, depositor, or shareholder can, on demand, turn in his claim at a price determined by a prespecified rule. For example, the shareholder of an open-end mutual fund can redeem his claim for the market value of his share of the fund's assets, while the whole life or endowment insurance policyholder, like the shareholder of a mutual savings bank, can redeem his claim for its specified value plus accumulated dividends.

The decision of the claim holder to withdraw resources is a form of partial takeover or liquidation which deprives management of control over assets. This control right can be exercised independently by each claim holder. It does not require a proxy fight, a tender offer, or any other concerted takeover bid. In contrast, customer decisions in open nonfinancial corporations and the repricing of the corporation's securities in the capital market provide signals about the performance of its decision agents. Without further action, however, either internal or from the market for takeovers, the judgments of customers and of the capital market leave the assets of the open nonfinancial corporation under the control of the managers.

2. *The Board of Directors.* Like other organizations characterized by substantial separation between decision management and residual risk bearing, the top-level decision control device in financial mutuals is a board of directors. Because of the strong form of diffuse decision control inherent in the redeemable residual claims of financial mutuals, however, their boards are less important in the control process than the boards of open nonfinancial corporations. The reduced role of the board is especially evident in mutual savings banks and mutual funds, which are not complex even though often large in terms of assets. Moreover, the residual claimants of mutuals show little interest in their boards and often do not have the right to vote for board members.[23] Outside board members are generally chosen by internal managers. Unlike open corporations, the boards of financial mutuals do not often impose changes in managers. The role of the board, especially in the less complex mutuals, is largely limited to monitoring agency problems against which redemption of residual claims offers little protection, for example, fraud or outright theft of assets by internal agents.

E. *Nonprofit Organizations*

When an organization's activities are financed in part through donations, part of net cash flows is from resources provided by donors. Contracts that define the share of residual claimants in net cash flows are unlikely to assure donors that their resources are protected from expropriation by residual claimants. In a nonprofit organization, however, there are no agents with alienable rights in residual net cash flows and thus there are no residual claims. We argue in "Agency Problems and Residual Claims" that the absence of such residual claims in nonprofits avoids the donor–residual claimant agency problem and explains the dominance of nonprofits in donor-financed activities.[24]

The absence of residual claims in nonprofits avoids agency problems between donors and residual claimants, but the incentives of other inter-

[23] See Edward S. Herman, Conflict of Interest in the Savings and Loan Industry, in A Study of the Savings and Loan Industry 789 (Irwin Friend ed. 1969), for documentation of such lack of interest. For example, he describes situations where in more than a decade only four depositors in total attended the annual meetings of two savings and loan associations and other situations where management did not even bother to collect proxies.

[24] Fama & Jensen, Agency Problems and Residual Claims, in this issue. See Henry B. Hansmann, The Role of Nonprofit Enterprise, 89 Yale L. J. 835 (1980), for a general discussion of nonprofits.

nal agents to expropriate donations remain. These agency problems between donors and decision agents in nonprofits are similar to those in other organizations where important decision managers do not bear a major share of the wealth effects of their decisions. Our hypothesis predicts that, like other organizations characterized by separation of decision management from residual risk bearing, nonprofits have decision systems that separate the management (initiation and implementation) and control (ratification and monitoring) of decisions. Such decision systems survive in donor nonprofits because of the assurances they provide that donations are used effectively and are not easily expropriated.

1. *Nonprofit Boards*. In small nonprofits delegation of decision management to one or a few agents is generally efficient. For example, in nonprofit cultural performing groups, an artistic director usually chooses performers, does the primary monitoring of their outputs, and initiates and implements major decisions. Nevertheless, the important decision agents in these organizations are chosen, monitored, and evaluated by boards of directors. Boards with similar decision control rights are common to other small nonprofits characterized by concentrated decision management, such as charities, private museums, small private hospitals, and local Protestant and Jewish congregations. Boards are also observed at the top of the decision control systems of complex nonprofits, such as private universities, in which both decision management and decision control are diffuse.

Although their functions are similar to those of other organizations, nonprofit boards have special features that are due to the absence of alienable residual claims. For example, because of the discipline from the outside takeover market, boards of open corporations can include internal decision agents, and outside board members can be chosen for expertise rather than because they are important residual claimants. In contrast, because a nonprofit lacks alienable residual claims, the decision agents are immune from ouster (via takeover) by outside agents. Without the takeover threat or the discipline imposed by residual claimants with the right to remove members of the board, nonprofit boards composed of internal agents and outside experts chosen by internal agents would provide little assurance against collusion and expropriation of donations. Thus, nonprofit boards generally include few if any internal agents as voting members, and nonprofit boards are often self-perpetuating, that is, new members are approved by existing members. Moreover, nonprofit board members are generally substantial donors who serve without pay. Willingness to provide continuing personal donations of wealth or time is generally an implicit condition for membership on nonprofit boards. Acceptance of this condition certifies to other donors that board members are motivated to take their decision control task seriously.

2. *The Roman Catholic Church.* To our knowledge the only non-profit organization that is financed with donations but lacks a board of important continuing donors with effective decision control rights is the Roman Catholic church. Parish councils exist in local Catholic churches, but unlike their Protestant and Jewish counterparts, they are only advisory. The clerical hierarchy controls the allocation of resources, and the papal system does not seem to limit the discretion of the Pope, the organization's most important decision agent.

Other aspects of the contracts of the Catholic clergy in part substitute for the control of expropriation of donations that would be provided by more effective donor-customer constraints on decisions. For example, the vows of chastity and obedience incorporated into the contracts of the Catholic clergy help to bond against expropriation of donations by avoiding conflicts between the material interests of a family and the interests of donor-customers. In addition, the training of a Catholic priest is organization-specific. For example, it involves a heavy concentration on (Catholic) theology, whereas the training of Protestant ministers places more emphasis on social service skills. Once certified, the Catholic priest is placed by the hierarchy. He cannot offer his services on a competitive basis. In exchange for developing such organization-specific human capital, the Catholic priest, unlike his Protestant and Jewish counterparts, gets a lifetime contract that promises a real standard of living. The organization-specific nature of the human capital of the Catholic clergy and the terms of the contract under which it is employed act as a bond to donor-customers that the interests of the Catholic clergy are closely bound to the survival of the organization and thus to the interests of donor-customers.

Although Protestantism arose over doctrinal issues, the control structures of Protestant sects—in particular, the evolution of lay councils with power to ratify and monitor resource allocation decisions—can be viewed as a response to breakdowns of the contract structure of Catholicism, that is, expropriation of Catholic donor-customers by the clergy. The evolution of Protestantism is therefore an example of competition among alternative contract structures to resolve an activity's major agency problem—in this case monitoring important agents to limit expropriation of donations.

There is currently pressure to allow Catholic priests to marry, that is, to drop the vow of chastity from their contracts. We predict that if this occurs, organizational survival will require other monitoring and bonding mechanisms, for example, control over allocation of resources by lay councils similar to those observed in Protestant and Jewish congregations.

3. *The Private University and Decision Systems in Complex Nonprofits.* In complex nonprofits we observe mechanisms for diffuse decision control similar to those of other complex organizations. For example, large private universities, like large open corporations, have complicated decision hierarchies and active internal agent markets with mutual monitoring systems that generate information about the performance of agents. Again, however, the decision control structures of complex nonprofits have special features attributable to the absence of alienable residual claims.

For example, a university's trustees are primarily donors rather than experts in the details of education or research. In ratifying and monitoring decision initiatives presented by internal decision agents (presidents, chancellors, provosts, etc.), and in evaluating the agents themselves, boards rely on information from the internal diffuse decision system—for example, reports from faculty senates and appointments committees—and on external peer reviews.

Moreover, the structure of internal diffuse decision control systems is a more formal part of a university's contract structure (its charter or bylaws) than in large for-profit organizations such as open corporations. For example, unlike corporate managers, university deans, department heads, provosts, and presidents are generally appointed for fixed terms. The end of a contract period activates a process of evaluation, with search committees chosen according to formal rules and with rules for passing their recommendations on to the board. A more formal structure of diffuse decision management and control is helpful to trustees who do not have specialized knowledge about a university's activities. It also helps to assure donors that the absence of discipline from an outside takeover market is compensated by a strong system for internal decision control.

V. Summary

The theory developed in this paper views an organization as a nexus of contracts (written and unwritten). The theory focuses on the contracts that (1) allocate the steps in an organization's decision process, (2) define residual claims, and (3) set up devices for controlling agency problems in the decision process. We focus on the factors that give survival value to organizational forms that separate what the literature imprecisely calls ownership and control.

A. *The Central Hypotheses*

An organization's decision process consists of decision management (initiation and implementation) and decision control (ratification and monitoring). Our analysis produces two complementary hypotheses about the relations between decision systems and residual claims:

1. Separation of residual risk bearing from decision management leads to decision systems that separate decision management from decision control.
2. Combination of decision management and decision control in a few agents leads to residual claims that are largely restricted to these agents.

B. *Combination of Decision Management and Control*

When it is efficient to combine decision management and control functions in one or a few agents, it is efficient to control agency problems between residual claimants and decision makers by restricting residual claims to the decision makers. This proposition gets clear support from the proprietorships, small partnerships, and closed corporations observed in small-scale production and service activities. These organizations are all characterized by concentrated decision systems and residual claims that are restricted to decision agents.

C. *Separation of Residual Risk Bearing from Decision Management*

1. *The Role of Specific Knowledge.* In contrast, most of the organizations characterized by separation of residual risk bearing from decision management are complex in the sense that specific information valuable for decisions is diffused among many agents throughout the organization. Thus in a complex organization separation of residual risk bearing from decision management arises in part because efficient decision systems are diffuse. Benefits from better decisions can be achieved by delegating decision functions to agents at all levels of the organization who have relevant specific knowledge, rather than allocating all decision management and control to the residual claimants. Control of the agency problems of such diffuse decision systems is then achieved by separating the ratification and monitoring of decisions (decision control) from initiation and implementation (decision management). The efficiency of such decision systems is buttressed by incentive structures that reward agents both for initiating and implementing decisions and for ratifying and monitoring the decision management of other agents.

2. *The Role of Diffuse Residual Claims.* In most complex organizations, residual claims are diffused among many agents. When there are many residual claimants, it is costly for all of them to be involved in decision control. As a consequence there is separation of residual risk bearing from decision control, and this creates agency problems between

residual claimants and decision agents. Separation of decision management and decision control at all levels of the organization helps to control these agency problems by limiting the power of individual agents to expropriate the interests of residual claimants. Thus diffusion and separation of decision management and control have survival value in complex organizations both because they allow valuable specific knowledge to be used at the points in the decision process where it is most relevant and because they help control the agency problems of diffuse residual claims.

3. *Common Features of Decision Control Systems.* What we call separation of residual risk bearing from decision management is the separation of ownership and control that has long bothered students of open corporations. We argue that separation of decision and risk bearing functions is also common to other organizations like large professional partnerships, financial mutuals, and nonprofits. Moreover, our central hypothesis about control of the agency problems caused by separation of residual risk bearing from decision management gets support from the fact that the major mechanisms for separating decision management and decision control are much the same across organizations.

The common central building blocks of the diffuse decision control systems of complex organizations of all types are formal decision hierarchies in which the decision initiatives of lower level agents are passed on to higher level agents, first for ratification and then for monitoring. Such decision hierarchies are found in large open corporations, large professional partnerships, large financial mutuals, and large nonprofits. Formal decision hierarchies are buttressed by less formal mutual monitoring systems that are a by-product of interaction that takes place to produce outputs and develop human capital.

The common apex of the decision control systems of organizations, large and small, in which decision agents do not bear a major share of the wealth effects of their decisions is a board of directors (trustees, managing partners, etc.) that ratifies and monitors important decisions and chooses, dismisses, and rewards important decision agents. Such multiple-member boards make collusion between top-level decision management and control agents more difficult, and they are the mechanism that allows separation of the management and control of the organization's most important decisions.

APPENDIX

Bibliography

Alchian, Armen A. "Uncertainty, Evolution and Economic Theory." *Journal of Political Economy* 58, no. 3 (June 1950): 211–21.

Alchian, Armen A., and Demsetz, Harold. "Production, Information Costs, and Economic Organization." *American Economic Review* 62, no. 5 (December 1972): 777–95.

Arrow, Kenneth J. "The Role of Securities in the Optimal Allocation of Risk Bearing." *Review of Economic Studies* 31, no. 86 (April 1964): 91–96.

Berle, Adolf A., and Means, Gardiner C. *The Modern Corporation and Private Property*. New York: Macmillan Publishing Co., 1932.

Blau, Peter M. *Bureaucracy in Modern Society*. New York: Random House, 1956.

Chandler, Alfred D., Jr. *The Visible Hand*. Cambridge, Mass.: Harvard University Press, 1977.

Chandler, Alfred D., Jr., and Daems, Herman. *Managerial Hierarchies*. Cambridge, Mass.: Harvard University Press, 1980.

Fama, Eugene F. *Foundations of Finance*. New York: Basic Books, 1976.

Fama, Eugene F. "Agency Problems and the Theory of the Firm." *Journal of Political Economy* 88, no. 2 (April 1980): 288–307.

Fama, Eugene F., and Jensen, Michael C. "Agency Problems and Residual Claims." *Journal of Law and Economics* 26 (June 1983): 327–49.

Fama, Eugene F., and Jensen, Michael C. "Organizational Forms and Investment Decisions." Managerial Economics Research Center Working Paper no. MERC 83-03. Rochester, N.Y.: University of Rochester, Graduate School of Management, 1983.

Hansmann, Henry B. "The Role of Nonprofit Enterprise." *Yale Law Journal* 89, no. 5 (April 1980): 835–901.

Hayek, Freidrich A. "The Use of Knowledge in Society." *American Economic Review* 35, no. 4 (September 1945): 519–30.

Herman, Edward S. "Conflict of Interest in the Savings and Loan Industry." In *A Study of the Savings and Loan Industry*, edited by Irwin Friend. Washington, D.C.: Federal Home Loan Board, 1969.

Herman, Edward S., *Corporate Control, Corporate Power*. Twentieth Century Fund Study. New York: Cambridge University Press, 1981.

Horngren, Charles. *Cost Accounting: A Managerial Emphasis*. Englewood Cliffs, N.J.: Prentice-Hall, Inc., 1982.

Jensen, Michael C. "Organization Theory and Methodology." *Accounting Review* 50, no. 2 (April 1983): 319–39.

Jensen, Michael C., and Meckling, William H. "Theory of the Firm: Managerial Behavior, Agency Costs and Ownership Structure." *Journal of Financial Economics* 3, no. 4 (October 1976): 305–60.

Jensen, Michael C., and Meckling, William H. "Rights and Production Functions: An Application to Labor-Managed Firms and Codetermination." *Journal of Business* 52, no. 4 (October 1979): 469–506.

Manne, Henry. "Mergers and the Market for Corporate Control." *Journal of Political Economy* 73, no. 2 (April 1965): 110–20.

Simon, Herbert A. "The Architecture of Complexity." *Proceedings of the American Philosophical Society* 106 (December 1962): 467–82.

Smith, Adam. *The Wealth of Nations*. 1776. Edited by Edwin Cannan, 1904. Reprint. New York: Modern Library, 1937.

Sowell, Thomas. *Knowledge and Decisions*. New York: Basic Books, 1980.

Stettler, Howard P. *Auditing Principles*. Englewood Cliffs, N.J.: Prentice-Hall, Inc., 1977.

Weber, Max. *The Theory of Social and Economic Organization*, edited by T. Parsons. Glencoe, Ill.: Free Press, 1947.

Williamson, Oliver E. *Markets and Hierarchies: Analysis and Antitrust Implications*. New York: Free Press, 1975.

Williamson, Oliver E. "The Modern Corporation: Origins, Evolution, Attributes." *Journal of Economic Literature* 19, no. 4 (December 1981): 1537–68.

[4]

THE STRUCTURE OF CORPORATION LAW*

*Melvin Aron Eisenberg***

A corporation is a profit-seeking enterprise of persons and assets organized by rules. Most of these rules are determined by the unilateral action of corporate organs or officials. Some of these rules are determined by market forces. Some are determined by contract or other forms of agreement. Some are determined by law.

This Article will consider the legal rules that directly concern the internal organization of the corporation and the conduct of corporate actors.[1] Viewed in terms of their form, these rules fall into three basic categories. *Enabling rules* give legal effect to rules that corporate actors adopt in a specified manner. *Suppletory* or *default rules* govern defined issues unless corporate actors adopt other rules in a specified manner. *Mandatory rules* govern defined issues in a manner that cannot be varied by corporate actors.[2]

The major purpose of this Article is to develop the normative principles that determine which of the legal rules that concern the internal organization of the corporation and the conduct of corporate actors should be enabling or suppletory, and which should be mandatory. Because the corporation is an economic institution that is owned and managed by human actors, the development of these principles rests for the most part on economic analysis, quantitative data, and the insights of psychology.

In practice, the application of these elements depends largely on the subject matter of the rule and the nature of the institutional setting. In terms of the nature of the institutional setting, I will distinguish between closely held corporations, publicly held corporations, and corpo-

---

** Koret Professor of Law, University of California, Berkeley. B.A., Columbia University, 1956; LL.B., Harvard University, 1959.

I thank Bernard Black, Bob Cooter, Merritt Fox, Ron Gilson, Bill Klein, Lewis Kornhauser, Roberta Romano, Dan Rubinfeld, Marshall Small, and Oliver Williamson for extremely helpful comments on drafts of this Article.

An early version of this Article was presented as a comment at a Conference on the Economics of Corporation Law at Harvard Law School in December 1986.

1. These rules do not exhaust corporation law. For example, some rules of corporation law concern the relationship between the corporation and its organs on the one hand, and the outside world on the other. A leading example is the rule that shareholders have limited liability. Rules of this type often have an indirect effect on the internal organization of the corporation, but will not be considered in this Article.

2. I do not consider in this Article the question which rules that are not mandatory should be enabling rules, and which should be suppletory or default rules. I also do not consider the principles that should govern the content of suppletory or default rules, and what form such rules should take. On these issues, see generally Ayres & Gertner, Filling Gaps in Incomplete Contracts: An Economic Theory of Default Rules (forthcoming 99 Yale L.J. (1989)).

rations that are about to go public. In terms of subject matter, I will distinguish between structural, distributional, and fiduciary rules. *Structural rules* govern the allocation of decisionmaking power among various corporate organs and agents and the conditions for the exercise of decisionmaking power; the allocation of control over corporate organs and agents; and the flow of information concerning the actions of corporate organs and agents. *Distributional rules* govern the distribution of assets (including earnings) to shareholders. *Fiduciary rules* govern the duties of managers and controlling shareholders. These three types of rules will be referred to collectively as *constitutive rules*, and that term will include both rules determined by law and rules determined by private action.

Part I will consider closely held corporations. In such corporations, constitutive rules are often determined by bargain. Whether the legal rules that govern such corporations should be enabling or suppletory on the one hand, or mandatory on the other, therefore depends in large part on the force and limits of the bargain principle. Given the force of that principle, structural and distributional rules should be enabling or suppletory at the core. Given the limits of that principle, fiduciary rules should be mandatory at the core.

Part II will consider publicly held corporations. In such corporations, constitutive rules are seldom determined by bargain. Whether the legal rules that govern such corporations should be enabling and suppletory on the one hand, or mandatory on the other, therefore depends in large part on the force and limits of noncontractual private ordering. Noncontractual private ordering may have considerable force in the absence of a conflict of interest. Accordingly, top managers should have power to determine the constitutive rules that govern the conduct of the corporation below their level, because it is in both their interests and the shareholders' interest to set such rules in an optimal fashion. In contrast, noncontractual private ordering by agents who have a conflict of interest is normally undesirable. Therefore, top managers in publicly held corporations should not have power to determine or materially vary the core fiduciary and structural rules that govern matters in which their interests may materially diverge from those of the shareholders. Furthermore, because of the defects in the proxy-voting process and the control over that process exercised by top managers, the core fiduciary and structural rules should not be subject to determination or material variation even with shareholder approval.

Finally, Part III will consider corporations that are about to make an initial public offering. Here too, the core fiduciary and structural rules should not be subject to variation, because variations in such rules might not be accurately priced, would be unfairly surprising, would lead to inefficiency in the capital markets, and might well lead to inefficiency in the national economy.

I. Closely Held Corporations

I begin with closely held corporations—corporations that have a small number of shareholders, most of whom either participate in or directly monitor corporate management.

A. *Structural and Distributional Rules*

In closely held corporations, shareholders often will bargain out at least some structural and distributional rules. It is a general principle of law that a bargain should normally be enforced according to its terms, without regard to whether it is reasonable or fair. One reason for this principle is that bargains have social utility because they create joint value through trade. Another reason is that a fully informed party is normally the best judge of his own utility or interest and, therefore, of the value to him of a bargained-for performance. The reasons for the bargain principle usually apply to bargains among the shareholders in a closely held corporation concerning the corporation's structural and distributional rules. Accordingly, at its core the law governing structural and distributional rules in closely held corporations should be enabling and suppletory, rather than mandatory.

This is essentially the position taken by modern corporate law. Modern case law has moved in the direction of enabling shareholders in closely held corporations to bargain out their own structural and distributional rules.[3] Many of the modern statutes explicitly validate such rules for those closely held corporations that elect special statutory treatment.[4]

At the periphery, however, a special type of mandatory legal rule should apply. The bargain principle is based partly on the proposition that a fully informed party is the best judge of his own utility. If a party is not fully informed, or lacks the sophistication to understand the implications of his bargain, the bargain principle loses some or all of its force. For example, the courts have traditionally refused to apply the bargain principle to liquidated-damages provisions, and instead have reviewed such provisions to determine whether they provided a reasonable forecast of the amount of damages foreseeable at the time the con-

3. See, e.g., Glazer v. Glazer, 374 F.2d 390, 411 (5th Cir.), cert. denied, 389 U.S. 831 (1967); Galler v. Galler, 32 Ill. 2d 16, 25, 203 N.E.2d 577, 583 (1964); Tschirgi v. Merchants Nat'l Bank, 253 Iowa 682, 690, 113 N.W.2d 226, 232 (1962); Peck v. Horst, 175 Kan. 479, 486, 264 P.2d 888, 893 (1953), aff'd on rehearing, 176 Kan. 581, 272 P.2d 1061 (1954); Petruzzi v. Peduka Constr., 362 Mass. 190, 193, 285 N.E.2d 101, 102 (1972); Henderson v. Joplin, 191 Neb. 827, 831–32, 217 N.W.2d 920, 923–24 (1974); Sternheimer v. Sternheimer, 208 Va. 89, 98–99, 155 S.E.2d 41, 48 (1967).

4. See, e.g., Cal. Corp. Code §§ 158, 300(b), 706(a) (West 1977 & Supp. 1989); Del. Code Ann. tit. 8, §§ 341–356 (1983 & Supp. 1988); Model Statutory Close Corp. Supp. §§ 3, 31 (1988), reprinted in 4 Model Business Corp. Act Ann. §§ 1803, 1810, 1845 (3d ed. Supp. 1989).

tract was made.[5] One major reason for this special treatment is that a contracting party will often fail to give his full attention to liquidated-damages provisions because he will focus on the contract terms governing his performance, which he expects to render, not on the contract terms governing breach, which he does not expect to commit. Furthermore, even if a contracting party does give such a provision his full attention, he will often fail to understand its implications because every contingency under which breach may occur cannot efficiently be conceived of (and indeed may not be conceivable) when a contract is made.

Within the last forty years, contract law has also developed and elaborated the principle of unconscionability, which serves as a limit on the bargain principle where one party's lack of information or sophistication is exploited by the other.[6] One of the most basic applications of this principle is the concept of unfair surprise, which renders unenforceable a term that one party knew or should have known would violate the other party's fair expectations.[7]

Still another problem, which contract law has only begun to address, involves long-term contracts.[8] John Stuart Mill, who argued that "laisser faire . . . should be the general practice" and "that every departure from it, unless required by some great good, is a certain evil,"[9] nevertheless singled out long-term contracts as appropriate for judicial intervention:

> [An] exception to the doctrine that individuals are the best judges of their own interest, is when an individual attempts to decide irrevocably now what will be best for his interest at some future and distant time. The presumption in favor of individual judgement is only legitimate, where the judgement is grounded on actual, and especially on present, personal experience; not where it is formed antecedently to experience, and not suffered to be reversed even after experience has condemned it. When persons have bound themselves by a contract, not simply to do some one thing, but to continue doing something . . . for a prolonged period, without any power of revoking the engagement . . . [any] presumption which can be grounded on their having voluntarily entered into the con-

5. See Restatement (Second) of Contracts § 356 (1981).

6. See Eisenberg, The Bargain Principle and its Limits, 95 Harv. L. Rev. 741, 769–73 (1982).

7. See, e.g., U.C.C. § 2-302 and Official Comment 1 (1987); Weaver v. American Oil Co., 257 Ind. 458, 464–65, 276 N.E.2d 144, 148 (1971); Johnson v. United Investors Life Ins. Co., 263 N.W.2d 770, 775–76 (Iowa 1978); C & J Fertilizer, Inc. v. Allied Mut. Ins. Co., 227 N.W.2d 169, 181 (Iowa 1975).

8. See A Schroeder Music Publishing Co. v. Macaulay, [1974] 3 All E.R. 616, 622 (five- to ten-year assignment of copyright to music publisher with no corresponding obligation to publish is unenforceable).

9. J. Mill, Principles of Political Economy 950 (W. Ashley ed. 1961).

tract . . . is commonly next to null.[10]

Mill's analysis is now further supported by evidence that there is a tendency to make systematic errors when comparing the value of present benefits and costs with future benefits and costs, and in particular, that there is a tendency to systematically underestimate risks.[11] Based on a review of the empirical evidence, Kenneth Arrow concluded, "[i]t is a plausible hypothesis that individuals are unable to recognize that there will be many surprises in the future; in short, as much . . . evidence tends to confirm, there is a tendency to underestimate uncertainties."[12] One reason for this is the representativeness heuristic, a characteristic judgment process in which small samples are often wrongly taken to be representative.[13] In particular, evidence based on the sample consisting of present events is often wrongly taken to be representative of future events. "The individual judges the likelihood of a future event by the similarity of the *present* evidence to it. There is a tendency to ignore both prior information . . . and the quality of the present evidence, for example, the size of the sample used to present evidence."[14] Another reason is that pallid evidence, such as a statement of probability, is unduly discounted in favor of vivid evidence, such as present events.[15]

These problems of systematic error apply with special force to bargains concerning closely held corporations. It is almost impossible for contracting parties to assess adequately the future costs and benefits in a fluid long-term relationship, because the tree of events will branch far beyond the ideas of the future that will be conceived when the contract is made. Furthermore, corporations by their nature involve a form of activity in which uncertainty plays an essential role. Because of the difficulty of predicting and planning for future events and their impact on a business enterprise, an opportunistic shareholder who controls one or more aspects of a closely held corporation will often find ways to exploit bargained-out structural and distributional rules that seemed both fair and complete at the time of the bargain.[16] It is almost impossible to deal adequately with this potential for ex post opportunism by ex ante contracting. Therefore, although the purpose of enforcing bar-

10. Id. at 959–60.

11. See T. Jackson, The Logic and Limits of Bankruptcy Law 232–40 (1986) (reviewing and synthesizing the literature).

12. Arrow, Risk Perception in Psychology and Economics, 20 Econ. Inquiry 1, 5 (1982).

13. Tversky & Kahneman, Belief in the Law of Small Numbers, *in* Judgment Under Uncertainty: Heuristics and Biases 23 (D. Kahneman, P. Slovic & A. Tversky eds. 1982).

14. Arrow, supra note 12, at 5.

15. See R. Nisbett & L. Ross, Human Inference: Strategies and Shortcomings of Social Judgment 55–59 (1980).

16. Moreover, closely held corporations involve personal relationships, which give rise to a special type of systematic error:

Typically, [closely held corporations] are founded by individuals who have a

gains is to protect expectations, the full enforcement of bargained-out structural and distributional rules in a closely held corporation may actually violate fair expectations. Accordingly, while the law governing the structural and distributional elements of closely held corporations should be largely enabling and suppletory, corporation law should also provide mandatory rules that empower the courts to override bargains concerning structural and distributional terms when necessary to prevent opportunism and protect probable fair expectations.

Modern corporation law has taken just this position. Both the courts and the legislatures have fashioned mandatory rules that limit the full force of bargains concerning structural and distributional rules in closely held corporations.

Some statutes simply limit the duration of such bargains. This approach has traditionally been taken to voting trusts,[17] and is now taken by a few states, including Delaware, with respect to shareholder agreements.[18]

A more widespread approach, reflected in both cases and statutes, provides for judicial intervention when enforcement of bargained-out structural and distributional rules would defeat a shareholder's fair expectations. The case law approaches this problem through the use of fiduciary principles. For example, in *Donahue v. Rodd Electrotype Co. of New England*,[19] the Massachusetts Supreme Judicial Court held that majority shareholders in a close corporation cannot use their voting power to authorize the purchase of shares from one of their number when an equal opportunity is not offered to the minority.[20] In *Wilkes v. Springside Nursing Home, Inc.*,[21] the same court held that majority shareholders in a close corporation cannot use their voting power to take a business ac-

---

> virtually complete identity of interests and strong feelings of trust and confidence for one another.
>
> Time and human nature may cause a divergence of interests and a breakdown in consensus, however. The nature of the enterprise may change so that the once-valued contributions of a shareholder-employee become irrelevant. The shareholder may become incapacitated. Personal relations with dominant shareholders may become strained to such an extent that the minority finds itself ignored. The interest of a deceased shareholder may pass to an heir who is unwilling or unable to participate actively in the business. Or a shareholder may simply come to believe that his talents and capital can be more profitably invested elsewhere.

Hetherington & Dooley, Illiquidity and Exploitation: A Proposed Statutory Solution to the Remaining Close Corporation Problem, 63 Va. L. Rev. 1, 2–3 (1977); see also Hillman, Private Ordering Within Partnerships, 41 U. Miami L. Rev. 425, 434–35 (1987) (discussing difficulty of anticipating future events in business relationships).

17. See, e.g., Del. Code Ann. tit. 8 § 218(a) (1983).

18. See id. § 218(c); 2 Model Business Corp. Act Ann. §§ 708–708.1 (3d ed. Supp. 1989) (nine states, including Delaware, impose a ten-year limit; two impose a twenty-year limit).

19. 367 Mass. 578, 328 N.E.2d 505 (1975).

20. Id. at 600, 328 N.E.2d at 519.

21. 370 Mass. 842, 353 N.E.2d 657 (1976).

tion that disadvantages the minority if the purpose of the action could be achieved through an alternative course of action that is less harmful to the minority.[22] In *Smith v. Atlantic Properties, Inc.*,[23] a Massachusetts appellate court held that if shareholders in a close corporation abuse a power of control over matters such as dividends or capital improvements, the court can determine the policies that will govern these matters.[24]

The statutes are equally far-reaching. A number of statutes give the courts authority to dissolve a corporation—and, thereby, any bargains concerning its constitutive rules—if those in control have acted oppressively or unfairly. Under the New York statute, for example, the court can order dissolution if those in control have been guilty of oppressive actions.[25] The statute directs the court to take into account whether liquidation is the only feasible means by which the complaining shareholders can reasonably expect to obtain a fair return on their investment.[26] In *In re Judicial Dissolution of Kemp & Beatley, Inc.*,[27] the New York Court of Appeals said that "oppression," in the context of such a statute, means "conduct that substantially defeats the 'reasonable expectations' held by minority shareholders in committing their capital to the particular enterprise."[28]

---

22. Id. at 851–52, 353 N.E.2d at 663.

23. 12 Mass. App. Ct. 201, 422 N.E.2d 798 (1981).

24. Id. at 210, 422 N.E.2d at 804. For additional cases holding that close corporation shareholders owe each other a fiduciary obligation, see Comolli v. Comolli, 241 Ga. 471, 475, 246 S.E.2d 278, 281 (1978); Cressy v. Shannon Continental Corp., 177 Ind. App. 224, 229–30, 378 N.E.2d 941, 945 (1978); 68th St. Apts., Inc. v. Lauricella, 142 N.J. Super. 546, 559, 362 A.2d 78, 85 (1976), aff'd per curiam, 150 N.J. Super. 47, 374 A.2d 1222 (1977).

25. N.Y. Bus. Corp. Law § 1104-a (McKinney 1986); see also Cal. Corp. Code §§ 1800(a)(2), (b)(4), 1804 (West 1977). Under the California statute, the courts are authorized to dissolve a corporation on the ground that those in control have knowingly countenanced persistent unfairness toward any shareholders. A petition can be brought on this ground by (i) shareholders who hold at least one-third of the corporation's shares, exclusive of those owned by persons who have personally participated in the actions under attack, or (ii) any shareholder of a statutory close corporation.

26. N.Y. Bus. Corp. Law § 1104-a(b)(1) (McKinney 1986). The section is confined to unlisted corporations, and a petition for dissolution under the section can be brought only by holders of 20% or more of the corporation's stock. Id. § 1104-a(a).

Many of the involuntary-dissolution statutes permit the corporation or the noncomplaining shareholders to avoid dissolution by purchasing the shares owned by the complainants at their fair value. See, e.g., Cal. Corp. Code § 2000(a) (West Supp. 1989); N.Y. Bus. Corp. Law § 1118(a) (McKinney Supp. 1989).

27. 64 N.Y.2d 63, 473 N.E.2d 1173, 484 N.Y.S.2d 799 (1984).

28. Id. at 72, 473 N.E.2d at 1179, 484 N.Y.S.2d at 805 (citations omitted). The court continued:

> A shareholder who reasonably expected that ownership in the corporation would entitle him or her to a job, a share of corporate earnings, a place in corporate management, or some other form of security, would be oppressed in a very real sense when others in the corporation seek to defeat those expectations and there exists no effective means of salvaging the investment.

The concept of a shareholder's fair expectations in corporation law parallels in part the concept of protecting against unfair surprise in contract law.[29] Also relevant is the contract-law doctrine that contracts must be performed in good faith.[30] However, the analogy to contract law has limits. Under the concept of unfair surprise, a court may disregard inconspicuous or unclear provisions of a written contract that eviscerate the fair expectations to which the contract's clear and prominent terms give rise, and then enforce the clear and prominent terms.[31] Under corporation law, in contrast, the court may derive fair expectations not only from a written agreement but from a broad range of circumstances, and may dissolve rather than enforce the shareholder's contract. For example, under the North Carolina statute the courts have power to liquidate a corporation if it "is reasonably necessary for the protection of the rights or interests of [a] complaining shareholder."[32] In *Meiselman v. Meiselman*,[33] the court held that a complaining shareholder's "reasonable expectations" are to be ascertained by examining the entire history of the participants' relationship. According to the Court, "[t]hat history will include the 'reasonable expectations' created at the inception of the participants' relationship; those 'reasonable expectations' as altered over time; and the 'reasonable expectations' which develop as the participants engage in a course of dealing in conducting the affairs of the corporation."[34]

Moreover, although the relevant statutes are rooted in the remedy

---

Id. at 72–73, 473 N.E.2d at 1179, 484 N.Y.S.2d at 805; see also Stefano v. Coppock, 705 P.2d 443, 446 n.3 (Alaska 1985); Fox v. 7L Bar Ranch Co., 198 Mont. 201, 209–10, 645 P.2d 929, 933 (1982); cf. Meiselman v. Meiselman, 309 N.C. 279, 298, 307 S.E.2d 551, 563 (1983) (dissolution allowed where "rights and interests of minority shareholders" were violated by majority shareholder); Masinter v. WEBCO, 164 W. Va. 241, 251–52, 262 S.E.2d 433, 440 (1980) (breach of fiduciary duty is " 'oppressive conduct' "). See generally Thompson, Corporate Dissolution and Shareholders' Reasonable Expectations, 66 Wash. U.L.Q. 193, 237–38 (1988) (remedy of dissolution and the reasonable expectations standard form effective substitute for private ordering).

29. See U.C.C. § 2-302 and official comment 1 (1987); Restatement (Second) of Contracts § 208 (1981).

30. See U.C.C. § 1-203 (1987); Restatement (Second) of Contracts § 205 (1981).

31. See, e.g., Frank's Maintenance & Eng'g, Inc. v. C.A. Roberts Co., 86 Ill. App. 3d 980, 991–93, 408 N.E.2d 403, 411–12 (1980); Collins v. Uniroyal, Inc., 126 N.J. Super. 401, 406, 315 A.2d 30, 33 (1973), aff'd, 64 N.J. 260, 315 A.2d 16 (1974); Gerhardt v. Continental Ins. Cos., 48 N.J. 291, 298–300, 225 A.2d 328, 332–34 (1966).

32. N.C. Gen. Stat. § 55-125(a)(4) (1982); see also N.Y. Bus. Corp. Law § 1104-a(b)(2) (McKinney 1986) ("[T]he court . . . shall take into account . . . [w]hether liquidation of the corporation is reasonably necessary for the protection of the rights and interests of any substantial number of shareholders . . . ."); Minn. Stat. Ann. § 302A.751, Subd. 3a (West Supp. 1989) ("In determining whether to order . . . dissolution . . . the Court shall take into consideration the duty which all shareholders . . . owe one another to act in an honest, fair, and reasonable manner . . . and the reasonable expectations of the shareholders . . . ."); N.D. Cent. Code § 10.19.1-115.3 (1985) (same).

33. 309 N.C. 279, 307 S.E.2d 551 (1983).

34. Id. at 298, 307 S.E.2d at 563; see also Fox v. 7L Bar Ranch Co., 198 Mont. 201, 210, 645 P.2d 929, 933 (1982) ("[C]ourts must determine the expectations of the share-

of dissolution, the courts usually have the power to impose, as an alternative remedy, a revision of constitutive rules that the parties clearly agreed to. In some cases, the statutes explicitly grant such power. The California statute, for example, provides that the court "may make such orders and decrees and issue such injunctions in the case as justice and equity require."[35] The North Carolina statute provides that in an action for dissolution the court may cancel or alter any provision in the corporation's articles of incorporation or by-laws.[36] Even where such power is not explicitly granted, it may be held to be implied. For example, in *Baker v. Commercial Body Builders*,[37] the Oregon court held that although the Oregon statute in terms authorized only the remedy of dissolution, a court also had authority to grant other forms of relief, such as a decree reducing and distributing capital, ordering the declaration of a dividend, or empowering minority shareholders to purchase additional stock on terms set by the court.[38] In *In re Judicial Dissolution of Kemp & Beatley, Inc.*,[39] the New York court construed the comparable New York statute in a similar way.[40]

B. *Fiduciary Rules*

Structural and distributional legal rules for closely held corporations should be enabling and suppletory at the core but mandatory at the periphery. In contrast, fiduciary legal rules for closely held corporations should be mandatory at the core but enabling and suppletory at the periphery. The reasons behind these principles are straightforward. The bargain principle assumes that contracting parties are fully informed, or at least not systematically underinformed. Parties who bargain over structural and distributional rules are likely to understand the consequences of their bargain in most cases, at least over the short term, and mandatory rules are therefore needed only as a backstop. However, bargains to relax materially the fiduciary rules set by law would likely be systematically underinformed even over the short term. Even if the shareholders understood the content of the rules whose protection they attempted to waive—which is unlikely—they still could

---

holders concerning their respective roles in corporate affairs."); Thompson, supra note 28, at 218–19.

35. Cal. Corp. Code § 1804 (West 1977 & Supp. 1989).

36. N.C. Gen. Stat. § 55-125.1(a)(1) (1982) (court may cancel or alter "any provision contained in charter or the bylaws"); see also Me. Rev. Stat. Ann. tit. 13-A, § 1123(3)(D) (1981) (same); S.C. Code Ann. § 33-14-310(d)(1) (Law. Co-op. 1976 & Supp. 1988) (same).

37. 264 Or. 614, 507 P.2d 387 (1973).

38. Id. at 631–33, 507 P.2d at 395–96.

39. 64 N.Y.2d 63, 473 N.E.2d 1173, 484 N.Y.S.2d 799 (1984).

40. Id. at 73, 473 N.E.2d at 1180, 484 N.Y.S.2d at 806. But see White v. Perkins, 213 Va. 129, 135, 189 S.E.2d 315, 320 (1972) (dissolution or appointment of custodian are exclusive remedies available to a minority shareholder under the Virginia dissolution statute).

not begin to foresee the varying circumstances to which such a waiver would be applicable. Any such waiver would therefore inevitably permit unanticipated opportunistic behavior.

Some bargained-out fiduciary rules do not present the dangers of systematic error and exploitation. Bargains to change a legal rule that is not congruent with current concepts of fairness or that does not afford any real protection to shareholders, such as the old rules that interested transactions were voidable without regard to fairness or that interested directors could not be counted in determining a quorum, fall into this category.[41] In some cases, a bargained-out fiduciary rule is specific, easily understood, and not easily susceptible to exploitation. A rule that clearly specifies a type of business venture that will not be considered a corporate opportunity may fall in this category.[42] Similarly, shareholder approval of a specific conflict-of-interest transaction usually does not present the dangers of systematically underinformed consent and exploitation, because the approval relates to a specific event rather than to an unknowable future. In these peripheral cases, bargained-out fiduciary rules should be enforceable.

The law reflects these principles. The core fiduciary rules which govern the close corporation are mandatory,[43] but private rules that do not present the dangers of systematic unforeseeability and exploitation—such as rules that allow an interested director to be counted toward a quorum—normally will be given effect.[44]

---

41. See Marsh, Are Directors Trustees?—Conflict of Interest and Corporate Morality, 22 Bus. Law. 35, 39–43 (1966).

42. See Principles of Corporate Governance: Analysis and Recommendations § 5.09(c) (Tent. Draft No. 7, 1987). On the other hand, a rule that permitted directors or officers to take opportunities that were derived from corporate information would present the dangers of unforeseeability and exploitation and, therefore, should be unenforceable. See id.

43. See Pappas v. Moss, 393 F.2d 865, 867–68 (3d Cir. 1968); Irwin v. West End Dev. Co., 342 F. Supp. 687, 701 (D. Colo. 1972), aff'd in part and rev'd in part on other grounds, 481 F.2d 34 (10th Cir. 1973), cert. denied, 414 U.S. 1158 (1974); Sterling v. Mayflower Hotel Corp., 33 Del. Ch. 293, 313–14, 93 A.2d 107, 118 (S. Ct. 1952); Abeles v. Adams Eng'g Co., 35 N.J. 411, 428–30, 173 A.2d 246, 255 (1961).

A number of recent statutes permit the certificate of incorporation to limit or eliminate personal liability of directors for simple duty-of-care violations. See, e.g., Del. Code Ann. tit. 8, § 102(b)(7) (Supp. 1988). Almost all of these statutes, however, are explicitly inapplicable to duty-of-care violations by officers and duty-of-loyalty violations by either directors or officers. See Principles of Corporate Governance: Analysis and Recommendations § 7.17, reporter's note 6 (Tent. Draft No. 9, 1989).

44. See Piccard v. Sperry Corp., 48 F. Supp. 465, 469 (S.D.N.Y. 1943), aff'd per curiam, 152 F.2d 462 (2d Cir.), cert. denied, 328 U.S. 845 (1946); Sterling v. Mayflower Hotel Corp., 33 Del. Ch. at 313–14 , 93 A.2d at 118; Hackett v. Diversified Chem., Inc., 180 So. 2d 831, 834–35 (La. Ct. App. 1965); Everett v. Phillips, 288 N.Y. 227, 233, 236–37, 43 N.E.2d 18, 20–22 (1942); Adams v. Mid-West Chevrolet Corp., 198 Okla. 461, 473, 179 P.2d 147, 160 (1947).

II. Publicly Held Corporations

I turn now to publicly held corporations, by which I mean corporations that have a large number of shareholders, most of whom neither participate in the management of the corporation nor directly monitor corporate management.[45] Typically, the number of managerial and nonmanagerial agents is also large, and for reasons of efficiency the business of the corporation is controlled and conducted by these agents. Under these conditions, bargaining among the shareholders, or between managers and the shareholders as a body, is virtually impossible. Accordingly, most of the constitutive rules of such corporations are determined not by contract, but by law or by private bureaucratic rulemaking—for example, by managerial orders, by board or committee resolutions, by board-adopted by-laws, or by board determination of governance terms in preferred stock, stock rights, or debt instruments.

In such corporations, therefore, the principles that determine which legal rules should be enabling or suppletory and which should be mandatory depend on the force and limits of forms of private ordering other than bargain and contract. The force and limits of these forms of private ordering in publicly held corporations, in turn, depend very largely on the impact of the potential self-interest of top managers of such corporations and on the extent to which this impact is controlled by market forces other than bargain and contract.

A. *Divergencies of Interest*

The interests of the shareholders and managers in publicly held corporations converge in many respects: in general, if the shareholders do well, so will the managers. As in any principal-agent relationship, however, the interests of shareholders and managers also diverge. All agents have a potential interest in working at a slack pace and in avoiding the effort and discomfort involved in adapting to changed circumstances, such as the emergence of new technologies. This is the problem known as *shirking*. All agents have a potential interest in diverting the principal's assets to their own use through unfair self-dealing. This is the problem of *traditional conflicts of interest*.

Top corporate managers differ from most other agents, however, in that they are legally and factually autonomous for many purposes. For example, under corporate law the shareholders normally cannot make ordinary business decisions, cannot make major structural decisions unless the directors concur, and cannot remove directors without cause.[46] Because of this relative autonomy, and the range of discretion

45. Corporations that are about to become publicly held are considered in Part III, infra.

46. See M. Eisenberg, The Structure of the Corporation 2-5 (1976). Indeed, because of their relative autonomy, some top corporate managers are not agents at all in

that it leads to, top corporate managers have the power to give expression to still a third potential divergence of interest: an interest in maintaining and enhancing their positions even at the shareholders' expense. I will refer to instances of this type of divergence of interest as *positional conflicts*.[47]

Positional conflicts may be expressed in a great variety of ways. For example, top managers may make it particularly difficult for anyone to objectively monitor their performance. They may impose high barriers to their own removal for inefficiency or other reasons. They may seek to increase corporate size as a way to maximize their power, prestige, and salary, even if an increase in corporate size does not increase shareholder wealth. They may seek to maximize the cash and other resources that they command, even when distributions to the shareholders would be more efficient. They may diversify the firm as a means to reduce the riskiness of their human-capital investments, even when diversification of the firm is not in the interest of shareholders because shareholders can diversify their own risks through portfolio management.[48]

In the real world, positional conflicts are much more important

---

the classical legal sense. See Clark, Agency Costs Versus Fiduciary Duties, *in* Principals and Agents: The Structure of Business 55, 58 (J. Pratt & R. Zeckhauser eds. 1985). Top corporate managers are, however, agents in the economic sense, because they are under both a moral and a legal obligation to manage the corporation in the interest of the shareholders. This moral and legal obligation is imposed because the shareholders are the owners of the corporation; because shareholder ownership is a critical element of corporate legitimacy; and because the shareholders' interest that the corporation maximize profits, within broad constraints, is largely coincident with the social interest.

47. The takeover movement is based in part on the results of positional conflicts. A bidder may be able to offer an above-market price for a target because the target's managers have prevented the installation of internal monitoring and removal devices, so that the target is being run by inefficient managers. Or the target's managers may have stressed growth over profits, so that a sell-off of the corporation's businesses (a bust-up takeover) will yield more value than its continued operation. On the other side of the equation, the bidder's management may be motivated by its own taste for size, as evidenced by the fact that bidders appear to make little or perhaps even no gains on acquisitions. See Jarrell, Brickley & Netter, The Market for Corporate Control: The Empirical Evidence Since 1980, J. Econ. Persp., Winter 1988, at 49, 53; Roll, The Hubris Hypothesis of Corporate Takeovers, 59 J. Bus. 197, 198 (1986).

48. See Shleifer & Vishny, Value Maximization and the Acquisition Process, J. Econ. Persp., Winter 1988, at 7, 7–9:

> Like the rest of us, corporate managers have many personal goals and ambitions, only one of which is to get rich. The way they try to run their companies reflects these personal goals. . . . Much corporate behavior seems best understood in terms of managers running the show largely as they please. . . . [I]n practice, non-value-maximizing behavior seems vastly to exceed what one would expect to observe under optimal incomplete information contracts. A wealth of evidence suggests that managers often take actions that dramatically reduce the value of the firm. . . . [I]t is important to recognize that a manager is likely to take whatever actions he can to make himself more valuable to the firm, and more costly to remove.

than either shirking or traditional conflicts of interest. Most top managers will probably refrain from shirking simply because their self-esteem is tied to hard work and accomplishment. Most top managers will probably refrain from unfair self-dealing simply because they have internalized the rules of social morality. However, self-esteem and morality may often be inadequate to curb positional conflicts.[49] The top manager's self-esteem often crucially depends on the maintenance and enhancement of his position, and conduct designed to maintain and enhance one's position may not be immoral in any obvious sense.

Of course, many top managers will not act in a manner that reflects positional conflicts, just as they will not work at a slack pace or engage in unfair self-dealing. However, top managers may fail even to recognize that positional conflicts exist. Inefficient top managers are unlikely to believe themselves to be inefficient. Top managers who enhance their positions through corporate growth, diversification, or the like, usually believe (often, but not always, correctly) that their actions are in the interest of the shareholders. Finally, top managers may have more difficulty in taming a taste for maintaining and enhancing their positions than in taming a taste for shirking or unfair self-dealing. It is at least in part through the appetite for position that top managers have achieved their place atop the corporate hierarchy. Thus, not only are moral restraints normally weaker in the case of positional conflicts than in the case of shirking or unfair self-dealing, but avoiding the expression of such conflicts may require the manager to control the very characteristics that put him where he is.

The divergencies of interest between corporate agents and shareholders, and the special problem of positional conflicts, explain why some constitutive rules that govern publicly held corporations should be enabling or suppletory while others should be mandatory. The legal rules that govern the internal organization of the corporation and the conduct of corporate actors *below the level of top managers* should by and large be enabling or suppletory. Top managers have both the self-interest and the power to install constitutive rules that will efficiently determine the roles, coordination, supervision, and monitoring of lower corporate agents and constrain those agents from giving expression to their own interests in preference to the interests of the shareholders.

In contrast, top managers of publicly held corporations have little incentive to adopt rules that put constraints on their own positions. On the contrary, the incentive of top managers may be to insulate themselves from such constraints. The core fiduciary and structural rules that govern material divergencies of interest of top managers in publicly held corporations, therefore, should be neither determined nor subject to material variation by the action of managers or managerial

49. Market forces are also inadequate, as demonstrated below. See Part II.E, infra.

organs.[50] The reason for this principle is not that legislatures or judges know more about such rules than top managers; they may or may not. Rather, the reason is that in this as in other areas of law, agents whose interests may materially diverge from the interests of their principals should not have the power to unilaterally determine or materially vary the rules that govern those divergencies of interest.

B. *The Limits of Shareholder Consent*

This first principle—that the core fiduciary and structural rules that govern material divergencies of interest of top managers in publicly held corporations should be neither determined nor subject to material variation by managers or managerial organs—spills into a second. Such rules should also normally not be subject to determination or material variation even with shareholder approval. Allowing such rules to be determined or materially varied on the basis of shareholder approval would effectively undercut the first principle, because, under current law and practice, shareholder consent to rules proposed by top managers in publicly held corporations may be either nominal, tainted by a conflict of interest, coerced or impoverished.[51]

1. *Nominal consent.* — Under current law and practice, an action proposed by managers may be legally deemed approved by shareholders who never consented to it in fact. For example, under Rule 14a-4(b)(1) of the Proxy Rules,[52] if a shareholder does not designate how he wants to vote on a given issue, management may vote the shareholder's proxy as it chooses, provided the form of proxy states how management intends to vote.[53] For many shareholders, the cost of reading and understanding each proposal in the proxy materials will exceed the likely economic effect of any given proposal. For such shareholders, it is rational not to read any proposals.[54] Shareholders receive a number of management proposals in proxy statements. Because the interests of managers and shareholders converge to a significant extent, and because many proposals relate to housekeeping details (such as approval of auditors), shareholders have reason to believe that the typical management proposal will be value-increasing. Therefore, unless a shareholder holds a very large amount of a given corporation's

---

50. This does not mean that all constitutive rules that concern top managers should be mandatory. Many or most of the constitutive rules that define and coordinate the tasks of top managers should be determined by private ordering, because many or most such rules do not involve divergencies of interest between top managers and shareholders.

51. Further reasons for this second principle are developed in Part III, infra.

52. 17 C.F.R. § 240.14a-4(b)(1) (1988).

53. Id.

54. See R. Clark, Corporate Law § 9.5.1 (1986); Easterbrook & Fischel, The Corporate Contract, 89 Colum. L. Rev. 1416, 1443 (1989); Gordon, Ties That Bond: Dual Class Common Stock and the Problem of Shareholder Choice, 76 Calif. L. Rev. 1, 43–44 (1988).

stock, he will probably conclude that the expected gains from analyzing all the management proposals he receives will be less than the expected costs. If the shareholder nevertheless signs and returns the form of proxy, solely for the purpose of reelecting incumbent directors, Rule 14a-4 allows management to vote his shares for a proposal of whose terms he was completely ignorant, and as to which he gave no consent.[55]

Similarly, shares that are held of record by a broker or broker's depository are often voted by the broker with no instructions from the beneficial owner. Although the Proxy Rules generally require an institutional holder of record to forward corporate soliciting material to the beneficial owner, they do not prohibit the institutional holder of record from voting the proxy on the beneficial owner's behalf in the absence of instructions from the beneficial owner.[56] When a beneficial owner's shares are registered in the name of a broker or a brokers' depository, the rules that determine how the broker can vote the shares are those of the stock exchanges and the National Association of Securities Dealers.[57] The rules of the New York Stock Exchange are dominant in this area, because of the importance of the corporations listed on that exchange and the dollar volume of trading. Under the Exchange's "ten-day rule," a broker can vote shares held in his name even though he has received no instructions from the beneficial owner how to vote the stock and did not inform the owner how he would vote the stock in the absence of instructions, as long as he solicited instructions from the owner at least fifteen days before the meeting and has not received instructions by the tenth day before the meeting.[58] Brokers receive instructions from the beneficial owners for only half the shares registered in broker name.[59] Brokers who vote without instructions from owners ordinarily vote in favor of management proposals.[60]

The power of a broker to vote without instructions under the Exchange's ten-day rule is subject to a number of exceptions,[61] but the exceptions fail to cover a number of important matters. For example, within the past several years many states have authorized corporations to adopt certificate-of-incorporation provisions that limit or eliminate directors' liability for breach of the duty of care.[62] Despite the impor-

55. 17 C.F.R. § 240.14a-4 (1988).

56. Rule 14b-1, 14b-2, 17 C.F.R. § 240.14b-1, 240.14b-2 (1988).

57. See, e.g., New York Stock Exchange Listed Company Manual ¶ 402.06(A), (D) (1986).

58. Id.

59. J. Heard & H. Sherman, Conflicts of Interest in the Proxy Voting System 22 (1987).

60. Id. at 22.

61. New York Stock Exchange Listed Company Manual ¶ 402.06(D) (1986).

62. See, e.g., Cal. Corp. Code § 204(a)(10) (West 1977 & Supp. 1989); Del. Code Ann. tit. 8, § 102(b)(7) (Supp. 1988); N.J. Stat. Ann. § 14A:2-7(3) (West 1969 & Supp. 1989).

tance of such provisions, the Exchange has permitted brokers to vote stock registered in their names on these provisions with no instructions whatsoever from the beneficial owners.[63]

2. *Consent that is tainted by a conflict of interest.* — Shareholder consent that is not nominal may nevertheless be tainted by a conflict of interest. Approximately fifty percent of the stock in publicly held corporations is owned by institutional investors.[64] Many institutional investors have ties to management that inhibit voting against a management proposal.[65] For example, if the trust department of a bank holds the stock of C Corporation in a pension portfolio, and C is also a client of the bank's commercial department, a trust officer will think long and hard before voting against a proposal made by C's management. Indeed, some corporate managers have begun to explicitly request their counterparts in other corporations to pressure pension-fund trustees to take a promanagement stance in casting their votes.[66] The same problem arises for insurance companies, which, like banks, often have extensive commercial contacts with corporations whose stock they hold in their investment portfolios.[67] Undoubtedly, institutional investors often vote in the interests of their beneficiaries despite such conflicts, but it seems equally clear that institutional investors often succumb to a conflict of interest in their voting decisions.[68]

Frequently, shareholder voting decisions are based on an even more direct conflict of interest. Managers often have significant holdings in their own corporations, and they are seldom if ever prohibited from voting their holdings in favor of a proposal that advances their own interests.[69] Even more to the point, in many corporations a controlling block is held by one or more corporate or individual shareholders whose interests may diverge from those of the noncontrolling

63. Telephone conversation with Paul Wyciskala, Managing Director of Operations & Policy Support, New York Stock Exchange, June 8, 1989. An exception is made if material litigation is pending. Id.

64. See W. Cary & M. Eisenberg, Cases and Materials on Corporations 195–96 (6th ed. 1988) (in 1986, 54% of total equity holdings held by institutional investors).

65. See generally J. Heard & H. Sherman, supra note 59, at 40–67; Herman, Commercial Bank Trust Departments, *in* Abuse on Wall Street: Conflicts of Interest in the Securities Markets 23, 72 (Twentieth Century Fund ed. 1980).

66. See J. Heard & H. Sherman, supra note 59, at 99.

67. See id. at 54.

68. See id. at 40–67.

69. The mean inside holding (including options that could be exercised within 60 days) of chief executive officers and their immediate families in 746 corporations, as published in the 1987 Forbes Executive Compensation Survey, was 2.42 percent, although the median holding was only .25 percent. What the Boss Makes: The People in Power, Forbes, June 15, 1987, at 162, discussed in M. Jensen & K. Murphy, Performance Pay and Top-Management Incentives, University of Rochester Managerial Economics Research Center Working Paper No. 89-08, at 14–15 (1989). Obviously, however, many chief executive officers own significantly more than the mean, and many top officers other than the chief executive also have significant inside holdings.

shareholders. In theory, voting by a controlling shareholder can be reviewed on a case-by-case basis under a fairness test.[70] In practice, however, the costs of bringing a suit based on fairness, and the difficulty of applying that test in this context, would make a case-by-case review of the fairness of votes cast by controlling shareholders an inadequate tool for regulating the conflicts of interest of controlling shareholders voting on variations in core fiduciary or structural rules that they have proposed.

3. *Coerced consent.* — Shareholder consent that is neither nominal nor tainted by a conflict of interest may nevertheless be coerced. For example, management may threaten to withhold approval of an action that is in the shareholders' best interests, such as an increase in dividends, unless the shareholders approve an unrelated management proposal.[71] Or, management may tie a proposal that shareholders might vote down if it stood alone to a proposal that shareholders will clearly favor.[72]

4. *Impoverished consent.* — Finally, and perhaps most importantly, shareholder consent that is neither nominal, tainted by a conflict of interest, nor coercive may nevertheless be impoverished. For example, shareholders may vote for a rule proposed by management even though they would prefer a different rule, because the proposed rule is better than the rule it replaces and management's control over the agenda effectively limits the shareholders' choice to the existing rule or the proposed rule.

Proposals concerning directors' liability for breach of the duty of care furnish an example. The recently adopted statutes permit adoption of a certificate amendment that either limits such liability or eliminates it entirely.[73] The duty of care is an important tool for ensuring managerial accountability. One factor that may have motivated the recent statutes was a great increase in the cost of directors' liability insurance.[74] Another is the real possibility that liability for duty-of-care violations will be hugely disproportionate both to directors' fees and to fault. This raises an issue not only of fairness but of efficiency, because the prospect of such disproportionate liability may deter qualified persons from accepting outside directorships and may make directors un-

70. Cf. Sterling v. Mayflower Hotel Corp., 33 Del. Ch. 293, 298, 93 A.2d 107, 110–11 (Sup. Ct. 1952) (review of self-interested merger for fairness).

71. This tactic has been especially prevalent in dual-class voting. See Lacos Land Co. v. Arden Group, Inc., 517 A.2d 271, 276–79 (Del. Ch. 1986); Gordon, supra note 54, at 48–53. For an analysis of the coercive effect of this tactic, see Ruback, Coercive Dual-Class Exchange Offers, 20 J. Fin. Econ. 153, 157 (1988).

72. See, e.g., Inco "Poison Pill" Tested in Canada, N.Y. Times, Dec. 7, 1988, at D8, col. 3 (poison pill and special $10 dividend combined in a single proposal).

73. See, e.g., Del. Code Ann. tit. 8, § 102(b)(7) (Supp. 1988).

74. See, e.g., Sing, More Firms Shielding Directors from Suits, L.A. Times, May 14, 1989, pt. 4, at 6, col. 1 (change in Delaware law permitting liability limitation "triggered in part by the high cost of directors liability insurance").

duly risk-averse. Both the cost and the disproportionality problems could be addressed by certificate amendments that limit directors' liability to a low fixed amount or to an amount equal to directors' fees for one or two years. The certificate amendments proposed by management under these new statutes, however, invariably call for director liability to be completely eliminated, not simply limited. Suppose shareholders believe the best rule would be to limit liability to a reasonable amount, thereby preserving accountability while both reducing insurance premiums and serving the fairness and policy goals that might be frustrated by disproportionate liability. The shareholders might nevertheless vote in favor of a management proposal to eliminate liability, because management control over the agenda effectively restricts the shareholders to a choice between the management proposal or the existing rule, and as between those two rules the management proposal may seem preferable.

More fundamentally, shareholder approval may be impoverished because many shareholders may have a weak, incomplete, or nonexistent understanding of a proposal for which they vote. To begin with, under the Proxy Rules, management can present proposals to the shareholders with a one-sided argument. The Proxy Rules do not enable a shareholder who opposes a management proposal to present the other side of the matter in the corporate proxy statement.[75] Of course, the management argument cannot be misleading,[76] but an argument that is not misleading may nevertheless be very one-sided.[77]

Even if the argument for a management proposal is balanced, many shareholders will rationally decide not to read it, for reasons that have already been canvassed.[78] And even if a shareholder does analyze a particular management proposal and does determine that the proposal would be value-decreasing, he is unlikely to mount a counter-solicitation unless his stake in the corporation is extremely large, because if he prevails other shareholders would not bear any of the costs of the counter-solicitation but would free-ride on most of its benefits.

Of course, the free-rider problem could be addressed by collective action, but the barriers to collective action are extremely high. A communication by a shareholder who seeks to alleviate the free-rider problem by forming a group to share the costs of a solicitation will probably itself be a solicitation subject to the Proxy Rules, unless the shareholder solicits less than eleven other persons to join his group.[79] Even if a

75. See Rule 14a-8(c)(9), 17 C.F.R. § 240.14a-8(c)(9) (1988).

76. Rule 14a-9, 17 C.F.R. § 240.14a-9 (1988).

77. See, e.g., the proxy statements of Schering Plough Corporation and RCA Corporation, excerpts from which are reprinted in 3 M. Lipton & E. Steinberger, Takeovers & Freezeouts G-3, G-20 (1989).

78. See supra note 54 and accompanying text.

79. Rules 14a-1(k)(iii), 14a-2(b)(6), 17 C.F.R. § 240.14a-1(k)(iii), 14a-2(b)(6) (1988).

group is successfully formed, shareholders who do not join the group will free-ride on its efforts and will therefore have an incentive not to join.[80]

Initiatives by shareholders are even less likely than counter-solicitations. Under most statutes, an amendment of the certificate of incorporation must be initiated by the board.[81] Accordingly, a shareholder cannot solicit for any change in a corporation's constitutive rules that would require certificate amendment. Instead, he would have to mount a campaign to oust the board, which is extremely expensive and in any event may not be his objective.

Even changes that can be accomplished without a certificate amendment face substantial impediments. Management can solicit proxies against a proposed change in the corporation's constitutive rules at no cost to itself, because it can charge the expenses of its soliciting activity to the corporation.[82] In contrast, a shareholder who proposes to solicit for a change must bear his own expenses, and will encounter the same free-rider problem and barriers to collective action that confront a shareholder who is considering a counter-solicitation.[83] Accordingly, even a very large shareholder in a publicly held corporation is unlikely to solicit for a change in the corporation's constitutive rules unless the change would be exceptionally wealth-maximizing for the shareholders of the individual corporation (for example, the elimination of a poison pill) or would have some sort of precedential value for other corporations in which he holds major investments.

The many limits on the meaningfulness of shareholder consent do not compel the conclusion that shareholder voting is never meaningful. Some individual holders may read the proxy statement and vote their own stock. Some institutional holders have no conflicting ties to management. Many institutional holders that do have conflicts of interest will nevertheless vote in the interests of their beneficiaries, either because of a sense of moral duty or because of legal pressures or pressures to maximize their returns. As a result, management proposals

80. Even if a shareholder's stake is large enough, and the expected negative impact is great enough, rationally to justify some expenditure against the proposal, the expenditure will be less than the optimum amount. See Gordon, supra note 54, at 44 n.143.

81. See, e.g., Del. Code Ann. tit. 8, § 242(b)(1) (1983); Revised Model Business Corp. Act § 10.03(a), (b)(1) (1984).

82. See M. Eisenberg, supra note 46, at 102–10.

83. Rule 14a-8, 17 C.F.R. § 240.14a-8 (1988), gives shareholders the right to require certain kinds of proposals to be included in the corporate proxy statement. However, the Rule is subject to a number of important exceptions that drastically limit its usefulness to shareholders who propose to solicit for significant changes. For example, under state law, mergers, sales of substantially all assets, amendments to the certificate of incorporation, and dissolution must normally be initiated by the board. Shareholder proposals to effectuate any such transactions would therefore normally be excludable from the proxy statement under Rule 14a-8(c)(1), 17 C.F.R. § 240.14a-8(c)(1) (1988), which permits exclusion of a proposal that is not a proper subject for action by shareholders under state law.

that will have obvious and very large value-decreasing effects are unlikely to be adopted by shareholders, and even proposals that have smaller negative effects may not always be adopted. Furthermore, it is entirely conceivable that with further increases in institutional ownership, and changes in the moral, legal, and financial pressures that affect voting by institutional owners, the significance of shareholder voting will change in the future. Under prevailing conditions, however, the limits on the meaningfulness of shareholder consent are so substantial that allowing those rules to be determined or materially varied by top managers with shareholder approval often would be functionally equivalent to allowing those rules to be unilaterally determined or materially varied by top managers.

C. *The Structure of the Law Governing Publicly Held Corporations*

The general principle, then, is that in publicly held corporations, mandatory legal rules should govern those core fiduciary and structural areas in which the interests of shareholders and top managers may materially diverge. The content of these rules should reflect the basic types of potential divergence. To deal with traditional conflicts of interest, mandatory rules should impose a duty of fair dealing, should provide for disclosure of self-interested transactions, and should establish an effective enforcement mechanism. To deal with the problem of shirking, mandatory rules should impose a duty of care. As to these matters, the principle that governs publicly held corporations is the same as the principle that governs closely held corporations: fiduciary rules should be mandatory at the core.

In the case of publicly held corporations, however, an additional principle comes into play to deal with positional conflicts, which involve the most serious of the divergencies of interest between top managers and shareholders. In such corporations, core structural rules double as fiduciary rules, because it is structural rules that address positional conflicts. Accordingly, in publicly held corporations core structural rules as well as core fiduciary rules should be mandatory.

These core structural rules fall into several categories. One set of mandatory structural rules should provide for the appointment and monitoring of senior executives by a governing organ (that is, a board of directors) that is elected by shareholders for a limited term of office, a majority of which is composed of members who are independent of the senior executives. A second set should require periodic disclosure of detailed financial data and information concerning material business and legal developments and should provide for institutional mechanisms to ensure that the financial data is reliable. A third set should concern the approval of, and dissent from, transactions that tend to raise positional conflicts. In general, shareholder approval should be required for any transaction in control to which the corporation is a party—that is, any corporate transaction that causes a change in control of the corporation, its assets, or its business. In the case of major transactions that characteristically involve either traditional or positional conflicts, create a significant potential for overreaching by controlling shareholders, or radically alter the structure of the corporation, dissenting shareholders should have the right to require the corporation to purchase their shares at fair value. A final set of mandatory structural rules should protect the integrity of shareholder voting.

The core mandatory rules should operate to check positional conflicts without preventing advantageous corporate transactions. To this end, the core structural rules should require mechanisms for accountability and disclosure for top executives, shareholder approval of certain transactions, and appraisal rights for certain transactions, but they should not regulate the content of corporate transactions. Because mandatory rules generally should not regulate the content of transactions, distributional rules should generally be enabling, except as required to protect the interests of creditors.

The legal rules that actually govern publicly held corporations correspond reasonably well to the legal rules that should govern such corporations.

Assume, for example, that a given corporation is publicly held, but has less than 500 shareholders and is not required to register its stock under Section 12(g) of the Securities Exchange Act.[84] Call such a corporation a small publicly held corporation. Suppose first that the corporation is incorporated in Delaware. Although Delaware is usually taken as the apotheosis of enabling states, and indeed has the least regulatory of the major corporations statutes, even under Delaware law the corporation will be governed by a number of mandatory legal rules. For example, the corporation's directors and officers have a duty of loyalty to the corporation that cannot be substantially altered.[85] The officers have a duty of care to the corporation that cannot be substantially altered.[86] Any shareholder who owned stock at the time of a breach of the duties of care or loyalty can bring suit against the wrongdoer on the corporation's behalf.[87] The corporation is required to have a board of directors or some comparable organ.[88] The term for which a director serves may not be longer than three years, and if the board is classified, one class must come up for election every year.[89] The corporation must have an annual meeting of shareholders for the election of directors.[90] The shareholders have a right to inspect a shareholder list

84. Securities Exchange Act § 12(g)(1)(B), 15 U.S.C. § 78*l*(g)(l)(B) (1982).

85. See authorities cited at supra note 43.

86. Id.

87. Del. Code Ann. tit. 8, § 327 (1983).

88. Id. § 141(a).

89. Id. § 141(d) (Supp. 1988).

90. Id. § 211 (1983).

within the ten days preceding a shareholders' meeting,[91] and a right to inspect the corporation's books and records at any time for a proper purpose.[92] The corporation's certificate of incorporation may be amended only with the approval of a majority of the outstanding shares.[93] Under a variety of circumstances, such an amendment must also be approved by separate classes of shareholders—even classes not entitled to vote under the certificate of incorporation.[94] The corporation may dissolve or sell substantially all of its assets only with the approval of a majority of the outstanding shares.[95] Shareholders who dissent from a merger generally have a right to be paid the fair value of their shares.[96] The shareholders have the power to amend the corporation's by-laws.[97] And so forth.[98]

In short, a small publicly held corporation will be governed by very extensive mandatory legal rules even in Delaware, which is probably the least regulatory of states. Furthermore, most small publicly held corporations will be incorporated not in Delaware, but in the state in which their principal office is located, because out-of-state incorporation will normally entail somewhat higher costs than local incorporation.[99] Since most states are more regulatory than Delaware, most small publicly held corporations will be governed by an even more extensive mandatory legal regime than that just described.

Suppose, for example, the corporation is incorporated under a

91. Id. § 219(a).
92. Id. § 220.
93. Id. § 242(b).
94. Id.
95. Id. §§ 271, 275 (1983 & Supp. 1988).
96. Id. § 262.
97. Id. § 109(a) (1983).
98. For example, the power to manage the business of the corporation or to supervise its management must be confided in a board or a comparable organ, and cannot be exercised by the shareholders. Id. § 141(a). A quorum for directors' meetings may not be less than one-third of the whole board. Id. § 141(b). A committee of the board may not be given power or authority to amend the certificate of incorporation or adopt an agreement of merger; may not recommend to the shareholders a dissolution or a sale of substantially all assets; and may not amend the by-laws. Id. § 141(c) (Supp. 1988). A quorum for shareholders' meetings may not be less than one-third of the shares entitled to vote. Id. § 216. A proxy to vote shares in the corporation may not be made irrevocable unless accompanied by an interest. Id. § 212(c) (1983). A voting trust of the corporation's stock may not exceed ten years in duration. Id. § 218. Restrictions on the transferability of stock may not be imposed on previously issued shares without the consent of the holder. Id. § 202(b). Shareholders are not liable for the corporation's debts. Id. § 102(b)(6) (Supp. 1988). Distributions are regulated within broad limits. Id. § 170 (1983).

I do not claim that all the rules that are presently embodied in the corporate statutes should be viewed as mandatory, or that all the rules that are presently mandatory should be so. For an exploration of this issue, see Coffee, The Mandatory/Enabling Balance in Corporate Law: An Essay on the Judicial Role, 89 Colum. L. Rev. 1618, 1618 n.1 (1989).

99. See W. Cary & M. Eisenberg, supra note 64, at 98.

state law that is based upon the Revised Model Business Corporation Act. It will then be subject not only to almost all of the mandatory rules that Delaware imposes, but also to many more. For example, the corporation must furnish its shareholders with annual financial statements, which must be prepared on the basis of generally accepted accounting principles if the corporation prepares its financial statements on that basis.[100] An amendment to the corporation's certificate of incorporation that increases the normal quorum or voting requirement must meet the same quorum requirement and be adopted by the same vote as the quorum or vote proposed.[101] Shareholders who dissent from a sale of substantially all assets, a merger, or certain types of amendment to the certificate of incorporation normally have a right to be paid the fair value of their shares.[102] And so forth.[103]

Some state statutes impose even more mandatory rules than the Model Act. Under the California Corporations Code, for example, the corporation will be subject to virtually all the mandatory rules of Delaware and the Model Act, and more. All directors must be elected annually.[104] Disclosure requirements are more extensive.[105] Stock-for-stock and stock-for-assets combinations normally can be effected only with shareholder approval.[106] And so forth.[107]

So much for the small publicly held corporation. Assume now that a corporation has 500 holders of a class of equity securities and more than $5 million in assets and thus must register under Section 12(g) of

100. Revised Model Business Corp. Act § 16.20(a) (1984).

101. Id. § 7.27(b).

102. Id. § 13.02.

103. For example, the corporation may not voluntarily indemnify a director in connection with a proceeding by or in the right of the corporation in which the director was adjudged liable to the corporation, or in connection with any other proceeding charging improper personal benefit to the director in which he was adjudged liable on that basis. Id. §§ 8.51(d), 8.58(a). (A *court* may order indemnification in some such cases if it determines that the director is fairly and reasonably entitled to indemnification in view of all the relevant circumstances. Id. § 8.54.) The corporation must report to its shareholders the indemnification of directors. Id. § 16.21. The corporation's articles of incorporation must authorize one or more classes of shares that together have unlimited voting rights and one or more classes of shares that together are entitled to receive the corporation's net assets on dissolution. Id. § 6.01(b).

104. Cal. Corp. Code § 301(a) (West 1977).

105. Id. § 1501.

106. Id. §§ 181, 1200, 1201.

107. For example, distributions are more tightly limited. Id. § 500.

A small publicly held corporation whose business is based in California may not be able to avoid the force of the California statute by incorporating elsewhere, even if it wishes to do so, because many provisions of the statute are applicable to corporations that do more than half their business in California and have more than half their record shareholders in California, regardless of their state of incorporation. Id. § 2115. On § 2115 and its exceptions, see 3 H. Marsh, Marsh's California Corporation Law § 24.15 (2d ed. 1982).

the Securities Exchange Act.[108] It will then be subject to a further and very extensive layer of mandatory rules concerning traditional and positional conflicts. For example, the corporation's directors, officers, and other employees may not trade in the corporation's securities on the basis of material undisclosed information.[109] Its directors, officers, and shareholders owning at least 10 percent of the voting securities must give up any profits from short-swing trades even if the trades were not based on inside information.[110] The corporation must file annual reports that include annual financial statements audited by an independent public accountant, a management report on the corporation's financial condition and results of operations, and additional disclosures concerning specified matters.[111] It must file quarterly reports that include quarterly financial data prepared in accordance with generally accepted accounting principles, a management report, and additional disclosures concerning specified matters.[112] It must file current reports that describe the occurrence of specified events.[113] Proxies may not be solicited by management unless the shareholders are furnished with a written proxy statement containing specified information concerning the transaction to be acted upon.[114] The proxy statement for an annual meeting at which directors are to be elected must make extensive disclosure concerning conflict-of-interest transactions and executive compensation.[115] Such a proxy statement must be accompanied by an annual report that includes audited balance sheets for the corporation's last two fiscal years, audited income statements and statements of change in financial condition for its last three fiscal years, and other specified information.[116] Shareholders must be permitted to

---

108. Securities Exchange Act § 12(g)(1)(B), 15 U.S.C. § 78*l*(g)(1)(B) (1982); Rule 12g-1, 17 C.F.R. § 240.12g-1 (1988).

109. Securities Exchange Act § 10(b), 15 U.S.C. § 78j(b) (1982); Rule 10b-5, 17 C.F.R. § 240.10b-5 (1988).

110. Securities Exchange Act § 16(b), 15 U.S.C. § 78p(b) (1982).

111. Rule 13a-13, 17 C.F.R. § 240.13a-13 (1988), and Form 10-K, 17 C.F.R. § 249.310 (1988). The specified matters include legal proceedings and defaults on senior securities. See 4 Fed. Sec. L. Rep. (CCH) ¶ 31,102 (Apr. 5, 1989).

112. Rule 13a-1, 17 C.F.R. § 240.13a-1 (1988), and Form 10-Q, 17 C.F.R. § 249.308a (1988). The specified matters include legal proceedings, executive compensation, and conflict-of-interest transactions. See 4 Fed. Sec. L. Rep. (CCH) ¶ 31,032 (Apr. 5, 1989).

113. Rule 13a-11, 17 C.F.R. § 240.13a-11 (1988), and Form 8-K, 17 C.F.R. § 249.308 (1988). The specified events include a change in control of the corporation, an acquisition or disposition of a significant amount of assets, and a change of accountants.

114. Rules 14a-2, 14a-3(a), 17 C.F.R. §§ 240.14a-2, 240.14a-3(a) (1988).

115. Schedule 14A, 17 C.F.R. § 240.14a-101 (1988). The proxy statement for such a meeting must also disclose whether the corporation has audit, nominating, and compensation committees, and if so, the number of meetings each committee held during the last fiscal year and the functions it performs. Id. Item 7.

116. Rule 14a-3(b), 17 C.F.R. § 240.14a-3(b) (1988).

include a wide variety of proposals in the corporate proxy statement.[117] The corporation's form of proxy must identify clearly and impartially each matter or group of related matters intended to be acted upon.[118] Shareholders must be afforded an opportunity to specify in the proxy a choice between approval, disapproval, or abstention with respect to each matter or group of related matters, and to withhold authority to vote for directorial nominees.[119] A proxy normally may not confer discretionary authority to vote on an issue unless it states in bold-face type how the shares represented by the proxy will be voted on the issue.[120] A proxy may not confer authority to vote at any annual meeting other than the next annual meeting.[121] And so forth.[122]

Finally, most very large publicly held corporations are listed on the New York Stock Exchange, which has had a virtual monopoly in the liquid trading market for the stock of such corporations and imposes a variety of constitutive rules on listed corporations. Among other things, corporations listed on that Exchange must have at least two outside directors, must have an audit committee composed of independent directors, and must obtain shareholder approval for most economically significant corporate combinations.[123]

In short, corporation law taken as a whole—that is, taken to include state law and federal law, and the rules of the New York Stock Exchange as a de facto legislator by virtue of its monopolistic power—contains a significant number of core mandatory rules to govern divergencies of interest between top managers and shareholders. And to a significant extent, these are just the mandatory rules that corporation law should contain.

D. *Alternative Descriptions of Corporation Law and the Corporation*

Three classes of argument may be made against the principle that the fiduciary and structural rules governing material divergencies in interest between top managers and shareholders in publicly held corporations should be and for the most part are mandatory. The first

117. Rule 14a-8, 17 C.F.R. § 240.14a-8 (1988).

118. Rule 14a-4, 17 C.F.R. § 240.14a-4 (1988).

119. Id. § 240.14a-4(b)(1) (1988).

120. Id.

121. Id. § 240.14a-4(d)(2) (1988).

122. For example, under Securities Exchange Act § 14(c), 78 U.S.C. § 78n(c) (1982), Regulation 14C, 17 C.F.R. § 240.14c-1-7 (1988), and Schedule 14C, 17 C.F.R. § 240.14c-101 (1988), a corporation that is registered under Securities Exchange Act § 12(g) must distribute an information statement and an annual report in connection with an annual meeting at which directors are to be elected, even if the corporation is not soliciting proxies.

123. New York Stock Exchange Listed Company Manual ¶¶ 303.00, 312.00 (1983). The monopoly position of the New York Stock Exchange, and with it the Exchange's power to impose constitutive rules, has been weakened, but not yet eliminated, by the development of NASDAQ.

argument, which will be considered in this section, is that both corporation law and the corporation are essentially contractual in nature. One branch of this argument is that *corporation law* is essentially enabling and suppletory—or, as it has been put by Professor Fischel, that "corporate statutes provide a set of standard-form terms, but firms are generally free to alter these terms in their charters or by-laws."[124] The second branch of the argument is that the *corporation* is a "nexus of contracts."[125] Both branches of the argument are descriptively erroneous.

The characterization of corporation law as a standard-form contract whose terms each firm is generally free to vary is belied by the great number of mandatory rules of corporation law.[126] It is true that most of a corporation's constitutive rules will be adopted by private action. That is because most of a corporation's constitutive rules concern the roles, coordination, supervision, and monitoring of corporate agents below the level of top managers, and such rules should and will be determined by private ordering. (Indeed, many or most of the constitutive rules that define and coordinate the tasks of top managers also should and will be determined by private ordering, because many or most such rules do not involve divergencies of interest between top managers and shareholders.) It is also true that many rules of corporation law are enabling or suppletory rather than mandatory.

What is not true is that corporations are "generally free" to vary the rules of corporation law. Many of the most important rules of corporation law—such as those dealing with unfair self-dealing, insider trading, proxy voting, and disclosure—are largely mandatory, at least for publicly held corporations. It is descriptively inaccurate to characterize corporation law as essentially either enabling and suppletory on the one hand, or mandatory on the other. Furthermore, for reasons

---

124. Fischel, Labor Markets and Labor Law Compared with Capital Markets and Corporate Law, 51 U. Chi. L. Rev. 1061, 1063 (1984); see also Easterbrook & Fischel, Voting in Corporate Law, 26 J.L. & Econ. 395, 401 (1983) ("The code of corporate law is a standard form contract for issues of corporate structure."); Fischel, The Corporate Governance Movement, 35 Vand. L. Rev. 1259, 1264 (1982) ("Fiduciary duties serve... as a standard form contractual term . . . .").

125. See, e.g., Fama & Jensen, Separation of Ownership and Control, 26 J.L. & Econ. 301, 302 (1983); Jensen & Meckling, Theory of the Firm: Managerial Behavior, Agency Costs and Ownership Structure, 3 J. Fin. Econ. 305, 310 (1976).

126. See supra text accompanying notes 5–28, 41–43, 85–123 (setting out some of these rules).

In his comment on this Article, Professor McChesney (like many other contractarians) recognizes that corporation law has many mandatory elements. McChesney, Economics, Law, and Science in the Corporate Field: A Critique of Eisenberg, 89 Colum. L. Rev. 1530, 1537 (1989). Having said that, however, he makes the following two wholly inconsistent arguments: (1) Corporation law should be radically reformed, by making it completely enabling and suppletory. Id. at 1534–35. (2) Those who propose reforms in corporation law have failed to demonstrate the existence of any problems in corporation law. Id. at 1539–40 & n.33 (quoting Fischel, The Corporate Governance Movement, supra note 124, at 1265).

already discussed,[127] a body of corporation law that *was* essentially enabling and suppletory would be normatively undesirable.

The characterization of the corporation as a nexus of contracts is also inaccurate. A corporation is a profit-seeking enterprise of persons and assets organized by rules. Some of these rules are determined by contract or other forms of agreement, but some are determined by law, and most are determined by the unilateral action of corporate organs or officials.

The problem with the nexus-of-contracts conception transcends its inaccuracy. For some commentators, the view of the corporation as a nexus of contracts carries heavy normative freight, because, having premised that the corporation is a nexus of contracts, they then argue that mandatory rules are anticontractarian.[128] Once it is understood that the premise of this argument is incorrect, because the corporation is not a nexus of contracts but an enterprise organized by rules, many or most of which are adopted by the unilaterial action of managers, the argument that mandatory rules are anticontractarian falls of its own weight.

To make up for the paucity of real contracts, it is sometimes argued that the corporation consists of a web of "implicit contracts."[129] The term "implicit contracts" is extremely misleading. It is borrowed from labor economics, and as used in that discipline it refers to relationships that are neither contracts nor bargains.[130] A contract is a legally enforceable bargain, or, at the least, a legally enforceable promise.[131] In contrast, in labor economics the term *implicit contract* refers to a state of affairs in which a worker chooses to accept a lower wage rate from Firm A than he could get from Firm B, with the expectation that for reasons of self-interest, fairness, or altruism—that is, for reasons other than the sanction of a contract or other legally enforceable obligation—Firm A will provide an advantage that Firm B would not. For example, workers may accept a lesser wage rate at Firm A because they believe, based on past practice, that there is a lower probability of being laid off at Firm A than at Firm B. More generally, "implicit contracts" are relationships that are marked *not* by a real bargain, let alone a legally enforceable commitment, but by a tacit expectation, or at most a tacit understanding. Such relationships are not unique to business; indeed, such relationships are ubiquitous in inti-

127. See supra Parts II.A, II.B. Further reasons are developed in Part III, infra.

128. See McChesney, supra note 126, at 1536.

129. See, e.g., Coffee, Shareholders Versus Managers: The Strain in the Corporate Web, *in* Knights, Raiders, & Targets 77, 85, 107, 110–12 (J. Coffee, L. Lowenstein & S. Rose-Ackerman eds. 1988).

130. See Rosen, Implicit Contracts: A Survey, 23 J. Econ. Lit. 1144, 1149 (1985) ("an implicit contract must be interpreted in the 'as if' sense of an explicit one").

131. See Restatement (Second) of Contracts § 1 (1981) ("A contract is a promise or a set of promises for the breach of which the law gives a remedy, or the performance of which the law in some way recognizes as a duty.").

mate settings like marriage and friendship. They are relationships in which for some reason—often, some very good reason—legal enforceability and explicit bargaining is deliberately avoided.

It is true that sometimes tacit understandings slide into implied-in-fact promises that do give rise to legally enforceable contracts,[132] and that sometimes tacit understandings provide a basis for legally enforceable fiduciary obligations.[133] These cases, however, involve a metamorphosis of the relationship, because it is a central characteristic of "implicit contracts" that they are *not* legally enforceable.[134] The use of "implicit contract" terminology in the corporate context screens out real and important differences between laid-down rules and real contracts. Contracts and bargains are forms of private ordering, but they are not the only such forms. "Implicit contracts" are forms of private ordering, but they are not contracts. Most of a corporation's constitutive rules are not determined by law, but neither are they determined by contract.

E. *The Effect of Markets and Other Forms of Private Ordering*

A second class of arguments that might be made against the principles developed so far is that market forces so adequately align the interests of top managers and shareholders and so adequately address the problem of managerial inefficiency that mandatory legal rules to address these issues are unnecessary and indeed undesirable.[135]

---

132. One unfortunate aspect of the term "implicit contract" is that it phonetically resembles the term "implied contract," while in fact the two terms describe two entirely different concepts. An implied contract may be either a real contract (a contract implied in fact) or a legal obligation that is not contractual but is denominated contractual for purely historical reasons (a contract implied in law). In contrast, an "implicit contract" is neither a real contract nor a legal obligation.

133. See, e.g., Meiselman v. Meiselman, 309 N.C. 279, 307–11, 307 S.E.2d 551, 567–70 (1983).

134. I owe this point to Ron Gilson.

135. Those commentators who argue that market forces make mandatory legal rules unnecessary do not claim that such forces completely eliminate the divergencies of interest between managers and shareholders. Rather, they claim that such forces so greatly reduce the divergence of interest between investors and managers that any attempt to reduce the remaining divergence even further by the use of mandatory legal rules would not be worth the costs. See, e.g., Fischel, The Corporate Governance Movement, supra note 124, at 1265.

Those who make such arguments are often somewhat ambiguous about the role of law. For example, Fischel claims that "[t]he combination of direct monitoring, market forces, *and legal rules* operate greatly to reduce the divergence of interests between investors and managers." Id. at 1265 (emphasis added). However, Fischel characterizes the legal rules as "a standard form contractual term," which "serves as an alternative or a supplement to . . . writing lengthy and complicated contracts." Id. at 1264. Presumably, this characterization is intended to mean that the legal rules, like the rules in other standard form contracts, are merely suppletory or default rules. See the statement by Fischel quoted supra, text accompanying note 124. If Fischel and other commentators who characterize legal rules as standard form contracts believe that legal rules are

Arguments of this type are on their face both descriptive and normative. They are descriptive insofar as they purport to set forth the outcomes of actual market forces. They are normative insofar as they claim that mandatory rules to govern divergencies of interest are undesirable because dependence solely on market forces would result in more efficient outcomes. None of the most prominent arguments that have been or may be made are persuasive in the present world.

1. *Product Markets.* — At the outset, it is occasionally argued that managers are severely inhibited from pursuing their own interests or acting inefficiently because product markets often will render insolvent any firm that does not minimize costs.[136] This argument seriously overstates the power of product markets.[137] Although a highly competitive market may have this effect, an imperfectly competitive market will not quickly convert unfair self-dealing or inefficiency into insolvency.[138] Most publicly held corporations have sufficient resources and market power to absorb substantial losses resulting from inefficiency, gross miscalculations, or unfair self-dealing.

2. *Management Compensation.* — A more weighty argument is that the interests of managers and shareholders are adequately aligned by executive compensation, because such compensation is closely tied to shareholder gain.[139] It seems likely that compensation has some alignment effect. Empirical studies have shown that there is indeed a statistically significant relationship on average between shareholder gain, measured by returns to common stock, and executive salaries and bo-

---

mandatory, their characterization is incorrect but their view of the rules would then be comparable to mine.

136. See Butler, The Contractual Theory of the Corporation, 11 Geo. Mason U.L. Rev., Summer 1989, at 99, 114; Dooley & Veasey, The Role of the Board in Derivative Litigation: Delaware Law and the Current ALI Proposals Compared, 44 Bus. Law., 503, 526 (1989); Fischel, The Corporate Goverance Movement, supra note 124, at 1264.

137. Cf. Jensen & Meckling, supra note 125, at 330 ("[T]he existence of competition in product . . . markets will not eliminate the agency costs due to managerial control problems. . . . If my competitors all incur agency costs equal to or greater than mine I will not be eliminated from the market by their competition.").

138. See J. Tirole, The Theory of Industrial Organization 277–303 (1988).

139. See, e.g., Coughlan & Schmidt, Executive Compensation, Management Turnover, and Firm Performance: An Empirical Investigation, 7 J. Acct. & Econ. 43, 46 (1985):

> [T]he existence of competition in capital markets makes the survival of corporations depend on the construction of incentive arrangements which encourage top management to act in the shareholders' interest. Firms which fail to compensate managers in this way will face higher costs and thus will not compete successfully with firms whose managers act in the shareholders' interest.

See also Fischel, The "Race to the Bottom" Revisited: Reflections on Recent Developments in Delaware's Corporation Law, 76 Nw. U.L. Rev. 913, 919 (1982) ("Various compensation packages such as stock option plans, which cause managers to share the risk bearing function with shareholders, provide managers with an incentive to maximize shareholders' wealth and keep stock prices high.").

nuses.[140] However, "significance" in statistics bears no necessary relationship to the ordinary meaning of significance—that something is important.[141] Although the relationship between compensation and corporate performance is *statistically* significant, it is not *economically* significant. Based on a study of 2,214 chief executive officers during 1974–86, Jensen and Murphy determined that on average the chief executive's salary and bonus changed only 1.4 cents for each change of 1000 dollars in shareholder wealth.[142] They illustrate the trivial nature of this relationship as follows:

> The [data implies] that a CEO receives an average pay increase of $31,700 in years when shareholders earn a zero return, and receives on average an additional 1.35 cents for each $1,000 increase in shareholder wealth. The median annual standard deviation of shareholder-wealth changes for firms in our sample is about $200 million, so the average pay change associated with a stockholder-wealth change two standard deviations above or below the normal (a gain or loss of $400 million) is $5,400. Thus, the average pay increase for a CEO whose shareholders gain $400 million is $37,300, compared to an average pay increase of $26,500 for a CEO whose shareholders lose $400 million.[143]

Jensen and Murphy also measured the relation between salary and bonus, and change in shareholder wealth based on stock performance, for the present and preceding year, rather than only the present year. This relationship was slightly stronger, but still trivial—2.2 cents, rather than 1.4 cents, for each change of 1,000 dollars in shareholder wealth.[144] If all benefits (other than those related to stock options) are taken into account, and the measurement is based on two years of lagged shareholder wealth rather than one, the relationship still amounts to only 3.3 cents in compensation per 1,000 dollars of change in shareholder wealth.[145]

140. See Coughlan & Schmidt, supra note 139, at 53–60; M. Jensen & K. Murphy, supra note 69, at 5; Murphy, Corporate Performance and Managerial Remuneration: An Empirical Analysis, 7 J. Acct. & Econ. 11, 32–37 (1985).

141. See Gould, Through a Lens Darkly, Nat. Hist., Sept. 1989, at 16. Gould illustrates: "Mouse tails may be 'significantly' longer in Mississippi than in Michigan—meaning only that average lengths are not the same at some level of confidence—but the difference may be so small that no one would argue for significance in the ordinary sense." Id. at 16.

142. M. Jensen & K. Murphy, supra note 69, at 5–6.

143. Id. at 5–6.

144. Id. at 5–7. The relationship between salary and bonus, and three years of lagged shareholder wealth, was little different than the relationship for two years of lagged shareholder wealth. Id. at 7.

145. Id. at 5, 7.

If it is assumed that all increments in salary and bonus are permanent and that all CEOs will receive the increments until age 70, the average present value of the cash flow resulting from the sum of the change in salary and bonus from the present year until the year of retirement would add or subtract 30 cents per 1,000 dollars to the average chief

Salary, bonus, and benefits are so little related to shareholder gain because managers want it that way. In theory, a chief executive's compensation is determined by the board on the recommendation of an independent compensation committee, which in turn acts on the recommendation of an independent personnel department and (often) an independent outside consulting firm, all without the chief executive's participation. In practice, however, "the chief executive often has his hand in the pay-setting process almost from the first step."[146] Person-

---

executive's wealth. Id. at 8–9. For present purposes, however, these assumptions seem both inaccurate and inappropriate. The assumptions seem inaccurate, because bonuses are supposed to be dependent on performance, and a change in bonus therefore should be transitory, not permanent. (Jensen and Murphy recognize this, but were forced to adopt the assumption because their data source aggregated salary and bonuses.) The assumptions seem inappropriate, because they produce only an average present value for all chief executives and are therefore of no relevance for chief executives who are about to retire, and of limited relevance for chief executives who are close to retirement.

See also Shleifer & Vishny, supra note 48, at 10 ("No study we know of indicates that the incentives provided by extant compensation contracts effectively discourage most non-value-maximizing behavior.").

146. Williams, Why Chief Executives' Pay Keeps Rising, Fortune, April 1, 1985, at 66, 67, see also id., (The CEO "generally approves, or at least knows about, the recommendation of his personnel executive *before* it goes to the compensation committee, and may take a similar pregame pass at the consultant's recommendations too."); Louis, Business is Bungling Long-Term Compensation, Fortune, July 23, 1984, at 64, 65 ("[T]he reality at most companies is that top management itself usually devises the executive compensation plan—hiring the consultants whose scheme is then ratified by the board of directors and shareholders . . . .").

Cf. Crystal, Where's the Risk in CEOs' Rewards?, Fortune, Dec. 19, 1988, at 62, 62–63:

> The implicit message of every broad-based incentive pay plan is, "We're all in this together. When the company prospers, we all do—and when it suffers, we suffer." Trouble is, in many companies that statement is obviously false. With a few notable exceptions, the CEOs suffer little or not at all no matter what happens to the company. . . .
>
> . . . .
>
> How did this odd situation develop? Mainly as a result of several factors operating together:
>
> Many CEOs receive huge base salaries. Remember that base salary is part of the CEO's aggregate remuneration, the part that, for practical purposes, is inert . . . .
>
> Many companies' short-term incentive plans begin to generate bonus pools at levels of performance that are ridiculously puny. This writer's study of 100 major companies' bonus plans conducted a few years back showed that the typical company began to generate bonus money once it achieved a triflingly low 6% return on equity. (Last year the median [return on equity] of the FORTUNE 500 was 14.4%.)
>
> Most executive bonus plans allow far too much discretion—and with discretion comes rationalization. It is amazing to see the clarity of vision demonstrated by CEOs and board compensation committees when it comes to spotting uncontrollable events that trigger downturns in company performance—events like rising oil prices, rising interest rates, hurricanes, and so forth. Yet it is equally amazing to see the cloudiness of vision demonstrated by the same CEOs and board compensation committees when it comes to spotting

nel executives who don't recommend what the chief executive officer wants may find that their jobs are at risk; consultants who don't recommend what the chief executive wants are unlikely to be invited back.[147]

The value of executive stock options is also related to shareholder gain measured by returns on common stock. Here again, however, the dollar significance of the relationship is virtually immaterial—a change of 15 cents in the value of the chief executive's stock options for each change of 1,000 dollars in shareholder wealth.[148] The value of stock options as a mechanism to align adequately the interests of shareholders and top managers is further limited by the fact that while shareholders invariably lose wealth if the stock price decreases, top managers with stock options may not, because when the price of the stock goes down the board often reduces the option price to match the fall in the market.[149]

In short, the argument that the interests of managers and shareholders are adequately aligned by executive compensation is descriptively inaccurate because the dollar amounts involved are trivial or immaterial. Moreover, this argument is based on a fallacy. The fallacy, which runs through a great deal of the literature on the alignment effect of market forces, is that mandatory rules are unnecessary because *on average* the interests of managers and shareholders are adequately aligned by market forces. I shall call this the average-manager fallacy.

The average-manager fallacy reflects a fundamental misunderstanding of the use of statistical evidence in determining whether mandatory legal rules are desirable. A statistically significant relationship between two variables, such as compensation and corporate performance, occurs when there is a high correlation between the two variables. The presence of a material number of cases that are not consistent with the overall relationship will not necessarily preclude a finding of statistical significance. Accordingly, a finding that a relationship between two groups of data is statistically significant—that there is a relationship between the two variables "on average"—may often mask

external events that spark upturns in company performance—events like falling oil prices, falling interest rates, and a booming economy. In the first case, compensation committees almost always cushion the CEO's pay from events that he arguably cannot control. But in the second case, those committees seem to assume that great performance is always a result of CEO brilliance: Therefore pay moves sharply upward.

147. Williams, supra note 146, at 66–67.

148. M. Jensen & K. Murphy, supra note 69, at 10–11, 45.

149. See, e.g., Cohen v. Ayers, 596 F.2d 733, 735–43 (7th Cir. 1979) (board of directors' decision to terminate and reissue overpriced options does not constitute waste); Michelson v. Duncan, 407 A.2d 211, 219–22 (Del. 1979) (shareholder ratification of plan to issue stock options was adequate to sustain directors' cancellation and reissue of options following sharp decline in stock price); Coffee, No Exit?: Opting Out, the Contractual Theory of the Corporation, and the Special Case of Remedies, 53 Brooklyn L. Rev. 919, 943 (1988).

the fact that many members of each group are not related in a manner consistent with the underlying relationship. This may not be a problem when statistical techniques are intended to *describe* certain social phenomena, or when prediction is an important objective. However, in determining whether conduct should be *prescribed* or *prohibited* by a mandatory legal rule, it is not enough to say that there is a significant overall relationship. Rather, all cases, including those that are not consistent with the observed relationship, must be taken into account. Conduct may be legally prescribed or prohibited *just because* not all conduct clusters around the norm. For example, even though most parents would send their children to school even in the absence of a legal rule, we prescribe mandatory education for children because some parents will not. Similarly, we make perjury a crime even though most witnesses would tell the truth in any event, because in the absence of a sanction some witnesses would not. Whether conduct should be prescribed or prohibited on the one hand, or left unregulated on the other, depends on a prudential, case-by-case judgment whether the cost of adopting a mandatory rule to govern the conduct of those who will not voluntarily conform to a desired norm exceeds the cost of failing to adopt the rule, and, in that connection, whether a mandatory legal rule will increase voluntary self-regulation by emphasizing the weight that society gives to the norm. This equation cannot be solved by looking only at average conduct.

Applying these principles to corporate law, even if a given market mechanism does align the interests of most top managers and shareholders in a statistically significant and material way, such a relationship does not in itself tell us that mandatory rules are unnecessary. For example, even if the correlation between executive compensation and shareholder gain was both very high and material (which it is not), that would provide only limited help in determining the shape of corporate law unless we also know the extent to which the relationship holds throughout the executive population.

3. *Inside Stock Ownership.* — Closely related to the argument that the interests of shareholders and managers are adequately aligned by executive compensation is the argument that those interests are adequately aligned by managers' inside stock ownership, that is ownership of stock in their own corporations. It is true that managers, or at least chief executive officers, do tend to hold significant dollar amounts of stock in their own corporations. For example, Jensen and Murphy studied 73 chief executive officers of manufacturing companies and found that the officers' inside stock ownership averaged $4.8 million, or $8.8 million if shares held as a trustee and by members of the chief executive's family were taken into account.[150] Jensen and Murphy concluded that the value of inside stock held by the average chief executive would change

150. M. Jensen & K. Murphy, supra note 69, at 12.

$1.31 or $2.40 (depending on the sample) for each $1,000 change in shareholder wealth.[151]

Certainly this data establishes that inside stock ownership is often large enough to have some alignment effect. What it does not establish is that inside stock ownership so adequately aligns the interests of the shareholders and managers that mandatory legal rules to control divergencies of those interests are unnecessary. For one thing, the median value of inside stockholdings has been decreasing dramatically. Based on the sample of 73 chief executive officers mentioned above, Jensen and Murphy found that the median value of chief executive officers' inside holdings had dropped from $3,531,000 in 1969–73 to $1,178,000 in 1979–83, while the median percentage of the firm owned by the chief executive officer (including members of his family and trusts) fell from .21% to .11%.[152] Similarly, a study comparing the inside holdings of the chief executive officers of the 120 largest corporations in 1938 and 1984 showed a drop in the average percentage of the firm owned by the chief executive officer from .30% to .03%.[153]

Much more importantly, the argument that inside holdings have the effect of adequately aligning the interests of shareholders and managers, like the argument that executive compensation has that effect, reflects the average-manager fallacy. The relevant questions include not simply the magnitude of average or median inside holdings, but the extent to which the relationship holds throughout the population. In fact, the relationship is extremely variable. A study by Jensen and Murphy of the inside holdings of 746 chief executives and their family members found that 40% had inside holdings worth less than $2.5 million, 20% had inside holdings of less than $700,000, and some had inside holdings worth less than $100,000.[154]

Moreover, even relatively significant inside holdings will have only a limited alignment effect in the three major areas in which the interests of top managers may diverge from those of shareholders. Take first the problem of unfair self-dealing. Assume that a manager who contemplates unfair self-dealing has a large inside holding. The manager's gain from the unfair self-dealing will nevertheless almost invariably swamp the resulting loss in the value in his stock, because the manager will normally realize the full value of the unfair self-dealing, but will lose only a fraction of the value of his stock. For example, suppose Corporation C has a net worth of $1 billion, and Manager M owns C stock worth $10 million. If M unfairly appropriates a corporate opportunity worth $1 million, he will net $990,000 even after taking into account the impact of his action on the value of his inside holdings.

151. Id. at 11, 13, 45.

152. Id. at 40–41. The measurement is in constant dollars.

153. Id.

154. Id. at 14; M. Jensen & K. Murphy, Are Executive Compensation Contracts Structured Properly? 28 (Oct. 14, 1987) (unpublished draft).

Inside holdings also will have little or no effect on efficiency. Few if any inefficient managers are likely to believe themselves inefficient. Accordingly, even the most inefficient managers will typically believe that their actions will increase the value of their inside holdings.[155]

Finally, inside holdings will have little or no effect on positional conflicts. Financial gain is only one incentive for top managers. Other and often far more important incentives include the sense of accomplishment, the self-esteem, and the power that accompany a top management position.[156] The combined financial and nonfinancial value that a top manager places on his position is almost certain to swamp any possible loss in his inside holdings that results from actions he takes to maintain and enhance that position, even in the unlikely event that he believes those actions to be value-decreasing.

4. *The Market for Managers, the Prospect of Promotion, and the Risk of Discharge.* — Still another device that is said to adequately align the interests of managers and shareholders, and adequately address the problem of managerial inefficiency, is the market for managers.[157] The idea here is that managers who perform poorly will find it difficult to market themselves.

There is in fact a market for middle and lower managers, although it is somewhat limited because of skill specificity and asymmetric information.[158] However, it is top managers with whom corporation law should be and is concerned, and for these actors the market for managers, such as it is, is of limited relevance. That market is not relevant to the chief executive officer, because he is almost invariably in his final period as a manager.[159] It is of limited relevance to top executives other than the chief executive officer, because their major concern is satisfying the chief executive. It is not relevant to outside directors, because outside directorships are normally sideline activities.

A mechanism related to the market for managers is the prospect of

155. It is sometimes argued that the mere fact that managers invest in their own corporation indicates that they do not intend to exploit investors in the corporation, because if they did, they would invest somewhere else. This argument is one more reflection of the average-manager fallacy, because it assumes that all managers own substantial amounts of stock in the corporations they manage. Furthermore, a manager could exploit a corporation without damaging its essential profitability. Finally, the argument fails to address unfair self-dealing that managers convince themselves is fair, inefficient conduct by managers who believe themselves efficient, and conduct that gives expression to positional conflicts.

156. Cf. the Shleifer and Vishny passage quoted supra note 48.

157. See Dooley & Veasey, supra note 136, at 526; Fama, Agency Problems and the Theory of the Firm, 88 J. Pol. Econ. 288 (1980).

158. The limited mobility of managers is suggested by the fact that the typical chief executive has had only one other corporate employer. M. Jensen & K. Murphy, supra note 154, at 33.

159. See id. at 31 (most chief executives leave office only after reaching normal retirement age).

promotion. This prospect, however, has no effect on directors or chief executive officers, because they cannot be promoted.

Another mechanism related to the market for managers is the risk of discharge. There is evidence that suggests a relationship between corporate performance and the discharge of chief executives,[160] and undoubtedly the risk of discharge has an alignment effect. However, the relationship between corporate performance and risk of discharge is weak. Because the discharge of a chief executive is usually masked as a voluntary separation, there is little or no evidence concerning discharge as such, but only aggregate evidence on departures for all reasons, including poor health, retirement, death, and takeover. A study by Weisbach of departures for all reasons of chief executives younger than age 64 concluded that in the highest-performing decile of corporations, 3% of chief executives probably would depart in any given year, while in the lowest-performing decile 6% would depart—a difference of only 3 percentiles.[161] Similarly, the difference between probable departures for all reasons in corporations whose performance was in the top and bottom quintiles was only two percentiles.[162] The difference between the median corporation and corporations in the lowest decile was also only two percentiles.[163]

Not only is the relation between departures and corporate performance weak, but the uniformity of the relationship is very low. The relation is apparently strongest for chief executives under age 50. For chief executives age 50–55 there is no significant relation.[164] For chief executives age 55–60 or past age 64 the relation is only marginally significant.[165] There is also no significant relation between departures and corporate performance in corporations in which 60% or more of the directors are either insiders or have significant relationships to management.[166]

As Jensen and Murphy conclude, "[t]he data suggest that CEOs

160. See Coughlan & Schmidt, supra note 139, at 60–65; Warner, Watts & Wruck, Stock Prices and Top Management Changes, 20 J. Fin. Econ. 461 (1988); see also Weisbach, Outside Directors and CEO Turnover, 20 J. Fin. Econ. 431 (1988) (boards dominated by outsiders more likely to remove CEO for poor performance than boards dominated by insiders).

161. Weisbach, supra note 160, at 440. Warner, Watts & Wruck, supra note 160, at 477–79, predicted a difference of 5.3 percentiles between top and bottom deciles, 2.55 percentiles between top and bottom quintiles, and 1.35 percentiles between the median and the bottom deciles. Coughlan & Schmidt, supra note 139, at 60–65, found higher spreads—8 percentiles between top and bottom deciles, 5 percentiles between the median and the bottom decile, and 5 percentiles between top and bottom quintiles. See also M. Jensen & K. Murphy, supra note 69, at 12–21.

162. Weisbach, supra note 160, at 443.

163. Id.

164. M. Jensen & K. Murphy, supra note 69, at 16–17.

165. Id.

166. Weisbach, supra note 160, at 435–41.

bear little risk of being dismissed."[167] This is not surprising. The chief executive can be discharged only by the board, and a majority of board members are often either subordinates of the chief executive or persons who have economic affiliations with the corporation that are under the chief executive's control.[168] Furthermore, it is often difficult for even the most objective and discerning directors to know whether poor corporate performance can properly be laid at the chief executive's feet, or is due instead to the decisions of his predecessors, exogenous circumstances, or the inefficiency of middle and lower managers.

5. *The Market for Corporate Control.* — Another market mechanism that has been claimed adequately to align the interests of shareholders and managers, and adequately to address the problem of managerial inefficiency, is the market for corporate control—that is, the takeover market. The now-familiar idea is that if the managers of a corporation act in their own interests rather than the shareholders' interests, or are inefficient, a third party can make gains by bidding for the corporation's stock at a price that is above the market price, but below the value the stock would have if the corporation was properly managed.[169]

It seems clear that some takeovers are motivated by the inefficiency of the target's management.[170] Therefore, at least some completed takeovers undoubtedly result in a substitution of more efficient managers for less efficient managers, or of more efficient allocations of resources for less efficient allocations. It also seems likely, although not uncontroversial, that the threat of takeover makes some managers more efficient, or causes some managers to allocate resources more efficiently than they otherwise would.[171] Nevertheless, the takeover market neither adequately aligns the interests of managers and shareholders, nor adequately addresses the problem of managerial inefficiency.

To begin with, the takeover market has very little impact on traditional conflicts of interest. A hostile takeover bid cannot succeed unless it includes a premium that is significantly above the market price, partly because all existing shareholders value their stock at a price

167. M. Jensen & K. Murphy, supra note 69, at 18.

168. See Principles of Corporate Governance: Analysis and Recommendations § 3.04, reporter's note 3 at 88–89 (Tent. Draft No. 2, Apr. 13, 1984); M. Eisenberg, supra note 46, at 144–48, 164–65.

169. See, e.g., Easterbrook & Fischel, The Proper Role of a Target's Management in Responding to a Tender Offer, 94 Harv. L. Rev. 1161, 1173–82 (1981); Manne, Mergers and the Market for Corporate Control, 73 J. Pol. Econ. 110, 113 (1965).

170. See Jensen, Takeovers: Their Causes and Consequences, 2 J. Econ. Persp., Winter 1988, at 21, 28.

171. The effects of takeovers on managerial efficiency are discussed in Jarrell, Brickley & Netter, supra note 47; Shleifer & Vishny, supra note 48, at 7, 18; Jensen, supra note 170; Scherer, Corporate Takeovers: The Efficiency Arguments, J. Econ. Persp., Winter 1988, at 69, 76.

higher than the market price,[172] and partly because the target's managers can create formidable obstacles to a takeover that can be overcome only by a substantial premium over market price. The premium for all takeovers runs between thirty and fifty percent over market price,[173] and in most cases it is probably impossible to make a successful hostile bid at less than a thirty percent premium. A hostile bidder must also pay very large fees to investment bankers, lawyers, and other professionals. Because of the need to expend these large premiums and fees, a takeover bid will almost never be economically justified if the bidder's only strategy is to end unfair self-dealing by incumbent managers. Furthermore, if a bidder acquires most of a target's stock, and the financial impact of past unfair self-dealing was reflected in the target's financial statements, the target will normally be barred by law from recovering the managers' gains from unfair self-dealing.[174]

The takeover market also has only a limited effect on positional conflicts. The threat of takeover will not cause managers to avoid taking actions to maintain and enhance their positions at the shareholders' expense. Indeed, just the reverse has occurred. The threat of takeover has led many managers to cause the adoption of constitutive rules that make their ouster even more difficult than it would otherwise have been. Furthermore, the central problem posed by positional conflicts is the problem of inefficient managers who do not realize they are inefficient, and do their best as they see it. The threat of takeover will not affect the behavior of such managers: they are already doing all they can.[175]

Even a manager who knows he is inefficient may not have too much to fear from the threat of a takeover. Takeovers are motivated by a variety of economic factors, of which inefficient management is only one, and not necessarily the most important.[176] As Jensen points out, "[m]ore than a dozen separate forces drive takeover activity, including

172. See Coffee, Regulating the Market for Corporate Control: A Critical Assessment of the Tender Offer's Role in Corporate Governance, 84 Colum. L. Rev. 1145, 1187–88 (1984).

173. See Jensen, supra note 170, at 22.

174. See Bangor Punta Operations, Inc. v. Bangor & Aroostook R.R., 417 U.S. 703, 710–11 (1974).

175. A distinction may be drawn between operating and resource efficiency. By *operating* efficiency, I mean the ability to manage the resources that the corporation holds in such a manner as to maximize the profits derived from those resources. By *resource* efficiency, I mean the ability to determine what resources the corporation should hold, and how those resources should be financed. The pressure of takeovers normally will not increase a manager's ability to operate the resources that the corporation holds, but it may force him to increase resource efficiency, as by selling off resources the corporation should not hold or refinancing the resources it continues to hold. I use the term "inefficient" in the text to mean operating inefficiency, that is, a failure to manage a corporation's existing resources so as to wring out maximum profits.

176. See Jensen, supra note 170, at 28; see also Shleifer & Vishny, supra note 48, at 16.

such factors as deregulation, synergies, economies of scale and scope, taxes, the level of managerial competence, and increasing globalization of U.S. markets."[177] A significant portion of the resources devoted to takeovers seems to be directed not at taking over poorly managed corporations, but rather at taking over well-managed corporations. Indeed, it seems likely that in some takeovers the target is better managed than the bidder.[178] Those resources that are directed at poorly managed corporations will probably not be directed at corporations that are managed in only a moderately inefficient way, because replacing a management that is only moderately inefficient will normally not produce sufficient gains to justify the huge premium and out-of-pocket costs required to mount a successful takeover.

In a well-known article,[179] Easterbrook and Fischel argued that managers should be prohibited from engaging in defensive actions against takeovers even if the purpose of the actions was to create an auction and thereby increase the premiums paid to the shareholders, on the ground that the need to pay high premiums interferes with the operation of the takeover market as an interest-alignment and efficiency-monitoring device.[180] This argument has not been accepted by either courts or legislatures. The courts have approved a variety of defenses and the promotion of bidding contests,[181] and state legislatures have made takeovers harder rather than easier.[182] Nevertheless, the argument is instructive. The premise of the argument is that if high premiums were eliminated, the takeover market would adequately align the interests of managers and shareholders and adequately address the problem of managerial inefficiency, and would thereby render mandatory legal rules to control these problems unnecessary. The negative implication is that if legal and business conditions result in a regime of high premiums, which they do, the divergencies of interests between managers and shareholders, and the problem of managerial inefficiency, will not be adequately dealt with by the market for managerial control. Instead, these issues must be addressed, at least in part, by mandatory legal rules. Indeed, mandatory rules that help prevent positional conflicts from interfering with the operation of the market for corporate control can be justified on the ground that they act to *protect* the operation of the market.

177. Jensen, supra note 170, at 28.

178. See Herman, The Limits of the Market as a Discipline in Corporate Governance, 9 Del. J. Corp. L. 530, 536–37 (1984).

179. Easterbrook & Fischel, supra note 169.

180. Id. at 1174–80.

181. See, e.g., Moran v. Household Int'l, Inc., 500 A.2d 1346, 1350 (Del. 1985) (defensive action against takeover threat upheld); Unocal Corp. v. Mesa Petroleum Co., 493 A.2d 946, 955 (Del. 1985) (same).

182. See, e.g., Del. Code Ann. tit. 8, § 203 (1983 & Supp. 1988); Ind. Code Ann. § 23-1-42 (Burns Supp. 1989); N.Y. Bus. Corp. Law § 912 (McKinney 1986 & Supp. 1989); Wis. Stat. Ann. § 180.726 (West Supp. 1988).

6. *The Market for Capital.* — Another market-forces argument is that the market for capital will adequately constrain managers from adopting constitutive rules that are in the managers' interests but against the shareholders' interests.[183] I shall refer to such rules as managerial rules. The idea of the argument is as follows: The adoption of a managerial rule would reduce the price of the corporation's stock. Reducing the price of the corporation's stock would increase the cost of the corporation's capital. Increasing the cost of the corporation's capital will lead either to bankruptcy of the corporation through the operation of the product market or ouster of management through the operation of the takeover market.

An analysis of the effect of the adoption of a managerial rule on the product and the capital markets shows that the capital market is unlikely to adequately align managerial and shareholder interests.

a. *Effect on the Product Market.* — To begin with, a corporation's ability to compete in the product market will not be impaired at all by the adoption of a managerial rule unless its out-of-pocket expenses are increased or its cash flow is reduced. However, many managerial rules are value-decreasing not because they increase present out-of-pocket expenses or decrease cash flow, but because they may lead to reduced profits at some point in the future or create the possibility of a future redistribution of corporate profits from shareholders to managers. Poison pills, for example, are normally value-decreasing only for these reasons. Adoption of a managerial rule may therefore have no present impact on out-of-pocket expenses or cash flow.

Of course, it can be argued that when a corporation that has adopted a managerial rule *does* go into the market to raise capital by the sale of stock, it will find that the price of its stock is lower, and therefore the price it must pay for capital is higher. However, although this impact may have an effect on the takeover market (an issue I consider below[184]), a potential impact at some point in the future may have little or no significance to present managers insofar as they are concerned with the ability of the corporation to compete in the product market.[185]

183. See Easterbrook, Managers' Discretion and Investors' Welfare: Theories and Evidence, 9 Del. J. Corp. L. 540, 556–57 (1984); Fischel, The Corporate Governance Movement, supra note 124, at 1264; Winter, State Law, Shareholder Protection, and the Theory of the Corporation, 6 J. Leg. Stud. 251, 275–76 (1977).

184. See infra note 201 and accompanying text.

185. In a comment on this Article, Winter criticizes this argument on the ground that

> [e]ven if the side payments will have an effect only in the future, investment analysts will know (if true) that the earnings of Delaware corporations are lower in the long run than the earnings of businesses incorporated elsewhere, and this recognition would have a present effect on investors. That effect will necessarily be of significance to managers.

Winter, The "Race for the Top" Revisited: A Comment on Eisenberg, 89 Colum. L. Rev. 1526, 1526–27 (1989). Winter erroneously conflates the operation of the product and takeover markets. I agree that the impact of the valuations of investment analysts

Furthermore, a value-decreasing managerial rule may have little or no impact on out-of-pocket expenses even in the future. To begin with, few publicly held corporations raise capital by issuing new stock. A primary source of capital for most corporations is internally generated cash.[186] Publicly held corporations issue new equity on average only once every eighteen years—"less often than locusts."[187] Between 1973 and 1982, net stock issues provided an annual average of 2.1% of corporate funding.[188] Many corporations almost never issue new equity.[189] To the extent a corporation finances itself from internally generated cash, the capital market will have no significant disciplinary effect through the product market.[190]

The capital market may also have no significant disciplinary effect through the product market if a corporation prefers to meet its capital needs by issuing debt, so long as the adoption of a managerial rule has no effect on profits or cash flow through the product market.[191]

---

may affect managers through the *takeover* market. However, they will not necessarily affect managers through the *product* market. The difference is important because of the huge premiums that are required to effect takeovers. See supra notes 172–174 and accompanying text.

186. Stout, The Unimportance of Being Efficient: An Economic Analysis of Stock Market Pricing and Securities Regulation, 87 Mich. L. Rev. 613, 648 (1988) (operating revenues finance an average of 61% of corporate expenditures; corporate borrowing provides 36%).

187. Id. at 647.

188. Id.

189. Id. at 647 n.185.

190. In a comment on this Article, Winter argues that

> [t]he cost of internal financing is the opportunity cost or the highest return available from investment outside the firm. If a corporation can earn 15 percent on an outside investment, then the cost of investing internally is also 15 percent.

Winter, supra note 185, at 1527. This argument is incorrect insofar as it implies that an opportunity cost is an out-of-pocket cost. An increase in out-of-pocket costs can drive a corporation into bankruptcy in the product market. An increase in opportunity costs cannot.

191. It has been argued that a corporation whose stock price is rising can borrow more, at a lower interest rate, than a corporation whose stock price is declining. See W. Baumol, The Stock Market and Economic Efficiency 81 (1969). Certainly there might be a marginal effect on the cost of debt where a lender bases its credit decision on the market value of the corporation's equity, rather than on profits, cash flow, and liquidation values. But

> [t]he flaw in the debt-to-equity ratio argument is that it assumes that banks evaluate leverage by measuring debt load against market equity prices, rather than against the value of the corporation's underlying earnings and assets. The bank that readily lends on the basis of high share value unsupported by assets or revenues is unlikely to stay in the banking business long. Nor would rational lenders be deterred by depressed stock prices if the assets and revenues to support the loan exist. Banking literature confirms that lenders prefer to measure risk by comparing outstanding debt against the value of a corporation's underlying assets, rather than the market price of its stock.

Stout, supra note 186, at 649–50; see also id. at 650 n.202 ("Many of the credit-scoring

Even in the relatively uncommon case in which a publicly held corporation prefers to finance itself by issuing new stock, the capital-market argument has little force. There is strong evidence that many significant changes in a corporation's constitutive rules do not have a statistically significant effect on the price of the corporation's stock. Weiss and White conducted an event study of the effect of seven major Delaware judicial decisions on stock prices of Delaware corporations.[192] Each of these decisions made important changes in significant constitutive rules: one commentator characterized four of the decisions as "radical departures from prior law"[193] and a fifth as breaking new ground.[194] Yet Weiss and White found that the market reaction to the decisions was almost uniformly not statistically significant.[195] In a comment on the Weiss and White data, Fox pointed out that even if changes in constitutive rules are negatively priced by the market, that pricing would not necessarily be discernible at a statistically significant level under the standard technique used in conducting event studies:

> For the price change that accompanies [an] announcement . . . to be considered statistically significant, it must be sufficiently different from zero that one can, with reasonable confidence, reject the "null hypothesis" that the true effect . . . is zero and that the observed change results solely from other chance factors. The "standard error" is a statistically derived estimate of the tendency of these other factors to cause the *observed* price changes to deviate from the *actual* effect . . . on prices. Assume for our example a standard error of 0.65, which is representative of the standard error in the Weiss and White tests. The observed adjusted price change would have to be at least 1.3% before we could reject the null hypothesis with 95% confidence. There is less than one chance in twenty

formulas used by commercial lenders to evaluate the creditworthiness of corporate borrowers do not consider stock price at all. . . . Those credit-scoring models that do consider market equity price consider it as only one out of five or more factors, and a lightly weighted one at that.").

192. Weiss & White, Of Econometrics and Indeterminacy: A Study of Investors' Reactions to "Changes" in Corporate Law, 75 Calif. L. Rev. 551, 569–602 (1987) (studying effect on share prices of: Unocal Corp. v. Mesa Petroleum Co., 493 A.2d 946 (Del. 1985); Lynch v. Vickers Energy Corp., 429 A.2d 497 (Del. 1981); Lynch v. Vickers Energy Corp., 383 A.2d 278 (Del. 1977)); Singer v. Magnavox Co., 380 A.2d 969 (Del. 1977); Weinberger v. UOP, Inc. 426 A.2d 1333 (Del. Ch. 1981), rev'd, 457 A.2d 701 (Del. 1983); Maldonado v. Flynn, 413 A.2d 1251 (Del. Ch. 1980), rev'd sub nom. Zapata Corp. v. Maldonado, 430 A.2d 779 (Del. 1981). The market's reactions to the Chancery and Supreme Court decisions in *Maldonado* were measured separately.

193. Fischel, supra note 139, at 942.

194. Fischel, The Appraisal Remedy in Corporate Law, 1983 Am. B. Found. Res. J. 875, 894–96.

195. Weiss & White, supra note 192, at 582. For one of the seven cases there were statistically significant positive returns to a Delaware portfolio on the fourth and ninth days after the announcement of the decision. Id.

The results for a non-Delaware portfolio were generally comparable. Id.

that an increase of 0.1% in the actual value of a sample portfolio will be accompanied by an observed change in prices sufficiently large, that is, 1.3%, to be considered statistically significant.[196]

Even a managerial rule that does have a measurable effect will not necessarily increase out-of-pocket costs. For example, suppose that because C Corporation has adopted a poison pill, C's stock sells for $49 instead of $50.[197] C wants to raise $500,000 in the capital market for equity. The poison pill will not raise C's out-of-pocket cost of capital: C simply issues 10,204 shares instead of the 10,000 shares it would have issued without the rule. Of course, the value of the stock held by existing shareholders may fall, which may effect C in the *takeover* market, but C's ability to compete in the *product* market will remain unaffected. (Dilution of the value of a corporation's stock is a cost, but the point is that this cost is typically borne by the shareholders rather than the managers, and in any event is not the kind of cost that will have a significant effect in the product market.)[198]

Suppose the managerial rule does increase out-of-pocket expenses or reduce cash flow. Because of the slack in most product markets, most corporations would not be at risk of failure in the product market unless out-of-pocket expenses were significantly increased or cash flow was significantly reduced. However, even those managerial rules that do have a measurable effect on stock prices are likely to have only a

196. Fox, The Role of the Market Model in Corporate Law Analysis: A Comment on Weiss and White, 76 Calif. L. Rev. 1015, 1036 (1988) (emphasis in original).

197. By way of comparison, Securities & Exchange Commission, Office of the Chief Economist, The Effects of Poison Pills on the Wealth of Target Shareholders 30–31 (Oct. 23, 1986), found that the adoption of a poison pill resulted in a negative return of .66% across the entire sample studied. For a subsample of companies where takeover speculation existed at the time the pill was adopted, the negative return was 1.74%. For a subsample of companies subject to takeover speculation that adopted a more effective type of pill, the negative return was 2.21%.

Similarly, Ryngaert, The Effect of Poison Pill Securities on Shareholder Wealth, 20 J. Fin. Econ. 377 (1988), found that announcement of the adoption of a poison pill resulted in a negative return of .34% across the sample studied. Id. at 391. For a subsample of companies where takeover speculation existed at the time of adoption, the negative return was 1.51%. Id. at 391–92. For a subsample of companies subject to takeover speculation that adopted a more effective type of poison pill, the negative return was 2.12%. Id. at 393–94.

198. In a comment on this Article, Winter objects that "[t]his hypothetical appears to be based on the assumption that share price is independent of the number of shares issued. That assumption is plainly unsound. If it were correct, C Corporation would issue 39 trillion shares at $49 instead of the 10,204 Eisenberg postulates." Winter, supra note 185, at 1527. This objection is somewhat difficult to understand, because the hypothetical assumes that the corporation only wants to raise $500,000. Putting that aside, the objection seems to mistake the operation of the takeover market with the operation of the product market. Suppose the corporation issued, say, 102,040 shares. And suppose that the shares were issued at less than $49. That would affect the corporation in the *takeover* market, but it would not affect the corporation in the *product* market.

relatively small effect.[199] Relatively small effects will not lead to bankruptcy in most product markets, particularly if, as is often the case, the corporation retains earnings and does not reenter the capital markets.[200]

In short, the adoption of a managerial rule would rarely lead to bankruptcy in the product market, because such a rule would rarely have any present impact on out-of-pocket costs and would often have no significant impact even on future out-of-pocket costs. Any impact that such a rule did have on out-of-pocket costs would normally be swamped by the slack in the product market.

b. *Effect on the Takeover Market.* — Although a managerial rule that has no impact on expenses or current cash flow may have no effect on the corporation's ability to compete in the product market, such a rule may cause the price of the corporation's stock to fall, which in turn could have an effect in the takeover market. But any decrease in the value of a corporation's stock that results from the adoption of a managerial rule will be typically either not measurable or relatively small[201]

---

199. See supra notes 196–198 and accompanying text.

200. See supra notes 186–189 and accompanying text.

201. Merritt Fox, in a comment on an earlier draft of this Article, worked out the effect of a small but measurable change on the price of a new issue as follows, employing the hypothetical set out at supra notes 196–200 and accompanying text:

> [S]uppose a corporation has assets that would produce a permanent cash flow available for shareholders of $500,000 per year (in other words its gross cash flow is sufficiently large to leave $500,000 after payment of operating expenses, interest on debt and the cost of purchasing new productive assets to replace those that have worn out during the year). The discount rate is 10%. The value of the equity of this firm, absent the managerial rule, would thus be $5 million. If there are 100,000 shares, they would be priced in an efficient market at $50 each. Imposition of the managerial rule reduces the net cash flow to $490,000, the value of the equity to $4.9 million and the share price to $49. If the cash flow is certain in this example, the corporation can continue operating under the managerial rule without the slightest risk of bankruptcy and would have no need to reenter the capital markets. . . .
>
> [A]ssume that the corporation wishes to raise $500,000 to invest in a project that will produce a net cash flow of $50,000 (i.e., a market rate of return) and with respect to which the managerial rule will not be imposed. . . . The net cash flow of the corporation after the expansion will be $540,000 and the value of the equity will be $5.4 million. If the corporation proposes to raise the $500,000 by offering 10,204 shares at $49, the public will willingly pay the price. The value of the equity will be $5.4 million and $5.4 million/110,204 = $49.00.
>
> [A]ssume now that the corporation wishes to raise the $500,000 to invest in [a new] project but that it plans to extend the managerial rule to these new operations . . . . The net cash flow of the corporation after the expansion will be $539,000 and thus the value of the equity will be $5.39 million. . . . Set E = $5.39 million (the value of the equity after the investment), I = $500,000 (the amount that must be raised for the new project) and S = 100,000 (the number of shares initially outstanding). Take p as the price at which the shares will be offered and [let] n be the number of shares that must be issued at p in order to raise I. An efficient capital market imposes the following conditions:

and relatively small effects on the market price of a corporation's stock will not trigger a hostile takeover because they will be swamped by the huge premium and fees required. Therefore, the capital market, operating through either the product or takeover markets, will seldom if ever prevent managers from adopting managerial rules.

That the financial effects of the market mechanisms considered so far will not in themselves adequately align the interest of managers and shareholders does not mean that managers will act only in their own interest except so far as constrained by law. Many or most managers will probably act in the shareholders' interests, even if not constrained to do so by market mechanisms, because they have internalized the moral principles of corporate stewardship. Those principles, however, have been significantly elaborated and supported by the legal rules that concern the powers and duties of corporate managers. Treating these rules as merely default rules would inevitably weaken the force of the principles they now support.

7. *The Market for Corporate Charters.* — A very different kind of market that is relevant to corporation law is the market for corporate charters. A corporation can incorporate in any state it selects, and under standard choice-of-law rules a corporation's internal affairs are normally governed by the law of the state in which it incorporates.[202] Under the rules of state taxation, if a corporation does business within a state, that state may tax the corporation on a basis that reflects the amount of that business, and if a corporation is incorporated in a state, that state may impose a tax for the privilege of incorporation even if the corporation does no business in the state.

Call the latter tax a franchise tax. A small state has a very strong financial incentive to design a corporate-law regime that will sell—that

---

$$p \times n = I$$
$$E/(n + S) = p \text{ (so that } p \text{ is a market clearing price)}$$

These conditions can be manipulated to get the value of p and n in terms of E, I, and S:

$$E/(n + S) = p = I/n$$
$$(n + S)/E = n/I$$
$$(I/E) \times (n + S) = n$$
$$(I/E) \times S = n \times (1 - (I/E))$$
$$\frac{(I/E)}{1 - (I/E)} \times S = n$$

Filling in the actual values of E, I, and S, $n = 10{,}224$ shares. Correspondingly, $p = \$48.90$, which is a market clearing price because \$5.39 million/110,224 = \$48.90.

Letter from Merritt B. Fox to author (December 12, 1988) (copy on file at the Columbia Law Review).

202. See Restatement (Second) of Conflict of Laws § 302(2) (1971); see also Davis & Cox v. Summa Corp., 751 F.2d 1507, 1527 (9th Cir. 1985) ("Claims involving 'internal affairs' of corporations, such as the breach of fiduciary duties, are subject to the laws of the state of incorporation."); accord Fry v. Trump, 681 F. Supp. 252, 255–56 (D.N.J. 1988).

is, a regime that will attract incorporation. If the state is successful in attracting incorporation, the resulting franchise-tax revenues can subsidize a large portion of its budget, because the out-of-pocket cost of maintaining such a regime will be negligible while the social and economic costs of any defects in the regime will be borne largely by the citizens of other states. In a large state, franchise taxes are likely to be swamped, and indeed may be legally offset, by revenues from the doing-business tax. Even a large state, however, has an incentive to design a regime that will attract incorporation, because the revenues of the local corporate bar may depend in part on the extent of local incorporation.[203]

Normally, it is uneconomical for a closely held corporation to incorporate in a state other than that in which its business is principally based.[204] Furthermore, states will normally derive significant franchise-tax revenue only from publicly held corporations. A state that wants to maximize its franchise tax will therefore focus not so much on attracting original incorporation as on attracting reincorporation by corporations that are or are about to become publicly held. In a landmark article,[205] William Cary argued that decisions to reincorporate publicly held corporations are effectively made by managers; that Delaware, a small state, has systematically attempted to generate huge franchise-tax revenues—which pay for about one-sixth of its budget[206]—by designing its corporation law to attract managers; and that Delaware has carried out its design by distorting its corporate law to favor managers, thereby leading a race to the bottom that other

203. See Court's Decision Against Tactic in Takeover Fight Is Upheld on Appeal, Wall St. J., Oct. 5, 1988, at A6, col. 3 ("New York Bar Association wouldn't be happy to see their big clients move to Delaware" in response to New York Court of Appeals decision invalidating some types of poison pills.).

204. A closely held corporation typically is a small enterprise that does most of its business in one state. If a corporation does most of its business in State *A*, but incorporates in State *B*, it is likely to end up paying higher legal fees, because its local counsel will probably be more familiar with the law of State *A* than with the law of State *B*, and therefore will either have to work to overcome its lack of familiarity, or retain local counsel in State *B*, when advising on corporation-law issues. Furthermore, if State *B* is selected, it will be "necessary [for the corporation] to pay not only organization fees and taxes in that state but . . . also [to] qualify the corporation to do business in [State *A*]. This will entail the filing of more papers and the payment of further fees and taxes." W. Painter, Corporate and Tax Aspects of Closely Held Corporations 21 (2d ed. 1981). Combined taxes in State *A* and State *B* may well be higher than would state taxes in State *B* alone, depending on the tax regimes of each state. The net result is that "it is generally less expensive, and certainly more convenient, to incorporate locally." W. Painter, supra, at 21.

205. Cary, Federalism and Corporate Law: Reflections Upon Delaware, 83 Yale L.J. 663 (1974).

206. See U.S. Dept. of Commerce, Bureau of the Census, Government Finances—State Government Finances in 1987 at 12 (1988). The figure includes franchise taxes, fees, and charges related to annual reports.

states feel constrained to join.[207]

A response to Cary's argument was formulated by Ralph Winter.[208] Winter agreed that managers of publicly held corporations effectively decide upon the state of incorporation, and that Delaware has systematically designed its law to attract managers. He distinguished, however, between attracting managers and unduly favoring managers, and argued that if Delaware unduly favored managers, shareholders in Delaware corporations would earn lower-than-normal returns and Delaware corporations would therefore have a higher cost of capital. This would either bankrupt Delaware corporations in the product markets or cause the ouster of management through takeover bids, and managers would therefore avoid incorporating in Delaware. Since Delaware is in fact by far the most popular state of incorporation for large publicly held corporations—forty-three percent of New York Stock Exchange firms are incorporated there[209]—Cary's argument that Delaware has led a race to the bottom must be wrong.[210] Indeed, Winter argued, the incentive to sell corporate law has actually led Delaware and other states to produce an optimal corporate-law regime,[211] because a state that offers the optimal, value-maximizing regime of corporate law will attract the most incorporation. As two later commentators put it, "managers of a firm take advantage of the competition among states to locate in a state which offers an efficient set of restrictions on the firm, given the firm's anticipated production-investment and financing decisions."[212] Each state therefore has a market incentive to create the optimal corporate-law regime.

The argument that market forces lead to optimal corporate law—sometimes referred to as corporate federalism—is not inconsistent with the thesis that in certain cases mandatory rules are more efficient than enabling or suppletory rules. Corporate federalism claims that state corporation law will be optimal because the state with optimal rules will sell its law to the most corporations. Corporate federalism, however, does not in itself suggest what mix of enabling, suppletory, and mandatory rules will be optimal.

Nevertheless, the issues staked out by Cary and Winter need to be addressed in any full examination of the structure of corporation law, because these issues concern fundamentals of corporation law, figure actively in the literature that stresses the alignment effect of market

207. Cary, surpa note 205, at 665–66, 668–72.

208. Winter, supra note 183.

209. See Macey & Miller, Toward an Interest Group Theory of Delaware Corporate Law, 65 Tex. L. Rev. 469, 478 (1987).

210. Winter, supra note 183, at 257, 258, 275–76.

211. Id. at 290.

212. Dodd & Leftwich, The Market for Corporate Charters: "Unhealthy Competition" Versus Federal Regulation, 53 J. Bus. 259, 282 (1980).

forces, and help to explain the structure of corporation law.[213]

Several commentators have attempted to resolve these issues through event studies designed to measure the effect of reincorporation in Delaware on the stock prices of reincorporating firms.[214] Such studies have only limited usefulness in this context. Even under Cary's analysis, it would be surprising if the mere announcement of reincorporation in Delaware had a significant negative effect on stock prices. If competition among the states results in a uniformly low-grade regime, as Cary argued it did, the announcement of a shift from one low-grade regime to another would not be a significant event.[215] Furthermore, Delaware has certain advantages for shareholders, such as a rich case law that increases predictability, that could offset the suboptimality of its rules. Perhaps most important, reincorporation in Delaware often accompanies other developments, such as an initial public offering or the initiation or expansion of a mergers-and-acquisitions program,[216] and the statistical noise from those developments would be likely to drown out any negative effect resulting from a switch to a less optimal legal regime. Finally, distortions in state law may take the form not of rules that invite exploitation, but of rules that remove checks on positional conflicts. If the managers of a reincorporating corporation are doing a reasonably good job at the time of reincorporation, the negative effect of removing checks on positional conflicts would be exceptionally difficult to value and might well be underestimated because of the representativeness heuristic.[217] It will be recalled that Weiss and White studied seven major Delaware decisions that changed the constitutive rules of Delaware corporations and found that none produced a statistically significant change in the price of the stock of Delaware corporations.[218] As Weiss and White point out, this data casts "considerable doubt on Winter's claim that investors' decisions concerning whether to buy the stock of Delaware or non-Delaware companies operate so as to preclude the development of unduly pro-manager systems of corporate law."[219]

213. See infra text accompanying notes 226–35.

214. See, e.g., Dodd & Leftwich, supra note 212; Romano, Law as a Product: Some Pieces of the Incorporation Puzzle, 1 J.L. & Econ. Organization 225 (1985) [hereinafter Law as Product]; Romano, The State Competition Debate in Corporate Law, 8 Cardozo L. Rev. 709 (1987) [hereinafter Competition Debate].

215. See Weiss & White, supra note 192, at 555, 559–60.

A corporation might want to switch to Delaware even if Delaware's rules were just as low-grade as those of the present state of incorporation because Delaware's case law is much richer and Delaware has more effectively committed itself to maintaining its regime. See infra text accompanying notes 230–31.

216. See Romano, Law as Product, supra note 214, at 250, 256.

217. See supra note 13 and accompanying text.

218. See supra note 192 and accompanying text.

219. Weiss & White, supra note 192, at 603; see also Fox, supra note 196, at 1042–43.

As Fox points out, "[w]hile a decision that [changes] the share value of Delaware

The two most important event studies on the effect of reincorporation in Delaware were conducted by Dodd and Leftwich and by Romano. Predictably, Dodd and Leftwich found that the announcement of reincorporation in Delaware did not have a statistically significant impact on stock prices.[220] Romano found that it had a positive significant effect, but that this effect was driven by the positive returns for firms that switched to Delaware in preparation for engaging in merger and acquisition activity.[221] Moreover, Dodd and Leftwich found that on average the firms in their sample had growing supranormal returns until reincorporating in Delaware, but that this growth stopped after reincorporation,[222] a pattern that is consistent with Cary's claim.[223]

Given the limitations of the data, a deeper economic analysis is required. Such an analysis shows that neither Cary nor Winter captured the actual dynamics of the charter market and leads to a position that is intermediate between those of Cary and Winter, although closer to Cary's.

To begin with, Winter's claim that all states have an economic incentive to adopt optimal corporate-law regimes will not withstand scrutiny. The claim is driven purely by the argument concerning the cost of capital—that if a state unduly favors managers, corporations incorporated in that state would either go bankrupt or be taken over. That argument is fatally defective for the reasons set out above:[224] Adoption of rules that are in the interests of managers but not shareholders will not necessarily have any effect on the ability of the corporation to compete in the product market, and any effect they do have is likely to be swamped by the slack in those markets. Adoption of such rules is also highly unlikely to result in a reduction in the value of a corporation's stock that is sufficient to trigger a takeover.

Winter's claim also fails to take account of basic agency-cost principles. Assume, with both Cary and Winter, that the state of incorpora-

---

firms by 0.1% has effects too small in general to be accompanied by statistically significant price changes . . . . the aggregate effect of the decision would be more than $1 billion." See Fox, supra note 196, at 1037–38.

220. Dodd & Leftwich, supra note 212, at 266, 272–75.

221. Romano, Law as Product, supra note 214, at 271.

222. Dodd & Leftwich, supra note 212, at 266, 272–75.

223. Cf. Fox, supra note 196, at 1043 (footnote omitted):

> [T]he Weiss and White results are damaging to the contractual theorists' empirical case against Cary's race to the bottom hypothesis. That case is based on the findings of Dodd and Leftwich that there is no statistically significant price reaction to reincorporation in Delaware. Weiss and White's failure to find statistically significant reactions to cases articulating major changes in Delaware law suggests that Dodd and Leftwich placed too high a burden of proof on Cary. Even if the market accurately evaluates the effects of Delaware reincorporations and these effects are negative in an amount that is economically important in aggregate, reincorporations may not be accompanied by statistically significant price changes.

224. See supra note 185–200 and accompanying text.

tion of a publicly held corporation is chosen by its managers, and that the only goal of a state is to maximize franchise-tax revenues. The state can then be viewed as a seller that deals largely with buyers represented by agents. A seller that deals largely with buyers represented by agents will normally maximize its returns if it can make side payments to the agents while providing a product that is acceptable even though not optimal to their principals (not optimal, because by hypothesis the cost of the product includes a side payment to the agent). A familiar example is provided by the airline industry. The airlines sell a significant portion of their tickets to firms, but the choice of airline is usually made by the traveling employee. The airlines therefore offer side payments to employees, in the form of mileage bonuses that are credited to the employees' personal accounts.[225] Competition between airlines results not in optimal prices to buying firms, but in side payments to employees and suboptimal prices to buying firms. Many chain-hotel and auto-rental companies—who, like airlines, deal largely with buyers represented by agents—follow the same course.

A state whose only goal is to maximize franchise-tax revenues will also follow that course. Rather than provide an optimal legal regime to corporate buyers, it will provide side payments to the agent-managers who make the actual decision concerning which state's legal regime the corporation will purchase. These side payments will take the form of managerial rules—rules that are in the interests of managers but not shareholders. The strongest managerial interests concern positional conflicts. A state whose only goal is to maximize franchise-tax revenues will therefore adopt legal rules that facilitate actions by top managers to maintain and enhance their offices. This is exactly the position the Delaware legislature took in the past, by adopting, for example, rules that permit staggered boards, allow economically significant corporate combinations to occur without shareholder approval, fail to require the distribution of information on managerial performance, and fail to regulate proxy voting.[226] Over the past ten or fifteen years, Delaware's

---

225. At one point, Continental Airlines was paying rebates to employees in cash. Continental Air's Cash Rebate: Promotion or Kickback?, Wall St. J., Dec. 5, 1988, at B1, col. 3. Cf. Travel Agents' Games Raise Ethics Issue, Wall St. J., Nov. 23, 1988, at B1, at col. 3 (special kickbacks by airlines to travel agents).

226. See Eisenberg, The Modernization of Corporate Law, 37 U. Miami L. Rev. 187 (1983).

In a comment on this Article, Winter concludes:

> My bottom line remains that, if Professor Cary is right, earnings per dollar of investment in Delaware corporations must be less than earnings per dollar of investment in corporations that do not permit such side payments. Indeed, the entire point of Professor Cary's article was that investors do worse under Delaware law than under other corporate codes.... It therefore follows that, unless the market for capital is indifferent to a firm's earnings, Delaware corporations will be at a disadvantage in raising capital. That is a consequence that is hardly likely to maximize Delaware's franchise tax revenues.

Winter, supra note 185, at 1528 (footnotes omitted). This misses the agency-cost point.

position on statutory innovations has been moderate, and often even statesman-like.[227] The Delaware legislature has not, however, significantly changed most of the managerial rules Delaware adopted in its bid for primacy prior to that time.

Winter and Cary also significantly oversimplified the nature and dynamics of the charter market. For example, both failed to address the complexity of the states' objectives in framing corporate law. Not all states are motivated solely by the goal of maximizing franchise-tax revenues. Many states are at least weakly motivated by the goal of maximizing the revenues of the local corporate bar.[228] The corporate-law rules that will maximize the revenues of the local corporate bar may differ from the corporate-law rules that will maximize franchise-tax revenues,[229] and the relative weight attached to these differences undoubtedly varies from state to state. Furthermore, legislatures are not private sellers, but public actors. Attracting the business of principals by making side payments to agents is a morally dubious enterprise. For some legislators, public morality will be an important constraint on the willingness to engage in that enterprise. The extent of that willingness also undoubtedly varies from state to state.

Furthermore, Winter and Cary both assumed that the states are like sellers in a perfectly competitive market. In fact, the charter market is not perfectly competitive. As the market has developed, Delaware has come to enjoy both a huge share of the market and a great amount of market power,[230] because it offers attractions (some of which are beneficial to both shareholdes and managers) that few other states can now match.[231] Among these are a rich body of case-law that facilitates planning and dispute-settlement; a geographical location that makes it easy for most non-Delaware corporate lawyers to consult with the Dela-

---

Even if the stock prices of Delaware corporations are negatively affected by Delaware law, managers may choose Delaware because the side payments Delaware makes to top managers outweigh the impact on them of that negative effect. Indeed, in a passage that could easily have been written by Cary, Winter himself says:

> [A state] takeover statute will . . . [negatively] affect share price and ability of relevant corporations to raise capital . . . . [However, losing] one's position as management will seem much less desirable than whatever injury may occur to the corporation as a result of a state takeover statute. Profit maximizing on behalf of the corporation in these circumstances . . . may not be in the economic self-interest of management.

Winter, supra note 183, at 288. But the same observation applies to *any* legal rule that will help prevent a manager from losing his position.

227. See Romano, Law as Product, supra note 214, at 231–42.

228. See Macey & Miller, supra note 209, at 491. Cf. id. at 472 (bar "most important interest group" driving changes in Delaware law).

229. For example, making it easier to bring derivative suits may increase the revenues of the litigating bar, but diminish the incentive to incorporate in the state.

230. See Macey & Miller, supra note 209, at 483.

231. See Romano, Competition Debate, supra note 214; Romano, Law as Product, supra note 214.

ware corporate bar; an established corporate address; and various rules, practices, and economic features—particularly its heavy dependence on the franchise tax—that serve as a bond for the faithful continuance of its regime.[232] These features serve as barriers to entry in the charter market.

One result of Delaware's attainment of market share and market power through the past adoption of suboptimal managerial rules is that Delaware now has a special incentive *not* to lead in the adoption of such rules: the desirability of avoiding massive federal intervention in corporate law. The incentives of the federal government on issues of corporate law differ considerably from those of the states. Because of its plenary power under the Supremacy Clause, the federal government has no incentive to compete for incorporation and no need to make side payments to managers. Furthermore, while any given state may view defects in its corporate-law regime as an externality whose effects fall almost entirely on the out-of-state population, the federal government, as the representative of the entire population, and as an entity whose own revenues are significantly based on corporate income rather than on a franchise tax based on nonincome elements, must internalize all defects in corporate law. The federal government therefore has a greater incentive than the states to be concerned with suboptimality. Because such intervention would be costly, the federal government should not and does not intervene to correct every suboptimal rule. If, however, state law became highly suboptimal, the risk of federal intervention would increase.

A state that has had little success in the charter market has much to gain and little to lose by offering innovative side payments. If the side payments attract incorporation, the state comes out ahead; if the side payments stimulate federal intervention, the state is no worse off. In contrast, if comprehensive national rules were established for publicly held corporations, over time Delaware would almost certainly lose a significant portion of its franchise-tax revenues. Therefore, precisely because of its historical success in the charter market, Delaware is more threatened by the possibility of comprehensive federal intervention than any other state. Furthermore, because of Delaware's massive market share, innovative side payments by Delaware are more likely to provoke federal intervention than innovative side payments by any other state. So, having achieved a huge market share in significant part because of its past leadership in offering side payments to managers, Delaware now has an incentive not to lead in the adoption of innovative managerial rules.

232. See Romano, Law as Product, supra note 214, at 240–42; Romano, Competition Debate, supra note 214, at 721–23.

Certainly it seems to be the case that within recent years Delaware has become relatively moderate in adopting statutory innovations.[233] It is no longer fair to say that Delaware is leading the race to the corporate bottom. Undoubtedly, Delaware's current posture is in significant part the result of the moderate views of its present corporate bar. It is nevertheless the case that while Delaware can now afford to be moderate, and even has an incentive to do so, it cannot ignore what other less moderate states may do. If an innovative side payment adopted by other states becomes so well established that Delaware's failure to respond in some way would call into question Delaware's resolve to match the market, Delaware falls under enormous economic pressure to adopt some version of the innovation.

In short, both Winter and Cary oversimplified the nature and dynamics of the market for corporate charters.[234] Cary was right in concluding that a state will not always seek to adopt laws that maximize shareholder wealth. A state whose only goal is to maximize franchise-tax revenues will find it in its interest to depart from an optimal corporate-law regime by making side payments to managers in the form of rules that fail to adequately address positional conflicts. However, Cary was wrong in concluding that Delaware and other states will not take the maximization of shareholder wealth into account. A state whose only goal is to maximize franchise-tax revenues will not depart from optimality *too far*, because, if it does, the value-decreasing effect of incorporating in the state could become so large as to invite takeovers or federal intervention.

Winter, on the other hand, was right in pointing out that states have an incentive to take optimality into account, but wrong in concluding that success in the charter market would turn solely on optimality, and that a state therefore would not deliberately adopt value-decreasing managerial rules in preference to optimal rules.

It can now be seen both why Delaware corporation law has many mandatory elements, and why it is less extensively mandatory than the law of most other states. Delaware law has many mandatory elements,[235] because mandatory elements are part of an optimal regime of corporation law. Delaware law is less extensively mandatory than most other states, because heavily dependent as Delaware has been on

233. See Romano, Law as Product, supra note 214, at 231–42. Romano studied innovation and responsiveness among all states by tracking the careers of four innovative laws. She found that

> [Delaware] leads all states on the responsiveness measure. . . . While it was the first state to enact only one of the four laws under study, it adopted the other three within four to seven years from their introduction in another jurisdiction, and as a result, it unambiguously outpaced the other states [in responsiveness].

Id. at 240.

234. Cf. Romano, Competition Debate, supra note 214, at 752–53.

235. See supra notes 85–98 and accompanying text.

franchise-tax revenues, historically its legislature was more willing than most other states to sacrifice optimality in favor of managerial rules.

It can also be seen why the federal government has intervened in corporation law, and why that intervention is generally limited to publicly held corporations. The federal government has intervened in corporation law because suboptimal state-law rules may affect both the welfare of the citizens of other states and the revenues the government derives from the income tax. Federal intervention is generally limited to large publicly held corporations because suboptimal rules for those corporations raise the most serious welfare and revenue issues for the federal government.

Finally, it can be seen why the New York Stock Exchange has historically regulated corporate governance. At least until recently, the Exchange virtually monopolized the liquid trading markets for the stock of very large publicly held corporations and, therefore, could attract listings from such corporations without making extensive side payments to managers. At the same time, the Exchange has an economic interest in the adoption of rules that maximize shareholder wealth and attract investment in stock. Accordingly, the Exchange has had both an interest in curing defects in state law and the power to do so.

F. *The Pricing Argument*

There is a third type of argument that may be made against the principle that mandatory legal rules should govern areas in which the interests of shareholders and top managers may materially diverge. This argument proceeds as follows: Under the efficient-market hypothesis, the market accurately prices all constitutive rules. Therefore, if a corporation adopts a constitutive rule that unduly favors the interests of top managers at the expense of shareholder interests, the effect will be impounded in the price of the corporation's stock. Accordingly, a shareholder in a publicly held corporation cannot fairly complain that any given rule unduly favors management interests, because even if it does, the shareholder has gotten what he paid for.

I will call this the pricing argument. The argument differs in three important ways from the arguments based on market forces considered above.

First, those arguments are rooted in an efficiency claim: that market forces adequately align the interests of shareholders and managers, so that mandatory legal rules are unnecessary and indeed costly. In contrast, the pricing argument is rooted in a fairness claim. The argument is not that market forces will adequately align the interests of shareholders and managers, but only that the stock of corporations in which such alignment is lacking will sell at an appropriate discount, so that buyers of the stock will suffer no unjust loss as a result of the lack of adequate alignment.[236]

Second, the market-forces arguments purport to describe the actual effects of existing market institutions. In contrast, the pricing argument is largely hypothetical, because most of the core fiduciary and structural legal rules that govern publicly held corporations are not in fact subject to substantial variation.

Third, the market-forces arguments claim that both existing market institutions both align the interests of top managers and shareholders in publicly held corporations, and address the problem of managerial inefficiency, so adequately that mandatory legal rules to address those issues are unnecessary. In contrast, the pricing argument applies to just those cases in which the constitutive rules of a corporation do *not* adequately align the interests of top managers and shareholders and address the problem of managerial efficiency.

The pricing argument has some force in the case of corporations that are about to go public,[237] but it will not withstand scrutiny in the context of publicly held corporations. The argument is that a shareholder who buys stock cannot fairly complain that the corporation has a suboptimal managerial rule, because even if it does, the shareholder has gotten what he paid for. By its terms, therefore, the argument has no application in cases where there are shareholders who own stock in a corporation *before* a suboptimal managerial rule is adopted, and do not meaningfully consent to the new rule. That would nearly always be the case in corporations whose stock is already publicly held.

III. Corporations That Are About to Go Public

Assume now that a corporation adopts a constitutive rule just as it is about to go public. Two very different claims can then be made. First, it can be claimed that the pricing argument is now relevant, because all public shareholders will buy their stock after the rule has been adopted. Second, a market-forces claim can be made, along the following lines: Suppose an owner-manager holds all of the corporation's stock, and he intends to sell all his stock to the public and drop his managerial position. He then has every incentive to adopt constitutive rules that will maximize the value of the corporation's stock, and no incentive to adopt rules that will decrease that value.

Admittedly, this is not the typical case. Usually, an owner-manager intends to retain some stock and his managerial position. Even in that case, it can be argued, an owner-manager would not have a financial incentive to adopt managerial rules that would decrease the value of the corporation's stock. Although he would reap the benefit of such

236. Cf. Fischel, The Corporate Governance Movement, supra note 124, at 1266 ("even if agency costs are substantial . . . shareholders will not be injured if relevant information is incorporated in market prices").

237. See infra text accompanying note 238.

rules in his managerial capacity, he would suffer the impact of those rules in his ownership capacity, because the rules would decrease both the value of the stock he retained and the price of the stock he sold.[238] By aggregating the pricing and market-force claims, the argument can be made that corporations that are about to go public should be permitted to vary core fiduciary or structural rules.

This line of reasoning, which I will call the initial-public-offering argument, does not prevail under current law. In general, the core fiduciary and structural rules that are mandatory for publicly held corporations[239] are no less mandatory for corporations that might attempt to vary those rules before going public. An examination of the limits of the initial-public-offering argument shows why this should be so.

To begin with, the argument assumes that such variations, if permitted, would be accurately priced. In fact, however, there is no direct evidence that all such variations would be accurately priced, and some direct evidence that they would not.[240] It must be borne in mind that the pricing and market for stock offered in an initial public offering ("IPO") may differ substantially from the pricing and market for stock that is already publicly traded. The price of stock that is already publicly traded is determined by the intersection of the valuations of a huge number of buyers and sellers, whose random biases may tend to cancel one another out.[241] In contrast, the price of stock offered in an initial public offering is typically determined by negotiation between the corporation and an underwriter on the basis of general market conditions and preliminary expressions of interest by potential investors,[242] many of whom would probably be unaware of the corporation's constitutive rules.[243] "Pricing is most difficult for issues of unseasoned stock. In these cases the underwriter has very little guidance as to the market

238. This argument was formulated in Jensen & Meckling, supra note 125, at 312–30. Jensen and Meckling carefully restricted their analysis to rules that constrain expenditures on managers' nonpecuniary benefits. They also argued that in some cases the incentive of owner-managers to adopt rules that favored shareholder interests would exceed the incentive to adopt rules that favored managers' interests, id. at 325–26, but that argument does not extend to all rules in all cases.

An owner-manager also might set a sufficiently high value on the nonfinancial benefits of maintaining and enhancing his position that he would be willing to accept a lower price for his stock in exchange for rules that protect that nonfinancial interest.

In the balance of this section, I will assume for convenience that a single owner-manager owns all of a corporation's stock. The analysis can be suitably modified where this is not the case.

239. See supra Part II. C.

240. See supra notes 192–196 and accompanying text (the Weiss and White data).

241. Gilson & Kraakman, The Mechanisms of Market Efficiency, 70 Va. L. Rev. 549, 581–82 (1984).

242. See Stout, supra note 186, at 651–52.

243. Cf. Coffee, supra note 149, at 935 (information concerning risks of managerial exploitation "approaches the unknowable.").

value of the security."[244] The pricing of initial public offerings is marked by extreme uncertainty.[245]

Accordingly, the price at which IPO stock actually trades reflects the relative lack of power of the mechanisms used to set the price at which such stock is actually issued. On average, there is fifty percent more variation in the price of such stock during a two-week period than the stock market shows in an entire year.[246] About half of all initial public offerings are significantly underpriced in relation to the price at which the stock actually trades; about one-fourth are significantly overpriced.[247]

A related assumption of the initial-public-offering argument is that purchasers of IPO stock will be informed investors who will know of and can properly value variations in core structural or fiduciary rules. In fact, however, it seems likely that many investors in IPO stock are relatively uninformed.[248] It is sometimes said that even if that is so, variations in core fiduciary and structural rules would be accurately priced because institutional investors, who would have the ability and incentive to price such variations, purchase a significant amount of IPO stock, and uninformed investors would free ride on their efforts.[249] There are several reasons why this is not necessarily true. For one thing, exploitation of a variation in a core fiduciary or structural rule might or might not occur, and if it did occur, would normally occur in the future. Given the difficulty of estimating the probabilities, and the need to discount any future loss by the time value of money, the effort required to price a variation often might not be justified,[250] particularly because any single institutional investor will normally be allocated only a limited amount of any given initial public offering.[251]

Moreover, even if an informed investor does set a value on such a

244. R. Brealey & S. Myers, Principles of Corporate Finance 306 (2d ed. 1984); see also id. at 331 (3d ed. 1988) ("Whenever any company goes public, it is very difficult for the underwriter to judge how much investors will be willing to pay for the stock.").

245. See Beatty & Ritter, Investment Banking, Reputation, and the Underpricing of Initial Public Offerings, 15 J. Fin. Econ. 213, 213–14 (1986); Rock, Why New Issues Are Underpriced, 15 J. Fin. Econ. 187, 188 (1986).

246. Stout, supra note 186, at 657; Cf. Ibbotson, Price Performance of Common Stock New Issues, 2 J. Fin. Econ. 235, 246–50 (1975) (average initial performance of new offering is positive but distribution of returns is skewed).

247. See Weiss, Initial Public Offerings and the Cost of Information 18–19 (unpublished PhD thesis, University of Florida, 1988) (excerpt on file at the Columbia Law Review).

248. See Rock, supra note 245, at 199; cf. Ibbotson, Sindelar & Ritter, Initial Public Offerings, 1 J. Applied Corp. Fin. 37, 43 (1988) (asymmetry of information among potential IPO investors).

249. See Gordon, The Mandatory Structure of Corporate Law, 89 Colum. L. Rev. 1549, 1557 (1989).

250. Black, Is Corporation Law Trivial? (forthcoming 84 Nw. U.L. Rev. (1989)).

251. See Beatty & Ritter, supra note 245, at 215 ("The majority of initial public offerings are subject to . . . quantity rationing.").

term, it might not always be able readily to introduce that valuation into the price at which the IPO stock is offered. In the case of stock that is already publicly traded, an investor who assigns a negative value to an obscure governance term could in theory profit from that information by selling short and then making a public announcement about the term and its value, which would cause the price of the stock to fall. In the case of initial public offerings, however, even this theoretical possibility may be unavailable. An investor who sold IPO stock short on the basis of its negative view of a governance term would often lose money even if it was right about the term, because on average such offerings are underpriced.[252] In any given case, therefore, informed investors might or might not be able to cause the price of IPO stock to be reduced by the negative value of a variation in core fiduciary or structural rules.

Even more important, although institutional investors may buy a significant number of shares of initial public offerings *on average*, it seems likely that there are many initial public offerings in which institutional investors do not play a major role. Many IPOs are too small to be of likely interest to institutional investors. In a sample of initial public offerings from 1975 to 1984, almost sixty percent of the offerings involved firms with sales of less than $5 million.[253] Some initial public offerings are sold almost exclusively to individual investors.[254] One entire class of initial public offerings, closed-end investment companies, is systematically and materially overpriced,[255] suggesting that there is a large pool of uniformed buyers to whom entire issues can be sold.[256]

Another argument sometimes made is that IPO investors will be protected against bad bargains by the interest of the underwriter in developing or maintaining a good reputation.[257] Again, this may well be true on average, but there is no evidence that it is true in all or even almost all cases. Reputation is one element that motivates firms, but it is not the only element.[258] In particular, underwriters have an interest in obtaining issues to underwrite, and that interest may sometimes re-

252. See id.

253. See Ibbotson, Sindelar & Ritter, supra note 248, at 42.

254. See Entrepreneur Remains Undeterred by Venture's Failure, Wall St. J., Aug. 21, 1989, at B2, col. 3.

255. K. Weiss, K. Lehn & D. Malmquist, The Post-Offering Price Performance of Closed-End Mutual Funds 11 (unpublished manuscript, The Office of Economic Analysis, Securities and Exchange Commission, July 1989) (on file at the Columbia Law Review) (closed-end mutual funds suffer an average cumulative index-adjusted return of − 15.054% in 120 days following IPO).

256. Weiss and her colleagues conclude that institutional investors are less active in purchasing shares in the initial public offerings of closed-end funds than in purchasing other IPOs. Id. at 23–24.

257. See Gordon, supra note 249, at 1558–59.

258. See, e.g., "Highly Confident" Morgan Stanley Backs Out, Wall St. J., Sept. 12, 1989, at C1, col. 4.

quire acquiescing in terms they believe to be inappropriate.[259]

Even assuming that despite all these problems variations in core fiduciary or structural rules would in fact be priced in an unbiased manner, that would not in itself be dispositive, because investors who purchased such stock without knowing about these variations would often be unfairly surprised. In this connection, Merritt Fox has drawn a useful distinction between lack of bias and accuracy. Market reactions are properly termed unbiased, he suggests, if on average they correctly measure actual changes in share value.[260] But, as Fox points out:

> lack of bias and accuracy are different concepts. Consider, for example, two investors, *X* and *Y*, who forecast the effects of court decisions on share value. Both forecasts might be unbiased, but *X* would be considered more accurate than *Y* if the average deviation of *X*'s estimates from the actual effects of the decisions (*X*'s forecast errors) was smaller than the average deviation of *Y*'s estimates.[261]

Under modern contract law, a contract term that is unfairly surprising is unenforceable even if the term is impounded in the contract price. For example, the courts routinely hold that unclear or inconspicuous terms in insurance contracts that violate the insured's fair expectations are unenforceable, without regard to whether the terms lowered the insured's premiums.[262] In one typical case, an insurer sold the

---

259. Compare Limited Partnership Are Often Faltering, to Investors' Dismay, Wall St. J., Aug. 17, 1989, at A1, col. 6:

> Many brokers complain that their bosses pushed them to sell questionable partnerships—in many cases, slighting their fiduciary responsibility to investors. Several present and former [Shearson Lehman Hutton] brokers say their bosses warned them not to waste time reading prospectuses, time that would be better spent selling to clients.
>
> ....
>
> In California . . . a third of investors' complaints lodged with the Department of Corporations allege that the general partners illegally commingled funds. Many of the syndicators took cash out of profitable partnerships to prop up failing ones . . . . Eventually, most of them crashed.
>
> ....
>
> Irwin Fisk, the chief investigator in the [Department of Corporations' Southern California branch] says that "we see maybe 50" cases of allegedly commingled funds a year, many of which "result in prosecutions and, usually, in convictions." But often, he laments, "the general partners' right to move money around [among different limited partnerhsips that they control] is written into the partnership agreement. That's a crazy thing to sign, but investors don't read it."

And, apparently, underwriters don't object to it.

Cf. Municipal Bond Trustees Hit by Growing Criticism, Wall St. J., May 23, 1988, at A21, col. 5 ("A [municipal bond] trustee who sees problems in a planned offering can request changes or decline the role of overseer. But trustees say the field is so competitive that in practice doing so means losing work.").

260. Fox, supra note 196, at 1027–28.

261. Id. at 1028.

262. See, e.g., Gray v. Zurich Ins. Co., 65 Cal. 2d 263, 274, 419 P.2d 168, 174–75,

owner of a department store a "Bodily Injury Liability" policy to cover premises operation. A term in the fine print of the policy excluded coverage for accidents in elevators on the premises.[263] The exclusion was held unenforceable because it violated the store owner's fair expectations. In another typical case,[264] an insurer sold a home owner a home owner's policy that included "Comprehensive Personal Liability (Bodily Injury and Property Damage)." A term in the fine print of the policy excluded injuries to a domestic employee. The exclusion was held unenforceable because it violated the home owner's fair expectations. It has never been thought a defense, in such cases, that in the absence of the exclusion the policy premium would have been higher.

One reason for this rule is that even a term that is priced may be inefficient if information is asymmetrical. For example, suppose there is competition among banks to attract consumers to open checking accounts. Assume that consumers focus primarily on interest rates, which are both the most salient and the most easily understood characteristic of checking accounts. In contrast, many other characteristics, such as the consequences of failing to detect and promptly report embezzlement, forgery, or mistakes in the account, are difficult to explain simply or understand fully, so that typically consumers are rationally ignorant about the terms that define the depositor's liability if these contingencies occur. It is then in the interest of each bank to increase interest rates up to the point where the additional revenue derived by attracting more consumers will equal the marginal cost of the interest rate and all other characteristics of the account.

One way to increase the interest rate is to reduce the costs of other characteristics by setting very unfavorable terms on those characteristics that are both less salient and less easily understood. All prices will then be based on the marginal costs attributable to the accounts. However, many consumers, if fully informed, might prefer to accept a slightly lower interest rate and have better terms on other characteristics, because, for example, they would prefer not to risk the massive loss that they might incur under the terms of the account if they fail to promptly report a forged check, an error, or the like. If so, competition will lead to an inefficient result, because consumers who were fully informed would have placed a higher value on products that they were not offered than on the products that they were offered. Similarly, insurance terms may be unfairly surprising even if the terms are impounded into the price, because the insured would have preferred

54 Cal. Rptr. 104, 110–11 (1966); Johnson v. United Investors Life Ins. Co., 263 N.W.2d 770, 776 (Iowa 1978); Gerhardt v. Continental Ins. Cos., 48 N.J. 291, 300, 225 A.2d 328, 333–34 (1966); Portella v. Sonnenberg, 74 N.J. Super. 354, 362, 181 A.2d 385, 390 (1962).

263. *Portella*, 74 N.J. Super. 354, 181 A.2d 385 (1962).

264. Gerhardt v. Continental Ins. Co., 48 N.J. 291, 298–99, 225 A.2d 328, 333 (1966).

paying a bit more rather than incurring the risk that the catastrophic event that the insured wanted covered, and believed would be covered, was in fact not covered.

In much the same way, variations of core fiduciary or structural rules might be both unfairly surprising and inefficient even if impounded into the price. What will be impounded into the price is the average likelihood that managers will exploit such a provision in a manner that will significantly decrease shareholder wealth. This average may be quite small, but many investors may well have preferred not to invest in a corporation whose stock was subject to significant losses as a result of substantial nonbusiness risks.[265]

It is no more likely that buyers in an initial public offering would know of variations in core fiduciary and structural rules than that buyers of insurance policies will know the fine print in their policies. Furthermore, even if the original buyers knew of the variations, subsequent buyers would not. Stock differs from ordinary consumer goods in that it is intended to be resold in pristine condition. It is not enough to say that original buyers of stock will know of a term if it is foreseeable that subsequent buyers will be unfairly surprised. Most shareholders who purchased a corporation's stock on the open market would be unfairly surprised to learn that the corporation had a rule that permitted senior executives to take corporate opportunities developed through the use of corporate information or assets or a rule that prohibited the board or the shareholders from removing the chief executive from office. If, as a result of such rules, an executive took a corporate opportunity worth twenty percent of the value of the corporation, or the corporation's earnings declined precipitously because of the chief executive's incompetence, it would be no answer to the shareholders to say that

265. See Brudney, Corporate Governance, Agency Costs, and the Rhetoric of Contract, 85 Colum. L. Rev. 1403, 1411 (1985):

> [I]f investors in fact are induced to "consent" to conditions of management discretion to serve itself that they do not understand, on price terms they would not accept if they understood the conditions, that [consent] . . . will not effect Pareto superiority or maximize efficiency. If investors understood the terms . . . as rational wealth maximizers they would demand other terms.

Cf. Jensen, supra note 170, at 42:

> [C]onsider the simple situation in which a principal (stockholder) hires an agent (managers and board of directors) to take some actions on his or her behalf. To effect this arrangement, the principal delegates to the agent a set of decision rights. . . .
>
> The principal may want to delegate a wide range of decision rights to the agent. In no event, however, will it be sensible for the principal to delegate the ultimate control rights to the agent: the rights to hire, fire, and set the compensation of the agent. . . .

If every investor was fully diversified, unfair surprise might be less of a problem, although even in that case some investors might simply be unwilling to take the risk of substantial losses that result from variation in core governance terms, if they knew of the variations. However, there is no strong evidence that all or even almost all stock is held by fully diversified investors.

although they were unfairly surprised by such events, the one-in-two-hundred chance that the events would occur was impounded into the price.

Furthermore, even if variations in core fiduciary and structural rules were known, shareholders would not meaningfully consent to them. Recall that even in closely held corporations, where true bargaining can occur, variations in core fiduciary rules should not be and are not enforceable, because consent to such variations would be systematically underinformed.[266] The quality of the consent to such variations would be even weaker in publicly held corporations, where true bargaining is almost impossible, and knowledge of the variation, let alone its meaning and implications, would typically be lacking. In publicly held corporations, the problem of systematically underinformed consent would apply not only to core fiduciary rules, but to core structural rules, because just as core fiduciary rules govern traditional conflicts of interest, so core structural rules govern positional conflicts.

Permitting owner-managers of publicly held corporations to vary core fiduciary and structural rules if they do so before their corporations go public could also lead to inefficiency in the capital markets. The problem is a special case of the market for lemons.[267] When the quality of a good is hard to determine, and sellers are likely to know the quality much better than buyers, buyers will only be willing to pay a price, P_{a1}, that reflects average quality. Persons who hold high-quality goods will generally refuse to sell at P_{a1}, since P_{a1} is less than the value of their products. But withholding high-quality goods from the market will drive down average quality and will therefore drive down the price to P_{a2}. This will cause more sellers to withhold, which will drive prices even lower, which will cause even more sellers to withhold, and so on until only low-quality goods are sold. All goods are then properly priced, but total utility is less than it would have been if sellers had been able to reliably signal the quality of their products.

Similarly, if core fiduciary or structural rules were subject to variation by certificate provisions adopted before an initial public offering, some publicly held corporations would be governed by core fiduciary and structural rules that are unduly favorable to top managers and some would not. Persons who proposed to buy stock in a publicly held corporation therefore would either have to expend resources to determine whether the corporation was subject to all the core rules that constrain unfair self-dealing, shirking, and positional conflicts by top managers, or assume that all corporations had adopted variations of those core rules. Either course of action would render capital markets less efficient, because investors would either put less of their money

266. See supra text accompanying notes 41–43.

267. See Pindyck & Rubinfeld, Microeconomics 592–97 (1989); Akerlof, The Market for "Lemons": Quality Uncertainty and the Market Mechanism, 84 Q.J. Econ. 488 (1970); Coffee, supra note 149, at 947–49.

into corporate securities or demand a higher return from such securities, than would otherwise be the case.

Indeed, if the initial-public-offering argument were to be accepted as law, managerial rules might well become the norm. If buyers assumed that all corporations had adopted "average" variations from the core rules that constrain unfair self-dealing, shirking, and positional conflicts by top managers, it would frequently be irrational for an owner-manager who proposed an initial public offering to fail to adopt variations. Assume the following: An owner-manager proposes to make an initial public offering of a large part of his stock, but to retain his top management position. The owner-manager's stock can be sold for $X per share. This price will not depend on whether the corporation has varied the normal constraints on unfair self-dealing, shirking, and positional conflicts, because buyers, acting on the lemon theory, will assume that average variations have been adopted. Adoption of variations in core fiduciary and structural rules would be worth $Y to the owner-manager in his managerial capacity. Under these assumptions, the owner-manager, if he is economically rational, will adopt the variations, because if he does, his wealth will be $X per share plus $Y, while if he does not, his wealth will be only $X per share.[268]

Finally, permitting publicly held corporations to vary core fiduciary and structural rules if they did so before they went public might well lead to inefficiency in the national economy. The American economy is a corporate system, in the sense that control of the economic factors of production and distribution is vested largely in the hands of privately appointed corporate managers. This system is legitimated on three major bases. The first is a belief that the shareholders, as the owners of the corporation, have the ultimate right to control it. The second is a belief that corporate managers are accountable for their performance. The third is a belief that placing control of the factors of production and distribution in the hands of privately appointed corporate managers, who are accountable for their performance and who act in the interest and subject to the ultimate control of those who own the corporation, achieves a more efficient utilization of economic resources than that achievable under alternative economic systems. The initial-public-offering argument is not that owner-managers will always prefer rules that adequately address the problem of managerial inefficiency,

268. The "market for lemons" problem might be ameliorated if corporations could reliably signal whether they had adopted variations from core fiduciary and structural rules. It seems unlikely, however, that an adequate signalling regime could be developed. For one thing, the regime would have to be very complex unless signals could be used only by corporations that had not adopted even a single variation. More important, it would be difficult to make the signals reliably visible in the aftermarket. Because few investors in that market are likely to read the initial prospectus or any other corporate legal documents, probably the only way to ensure the visibility of the signals would be to attach them to the corporation's name—an unlikely prospect even if a simple signal were developed, and an almost impossible prospect if the signals were complex.

but only that they will often be indifferent between rules that do and do not address that problem. If, in pursuit of this argument, publicly held corporations could have governance structures determined by the decisions of owner-managers long gone from the scene who imposed rules that did not constrain positional conflicts, a significant portion of our national economy could eventually come to be vested in the hands of corporations in which inefficient managers were not effectively accountable and could not easily be removed. Such a regime could both jeopardize the efficiency of the economy and put the legitimacy of the corporate system into question.

Conclusion

The efficacy of enabling and suppletory rules depends on the institutions of private ordering. These institutions have substantial force. Often, however, they have substantial limits as well, sometimes subsumed under the heading of market failure. Mandatory rules also have substantial limits, sometimes subsumed under the heading of regulatory failure. Determining the balance between the costs and benefits of private ordering and mandatory rules in any given case is a matter for the exercise of prudential judgment, informed by economic analysis, quantitative data, the insights of psychology, and other empirical propositions.

In the case of closely held corporations, where constitutive rules are often determined by bargaining, prudential judgment suggests that the shareholders should be allowed to determine their own rules, subject to the limits on the bargain principle in areas where consent is likely to be systematically underinformed and even bargained-out rules would be subject to opportunistic exploitation.

In the case of publicly held corporations, where private ordering seldom takes the form of bargains, a different calculus prevails. Publicly held corporations have survived and prospered in this country, despite the potential divergencies of interests of top managers and shareholders, because these divergencies have been constrained by market forces, moral principles, and legal rules. Mandatory legal rules do double duty in this regard. They are important not only in themselves, but because they serve to emphasize and make particular the general moral principles of stewardship. It would be a descriptive mistake to think that either corporate law or the corporation is contractual in nature. It would be a normative mistake to think that under prevailing circumstances (including the current rules and practices concerning shareholder voting and the structure of share ownership), publicly held corporations would continue at their present level of success if the legal constraints on traditional and positional conflicts that have contributed to that success were removed.

It is sometimes said that arguments for mandatory rules reflect the Nirvana Fallacy, which consists of believing that just because markets are not perfect, mandatory rules would be better. It is of course true that just because markets are imperfect does not mean that mandatory rules would be better. However, the converse proposition is also true: just because mandatory rules are imperfect does not mean that markets would be better. Commentators who stress the Nirvana Fallacy are almost invariably themselves guilty of a mirror-image mistake which might be called the Heavenly Market Fallacy. This is the erroneous belief that because regulation is imperfect, any market, no matter how terribly flawed, is heavenly, and therefore to be preferred to a mandatory legal rule. The brute facts are that most markets are not perfect and most mandatory rules are perfect; that even imperfect markets and legal rules may have positive effects; and that the question in any given case is to determine which of these imperfect mechanisms is better, or, if possible, to determine how these two imperfect mechanisms can be shaped to reinforce each other. Taken separately, neither markets, morals, nor law are in themselves sufficient to curb traditional and positional conflicts. Taken together, however, markets, morals, and law have shown themselves capable of achieving that objective.

[5]

Bank Control, Owner Control, or Organizational Dynamics: Who Controls the Large Modern Corporation?[1]

Neil Fligstein
University of California, Berkeley

Peter Brantley
University of Arizona

There has been a long-standing debate over who controls the large American corporation. The results presented here indicate that existing power relations within the firm, the conception of control that dominates the firm's actions, and the actions of competitors account for the economic actions undertaken by large firms, while the differences in manager or owner or bank control and the presence of bank interlocks do not. A sociology of markets is therefore more likely to account for the courses of actions of large firms by considering these relations, rather than focusing on the construction of interests by bankers, owners, or board interlocks.

INTRODUCTION

The question of who controls the large modern corporation is one of the most enduring of modern social science. Sociologists who have studied the issue have gone in two directions: they have been interested in detecting a capitalist class and discovering the nature of its cohesion (Zeitlin 1974; Useem 1984) or they have tried to use organizational theory to account for the structure of the relations between large-scale business organizations (Burt 1983; Mintz and Schwartz 1985; White 1981; Fligstein 1990; Baker 1984, 1990). Economists have approached the question by being concerned about the possible negative effects of the separa-

[1] This article is based on a paper prepared for the 1989 meetings of the American Sociological Association in San Francisco. We would like to thank Wayne Baker, Paul DiMaggio, Mark Mizruchi, Charles Perrow, and the Yale Social Organization Colloquium for their useful comments and David Chang for his help in collecting the data. We would also like to thank the *AJS* reviewers for their comments. Correspondence may be addressed to Neil Fligstein, Department of Sociology, University of California, 410 Barrows Hall, Berkeley, California 94720.

0002-9602/93/9802-0002$01.50

tion of ownership from control in maximizing profits (Williamson 1964, 1985; Marris 1964; Jensen and Meckling 1976; Fama and Jensen 1983*a*, 1983*b*; Holmstrom 1988; MacNeil 1985). What is at stake in this debate is our understanding of how large corporations operate and the nature of the worlds that are constructed around them.

Much of the evidence for the effects of owner versus management versus bank control and the composition of boards of directors on the financial performance of corporations is mixed or negative (Burt 1983; Herman 1981; for evidence that supports some effect see Pennings [1980]; for a review, see Scherer [1980]). These analyses have a number of problems. They use different measures of control and generally use only one measure of performance (profits) with a cross-sectional research design. Even more important, there are almost no attempts to model the effects of the various forms of control on important strategic decisions, such as product mix, mergers, and which subunit dominates firms (for an exception, see Palmer et al. [1987]).

The major empirical contribution of this article is to expand these tests in a number of ways. First, we test a number of measures of forms of control simultaneously in order to assess if any has particular advantages. Second, in addition to a cross-sectional design, we utilize a panel design to assess whether control forms affect outcomes over time. Third, we model a larger number of important organizational outcomes, thereby extending attempts to test versions of control theory to other variables. Finally, we contrast control theory with a political/cultural view that focuses on interorganizational factors as predictors of outcomes.

Our major substantive conclusion is that differential ownership and the presence of bank interlocks are not important determinants of the strategic and financial outcomes of large firms. A far more plausible model is that the actors who control corporations use what occurs in their organizations and organizational fields as cues to guide their behavior. Family owners, bank owners, managers, and bank directors behave according to the dictates of the organizational field in which the firm is embedded and the internal dynamics of their organizations.

Economic sociologists have been debating the nature of the sociological embeddedness of markets for over 10 years. Much of the work has focused on network analyses (Burt 1983; Granovetter 1985; Baker 1984), and a fair amount of that work has concentrated on using boards of directors and bank interlocks as the basis of the network data (Burt 1983; Mintz and Schwartz 1985). Our results here suggest that American firms are neither constrained nor enabled by this form of network embeddedness. Therefore, the social structure of American firms may be studied more adequately by targeting the existing distribution of power in the firm, the behavior of competitors in the organizational field (White 1981), and the relations of firms to the government (Fligstein 1990). Further, it is the substantive content of those relations (i.e., the background of chief executive officers [CEOs] and the existing conceptions of action that dominate competitors) that are the strongest predictors of any given firm's actions—not the mere existence of social relations between them.

REVIEW OF THE LITERATURE

In this section, we consider the relevant literature from three perspectives, (1) management control versus family or individual control, (2) the potential for bank control, and (3) the findings of the recent organizational literature. Much of the sociological literature has tried to establish the existence of an economic elite or capitalist class and has therefore been uninterested in differences in the economic behavior of corporations (Zeitlin 1974; Allen 1974; Useem 1983). We do not address the concern of that literature here, nor do we focus on the translation of elite interests into political action (Mizruchi 1989). Our purpose is to examine the determinants of the strategic behavior of large firms and their relation to the control debate.

Corporate control will be defined as the power to determine the broad policies guiding the corporation, including decisions regarding capital structure (such as equity, debt, profits, and cash flow), geographic expansion, product diversification, corporate structure, and mergers (see Herman [1981] for a similar definition). Our question here is whether differences in ownership patterns and bank linkages actually affect the actions that firms undertake. The review suggests why groups might have varying interests that would cause them to make strategic decisions differently.

Management versus Owner Control

Economists have been interested in the control debate ever since Berle and Means (1932) asserted that there was an increasing separation between the ownership and control of the largest firms (theoretical arguments for the relation are presented in Marris [1964] and Williamson [1964]). Their concern is the degree to which managerial discretion causes firms to fail to pursue profit maximization. The theory suggests that managers try to protect their jobs by avoiding courses of action that could potentially threaten them, whereas owners would act in a more entrepreneurial fashion. The alternative tactics pursued by managers could include settling for lower but more stable profits by aiming for growth in sales and assets over profits, acting for the public interest instead of shareholder interests, increasing their salaries and perquisites, and implementing strategies that involve low risk-taking behavior. Managers would thus be more likely than owners to diversify product lines in their efforts to spread risk. They would also use mergers for corporate growth because buying an already existing company is less risky than entering a new business.

Several theoretical advances in economic theory have altered this debate. Williamson (1985, pp. 311–22), extending a transaction-cost perspective, has argued that the governance structure of joint-stock corporations has been set up to minimize managers' opportunism. This opportunism arises from information asymmetries between boards of directors and top managers. Boards of directors act to control this by writing contracts for top managers that bond their interests to those of the shareholders. The multidivisional form is also a control mechanism that makes managerial opportunism more difficult (Williamson 1985, pp. 320–22). While Williamson thinks these devices align interests, he also argues that managerial discretion and the possibility for opportunism always exist.

Agency theorists make a similar case.[2] The basis of their analysis is the principal-agent model that emphasizes that one common feature of economic life is that individuals (principals) engage others (agents) to perform some service. The problem is that the interests of the two will not always coincide, and so the principal must establish appropriate incentives and monitor the behavior of the agent in order to ensure that the agent acts in the principal's interests (Jensen and Meckling 1976, p. 308). In the context of the large corporation, agency theory seeks to explain why the joint-stock corporation exists, how the principal-agent relation between owners and managers is structured, and how it can go astray.

Agency theorists consider the firm to be a fictitious entity. They see the firm as a governance structure made up of contracts and claims on the assets and cash flows of the organization (Jensen and Meckling 1976). The form of that governance structure will reflect the organization's special agency problems and will be selected as an efficient solution to them. Fama and Jensen (1983*b*) argue that the joint-stock corporation comes into existence in situations where technology requires a large amount of capital, there is a demand for specialized agents to utilize economies of scale, and a large pool of capital is needed to bond contracts and specific assets of the organization. As they put it, "The benefits of unrestricted common stock residual claims in activities where optimal

[2] It should be noted that there are a number of versions of agency theory (i.e., Ross 1978; MacNeil 1985; Holmstrom 1988). Here, we develop only enough of the general points so as to acquaint the reader with the perspective.

organizations are large and complex offset the agency costs resulting from separation of decision functions and residual risk-bearing" (Fama and Jensen 1983*b*, p. 346).

The principal-agent relation between managers and owners is mediated through boards of directors and financial markets. Boards function to monitor managers' decisions and are backed up by contracts that reward managers for performance. Financial markets monitor management teams by providing owners with current information about the firm's prospects (i.e., the price of the stock) and the ability to sell the stock at low cost. The market for corporate control provides the final backup to ensure that managers act in the interests of principals. If the fortune of the firm declines substantially, competing groups of managers can bid to take control (Fama and Jensen 1983*a*; Jensen and Ruback 1984).

The principal-agent relation between boards of directors and managers can go awry when boards lack the will or information to enforce discipline on managers. This will occur most frequently when stock ownership is diffused or institutional investors dominate (Jensen 1989; for an analysis of other dependent variables that use a similar argument, see Graves [1988] and Fombrun and Stanley [1990]). An oft-used measure of managerial discretion is free cash flow, which indicates whether managers are holding capital instead of distributing it to shareholders. Other firm strategies that reflect managerial control include diversification and growth in sales and assets with little change in profits. Diversification can represent a tactic to hold onto free cash flow and enter less profitable businesses (for a dissenting view, see Amit and Wernerfelt [1990]). Managerial salaries tend to be tied to firm growth and examining the determinants of variables like the ratio of profits to sales and assets would suggest whether or not managers were sacrificing profits for growth.

Bank Control

The issue of financial control over the largest firms has lurked in the social science literature since the turn of the century. The role of financiers in the merger movement of 1895–1905 is well known (Lamoreaux 1985; Mizruchi 1982). The literature on bank control has recently focused on the extent of that control and its effects on the behavior of large firms. Banks, insurance companies, mutual funds, and pension funds have all increased their holdings in large industrial firms (Herman 1981). The interesting question is whether they extended their involvement to active control over strategic decisions and if so, in what direction? Those who argue for bank control can be divided into three camps, in which they espouse bank control either through ownership, through bank hegemony achieved by their key position in the financial system, or through the potential for bank influence because of financial dependence.

The strongest advocate of direct bank control is Kotz (1978). He argues that finance-controlled firms are more likely to take on external debt than nonfinance-controlled firms and thus their debt/equity ratio should be higher. This propensity to assume debt also makes them more likely to engage in mergers than nonfinance-controlled firms. The presence of finance control throughout an entire industry which can be indexed by the degree of bank interlocks should lower competition and raise profits. Hence, finance control would lead to higher profitability for firms.

Mintz and Schwartz (1985) argue that banks exert hegemony in the industrial system by virtue of their key control of the capital markets. This structural position has two effects. First, bankers intervene in corporations under conditions of crisis and replace managements who are not providing profitable returns. Second, bankers are at the center of corporate interlocks, and can use this influence to help firms collude or cooperate.

Unfortunately, it is usually difficult to ascertain the direction of influence between bankers and internal corporate representatives. Indeed, there is evidence that bankers are invited onto the board to co-opt them into making loans to the firm (Burt 1983; for a debate see the exchange by Herman [1979, 1980] and Kotz [1980]). Bankers may also be brought onto boards of directors when firms are in financial trouble (Mizruchi and Stearns 1988). The evidence above suggests that bankers, themselves, are being used as much as they are influencing the course of the organization.

These problems have led to a third position that posits a more complex relation between banks and firms. Because bankers often play many roles, one would expect that their influence would depend on the situation and their relative power. Bankers brought onto boards because of the financial dependence of a firm would be the most likely to have influence over the firm's financial structure and choice of debt instruments (Hirsch 1989). But bankers could be brought on the board for numerous reasons, including co-optation, prestige, or social and political connections (Herman 1981). This explains why, historically, banks have been at the center of firm interlocks, but different banks have occupied these positions over time (Mizruchi 1982), and why board of director interlocks are notoriously unstable and renewed less than 15% of the time (Palmer 1983).

Organizational Dynamics and Management Control

The organizational literature has increasingly focused on organizational fields (DiMaggio 1985). It is believed that organizations' actions are shaped by the links between any given organization and its surrounding organizations. Two literatures are relevant: the external control of organizations approach (Pfeffer and Salancik 1978; Burt 1983) and what can be called a political/cultural approach (Fligstein 1985, 1987, 1990). Each has a different perspective on important mechanisms governing organizational embeddedness.

Organizations exist in organizational fields, within which they are dependent on other organizations for inputs and the consumption of outputs. The view that organizations are externally controlled suggests that actors who can make claims on delivering inputs or outputs are likely to have a disproportionate say in the internal allocation of resources (Pfeffer and Salancik 1978). Burt (1983) has used this perspective to argue that boards of directors are used by firms as mechanisms to co-opt organizations in the environment. His analysis shows that outside directors are often representatives of firms who are important customers or suppliers. The presence of bankers on boards of directors can be explained by the need to generate capital. Unfortunately, Burt was unable to show that these ties actually produce additional profits for the firm, which would seem to undermine the claim that this co-optation has positive effects.

The political/cultural approach expands on the insights suggested by institutional theory (Meyer and Rowan 1978; DiMaggio and Powell 1983) and the work of White (1981) on the structuring of markets by focusing on how the intraorganizational power struggle is structured in large organizations and how it is affected by and affects organizational fields (Perrow 1970; Fligstein 1987, 1990). This sociological view offers explicit hypotheses about the links between firms, their organizational fields, and the structuring of their behavior.

The issue for any given organization is what courses of action to pursue. Since a priori the actual effect of any given strategy may be difficult to assess, there arises the possibility that there will be conflict over the goals of the organization. There are two bases for control: ownership and authority. To the degree that owners control large-scale organizations, they will be able to direct the course of those organizations; but even ownership groups will have to formulate a view of the world in order to act.

The basic problem for organizational actors is to create a stable world so the organization will continue to exist. This necessitates the construction of an organizational field where actors take each other's actions into account in the framing of their own actions. The two problems involved in creating a stable organizational field are the necessity for understandings that are general and enforceable and the problem of legitimation of those understandings by the government. Fligstein (1990, chap. 1) calls such a set of understandings a conception of control.

One interesting question is: Where do conceptions of control come from? Since conceptions of control require a perspective on the world, these perspectives can have two sources: they may be borrowed from other organizations or organizational fields, or they can be embedded in how the different subunits of an organization conceptualize its problems and solutions. Subunit background provides actors with a way of seeing the world. A conception of control implies a filter that actors use in viewing their internal and external problems and in defining their actions to solve those problems. Effective conceptions of control will diffuse and eventually dominate and define organizational behavior in organizational fields. In this way they operate both as a cultural template for structuring new actions (i.e., what behaviors make sense) and a set of structures limiting the possibilities for action (i.e., what others are doing, thereby structuring what reactions are possible).

Intraorganizational groups gain and maintain power as a function of their ability to promote organizational survival and create stable organizational fields. From this perspective, organizational fields are more than socially constructed meanings, they are systems of power. The largest organizations generally control the fields and dictate their rules. Smaller organizations benefit from this system as long as they fall in line with the organizations setting the rules. All participants in the field come to see the world similarly and react to each other's moves from this perspective. This theoretical approach can be termed political/cultural because it focuses on the intra- and interorganizational power struggles and suggests that the goal of such struggles is to create shared meanings, that is, local cultures that operate to produce stable interactions. The approach is also political because the state can enter into and regulate actions in any given organizational field.

Today, most large American corporations are dominated by the finance conception of control that views the firm as a bundle of assets that are deployed in order to maximize short-term earnings (Fligstein 1990, chap. 6). The finance conception of control originated with executives trained in finance methods who had been primarily financial officers in their companies. Their balance-sheet approach implies that the firm is no longer in the business of producing commodities, but instead operates as a set of assets, whereby divisions of the firm that do not perform up to expectations are sold off and new ones purchased. A central tactic is the use of mergers (and divestitures), often for diversification, to achieve growth.

The finance conception of control displaced the sales and marketing conception during the 1960s and early 1970s. Sales and marketing executives favor policies that boost sales by increasing marketing, differentiating products, and diversifying product lines. The finance conception emerged in the postwar era as a function of the increasingly diversified nature of the firm and the aggressive antitrust policies of the Truman and Eisenhower administrations (Fligstein 1990, chap. 6). Subsequently, many of the largest firms have become dominated by finance personnel espousing a finance conception of control (Fligstein 1987). Their claim to expertise is based on their ability to evaluate the profitability of different product lines and hence manage the large firm as an investment portfolio. Their claim to power is derived from the relative success of such a point of view in generating growth in the firm. One of the key hypotheses that this implies is that those acting with a finance conception are able to produce growth in sales, assets, or profits, mainly through mergers and diversification.

During the merger movement of the 1960s, two of every five firms that had assets of more than $10 million were merger targets (Fligstein 1990, chap. 7). If the field of a firm was invaded by firms using the finance conception of control, then that firm had to either adopt a similar view or risk becoming a target for merger. In this way, the organizational fields of many of the largest corporations were reorganized by the finance conception of the corporation.

HYPOTHESES

The critical issue in these literatures is how the agents of control affect the actions of the largest corporations. The political/cultural approach stresses the current structure of the situation, both internal and external to the organization, as the wellspring of action. The owner/management/bank debate suggests that the goals of specific interest groups, as owners and creditors, will differ and cause the organization to act differently, net of its internal configuration and its links to its field.

The dependent variables studied here are of two types: financial and strategic. Financial outcomes are to some extent strategic choices. If firms have cash surpluses, then they must decide how much to retain or disburse to shareholders. Firms might retain cash flow because they want to invest in new projects, or use it as a cushion against unforeseen events, or managers might hold excessive cash in reserve for opportunistic reasons. Three other types of strategic decisions are modeled: whether firms undertake mergers, whether firms have diversified their products, and who gets to be the corporate CEO. These actions reflect strategic policies of the organization. The use of mergers is an important decision regarding the allocation of capital. The decision to diversify the product mix reflects the actual definition of the organization in terms of its goals. The background of the incumbent CEO is an indication of which organizational subunit is responsible for determining firm strategy (Pfeffer 1981).

The management-control literature, as opposed to the owner-control literature, predicts that manager-controlled firms are more likely to increase equity over debt, decrease the ratios of returns to assets and sales, have relatively low returns on equity, relatively high price/earnings ratios (because of low payouts), and relatively high levels of free cash flow. The return on assets and return on sales variables reflect how much managers are trading off earnings for assets or sales. Manager-controlled firms also favor mergers and diversification. All of these actions reflect management's propensity to retain or reinvest earnings rather than disburse them to shareholders.

There are a number of indicators of management control, including a low percentage of stock held by a single family, individual, or bank, or a high percentage of stock held by institutional investors, a gauge of shareholder passivity (Jensen 1989). Product diversification is another indicator of management control as managers tend to diversify rather than disburse earnings. From the transaction-costs perspective, the presence of a multidivisional form suggests that managers are more constrained in their actions.

Bank control is indexed by the percentage of voting shares held by the largest bank and the number of bank interlocks on the board of directors. The bank-control literature predicts that firms controlled by banks are more likely to pursue merger strategies in order to increase the banks' power. They should also be more likely to have higher returns on equity and higher debt/equity ratios. The predictions of the financial hegemony perspective are indeterminate, although interlocks could be associated with higher returns on equity and higher debt/equity ratios. The financial dependence perspective suggests that the presence of bank control would make firms more likely to engage in mergers and to have high debt/equity ratios. Network views that see boards of directors as co-optive devices to lessen resource dependence would predict that bankers on the board and bank interlocks should enhance financial performance.

The political/cultural perspective stresses three types of factors that govern the financial and strategic choices of firms: the behavior of competitors who form an organizational field, defined here in terms of the other large firms that occupy the same industry (specified at the two-digit Standard Industrial Classification [SIC] level), the already existing strategies and structures in place, and which subunit controls the organization. The major hypotheses of the political/cultural perspective focus on how much an organization and its organizational field are dominated by the finance conception of control. If other firms in the same field are diversifying or merging, indicating the dominance of the finance conception of control, a firm is more likely to engage in those activities also.

The existing strategy of the firm is a powerful determinant of many outcomes, including growth and mergers, and reflects entrenched systems of power. Finance-controlled firms will be diversified and should be more likely to engage in mergers and show higher growth rates and returns than nondiversified firms. This prediction runs counter to that of agency theory, which views diversification as lowering returns on assets and sales. The multidivisional form will be the favorite structural vehicle for finance-oriented diversification and mergers, and its presence should positively affect growth in sales, assets, and profits.

The subunit that controls the CEO of the firm also operates as an indicator of the conception of control that dominates the firm (Fligstein 1987). Sales and marketing and finance CEOs will be more likely to lead firms that are diversified than will manufacturing CEOs; they will also be more likely to engage in mergers. It is probable that sales and marketing CEOs will lead firms with lower returns on assets and sales, reflecting their preference for sales growth over asset and profit growth. They will also be less likely to engage in product-unrelated diversification and more likely to engage in product-related diversification. Finance CEOs are expected to be adept at producing profits for all measures, including returns on assets, sales, and equity.

The growth of large firms will be determined, to some degree, by the rise or fall of the firm's specific industry. If the industry is expanding, then we expect sales, assets, and profits of a given firm to increase. This is not, of course, an effect of the social organization of a given field, but a purely economic variable.

It should be noted that a number of our variables index items for multiple theories but that the theories predict different effects (e.g., the measures of diversification). Additionally, agency theory and transaction-cost theory are probably impossible to falsify. If it turns out that management-controlled firms do not use managerial discretion to lower profits, that implies that the mechanisms to control managerial opportunism work. On the other hand, if evidence exists that managers do not favor profit maximization, then the mechanisms have failed. Therefore, the theory cannot be proved incorrect and can only be used to suggest if opportunism exists.

DATA AND METHODS

The selection of a data set and a time frame is hampered by a number of problems, largely stemming from the character of the existing measures of control. First, many of the available data that attempt to measure control were collected at different time points ranging from the mid-1960s to the early 1970s. Second, almost all of the control measures have focused on the largest industrial corporations. This is understandable, given their important role in the U.S. economy. However it means that there are no data on control forms for a large number of firms in any given industry.

Given these limitations, we focus here on the 100 largest industrial corporations in the United States in 1969 and the firms that entered the list of the 100 largest industrial corporations between 1969 and 1979. These data were obtained from *Fortune* magazine (1970, 1980). This design was chosen to create a panel study of large firms (in essence, the *population* of the largest). The panel design allows us to test how the initial conditions that include the control types and the organizational factors affect the behavior of the firm over a subsequent period of time. The decade-long time frame allows for the slow accumulation of strategic changes and effects of control in the largest corporations. By modeling such change over long periods, we are more likely to observe such effects. For the financial measures, 10 years stabilizes the effects of year-to-year fluctuations. We chose 1969 as the initial year because many of the control and organizational variables had available measures for this year. One problem created by this choice is that the financial data refer to 1969 and 1970, years when the economy and stock market were depressed.

The measures of forms of control are not straightforward to operationalize. Indeed, proponents have not been able to agree on how to measure them, and there is substantial disagreement on which firms fall into bank, owner, or management control. Our approach is to operationalize measures of control that might be general to all theories.[3] We measured the percentage of stock held by the largest family or individual (Herman 1981), the largest percentage of stock with voting rights held by a bank (U.S. House of Representatives 1971; U.S. Senate 1973), and the percentage of the stock held by institutional investors in 1969 (U.S. House of Representatives 1971). The number of bank interlocks through boards of directors (U.S. House of Representatives 1969) was operationalized as well. There were substantial missing data for the bank data (25%) and the interlock data (37%).

In order to maximize the number of cases in the analysis, we created two dummy variables, coding them "0" if data were missing for the case and "1" if data were available. The observations with missing data for the bank and interlock variables were then recoded "0." If there is some systematic bias in how the data on control are related to the outcomes,

[3] The various measures of control proposed by Herman (1981), Larner (1971), Burch (1972), and Kotz (1978) were operationalized as dummy variables in unreported analyses. These analyses provide results that are very similar to the results presented here: i.e., a lack of effect for the control measures. Since each author bases these measures on very different criteria, we thought that using the actual percentages of the stock controlled by various groups was a more effective measure of the general control concept.

the dummy variables will be statistically significant. We estimated 32 separate coefficients for these dummy variables and only two are statistically significant. By chance, one would expect one or two of the coefficients to have statistical significance related to the outcomes and, therefore, we conclude that selectivity of missing data on these two variables is not a serious problem.

The measures of forms of control suffer from two kinds of problems. First, they may or may not tap into control. Since these are our only measures of stock-ownership patterns, we must accept them as face valid. Second, we only measure control at one point in time. Because we use the control variable to predict change over a substantial period (10 years), control may have shifted over the period. We know little about the stability of the control variables because they have not been systematically measured over time. In order to maximize the possibility of discovering control effects, we have run the models for each of the dependent variables at the first time point (i.e., the cross section) as well as looked for effects of control over time. It should be noted that most of the organizational variables have also been measured only at the first time point, and they may have similar problems. One advantage in this is that there is no confusion of the causal order of important relationships. Since the exogenous variables are measured at the first time point, they are clearly causes of outcomes during the decade.

We used a large number of dependent variables in this analysis. First, we analyzed free cash flow, market value, price/earnings ratio, return on assets, after-tax profit margin (return on sales), return on equity, and the debt/equity ratio in 1970 (Compustat 1989).[4] These variables were taken from corporate reports and 10-K forms and coded by Compustat. Free cash flow could not be adequately constructed by its standard definition for the first time period (1970) because of the unavailability of requisite data. Consequently, we approximated it by subtracting current liabilities from current assets for both time periods. The calculations for all variables appear in the Appendix. We also analyzed the 1980 levels of these variables plus the 1980 value of assets and sales. Dollar amounts were adjusted to 1967 levels. In the panel analysis we included the level of each of the dependent variables at the first point in time as a regressor.[5]

[4] The years 1970 and 1980 were chosen because many firms begin and end their fiscal years at different times. Therefore, the data may include part of the years 1969 and 1979 as well as those of 1970 and 1980. If 1969 had been selected as the year to predict results, then some of the data would refer to 1968, and this might have created problems of time ordering.

[5] Financial reporting can be uneven. Different firms can calculate these measures in different ways and so we must be cautious in accepting the definitions of the accounting terms across all organizations and time. Of course, we hope that such variations are random.

Corporate strategy was coded into three categories: product dominant, product related, and product unrelated. We used Rumelt (1974) and *Moody's Manuals* (1970, 1980) to code these categories. Product dominant implies that firms produce more than 70% of their revenues in a single product line. Product related implies that firms produce multiple products that were related or market extensions (e.g., chemical companies that produced paint and explosives), with no single line accounting for more than 70% of output. Product-unrelated strategies imply that firms depend on unrelated businesses for a substantial portion of their revenue (no product could account for more than 70% of revenue). Two dummy variables were coded indicating whether a firm had a product-related strategy (coded "1" on one of the dummy variables) or a product-unrelated strategy (coded "1" on the other dummy variable). They refer to 1969.

Corporate structure refers to the existence of a multidivisional form. A dummy variable was coded "1" if a firm had a multidivisional form as its structure in 1969. These data were coded from Rumelt (1974) and *Moody's Manuals* (1970).

Mergers were coded using the Federal Trade Commission's *Report on Mergers and Acquisitions* (1981). The total number of mergers from 1969 to 1979 was summed for each firm. On examination of the variable, we found that a distinction between firms who engaged in mergers and those who did not best captured the skewed distribution. Therefore, this variable is coded "0" if firms did not engage in mergers and "1" if they did. The variable indicating firms' previous merger behavior is the total number of mergers engaged in during 1959–69. This variable did not require dichotomization.

The subunit background of the corporate chief executive officer was coded for 1969 and 1979. Once the name of the CEO was collected from *Moody's Manuals*, we pursued it in *Who's Who in America, Who's Who in Finance and Industry,* and other sources. From the description of each CEO's career, a decision was made, on the basis of previous job titles, as to how the person came up through the firm. If the person switched firms, the subunit background was decided on the basis of job titles across the career. The following categories were coded: manufacturing, sales and marketing, finance, entrepreneur, lawyer, general management, other, and "unable to ascertain." The general management category reflects whether a person held different titles in different parts of the firm (e.g., plant manager and vice-president in charge of finance). In the data analysis presented here, we have collapsed the measure into three dummy variables indicating whether the CEO was a manufacturing person, a finance person, or a sales and marketing person. The omitted category is all others.

The organizational field variables all refer to the year 1969 and were based on the characteristics of the major industry of the firm (two-digit SIC). The change in the growth in assets from 1969 to 1979 in the industry was used as a measure of industry growth, with the change in assets for each firm in the analysis subtracted from the industry's change in order to remove any spurious relation between the measures. This variable serves as a rough measure of increase in demand. The percentages of other large firms who had product-related and product-unrelated strategies in the industry were coded to predict whether a given firm also had a product-related or unrelated strategy. Similarly the percentages of the other large firms in the industry whose CEOs had been in finance, sales and marketing, and manufacturing in 1969 was used to predict the CEO in 1979.

These measures have a number of potential problems. They assume that the relevant organizational field is composed of direct competitors, which are also large firms. If these measures do predict outcomes, then we can assert they have predictive validity. It could be argued that these measures tap into what is economically efficient for firms of a given type and that any association is merely due to the correlation between what is efficient and what others are doing. This criticism is less easy to answer and implies that there is a need for caution in accepting the organizational field interpretation of these variables.

We used two techniques to analyze the data: a least squares regression was used to analyze the level and change in the financial measures; logit analysis was used to determine whether or not a firm engaged in a merger, to analyze whether a firm had a product-dominant, product-related, or product-unrelated strategy (product dominant was the left-out category), and to predict the background of the CEO in 1979 ("other" was the left-out category). This procedure is appropriate because these are qualitative dependent variables. All calculations were performed using SAS.

RESULTS

We will discuss the hypotheses by first examining the effects of the control, industry, and organizational variables on the financial performance measures in 1970. Then we will discuss the results for the decade 1970–80. Finally, we will consider the determinants of the organizational variables. The means and standard deviations for the variables used in the analyses are presented in table 1.

Table 2 contains the results for the regression analyses of the various measures of financial performance in 1970. Our models do not explain a lot of the variation in financial performance in 1970, and the measures

TABLE 1

MEANS AND STANDARD DEVIATIONS FOR VARIABLES USED IN THE ANALYSIS (N = 120)

Variable Label	Description	Mean	SD
MERGER1	Merger activity, 1959–69	1.69	2.17
MERGER2	Merger activity, 1969–79	.56	.76
INDGROW	Growth of industry	4.94	4.98
RELN	Product related strategy, 1969	.55	.49
UNRELN	Product unrelated strategy, 1969	.20	.40
MDF1	Multidivisional form, 1969	.73	.44
SALEPR	Sales president, 1969	.19	.39
MANPRES	Manufacturing president, 1969	.24	.42
FINPR	Finance president, 1969	.22	.41
PERREL	% of firms with related strategy	47.43	26.58
PERUNREL	% of firms with unrelated strategy	18.16	16.12
SINDPER	% of firms with sales president	17.08	8.34
MINDPER	% of firms with manufacturing president	19.26	16.90
FINDPER	% of firms with finance president	25.13	20.51
FCF80	Free cash flow, 1980	437.79	568.19
MV80	Market value, 1980	.21	.31
PE80	Price/earnings ratio, 1980	3.76	2.94
ROA80	After tax return on gross assets, 1980	2.02	1.79
PM80	After tax profit margin, 1980	2.12	1.93
ROE80	After-tax return on common equity, 1980	12.75	70.95
DE80	Debt/equity ratio, 1980	.18	1.18
ASSETS80	Assets, 1980	5,137.83	7,961.98
SALES80	Sales, 1980	4,926.26	6,699.99
FCF70	Free cash flow, 1970	403.85	454.63
MV70	Market value, 1970	2,615.13	4,701.90
PE70	Price/earnings ratio, 1970	13.57	24.60
ROA70	After tax return on gross assets, 1970	3.52	2.63
PM70	After tax profit margin, 1970	4.97	3.34
ROE70	After tax return on common equity, 1970	8.35	7.24
DE70	Debt/equity ratio, 1970	.54	.80
ASSETS70	Assets, 1970	3,987.13	6,301.19
SALES70	Sales, 1970	2,573.08	2,928.85
ILOCK	Bank interlocks, 1969	2.71	2.81
BANK	Largest bank shareholder, 1969	3.05	3.78
FAMILY	Largest family shareholder, 1970	4.95	10.46
ILOCK-D	Missing data-interlocks	.25	.43
BANK-D	Missing data-bank shareholder	.36	.48
INSTIPER	% shares held by institutions	.11	.06

NOTE.—Data sources and coding are discussed in the text.

TABLE 2

REGRESSION ANALYSIS OF THE DETERMINANTS OF VARIOUS MEASURES OF FINANCIAL PERFORMANCE, 1970 (N = 109)

INDEPENDENT VARIABLES	DEPENDENT VARIABLES													
	FCF70		MV70		PE70		ROA70		PM70		ROE70		DE70	
	b	SE(*b*)	*b*	SE(*b*)	*b*	SE(*b*)	*b*	SE(*b*)	*b*	SE(*b*)	*b*	SE(*b*)	*b*	SE(*b*)
MERGER1	24.35	23.12	6.24	233.21	−.01	1.27	.02	.11	.12	.15	.38	.36	.01	.04
MDF1	101.85	110.49	1,602.48	1,114.43	−.03	6.07	−.14	.57	.38	.74	−1.49	1.74	.13	.19
RELN	−34.93	115.22	−681.45	1,162.16	16.14**	6.33	.92	.59	1.21	.77	3.68*	1.82	−.06	.20
UNRELN	−101.62	161.86	−2,673.03	1,632.52	17.11*	8.89	−.54	.83	−1.83*	1.08	−1.08	2.56	.70**	.29
MANPRES	−72.73	124.40	933.30	1,254.75	2.50	6.83	−.35	.64	1.79*	.83	−.58	1.97	−.10	.22
SALEPR	167.88	130.58	2,830.78*	1,317.01	−.36	7.17	.52	.67	.28	.87	1.28	2.06	.10	.23
FINPR	−16.68	128.00	200.75*	91.03	−9.06	7.03	.91*	.36	.49*	.25	−1.24	2.02	−.12	.23
INSTIPER	−756.54	872.64	−22,549.00**	8,801.20	−23.53	47.95	−10.45*	4.52	−10.15*	5.85	−6.18*	3.81	−.54	1.57
ILOCK	31.99	20.30	61.79	204.78	−2.43*	1.11	−.27*	.10	−.40**	.13	−.53*	.32	−.00	.03
BANK	−20.56	15.13	−205.41	152.66	−.41	.83	.05	.07	.04	.10	.25	.23	−.04	.02
FAMILY	8.62	5.88	−20.98	59.31	−.06	.32	.01	.03	−.00	.03	.12	.09	.00	.01
ILOCK-D	−173.02	139.13	−1,666.51	1,403.30	−13.87	7.64	−.65	.72	−1.33	.93	−.09	2.20	.03	.25
BANK-D	−316.70*	122.97	−3,493.67**	1,240.27	1.66	6.75	−.30	.63	−.57	.82	.17	1.94	−.29	.22
INTERCEPT	499.77*	217.33	6,059.23**	2,191.98	15.79	11.94	4.86**	1.12	5.96**	1.45	7.71*	3.44	.66*	.39
R^2	.08		.14		.16		.05		.16		.05		.07	

NOTE.—See table 1 for description of variables.
* $P > .05$.
** $P > .01$.

of forms of control fare poorly. It is useful to consider the specific hypotheses more closely. There is no evidence that bank or family shareholding affects any of the measures of financial performance. The lack of these effects suggests that, in situations where bank or family shareholding is not large, managers do not generate excesses of free cash flow, reduce the firm's market value, increase equity over debt, or favor assets and sales to profits. Further, bank ownership did not make firms more profitable (by any measure of profits) nor did it make firms more likely to favor debt over equity. Highly interlocked firms were actually less profitable in terms of returns on assets, sales, and equity, contradicting the bank-control hypothesis that firms with interlocks would be more profitable. One plausible explanation for this result is that firms in troublesome environments (those with low profitability) reduce their dependence by interlocking (Burt 1983). That there is also no effect of the multidivisional form on the financial performance of firms undermines transaction-costs arguments. This result could be because the multidivisional form has already spread to those firms who would benefit from it and, hence, it has little effect. Armour and Teece (1978) demonstrate that early movers to the multidivisional form benefit, relative to late adopters, but that, once diffused, the form has no impact on profits. Agency or transaction-cost theorists could conclude that managers were sufficiently constrained during 1970 so as not to act against the interests of shareholders. For bank- or family-control theorists, there is no evidence to support the view that either group affected the financial performance of firms.

What effects did predict financial performance? Generally, the more shares held by institutional investors, the more poorly the firm performed in terms of returns on assets, sales, equity, and market value. We can interpret this result in two ways. First, this is evidence that there was a problem of separation of ownership from control. Alternatively, 1970 was a bad year for the stock market, and many stocks lost a lot of value. It is possible that firms held by institutional investors fared more poorly during the downturn because these investors had overbought certain stocks during the boom from 1967 to 1969. If these results hold up in the panel analysis, then this will be evidence for the thesis that managers control firms with a large percentage of stock held by institutional investors and act to increase variables other than profits.

Several of the political/cultural variables also predicted financial performance. There is evidence that diversified firms had a higher return on equity and a higher price/earnings ratio. This suggests that the agency-theory view that diversification reflects management control and an unwise use of a firm's resources is flawed. Instead, diversification proved profitable. Firms with unrelated-product mixes also held higher debt, reflecting the acquisitive conglomerates' strategy of using debt to diversify. This also undermines the view that management-controlled firms are likely to favor the issuance of equity over debt.

Finally, there is evidence that the background of the CEO affected financial performance. Finance CEOs were able to improve firms' balance sheets; their firms had higher returns on assets and sales and higher market value than firms headed by other types of CEOs. Sales and marketing CEOs also were able to increase the market value of their firms. We interpret these effects as the operation of the special expertise of these types of CEOs who aimed at improving their firms' performance on exactly these measures. It also could be that finance CEOs have greater legitimacy in the institutional environment.

The evidence for the effects of forms of control on changes in financial performance are in table 3. The panel results parallel the cross-sectional results. Because the previous level of performance is included as a regressor in these equations, the rest of the parameters can be interpreted as predictors of change in the dependent variables (Kessler and Greenberg 1981, chap. 2). Firms that were linked by bank interlocks generally underperformed other firms, showing lower returns on assets, sales, and equity and a lower price/earnings ratio. Thus, being networked into the financial system did not prove to be a benefit. Further, firms that were interlocked had lower debt/equity ratios, suggesting that these firms favored equity over debt. None of these predictions supports a view that, during the decade, bank control directed profits toward banks. There was no direct effect of banks being significant shareholders on the financial performance of firms. Firms that had large numbers of bank shareholders did no better or worse than anyone else.

There are several effects of family holdings on performance. Family-controlled firms had lower returns on assets and sales and a lower price/earnings ratio. They also experienced less growth in sales over the decade. The higher the share of family holdings, the less well firms performed. This contradicts all of the theories of managerial control and suggests that during the turbulent economic times of the 1970s family control was not a good way to increase shareholder value.

The percentage of shares held by the institutional investors did not affect the change in the financial performance of firms, indicating that the results for 1970 were probably an artifact of the poor performance of firms whose stock was disproportionately held by institutional investors during the 1970s and not an effect of managerial control.

The most systematic predictor of change in financial outcomes during the 1970s was the asset growth of the industry. This variable positively affects growth in return on assets, growth in assets, sales, and market

TABLE 3

REGRESSION ANALYSIS OF THE DETERMINANTS OF VARIOUS MEASURES OF FINANCIAL PERFORMANCE, 1970–1980 (N = 106)

Independent Variable	Dependent Variable																	
	FCF		MV		PE		DE		ASSETS		SALES		ROA		PM		ROE	
	b	SE(*b*)	*b*	SE(*b*)	*b*	SE(*b*)	*b*	SE(*b*)	*b*	SE(*b*)	*b*	SE(*b*)	*b*	SE(*b*)	*b*	SE(*b*)	*b*	SE(*b*)
LAG[a]	.97**	.10	.52**	.03	−.00	.01	.42**	.15	1.20**	.04	1.86**	.13	.30**	.06	.31**	.05	.00	1.11
MERGER1	−6.62	22.30	−129.11	83.35	−.01	.14	.01	.06	−85.40	102.40	−190.02	165.01	.00	.07	.03	.07	−1.68	4.06
MDF1	−22.29	107.04	63.74	402.23	−.31	.69	−.33	.30	−68.51	487.28	29.56	86.99	−.15	.34	−.22	.36	26.48	19.36
INDGROW	15.07	9.64	252.34**	35.53	−.03	.06	.00	.02	171.12**	44.87	531.80**	72.02	.07**	.03	−.01	.03	−.08	1.72
RELN	18.91	106.78	−175.68	398.92	−.19	.71	.49*	.20	290.15*	144.28	−112.46	202.63	.17	.34	.40	.36	35.78*	19.79
UNRELN	4.91	156.10	109.38	586.58	−.27	1.03	.68*	.35	−71.23	112.41	−54.56	155.22	.68	.50	.70	.53	−38.80	28.36
MANPRES	188.54	121.95	10.44	456.85	.50	.79	.25	.34	−48.53	62.23	94.04	92.90	−.03	.39	−.13	.42	−7.39	22.12
SALEPR	34.83	126.35	−111.05	478.13	−1.15	.80	.35	.35	569.53*	274.53	502.82*	234.28	−.39	.39	−.62	.42	−8.47	22.54
FINPR	23.54	118.99	129.34**	44.38	.17	.78	−.49	.34	413.74**	172.63	476.66**	187.26	.72*	.38	.72*	.40	42.27*	21.63
INSTIPER	276.32	816.04	63.18	3,145.90	3.67	5.31	1.32	2.32	−5,103.50	3,842.90	1,074.97	2,331.62	1.60	2.70	1.68	2.79	22.52	148.04
ILOCK	−33.32	19.72	−3.82	73.25	−.26*	.13	−.15**	.05	−71.43	88.84	−266.92	147.62	−.23*	.06	−.19*	.06	−10.80*	3.63
BANK	−20.11	14.27	−2.88	53.40	−.05	.09	.01	.04	−53.43	65.10	−61.61	106.28	−.00	.04	.01	.04	−.24	2.58
FAMILY	−9.28	5.52	−31.62	20.36	−.06*	.03	−.00	.01	−7.22	25.35	−73.98*	41.51	−.05*	.01	−.04*	.01	.38	.99
ILOCK-D	−65.88	132.98	−397.35	494.75	.06	.86	−.19	.37	−431.11	605.71	−296.48	278.34	−.60	.42	−.13	.45	35.85	23.77
BANK-D	−97.49	121.05	−115.83	454.77	.36	.75	.18	.33	−372.44	546.71	−519.57	620.54	.16	.37	.23	.39	2.44	21.14
INTERCEPT	164.09	210.44	115.60	798.03	4.85**	1.35	−.08	.60	634.81	558.58	−566.42	1,602.26	1.56*	.72	1.23	.75	−21.63	38.38
R^2	.52		.78		.03		.14		.94		.80		.41		.43		.15	

[a] Each dependent variable was lagged to its 1970 value.
* $P > .05$.
** $P > .01$.

value of the firm. From an investor's point of view, the best type of firm to own stock in was one that was located in a growing industry.

The political/cultural variables also predict changes in outcomes in the 1970s. Sales and marketing CEOs produced growth in assets and sales for their firms. Finance CEOs produced growth in assets, and returns on assets, sales, and equity, as well as in market value. Firms with product-related strategies were likely to increase their return on equity while firms with product-unrelated strategies did no worse or no better than firms with product-dominant strategies. Firms with product-related and unrelated strategies were also likely to carry higher debts than product-dominant firms, reflecting their merger growth strategies of the 1960s and 1970s.

Taken together, the results suggest that forms of control were generally not important predictors of the financial performance of large corporations, either in the cross section or over time. Instead, the growth of the industry, the product strategy, and the background of the CEO were the most important predictors of performance. Managerial firms not only did not underperform either bank- or family-controlled firms; they outperformed them.

One interesting question is: What determined the strategies of firms? The results in table 4 explore the evidence that control types affected strategic decisions beyond financial performance. None of the control measures predict whether a firm engaged in a merger in the 1970s. Similarly, bank interlocks did not make firms more likely to engage in mergers. The only measures that did predict mergers are the political/cultural ones. If a firm had engaged in mergers in the 1960s, it was more likely to engage in mergers in the 1970s. Firms with product-related and product-unrelated strategies were more likely than firms with a product-dominant strategy to participate in mergers. Finally, firms with a finance CEO were more likely to have a merger in the 1970s. These results suggest that mergers as a strategy were entirely the product of organizational factors and unaffected by the measures of forms of control.

The equation predicting firm product mix in 1980 is also shown in table 4. None of the control measures predict whether firms are diversified; thus, there is no evidence that diversification is undertaken by managers who act on their own behalf and against the interests of owners. Instead the evidence suggests that diversified firms performed better than nondiversified firms (see tables 2 and 3) and that these firms undertook diversification for organizational, not control, reasons. Three sorts of political/cultural variables affected whether a firm was diversified in 1980: if it had engaged in a merger during the 1960s, if it had a finance CEO in 1969, and if a firm was in an industry with high percentages of firms with product-related and product-unrelated strategies.

TABLE 4

LOGISTIC REGRESSION ANALYSIS OF THE DETERMINANTS OF VARIOUS ORGANIZATIONAL CHARACTERISTICS (N = 110)

INDEPENDENT VARIABLES	DEPENDENT VARIABLES											
	MERGER2, 1969–79		Strategy, 1980				President's Origins, 1980					
			Related		Unrelated		MANPRES		SALEPR		FINPR	
	b	SE(*b*)	*b*	SE(*b*)	*b*	SE(*b*)	*b*	SE(*b*)	*b*	SE(*b*)	*b*	SE(*b*)
MERGER1	.23*	.12	1.59**	.48	.27*	.13	.27	.17	.42*	.23	.05	.18
RELN	1.38*	.65					.04	.39	.24*	.12	.05	.39
UNRELN	1.97*	.86					.53	.53	1.65*	.87	.60*	.24
MANPRES	.72	.61	.20	.54	.20	.43						
SALEPR	.73	.64	.02	.57	.02	.37						
FINPR	1.21*	.65	.18	.53	.31*	.14						
MDF1	−.79	.57					−.04	.36	1.57**	.61	.68*	.33
INSTIPER	−.66	4.29	3.81	7.25	1.43	5.61	.63	.37	.50	.75	.75	.79
BANK	.05	.08	.03	.13	.04	.12	.02	.08	−.27	.17	−.28*	.13
FAMILY	−.03	.03	.09	.06	.04	.06	.03	.03	−.04	.06	−.03	.03
ILOCK	.04	.10	.03	.16	−.03	.13	−.14	.15	.08	.17	−.08	.13
BANK-D	.80	.61	−.05	.53	−.09	.40	.14	.40	.42	.60	.94	.43
ILOCK-D	.73	.70	.34	.61	.30	.43	.03	.47	.60	.66	.51	.48
PERREL			.03**	.01	.00	.01						
PERRUNREL			−.07**	.02	.06**	.02						
FINDPER							.01	.05	.02	.05	.04*	.01
SINDPER							−.01	.03	.06*	.02	.01	.03
MINDPER							.05*	.02	−.04	.03	−.01	.02
INTERCEPT	−2.29**	1.18	3.60**	1.67	2.03*	1.14	−.34	1.52	−3.27	2.47	−.82	1.57
χ^2 (*df*)	22.65 (13)		56.72 (29)				147.70 (54)					

* $P < .05$.
** $P < .01$.

Finally, we consider the determinants of what types of CEOs were in place in 1980. Some of the control variables have interesting effects. For instance, family-controlled firms were less likely to have finance CEOs. Given that finance-CEO-led firms outperformed other firms in the 1970s, this proved to be a mistake. Second, firms with a high percentage of stock held by institutional investors tended to have sales and marketing or finance CEOs. This can be interpreted as an effect of manager control; that is, managers tended to control these types of firms, and they selected CEOs from power bases that were in ascendance.

There are clear organizational effects on who is made CEO. Firms that had mergers or product-diversified strategies were more likely to have sales and marketing or finance CEOs, consistent with the argument made earlier. Furthermore, industries with high percentages of finance or sales and marketing CEOs tended to affect the firm's propensity to have finance or sales and marketing CEOs. This clearly reflects an isomorphic process (DiMaggio and Powell 1983).

DISCUSSION AND CONCLUSIONS

Overall, the agency theorists and the sociological theorists who have focused on forms of control, either family, management, bank, or resource dependence through bank interlocks do not do a good job of explaining how large corporations performed or how they behaved strategically. Bankers, owners, and managers live in organizations that are systems of power located in organizational fields that help define successful behavior. If they attempt to construct their actions outside that context, then they threaten to undermine the organization that is producing wealth for them. The controlling force that determines courses of successful action is thus emergent in organizational interaction. The theory that accounts for these patterns most effectively is the political/cultural approach.

We might be tempted to argue that the political/cultural approach is generally consistent with a standard economic view that the market signals to managers about what works, and they follow the signals. One problem with the economic view is that it can only specify strategies after the fact. The political/cultural approach considers how competing conceptions of control can be compared in terms of their efficacy in producing outcomes. Put another way, economic theory could not theorize these variables precisely because they are not concerned with capturing firm or organizational field differences in conceptions of control. It is also true that these effects exist net of the growth of the industry (a rough indicator of the demand for the product), and therefore, they cannot have a purely economic interpretation.

Agency or transaction-costs theorists could interpret these results as evidence that managers were sufficiently constrained by boards of directors, contracts, and financial markets. Indeed, there is evidence that professional managers actually outperformed their counterparts in family-owned firms. But, to the degree that these perspectives are testable, there is little evidence in their favor. First, it is clear that managers do not favor free cash flow. Diversification, which was supposed to be bad, generally had positive effects. The data analyses show that the conventional wisdom about the 1970s was wrong as well: financially oriented executives who ran diversified firms and engaged in mergers outperformed their brethren, on the average.

It is useful to consider these results and what they imply about the causes of the 1980s merger movement. Jensen (1989), an agency theorist, has argued that inefficient managers held onto cash flow and made poor investment decisions by favoring diversification, provoking others to engage in mergers in the 1980s. The evidence presented here is that managers, particularly finance CEOs, did pretty well in the 1970s, considering the turbulent economic times. Two other hypotheses about the merger movement of the 1980s are more consistent with this evidence.

Friedman (1985), a finance economist, has argued that the primary cause of the 1980s merger movement was the high inflation of the 1970s that kept interest rates high, stock prices low, and inflated the value of corporate assets. Fligstein and Markowitz (1992) have argued that the lax Reagan-era antitrust policy and the 1981 tax cuts gave firms incentive and money to engage in mergers. They also have shown that firms that were diversified and led by finance CEOs were more likely to engage in all forms of financial reorganization (mergers, divestitures, and the repurchase of stock) and were less likely to be the targets of mergers.

This suggests an alternative interpretation of the 1980s merger movement that focuses on how managers were able to deal with the inflated value of their assets. Finance-oriented managers maintained control by recognizing their assets were undervalued and taking actions to prevent their being deposed, while non-finance-oriented managers were targets of mergers. It was not that the managers were systematically working against the interests of shareholders but, instead, that a select number of them were able to analyze the cause of their problem (undervalued assets) and act.

There has been a lot of interest in the recent literature in creating a sociology of markets, and much of that discussion has focused, and we believe rightly so, on the problem of social embeddedness (Granovetter 1985). The theoretical difficulty is deciding what that embeddedness consists of. The results presented here suggest two things. First, organizational and not financial or ownership embeddedness is likely to be a more important cause of actions of firms than anything else. This means we should concentrate efforts on specifying models of the relations between firms that focus on intra- and interorganizational processes, such as the construction of strategic action and the cultural frames by which such a construction makes sense.

Second, the type of embeddedness we choose should be relevant to the problem. The connections between firms, banks, owners, and managers just do not significantly predict much that is interesting in the strategic choices of firms, and, therefore, our theoretical focus should be on what does. In our particular case, most of the financial interlocks appear to reflect co-optation by managers and not control by bankers. This result is consistent with the general view proposed here that the relevant focus of attention should be the firm. We should abandon our concentration on board of directors as a source of network data, in general, and financial linkages across boards of directors, in particular, unless their possible relevance can be specified theoretically (for an example that explicitly concerns investment banks, see Baker [1990]). More relevant network data would focus on how firms obtain knowledge of competitors (trade publications, associations, meetings, and market research) and how they filter their use of that information.

The above does not imply that elites do not exist, nor that they do not organize to achieve collective political ends. Instead, it implies that the substantive content of economic actions taken by elites who control the large corporation will not be determined by a narrow view of what their interests are. Those interests will be determined by the context of their actions; that is, the organizational situations in which they find themselves. Organizational theory provides an alternative sociological view that forces us to take seriously the nature of the relations between large-scale corporations, their internal structuring, and the problem of constructing courses of action. In short, we think that a real sociology of markets will need to focus on some of the elements that have proved to be important here: inter- and intraorganizational politics and the specification of cultural frames that define the social relations between actors.

So short an article is not the place to develop a full-blown theory of the organization of markets, and the results we present are only suggestive of such an approach. However, we have tried here to push this debate by showing the usefulness of such notions as conceptions of control, organizational fields, and firms as structures of power, in order to understand how actors who control firms structure the behavior of those firms.

Controlling the Large Modern Corporation

APPENDIX

TABLE A1

CONSTRUCTION OF FINANCIAL MEASURES

Financial Measure	Component Parts
Market value	Stock price (at close) × common shares outstanding
Price/earnings ratio	Stock price (at close)/earnings per share excluding extraordinary items
Return on assets	100 × income before extraordinary items/(total assets + total gross property, plant, and equipment − total net property, plant, and equipment)
Profit margin	100 × income before extraordinary items/net sales
Return on equity	100 × income before extraordinary items adjusted for common stock equivalents/total common equity
Debt/equity ratio	Total long-term debt/total common equity
Assets	Total assets + (total gross property, plant, and equipment − total net property, plant and equipment)
Sales	Net sales
Free cash flow	Current assets − current liabilities

NOTE.—Measures were run using data from Compustat (1989).

REFERENCES

Allen, M. 1974. "The Structure of Interorganizational Elite Cooptation: Interlocking Corporate Directorates." *American Sociological Review* 39:393–406.

Amit, R., and B. Wernerfelt. 1990. "Why Do Firms Reduce Business Risk?" *Academy of Management Journal* 33:520–33.

Armour, H., and D. Teece. 1978. "Organizational Structure and Economic Performance: A Test of the Multidivisional Hypothesis." *Bell Journal of Economics* 90:106–22.

Baker, W. 1984. "The Social Structure of a Securities Market." *American Journal of Sociology* 89:775–811.

———. 1990. "Market Networks and Corporate Behavior." *American Journal of Sociology* 96:589–625.

Berle, A. A., and G. C. Means. 1932. *The Modern Corporation and Private Property.* New York: Commerce Clearing House.

Burch, P. 1972. *The Managerial Revolution Reassessed.* Lexington, Mass.: Heath.

Burt, R. 1983. *Corporate Profits and Cooptation.* New York: Academic Press.

Compustat. 1989. *Compustat II.* New York: Standard & Poor's.

DiMaggio, P. 1985. "Structural Analysis of Organizational Fields." *Research in Organizational Behavior* 7:335–70.

DiMaggio, P., and W. W. Powell. 1983. "The Iron Cage Revisited: Institutional Isomorphism and Collective Rationality in Organizational Fields." *American Sociological Review* 48:147–60.

Fama, E., and M. Jensen. 1983*a*. "Separation of Ownership and Control." *Journal of Law and Economics* 26:301–26.

———. 1983*b*. "Agency Problems and Residual Claims." *Journal of Law and Economics* 26:327–50.

Federal Trade Commission. 1981. *Report on Mergers and Acquisitions*. Washington, D.C.: Government Printing Office.

Fligstein, N. 1985. "The Spread of the Multidivisional Form." *American Sociological Review* 50:377–91.

———. 1987. "The Intraorganizational Power Struggle: The Rise of Finance Presidents in Large Corporations." *American Sociological Review* 52:44–58.

———. 1990. *The Transformation of Corporate Control*. Cambridge, Mass.: Harvard University Press.

Fligstein, N., and L. Markowitz. 1992. "The Finance Conception of the Corporation and the Causes of the Financial Reorganization of Large Corporations, 1979–1988." In *Sociology and Social Policy*, edited by W. J. Wilson. Beverly Hills, Calif.: Sage. Forthcoming.

Fombrun, C., and M. Stanley. 1990. "The Determinants of Corporate Reputation." *Academy Management Journal* 33:233–58.

Fortune Magazine. 1970. "The *Fortune* Directory of the 500 Largest Industrial Corporations" (May): 182–212.

———. 1980. "The *Fortune* Directory of the 500 Largest Industrial Corporations" (May 5): 274–95.

Friedman, B. 1985. "The Substitutability of Debt and Equity Securities." Pp. 274–95 in *Corporate Capital Structures in the United States*, edited by B. Friedman. Chicago: University of Chicago Press.

Granovetter, M. 1985. "Economic Action, Social Structure, and Embeddedness." *American Journal of Sociology* 91:481–510.

Graves, S. 1988. "Institutional Ownership and Corporate R&D in the Computer Industry." *Academy Management Journal* 31:417–28.

Herman, E. 1979. "Kotz on Banker Control." *Monthly Review* 31:46–57.

———. 1980. "Reply to David Kotz." *Monthly Review* 32:61–64.

———. 1981. *Corporate Control, Corporate Power*. Cambridge: Cambridge University Press.

Hirsch, P. 1987. *Pack Your Own Parachute*. Reading, Mass.: Addison-Wesley.

Holmstrom, B. 1988. "Moral Hazard in Teams." *Bell Journal of Economics* 18:324–40.

Jensen, M. 1989. "Eclipse of the Public Corporation." *Harvard Business Review* 67:61–73.

Jensen, M., and W. H. Meckling. 1976. "Theory of the Firm: Managerial Behavior, Agency Costs, and Ownership Structure." *Journal of Financial Economics* 3:305–60.

Jensen, M., and R. S. Ruback. 1983. "The Marker for Corporate Control: The Scientific Evidence." *Journal of Financial Economics* 11:5–50.

Kessler, R., and D. Greenberg. 1981. *Linear Panel Analysis*. New York: Academic Press.

Kotz, D. 1978. *Bank Control of Large Corporations in the United States*. Berkeley: University of California Press.

———. 1980. "Reply to Edward Herman." *Monthly Review* 32:57–60.

Lamoreaux, N. 1985. *The Great Merger Movement in American Business, 1899–1904*. New York: Cambridge University Press.

Larner, R. J. 1971. *Management Control and the Large Corporation*. New York: Dunellen.

MacNeil, L. 1985. "Relational Contracts." *Wisconsin Law Review* 54:483–525.

Marris, R. 1964. *The Economic Theory of Managerial Capitalism*. Glencoe, Ill.: Free Press.

Meyer, J., and B. Rowan. 1977. "Institutionalized Organizations: Formal Structure as Myth and Ceremony." *American Journal of Sociology* 83:340–63.

Mintz, B., and M. Schwartz. 1985. *Power Structure of American Business*. Chicago: University of Chicago Press.

Mizruchi, M. 1982. *The American Corporate Network, 1904–1973*. Beverly Hills, Calif.: Sage.

———. 1989. "Similarity of Political Behavior among Large American Corporations." *American Journal of Sociology* 95:401–24.

Mizruchi, M., and L. Stearns. 1988. "A Longitudinal Study of the Formation of Interlocking Directorates." *Administrative Science Quarterly* 33:194–210.

Moody's Manuals. 1970. "Industrials." New York: Moody's Investor Service.

———. 1980. "Industrials." New York: Moody's Investor Service.

Myers, S., and N. Majluf. 1984. "Corporate Financing and Investment Decisions When Firms Have Information That Investors Do Not Have." *Journal of Financial Economics* 13:187–221.

Palmer, D. 1983. "Broken Ties: Interlocking Directorates and Intercorporate Coordination." *Administrative Science Quarterly* 28:40–55.

Palmer, D., R. Friedland, P. D. Jennings, and M. Powers. 1987. "The Economics and Politics of Structure: The Multidivisional Form and the Large U.S. Corporation." *Administrative Science Quarterly* 32:25–48.

Pennings, J. 1980. *Interlocking Directorates*. San Francisco: Jossey Bass.

Perrow, C. 1970. "Departmental Power and Perspectives in Industrial Firms." Pp. 59–89 in *Power in Organizations*, edited by M. Zald. Nashville: Vanderbilt University Press.

Pfeffer, J. 1981. *Power in Organizations*. Marshfield, Mass.: Pittman.

Pfeffer, J., and H. Salancik. 1978. *The External Control of Organizations*. New York: Harper & Row.

Ross, S. 1978. "The Economic Theory of Agency: The Principal's Problem." *American Economic Review* 62:134–39.

Rumelt, R. 1974. *Strategy, Structure, and Economic Performance*. Boston: Harvard Business School.

Scherer, F. 1980. *Industrial Market Structure and Economic Performance*. Chicago: Rand McNally.

Useem, M. 1984. *The Inner Circle*. New York: Oxford University Press.

U.S. House of Representatives. 1969. House Banking and Currency Committee. "Commercial Banks and Their Trust Activities." 91st Cong., 2d sess.

———. 1971. House Committee on Interstate and Foreign Commerce. "Institutional Investor Study Report." 92d Cong., 2d sess.

U.S. Senate. 1973. Senate Committee on Government Operations. "Disclosure of Corporate Ownership." 93d Cong., 2d sess.

White, H. 1981. "Where Do Markets Come From?" *American Journal of Sociology* 87:517–47.

Williamson, O. 1964. *The Economics of Discretionary Behavior*. Englewood Cliffs, N.J.: Prentice-Hall.

———. 1985. *The Economic Institutions of Capitalism*. New York: Free Press.

Zeitlin, M. 1974. "Corporate Control and Ownership: The Large Corporation and the Capitalist Class." *American Journal of Sociology* 79:1073–119.

[6]

A POLITICAL THEORY OF AMERICAN CORPORATE FINANCE*

*Mark J. Roe***

Introduction

Why is the public corporation—with its fragmented shareholders buying and selling on the stock exchange—the dominant form of enterprise in the United States? Since Berle and Means, the conventional corporate law story begins with technology dictating large enterprises with capital needs so great that even a few wealthy individuals cannot provide enough. These enterprises consequently must draw capital from many dispersed shareholders. Shareholders diversify their own holdings, further fragmenting ownership. This combination of a huge enterprise, concentrated management, and dispersed, diversified stockholders shifts corporate control from shareholders to managers. Managers can pursue their own agenda, at times to the detriment of the enterprise.[1]

In the classic story, the large public firm survived because it best balanced the problems of managerial control, risk sharing, and capital needs. In a Darwinian evolution, the large public firm mitigated the managerial agency problems with a board of directors of outsiders, with a managerial headquarters of strategic planners overseeing the operating divisions, and with managerial incentive compensation. Hostile takeovers, proxy contests, and the threat of each further disciplined managers. Fragmented ownership survived because public firms adapted. They solved enough of the governance problems created by the large unwieldy structures needed to meet the huge capital needs of modern technology. In the conventional story, the large public firm evolved as the efficient response to the economics of organization.

I argue here that the public corporation is as much a political adaptation as an economic or technological necessity. The size and technology story fails to completely explain the corporate patterns we observe. There are organizational alternatives to the fragmented ownership of the large public corporation; the most prominent alternative is concen-

** Professor of Law, Columbia Law School. I benefited from presentations at Berkeley, Chicago, Columbia, Harvard, McGill, and UCLA, and from comments from Lucian Bebchuk, Bernie Black, Victor Brudney, Marvin Chirelstein, Jack Coffee, Alfred Conard, Jeffrey Gordon, Joe Grundfest, Cliff Holderness, Howell Jackson, Michael Jensen, Lou Lowenstein, Henry Manne, Robert Mundheim, Roberta Romano, Andy Rutten, Susan Tobias, and John Wiley.

1. A. Berle & G. Means, The Modern Corporation and Private Property (rev. ed. 1967) (original edition published in 1932).

trated institutional ownership, a result prevalent in other countries. But American law and politics deliberately diminished the power of financial institutions to hold the large equity blocks that would foster serious oversight of managers, making the modern American corporation adapt to the political terrain. The modern corporation's origin lies in technology, economics, *and* politics.

Shareholder control of managers arises when the owner holds a large block of stock. Individuals rarely have enough money to buy big blocks. Institutional investors do. But law creates barriers to the institutions' taking big blocks. Banks, the institution with the most money, cannot own stock. Mutual funds generally cannot own control blocks of stock. Insurance companies can put only a fragment of their investment portfolio into the stock of any one company. Pension funds own stock, but they also face restrictions. More importantly, corporate managers control private pension funds, not the other way around.

And we have just exhausted the major financial institutions in America; none can readily and without legal restraint control an industrial company. That is the first step of my argument: law prohibits or raises the cost of institutional influence in industrial companies.

The second step is to examine the politics of corporate financial structure. Many legal restraints had public-spirited backers; some rules would be those that wise regulators, unburdened by politics, would reach. But many important rules do not fit into this public-spirited mold. Examining financial regulation through the lens of the new public choice literature reveals a complex and new political story, of law repeatedly foreclosing alternatives to the Berle-Means corporation.

Opinion polls show Americans mistrust large financial institutions with accumulated power and have always been wary of Wall Street controlling industry. Politicians responded to that distrust by enacting rules restricting private accumulations of power by financial institutions. Various interest groups also benefited from fragmentation; Congress and the administrative agencies also responded to them.

During the SEC's formative years, its chairman said:

> [T]he banker . . . [should and will be] restricted to . . . underwriting or selling. Insofar as management [and] formulation of industrial policies . . . the banker will be superseded. The financial power which he has exercised in the past over such processes will pass into other hands.[2]

An inquiry into the interplay of political ideology and financial institutions follows. We shall examine the ideas of opinion leaders and political actors, and the content of major political investigations, leading us to speculate on a political explanation for corporate structure:

---

2. W.O. Douglas, Democracy and Finance 32, 40–41 (1940) (Douglas stunned his audience of nearly every important Wall Street investment banker when he gave this speech in 1937).

Main Street America did not want a powerful Wall Street. Laws discouraging and prohibiting control resulted.

I. Berle and Means

A. *The Classic Story*

Berle and Means' vision is central to corporate law scholarship. Their story is straightforward: "[T]he central mass of the twentieth-century American economic revolution [is a] . . . massive collectivization of property devoted to production, with [an] accompanying decline of individual decision-making and control[, and a] massive dissociation of wealth from active management."[3] This restructuring turns corporate law on its head: stockholders, the owners, become powerless. The stockholder's vote "is of diminishing importance as the number of shareholders in each corporation increases—diminishing in fact to negligible importance as the corporations become giants. As the number of stockholders increases, the capacity of each to express opinions is extremely limited."[4] As a result, corporate wealth is held by shareholders as a "passive" investment while managers control the corporation.

The problem is not solely the separation of shareholders from managers or, as Berle and Means put it, the "massive dissociation of wealth from active management." The problem is atomization. Most public companies are held by thousands of shareholders, each with only a small stake. As a result, an active shareholder cannot capture all of the gains from monitoring managers. The costs of monitoring are borne by the shareholder who becomes involved, studies the enterprise, or sits on the board of directors and thereby takes the risk of enhanced liability. But since monitoring gains would be divided among all shareholders, most fragmented shareholders rationally forego involvement.

This disincentive to monitor has costs: enterprises are run imperfectly as managers pursue their own agenda. Managers want high salaries, nice offices, and, if the firm is large enough, corporate jets. Occasionally they take corporate opportunities for themselves. Much more perniciously, many managers pursue operating policies that diminish social wealth. They want the enterprise to grow beyond an efficient size for the prestige, power, and salary that comes with running a larger organization. Too large, the enterprise slows down; it runs less efficiently.[5]

A large shareholder might make a difference: a shareholder with 25% of the company's stock could veto empire-building acquisitions,

---

3. A. Berle & G. Means, supra note 1, at xxv; see id. at 4–7.

4. Id. at xix.

5. See id. at 112–14; O. Williamson, The Economics of Discretionary Behavior: Managerial Objectives in a Theory of the Firm 34–35, 79 (1964).

question managerial performance, and in the extreme instance replace the managers. Since it could capture a quarter of the gains, the large shareholder would often have the incentive to act, an incentive fragmented shareholders lack.

B. *Modern Complaints About the Berle-Means Corporation*

Modern writers blame corporate mismanagement on shareholders, who they say value short-run profits excessively, to the detriment of the nation. They claim that managers would take the long-view but are stymied by Wall Street's short-run goals; companies shun long-term investment, and industry underinvests in research and development.[6]

The long/short controversy posits a market failure. After all, institutions should know how to discount long-term value to present value. While no one has *demonstrated* that the long/short phenomenon exists, consider the effect of fragmentation. Fragmentation diminishes the value to a single shareholder of assessing long-run soft information not reflected in the hard numbers of current financial statements. To assess long-term research and development plans often requires staff or consultants with specialized expertise. If there are scale economies in evaluation, then a fragmented shareholder may rationally decline to incur the cost.[7] Theoretically, the investor would invest in research and buy up undervalued stocks. That is, the *size* of shareholding would increase to reflect any scale economies in information. But, as I shall document in Part II, institutions have ceilings on their stock positions.[8]

Consider the difficulty in conveying soft long-term information to a fragmented marketplace; dispersed investors cannot cheaply distin-

6. See, e.g., L. Lowenstein, What's Wrong With Wall Street 1, 5–6, 9, 56–63, 76 (1988); Hayes & Abernathy, Managing Our Way to Economic Decline, Harv. Bus. Rev., July–Aug. 1980, at 67, 68–70; Lipton, Corporate Governance in the Age of Finance Corporatism, 136 U. Pa. L. Rev. 1, 7–9, 23–25 (1987); Dobrzynski, More Than Ever, It's Management for the Short Term, Bus. Wk., Nov. 24, 1986, at 82; Drucker, A Crisis of Capitalism, Wall St. J., Sept. 30, 1986, at 32, col. 3; Altman & Brown, A Competitive Liability, Ridding Wall Street of a Short-Term Bias, N.Y. Times, June 1, 1986, § 3, at 3, col. 1 (former Assistant Secretary of the Treasury decries "a new cadre of professional money managers . . . [who push] corporate management to focus on short-term results.").

7. Cf. Wilke, Among Those Baffled by Technology Are Lots of Stock Analysts, Wall St. J., Sept. 28, 1989, at A1, col. 6 (stock analysts have trouble evaluating long-term research).

8. Furthermore, managers may feel constrained to follow *average* shareholder opinion, for fear that the average will sell out and prompt a change in control. An isolated institution with a *small share* of the enterprise will accordingly be unable to "protect" managers from other shareholders; both managers and the fragmented institution seeing an undervalued long-term opportunity will fear that other shareholders will force termination of the good long-term project. See T. Hoshi, A. Kashyap & D. Scharfstein, Corporate Structure, Liquidity, and Investment: Evidence from Japanese Panel Data 9–15, 19–25 (MIT Working Paper No. 2071-88, Sept. 1988) (data suggests industrial firm affiliation with banks in Japan mitigates some informational defects of securities markets).

guish egoistic empire-building from a high net present value project. And managers are wary of revealing proprietary information to scattered shareholders;[9] without good information, even highly paid, technically competent analysts cannot evaluate long-term research and development. In contrast, financial analysts with generic skills can easily evaluate short-term financial data.

Complaints also are heard that shareholders do not monitor managers. Managers build empires and pursue bad strategies without shareholder intervention until matters are so out-of-hand that the violence of the hostile takeover or the instability of the leveraged buyout results. Persistent shareholder involvement could lead to intervention before bloodshed.

These pernicious monitoring and information stories depend on the Berle-Means corporation. Imploring an owner of $10 million of the stock of a $10 billion industrial firm to be an active shareholder is useless. The shareholder can capture only 1/1,000 of the corporation's gain. The shareholder should rationally decline to invest $100,000 of his or her time and wealth, even if that $100,000 would yield a $100 million gain *for the corporation*.

But a 25% shareholder could invest millions of dollars in monitoring and in costly evaluation of soft research and development information. Beneficial monitoring does not even depend on the monitors being *better* than managers at most tasks, as I discuss in Part IV. The 25% shareholder could in fact generally be worse, but could still help if it were smart enough to resist intervention until corporate results were poor, and had some skill in assessing whether the poor results were due to poor management.

Moreover, management would more willingly reveal proprietary information to the large long-term shareholder, who has the incentive to maintain secrecy. The large shareholder would protect secrets *and* protect managers from outsiders who would second guess truly profitable long-run investments. If an owner could take 25% stock positions in a few firms, it might find it worthwhile to assemble a staff with the expertise to monitor effectively. Finally, managerial motivation to pursue wealth-maximizing operating policies could change for the better if managers knew that a 25% block was already assembled, even if the owner was inactive day-to-day; managers would realize that deviation from long-run profitability could activate the large-block holder, or activate an outsider who would find it easy to buy the control block. Financial economists argue that large block shareholding improves corporate operations.[10]

9. See O. Williamson, Markets and Hierarchies: Analysis and Antitrust Implications 35–37, 97–98 (1975).

10. See Holderness & Sheehan, The Role of Majority Shareholders in Publicly Held Corporations, 20 J. Fin. Econ. 317, 333–45 (1988); Wruck, Equity Ownership Concentration and Firm Value, 23 J. Fin. Econ. 3, 14–16, 23–24 (1989). But see Demsetz &

Few of the largest public firms are controlled by a holder of a substantial block of shares.[11] Few individuals have the wealth to take that large a position. Although banks, insurance companies, mutual funds, and pension funds have enough money, they do not take large positions.

Possibly financial institutions do not because they believe they would fail to be effective. But examples from the past offer tantalizing prospects. General Motors—the largest American industrial corporation—today has no controlling shareholder. But once it had one. Du Pont owned 25% of GM until the courts ordered antitrust divestiture. In the 1920s, an ineptly managed GM neared bankruptcy. Its management was reinvigorated by neither a proxy fight, nor a hostile takeover, nor a leveraged buyout in reaction to the prospect of a takeover, but by the intervention of its large shareholder. Pierre du Pont moved to Detroit, reorganized the company, and installed new managers.[12] Similarly, the J.P. Morgan investment bank monitored many of the country's railroads when reorganizing them at the turn-of-the-century.[13]

Certainly concentrated control by financial institutions is imaginable: Japanese and German corporate ownership is quite concentrated; their financial institutions are more actively involved in their companies than are financial institutions in the United States.[14] Daimler-Benz, the automotive concern that is the largest German industrial company, has a 28% shareholder, Deutsche Bank. When managerial infighting recently left the company without clear direction, the bank replaced Daimler-Benz' senior management without the organizational violence of a hostile takeover.[15] The result in Germany—like GM during the du Pont intervention—should be contrasted with the recent result in the United States when financial institutions (in this instance, public pension funds) sought to influence the selection of the next chairman of GM; GM management rebuffed them.[16] If American financial institutions had a stake in GM approaching that controlled by Deutsche Bank in Daimler-Benz, that rebuff would have been difficult.

Lehn, The Structure of Corporate Ownership: Causes and Consequences, 93 J. Pol. Econ. 1155, 1173–76 (1985) (comparing companies with fragmented shareholders to companies with concentrated stockholders).

11. M. Eisenberg, The Structure of the Corporation: A Legal Analysis 45–52 (1976) (studies show that 10% blocks, while not unheard of, were found in no more than one-third of the various samples of large firms).

12. A. Chandler & S. Salsbury, Pierre S. du Pont and the Making of the Modern Corporation 457–560 (1971).

13. See V. Carosso, The Morgans: Private International Bankers 1854–1913, at 371–72 (1987); R. Chernow, The House of Morgan 44 (1990).

14. See Aoki, Toward an Economic Model of the Japanese Firm, 28 J. Econ. Literature 1, 14 (1990); Ingersoll, The Banker Behind the Shakeup at Daimler-Benz, Bus. Wk., July 27, 1987, at 36.

15. Ingersoll, supra note 14, at 36.

16. Lorsch, Funds Should Flex Their Muscle, N.Y. Times, Feb. 11, 1990, § 3, at 13, col. 2.

Natural selection suggests that if the separation of ownership from control created agency problems, the organization that survived found adaptive mechanisms to mitigate the agency costs. Survival of the fittest organizational structures makes the modern corporation as efficient as it can be.[17] The political perspective raises doubts, since as I argue next, important organizational forms are prohibited or made costly in the United States. At best, the modern corporation is "as efficient as it can be" only within powerful political constraints.

I do not here argue that institutional control would have been better for the United States. Serious disadvantages would arise as well.[18] Rather than prescription, I want first to understand how politics determined corporate structure.

II. The Financial Institutions: Who Has the Money and What Can They Do with It?

Four types of financial institutions dominate: commercial banks, mutual funds, insurance companies, and pension funds. They have assets, respectively, of $3.2 trillion, $548 billion, $1.8 trillion, and $1.9 trillion.[19]

Clearly these financial institutions have enough assets to influence large corporations. But portfolio rules, anti-networking rules, and other fragmenting rules disable them from systematically taking control blocks. Demonstrating this requires regulatory detail, but the rules can be summarized quickly for those who do not want the detail: Banks and bank holding companies were repeatedly prohibited from owning control blocks of stock or from affiliation with investment banks that did. Insurance companies were for quite some time prohibited from owning any stock, and portfolio rules still restrict their ability to take control. Mutual funds cannot deploy more than a fraction of their portfolio in a concentrated position; buying more than 5% of a company triggers on-

17. See, e.g., Stigler & Friedland, The Literature of Economics: The Case of Berle and Means, 26 J.L. & Econ. 237, 258-59 (1983).

18. See infra Part IV (conflicts of interest, banking instability, politically intolerable accumulations of power, "capture" by management). And do not think that there were halcyon days of institutional monitoring that have ended. Most institutions never could take a large stock position. For the few that could, some damaged shareholders by "siphoning" off value, or helped shareholders only by organizing monopolies and cartels. See L. Brandeis, Other People's Money—And How the Bankers Use It 33 (1914); infra Part III.

19. Board of Governors of the Federal Reserve System, Flow of Funds Accounts: Financial Assets and Liabilities (Mar. 1990) (preliminary figures for year-end 1989). Bank assets are only those of FDIC-insured commercial banks, not savings associations, which have another $1.7 trillion. These institutions account for nearly 90% of the assets in financial intermediaries. See Board of Governors of the Federal Reserve System, Balance Sheets for the U.S. Economy 1945-1989, at 42, line 4 (Apr. 1990). Mutual funds exclude closed-end and money market mutual funds. Banks also had $679 billion in discretionary trust funds at year-end 1988. Federal Financial Institutions Examination Council, Trust Assets of Financial Institutions: 1988, at 33 (1989).

erous rules. Pension funds are less restricted, but they are fragmented; rules make it difficult for them to operate jointly to assert control. Private pension funds are under management control; they are not constructed for a palace revolution in which they would assert control over their managerial bosses.

Do not be deceived by the detail that follows: A pattern is there that emerges with clarity in Part III when we look at legislative history, popular ideology, the power of interest groups, and the views of opinion leaders. Politics never allowed financial institutions to become powerful enough to control operating companies. American politics destroyed the most prominent alternative to the Berle-Means corporation: concentrated institutional ownership.

A. *Banks and Commerce*

Banks have *half* of the financial assets available for investment. They are still where the money is. But legal analysis of bank power in industrial ownership is simple: Banks cannot own stock.

1. *The Historical Separation of Banks from Commerce.* — Some early American banking charters expected banks to be in commerce. The Manhattan Bank was also a waterworks; some manufacturers had corporate charters that included the right to open a bank. But other chartering authorities just copied English charters, which separated banks from commerce. By the mid-nineteenth century, separation was the norm.[20] The important National Bank Act of 1863 gave national banks only limited powers. Control of an industrial company was out of the question. When controversy arose over whether banks could own stocks, the Supreme Court resolved that question against the banks: the power to own stock was not listed, accordingly it was not granted.[21]

2. *The Glass-Steagall Act.* — To avoid the direct prohibition on stock dealing, commercial banks dealt in securities through affiliates. In 1933, Congress believed that the failure of these stock affiliates damaged banks, and the resulting bank failures caused, not reflected, the Depression. The resulting Glass-Steagall Act of 1933 prohibited bank affiliates from owning and dealing in securities, thereby severing commercial banks from investment banks.[22] Today, prohibitions on commercial banks' underwriting and affiliation with companies *dealing* in securities are breaking down.[23] But the prohibition on bank ownership

20. B. Hammond, Banks and Politics in America from the Revolution to the Civil War 149–55 (1957).

21. California Bank v. Kennedy, 167 U.S. 362, 366–67 (1897); National Bank Act of Feb. 25, 1863, § 11, 12 U.S.C. § 24 (seventh) (1988). State member banks of the Federal Reserve System were later similarly restricted. Banking Act of 1933 (Glass-Steagall), § 5(c), 12 U.S.C. § 335 (1988).

22. Banking Act of 1933 (Glass-Steagall), § 16, 12 U.S.C. § 24 (seventh) (1988).

23. Securities Indus. Ass'n v. Board of Governors of the Fed. Reserve Sys., 468 U.S. 207, 214–21 (1984) (upholding FRB's authorization of Bank of America to acquire

of equity remains stable.

Bank trust departments are commercial banks' only remaining direct link to equity. Rules fragment trust fund investments: no more than 10% of a bank's trust funds may be invested in the stock of any single corporation.[24] The regulation first came down a few years after the Patman Report warned against the growing power of bank trust departments.[25] Other trustee laws foster a hyper-fragmentation of the bank trust portfolio, well beyond that which financial economists say is needed for diversification.[26]

3. *The Bank Holding Company Legislation.* — Many bank owners wished to operate from several locations or to chain several banks together. However, many states prohibit banks from branching and prohibit out-of-state banks from operating locally. In the 1950s, banks reincorporated themselves as holding companies, each owning several separately incorporated banks. The holding company had other regulatory advantages: it was not subject to the same stringent regulation of activities as were the bank subsidiaries—the holding company could own businesses and stock, including control blocks.[27] In response, Congress enacted the Bank Holding Company Act of 1956, restricting a holding company's activities to those closely related to banking. A bank holding company cannot own more than 5% of the voting stock of any nonbanking company and cannot otherwise control an industrial firm.[28] Holding companies can own more than 5% (up to 25%), but only if the additional stock is nonvoting.[29]

Schwab, a securities dealer); see also J.P. Morgan & Co., [1988–1989 Transfer Binder] Fed. Banking L. Rep. (CCH) ¶ 87,554 (Jan. 19, 1989) (FRB approves application of commercial bank to establish underwriting affiliate); Bankers Trust New York Corp., 75 Fed. Reserve Bull. 829 (Oct. 30, 1989) (FRB approves application of commercial banks to engage in some brokerage activities).

24. 12 C.F.R. § 9.18(b)(9)(ii) (1990).

25. 1 Staff of House Subcomm. on Domestic Finance, Comm. on Banking and Currency, 90th Cong., 2d Sess., Commercial Banks and Their Trust Activities: Emerging Influence on the American Economy 1–4 (Comm. Print 1968) [hereinafter Patman Report].

26. See Roe, Institutional Fiduciaries in the Corporate Boardroom, *in* Institutional Investors: Challenges and Responsibilities (A. Samsetz & J. Bicksler eds. 1991) (forthcoming).

27. Clair & Tucker, Interstate Banking and the Federal Reserve: A Historical Perspective, Fed. Reserve Bank of Dallas Econ. Rev., Nov. 1989, at 1, 6–12.

28. Bank Holding Company Act of 1956, § 4(c)(4)–(5), 12 U.S.C. § 1843(c)(5)–(6) (1988). Shares acquired in a fiduciary capacity are not included in the 5% limitation. Id.

29. Id.; P. Heller, Federal Bank Holding Company Law § 4.03[2][b] (1990). Authority to own nonvoting stock of *public* companies was until recently largely illusory. Public companies could not issue nonvoting stock for most of the post-1956 era because of one-share, one-vote rules. New York Stock Exchange, New York Stock Exchange Listed Company Manual 3-11–3-14 (Feb. 1990).

B. *Mutual Funds*

Mutual funds pool the investment funds of hundreds of investors, thereby enabling the investors both to diversify and to buy the investment expertise of the fund's managers. If mutual funds could have taken large blocks, they might have found monitoring worthwhile. In theory, they could have evolved into the missing monitoring link between fragmented investors and large operating firms.

However, Congress was suspicious of mutual funds' potential to control industrial companies. A 1934 Senate securities report distinguished two functions: investment and management control. Only unscrupulous financiers mixed investment with control: "The investment company [has] bec[o]me the instrumentality of financiers and industrialists to facilitate acquisition of concentrated control of the wealth and industries of the country."[30] As a consequence, Congress must "prevent the diversion of these [investment] trusts from their normal channels of diversified investment to the *abnormal* avenues of control of industry."[31] Congress might have "to completely divorce investment trusts from investment banking."[32] Mutual funds should invest only passively; holding companies were organized for control and they were denigrated, because conflicts of interest damaged outsider shareholders. Congress directed the SEC to draft legislation.[33]

1. *The Investment Company Act of 1940.* — The SEC understood its marching orders from Congress. Its bill declared that "the national public interest . . . [is] adversely affected . . . when investment companies . . . [have] great size . . . [and] have excessive influence in the national economy."[34] The SEC wanted mutual funds' directors and employees off the boards of all portfolio companies, essentially a Glass-Steagall-type severance.[35] Enactment ultimately entailed compromise with the industry, but the SEC achieved much of its severance goal.

A mutual fund cannot advertise itself as diversified if the regulated part of its portfolio has more than 10% of the stock of any company, even if that stock is a small portion of the fund's portfolio.[36] (Only

30. Comm. on Banking and Currency, Stock Exchange Practices, S. Rep. No. 1455, 73d Cong., 2d Sess. 333–34 (1934) [hereinafter Pecora Report, in reference to its final chief counsel].

31. Id. at 333 (emphasis added); see also Investment Trusts and Investment Companies, Hearings on S. 3580 Before a Subcomm. of the Senate Comm. on Banking and Currency, 76th Cong., 3d Sess. 36 (1940) [hereinafter 1940 Act Hearings] (statement of Robert E. Healy, Comm'r, Sec. and Exchange Comm.) (quoting Pecora Report).

32. Pecora Report, supra note 30, at 393.

33. Public Utility Holdings Company Act of 1935, § 30, 15 U.S.C. § 79a-4 (1988).

34. 1940 Act Hearings, supra note 31, at 2. The statement of purpose also showed concern for efficient investment management and protection of investors. Id.

35. Id. at 216–20.

36. Investment Company Act of 1940, § 5(b), 15 U.S.C. § 80a-5(b) (1988) [hereinafter 1940 Act].

one-quarter of the portfolio is unregulated.[37]) The SEC wanted that restriction to disable control.[38] Some mutual funds might have competed as monitors owning large blocks of stock. That prospect was cut off for diversified investment companies by the 1940 Act, and for other investment companies by the tax requirements I discuss in the next section.[39] Virtually all mutual funds call themselves diversified; they cannot control public firms.

The 1940 Act also prohibits a "diversified" mutual fund from putting more than 5% of its regulated assets in the securities of any one issuer.[40] As a diversification standard this prohibition is crude but defensible. Mutual funds are designed for unsophisticated investors who cannot assemble a diversified portfolio or evaluate the mutual fund's portfolio.[41] By requiring some standard of fragmentation if the fund chooses to call itself diversified, the 1940 Act helps make sure that investors get what they were promised.

But the *10%* restriction (no more than *10%* of the *portfolio* company's stock) is unnecessary for true diversification. Obviously, a large investment company could have a small portion of its assets in a single firm, but if the portfolio firm were mid-sized the investment company could have an influential block of stock.

2. *Subchapter M of the Internal Revenue Code.* — The tax penalties for not being "diversified" are considerable. The mutual fund that would control industry would be taxed unfavorably on its *entire* portfolio, since the tax code allows only *diversified* mutual funds to pass income through to shareholders, untaxed to the conduit mutual fund. And the tax code's notion of "diversification" parallels that found in the 1940 Act; it only faintly resembles the diversification concept taught in today's business schools. Under the tax code, mutual funds must have at least half of their investments in companies constituting no more than 5% of the portfolio *and* constituting no more than 10% of the *portfolio company's* outstanding stock; for the other half, no more than 25% of the fund's total assets can go into a single company's stock.[42]

37. Id.

38. See 1940 Act Hearings, supra note 31, at 188, 192 (statement of David Schenker, Chief Counsel, SEC Investment Trust Study); Pecora Report, supra note 30, at 348–51; 1 T. Frankel, The Regulation of Money Managers § 33.1, at 343 (1978).

39. The SEC wanted more stringent control restrictions, including a bar on any fund exceeding $150 million in assets. The SEC also resisted recommending expanding the Internal Revenue Code's tax advantage for diversified funds (which could not own control blocks) to nondiversified funds (which could) and wanted to prohibit mutual fund directors from serving as directors of any portfolio company. 1940 Act Hearings, supra note 31, at 375, 400–01, 412.

40. 1940 Act, § 5(b)(1), 15 U.S.C. § 80a-5(b)(1) (1988).

41. See Pecora Report, supra note 30, at 348–51 (congressional criticism of mutual fund that put 19% of its assets into a railroad stock).

42. I.R.C. § 851(b)(4) (1988). Subchapter M is available only to companies that derive 90% of their income from investment in stocks, bonds and other securities. Id. § 851(b)(2) (1988). On the statute's face, there is a serious question whether a public

If the fund chose not to be "diversified" under the tax code or the 1940 Act, its income would be taxed at the ordinary corporate tax rate, destroying the fund by a triple taxation of its income. Income received by the noncomplying fund as dividends would be taxed twice, once at 34% when earned by the portfolio company, and then again when received by the fund. True, the noncomplying mutual fund could exclude 70% of the dividends received, netting out to an effective tax rate of 10% on dividends. Capital gains would be taxed at 34%. And the income would be taxed a third time when realized by shareholders.

This triple taxation deters most ordinary corporations from acting as long-term, undiversified monitors (and deters most mutual funds from losing their "diversified" status). A corporation might accept the unfavorable tax status in the short-run, as a prelude to a takeover and restructuring, but the corporation asserting control over the long-term would have to be confident it had unusually acute monitoring skills. After all, if the corporation received half of its income in capital gains and half in dividends, then it would pay approximately 20% of its income in taxes. A great deal of effective monitoring would be needed to make up for that initial penalty; only unusually able monitors could overcome it. Nor could a public fund organize itself as a partnership to pass through its income to owners without itself paying tax. To get pass-through tax status, a publicly-traded partnership *must* also comply with subchapter M's portfolio restrictions.[43]

Thus, if a mutual fund wished to sell services as an intermediary/monitor, dividing its portfolio into three or four stocks, it could not get the advantage of subchapter M. And no subchapter M mutual fund could *ever* threaten a portfolio company that the fund would devote more than a quarter of its assets to obtain a majority of the portfolio company's stock and oust management. That threat, and the influence it would yield, is prohibitively expensive for a mutual fund.[44]

3. *Other Restrictions on Control.* — For that quarter of the fund that could be concentrated, other restrictions apply. If a mutual fund owned 5% of a portfolio company's stock or sat on its board, the portfolio firm would become a statutory affiliate of the mutual fund *and* of the mutual fund's principal underwriter.[45] Many mutual funds are sponsored by investment banks. A sponsoring investment bank could

company that intended to make most of its income from *management*, as opposed to passive investment, could obtain subchapter M pass-through at all.

Venture capital firms, which would provide monitoring for *small* firms, not the large firms that are our subject, are partially exempt from the no-control provision. Id. § 851(e) (1988).

43. The "triple taxation" rules and the partnership rule are in id. §§ 243, 1201 & 7704(c) (1988).

44. Id. § 851(b)(4)(B) (1988). Nor can mutual funds readily issue senior securities to enhance absolute size, and hence the size of its holding of any single company. 1940 Act, § 18(a), 15 U.S.C. § 80a-18(a) (1988).

45. 1940 Act, § 2(a)(3), 15 U.S.C. § 80a-2(a)(3) (1988); 17 C.F.R. 270.17a-6 (1990).

not sell securities to the affiliate industrial company without an SEC exemptive order. Moreover, if the mutual fund wanted to assert control jointly with any affiliate—defined as any company also owning 5% of a portfolio company—it would need prior SEC approval.[46] The rule thereby discourages financial networks.

C. *Insurance Companies*

About twenty-five years ago, an historian of the insurance industry wrote:

> [Insurance companies are] at the highest level of the nation's business structure. If size counts, and money talks, they should be among the most potent institutions of this society. Yet the large life insurance companies play a curiously limited role in American life. [After fifty years of prohibition on stock ownership, they finally] control increasing amounts of corporate stock, but they do not systematically and purposefully use their voting strength. . . . In many ways, they are giants without power.[47]

In 1906, New York prohibited life insurance companies from buying stock.[48] The prohibition affected most insurance companies, since more than half of insurance assets were in New York insurers.[49] In 1951, a small wedge opened: 3% of the company's assets could go into stock.[50] Today 20% of a life insurer's assets, or one-half of its surplus, can go into stock.[51]

But even today insurers cannot take influential blocks; New York life insurers cannot put more than 2% of the insurance company's assets into the stock of any single issuer,[52] and property and casualty in-

46. 1940 Act, § 17(a)(1)–(2), 15 U.S.C. § 80a-17(a)(1)–(2) (1988). There are some exceptions. See id., § 17(b), 15 U.S.C. § 80a-17(b) (1988).

47. M. Keller, The Life Insurance Enterprise, 1885–1910: A Study in the Limits of Corporate Power ix (1963).

48. Act of Apr. 27, 1906, ch. 326, 1906 N.Y. Laws 763, 797.

49. At the turn of the century, common stocks were an increasing part of large insurer's portfolios. M. Keller, supra note 47, at 129. Prudent person rules also restrained insurers from heavy investment in common stock.

50. More precisely, the lesser of 3% of assets or one-third of surplus could go into common stock; investment in a particular company was limited to 2% of the portfolio company's stock and one-tenth of 1% of the insurer's assets. Act of Mar. 31, 1951, ch. 400, § 5, 1951 N.Y. Laws 1065, 1070. In 1951, New York law governed 85% of the insurance industry's assets. Bell & Fraine, Legal Framework, Trends, and Developments in Investment Practices of Life Insurance Companies, 17 Law & Contemp. Probs. 45, 46 (1952).

51. N.Y. Ins. Law § 1405(a)(6), (8) (McKinney 1985 & Supp. 1990).

52. Id. §§ 1405(a)(6)(i), 1705(a)(1)–(2). In the 1980s, New York expanded the permissible activities of life insurer subsidiaries. But portfolio rules still limit them: a subsidiary's goodwill is carved out from coverage tests (id. §§ 1302(a)(1), 1414(f)), no more than 2% of a life insurer's assets can go into any subsidiary, and no more than 5% of a life insurer's assets can go into non-New York subsidiaries. (Another 5% can go into New York subsidiaries.) Ownership of as little as 5%+ of the portfolio company could

surers cannot control a noninsurance company.[53] Although the state of incorporation sets the major rules in corporate law, the state where the policy is sold sets insurance law. State insurance law has two implications here. First, reincorporating an insurer in a small state with more favorable rules does little good, since the small state has few buyers of the insurance. Second, insurers are often governed by several states and insurance companies must comply with the most restrictive regulation.[54] New York law governs 58% of the life insurance industry's assets and 82% of the property and casualty industry's assets.[55] And other states have similar rules. California, Illinois, and Texas prohibit life insurers from investing more than 10% of the insurer's capital and surplus in any single company.[56] Approximately forty states limit stock to between 2% and 25% of the insurer's assets.[57]

D. *Pension Funds*

Pension funds are the newest, least regulated of the financial institutions. Although they have fewer assets under their control than banks and insurers, a large portion is in common stock. Nevertheless, the structure of pension funds inhibits them from acting as monitors.

Pension funds are themselves fragmented; each company typically sets up its own fund, often giving money to several managers, who re-

---

trigger classification as a subsidiary, thereby triggering the goodwill carve-out and the overall 5% limit on deployment of the life insurer's assets. Id. § 107(a)(40). And finally, networking with banks is limited, since insurance companies cannot own banks. Id. § 1701(a). But since it is at least *possible* to take control now, insurance companies might emerge from their historical passivity.

Even if law did not restrict life insurers' investments, they would prefer debt to equity. With their payment obligations actuarially fixed, insurers would presumably prefer debt so that their investment returns track their obligations.

53. Id. §§ 107(a)(40), 1403(c), 1404(a)(13)(B)(i) (no more than 5% of portfolio company's voting stock), 1407(a)(4), 1600–12 (only insurance subsidiaries).

Three prominent investors, Laurence Tisch, Saul Steinberg, and Warren Buffett, are associated with insurance companies and often take control positions. How, given New York's restrictions? Tisch and Steinberg do not funnel control investments through their insurance company, but use a holding company. Buffett is as unusual in his organizational structure as he is in his investment success. His Nebraska-based insurance companies make large stock investments, but apparently do not do business in New York; they obtained a change in Nebraska's portfolio rules to allow concentrated investments. Neb. Rev. Stat. § 44-311.04 (1988).

54. See N.Y. Ins. Law § 1413 (McKinney 1985 & Supp. 1990) (non-New York insurers must substantially comply with New York law if the insurer wishes to sell policies to New Yorkers). New York also became the model state for insurance company investment regulation. M. Keller, supra note 47, at 121–22.

55. The New York-governed statistic came from the Bureau of Research of the New York Insurance Department. Aggregate assets came from A.M. Best's information department.

56. Cal. Ins. Code §§ 1198, 1199 (West 1972); Ill. Ann. Stat., ch. 73, § 737.12(a)(c) (Smith-Hurd Supp. 1990); Tex. Ins. Code Ann. § 3.39.C.3 (Vernon 1981).

57. McCown & Martinie, State Regulation of Life Insurance Companies, 27 A. Life Ins. Couns. Proc. 8 (1988).

ceive money from several companies. Since ERISA (the Employee Retirement Income Security Act of 1974) generally requires each fund to be diversified,[58] there is little room for an influential position in an operating company. ERISA allows deviation from diversification only if "*clearly* prudent not [to minimize] the risk of large losses."[59]

Prudence is not what a business school graduate might first expect—maximization of net present value, with due regard to risk. Commentators suggest that the rule looks to prevailing investment practices, to the average, but with a substantial conservative drag: preservation of principal, even in the face of reduced return, is critical. Innovation risks liability.[60] While financial economists tell us that just about all of the possible diversification comes with the first sixteen stocks,[61] fund managers expect diversification to require investment in hundreds of issuers.

Onto this baseline of average opinion, tilting toward safety, ERISA enhances the standard of care for plan operators to that of an expert: they must act "with the care, skill, prudence, and diligence . . . that a prudent man acting in a like capacity and familiar with such matters would use in the conduct of an enterprise of a like character and with like aims."[62] As such, a plan operator could not get very far in front of the pension manager crowd. Pension managers who took seats on the boards of portfolio companies would run the risk that their actions would be judged in a lawsuit by beneficiaries not by the low-level scrutiny of the business judgment rule, but by ERISA's higher standard of care.[63]

Of greater significance is the control that a plan sponsor's management has over the investment managers of the pension fund. Senior managers hire the people who run the company's pension. Pension managers who took an active role in overseeing the operating managers of another company could expect to incur the ire of their own company's senior managers.[64] The senior managers' control of their com-

58. ERISA § 404, 29 U.S.C. § 1404 (1988).

59. ERISA § 104(1)(C), 29 U.S.C. § 1104(1)(c) (1988) (emphasis added).

60. B. Longstreth, Modern Investment Management and the Prudent Man Rule 21, 29, 39–40 (1986).

61. See J. Lorie, P. Dodd & M. Kimpton, The Stock Market: Theories and Evidence 85 (2d ed. 1985).

62. ERISA § 104(1)(B), 29 U.S.C. § 1104(1)(B) (1988).

63. See B. Krikorian, Fiduciary Standards in Pension and Trust Fund Management 290–91 (1989).

64. See Senate Subcomm. on Oversight of Government Management of the Comm. on Governmental Affairs, The Department of Labor's Enforcement of the ERISA, S. Rep. No. 144, 99th Cong., 1st Sess. 53–58 (1986); Pound, Proxy Contests and the Efficiency of Shareholder Oversight, 20 J. Fin. Econ. 237, 242–44 (1988). That ire might come directly or through politics. A business-labor task force, chaired by a leading member of the New York bar, recently proposed prohibiting New York *public* pension systems from financing hostile takeovers. White, Panel Seeks to Curb New York State Funds, Wall St. J., June 22, 1989, at C1, col. 3.

pany's pension managers limits the ability of private pension funds to control companies.

Thus, the one institution that is substantially unregulated in its ability to invest in large blocks of equity securities is controlled by operating company managers. This confluence might not be accidental. I suggest in Part III that some restrictions that stopped banks, insurance companies, and mutual funds from influencing operating companies arose and persisted because of a populist, anti-Wall Street sensibility that allied with the interests of small banks and industrial managers. Pension funds are not likely to be the target of either political interest: they are not directly connected with Wall Street, but are for the benefit of employees. And since managers control their company-sponsored pensions, private pensions do not pose a direct threat to operating company managers.

E. *Joint Ventures and General Restrictions on Control*

Despite these legal roadblocks, I suspect some financial institutions determined to control or influence an industrial company could acquire a large block. True, banks could not. True, diversified mutual funds can devote only a portion of their assets to a single company, but 25% of a large mutual fund is a lot, even 2% of a huge New York-regulated insurance company's assets might be enough, and ERISA allows deviation from diversification when clearly prudent. And financial institutions could form joint ventures to manage the ownership. The SEC once concluded that for many large companies, a *group* of institutions owned enough stock to put together an influential block if they acted jointly.[65]

However, four problems would afflict such joint ventures. First, not all organizational forms succeed. Second, legal restrictions on joint activity and control make many actions futile or costly. Third, institutions fear that their control would be publicized and criticized, and induce a reaction of increased regulation. Fourth, some financial institutions expect to make profits by trading; the securities laws inhibit trading by large blockholders who manage.

1. *Organizational Fragility.* — Despite much study of organizational forms, we do not fully understand why some work, and others fail.[66] Joint action has costs. Coordination among institutionally separate owners would be necessary; mistrust among several players might arise; and agency problems might not be controllable at low enough cost. When the costs of joint action are too high, joint monitoring fails.

65. SEC, Institutional Investor Study Report, H. Doc. No. 64, 92d Cong., 1st Sess., pt. 5, at 2561 (1971).

66. Cf. R. Coase, The Firm, the Market, and the Law 30–31 (1988) (choice of economic institutions matters because transactions costs vary among different forms of organization). When the costs of control are raised, even if not by much, a substitute institutional form takes over. See infra Part IV.B.

2. *Regulatory Costs.*

a. *Sections 13 and 14 of the Securities Exchange Act of 1934: Controlling Persons.* — When a 5% shareholder group is formed, the Securities Exchange Act of 1934 requires that the group make a public filing, outlining the group's plans and revealing its ownership and sources of financing.[67] Were it only a single piece of paper that had to be filed, the requirement would be a limited deterrent. But filings often require information that the institution wishes to keep confidential, sometimes require a statement of intention when the plans are vague (the institution wants to talk with other institutions *to form* a plan of action), and have been the basis for nasty litigation in the takeover wars as target firm managers seek to wear down the morale of those who would assert control. Institutional investors avoid that kind of litigation and publicity.[68] They seek to avoid conflict and routinize administration.

Group formation requires communication. But if an institution contacted enough other institutions, the communications would be deemed a proxy solicitation and would have to proceed under section 14 of the 1934 Act.[69] Filings would have to be made; those contacted must be given the information specified in schedule 14A.[70] The securities acts also trigger liability of controlling persons.[71] Groups that control could be liable for the misdeeds of the controlled portfolio company.

b. *Short-Swing Profit Liability.* — The control group probably would also be liable for profits made on trades of stock held six months or less, regardless of whether the profits were made on material inside information.[72] A control group filing a schedule 13D would be subject to section 16(b).[73]

67. Rules 13d-1, -5(b)(1), 17 C.F.R. § 240.13d-1, -5(b)(1) (1990). Institutional investors are ordinarily allowed to file fewer papers, less frequently, but *not* if they intend to influence control of the issuer. Rules 13d-1(b)(1), -5(b)(2), 17 C.F.R. § 240.13d-1(b)(1), -5(b)(2) (1990). Conard and Black critique these control rules as applied to institutional investors. Conard, Beyond Managerialism: Investor Capitalism?, 22 U. Mich. J.L. Ref. 117, 162 (1988); Black, Shareholder Passivity Re-Examined, 89 Mich. L. Rev. 521 (1990) (forthcoming); cf. 1940 Act Hearings, supra note 31, at 510–11 (directors of one mutual fund could not, in proposed mutual fund bill, be directors of another mutual fund because in combination the group might control an industrial company).

68. See Conard, supra note 67, at 162.

69. Rule 14a-1(l), 17 C.F.R. § 240.14a-1(l) (1990). This rule dates back to the SEC's early structuring of the proxy rules under the 1934 Act. SEC Release No. 3347 (1942).

70. Rules 14a-2(b)(1), (a), 17 C.F.R. § 240.14a-2(b)(1), -3(a) (1990).

71. Securities Act of 1933, § 15, 15 U.S.C. § 77o (1988); Securities Exchange Act of 1934, § 20, 15 U.S.C. § 78t (1988).

72. Securities Exchange Act of 1934, § 16, 15 U.S.C. § 78p (1988); cf. Feder v. Martin Marietta Corp., 406 F.2d 260 (2d Cir. 1969) (deputized director triggers principal's 16(b) liability), cert. denied, 396 U.S. 1036 (1970).

73. The SEC wants this requirement explicit. Exchange Act Release Nos. 34-26333, 35-24768, IC-16669, 26,333, 42 SEC Dock. 464, 471 (1988); see Exchange Act Release No. 18,113, 23 SEC Dock. 856, 857 (1981).

If an investor is certain that it will be a long-run player with the portfolio company, then section 16(b) might seem unimportant. But as a member of the group, 16(b) presents a problem. Nasty questions would arise if another member sells within six months of one group member's purchase. Does that trigger 16(b) liability? Of the group? Or of the seller only? Even if the seller had less than 10%, but the group had more than 10%?

Also, institutions must consider their relative advantage. Institutions often believe they can get word of bad news about a portfolio company before individuals do. A group or single institution with 16(b) and 10b-5 insider trading responsibilities would have to forego that advantage. Institutional investors in general, and mutual funds in particular, do not want to be "locked in" to any investment; if they took a big block, 16(b) would lock them in.

When an investor or group controls a portfolio company, its resales of the security require registration or an exemption under the 1933 Act. The expense and inconvenience of registration is one more reason to avoid control. The combination of trading restrictions and registration requirements may be decisive for many financial institutions. An open-end mutual fund in particular must be ready to redeem shares immediately; the cost of legally-inspired illiquidity may be too great for the mutual fund to bear.[74]

3. *Fear*. — Of equal consequence is the institutional investors' historical *fear* of greater political controls and their social view that institutional control of management was improper. Although difficult to document, institutional investors have considered joint action to affect management and, I understand, an important consideration militating against joint action was fear that political regulation would follow. Some institutional investors believe not only that regulation may follow, but that joint action is already illegal.[75]

The SEC concluded in its institutional investor study that:

> [I]nstitutions appear to believe that participation may be illegal or unethical. . . . The concern may [really] be political; that laws may be enacted or regulation imposed out of fear of financial power that would inhibit their existing relative invest-

74. See Symposium, Mutual Funds as Investors of Large Pools of Money, 115 U. Pa. L. Rev. 669, 677–78 (1967) (statement by Fred E. Brown, President of Broad Street Investing Corp.).

75. The director of the Division of Investment for the state of New Jersey and co-chair of the Council of Institutional Investors said:

> Observors . . . speculate on whether a handful of large investors might act in collusion in order to control corporations. I believe that, under existing state and federal law, such collusion is illegal. . . . [A]s fiduciaries for the funds under their supervision, institutional investors cannot delegate that responsibility to any other group or individual.

Machold, The American Corporation and the Institutional Investor: Are There Lessons From Abroad?, 3 Colum. Bus. L. Rev. 751, 757 (1988).

> ment freedom. . . . Institutions are particularly sensitive to . . . joint participation by a group of institutions with common objectives. Existing antitrust laws and the 1968 tender offer provisions in the Exchange Act appear to have the effect of impeding frank discussion of concerted action by institutions, if not of precluding such action.[76]

An official of CREF (the College Retirement Equities Fund, a huge investor in the stock market) said he felt

> perfectly confident that some day I will be sitting in the witness chair before a Congressional committee defending the record of our fund, as to portfolio company relations. [If we were too active, it might be] Wright Patman . . . attacking us for abusing our position of power by the use of excessive influence.[77]

Mutual funds held the decisive votes in the 1967 proxy fight to control MGM. Senator Sparkman, chairman of the Senate Banking Committee, asked the undecided funds what their policy was in proxy contests, to side with management or not. One fund announced that it would vote for management. Sparkman pointedly omitted that fund from his inquiry. The mutual fund industry viewed Sparkman as threatening restrictive legislation if they voted against management. One of the undecided funds, unable to sell at an attractive price soon enough, tilted the balance by voting with management.[78]

Institutions typically use the "Wall Street Rule": either vote with management or, if unhappy, sell. The SEC attributed the Wall Street Rule to the institutions' sense that they *ought* to make only investment decisions and "an effort to [influence management] would subject them to criticism."[79] The SEC left unclear from whom that criticism would come. It could come from the institution's employer, from the portfolio company, or from political and regulatory actors. It could also come from peers, critical of the "socially improper" control activities.

Fear of regulation should be analyzed. A normal economic prediction would be that atomized institutions would take the plunge, *if it were immediately profitable*, and let the regulation come later. The costs would be borne by all, the benefits appropriated by the first mover. But, the actor's *own* expected costs of "over"-regulation might be high enough to deter action. And monitoring would have large start-up costs because the monitor would have to build a new organizational structure.

---

76. SEC, Institutional Investor Study Report, supra note 65, at 2760.

77. Note, Mutual Funds, Portfolio Companies and the Small Investor: The Role of Institutional Influence, Colum. J.L. & Soc. Probs., Aug. 1969, at 69, 80–81.

78. The Battle, Not the War, Forbes, Mar. 15, 1967, at 25, 25–27; The Senators, the Funds, and the Law, Fortune, May 1967, at 152, 152–53; Sen. Sparkman Polls Mutual Funds Holding MGM Stock to Learn Proxy-Fight Policies, Wall St. J., Jan. 19, 1967, at 3, cols. 2–3.

79. SEC, Institutional Investor Study Report, supra note 65, at 125 (summary volume).

The short-run profit might not exceed the start-up costs, and the institution might well believe that in the long-run regulation would kill the financial monitoring process anyway.

4. *Trading and Monitoring.* — Diversification requirements dampen influence. Peter Lynch successfully managed the $11 billion Magellan Fund, a diversified mutual fund. Imagine his organizational problem if he had wanted to take a few controlling positions. Three-quarters of the portfolio could not have been used for control under the 1940 Act's restrictions (one-half of the portfolio under the tax code). Excellent stock pickers for the noncontrol part of the portfolio would not be enough. The fund's managers would have had to acquire *another* skill, in monitoring, to manage the quarter of the portfolio devoted to control. Lynch would have needed to split expertise, but the two skills and cultures may not match.

The diversification requirements would also have denied him other means of influence. When Carl Icahn takes a 13% position in USX Corporation, he obtains power and influence from two sources: his actual stock position itself plus the threat that he will increase it and oust management. That threat entitles him at least to have dinner on a regular basis with the USX chairman. Peter Lynch could not have made that threat. Indeed, when Lynch recently joined a public firm's board (before resigning from Magellan), the mutual fund he managed divested itself of the company's stock.[80]

F. *Creditors in Control*

A creditor in control will be subject in bankruptcy to subordination of its loans: it will be paid last, which often means not paid at all. The doctrinal standard for subordination in bankruptcy—control accompanied by action solely for the benefit of the creditor, not the enterprise—seems innocuous, but, fearing the doctrine's application to murky fact settings, creditors shy away from control.[81] And bankruptcy is not a sine qua non of such control liability. Bankers fear liability to a controlled solvent firm.[82] Accordingly, even if banks could overcome diversification rules for their discretionary trust funds and make control investments,[83] they would fear the effect of control on their commercial loans to the same company. Control might also create RICO liability or veil-piercing liability for the general debts of the controlled entity.

80. Cowan, A Savvy Outsider Ventures Inside, N.Y. Times, Aug. 3, 1989, at D8, col. 3.

81. See Douglas-Hamilton, Creditor Liabilities Resulting from Improper Interference with the Management of a Financially Troubled Debtor, 31 Bus. Law. 343, 365 (1975); Taylor v. Standard Gas & Elec. Co., 306 U.S. 307 (1939).

82. See State Nat'l Bank of El Paso v. Farah Mfg. Co., 678 S.W.2d 661 (Tex. Ct. App. 1984).

83. See supra text accompanying notes 24–26.

G. *Conclusion: The Uneasy Accommodation*

The conclusion of all this is that legal decisions deeply influenced corporate structure. Some influence was direct: prohibitions on banks and bank holding companies—the institutional players with half of the money—from owning and controlling, prohibitions on insurance companies from owning stock for a half-century and now limiting their ownership, and tax penalties on mutual funds owning control blocks. And some influence was indirect: (1) fragmented investors talking to one another must act through the SEC's proxy machinery; (2) schedules have to be filed with the SEC; (3) groups that own 10% or more of an industrial company's stock risk imposition of 16(b) liability, forcing disgorgement of any short-swing profits; and (4) an institution wishing to obtain influence and control will be subject to enhanced duties and liabilities.

Just as important as these prohibitions and costs are social constraints and *fear*: fear that a successful effort at control will trigger a political reaction. If the political system will turn on the controllers anyway—and worse yet, if control would risk overregulation in response—then those who might overcome the legal obstacles could decline the added risk of political reaction. Social constraints—the view that control by institutional investors is improper—also have a role. These social constraints may themselves be the result of political and legal conditioning.

Furthermore, when the Glass-Steagall Act and the 1940 Act severed financial institutions from one another, the law eliminated an easy coordinating link. Influence on operating companies could have come through internal coordination in a financial institution that would (1) underwrite the industrial company's securities, (2) own a big block of its stock directly, (3) own a big block of stock indirectly through an affiliated commercial bank's trust department, (4) own stock through a sponsored mutual fund, (5) own stock through an affiliated life insurance company, and (6) also own stock in a pool of pension fund assets managed by the financial institution. Such financial supermarkets are impossible to build in the United States.

That nexus of relationships does exist in Japan and Germany; elements of that nexus appeared in the banking networks of J.P. Morgan, Chase, and National City during the beginning of this century.[84] Indeed, an internal network might function better than an external network of several financial institutions talking to one another, or acting jointly through a leveraged buyout fund. Monitoring requires staff and specialized expertise; when the institutions fragment, they lose scale economies of staff and expertise.

Whether these internal networks are good or bad is worthy of discussion: the networks could siphon resources for banker profit and still

84. See G. Edwards, The Evolution of Finance Capitalism 171 (1938).

fail to monitor managers effectively. Or, the networks could represent politically intolerable concentrations of economic power. But the point here is not to evaluate the networks. The point is that politics either makes them costly or prohibits them.

Hence, the first step in my argument is that portfolio rules guide the uneasy relationship between financial institutions and industrial companies: financial institutions can shuttle capital in and out of industrial companies, but rarely can they exercise controlling influence.

III. Elements of a Political Theory

The second step in my argument is that these portfolio rules are not solely the result of political drift or public-spirited laws; behind them lies an array of political forces that helped determine and maintain them. Public choice theory helps explain the ownership structure of the public corporation. There were winners in fragmenting financial institutions. These winners had a large voice in Congress and their goals matched public opinion.

Public choice is about politicians making decisions. Politicians advance their careers, their ideologies, their chance to win the next election by the decisions they make. Popular ideology made it easy for politicians to fragment financial institutions; if the politician believed that was the best result, the voters would impose no penalty. Interest groups also pressured politicians to fragment financial institutions.

The simplified political picture I shall use is of politics as the interplay between selfish economic interests and ideology on the playing field of the nation's institutions. Policy choices depend on ideology and interest group power, each of which is impeded or enhanced by existing political institutions. American federalism magnified the power of fragmented financial institutions; fragmented financial institutions did not want to compete with large, powerful financial institutions; politics helped small financial institutions maintain themselves as winners. Neither interest group power nor ideology alone appears strong enough to have fragmented ownership patterns. Together they achieved financial fragmentation.

Ideology is not central in the public choice stories about financial rules. This is understandable, but incorrect. Ideology—the opinions of average people without a direct economic stake in the political outcome—*is* often irrelevant in politics. People are confused and uninterested; those with opinions have differing, weakly-held opinions that often cancel each other out. Politicians obviously want votes and ideologies can influence votes, but when the political issue at hand evokes cross-cutting ideological preferences, confusion, and disinterest, politicians can safely ignore ideology. The implicit public choice assumption that ideology doesn't count, or doesn't count much, is usually correct. But when the broad mass of average people have *even a weak preference, and that preference is the same* for most people, then ideology does matter.

For fragmenting financial institutions, broad public preferences mattered.

Rather than tell the story chronologically, and repetitively recite the political elements behind each restriction, I shall tell it abstractly, separately discussing each element of financial politics. To understand why we have fragmented finance, legislative history is not enough. We must also understand why the laws once passed have remained stable, for a half-century in many cases, for a century in others. Again, ideology and interest group power help explain some of the stability. Even if populist ideology fully explains passage of a financial law, interest group power (that is, for the most part, the preferences of Main Street's small financial institutions) is necessary to explain its stability. Odd as it may at first seem, "history" occurs after passage.

Several rules are public-spirited; several are sound policy, for which there is no good alternative. Surely, for example, we want some level of diversification for financial institutions in which the average citizen deposits her money. But even that does not eliminate the interest group explanation. If other means were found to effectuate the public interest and to allow for greater institutional influence in industry, opposition would still arise. Congress does not always adopt and maintain public-spirited rules; I suspect we need interest group support and popular opinion to explain even the soundest of the fragmenting rules. A wholesale effort to reverse the fragmentation could be expected to induce the opposition of managers and financial institutions with a stake in the status quo.

I do not claim to have the massive historical expertise needed to fully demonstrate every detail that follows; a few of the political stories could even be false without defeating my central thesis. These political and historical elements, some of which are familiar, have not yet been brought to bear on our understanding of the Berle-Means corporation. We cannot understand corporate finance through deductive economics alone; it is the result of multiple historical forces, of interest groups and populism colliding to restrict the terrain on which the corporation could evolve.

A. *The Political Story: Ideology*

1. *Populism.* — Americans prefer that no institution acquire significant power. Polling data show that Americans have an abiding distrust of concentrations of power, inside or outside of government.[85]

Anger at large institutions that seem to control the average person's life is one element of the political story. In recent decades anger against large institutions has been directed at government, particularly government in Washington. Earlier it was directed at financiers, partic-

85. S. Lipset & W. Schneider, The Confidence Gap: Business, Labor, and Government in the Public Mind 5–6 (rev. ed. 1987).

ularly Wall Street financiers, and big business. At the end of the nineteenth century the populist movement, which had farmers at its core, gave the impetus to passage of the Sherman Antitrust Act, formed its own political party, and captured the Democratic Party. It reflected deep, widespread sentiments.

Some people want small institutions, even if smallness does not benefit them other than to satisfy their sense that institutional scale should be small. Obviously some populists—small-town bankers, for example—directly benefited from fragmenting financial legislation. For these people, their populist ideology masked self-interest.

By populism, I mean more than the 1890s political movement. I mean to refer to a widespread attitude that large institutions and central accumulations of economic power are inherently undesirable and should be reduced, even if the concentration serves a useful productive function. That notion of populism is familiar to students of antitrust, and has been an important American ideology from nearly a century before the populists—first called Jeffersonians—to today.

This part of the political story will be familiar to many readers. But I suspect that its familiarity comes from antitrust, which has always had a large dose of politics and populism. Antitrust policy historically sought to reduce the scale of economic organization, to give small firms a comparative advantage, and to promote consumer choice and autonomy. Whether such political goals were always primary, and whether they should be submerged to new economic understandings of efficiency have been debated.[86] But no one denies that historically antitrust has a political component. Less well understood is that populism was also a basis for rules governing the range and size of financial institutions.

The populist image has become ingrained in our democratic tradition. In Frederick Jackson Turner's well-known "Frontier Thesis," American democracy was formed on the frontier:[87] "Democracy, in our traditions, has rich connections with the yeoman farmer (involving . . . freedom from the urban banker) . . . ."[88] Politicians evoked similar images. William Jennings Bryan stated, in his Cross of Gold speech: "[O]n the one side stand the . . . moneyed interests, aggregated wealth and capital, imperious, arrogant, compassionless. . . . On the other side stand an unnumbered throng."[89]

86. See R. Bork, The Antitrust Paradox: A Policy at War with Itself 15–71 (1978); H. Thorelli, The Federal Antitrust Policy 164–232 (1964); Blake & Jones, In Defense of Antitrust, 65 Colum. L. Rev. 377, 382–84, 394–400 (1965); Pitofsky, The Political Content of Antitrust, 127 U. Pa. L. Rev. 1051, 1051–75 (1979).

87. F. Turner, The Frontier in American History 30 (1920).

88. Elkins & McKitrick, A Meaning for Turner's Frontier, Part I: Democracy in the Old Northwest, 69 Pol. Sci. Q. 321, 324 (1954); see also F. McDonald, Novus Ordo Seclorum 130–31, 140 (1985) (founders other than Hamilton mistrusted banking, which unlike agriculture was unproductive).

89. R. Hofstadter, The Age of Reform: From Bryan to F.D.R. 65 (1955).

The 1890s' populists were not alone in loathing Wall Street; the Progressive movement did as well. Businesspeople preferred to be uncontrolled. Elites who were not associated with Wall Street or the emerging industries of the early twentieth century feared a Wall Street that would displace their power and status.[90] Senator Robert La Follette, in a prominent speech, argued that less than one hundred people controlled the nation's major businesses.[91] A market for capital was needed, said La Follette, but centralized banking concentrations must be opposed; small business must have a chance.[92] In 1911, Congress launched a widely followed investigation into the financial workings of Wall Street. The Pujo investigation, as it was called, seemed to confirm the popular judgment that the Morgan interests had their fingers everywhere in corporate America.[93]

At the core of the Progressive movement was the sense that individuals must be protected against the large institutions then forming in business and government; "the Progressive movement was the complaint of the unorganized against the consequences of organization."[94] The Populist and the Progressive movements, different in most respects, had in common a mistrust of the Eastern seaboard and its economic capital, Wall Street. Neither the heroic yeoman farmer, cultivating the land without economic complexities, nor the self-reliant small businessperson or white collar reformer had any use for a Wall Street stretching its tentacles out from the urban Eastern seaboard into the hinterland. An organized corporate/financial nexus exploited a divided and helpless citizenry of small farmers and businesspeople.[95] Such sentiments made it easy for politicians to pass laws to fragment the ownership interests of Wall Street.

The attitude persisted. Floor debates over the securities legislation of the 1930s show the House of Representatives applauding calls to limit the power of bankers:

> [T]he failure of many of our great industrial corporations is due to investment-banker management. . . . [B]anker directors living remote from the properties operated have no understanding of the . . . industry they direct. . . . The deplorable situation of many of our great industrial corporations is directly due to their banker management. . . . Congress must make it unlawful for any person to act as a director . . . who

90. Id. at 92–93.

91. Id. at 232.

92. See J. Weinstein, The Corporate Ideal in the Liberal State: 1900–1918, at 157–58 (1968).

93. See Money Trust Investigation: Hearings on H. Res. 429 & H. Res. 508 Before the Subcomm. of the House Comm. on Banking and Currency, 62d Cong., 3d Sess. 1011–20 (1913) [hereinafter Money Trust Investigation].

94. R. Hofstadter, supra note 89, at 214; see id. at 6–7, 10–11.

95. Id. at 20–21, 24, 65 & n.8; R. Wiebe, The Search For Order 52–53 (1967).

shall also be [an] investment-bank[er] . . . .[96]

And the Pecora hearings of the early 1930s showed bankers often were dominating directors of industrial companies. Control of business wealth was concentrated in too few hands.[97]

One major historian summarized these ideologies: "[T]he ordinary American's ideas of what . . . economic life ought to be like had long since taken form under the conditions of a preponderantly rural society with a broad diffusion of property and power. In that [rural] society large aggregates had played a minor role."[98] The average citizen expected to participate in both political and economic decisions.

Anchoring may play a role.[99] Fragmented economic groups, like farmers, dairy producers, or local bankers, can achieve large political influence.[100] But the popular mind disbelieves that many farmers are more powerful politically than one large bank or insurance company. The money center bank *looks* large, inhuman, inaccessible, not amenable to persuasion. Political restraints are therefore necessary.

"The great monopoly in this country," Woodrow Wilson said in a phrase that reverberates in financial populism, is "the money monopoly," whose control over capital had destroyed the "old variety and freedom and individual energy of development."[101] This phrase was the opening passage of Louis Brandeis' *Other People's Money*; members of Congress quoted it two decades later when the reformation of financial institutions began.[102] Although the evidence is that by the 1920s commercial power had already shifted to managers, who by then had many sources of capital, Wilson's attitude against the money trust apparently continued to be popular.[103]

Certainly the 1930s' Congress was hostile to "the concentration of control of the public's money" that the mutual funds facilitated.[104] Such control "serv[ed] no productive function[, served] merely to pervert the use of controlled companies [and was] detrimental to the public welfare."[105] The SEC's statement of purpose "declared that the national public interest . . . [is] adversely affected . . . when investment

96. 77 Cong. Rec. 2933–34 (1933) (remarks of Rep. Marland).

97. Pecora Report, supra note 30, at 385–91.

98. R. Hofstadter, supra note 89, at 215; see R. Wiebe, supra note 95, at 52, 54–55; Elkins & McKitrick, supra note 88, at 321.

99. See Tversky & Kohneman, Judgment Under Uncertainty: Heuristics and Biases, *in* Judgment Under Uncertainty: Heuristics and Biases 3, 14–18 (D. Kahneman, P. Slovic & A. Tversky eds. 1982).

100. See generally W. Jones, Corporate Size and Corporate Power: The History of a Myth, 1929–1979 (1987) (unpublished manuscript) (on file with Columbia Law Review).

101. E. Hawley, The New Deal and the Problem of Monopoly 304 (1966).

102. 77 Cong. Rec. 2929 (1933) (remarks of Rep. Pettengill); id. at 2932 (remarks of Rep. Marland).

103. E. Hawley, supra note 101, at 305.

104. Pecora Report, supra note 30, at 339.

105. Id. at 394; see id. at 363.

companies . . . attain . . . great size."[106]

Nor should this populist opinion be thought of as solely a historical phenomenon. During the 1955 bank holding company hearings, senators discussed concentration of economic power as a justification for regulation.[107] A decade later, the Patman Report began by reciting the Wilson money monopoly quotation and warned that banks, through their trust fund investments, have an "enormous potential power, for good or evil, over important parts of the nation's corporate structure."[108]

In the 1960s, the SEC staff cited classical antitrust imprecations against size to support its view that mutual fund control of portfolio companies was wrong.[109] In the 1980s, the chair of the Senate's Banking Committee, William Proxmire, in a comment that could have been populist, public-regarding, reflective of the power of small bankers, or some combination of all three, said: "The genius of American banking is competition. And the more competition, the better. You look at every other major country, and they only have a handful of banks that account for most of the business."[110] And populist sentiment helped fuel recent antitakeover legislation; managers are the happy beneficiaries of a public opinion that helps insulate them from takeover.[111]

2. *Political Investigations: Armstrong, Pujo, and Pecora*. — Repeated investigations into the activities of financial institutions and the thoughts of several opinion leaders show an ideology that ebbs and flows but has always been part of the American scene.

a. *Armstrong and the Insurance Companies.* — By the turn of the century, life insurance was an important component of middle class savings. A scandal and managerial dispute arose inside one insurance company, inducing the New York legislature to investigate the industry.

106. 1940 Act Hearings, supra note 31, at 2.

107. Control of Bank Holding Companies: Hearings Before a Subcomm. of the Senate Comm. on Banking and Currency, 84th Cong., 1st Sess. 98 (1955) (comments of Sen. Douglas) [hereinafter Senate Bank Holding Company Hearings].

108. Patman Report, supra note 25, at 3; see also id. at iv, 9 (recommending prohibition on trust department owning more than 10% of the stock of any company). The Comptroller adopted restrictive regulation a few years later. See supra text accompanying note 25.

109. Maseritz, The Investment Company: A Study of Influence and Control in the Major Industrial Corporations, 11 B.C. Indus. & Com. L. Rev. 1, 15 (1969) ("It is possible, because of its indirect social or moral effect, to prefer a system of small producers . . . to one in which the great mass of those engaged must accept the direction of a few. [G]reat industrial consolidations are inherently undesirable, regardless of their economic results.") (quoting United States v. Aluminum Co. of Am., 148 F.2d 416, 427–28 (2d Cir. 1945)).

110. Naylor, Proxmire to Seek Bank Size Limits, Am. Banker, Dec. 10, 1986, at 1.

111. See Romano, The Political Economy of Takeover Statutes, 73 Va. L. Rev. 111, 121–22, 138–41 (1987); Ryngaert & Netter, Shareholder Wealth Effects of the Ohio Antitakeover Law, 4 J.L. Econ. & Org. 373, 376 (1988); Wayne, Takeovers Face New Obstacles, N.Y. Times, Apr. 19, 1990, at D1, col. 3.

The Armstrong investigation, named after its legislative chairman, revealed *sub rosa* political contributions and stoked popular flames of fear that the financial interests had too much influence.

The insurance companies' internal practices and political contributions triggered the inquiry. But the insurance companies were also condemned because their executives "thought of themselves more as financiers than as insurance [people]."[112] The Armstrong investigation's recommendation to prohibit stock ownership can be seen in context: eliminating the insurance companies' authority to make political contributions would reduce their political power, and eliminating their authority to own stock would reduce insurance companies' economic influence, confining them to insurance and keeping them out of finance.[113] New York's prohibition was adopted when half of the nation's insurance assets were in New York-regulated insurers, and it was widely copied by other states.[114]

Popular conclusions reached further: Insurance companies had "resources . . . so vast [that] their management, if permitted to grow unrestrained, will soon become a serious menace to the community."[115] Insurance commissioners were told at their annual convention that "life [insurance] companies are becoming vast financial corporations, and may become a source of danger to the commonwealth by reason of the vast money power lodged in the hands of a few men."[116] The Massachusetts commissioner feared that some bold manipulator would control a life insurer's assets and use that control to "financ[e] large enterprise and promot[e] all kinds of corporate consolidations."[117] All these fears arose although at the time insurers did not own much common stock. They mostly made mortgages, lent money, and bought corporate bonds. Only the very largest of the insurers had as much as 12% of their investments in stock.[118]

b. *Pujo.* — The eight-month 1912 Congressional investigation was said to have "frightened the nation with its awesome, if inconclusive statistics on the power of Wall Street over the nation's economy. [T]he

112. M. Keller, supra note 47, at 253.

113. N.Y. Assembly Doc. No. 41, Joint Comm. of the Senate and Assembly Appointed to Investigate the Affairs of Life Ins. Companies 381–88, 393 (1906) [hereinafter Hughes Report] (Charles Evans Hughes was chief counsel to the investigation). By owning stock in other companies, insurers faced two equally objectionable problems. Either they were minority shareholders subject to the risks of stock ownership and were at the mercy of the majority, or they took so much stock that they became controlling stockholders so that "the insurance corporation is not only engaged in a different enterprise, but directly undertakes its management." Id. at 393.

114. Act of Apr. 27, 1906, ch. 326, 1906 N.Y. Laws 763, 797; M. Keller, supra note 47, at 254–59 (reactions of other states); M. Pusey, I Charles Evans Hughes 140–68 (1951).

115. M. Keller, supra note 47, at 253–54.

116. Id. at 136.

117. Id.

118. Id. at 158–60.

nation was suitably frightened into realizing that reform of the banking system was urgent—presumably to bring Wall Street under control."[119] Counsel to the committee attacked J.P. Morgan for his bank's representation on corporate boards and for its hand in selecting managers.[120]

c. *The Pecora Hearings.* — The New Deal began with a seventeen-month investigation of banking and securities practices on Wall Street. The defensive tone of the bankers was set early. The second J.P. Morgan testified: "I consider the private banker a national asset *and not a national danger*. [Despite accusations to the contrary, the Wall Street banker has not] become too powerful. . . ."[121] But Ferdinand Pecora, counsel to the Senate Banking Committee for the hearings, later reflected the national mood: "[T]he terrific concentration of power in [bankers'] hands from many sources [*was*] *threatening*. . . . The bankers were neither [just] a national asset nor [just] a national danger—*they were both*."[122] Investment bankers' control over industrial companies was again denounced;[123] representation of banking interests on the boards of industrial companies perniciously magnified banker power.[124]

The Pecora hearings were a conduit for populist sentiment to punish Wall Street, presumably with legislation such as the Glass-Steagall Act and the Investment Company Act of 1940:

> The financial skulduggery so often translated to rural voters by Bryan and the Populists as "Wall Street's grip on the farmer" impelled many demands for punitive measures by Congressmen from agrarian districts. Western and southern Representatives were particularly insistent after the Pecora revelations that the transgressors be dealt with harshly.[125]

3. *Ideological Leaders and a Conceptual Framework for Political Restraints: Brandeis, Wilson, and Douglas.* — The Pujo investigation gathered data and concluded that a Wall Street money trust dominated industrial America. But historians believe that the investigation might not have influenced later legislation had Louis Brandeis not picked through the

119. G. Kolko, The Triumph of Conservatism 220 (1963).

120. Money Trust Investigation, supra note 93, at 1019–20.

121. Stock Exchange Practices: Hearings Before the Senate Comm. on Banking and Currency, 73d Cong., 1st Sess. 5–6 (1934) (emphasis added).

122. F. Pecora, Wall Street Under Oath: The Story of Our Modern Money Changers 6 (1939) (emphasis added).

123. Voting trusts, for example, were denounced because they were used "to dominate the management if [the trustees] thought it necessary." Stock Exchange Practices: Hearings Before the Senate Comm. on Banking and Currency, supra note 121, at 3836 (testimony of Harley Clarke, Chase Securities Corp.); see also F. Pecora, supra note 122, at 59, 208 (prominent investment banker agrees that voting trusts were "inventions of the devil"). Since shareholder control was unlikely, as Berle and Means were demonstrating, the alternative to banker control was managerial control. Neither bankers nor interrogator discussed this.

124. F. Pecora, supra note 122, at 37.

125. R. De Bedts, The New Deal's SEC: The Formative Years 196 (1964).

data and quickly published popular magazine articles and a book, providing both an ideology and a plan for action.[126] Brandeis wrote: "The dominant element in our financial oligarchy is the investment banker. Associated banks, trust companies and life insurance companies are his tools."[127] Return bankers to their proper role as middlemen and eliminate the interlocking of financial institutions; that would end the evils of the oligarchy.[128]

Woodrow Wilson believed small groups of people in large corporations made autocratic decisions, concentrating in their own hands the "resources, the choices, the opportunities, in brief, the power of thousands."[129] Moreover, trusts were growing in size and power. What if there arose a "combination of the combinations?" he asked. *Investment bankers* could or would organize the combination of the combinations. The "combination of the combinations" might act covertly and, due to its "community of interest," could be "more formidable than any conceivable single combination that dare appear in the open." Such a combination could buy up the political process, ending democracy. "If there are men in this country big enough to own the government of the United States, they are going to own it."[130] Since, as Wilson stated, investment bankers could organize the combination of the combinations that could subvert democracy, then, the conclusion is inexorable: democracy must strike first and end banker domination of the trusts. The idea of a preemptive strike was echoed by Brandeis: "We must," he said, "break the money trust or the money trust will break us."[131]

William O. Douglas had a pivotal role in the regulation of financial institutions, as commissioner and chair of the SEC in the 1930s. During his days as commissioner, the SEC proposed the Investment Company Act and formulated rules limiting joint action. Undoubtedly reflecting the concepts and prejudices of many during that crucial time, Douglas *wanted* to destroy any Wall Street control of Main Street:

> [T]he banker *will* [be] restricted to . . . either underwriting or selling. Insofar as management [and] formulation of industrial policies . . . are concerned, it is my belief that *the banker will be superseded*. The financial power which he has exercised in the past over such processes will pass into other hands.[132]

"Remote control by an inside few of these fundamental economic and

126. V. Carosso, supra note 13, at 639–40; see also F. Pecora, supra note 122, at 39 (favorable senatorial thoughts about *Other People's Money* during Pecora hearings).

127. L. Brandeis, supra note 18, at 3.

128. Id. at 3, 5, 47.

129. Wilson, The Lawyer and the Community, 192 N. Am. Rev. 612, 617–18 (1910); see also W. Diamond, The Economic Thought of Woodrow Wilson 67 (1943) (financiers, argued Wilson, control railroads and industry to detriment of the nation).

130. W. Wilson, The New Freedom 187, 286 (1913).

131. L. Brandeis, supra note 18, at 137.

132. W.O. Douglas, supra note 2, at 40–41 (emphasis added).

human matters is fatal," Douglas said. "There can be in our form of corporate and industrial organization no royalism which can long dictate or control these basic matters."[133] The power of Wall Street must be held at bay: "[F]inance moves into the zone of exploitation whenever it becomes the *master* rather than the faithful and loyal *servant* of investors and business. To make finance such a *servant* rather than a *master* becomes a central plank in any platform for reform."[134] Investigators of administrative activity in the 1930s concluded that the SEC, "[i]nstead of wreaking vengeance [for a discredited securities market], set out to restore legitimacy to Wall Street's essential function of channeling investment capital into enterprise."[135]

Moreover, Douglas thought that people who dominate financial markets have "tremendous power . . . . Such men become virtual governments in the power at their disposal. . . . [Sometimes it is] the dut[y] of government to police them, at times to break them up, to deter their further growth."[136] "The needs of a small Middle Western community are apt to be better served by a banker at the head of a small local bank than by the same banker at the head of the nation's biggest bank."[137]

In short, bankers should provide and direct the flow of capital, but not control the enterprise after the capital has flowed to it.[138] Douglas was not alone in this view among the key players at the 1930s SEC; its first chair, Joseph Kennedy, agreed.[139] And this view is not just historical. In 1980, the Senate Government Affairs Committee's staff examined corporate ownership and reported that "Congress [has been] concerned that the tremendous growth in securities held . . . by the larger banks, insurance companies, pension funds, and investment advisors might result in a concentration of economic power by a few institutional traders . . . *over the managements of the companies whose stock they held, and indeed over American industry itself.*"[140]

4. *Ideology: Public-Regarding Goals.* — Neither populist ideology nor interest group power explains everything; fragmentation had public-regarding justifications. The first key point here is that law helped deter-

133. Id. at 44.

134. Id. at 10.

135. McCraw, The Public and Private Spheres in Historical Perspective, *in* Public-Private Partnership 31, 81–82 (H. Brooks, L. Liebman & C. Schelling eds. 1984).

136. W.O. Douglas, supra note 2, at 15.

137. Id. at 14. Senator Carter Glass had similar thoughts. Bank involvement in securities diverted funds away from local businesses in need of credit. See Langevoort, Statutory Obsolescence and the Judicial Process: The Revisionist Role of the Courts in Federal Banking Regulation, 85 Mich. L. Rev. 672, 694 (1987).

138. W.O. Douglas, supra note 2, at 44–45.

139. See Carosso, Washington and Wall Street: The New Deal and Investment Bankers, 1933–1940, 44 Bus. Hist. Rev. 425, 444–45 (1970); Kennedy, Big Business, What Now?, The Saturday Evening Post, Jan. 16, 1937, at 10, 11.

140. Staff of Senate Comm. on Governmental Affairs, 96th Cong., 2d Sess., Structure of Corporate Concentration: Institutional Shareholders and Interlocking Directorates Among Major U.S. Corporations 2 (Comm. Print 1980) (emphasis added).

mine corporate structure. The next step is that popular opinion made it easy for politicians to fragment financial institutions, whether politicians' actions were public-spirited or due to interest group pressures.

What were the public-spirited rationales?

a. *Protecting Depositors, Policyholders, and Mutual Fund Shareholders.* — In the nineteenth century, some states found the mixture of banking and commerce too risky for their banks.[141] Similarly, sponsors of Glass-Steagall argued that speculative stock activities misused commercial bank resources.[142] After 1933, a bank failure drains the government's insurance fund. Keeping banks out of risky assets such as common stocks seemed to reduce the riskiness of their investments, thereby reducing the chance of bank failure. Similar considerations of policyholder protection and ease of government supervision justify limiting insurance company investment in stocks.

As for mutual funds, Congress feared unsophisticated investors would invest in mutual funds expecting diversification, but be unable to evaluate the portfolio. The SEC testified that a mutual fund's *only* positive function was to provide diversification; any extension risked thievery.[143] Keeping mutual fund managers out of controlling positions kept them free from conflicts of interests. The funds' investment adviser, often an investment bank, would use the control exerted by the mutual fund to obtain securities underwriting business from the controlled portfolio company.[144]

b. *Conflicts of Interest, Tying.* — Elimination of the potential for conflicts of interest was another public-spirited justification for fragmentation. Banks with nonbanking affiliates would be difficult to examine, and problem assets could be shunted between bank and operating company.[145] Conflicts of interest and monopoly power could be reduced by restricting the activities of bank affiliates. Banks that owned industrial enterprises might tie their loans to purchases of stock from the industrial company, as occurs in Germany where banks own stock and often expect their companies to be borrowers. Such economic dictates were to be prohibited in the United States. And, since prohibiting the

141. See, e.g., B. Hammond, supra note 20, at 153–55; E. Symons & J. White, Banking Law: Teaching Materials 8–11, 33–34 (2d ed. 1984).

142. See, e.g., S. Rep. No. 77, 73d Cong., 1st Sess. 1, 8–12 (1933); 75 Cong. Rec. 9904–06 (1932) (remarks of Sen. Walcott); id. at 9910–11 (remarks of Sen. Bulkley). Bank affiliate speculation, said Senator Glass, had led to "unprecedented disaster which has caused this almost incurable depression." Id. at 9882–89, 9915 (remarks of Sen. Glass).

143. 1940 Act Hearings, supra note 31, at 131, 132 (statement of George Mathews, Member of the SEC); id. at 807 (reiteration by David Schenker, Chief Counsel, SEC Investment Trust Study).

144. See Pecora Report, supra note 30, at 333; 1940 Act Hearings, supra note 31, at 36; id. at 207 (statement of L.M.C. Smith, Associate Counsel, SEC Investment Trust Study).

145. See Senate Bank Holding Company Hearings, supra note 107, at 360 (statement of Rep. Multer).

practice might not stop implicit understandings, bank ownership of operating companies had to end.[146]

c. *Antitrust*. — Some politicians and the general public believed that monopoly capital restricted new ventures, and that the best way to open the bottlenecks was to eliminate banker control of industry. A handful of investment bankers controlled the spigots of finance. The market access objections could have been solved with other mechanisms, such as destroying financial ties not with *all* industry but just with *concentrated* industry. It might have been weak empirically, since American capital markets are usually seen as intensely competitive.

Historical evidence suggests that capital sources *were* concentrated at the turn of the century;[147] thereafter they dissipated, partly due to competition and partly due to the very legislation that is the subject of this Article. We can view antitrust, labor protection, and financial fragmentation as part of one large movement in American society to tame capital: through antitrust industrial monopolies would be shattered; through prohibitions on interlocking directors cartelization by banker coordination would be stymied; through labor law the range of profitable actions of capital would be limited; and through financial regulation the ties between those who gather capital and those who use capital would be frayed.

d. *Political Stability*. — Savvy social engineers might have had a strategic rationale for fragmenting finance. The social turmoil induced by pitting populist antibank sentiment against financial institutions that owned industry could have been too much for American politics to han-

146. See, e.g., id. at 64 (testimony of J.L. Robertson, member Fed. Reserve Board); id. at 66 (comments of Sen. Douglas) ("if there are not alternative sources of credit [the bank] can use [its] control of credit to get control over manufacturing, too."); id. at 106 (statement of W.J. Bryan, Indep. Bankers Ass'n of Am.) ("What chance does free enterprise have if people with ideas and ability cannot obtain capital with which to implement them?"). The populist fear of bank power is similar to this tying/economic opportunity perspective, but with a different vocabulary. Bank fragmentation might also be likened to the classical antitrust hostility towards vertical restraints. At first, few benefits were seen, so the practice was easy to condemn once some detriment was found, such as foreclosure or a threat to autonomy. Later, the vertical restraints story was seen to be more complicated.

During modern hearings on Bank Holding Company Act amendments, the Assistant Attorney General for Antitrust argued that restricting banks' nonbanking affiliations was necessary because banks had local monopolies (due to the government's chartering restrictions) that would expand when affiliates entered nonbanking markets. With vast financial resources banks could "become the centers of much larger industrial-commercial groups, [as they are in] Japan and a number of other countries." Bank Holding Company Act Amendments: Hearings Before the House Comm. on Banking and Currency, 91st Cong., 1st Sess. 91, 93 (1969) (testimony of Richard McLaren, Assistant Att'y Gen. for Antitrust). Accordingly, their nonbanking activities had to be restricted.

147. See J.B. De Long, How Did J.P. Morgan's Men Add Value?: A Historical Perspective on Financial Capitalism 2 (Nat'l Bureau of Econ. Res. Working Paper No. 3426, 1989).

dle.[148] By fragmenting finance, politicians moved issues of public ownership and class divisions off the political agenda. FDR himself said:

> It is time to . . . reverse that process of the concentration of power which has made most American citizens, once traditionally independent owners of their own businesses, helplessly dependent for their daily bread upon the favor of a very few, *who, by devices such as holding companies,* have taken for themselves unwarranted economic power. I am against private socialism of concentrated economic power as thoroughly as I am against government socialism. The one is equally as dangerous as the other; *and destruction of private socialism is utterly essential to avoid government socialism.*[149]

A prominent historical view is that at crucial times in American history, business interests became so powerful that a political counterweight had to arise. Before business could crush others in the economic system, politicians saved the nation from injustice by checking the business interests. The genius of American politics was, in this view, that business interests were checked, but not destroyed. First, it is said, Andrew Jackson rose to destroy the Second Bank of the United States, checking the crushing weight of eastern finance on the average American.[150] Then, Woodrow Wilson created a Federal Reserve System, taking power away from Morgan who had become the nation's de facto central banker.[151] And then, in the Great Depression, Franklin Roosevelt built an administrative structure as a counterweight to financial interests that were said to have brought on the Depression.[152] Certainly, leading politicians believed they were fighting for the country's soul against a Wall Street conspiracy. FDR wrote:

> The real truth . . . is, as you and I know, that a financial element in the larger centers has owned the Government ever since the days of Andrew Jackson—and I am not wholly excepting the administration of W[oodrow] W[ilson]. The coun-

148. See Blake & Jones, supra note 86, at 383 (weakening antitrust might create political backlash).

149. E. Hawley, supra note 101, at 281 (emphasis added).

150. A. Schlesinger, The Age of Jackson 97–114, 334–39, 505 (1945). But see B. Hammond, supra note 20, at 155 (attributing bank crisis to other forces).

151. A. Link, Woodrow Wilson and the Progressive Era, 1900–1917, at 45–53 (1954).

152. A. Schlesinger, The Age of Roosevelt: The Crisis of the Old Order, 1919–1933, at 289–90 (1957); A. Schlesinger, The Coming of the New Deal 489–91 (1959). These historical/economic interpretations seem at odds. In one view politicians are populists or tools of interest groups; in the other view politicians are heroic figures saving America from powerful business interests. But the two views can be reconciled for our purposes. In one vision, the social justice vision, right-hearted politicians save farmers and workers from the onslaught of capital. In the other vision, cynical politicians check capital to benefit favored groups such as small-town bankers. The *factual* story for each historical vision is roughly similar. The spin, the connotation, the sense of rightness, is what is variant. Such differences I will leave to the historians to settle, or to battle.

> try is going through a repetition of Jackson's fight with the Bank of the United States—*only on a far bigger and broader basis*.[153]

In the 1936 campaign, roughly contemporaneous with passage of the tax code that first disabled mutual funds from corporate control, Roosevelt denounced "economic royalists" who gathered "other people's money"—that phrase again—to impose a "new industrial dictatorship."[154] Roosevelt closed the campaign with a powerful speech: "[O]rganized money . . . hate[s] me. . . . I should like to have it said of my first Administration that [the forces of organized money] met their match. . . . [And] I should like to have it said of my second Administration that in it these forces met their master."[155]

Thus, one can see the historical bargain between the polity and financial institutions as this: unleashed capital, with disciplined control of the enterprise had to have a political counterweight. Either government would ultimately have to own companies directly or it would place strict public controls on them. Relations with workers, customers, and competitors would be regulated. The American choice was to reject intense regulation, and instead fragment the industrial market.[156] And we surely can see a pattern in American history: we have, at least in the rhetoric of antitrust, preferred industrial monopolies of small local producers to large central producers like Standard Oil or Alcoa; we have preferred a series of local banking monopolies to concentrated banking; and we have preferred to deny power over industrial operations to financiers, leaving that power in the hands of scattered managers.

Fragmentation of finance can thus be seen not as a stray piece of history but as a necessary part of American government and society. America has had a less regulated society than it could have had; certainly it is less regulated than other industrialized nations. Germany and Japan again come to mind. Regulation can take multiple forms. It can dictate the details of what can and cannot be done in the workplace under a labor regulation or a union rule. It can be in general governance mechanisms, such as German codetermination in which labor sits on the board of directors, right next to the bankers who control a large portion of the company's common stock. It can be in cultural understandings, such as those in the largest Japanese firms in which financial institutions have great influence and severe cultural norms restrain managers from failing to provide lifetime employment to most workers. Whether or not these institutional arrangements *must* be package deals we need not decide; suffice it to say that key actors—none could be

153. Letter from Roosevelt to Colonel House (Nov. 21, 1933), reprinted in W. Leuchtenburg, Franklin D. Roosevelt and the New Deal, at 80 (1963) (emphasis added).

154. Id. at 183–84.

155. Id. at 184.

156. Cf. Blake & Jones, supra note 86, at 382–83 (similar theme applied to antitrust).

more key in the 1930s than FDR—said they were necessary protections to the stability of American politics.

Once again I emphasize that I am not arguing that the American fragmentation result is necessarily wrongheaded; the sharp point is precisely that through politics America chose, perhaps wisely, to fragment financial institutions. That fragmentation induced, partly unintentionally, a shift in operating power from financial institutions to the managers of the largest corporations. Other countries have chosen (or accidentally evolved) to have power shared in the boardroom or to have severe restrictions on the range of acceptable actions by managers. The essential point is that the Berle-Means corporation is a product of American politics, not just American economics.

B. *The Political Story: Interest Groups*

I first sketched populist antibank sentiment for a reason. It is the backdrop to the interest group pressures for fragmentation. Popular opinion might not have been strong enough to generate and preserve fragmenting rules, but policy makers could see that fragmentation would foster plausibly public-spirited goals and interest groups could press their advantage. A politician who sought fragmentation, whether to implement public goals or to deliver to an interest group, would not meet public resistance.[157]

Interest group pressures were critical. Small financial institutions were the most important interest group militating for fragmenting finance. Small banks wanted to fragment large money-center institutions. Small businesses also wanted fragmentation, believing that small banks served them better than large ones.[158] These groups have had great weight in Congress.

Modern eyes search for managers and labor behind the passage of fragmenting legislation, as they can be found behind modern antitakeover legislation. While we see them here and there, their role in fragmenting finance at the time of legislative passage is pale. True, their interest is clear: managers do not want a financial boss. Managers forced to go to Wall Street for equity could be expected to prefer not to have institutional overseers. Sociologists say local business elites deeply resented their relative loss of economic power and status to out-

157. See Denzau & Munger, Legislators and Interest Groups: How Unorganized Interests Get Represented, 80 Am. Pol. Sci. Rev. 89, 91–92 (1986).

158. Cf. Langevoort, supra note 137, at 697 (popular theory was that bank involvement in stock channeled credit away from small business: "[i]f any special interest group was instrumental in [passage of the Glass-Steagall Act,] it was probably the smaller businesses and farmers (not surprisingly, [Senator] Glass' Virginia constituents) who considered the unavailability of credit at least partially responsible for their [Depression] woes").

siders.[159] New Deal legislation as a combination of attacks on Wall Street and pressures of organized industry is the picture one leading historian paints of the era.[160]

Perhaps historians one day will find plausible loose 1930s' support for fragmentation from managers, local controlling stockholders, who wanted equity capital without losing control to Wall Street, and labor. But whether or not such a coalition produced fragmentation, once fragmenting legislation passed, even if it passed without managers as necessary supporters, the *subsequent* stability of fragmentation probably has been due to managers as an interest group. Decades after passage, managers would oppose changes in fragmenting laws and would throw their weight in the way of change. When large financial institutions clash with managers, managers call upon politicians for aid, as they did when proxy contests heated up in the 1950s.[161] Managers appealed to politicians to raise the costs of proxy contests, the Senate held hearings, and the SEC responded by promulgating rules that pulled informal joint discussions among institutions into the proxy ambit. News reports showed managers' complaints getting a sympathetic response from journalists and politicians.[162] Modern political inquiry suggests that managers, sometimes allied with labor, are moving forces behind many antitakeover statutes.[163]

We might also search for labor behind the fragmenting legislation, a role labor has played in some modern antitakeover legislation. But for labor also, the modern interest group story is weak. How does labor benefit from weakening the ties that bind managers to sharehold-

159. See Lipset & Bendix, Social Status and Social Structure: A Re-examination of Data and Interpretations, 2 Brit. J. Soc. 230, 233 (1951).

160. E. Hawley, supra note 101, at 16.

161. See supra text accompanying note 78 (Sen. Sparkman bullies mutual funds into supporting incumbent management in proxy fight). Similarly, investment bankers have lobbied to slow down the erosion of Glass-Steagall's prohibitions on commercial bank involvement in securities underwriting. Bank market sharing could explain the *passage* of the legislation, as commentators argue, see Macey, Special Interest Groups Legislation and the Judicial Function: The Dilemma of Glass-Steagall, 33 Emory L.J. 1, 17–20 (1984). But even if interest groups do not explain *passage* of the legislation, interest politics contributed mightily to its *preservation*.

162. See, e.g., Stock Market Study (Corporate Proxy Contests): Hearings Before a Subcomm. of the Comm. on Banking and Currency on S. 879, 84th Cong., 1st Sess. pt. 3 (1955–1956); Dakin, Battle by Proxy: Henceforth New Ground Rules Will Govern These Contests, Barron's, Feb. 20, 1956, at 5; Coffin, Proxy Warfare May Provoke Tighter Government Rules, Nation's Bus., July 1955, at 32 ("stormy fights in the past two years [and] bruised contestants [have provoked a] Senate inquiry"); J. Pound, Proxy Voting and the SEC: Democratic Ideals Versus Market Efficiency 22 (1989) (unpublished manuscript) (on file with Columbia Law Review).

163. Romano, supra note 111, at 121–22, 138–41; Ryngaert & Netter, supra note 111, at 377–78 (Goodyear management's interest in passing Ohio antitakeover statute); Wayne, supra note 111 ("Pennsylvania business groups supporting the bill *are aligned with unions seeking to protect . . . their members* and local politicians worried about the impact of corporate takeovers on communities.") (emphasis added).

ers? Once workers are inside the system, once they have something akin to tenure, their interest, like that of managers, is *also* to loosen ties with capital. Capital could seek profits by getting highly motivated managers who seek innovation; managers might also obtain those higher profits by sweating their labor force. When law creates gaps in the responsiveness of managers to capital, then managers have less incentive to squeeze every penny of production out of labor.

Labor's principal representative in the 1930s' Senate, Robert Wagner, made this point: "In order that the strong may not take advantage of the weak, every group must be equally strong."[164] Since financial capital was strong and labor weak, law must fragment finance (via Glass-Steagall and the 1940 Act) and facilitate strengthening labor (via collective bargaining). Labor's representatives sought institutional financial fragmentation.[165]

One can see a historical sweep to this. Once a position is obtained, whether by the beneficiaries' own doing or as the incidental beneficiary of other political forces, the occupants of those positions seek through politics to maintain and extend that position. So one could expect to see managers and labor seeking to loosen the disciplinary restraints that capital would impose upon them. Or, more subtly and more realistically, laws that would loosen the control capital would have on managers and labor have survival properties; their repeal would be unpopular, and would lose the politician votes.[166] Those laws remain stable, shielding managers and workers from the raw and unpleasant consequences of an unrestrained market.

Small businesspeople are, like managers, politically influential. They have money and status and are spread among the states; dispersion with local power makes many in Congress responsive to their needs. Wall Street is geographically concentrated, and therefore is less likely to have the ear of many members of Congress. A well-known analogue to the local power of small businesspeople and managers is the power of savings and loan associations and the real estate lobby; they obtained beneficial legislation for decades.[167]

Small business representatives wanted to limit bank holding company control of business.[168] Retailers told the Senate: "Bank holding

164. W. Leuchtenburg, supra note 153, at 89; see id. at 109.

165. 1940 Act Hearings, supra note 31, at 333–37 (comments of Sen. Wagner).

166. This is one version of Karl Polanyi's famous thesis. K. Polanyi, The Great Transformation: The Political and Economic Origins of Our Time (1944).

167. See Senatorial Shills, Wall St. J., June 13, 1989, at A20, col. 1 (insolvent savings bank gets five influential Senators to intervene with regulators to slow shutdown).

168. Members of the National Federation of Independent Businesses (100,000 small and medium businesses) wished to "compel bank holding companies to get rid of nonbanking interests." They believed that "independent business prospers best when sources of financing are free, independent, local and many." See Senate Bank Holding Company Hearings, supra note 107, at 279 (letter of George Burger, Vice President, Nat'l Fed'n of Indep. Businesses).

companies, operated out of New York, cannot possibly know local conditions similar to the hometown independent banker."[169] Small bankers opposed allowing bank holding companies to control industry.[170]

This interest group effect need not reflect *conflict* between *operating* managers and *financial* managers. Financial managers themselves might have been happy to accept limitations. Monitoring is hard work; if all financial managers were precluded from the task, their job would be easier. Indeed the interest group effect can reflect conflict *among* financial institutions. Glass-Steagall's separation of investment from commercial banking has been explained as resulting from the power of: (a) investment bankers, who wanted to thwart commercial bankers, (b) commercial bankers, who wanted to thwart investment bankers, (c) small-town bankers, who wanted to thwart money-center bankers, and (d) upstart, transaction-oriented money-center investment bankers, who wanted to thwart established money-center investment bankers.[171] Indeed, once the legislation preventing financial institutions from taking influential blocks of stock is in place, the *regulated* could *themselves* resist easing of the regulation. Deregulation would allow competition on bases for which the incumbents lack an advantage.

C. *The Political Story: The Preexisting Institutions of Federalism, Congress, and the Bureaucracies*

American politics created elements of its fragmented financial system unintentionally. Federalism fragmented banks; and federalism and the structure of Congress enhanced the political power of those that would further fragment finance. The ideological forces and the interest groups pressures played out in a political system that already had fragmented the banks.

169. Id. at 280 (George H. Frates, Nat'l Ass'n of Retail Druggists).

170. See id. at 104, 109 (statement of W.J. Bryan of the Indep. Bankers Ass'n of Am.); id. at 238 (statement of F. Guy Hitt, President of Bank of Benton, part of a bank holding company) ("While the sponsors of [the Banking Holding Company Act] claim that they are fighting to preserve the American system of banking and to eliminate the threat of monopoly, the fact is the exact reverse. Their principal objective is to stifle competition by destroying bank holding companies."); id. at 280 (letter of Ben DuBois, Secretary, The Indep. Bankers Ass'n) ("We cannot afford to have the credit machinery of this country in few hands; it is too vital to our well-being"); id. at 317 (statement of J. Cameron Thomson, President Northwest Bancorporation) ("this legislation has taken so much of the time of Congress . . . due to the proponents' [including the Independent Bankers Association's] refusal to recognize . . . the record of performance of the bank holding companies. They have attempted to force Congress to pass legislation based on their own ideology . . . regardless of the . . . needs of their communities.").

171. See (a) Macey, supra note 161, at 17–19, (b) Shughart, A Public Choice Perspective of the Banking Act of 1933, *in* The Financial Services Revolution: Policy Directions for the Future 87, 88–89 (C. England & T. Huertas eds. 1988), (c) Langevoort, supra note 137, at 697, and (d) Ferguson, From Normalcy to New Deal: Industrial Structure, Party Competition, and American Public Policy in the Great Depression, 38 Int'l Org. 41, 70–72 (1984).

1. *Federalism.* — America's fragmented federal political system induced a fragmented banking system. Each state regulates its own state banks; national banks are regulated under the National Bank Act of 1863. Until the 1980s, most states protected local bankers from out-of-state entry. So when large enterprise emerged in the nineteenth century, few banks then had the resources to finance large enterprises. Thus, fragmented politics induced fragmented banking, making far-flung stockholders and not banks the best source of risk capital at the turn of the century. Law then reduced the chances of consolidation in financial institutions that might provide concentrated risk capital. Moreover, the fragmented banking system created interest groups—local bankers with money in their pockets and political influence—who wanted to maintain the status quo.

Similarly, the federal structure favored the political forces that wanted fragmentation. Farmers and small-town bankers have been disproportionately represented in the Senate. Their economic interests and ideology made them favor financial fragmentation. And for decades the congressional committee structure made southern politicians powerful. Many combined a conservative ideology of mistrust of central power in Washington with a populist ideology of mistrust of concentrated private financial power. Senator Carter Glass of Virginia and Representative Wright Patman of Texas had a large voice in the fragmentation of finance due to the structure of American politics.

2. *Bureaucracy.* — A political elite in Washington, of agency bureaucrats and some members of Congress, might have wished to fragment business elites. If Wall Street could not control industrial enterprises, political elites in Washington would have more room to maneuver. Politicians might have recognized that a financial-industrial coalition would have been powerful. If at crucial moments political actors had the upper hand and could permanently change the rules and sever finance capital from industry by making financial control difficult or impossible, financial-industrial coalitions would be weaker.[172] William O. Douglas, a central bureaucratic actor during the SEC's formative years, later wrote: "*Power that controls the economy should be in the hands of elected representatives of the people* . . . . Industrial power should be decentralized. It should be scattered into many hands . . . .[173] FDR had similar sentiments.[174] A bank or mutual fund with a small ownership interest in a midwestern industrial company would have little in-

172. Cf. W. Niskanen, Bureaucracy and Representative Government 39 (1971) (bureaucracies with discretion will seek their own ends); Ulen, The Market for Regulation: The ICC from 1887 to 1920, 70 Am. Econ. Rev., Papers & Proc. 306, 310 (1980) (after 1920, none of the originally dominant interest groups still "had a clear interest in extending and tightening the regulation. . . . The only group [with a] sustained interest . . . was the ICC itself.").

173. United States v. Columbia Steel Co., 334 U.S. 495, 536 (1948) (Douglas, J., dissenting) (emphasis added) (antitrust opinion).

174. W. Leuchtenburg, supra note 153, at 89–90 & n.76.

centive to lobby Washington for legislation favorable to the industry. More important for political elites would be the generalization: finance capital might withdraw some of their interest from politics.

Ferdinand Pecora, counsel to the Senate Banking Committee for the 1933–1934 hearings, concluded:

> Defeated at the polls, big business and finance still have their own crushing economic weapons of pressure and retaliation. In Europe, one may observe the process with the utmost clearness. The manner in which the Labor Government of Great Britain, for example, or the "Popular Front" administration in France was allegedly driven from office by the financial operation of the money powers of those countries, has attracted frequent comment. In the United States, fortunately, matters have not been carried to such an extreme.[175]

Bureaucratic incentives also played a role. The current system makes bank regulators important people, running important institutions. But regulating institutions that each controlled a few industrial companies would be different from regulating banks. Change in the regulated institution might change the identity or power of the regulating institution.[176] Moreover, in a reconstituted banking system, the Federal Reserve might be unable to mobilize politically powerful small bankers, as it can and does to its own bureaucratic advantage.

In 1954, when Wright Patman introduced a serious bill to audit the Federal Reserve, bank holding company legislation began to wind through Congress.[177] The audit and budget bill would have compromised the institutional autonomy of the Federal Reserve.[178] Meanwhile, small bankers wanted the holding company bill. The Fed mobilized these small banks to defeat Patman's audit bill, a matter of no small institutional significance to those running the Fed. The Federal Reserve then lobbied to confine banks to banking, and became the

175. F. Pecora, supra note 122, at 290–91.

176. See generally Friedman, Monetary Policy: Theory and Practice, *in* Central Bankers, Bureaucratic Incentives, and Monetary Policy 11, 28 (E. Toma & M. Toma eds. 1986) (Federal Reserve wants more banks in Federal Reserve System not for Fed's monetary function but because of "the prestige, sense of importance, power, and effective lobby that the system gains by supervising many thousands of banks and other financial institutions").

177. See H.R. 7602, 83d Cong., 2d Sess. (1954); Federal Reserve Act Amendments: Hearings Before the House Comm. on Banking and Currency, 83d Cong., 2d Sess. 5–7 (1954) (testimony of William McC. Martin, Chairman of Federal Reserve Board); Skaggs & Wasserkrug, Banking Sector Influence on the Relationship of Congress to the Federal Reserve System, *in* Central Bankers, Bureaucratic Incentives, and Monetary Policy, supra note 176, at 169, 175.

178. The Federal Reserve makes money in its open market operations. Unlike other federal agencies it has not been subject to the budget and appropriations process. Accordingly, it has more autonomy, which it has vigorously sought to keep. In the mid-1950s, the Federal Reserve had just freed itself from a political accord that had made it an adjunct to the Treasury Department.

principal regulatory agency for holding companies despite that one "capture" theory would indicate they would want large banks free to do more. The Federal Reserve might have chosen *who* would capture the agency (small banks with a diffuse but *politically* powerful congressional constituency instead of large economically powerful banks), in an implicit trade-off with Wright Patman.[179]

3. *Inertia.* — Social phenomena can occur without an apparent *intentional* causative agent. A rule must be chosen, so this rule is chosen. The exact contrary also could have been chosen. For example, Senator Carter Glass changed his mind a few years after the Glass-Steagall Act severed investment from commercial banking. Investment banks, he then thought, could not satisfy industry's capital needs without an affiliated commercial bank. Evidence suggests that populists and the forces of small-town bankers in Congress in 1933 really wanted federal deposit insurance, not severance. In the hope of defeating deposit insurance, various money-center bankers and politicians supported severance, not because they really wanted it but because they hoped to head off deposit insurance.[180] What if Carter Glass had changed his mind before Glass-Steagall passed, or the deposit insurance negotiations had taken a different path?

Many argue that the initial severing of American banks from commerce was copied without reflection from English precedent. When banking legislation was first adopted in the United States, legislators copied the 1694 charter of the Bank of England,[181] a royal institution that, unlike private English banks, Parliament circumscribed from wide commercial activity.[182] Legal elites lack imagination to create and prefer to borrow legal frameworks.[183] In the nineteenth century, England was the obvious place for American lawmakers to look to borrow commercial law. But the long-run consequence of separating banks from commerce was apparent neither in England in 1694 nor when copied and recopied in America, because the large firm had yet to emerge.

179. Seen slightly differently: Wright Patman's populists wanted the Fed under direct congressional control *and* wanted a fragmented banking system with banks unable to control industrial companies. Perhaps a politically agile Federal Reserve defeated the populist sentiment that threatened it by capitulating to the populist sentiment to fragment financial control.

180. Langevoort, supra note 137, at 695–97, 698 n.93.

181. B. Hammond, supra note 20, at 128–29; Halpert, The Separation of Banking and Commerce Reconsidered, 13 J. Corp. L. 481, 491 (1988).

182. R. Litan, What Should Banks Do? 13–14 (1987); Shull, The Separation of Banking and Commerce: Origin, Development, and Implications for Antitrust, 28 Antitrust Bull. 255, 274 (1983); see A. Andreades, History of the Bank of England 65 (1909); 3 E. Lipson, The Economic History of England 240–41 (2d ed. 1934).

183. A. Watson, Sources of Law, Legal Change, and Ambiguity (1984); see Samuelson & Zeckhauser, Status Quo Bias in Decision Making, 1 J. Risk & Uncertainty 7, 47–48 (1988).

D. *Summarizing the Political Story*

Thus we have several different but not inconsistent elements to the political story. No single political element alone determined any single regulation, nor was every element present at the creation of each. Like fragments in a kaleidoscope, they combined and recombined in various patterns to affect the outcome.

First, American public opinion has always mistrusted large institutions. That populist story is well known as part of antitrust attacks on big business that endured beyond the populist politics of the 1890s. Less well known is that a similar sentiment militated in favor of fragmenting financial institutions.

Second, interest group politics were important. Confining financial institutions produced winners, usually small financial institutions, small business, and eventually managers. Once banking interests were fragmented, there was a powerful, influential interest group that would resist financial concentration, namely the already fragmented small bankers. Public-spirited reasons to keep financial institutions from owning stock were also in play: reducing the risk of institutional insolvency, avoiding conflicts of interest, and breaking up perceived financial monopolies.

The third determinative role belongs to American political institutions. Federalism helped fragment finance. The structure of Congress gave interests seeking fragmentation a large voice. And political elites, wary of Wall Street, and bureaucracies seeking to preserve power each had incentives to fragment financial institutions.

Populists might well have wished to destroy all banks, both local and money-center, perhaps by setting up farmer-worker bank collectives. But politics would not let them, the forces arrayed against them were too strong. Small-town bankers might have wished to destroy the money-center banks. But politics would not let them. Agile politicians though might have seen that fragmenting the money-center banks' ability to control industrial corporations would both appease populist ideology and satisfy small-town bankers. And the structure of Congress put these politicians in important positions.

A few general comments on the mixture of elements are in order. Surely the need to control conflicts of interest was important. It would be naive to deny the fact of banker greed. But conflicts arise in other settings, such as dealings between corporate officers and their company, or between partly owned corporations and their controlling corporate parent. The law does not prohibit the relationship; abuses are subjected to case-by-case lawsuits. Something more than a conflict of interest is needed to induce prohibition; that something more was provided by populism and interest group power.

And popular animus toward large financial institutions can take many forms: it can prohibit institutions in their entirety—as it did the Second Bank of the United States; it can prohibit institutions from controlling industrial corporations—as banks are prohibited; it can limit an institution's size or range of operations—as occurs in unit banking states and as the SEC proposed in 1940 for mutual funds; or it can restrict the range of an institution's control activities. Populist sentiment against concentrations of economic power seems continuous, but legal change required a political catalyst, such as the insurance company scandals of 1906 or interest group demands or the Great Depression or the bureaucratic incentives of the Federal Reserve in 1956.

Nor can we be sure that the *articulated* mix of reasons reflects the real mix. Blatant appeal by an interest group to its self-interest and recitation to Senators of the interest group's political clout is unfashionable. Crude articulations of power will attract attention, generating a countervailing coalition. The appeal must be dressed in the garb of public interest; if no plausible public interest rationale is available, interest group legislation could fail.[184] Conversely, genuinely public-minded Senators still would mobilize the support of benefited interest groups.

IV. An Evaluation

My main purpose here is to show that political constraints deeply influenced the evolution of the Berle-Means enterprise, and not to argue that the constraints were a mistake. People might prefer fragmentated ownership, even at economic cost. And if left unfragmented, the nexus of financial institutions and industrial firms could have become a political coalition that the system could not resist. Or, if a *modus vivendi* between populism and large enterprise were not reached, the resulting political turmoil might have been intolerable. Concentrated economic power may not work well if the government reflects competing interests and the state is not sufficiently strong to be a separate and controlling actor. Moreover, fragmentation might be of no *economic* consequence if the substitutes that developed monitor as effectively as would financial institutions, or because financial institutions would fail as monitors.

Resolution of these questions is best left for future research, but I can in this Part sketch a few of the potential costs and some other possible benefits of the constraints. I discussed benefits in Part III as bases for the restrictions. My main goal in this Part is to identify some costs of the restrictions, and not to argue that the costs outweigh the benefits. I want to show the possibility that there are costs to fragmenta-

184. See Noll & Owen, The Predictability of Interest Group Arguments, *in* The Political Economy of Deregulation: Interest Groups in the Regulatory Process 53, 64 (R. Noll & B. Owen eds. 1983); Tullock, Future Directions for Rent-Seeking Research, *in* The Political Economy of Rent-Seeking 465, 473 (C. Rowley, R. Tollison & G. Tullock eds. 1988) ("[Most citizens] realize that the government can be expected to do things in their personal interest only if it at least superficially fits the public image."); cf. Macey, supra note 161, at 17–18 (judicial disbelief that Glass-Steagall Act was special interest piece of legislation).

tion—that large companies *might* operate better with powerful financial institutions as partial owners. The obvious instrumental objections to institutional monitoring are not show-stoppers.

A. *Problems and Comparisons*

True, no one should believe that unleashed institutional investors would surely tighten managerial slack. Unleashed institutions may interfere unwisely in the workings of the corporation, do nothing, seek collateral benefits, or be captured by management. But the economic question is whether at the margin they would improve business results enough and whether the detrimental effects could be held to a minimum.

1. *Enhancement of Managerial Control?* — Some studies suggest managers have *greater* control if institutions are the dominant stockholders.[185] Conflicts of interest tilt some institutions toward management. Institutions with something to sell to managers, such as loans or pension plans, are apt to succumb to managerial control. But the evidence is mixed.[186] Institutions without anything to sell to managers operate more independently. And, while we can predict from current data that managers will dominate a 5% owner with something to sell, we should expect a 30% investor to be able to dominate management.

Auditing poses an analogous problem. Investors want reliable information. They mistrust management and insist upon reports of outside auditors. But auditors sometimes succumb and are pulled into the managerial fraud. Nevertheless, the institution of the audit is so basic that few would question its usefulness simply because it *sometimes* fails.

2. *Shareholder Wealth Maximization.* — Three mechanisms could enhance shareholder wealth: (1) operating more efficiently, (2) enhancing cartel activity, and (3) stealing from others inside the corporation. Only the first is socially beneficial. Investment bankers controlled some operating companies at the turn of the century. When they did, they sought the private, antisocial gains of cartels and monopolies. They maximized shareholder wealth, but at the expense of the rest of society. Similarly, financial scandals suggest that a powerful financial institution might form powerful networks to control managers, not for the purpose of monitoring managers, but to force managers to pay tribute out of their corporation to the corrupt agents of the controlling financial institution, or to the financial institution itself.

The political belief that bankers promoted cartels and monopolies helped induce the fragmenting financial legislation. The public and

185. J. Heard & H. Sherman, Conflicts of Interest in the Proxy Voting System 40–49 (1987); Pound, supra note 64, at 242–43.

186. See Brickley, Lease & Smith, Ownership Structure and Voting on Antitakeover Amendments, 20 J. Fin. Econ. 267, 276–79 (1988).

Congress responded to monopoly and cartel problems both by passing antitrust laws *and* by fragmenting the financial interests that seemed to promote the trusts. The soundness of this double-barrelled policy I leave for others to evaluate. But today other mechanisms can deal with the antitrust issues; the melding of the United States into a single market and the internationalization of many markets each makes the antitrust rationales for financial fragmentation anachronistic.

There is another economic risk from widespread institutional control. Even if some companies would be better off with institutional control, widespread institutional control could concentrate economic decisions in too few hands; without decentralized decision making, economic progress might lag. In theory, dispersed stock market ownership for most large public companies could persist while only some had concentrated control. Competition between institutionally controlled firms and fragmented public companies should in theory enhance economic performance. But perhaps the two structures could not coexist; maybe we must pick one over the other and cannot get the benefits of both.

3. *The Mechanisms of Monitoring.* — I should briefly sketch how institutional monitoring might work. After all, the monitoring financial institutions of which we speak are themselves Berle-Means corporations. Why should they not succumb to the same agency problems that affect the Berle-Means industrial corporation?

Realistically, they often will succumb. But as long as their agency difficulties do not correlate with those difficulties afflicting the industrial companies in which they own stock, beneficial monitoring could occur. The auditing analogy is again instructive: an outside monitor without daily operational involvement can provide a check often enough to be worthwhile.

Even if the monitoring institution would usually be *worse* than the industrial company in making corporate decisions, monitoring still could improve performance, if the monitor specialized, only intervening when it was likely to be better than the operating firm managers. I categorize three potentially beneficial forms of monitoring: hierarchal, collegial, and probabilistic.

Hierarchal monitoring could occur if specialized units of financial institutions have industry expertise. The managerial literature suggests that managers overbuild enterprises for prestige and power. But financial institutions controlling an oil company, for example, might well be less susceptible to continuing to drill for oil when it was no longer profitable. The financial institutions could be concerned more directly than the oil company managers with the cash flowing out of the enterprise; the oil company managers might be more concerned with the power and size of their company. If the managers at the financial institution did not themselves become infected by the day-to-day excitement of the oil business, they might then make more objective decisions that would reduce the operating managers' wastefulness.

Collegial monitoring is different. No financial institution commands the operating company; instead, operating managers and financing managers seek consensus. The financing monitor does not need to have superior information, or less bias when evaluating the available information. Collegial monitoring does not assume that the operating managers are inferior to the financial monitors. As such it is more realistic than hierarchical monitoring, since one would expect senior operating managers to be systematically better in most operating tasks than distant financial monitors.

Collegial monitoring seems to occur in Japanese conglomerates, where banks and industrial companies own one another and meet regularly to exchange ideas to reach consensus. In an American context, collegial monitoring might help resolve the long/short, research and development difficulties discussed in Part II. A single large shareholder would find it more worthwhile to understand the value of the portfolio company's investments than do the stock market's scattered shareholders.

Probabilistic monitoring is generally nonintrusive. Day-to-day the financial institution does nothing. When operating results are poor, the monitor judges whether managerial misfeasance has caused the poor results. If so, the monitors would obtain the early retirement of the responsible managers. For probabilistic monitoring to be worthwhile, the monitors need not fully understand the industry. They must only be able to identify poor results and understand whether poor management probably caused the poor results. The replacement mechanism might be direct—a conversation with senior managers, in which the financial institution suggests early retirement—or indirect through a takeover. Takeovers to replace management are easier when a large block is preassembled and the offering company can negotiate with large blockholders over the terms of transfer.[187]

Institutional monitoring can be useful even if it would not improve the management of all corporations. Many companies would find institutions insufficiently entrepreneurial; institutions could be worse managers on average, as I suspect they would be. But as long as institutional monitoring would *sometimes* be superior, its prohibition and regulation is costly. Corporations and monitors should sort themselves out: those corporations that would benefit from institutional monitoring would tend to be monitored by institutions; those needing entrepreneurial leaders should tend not to be institutionally controlled.[188]

187. See Shleifer & Vishny, Large Shareholders and Corporate Control, 94 J. Pol. Econ. 461, 464 (1986).

188. See Demsetz & Lehn, supra note 10, at 1176.

4. *Weaknesses in the Securities Markets.* — Thus far I have treated the operating firm as the weak link, and raised the prospect that strong financial institutions might beneficially monitor the firm. But the efficiency issues are not solely those of monitoring. The *securities markets* might be the weak link. The fragmentation of institutions and their portfolios may weaken the securities markets and their debilities might be transmitted to operating firms, weakening them.

I have already given one possibility in Part II. Scale economies in securities research could plausibly debilitate securities markets from accurately assessing operating firm's long-term outlook. If expertise and staff are needed, a large holding might be necessary over which the costs of research would be spread. But if portfolio rules put a ceiling on the size of holdings, that staff may never be assembled. Large blocks would facilitate the flow of soft, technological information from the company to the large blockholder. If the securities markets undervalue long-term research and development because they cannot understand it, for example, then so will many managers who fear a takeover. Rules that prohibit or make costly the long-term positioning of large blocks of stock make it difficult for institutional shareholders and their companies to develop stable relations; shareholders become homeless.

5. *The Conglomerate.* — Has the owner as monitor already been tried, and did it fail? Was the conglomerate movement of the 1960s and 1970s—now largely discredited—functionally the same as institutional block ownership? In large part, yes. The managers of the conglomerate were said to run a mini-capital market, pulling cash away from the managers of subsidiaries no longer in growing industries, sending that cash into the companies in growing industries, and monitoring managers of all the subsidiaries.[189]

But the structures do *appear* to be different. The conglomerate typically owned *100%* of many companies. The institutional owner would typically have a large block, but would lack complete ownership. Does more than form distinguish the two?

Let's begin with the simplest monitoring paradigm. The monitor does *nothing* until it receives a signal of substandard performance, then it tries to identify whether managerial missteps caused the poor results. If those missteps are likely to continue, the monitor requires early retirement of the senior managers and promotion of the next rung of managers.

Where does the conglomerate monitor get the signal of faulty performance in its subsidiary? Principally from accounting data. The outside blockholder could also get that signal. But the blockholder could get *other* signals. Before the accounting numbers show a decline, the stock price set by traders should register *the market's expectations* of future trouble. A steep decline in stock price or underperformance of

189. O. Williamson, supra note 5, at 43–48.

Figure 1: A conglomerate with wholly-owned subsidiaries compared to partial ownership of financial institutions owning large blocks.

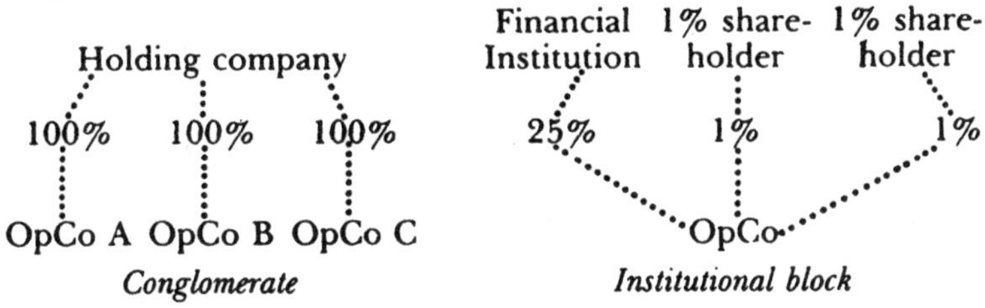

Figure 1 compares a typical conglomerate with what might be a typical block held by an unregulated financial institution. The conglomerate subsidiaries are wholly-owned; but the operating company controlled by an unregulated financial institution also has scattered shareholders buying and selling stock through one of the stock exchanges.

the stock compared to industry averages could trigger blockholder action. Financial economists argue that internal managerial changes are more likely when *stock* price lags industry averages.[190] A financial monitor could be beneficial even if it did no more than filter out poor market signals and force managers to listen to a few of the good ones; conglomerates owning 100% of a subsidiary lack the benefit of market signals. Firms with outside large shareholders who *lack* vise-like control perform well, according to data from the financial economists.[191]

Agents' incentives might be different. The *extreme* hierarchical structure of the conglomerate could exacerbate empire-building. The outside blockholder is a financial manager and plausibly would be less susceptible to the urge to build an empire. Also, compensation in marketable stock might help motivate managers. "Phantom" options and phantom stock ownership of a wholly owned subsidiary, based on multiples of earnings or sales, might not work as well as actual stock because the accounting-multiple compensation does not register *expectations* about future performance as well as does stock data.

Some monitors will be better than others; markets for monitors could develop. But the conglomerate would tend to stifle monitoring markets. Public information about a conglomerate's divisions and wholly-owned subsidiaries is not readily available, making unsolicited offers difficult and reducing the ability of the conglomerate managers

190. Morck, Shleifer & Vishny, Alternative Mechanisms for Corporate Control, 79 Am. Econ. Rev. 842, 845–46 (1989).

191. See sources cited supra note 10; Morck, Shleifer & Vishny, Management Ownership and Market Valuation: An Empirical Analysis, 20 J. Fin. Econ. 293, 311–14 (1988) (incentive effects improve performance as block size increases, but very large blocks create detrimental and overpowering entrenchment effects).

to sell, since the buyer has to contend with a risky informational base. This debility would be less prominent for financial institutions owning a large fraction of a public company's stock. With information readily available for public companies, some monitors will offer to buy the block from other, less able monitors. Similarly, there is now evidence that takeovers are easier when there are prepositioned large blocks than when the stock is in scattered hands.[192]

Hybrids stronger than either of their forebears, amalgams stronger than any of their constituents are not unheard of in biology, chemistry, or, I suspect, corporate governance. But if there were these advantages to the amalgam of partial control and marketplace signalling, why did the conglomerates not become amalgams, owning only part of their companies? Perhaps they would have evolved there, if they could have. But once the portfolio of the conglomerate was 40% devoted to partial ownership, the conglomerate would be a presumptive investment company, subject to the panoply of 1940 Act regulation.[193] Once again, partial control, partial vertical integration between industry and capital, is prohibited. Also, unlike qualifying mutual funds, conglomerates could not pull cash out of their less than 80%-owned subsidiaries without tax penalty.[194]

And perhaps conglomerates were not so bad after all. But as often happens with anything new and initially successful, success turned to excess. Conglomerates got too big, too many operating managers tried to diversify their company unwisely. Maybe conglomerates are still a good managerial tool, but in their place, only so much, only in related industries, and only if disciplined by a corporate control market. Nevertheless, we cannot yet reject the possibility that institutional monitoring would systematically fail, as the conglomerates did.

6. *National Comparisons: Germany and Japan.* — Banks are more heavily involved in commerce in other nations than in the United States. Despite the American military occupation's suppression of the Japanese zaibatsu,[195] major Japanese firms have a quarter of their stock controlled by large shareholders, typically life insurance companies and

---

192. See Shleifer & Vishny, supra note 187, at 470.

193. 1940 Act, § 3(1)(3), 15 U.S.C. § 80a-3(a)(3) (1988). If the conglomerate was not engaged in the investment business, but through *majority*-owned subsidiaries was engaged *primarily* in the business of its subsidiaries, then it might obtain an SEC exemption from the 1940 Act. Id. § 3(b)(1), (c)(6), 15 U.S.C. § 80a-3(b)(1), (c)(6) (1988); 1 T. Frankel, supra note 38, at 378–80.

194. I.R.C. §§ 243(b), 1504(a)(1), (2)(A) (1988).

195. The occupation limited bank ownership to 10% of a company, and Japan later reduced this to 5%. But other devices enabled greater Japanese bank control of the commercial firm. Cross-ownership of the banks and the related industrial firms cements ties between the financial and the industrial. See W. Ouchi, The M-Form Society 69–81 (1984); Goodman, Cumming & Kumekawa, Product Line Regulations for Financial Institutions: A Cross Country Comparison, *in* Proceedings of a Conference on Bank Structure and Competition 79, 102 (Fed. Reserve Bank of Chicago 1984).

banks; major American companies have only one-twelfth of their stock controlled by large shareholders, which more so than in Japan tend to be individuals.[196]

German banks also influence industrial companies, by block voting of shares they own directly, shares they hold as custodian, and shares they manage for pensions. Bankers sit on the boards of portfolio companies. Although passive in day-to-day affairs, they intervene when there is trouble. Banker control is quite concentrated; three banks control 40% of the stock.[197] Government in Germany and in several other continental nations is said to have *wanted* banks to become engines of development, gathering long-term capital and influencing the industries and managers to which that capital was allocated.[198] Recently a German political reaction to banker power arose, similar to that which I have described in the United States. The government is considering whether to limit bank control of industry.[199]

Parts II and III showed that American politics militated toward fragmentation of ownership by financial institutions. But undeniably scale economies and technology pushed toward large organizations, and shareholder diversification and liquidity needs pushed toward owners' fragmentation. Stock in large blocks makes a portfolio more risky and less saleable; even without mandated diversification, many institutions would want some. The question remains whether financial institutions, if permitted to take influential positions in the United States, would do so. Foreign experience provides strong evidence that they would.

American financial institutions have sought transactional end-runs around and amendment of the prohibitions and restrictions. This also suggests that the legal limits are real constraints: During the early twentieth century, banks sought to avoid the prohibition against engag-

---

196. See W. Ouchi, supra note 195, at 74; J. Scott, Capitalist Property and Financial Power: A Comparative Study of Britain, the United States, and Japan 75, 178–80 (1986). Japanese enterprises that falter are reorganized by their banks, not via a takeover. See Peck, the Large Japanese Corporation, *in* The U.S. Business Corporation: An Institution in Transition 21, 37 (J. Meyer & J. Gustafson eds. 1988).

197. Grossfeld, Management and Control of Marketable Share Companies, 13 Int'l Encyclopedia Comp. L. §§ 4-236 to 4-240, at 98–99 (1973); Kallfass, The American Corporation and the Institutional Investor: Are There Lessons From Abroad?, 3 Colum. Bus. L. Rev. 775, 782–83 (1988); Vagts, Reforming the "Modern" Corporation: Perspectives from the German, 80 Harv. L. Rev. 23, 55–58 (1966); Roth, German Banks Maintain Grip on Nation's Corporations, Wall St. J., Sept. 30, 1987, at 32, col. 1; Ingersoll, supra note 14, at 36 (replacement of Daimler-Benz management).

198. See A. Gerschenkron, Economic Backwardness in Historical Perspective 12, 14–15 (1962). But see Gille, Banking and Industrialisation in Europe 1730–1914, *in* 3 The Fontana Economic History of Europe: The Industrial Revolution 255, 297 (C. Cipolla ed. 1973) (German industrialists said to dominate banks).

199. Roth, West German Banks Face Threat of Reduced Influence in Industry: Bonn Will Consider Rules To Curb Their Holdings and Seats in Boardrooms, Wall St. J., July 18, 1989, at A20, col. 5.

ing in commerce by establishing securities affiliates. Glass-Steagall ended that. After the Depression and World War II, banks made another foray into commerce, that time via bank holding companies. The Bank Holding Company Act of 1956 ended that. In the 1980s, bank holding companies often go the maximum stock holding during leveraged buyouts. And in the 1950s, insurance companies sought to have New York inch away from the complete ban on stock ownership. Over the succeeding three decades, they obtained incremental easing. All these efforts suggest that financial institutions would, if permitted, take larger blocks of stock.

To be sure, they might not take stock to monitor, but to force controlled companies to take loans or do deals.[200] Or they might take stock because it yields higher returns than do other investments. And even if we were sure that foreign financial systems are efficient—which we are not—that would not necessarily recommend importation. If American financiers are more opportunistic, heightening the chance of scandal and abuse, or if government regulation is needed to stabilize financial power, and American government cannot regulate effectively, then foreign finance cannot be successfully grafted. And, if what we really want in America is fragmentation of power, then powerful financial institutions will give us less of what we really want.

7. *A Research Agenda.* — I obviously want to open up a large new area for research. First, more detailed studies of the legislation are needed. While we now have studies of the Glass-Steagall Act's passage and effects on underwriting competition, little has been done to examine its effects on monitoring, and there are few studies of the forces behind passage of ERISA, the 1940 Act, or the Bank Holding Company Act. We also need to know more about how financial institutions can enhance or weaken managerial performance.[201]

The political explanations can be deepened. The history available suggests that federalism, small financial institutions as interest groups, and populism largely explain fragmentation. Confirming studies can be made.[202]

---

200. See Anders, Captive Client: Morgan Stanley Found a Gold Mine of Fees by Buying Burlington, Wall St. J., Dec. 14, 1990, at 1, col. 6 (investment banker said to use control of industrial company to draw "off millions, load . . . Burlington with debt, then quietly bow . . . out").

201. As far as I can tell, only Jensen, Ouchi, and Thurow have asked whether portfolio restrictions seriously limit shareholder activity, and they devote only a few paragraphs in asides to other arguments. See Jensen, Eclipse of the Public Corporation, Harv. Bus. Rev., Sept.-Oct. 1989, at 61, 65; W. Ouchi, supra note 195, at 82, 89; L. Thurow, The Zero Sum Solution 164 (1985).

202. A few examples: (1) Event studies could track the effect of legislation on stock prices of companies likely to be affected by the legislation. (Since much of the legislation passed before the financial institutions were powerful, detecting stock price effects may require especially able econometricians.) (2) To test whether populism was important, we could find a proxy for populist sentiment that breaks down by congressional districts. Sponsorship of indubitably populist legislation could be a proxy. Then one

We should also want comparative studies to learn when the close ties between banks and industry in Japan and Germany are beneficial and when they are detrimental. Public choice studies of Japan and Germany would also be useful.

8. *Refutable Implications.* — Are there refutable implications to the story? Like other theories trying to explain history, mine is hard to verify; history cannot be replayed without the explanatory politics to see if the resulting corporate structure is different. The political theory is one of joint causation—ideology and interest groups against the background of prevailing governing institutions of federalism. Joint causation theories are difficult to disprove, especially since I think the force of the constituent elements varied from statute to statute. But difficult to refute and irrefutable are quite different. If we regularly observed managers lobbying to increase the ownership limits and power of financial institutions, if we saw managers bemoaning the lack of muscular financial institutions, if we regularly (or ever) observed small-town bankers lobbying to unleash money-center banks, if we saw opinion polls showing that the average American thought that money-center financial institutions had too little power over the economy and should be unshackled, then I would have to reconsider and probably reject the political theory.[203] That said, we still cannot yet reject alternative theories explaining the large public corporation: that most of the regulation is efficient and that even if politics induced adoption, the regulation survived because on balance most fragmenting of finance is efficient.

B. *Substitutes*

Post-World War II corporate history can be seen as an effort to find substitutes for the direct monitoring that politics disallowed. The failed proxy system gave way to the conglomerate. The conglomerate gave way to the takeover. And at the end of the 1980s, the takeover began to share center stage with the leveraged buyout.

1. *Emergence of Monitoring Intermediaries Despite the Prohibitions on Financial Institutions.* — How would a monitoring intermediary emerge? And how would the body politic allow emergence? Repeal of the prohibitions on financial institutions holding equity control is one way, the most direct. Or an unregulated firm might somehow acquire monitoring expertise and obtain financing from the regulated and disabled

could test the congressional voting patterns on the fragmenting legislation to see if there is a correlation. (3) The interest group theories could also be tested. We could find congressional districts that had corporate headquarters where Wall Street played a role—railroad headquarters before Glass-Steagall might be a first approximation, for example. Then one could see whether representatives from these districts favored Glass-Steagall more than those from otherwise similar districts that lacked the corporate headquarters.

203. See J. Buchanan & G. Tullock, The Calculus of Consent 300 (1962).

financial institutions. Such private funds are now forming on Wall Street. The economic destruction of many small banks in the 1980s could change the political balance. If politics would leave the new intermediary unregulated, the fragmented structure of American shareholding would be changed.

LBO firms can be seen as substitutes that developed partly due to institutional restrictions. The commercial bank cannot own stock. The investment bank cannot pool funds to control industrial firms by controlling big blocks of stock in a group of financial institutions such as commercial banks, bank trust funds, mutual funds, and pension funds. Separation of commercial from investment banking severs internal capital links; portfolio rules fragment the blocks; and securities rules make group formation costly. But the severed banks can be reunited in the leveraged buyout. The LBO firms obtain their equity and debt funding from the control-disabled, such as pension funds, insurers, and banks, and then the LBO firm takes board control. Financial institutions that could not take control directly have now found a way to weave around the regulations and prohibitions. (To be sure, not all LBOs can be attributed to better monitoring. Some surely result from tax benefits or from agency problems as managers buy companies when they have superior information about future results.)

2. *Contemporary Resonance.* — The political history I have offered resonates with the contemporary corporate controversies. Takeovers threaten managers. Political explanations similar to those I have sketched here lie behind the Williams Act and state antitakeover legislation. In state after state, influential managers have obtained, often with labor backing and popular support, legislation that impedes takeovers. Public opinion is suspicious of takeovers and their financiers. Wall Street greed has reentered the public's consciousness. Look at the recent debate in Pennsylvania before a sweeping antitakeover message passed. There the political forces were not hidden. The press reported that:

> Behind the debate [on the merits] in Pennsylvania is a power struggle between the shareholders . . . and the directors and managers. . . . Pennsylvania business groups supporting the bill are aligned with unions seeking to protect the jobs of their members. . . . The bill's supporters point to a wave of populist revulsion with the takeover boom of the 1980's . . . .[204]

And in New York, the Governor appointed a business-labor task force, which proposed that New York public pension systems be prohibited from financing hostile takeovers.[205] Once again, politics and not economics weakens ties between shareholders and managers.

Managers are not the primary force behind original passage of the

204. Wayne, supra note 111, at A1 (New York Times report).

205. Governor's Task Force on Pension Fund Investment, Office of Mario M. Cuomo, Governor of the State of N.Y., Our Money's Worth 47 (June 1989).

fragmenting financial legislation. Although the key players in the public corporation are managers and scattered shareholders, they are *secondary* players in the early politics of financial fragmentation. Federalism, small financial institutions, and popular opinion are primary. A first political hypothesis might have been that managers sought the fragmentation that would give them power, that the beneficiaries of fragmentation sought to obtain the benefit. But that story seems wrong. Small financial institutions and public opinion fragmented finance, thereby incidentally making managers the central players in the largest public corporations. The absence of managers and shareholders from the early politics of fragmentation helps explain why the political theory I offer here is not yet part of the common understanding of American corporate finance.

3. *Incompleteness as Substitutes.* — Substitutes for direct monitoring by financial institutions with large blocks of stock have arisen. These substitutes help explain why restrictions that raise the costs of control but do not completely prohibit it nevertheless deter financial institutions. When costs are raised, a substitute, such as the M-form conglomerate, the tender offer, or the LBO, becomes comparatively attractive. No one form is inherently superior to another; each sometimes mitigates agency problems.

The point here is not that the substitutes are *always* solutions to agency problems; often they *result* from agency problems as managers build empires and managers sometimes sought below-market bargains. But at least some, and maybe many conglomerates, tender offers, and LBOs have been responses to agency/monitoring problems. As such they are substitutes for direct monitoring by financial institutions owning a large equity block.

Even if takeovers, LBOs, and conglomerates were perfect substitutes, we now understand why these monitors developed in the United States and not in Germany and Japan, where financial institutions are the central players. They developed, whether as perfect or imperfect substitutes, because politics precluded institutional concentrated ownership as an alternative. Politics confined the terrain on which the large enterprise could evolve.

Development of a monitoring financial institution might not now be easy. Conditioned by legal restrictions, Wall Street's culture of financial speculation may be too deeply embedded to change readily. People go to business school, are trained, and become partners in investment banks or officers of commercial banks without understanding how to operate an industrial concern or, more to the point, how to check those operating an industrial firm. Carl Icahn, Kohlberg Kravis Roberts, and others began as financial players who became monitors; we do not know how quickly financial institutions could be transformed.

We do not even know *whether* they could be transformed: small investment partnerships that reap large gains may monitor better than large institutions where gains are diffusely distributed. Portfolio managers might have to be compensated differently.

The political perspective offers pessimism even if powerful financial institutions could improve corporate performance. If the alternatives are imperfect substitutes, then we have put ourselves at a national disadvantage by foregoing an institutional arrangement that other nations tolerate. History shows that this nation would have difficulty reconciling itself with such concentrations of financial power, *even if* legal reforms would properly enhance the role of institutional investors. Managers would prefer not to see financial institutions with significant ownership, popular attitudes would support managers, and tradition would make reforms seem abnormal, resulting in inertial drag. Other goals—generally of avoiding conflicts of interest—would be disrupted. In the political balance, the operational question of *whether* reforms would really enhance corporate performance would be lost. For now, I would expect politics will continue to restrain institutional action. If more institutions act, as a few now are, a confrontation may ensue.[206]

Conclusion

The result is fundamental: the modern public corporation is not an inevitably natural consequence of technology that demands large inputs of capital. If the premises of economists and legal academics have been that the demands of technology combined with the diversification demands of investors as the primary causes of the fragmented ownership of the public firm, those premises must be rethought. Politics confined the terrain on which the large enterprise could evolve. *That* confinement allowed the fragmented public corporation, and not some other organization, to evolve.

The fragmentation of institutional capital meant that owners' power would shift somewhere. It shifted to managers, who obtained their power partly by default: The public would not permit large, powerful financial institutions, but the power to direct large corporations had to go somewhere, so it went to managers. Managers may not be political heroes to the average voter, but they are dispersed, which makes them less identifiable targets than financial institutions. And managers obtained and kept some of that power because they themselves have political influence.

So, my argument has two steps: One, the legal system limited control by financial institutions. Limitations came in three types: (1)

206. Or perhaps the future prediction is that *democracy* produces the impulse to fragment financial institutions, and that politics in Germany and Japan, neither of which have had two centuries of democracy, eventually will fragment their financial institutions. See Protzman, Mighty German Banks Face Curb, N.Y. Times, Nov. 9, 1989, at D1, col. 9.

prohibitions—for banks, (2) fragmentation of financial institutions—they often cannot own one another and cannot readily network their portfolios to assert control jointly, and (3) fragmentation of institutional portfolios. Two, these prohibitions, restrictions, and fears have a political explanation.

I have sketched the ideas of representative actors—Woodrow Wilson, Louis Brandeis, William Douglas—and examined the political analogues—the Armstrong investigation, Pujo Commission, the Pecora Hearings, and surveys of public opinion. They indicate a pervasive mistrust of financial power. Small financial institutions at first and later managers lobbied for restrictions. These ideas, investigations, and interests resulted in laws that prohibited banks from owning stock, prohibited bank holding companies from owning any influential block of stock in an industrial company, restricted mutual funds from buying controlling blocks of industrial companies, and prohibited and then limited insurance companies from owning stocks. In a conservative era, when popular mistrust of accumulated power on the eastern seaboard is directed more at Washington than at Wall Street, it is easy to forget the deep mistrust that divided Main Street and Wall Street.

Perhaps it is all quite simple. Concentrated financial capital does not mix well with a broad-based egalitarian democracy in which interest groups can acquire great influence; one should not be surprised to see democracy influencing the structure of corporate finance. But I have tried here to inquire more deeply into the politics of the limiting legislation. The story has five elements: (1) inertia and the federal political structure, (2) pursuit of public goals, (3) interest group politics, (4) political elites' desire to shatter economic elites, and (5) a populism that has sought to fragment power in the economy.

This history opens up two policy perspectives. A widespread academic view is that the public corporation represents the natural selection of the fittest organizational adaptation to the economies of scale, difficulties of agency costs, and problems of technology. The historical demonstration suggests that the natural selection analogues are incomplete. Politics molded the modern corporation, at least in important part, and it is worthwhile for academics to begin to consider whether alternative financial and organizational forms would better resolve agency questions. While it does not follow from the existence of political limitations that these limitations are for the worse, it is an open question whether we have achieved the best.

The second policy perspective confines the first. While I have shown to my own satisfaction that it is an open *academic* question whether politics allowed the best organizational configuration to control agency costs, to reduce conflicts of interest, and to reduce cartel and monopoly organization, history shows that American politics would resist enhancing the power of financial institutions. If these political forces persist, then efforts to resolve the agency problem with outside financial control must somehow defeat or elude the political restrictions.

But we need not now assess the relative strength of these political explanations. Nor need we conclude whether the restrictions are beneficial, or whether other rules could have facilitated monitoring without deterring other valuable goals. None of this is necessary to understand the more central and until now neglected point: Politics heavily influenced corporate ownership structure. By restricting the terrain on which the large enterprise could evolve, politics created the fragmented Berle-Means corporation and the substitutes that have emerged, every bit as much as have natural laws of economy and technology. The Berle-Means corporation is an adaptation, not a necessity.

Part III
Corporate Law and the Role of the State

[7]

ARTICLES

FEDERALISM AND THE CORPORATION: THE DESIRABLE LIMITS ON STATE COMPETITION IN CORPORATE LAW

*Lucian Arye Bebchuk**

Corporate law scholars have long debated whether state competition for corporate charters is a "race for the bottom" or a "race for the top." In this Article, Professor Bebchuk offers an analysis of the dynamics and performance of state charter competition. He shows how the presence of managerial opportunism and externalities may lead states to adopt undesirable corporate law rules. Professor Bebchuk identifies the various issues with respect to which state competition is likely to fail, and he advocates an expansion of federal regulation to govern all of these issues. He also connects the state competition question with the question of contractual freedom in corporate law and argues that many scholars should reconsider their inconsistent views regarding these two questions. Finally, Professor Bebchuk concludes by addressing potential objections to the expansion of federal corporate regulation.

THIS Article addresses a fundamental question in the law of corporations: What is the desirable role of state competition in shaping corporate law? The Article puts forward a new framework for examining this longstanding question. It analyzes the dynamics and effects of state competition and identifies the areas of corporate law in which state competition works well and the areas in which it works poorly. In particular, it shows that state competition is likely to fail with respect to certain important issues that state corporate law has traditionally governed. Based on this analysis, the Article advocates a substantial expansion of the role of federal law in shaping corporate law rules.[1]

---

* Professor of Law, Harvard University. I wish to express my gratitude to my teacher Victor Brudney, who long ago got me interested in the subject of state competition in corporate law and who has much influenced my approach to it. I also would like to thank Christine Jolls for her invaluable assistance. For their very helpful comments, I am grateful to Ian Ayres, Stephen Choi, Robert Clark, Richard Epstein, Marcel Kahan, Louis Kaplow, Henry Hansmann, Michael McConnell, Roberta Romano, Frederick Schauer, Cass Sunstein, Detlev Vagts, Jay Westbrook, and participants in workshops at Harvard, Stanford, and the University of Chicago. Finally, for financial support, I am grateful to the National Science Foundation and to the Harvard Law School Program in Law and Economics, which is funded by the John M. Olin Foundation.

[1] Throughout this Article, the term "rules" refers to all types of rules, including statutory provisions, judge-made doctrines, and regulations. Similarly, the term "law officials" (whether federal or state) refers to all those who play a role in the adoption of rules, including legislators, judges, and regulators.

The American legal system accords primary responsibility for regulating corporate affairs to the states.[2] To be sure, federal law governs some important issues, including insider trading, disclosure, and the making of tender offers.[3] Nevertheless, much of the law regulating a corporation's affairs stems from its state of incorporation.[4] State law governs such major corporate matters as the allocation of power between managers and shareholders, fiduciary duties owed to shareholders, and fundamental corporate changes such as mergers and dissolutions.[5]

The important role of state law in the governance of corporate affairs makes critical to any corporation the corporate law rules of its state of incorporation. Because corporations are relatively free to select their states of incorporation,[6] and because states benefit from having corporations incorporate within their boundaries,[7] states are likely to compete to attract incorporations. The widely recognized leader in the state charter competition is Delaware.[8] Indeed, a major fraction of publicly traded companies in the United States is incorporated in Delaware and thus governed by Delaware corporate law.[9]

While the central role of state law has long been a familiar feature of American corporate law, it also has been the subject of vigorous debate in corporate law scholarship. On the one hand, critics of state competition view it as a "race for the bottom," in which Delaware and other states are driven to offer rules that benefit managers at the expense of shareholders.[10] According to this view, state competition

---

[2] *See* Roberta Romano, *The State Competition Debate in Corporate Law*, 8 Cardozo L. Rev. 709, 709 (1987).

[3] *See* ROBERT C. CLARK, CORPORATE LAW § 8.1, at 265 (1986) (discussing insider trading); *id.* § 9.2, at 366, § 10.2.3, at 413 (discussing disclosure); *id.* § 13.32, at 549 (discussing tender offers).

[4] *See* Curtis Alva, *Delaware and the Market for Corporate Charters: History and Agency*, 15 DEL. J. CORP. L. 885, 887 n.6 (1990); Ralph K. Winter, Jr., *State Law, Shareholder Protection, and the Theory of the Corporation*, 6 J. LEGAL STUD. 251, 252 (1977).

[5] *See generally* CLARK, *supra* note 3, § 3 (discussing the allocation of power between managers and shareholders); *id.* §§ 4–7 (discussing fiduciary duties); *id.* §§ 10–11 (discussing fundamental corporate changes).

[6] *See* Alva, *supra* note 4, at 887; Winter, *supra* note 4, at 252.

[7] *See infra* notes 24–25 and accompanying text.

[8] *See* Alva, *supra* note 4, at 887–88; Leo Herzel & Laura D. Richman, *Delaware's Preeminence by Design*, *Foreword* to R. FRANKLIN BALOTTI & JESSE A. FINKELSTEIN, THE DELAWARE LAW OF CORPORATIONS AND BUSINESS ORGANIZATIONS, at F-1, F-1 (2d ed. 1990); Romano, *supra* note 2, at 709.

[9] *See* Alva, *supra* note 4, at 889; *see also infra* notes 29–31 and accompanying text (citing statistics that indicate Delaware's dominance in the state charter competition).

[10] *See* William L. Cary, *Federalism and Corporate Law: Reflections Upon Delaware*, 83 YALE L.J. 663, 665–66 (1974); Melvin A. Eisenberg, *The Modernization of Corporate Law: An Essay for Bill Cary*, 37 U. MIAMI L. REV. 187, 188–91, 196–98, 202–09 (1983); Donald E. Schwartz, *Federalism and Corporate Governance*, 45 OHIO ST. L.J. 545, 548–51 (1984).

works poorly and should be curtailed.[11] On the other hand, supporters of state competition regard it as a "race for the top."[12] According to this view, charter competition drives Delaware and other states to offer rules that maximize shareholder value;[13] consequently, the regulation of corporate affairs should be left to the states.[14]

The question of state competition arises not only in the United States but also in any federal system in which companies incorporated in one state can operate without difficulty in the federation's other states. Accordingly, the European Economic Community has also confronted this question. The direction that the Community has thus far pursued is one of imposing more substantial constraints on state competition than the constraints existing in the United States.[15] Indeed, the founders of the Community seem to have taken for granted the need to prevent the largely unrestricted state competition that prevails in the United States.[16]

---

[11] *See, e.g.*, Cary, *supra* note 10, at 701 (proposing the adoption of a minimum federal standard "in order to remedy the Delaware syndrome").

[12] *See* Peter Dodd & Richard Leftwich, *The Market for Corporate Charters: "Unhealthy Competition" Versus Federal Regulation*, 53 J. BUS. 259, 260–61 (1980); Frank H. Easterbrook, *Managers' Discretion and Investors' Welfare: Theories and Evidence*, 9 DEL. J. CORP. L. 540, 549–50 (1984); Frank H. Easterbrook & Daniel R. Fischel, *Voting in Corporate Law*, 26 J.L. & ECON. 395, 398 (1983); Daniel R. Fischel, *The "Race to the Bottom" Revisited: Reflections on Recent Developments in Delaware's Corporation Law*, 76 NW. U. L. REV. 913, 919–20 (1982); Winter, *supra* note 4, at 256–57.

[13] *See* Dodd & Leftwich, *supra* note 12, at 282; Easterbrook, *supra* note 12, at 571; Fischel, *supra* note 12, at 919–20; Winter, *supra* note 4, at 256–57. Indeed, the belief that state competition tends to produce value-maximizing rules has led some commentators to adopt a strong presumption that state corporate law rules are efficient. *See* sources cited *infra* notes 45, 198.

[14] *See* Dodd & Leftwich, *supra* note 12, at 282; Fischel, *supra* note 12, at 921–23; Winter, *supra* note 4, at 290–92.

[15] For an overview of the Community's developing program of "harmonization" (as the program of adopting uniform minimum standards has come to be called), see Alfred F. Conard, *The European Alternative to Uniformity in Corporation Laws*, 89 MICH. L. REV. 2150, 2151 (1991); and Manning G. Warren III, *Global Harmonization of Securities Laws: The Achievements of the European Communities*, 31 HARV. INT'L L.J. 185, 197–98 (1990). The Constitution of the European Community expressly authorized the Community to establish "minimum standards" for corporate law issues. *See* TREATY ESTABLISHING THE EUROPEAN ECONOMIC COMMUNITY [EEC TREATY], art. 54, § 3, cl. g. The Community has thus far issued nine directives, and several others have been proposed and seem likely to be adopted. The existing and proposed directives govern many important corporate law issues that in the United States are left to state law, such as incorporation, creation and maintenance of capital, mergers, corporate governance (including the voice of labor), and takeover defensive tactics. *See* Conard, *supra*, at 2153–54.

[16] *See* Conard, *supra* note 15, at 2154. When the Community's harmonization program was started, there was rivalry for the administration of the program but no opposition to the concept of harmonization itself. Indeed, the case for harmonization was so much taken for granted that there was initially little express discussion of the reasons for it. Only later did commentators start to discuss the arguments for and against the Community's program of harmonization. *See*,

This Article puts forward a new approach to the question of state charter competition. My analysis indicates that this competition works well in some areas of corporate law but poorly in others; that is, state competition produces a race for the top with respect to some corporate issues but a race for the bottom with respect to others. More importantly, my analysis identifies those issues with respect to which state competition is likely to produce undesirable rules. This analysis provides workable criteria that I use to delineate the desirable limits on state competition and advocate a significant expansion of federal corporate law.[17]

Part I of the Article provides background necessary for understanding the state competition question and my analysis of this question. After providing some basic facts about the state charter competition, it critically reviews existing theories about the desirability of this competition. It then surveys the empirical evidence on state competition and explains why this evidence does not resolve the debate over the merits of state competition. Next it discusses the premises concerning states' objectives that underlie my analysis as well as the analyses of both supporters and critics of state competition. Finally, Part I outlines briefly the shortcomings of state competition.

The Article's analysis of the shortcomings of state competition is carried out in Parts II and III. Part II analyzes the ways in which divergence of interests between managers and shareholders may lead state competition to produce corporate law rules that reduce shareholder value. States competing to attract incorporations have an incentive to offer rules that are attractive to managers, who have substantial influence on incorporation decisions. To be sure, because the interests of managers and shareholders are somewhat aligned, there are many corporate issues with respect to which managers seek, and states in turn have an incentive to provide, rules that enhance share-

---

e.g., RICHARD M. BUXBAUM & KLAUS J. HOPT, LEGAL HARMONIZATION AND THE BUSINESS ENTERPRISE 8–11 (1988).

For an analysis of the advantages and disadvantages of allowing state competition in the Community, see David Charny, *Competition Among Jurisdictions in Formulating Corporate Law Rules: An American Perspective on the "Race to the Bottom" in the European Communities*, 32 HARV. INT'L. L.J. 423, 441–55 (1991). Charny's views on the shortcomings of state competition are similar to those presented in this Article.

17 My analysis of the dynamics of state competition builds upon an earlier framework that I developed for analyzing the desirability of allowing companies to opt out by charter amendment of the legal rules that would otherwise govern their affairs. *See* Lucian A. Bebchuk, *The Debate on Contractual Freedom in Corporate Law, Foreword* to Symposium, *Contractual Freedom in Corporate Law*, 89 COLUM. L. REV. 1395, 1399–1404 (1989) [hereinafter Bebchuk, *Foreword*]; Lucian A. Bebchuk, *Limiting Contractual Freedom in Corporate Law: The Desirable Constraints on Charter Amendments*, 102 HARV. L. REV. 1820, 1822–27 (1989) [hereinafter Bebchuk, *Limiting Contractual Freedom*]. This Article carries out the project anticipated in my foreword to the *Columbia Law Review* symposium. *See* Bebchuk, *Foreword*, *supra*, at 1414–15. The connection between my and others' work on contractual freedom and the question of state competition is discussed in Part V below.

holder value. As the analysis shows, however, the operation of market forces and the requirement of shareholder approval of reincorporations are insufficient to ensure that managers seek value-maximizing rules with respect to corporate law issues in general. Rather, with respect to certain issues, managers are likely to seek — and states in turn may well adopt — rules that serve the private interests of managers even if these rules are value-decreasing.

The analysis of Part II identifies three types of issues with respect to which managers' opportunism may well lead to undesirable state law rules. First, state competition is likely to produce such rules with respect to issues that involve a potential transfer of significant value from shareholders to managers. Such issues include self-dealing transactions, taking of corporate opportunities, and insider trading. Second, state competition is likely to fail with respect to issues that directly affect the strength of market discipline, such as the regulation of takeover bids and proxy contests. Third, state competition is likely to yield undesirable rules with respect to issues that involve potential transfers between public shareholders and controlling shareholders, such as the regulation of going-private and parent-subsidiary freeze-outs. I argue that all of these issues, some of which are and traditionally have been governed by state corporate law, should be subject to federal rules or, at least, to federal minimum standards.

Part III analyzes the ways in which state charter competition leads to socially undesirable rules in the presence of externalities. In designing corporate law rules, states competing to attract incorporations will have an incentive to focus on the interests of managers and shareholders and to ignore the interests of third parties not involved in incorporation decisions. Therefore, whenever significant externalities are present, states will tend to provide corporate law rules that differ from the socially desirable ones in a direction that systematically disfavors such third parties. Furthermore, the analysis shows that significant externalities are present in important areas of corporate law, including the regulation of takeover bids, proxy contests, and corporate disclosure and the protection accorded to creditors and other non-shareholder constituencies. I argue that federal law should be expanded to govern — or at least set minimum standards for — all aspects of these areas of corporate law.

Part IV of the Article discusses the connection between the question of state charter competition and the question of contractual freedom in corporate law. The contractual freedom question concerns the degree to which companies should be allowed to opt out of corporate law rules by adopting charter provisions to that effect. Commentators of all stripes have expressed stronger support for limits on the contractual freedom of companies than for limits on state competition. As Part IV shows, however, the desirability of contractual freedom and the desirability of state competition depend on the same set of considerations. Whatever concerns may lead one to support a mandatory rule with respect to a given corporate law issue should also lead one to support federal law rules for the same issue. This conclusion suggests that many commentators should reexamine their uncritical views of state competition.

While the focus of the Article is on the shortcomings of state competition, Part V offers some brief notes on issues that federal regulation raises. Part V discusses the possible imperfections of the federal law process and then explains the considerations that lead me to believe that, with respect to the issues identified by the analysis in Parts II and III, the federal process would not perform worse than state competition. Part V also discusses the implications of international charter competition for any program of federal regulation.

Finally, before proceeding, it is worth noting that the focus of this Article is on publicly traded companies. The decisionmaking process of close corporations differs substantially from that of publicly traded companies and requires a separate analysis.[18] Moreover, because close corporations generally incorporate in the states in which their principal places of business are located,[19] the state competition debate has naturally focused on publicly traded companies.[20]

I. The State Competition Question

A. Factual Background

American corporate law has always been largely the province of the states. Federal law was totally silent on the internal governance of corporations until the enactment of the Securities Act of 1933. Although federal securities law now plays a significant role in regulating corporate affairs, states still retain primary responsibility for corporate regulation, and state law governs the major aspects of corporate law.[21]

A corporation is governed for corporate law purposes by the law of its state of incorporation, regardless of where it conducts its business operations.[22] Therefore, corporations can shop around for attractive

---

[18] *See* Victor Brudney & Robert C. Clark, *A New Look at Corporate Opportunities*, 94 HARV. L. REV. 997, 1000–06 (1981).

[19] *See* WILLIAM L. CARY & MELVIN A. EISENBERG, CASES AND MATERIALS ON CORPORATIONS 98 (6th ed. 1988); Ian Ayres, Judging Close Corporations in the Age of Statutes 13–19 (Oct. 1991) (unpublished manuscript, on file at the Harvard Law School Library).

[20] For a recent analysis of the development of state law with respect to close corporations, see Ayres, *supra* note 19.

[21] *See* Cary, *supra* note 10, at 663; Romano, *supra* note 2, at 709; Winter, *supra* note 4, at 252–53; *see also* sources cited *supra* notes 4–5 (discussing the many aspects of corporate law that state law governs).

[22] *See* Alva, *supra* note 4, at 887 n.6; Winter, *supra* note 4, at 252.

corporate domiciles by comparing the legal regimes offered by different states.[23] States, in turn, have an interest in having companies incorporated within their boundaries. Incorporations yield franchise tax and fee revenues[24] and also provide patronage for local law firms, corporation service companies, and other businesses.[25] The ability of corporations to incorporate in states whose legal regimes they find attractive, together with the eagerness of states to attract incorporations, result in state competition for corporate charters.

Since its inception, the competition between states has always been characterized by the dominance of a particular state. The early leader was New Jersey.[26] In 1896, New Jersey adopted the first of the modern liberal corporation statutes, and it subsequently became home to many of the largest corporations of that time.[27] After restrictive amendments to its corporation law were made in 1913, New Jersey lost the leading role to Delaware, whose corporation law was at the time a close copy of New Jersey's original statute.[28] Delaware is at present the domicile of more than half of all Fortune 500 companies and more than forty percent of all companies listed on the New York Stock Exchange.[29] It is also the leading destination of companies that reincorporate: Delaware attracted eighty-two percent of publicly traded firms that reincorporated in the past three decades[30] and ninety percent of the New York Stock Exchange-listed companies that reincorporated between 1927 and 1977.[31]

Delaware's dominance of the state charter competition has resulted in the widespread diffusion of its law. Other states, anxious to stem the exodus of corporations from their jurisdictions, have followed Delaware in adopting various legal rules.[32] Delaware has played a

---

[23] *See* Alva, *supra* note 4, at 887–88.

[24] *See id.* at 888; Cary, *supra* note 10, at 668–69; Winter, *supra* note 4, at 255. In Delaware, the dominant state for incorporations, corporate franchise taxes and fees accounted for approximately 20% of general fund revenues in 1990. *See* Alva, *supra* note 4, at 888 & n.8.

[25] *See* Cary, *supra* note 10, at 668; John C. Coffee, Jr., *The Future of Corporate Federalism: State Competition and the New Trend Toward De Facto Federal Minimum Standards*, 8 CARDOZO L. REV. 759, 762 (1987); Jonathan R. Macey & Geoffrey P. Miller, *Toward an Interest Group Theory of Delaware Corporate Law*, 65 TEX. L. REV. 469, 492–93; Roberta Romano, *Law as a Product: Some Pieces of the Incorporation Puzzle*, 1 J.L. ECON. & ORG. 225, 240–41 (1985).

[26] *See* Cary, *supra* note 10, at 664.

[27] *See* Herzel & Richman, *supra* note 8, at F-1 to -2.

[28] *See* Cary, *supra* note 10, at 664–65; Herzel & Richman, *supra* note 8, at F-1 to -2.

[29] *See* Alva, *supra* note 4, at 887; Herzel & Richman, *supra* note 8, at F-1; Macey & Miller, *supra* note 25, at 483.

[30] *See* Romano, *supra* note 25, at 242, 244.

[31] *See* Dodd & Leftwich, *supra* note 12, at 263.

[32] *See* Cary, *supra* note 10, at 671 (noting Delaware's influence on statutory modernization and on case law in other states); *id.* at 666 n.18 (remarking that the intent of Michigan's new corporation code was, in the words of one of its sponsors, to "out-Delaware Delaware"); Winter,

major role in the spread of innovations concerning a range of corporate law issues, including election of directors, charter amendments, shareholders' meetings, appraisal rights, dividend policy, mergers, indemnification of officers, and antitakeover defenses.[33] Whether the widespread adoption of these and other innovations has harmed or benefitted shareholders is the critical point of contention in the state competition debate.

B. Existing Theories of State Competition

1. The Race for the Bottom. — The race for the bottom theory claims that state competition for corporate charters harms shareholders by driving states to adopt corporate law rules that are too lax with respect to managers and controlling shareholders.[34] William Cary forcefully advanced the argument that state competition is "a race for the bottom," noting that Delaware was both the consistent leader in loosening constraints on managers[35] and the indisputable winner of the state charter competition.[36] In Cary's view, Delaware (and, to varying degrees, other states) successfully used corporate law rules that disregard shareholders' interests to attract managers responsible for incorporation decisions.[37] Cary concluded that substantive federal regulation of corporations' internal affairs was necessary to protect shareholders from exploitation by managers.[38]

The problem with the race for the bottom analysis is its failure to consider the existence of market constraints on managers' behavior. Cary viewed corporate law as the sole source of protection for share-

---

supra note 4, at 255 (concluding that statutory changes were national in scope and that Delaware law was no longer significantly different from that of other states); *see also* Alva, *supra* note 4, at 889–90 (arguing that if Delaware adopts a provision attractive to corporations, then other states wishing to retain the companies incorporated within their boundaries will have to follow).

Delaware is not always the first state to provide innovative corporate law rules. *See* Romano, *supra* note 25, at 233, 240 (finding that of four major corporate law changes — explicit standards for director and officer indemnification, mergers without stockholder vote under certain circumstances, elimination of appraisal rights when shares are traded on a national exchange, and antitakeover statutes — only one was first adopted by Delaware). However, in cases in which Delaware is not the first state to change its law, it follows the innovator's lead quicker than any other state. *See id.* at 240.

[33] *See* Romano, *supra* note 25, at 233; Winter, *supra* note 4, at 254–55.

[34] *See* Cary, *supra* note 10, at 672; Eisenberg, *supra* note 10, at 188–91, 202–09; Schwartz, *supra* note 10, at 550.

[35] *See* Cary, *supra* note 10, at 669–70 (describing the Delaware statutory provisions that free managers from shareholder interference); *id.* at 670–84 (reviewing the Delaware judicial decisions that "create[d] a 'favorable climate' for management").

[36] *See id.* at 668–69; *supra* notes 29–31 and accompanying text.

[37] *See* Cary, *supra* note 10, at 665–66.

[38] *See id.* at 701.

holders.[39] As critics of the race for the bottom view were quick to point out, however, market forces must be taken into account in any analysis of state charter competition.

2. The Race for the Top. — The race for the top theory holds that state charter competition benefits shareholders by driving states to adopt corporate law rules that enhance shareholder value. Pointing to the existence of market forces that check management opportunism, Ralph Winter, Frank Easterbrook, Daniel Fischel, and others have rejected the conclusions of the race for the bottom theory.[40] These scholars do not dispute Cary's initial contention that Delaware and other states have successfully used liberal corporate law rules to influence the incorporation decisions of managers.[41] Instead, they quarrel with the presumed divergence between these decisions and shareholders' interests.

Market forces, the argument runs, will discourage managers from seeking incorporation in states with legal rules that permit managers to "exploit" shareholders. Incorporation in such states would increase the company's vulnerability to takeovers (which threaten managers' jobs), lower managers' compensation and other employment-related benefits, and harm managers' present and future job prospects.[42] In other words, the operation of various market forces aligns managers' interests with those of shareholders insofar as the incorporation decision is concerned. State competition for corporate charters is therefore a race not for the bottom, but for the top; states vie for incorporation business by offering corporate law rules that maximize shareholder value.[43] Delaware's dominance is thus attributable to its adoption of optimal rules.[44]

An important implication of the race for the top theory is that existing state corporate law rules, which result from a competitive race for the top, should be regarded as presumptively efficient.[45]

---

[39] In particular, Cary argued that the willingness of investors to entrust their funds to public companies could be maintained only by mandating disclosure and management accountability, and by providing opportunities for derivative or direct shareholder action. *See id.* at 671.

[40] *See* Dodd & Leftwich, *supra* note 12, at 261; Easterbrook, *supra* note 12, at 549–50; Easterbrook & Fischel, supra note 12, at 398; Fischel, *supra* note 12, at 915, 920–21; Winter, *supra* note 4, at 254.

[41] *See* Easterbrook, *supra* note 12, at 549–50; Winter, *supra* note 4, at 254.

[42] *See* Fischel, *supra* note 12, at 919; Winter, *supra* note 4, at 256, 264–66; *see also* Easterbrook, *supra* note 12, at 564 (arguing that the market for corporate control generally aligns managers' and shareholders' interests in corporate decisions); *id.* at 554 (arguing that compensation considerations induce managers to serve shareholders' interests).

[43] *See* Dodd & Leftwich, *supra* note 12, at 281–82; Easterbrook, *supra* note 12, at 571; Fischel, *supra* note 12, at 919–20; Winter, *supra* note 4, at 256.

[44] *See* Fischel, *supra* note 12, at 919–20; Winter, *supra* note 4, at 258.

[45] *See* Easterbrook, *supra* note 12, at 545; Fischel, *supra* note 12, at 919–20; Winter, *supra* note 4, at 256. For applications of this presumption by scholars subscribing to the race for the top view, see sources cited *infra* note 198.

Accordingly, the adoption of antitakeover measures by many states presents a puzzle for race for the top adherents, who generally believe that impediments to takeovers are inefficient.[46] If antitakeover measures are inefficient, then race for the top logic predicts that states will not adopt them. Nonetheless, states have done so overwhelmingly.[47] This divergence between the theory's prediction and the actual practice of states has not gone unnoticed.[48]

Whatever its shortcomings, the race for the top theory has contributed to the state competition debate by highlighting the effect of market discipline on managers' incorporation decisions. As this Article will demonstrate, however, the various market forces upon which the race for the top theory relies cannot discourage managers from seeking certain undesirable corporate law rules. State antitakeover statutes are not an anomaly but simply one manifestation of this phenomenon.[49]

3. The Race for Predictability and Stability. — According to both the race for the bottom and race for the top theories, states' performance in the competition for incorporations is determined by the substantive content of their legal rules. An alternative view, developed by Roberta Romano, is that a state's success in the state charter competition depends on its ability to offer corporations a credible commitment to predictability and stability.[50] Romano's analysis is motivated by Delaware's sustained ability to dominate the competition for charters, notwithstanding the similarity in content between Delaware's and other states' corporate law rules and the high tax burden associated with incorporation in Delaware.[51] Romano suggests that

---

46 *See* Amanda Acquisition Corp. v. Universal Foods Corp., 877 F.2d 496, 500 (7th Cir.) (Easterbrook, J.), *cert. denied*, 493 U.S. 955 (1989); Frank H. Easterbrook & Daniel R. Fischel, *The Proper Role of a Target's Management in Responding to a Tender Offer*, 94 HARV. L. REV. 1161, 1164 (1981); Winter, *supra* note 4, at 287–89.

47 For descriptions of the widespread adoption of state antitakeover statutes, see Roberta Romano, *The Political Economy of Takeover Statutes*, 73 VA. L. REV. 111, 113–14 (1987); and Romano, *supra* note 2, at 725. For an example of a judicial decision facilitating antitakeover tactics, see Paramount Communications, Inc. v. Time, Inc., 571 A.2d 1140, 1142 (Del. 1990).

48 *See, e.g.*, Romano, *supra* note 25, at 265–66 (noting the serious inconsistency in the logic of the position that, on the one hand, state competition induces efficient corporate law rules and, on the other hand, antitakeover measures are inefficient); Romano, *supra* note 2, at 726 (same). The puzzle posed by the clash between race for the top logic and states' adoption of antitakeover measures is discussed in more detail in section II.C below.

49 State antitakeover statutes will be discussed in section II.C and subsection III.B.4 below.

50 *See* Romano, *supra* note 25, at 273–79, 280–81; *see also* Romano, *supra* note 2, at 720–25 (discussing Delaware's dependency on a responsive relationship with corporations and the constraints that make a less responsive climate unlikely).

51 *See* Romano, *supra* note 25, at 226. Romano and other commentators have noted the similarity of states' corporate law rules. *See* Coffee, *supra* note 25, at 768 (noting that, in the competition among states, "the competitors are seldom that far apart"); Romano, *supra* note 25, at 235 (describing the empirical evidence of the diffusion of innovative corporate law rules through the states); Romano, *supra* note 2, at 709 (finding "substantial uniformity across the

Delaware's continued dominance stems from several factors that enable it to guarantee predictable and stable legal rules.[52] First, Delaware depends more heavily than its competitors on incorporation revenues — including receipts from franchise taxes and fees and the income of local service firms — and thus can be counted on to maintain the predictability and stability sought by incorporation decisionmakers.[53] Second, Delaware's corporation code can be revised only by a two-thirds vote of both houses of the state legislature and is therefore likely to be stable.[54] Finally, the substantial body of Delaware precedent, along with the small size and corporate expertise of Delaware's judiciary, ensure predictable outcomes for corporate litigation.[55]

But, even if the predictability and stability of Delaware's legal rules are attractive to corporations, the question whether state competition is desirable remains unanswered. For the features of predictability and stability hardly amount to a complete characterization of Delaware law. Clearly a critical dimension of Delaware's corporate law is the substantive content of its rules. Consider, for example, two alternative legal rules for the governance of a given corporate law issue (for example, managerial self-dealing). While both rules might be characterized by predictability and stability, they may differ significantly in their substance and thus in their effect on shareholder value. Accordingly, the question remains whether Delaware's (predictable and stable) corporate law rules are value-maximizing or, instead, diverge systematically from the value-maximizing rules (say, by treating managers too laxly).

Furthermore, even if the predictability and stability characterizing Delaware's corporate law are attractive features, this does not tell us whether state competition is desirable. Federal corporate law could provide predictability and stability as well. A federal corporate law system would offer a large body of precedent upon which it could

---

states"); *see also supra* note 32 and accompanying text (discussing the influence and spreading of Delaware corporation law). For figures indicating the weight of the tax burden in Delaware relative to other states, see Macey & Miller, *supra* note 25, at 492 n.86; and Romano, *supra* note 25, at 255–56, 257 & tbl. 7, 258.

[52] *See* Romano, *supra* note 25, at 273–79; Romano, *supra* note 2, at 721–22.

[53] *See* Romano, *supra* note 25, at 240, 242; Romano, *supra* note 2, at 721–22.

[54] *See* Romano, *supra* note 25, at 241; Romano, *supra* note 2, at 722. As Romano acknowledges, the supermajority requirement could impede Delaware's adoption of desirable corporate law innovations. *See* Romano, *supra* note 25, at 241; Romano, *supra* note 2, at 722. But if corporations follow a risk-averse strategy in their incorporation decisionmaking, Romano reasons, then the constitutional provision making legislative change more difficult by mandating a two-thirds vote of approval for all corporate law changes will "be a desirable feature," because the provision "increases the likelihood that [Delaware law will] be no worse than it was at the time of incorporation." Romano, *supra* note 25, at 241.

[55] *See* Romano, *supra* note 25, at 277–78; Romano, *supra* note 2, at 772.

draw, as all cases would be brought under the same set of legal rules. Moreover, judicial expertise could be ensured through a special court that would hear only corporate law cases. Thus, the main difference between a state competition system and a federal corporate law system is that competitive pressures shape the choice of substantive rules in the former system but not in the latter. Whether such competitive pressures are beneficial or detrimental is precisely the question that needs to be answered.[56]

C. *Empirical Evidence*

Empirical work on the state competition question has focused on identifying how reincorporations affect a corporation's stock price. Event studies by Peter Dodd and Richard Leftwich and by Roberta Romano found that the stock of reincorporating companies does not

[56] The three major theories of state competition described in this section focus on what might be called the "demand side" of this competition. That is, they focus on the preferences of incorporation decisionmakers as the determinants of state corporate law arrangements. Several commentators have also considered the "supply side" of the competition for charters. *See* Coffee, *supra* note 25, at 762–64; Macey & Miller, *supra* note 25, at 498–509. These commentators argue that Delaware's corporate law arrangements are determined not only by Delaware's desire to attract incorporators, but also by interest-group pressure exerted by the Delaware bar.

Indeed, the Delaware bar's apparent influence on the Delaware rules that concern the ability of shareholders to sue has been widely recognized. *See* Cary, *supra* note 10, at 686–88; Coffee, *supra* note 25, at 763; Macey & Miller, *supra* note 25, at 512. For example, under Delaware law, shareholder-plaintiffs need not post security for expenses, and they can bring suits against non-resident directors relatively easily. *See* Cary, *supra* note 10, at 686–87; Coffee, *supra* note 25, at 763; Macey & Miller, *supra* note 25, at 511–12; Winter, *supra* note 4, at 274–75 & n.72. Because the Delaware rules that facilitate suits against Delaware corporations do not appear to be aimed at attracting incorporations, commentators have viewed these arrangements as a consequence of interest-group pressure exerted by the Delaware bar. *See* Cary, *supra* note 10, at 687; Coffee, *supra* note 25, at 763; Macey & Miller, *supra* note 25, at 510–13.

In considering the view that the interests of the Delaware bar influence Delaware corporate law, it should be first noted that interest group pressure can come into play only to the extent that Delaware has "market power" in the state charter competition. If Delaware had no market power, it would not be able to adopt rules that sacrifice the interests of incorporation decisionmakers for the interests of the Delaware bar without producing a migration en masse from Delaware to friendlier grounds. Delaware probably has some degree of market power for the reason proposed in Romano's analysis, that is, Delaware's ability to offer predictable and stable corporate law rules. *See supra* notes 50–52 and accompanying text.

More important for our purposes, however, the litigation-friendly tendencies of Delaware law — to the extent such tendencies exist — are just one dimension of Delaware's corporate law. As I pointed out in discussing Romano's thesis, the content dimension of Delaware's rules remains critical. Consider again the example of two alternative rules that Delaware might adopt for the governance of managerial self-dealing, one allowing little or no such self-dealing and the other allowing a great deal of such behavior. While the rules might encourage litigation equally (and, accordingly, benefit the Delaware bar equally), they might differ significantly in their effect on shareholder value. The critical question is whether Delaware will choose the rule that better serves shareholders' interests.

decline in value when the reincorporation plans become public.[57] Race for the top adherents have pointed to these results as evidence that confirms their view.[58]

The results of these event studies, however, do not resolve the debate over the desirability of state competition. To start with, stock price movements around the time of reincorporation may reflect the market's reaction not to the reincorporation itself, but rather to other developments that coincide with, or even were signalled by, the decision to reincorporate.[59] Managers may well systematically choose to reincorporate when they have favorable information about the future of their company.[60] In such a case, the market may, around the time of the reincorporation decision, receive this favorable information or even infer it from the managers' decision to reincorporate. Consequently, even if the market did view the effect of the reincorporation itself to be negative, the market's reaction to the favorable information about the company may outweigh this negative effect, and the stock price may not decline around the time of reincorporation.

Second, and perhaps more importantly, the absence of negative returns upon reincorporation may indicate not that the legal rules of the destination state are beneficial to shareholders but rather that the legal rules of the original state and the destination state are equally harmful to shareholders. This observation is consistent with the failure of the empirical studies to uncover significant positive or negative returns in most cases[61] and with the degree to which states' corporate

---

[57] *See* Dodd & Leftwich, *supra* note 12, at 281–86; Romano, *supra* note 25, at 279–81. Events that might cause a company's reincorporation plans to become public include the approval of the reincorporation by the company's board of directors, incorporation of a shell successor corporation in the destination state, signing of a merger agreement between the company and its successor-subsidiary, mailing of proxy materials to shareholders, shareholder approval of the company's merger with the shell successor corporation, and/or publication of a *Wall Street Journal* article concerning the company's domicile change.

[58] *See* Dodd & Leftwich, *supra* note 12, at 281–82; Easterbrook, *supra* note 12, at 550; Fischel, *supra* note 12, at 920–21.

[59] *See* Romano, *supra* note 25, at 267 & n.58; Coffee, *supra* note 25, at 767–68.

[60] Indeed, in order to avoid experiencing a price decline, managers might systematically prefer to schedule a reincorporation decision at a time when they have such favorable information. In addition, incorporation in a state with favorable corporate law rules might increase in importance when the company seems to be on the road to success and growth that might produce a higher volume of corporate litigation.

[61] *See* Dodd & Leftwich, *supra* note 12, at 277 (finding no market reaction); Romano, *supra* note 25, at 271 (finding no significant abnormal returns for reincorporations that were motivated by antitakeover and tax considerations). Although Romano found significant abnormal returns for reincorporations motivated by planned acquisition programs, *see id.* at 271, this result may be attributable to stockholders' positive response to the signalling of the planned acquisition programs, *see* Coffee, *supra* note 25, at 767; Romano, *supra* note 25, at 267–68.

law rules are similar.[62] As long as there is little difference between the legal rules of the corporation's original state of incorporation and its state of reincorporation, the decision to reincorporate is likely to affect shareholders only minimally. Whether this similarity in state corporate law rules reflects a race for the top or a race for the bottom remains an open question.[63]

Finally, even if the event studies did show that a company's decision to reincorporate does not reduce its value overall, such a showing still would not rule out the possibility that state competition produces desirable results with respect to some corporate issues but not with respect to others.[64] This observation is not just a fine point; as Parts II and III will demonstrate, state competition can indeed be expected to yield such differential effects.

In addition to the event studies of reincorporation decisions, the body of empirical work concerning state competition includes a study of the effect that major changes in Delaware law had on the stock market price of Delaware corporations.[65] The study "found no statistically significant market reaction to any" one of seven major Delaware court decisions, "all of which appeared to make significant, unanticipated changes in Delaware corporate law."[66] This finding, however, also cannot resolve the state competition question. It is difficult to predict in advance which particular companies will be affected in the future by a given precedent. Therefore, it is not surprising that the rendering of any particular precedent has little impact on companies' stock prices. Moreover, even if a particular change in the law were found to have caused a significant increase or decrease in companies' value, such a finding would shed little light on the question of the *systematic* effects of state competition. It is possible that Delaware has produced one or more decisions that advanced shareholders' in-

---

[62] *See* Coffee, *supra* note 25, at 768; Romano, *supra* note 25, at 235, 238; Romano, *supra* note 2, at 709; *see also supra* notes 32–33 and accompanying text (describing the diffusion of innovative corporate law rules through the states).

[63] *See* Coffee, *supra* note 25, at 768 (stating that event studies of reincorporations can, at best, show only "the margin at any given time that separates [Delaware] from its nearest rival," and that they cannot show the "total distance that [state charter] competition [has taken us] from the legal regime that would result absent such competition").

[64] Suppose that a company migrates from state *A* to state *B* and that state *B* has a value-decreasing legal rule for the governance of a particular corporate law issue *X*. The move to *B* will not decrease the company's overall value if the desirability to shareholders of *B*'s rules with respect to issues other than *X* outweighs the undesirability to them of *B*'s legal treatment of *X*. It follows that, even if reincorporations could be shown not to decrease shareholder value overall, such a showing would not demonstrate that state competition produces value-maximizing rules with respect to *all* types of corporate law issues.

[65] *See* Elliott J. Weiss & Lawrence J. White, *Of Econometrics and Indeterminacy: A Study of Investors' Reactions to "Changes" in Corporate Law*, 75 CAL. L. REV. 551 (1987).

[66] *Id.* at 553.

terests but nonetheless has various legal rules that are harmful to these interests.

In sum, the body of empirical evidence that addresses the state competition question is inconclusive. Moreover, the preceding discussion of the existing work suggests that additional event studies would be unlikely to shed much light on the desirability of state competition. As the remainder of this Article will suggest, however, the potential for progress using theoretical analysis has not been exhausted.

D. *What States Maximize*

The analysis of this Article is premised on the assumption that, in designing corporate law rules, states — at least those that are successful in the competition for corporate charters — seek to maximize the number of companies incorporated within their boundaries. Both the race for the bottom and the race for the top theories make this assumption, at least implicitly.[67] But possible objections to this premise have not been explored; therefore, before proceeding, it is important to examine these objections.

States clearly derive benefits from in-state incorporations. Incorporations bring with them franchise tax and fee revenues as well as patronage for in-state law firms, corporation service companies, and other businesses.[68] Thus, states have an interest in increasing in-state incorporations. But the assumption that states design their corporate law rules to maximize the number of in-state incorporations might still be challenged on the ground that it does not accurately represent the complex reality of the state lawmaking process. I discuss below the three main ways in which this assumption might fail to capture the full spectrum of factors affecting states' behavior, and I explain why the assumption is nonetheless appropriate for the purpose of analyzing the effects of state competition on corporate law.

The first objection might be that although states have an interest in having more companies incorporated in-state, they also may have other interests that are directly affected by the content of the states' corporate law rules. In particular, a large state (for example, New York) may have among its citizens a significant fraction of the shareholders of its in-state corporations. Such a state, so the argument goes, may have a direct interest in the substantive content of its corporate law — in particular, in the effects of this law on shareholder

---

[67] *See* Romano, *supra* note 25, at 228 (stating that in both the race for the bottom and the race for the top theories, a state's objective is revenue-maximization, and revenue is thought to depend directly upon the volume of domestic incorporations).

[68] *See* Alva, *supra* note 4, at 888 & n.8; Cary, *supra* note 10, at 668-69; Macey & Miller, *supra* note 25, at 492-93; Romano, *supra* note 2, at 710.

value — and not only an interest in how this law affects incorporation decisions.[69]

In considering this objection, it should first be noted that the leader in the state charter competition is, and always has been, a relatively small state.[70] Delaware, the current leader, is sufficiently small to make it likely that Delaware citizens hold an insignificant fraction of the shares of Delaware companies. Consequently, Delaware does not have a significant *direct* interest in the consequences of its corporate law for shareholder value; it has a major interest only in how these consequences affect incorporation decisions. Note that the small size of the winning state is no coincidence. Rather, there are structural factors that give us reason to expect that the leader of the competition among states will be a small state like Delaware.[71]

Moreover, while a large state like New York may have a significant direct interest in having in-state companies governed by value-maximizing rules, it does not follow that the state's design of corporate law rules would not be substantially influenced by the desire to make these rules attractive to those who make incorporation decisions. For example, suppose that New York seeks to further the interests of its citizen-shareholders and disregards the interests of those who make incorporation decisions.[72] To the extent that companies respond by incorporating elsewhere, the state's adoption of rules that maximize shareholders' welfare would not help the state's citizen-shareholders. That is, because a given state's corporate law governs only companies incorporated in-state, the law's effect on the number of in-state incorporations is bound to be given much weight.

A second objection to the assumption that states seek to maximize in-state incorporations might be that, even if such maximization is a state's goal, not all of the individuals involved in the lawmaking process will necessarily focus on this goal. Legislators, judges, members of bar committees, and many other individuals influence and

[69] Of course, if the race for the top logic is correct, then the state's interest in serving its shareholder-citizens and the state's interest in attracting incorporations would coincide, as both interests would lead it to adopt value-maximizing corporate law rules.

[70] The original leader was New Jersey, and the leader since New Jersey's demise has been Delaware, *see supra* p. 1443.

[71] Delaware's small size is central to Romano's explanation of the state's dominance of the state charter competition. In particular, Romano identifies two factors particularly important to Delaware's success — the importance of incorporation-related revenues in light of Delaware's otherwise small revenue base, and the small size of the Delaware judiciary. *See* Romano, *supra* note 25, at 240, 277–78; Romano, *supra* note 2, at 721–22. Other commentators have emphasized the lack of competing political lobbies in Delaware as a determinant of Delaware's charter competition success. *See* Alva, *supra* note 4, at 918–19; Coffee, *supra* note 25, at 762–63.

[72] The analysis in the text focuses on a case in which the state's interest in fostering shareholders' welfare conflicts with its interest in attracting incorporations. If the two interests coincide, then the assumption that states choose corporate law rules to attract incorporations is unquestionably appropriate.

participate in the development of a state's corporate law.[73] These actors may not have a single-minded focus on maximizing in-state incorporations. In particular, individual players may be influenced in part by public-regarding aims, their conceptions of shareholders' and society's interests, or personal considerations.[74]

---

[73] For a recent description of the role of individuals in the formation of Delaware's corporate law, see Alva, *supra* note 4, at 917–19.

[74] It might be argued that the above discussion applies only to members of state legislative and executive branches and not to the judicial branch. State judges, so the argument goes, are insulated from the forces of influence and pressure to which members of other branches are subject, and consequently the judges will not be concerned about the state's interest in attracting incorporations. The judges will be guided solely by their sense of integrity — by their desire to do what is right. Consequently, the argument concludes, although state competition and the desire to attract incorporations are likely to affect state statutory provisions, they are unlikely to have an effect on judge-made law.

It is far from clear, however, that even state judges of great integrity — judges solely concerned with doing the right thing — will ignore the state's interest in attracting incorporations. Rather, it is quite possible that, when such a judge uses her discretion to form judge-made law, she will take this state interest into account. First, the judge may believe that considering legislative intent is part of the "right" interpretive strategy. For example, when a Delaware judge applies and interprets the Delaware corporate code, she may well be aware, and accept as her working assumption, that the code was designed with the intent of attracting and maintaining in-state incorporations. Second, the judge may view it as "right" to use her discretion in a welfare-enhancing way and, furthermore, may believe that the "right" welfare calculus is one that attaches less weight (if any at all) to the interests of out-of-state citizens than to the interests of the state's citizens. Such a judicial strategy will again lead the judge to give weight to the state's (and the state citizens') interest in attracting incorporations.

Furthermore, state judges might not be completely insulated from the forces of influence and pressure that make members of other branches concerned about the state's interest in attracting incorporations. To be sure, judges are undoubtedly much less affected by such forces than members of other branches. But judges might to some extent be affected by the preferences of members of the other branches and thus, in turn, by the forces of influence and pressure to which these members are subject. For example, the judges of the Delaware Chancery Court and the Delaware Supreme Court are appointed by the state governor, with the consent of the state senate, for a period of twelve years. *See* DEL. CONST. art. IV, §3; Macey & Miller, *supra* note 25, at 500. It is only human for judges, at least sometimes and on the margin, to not want to disappoint those who are responsible for their appointment. Furthermore, Delaware judges might well be aware that if they rendered decisions that produced a prospect of corporate migration, their decisions would likely be wholly or partly reversed by the legislature. Thus, for example, when the Delaware Supreme Court decision in Smith v. Van Gorkom, 488 A.2d 858, 874–78, 881 (Del. 1985), was perceived to create increased liability of directors and consequently the prospect of out-of-state migration by Delaware companies, the Delaware legislature reacted by adopting section 102(b)(7) of the Delaware Corporation Code, *see* DEL. CODE ANN. tit. 8, § 102(b)(7) (1991), to enable companies to limit the liability of directors. Whether or not a judge views the avoidance of such reversals as part of doing her job "right," it is only human to expect that she will prefer to avoid reversals.

For all of the above reasons, I conclude that not only state legislators and executives, but also state judges are affected by the state's interest in attracting incorporations. Consequently, state competition is likely to have an effect not only on state statutory provisions, but also on state judge-made law. In particular, to the extent that we find that states' interest in attracting incorporations would be served by having undesirable rules with respect to a given issue, we can conclude that state competition is also likely to have a detrimental effect on the judge-made

For the purpose of analyzing the effects of state competition on corporate law, however, the appropriate assumption is that a state's interest in attracting incorporations shapes the behavior of the individuals actually involved in the state's lawmaking process. If a state's interest in attracting incorporations plays no role in shaping the behavior of such individuals, then state competition has neither a good nor a bad effect on corporate law rules; it is irrelevant. Accordingly, if we assume that state competition has *some* effect and set out to analyze whether this effect is good or bad, then the appropriate assumption for the analysis is that the individuals involved in the lawmaking process are at least partially moved by the state's interest in attracting incorporations. It follows that, to the extent that we find that a state's interest in attracting incorporations will be served by adopting undesirable rules, we can conclude that state competition is detrimental. In this case, to be sure, the fact that the individuals involved in the lawmaking process may be moved only partially by the state's interest in attracting incorporations is some consolation; for it implies that the undesirable effect of state competition is less severe than it would be if these individuals all focused solely on the state's interest. But this refinement would not change at all the basic conclusion that state competition has certain systematic undesirable effects on corporate law.

Finally, a third objection to the premise that states seek to maximize in-state incorporations might be that successful states (such as Delaware) may consider in their lawmaking not only the response of incorporation decisionmakers, but also the response of federal lawmakers (courts, legislators, and agencies). That is, Delaware may elect not to adopt certain value-decreasing rules even if they are desired by incorporation decisionmakers, because adopting such rules might trigger federal intervention.[75] For example, some commentators have suggested that the decision by the Delaware Supreme Court in *Singer v. Magnavox Co.*,[76] which changed earlier case law and sig-

---

law (if any) that applies to this issue. To be sure, as discussed above, judges may be less affected by the state's interest in attracting incorporations than are state legislators and executives. In this case, the undesirable effect of state competition on judge-made law will be less severe than on state statutory law. But again, this refinement would not undermine the validity of the basic conclusion — that state competition has certain systematic, undesirable effects on both statutory and judge-made state law. For this reason, I use the term "rules" throughout to refer to rules established by *all* state law officials, including judges.

[75] In some sense, the state's interest in attracting incorporations without triggering federal intervention is just a refinement of its interest in maximizing the number of in-state incorporations. This is because *long-run* maximization of in-state incorporations requires states not only to provide corporate law rules attractive to incorporation decisionmakers, but also to avoid a situation in which federal law intervenes and stops the game altogether.

[76] 380 A.2d 969 (Del. 1977), *overruled by* Weinberger v. UOP, Inc., 457 A.2d 701 (Del. 1983).

nalled a willingness to apply close scrutiny to freezeouts, was motivated by a desire to avoid an expansion of federal law into this area.[77]

Again, although states such as Delaware may well be guided in part by their interest in avoiding federal intervention, for the purpose of analyzing the effects of state competition, the appropriate assumption remains that state law is shaped by states' desire to attract incorporations. To be sure, the fear of federal repercussion imposes a constraint on states. In particular, it imposes an upper bound on the degree of apparent harm that Delaware's corporate law rules can cause. But within the range of options that can be chosen without triggering federal intervention, states can be expected to choose the rules that are most attractive to incorporation decisionmakers. Thus, if we concluded that state competition tends to produce undesirable rules for the governance of certain issues, then the constraint imposed by the fear of federal intervention would only mitigate somewhat the magnitude of the identified adverse effect of state competition. It would not change the basic conclusion that state competition has such an adverse effect.

E. Toward a New Theory

Before proceeding to my analysis of the shortcomings of state charter competition, I wish to outline this analysis and explain briefly how it relates to the two opposing schools of thought, the race for the bottom theory and the race for the top theory. While the two theories differ on whether state competition produces desirable corporate rules, they do share certain basic premises. Both theories view the socially desirable rule with respect to any given corporate law issue as the rule that maximizes shareholder value.[78] Moreover, both theories assume that, in designing corporate law rules, states seek to make their law attractive to managers who make incorporation decisions.[79]

---

[77] *See* CLARK, *supra* note 3, § 12.3, at 520–21.

[78] *See, e.g.*, Cary, *supra* note 10, at 666, 671–72 (arguing that state charter competition is undesirable because it harms shareholders' interests); Fischel, *supra* note 12, at 921–22 (arguing that state competition is desirable because it induces corporate law rules that maximize shareholder value); *see also* Winter, *supra* note 4, at 256 (emphasizing that Cary's claim is not that state corporation law ignores overriding social goals, but rather "that Delaware is preventing *private* parties from optimizing their *private* arrangements" (emphasis in original)). Winter, for one, states explicitly that his analysis is directed at cases in which no third-party effects are involved. *See* Winter, *supra* note 4, at 253, 259.

[79] That managers make incorporation decisions and, accordingly, drive the adoption of state corporate law rules is stated explicitly in the work of race for the top theorists. *See* Easterbrook, *supra* note 12, at 545; Fischel, *supra* note 12, at 919–20; Winter, *supra* note 4, at 252. It is also clearly implicit in Cary's statement of the race for the bottom position. *See* Cary, *supra* note 10, at 668, 671–72; *see also* Macey & Miller, *supra* note 25, at 474 (noting that Cary's theory of state competition is an outgrowth of Berle and Means' recognition that managers, not shareholders, control corporate decisionmaking).

The race for the bottom and race for the top theories differ only with respect to the question of which rules are attractive to managers — that is, whether managers may seek rules that provide them with private benefits at the expense of shareholders or, instead, generally seek rules that maximize shareholder value.[80]

My analysis of the possible shortcomings of state charter competition is divided into two parts. Part II of this Article focuses on the problems that result from the possible divergence between managers' and shareholders' interests. To focus on these problems, Part II assumes, as have the existing theories of state competition, that the socially desirable rules are those that maximize shareholder value. I analyze the extent to which the existing checks on managers imposed by market forces and by the requirement of shareholder vote for reincorporation lead managers to seek (and states in turn to provide) rules that maximize shareholder value. The analysis shows that these checks have some, but far from total, effectiveness. Furthermore, the effectiveness of these checks varies widely from one area of corporate law to another. Consequently, managers are likely to seek rules that maximize shareholder value with respect to certain identifiable issues but not with respect to certain other identifiable issues.

Part III of this Article explores the possibility that state competition may produce undesirable rules because some corporate law issues involve externalities (with respect to creditors, potential buyers, or other third parties). This is a possibility to which both the race for the bottom adherents and the race for the top theorists have paid little attention.[81] When externalities are present, state competition raises serious concerns wholly apart from any problems that may arise from a divergence between managers' and shareholders' interests. In the presence of externalities, the social desirability of a corporate law rule depends not only on its effect on shareholders' interests, but also on its effect on other parties. Consequently, even if managers seek (and states in turn provide) rules that maximize shareholder value, the presence of externalities implies that these rules may well diverge from the socially desirable ones. Part III identifies certain corporate law issues that are likely to involve significant externalities. Accordingly, state competition may well produce socially undesirable results regardless of the effectiveness of the existing market checks on managerial decisions.

---

[80] Indeed, apart from the type of corporate law rules thought to attract managers and "the adjective selected to characterize state laws," the theories of state competition put forth by the two sides are difficult to distinguish. *See* Romano, *supra* note 25, at 228. As Romano puts it, "critics of the federal system agree with [the race to the top view] of the behavior of states and firms but substitute the phrase 'manager utility' for 'firm value,' as the object furthered by corporation codes, and 'permissive' or 'worst' for 'optimal' or 'most efficient,' as the characteristic outcome of the competitive legislative process." *Id.* at 229.

[81] *See* sources cited and discussed *supra* note 78.

At the outset, I wish to emphasize that, in my view, the appropriate starting point for the analysis that follows is a presumption that, absent some reasons to the contrary, state competition is more likely to produce an efficient rule than federal regulation.[82] As this Article shows, such reasons to the contrary do exist with respect to many important corporate law issues. But this presumption does provide a useful analytical starting point, and it is justified by the significant advantages that state competition offers whenever distorting biases are absent.

To start with, a regime of state corporate law is characterized by competitive pressure to produce the legal rules most attractive to those making incorporation decisions. By contrast, federal law officials are not subject to the discipline of such competitive pressure. Clearly, when the rules desired by those making incorporation decisions are indeed the socially desirable ones, such competitive pressure is beneficial.[83]

Moreover, state competition may yield informational advantages. State law officials are likely to have more information than would federal law officials with respect to the rules that are attractive to those making incorporation decisions. Incorporation decisions serve as an automatic feedback mechanism that supplies information about the relative attractiveness of various sets of rules.[84]

These benefits of state competition are simply a special case of the familiar point that, as long as competition operates to reward producers of the best product, competition is socially desirable. Thus, in

---

[82] *Cf.* Winter, *supra* note 4, at 291–92 (stating that federal intervention should be undertaken only after the need for such intervention has been clearly shown).

[83] *See, e.g.*, Fischel, *supra* note 12, at 922 (stating that federal intervention would destroy the healthy effects of state charter competition and replace the current system of fifty states striving to achieve the climate sought by companies with a "scheme of regulation by fiat").

[84] As Winter stressed, there is no effective mechanism at the federal level for evaluating the reaction of companies to corporate law rules. *See* Winter, *supra* note 4, at 290.

A third advantage of a state competition regime is that it enables different rules to coexist. A single rule may not be optimal for all publicly traded companies. A regime of state competition can offer a variety of rules, and companies can sort themselves out according to their particular needs. *See* Barry D. Baysinger & Henry N. Butler, *The Role of Corporate Law in the Theory of the Firm*, 28 J.L. & ECON. 179, 179, 184–90 (1985) (offering data to support the theory that firms "will select their state of incorporation adaptively"); *cf.* Frank H. Easterbrook, *Antitrust and the Economics of Federalism*, 26 J.L. & ECON. 23, 28 (1983) (discussing the competition among the states in the context of state antitrust law). Although I agree that this advantage is theoretically valid, in my judgment it should not be given much weight. As indicated earlier, *see supra* pp. 1443–44, 1446, there is in fact a great degree of uniformity among the rules provided by different states. This uniformity suggests that it is far from clear that public companies — or at least those who make incorporation decisions — differ all that much in the rules they seek. Moreover, and most importantly, to the extent that having several options for companies to choose from is desirable, one can contemplate a federal arrangement that provides several such options. The federal-state choice hinges upon whether federal or state law officials should determine the options among which companies will be able to choose.

the corporate context, we should limit charter competition only in those instances in which competition works to reward not those who provide the best product but rather those who provide a product with certain undesirable characteristics. It is to the identification of these instances that I now turn.

II. State Competition and Managers' Opportunism

This Part analyzes the ways in which divergence between the interests of managers and shareholders leads state competition to produce undesirable corporate law rules. To focus on the problems resulting from managers' opportunism, I assume in this Part that corporate law rules have no externality effects. Consequently, the socially desirable rule with respect to any given corporate issue is that which maximizes shareholder value. Accordingly, state charter competition works well if it produces rules that maximize shareholder value. As the analysis shows, however, state competition may well fail to do so with respect to certain issues. With respect to the identified issues, states seeking to attract incorporations may adopt rules that serve managers' and dominant shareholders' interests even if the rules are value-decreasing.[85]

A. The Managerial Opportunism Problem

1. The Centrality of Reincorporation Decisions. — Public companies make incorporation decisions at different stages in their corporate lives. They are incorporated in a particular state when they first go public, but may later reincorporate in another state. Reincorporation is generally achieved by merger or consolidation with a newly-formed company incorporated in the destination state and created expressly for reincorporation purposes.[86] Reincorporation generally requires a decision by the company's board and approval by the company's shareholders.[87]

As explained above, the appropriate premise for an analysis of the desirability of state charter competition is that states — at least those that are successful in the charter competition — design their corporate law rules to maximize the number of in-state incorporations. States therefore have an interest both in initial incorporation decisions and in subsequent incorporation decisions, and my analysis will take both

[85] The term "managers" is used in the analysis below to refer generally to those individuals — whether executives or directors — who can bring about a decision by a company's board to reincorporate. Although companies differ in how influence is divided among executives, inside directors, and independent directors, this division is not important for our purposes.

[86] *See* Dodd & Leftwich, *supra* note 12, at 263; Romano, *supra* note 25, at 248 n.38.

[87] *See* Clark, *supra* note 3, § 10.2.4, at 416–17 (stating that under state corporation law, mergers must be approved by board resolution and shareholder vote).

types of decisions into account. It should be emphasized at the outset, however, that states seeking to attract incorporations will focus largely on making their corporate law rules attractive to those making *reincorporation* decisions.

States tend to focus on reincorporation decisions because the number of explicit or implicit reincorporation decisions that public corporations make in any given period of time is greater than the number of initial incorporation decisions that companies going public for the first time make in the same period. During any given year, the number of initial incorporations is fairly limited. By contrast, during the same period, every public company makes an explicit or implicit reincorporation decision. That is, because an existing corporation can reincorporate with relative ease,[88] it may be viewed as making in any given period of time either an explicit decision to move elsewhere or an implicit decision to remain in its home state.

Considering the situation of Delaware, the dominant state in the charter competition, may illustrate the importance of reincorporations in states' calculus. In choosing its corporate law rules, Delaware undoubtedly considers the effect that its choices will have on its ability to attract initial incorporations. But Delaware will be much more concerned with retaining companies already chartered in Delaware and with inducing companies incorporated elsewhere to relocate to Delaware. Accordingly, Delaware's choice of corporate law rules will be determined primarily by its desire to ensure that its rules are attractive to those making explicit or implicit reincorporation decisions.

Given that states are likely to focus on the effect that their corporate law rules will have on reincorporation decisions, this Part initially assumes, for simplicity of exposition, that states are concerned *solely* with reincorporation decisions. Section II.F adds initial incorporations to the picture and shows that the conclusions of the analysis remain valid.

2. *Reincorporations and Managers.* — For purposes of analyzing companies' reincorporation decisions, it is useful to distinguish situations in which companies are controlled by dominant shareholders at the time the reincorporation decision is made from situations in which companies are not under such control at the time of the reincorporation decision. The analysis of this Part initially focuses on companies not controlled by a dominant shareholder at the time of the reincorporation decision. In the absence of a dominant shareholder, ownership (divided among a dispersed body of shareholders) is divorced from control, which is in the hands of the managers. Section II.E

---

88 *See* Roberta Romano, *Answering the Wrong Question: The Tenuous Case of Mandatory Corporate Laws*, 89 COLUM. L. REV. 1599, 1599–1600 (1989).

extends the analysis and considers the case of companies controlled by a dominant shareholder.

Focusing then on companies with a dispersed body of public shareholders, it is important to recognize that managers of such companies have considerable influence over reincorporation decisions. While this point will be elaborated and supported by the analysis that follows, the basic reasons for this point can be stated up front quite simply. To start with, if the managers seek to maintain the current state of incorporation, they can easily have their way; a company cannot move to another state if its managers do not bring a reincorporation proposal to a shareholder vote. Managers thus have a veto power over corporate migration. Consequently, as long as the managers of Delaware companies continue to be pleased with Delaware law, Delaware will have incorporated in-state at least the number of companies currently incorporated in Delaware. Furthermore, even if the managers would like to have the company migrate to some other state, the managers are also likely to have their way. To be sure, in this case the managers will have to obtain shareholder approval. As section II.D will explain, however, the requirement of shareholder approval is frequently an ineffective constraint because of problems of information, collective action, and distorted choice.

Thus, a state focusing on reincorporation decisions will pay substantial attention to the desires of managers. The question, of course, is which legal rules will make the law of a state attractive to managers who make (explicit or implicit) reincorporation decisions. Consider a given corporate issue X, and suppose that there are two possible rules for the governance of this issue, A and B, and that A is the value-maximizing rule. The question is whether A is necessarily the better choice for a state seeking to make its law attractive to managers making reincorporation decisions.

In examining this question, it is useful to divide the issues governed by corporate law into two groups: issues that do not involve a potential transfer of value from shareholders to managers and issues that do involve such a potential transfer. When an issue does not involve a potential transfer, there is no divergence of interest between managers and shareholders, and, thus, there is no reason for managers to prefer a value-decreasing rule. After all, there is no question that, although managers may well have some private interests, the interests of managers and shareholders are somewhat aligned, and managers accordingly prefer, all other things being equal, to have a higher share value.[89] Thus, whenever a given corporate law issue does not implicate managers' private interests, managers will undoubtedly want to

---

[89] *See infra* subsections II.B.1–II.B.4 (describing market forces that somewhat align managers' and shareholders' interests).

have the issue governed by the value-maximizing rule, and states will have an incentive to offer this rule.

Therefore, the analysis below focuses on those corporate law issues that do involve a potential transfer between shareholders and managers. With respect to such "redistributive" issues, the question arises whether states, seeking to make their law attractive to managers making incorporations decisions, may elect to provide rules that serve managers' private interests even if such rules are value-decreasing.

In addressing this question, two possible constraints on managerial discretion must be considered. One constraint, examined in section II.D, is the requirement that reincorporation be approved by shareholder vote. The main constraint that is stressed by supporters of state competition, however, is the disciplinary force exerted by various markets — the market for corporate control, the managerial labor market, the market for additional capital, and the product market.[90] Market discipline, it is argued, generally leads managers to prefer value-maximizing rules even when alternative rules seem to serve better the private interests of managers. When a rule is value-decreasing, so the argument goes, its adverse effect on shareholder value — operating through various market mechanisms — makes it on the whole unattractive to managers.

The effectiveness of market discipline, however, varies greatly across issues. In particular, there are two types of issues with respect to which market discipline can hardly be relied on to induce managers to seek value-maximizing rules. These two types of issues are those that are "significantly redistributive" and those that directly affect the strength of market discipline. The next two sections will demonstrate in turn the ineffectiveness of market discipline with respect to each of these two types of issues.

B. Significantly Redistributive Issues

With respect to redistributive issues, the effectiveness of market discipline in discouraging managers from seeking value-decreasing rules depends on the relationship between the size of the potential transfer involved (the distributive element) and the magnitude of the potential effect on overall value (the efficiency element). An issue is "insignificantly" redistributive if the distributive element is very small relative to the efficiency element — for example, the potential direct transfer to managers is $1, whereas the effect on shareholder value is $1,000. By contrast, an issue is "significantly" redistributive if the distributive element is significant relative to the efficiency element — for example, the potential transfer is $200, whereas the effect on

[90] *See* Easterbrook, *supra* note 12, at 543–46, 553–57, 564; Fischel, *supra* note 12, at 919; Winter, *supra* note 4, at 256–58, 262–66.

shareholder value is $1,000. As this example indicates, for an issue to be classified as significantly redistributive does not require that the potential transfer exceed in size the potential efficiency effect; the transfer need only constitute a significant fraction of this effect. Clear examples of significantly redistributive issues are managerial self-dealing, taking of corporate opportunities, and insider trading.

Below I examine the operation of the various markets that may affect the decisions of managers. I show that, although market discipline will probably discourage managers from seeking inefficient rules with respect to insignificantly redistributive issues, it is unlikely to have such an effect with respect to significantly redistributive issues.

1. Market for Corporate Control. — Race for the top adherents regard the market for corporate control as exerting a powerful disciplinary force. In their view, the fear of losing control induces managers to seek, and states in turn to provide, value-maximizing rules.[91] If a company reincorporates in a state that provides a certain value-decreasing rule, the company's share price will decline to reflect the loss associated with this rule. Consequently, the company will become more vulnerable to a takeover bid or a proxy contest.[92] Because a takeover bid or a proxy contest may wrest from managers the control that is valuable to them, so the argument goes, the prospect of such a bid or contest discourages managers from seeking value-decreasing rules.[93]

Because the threat of a takeover bid or a proxy contest provides managers with incentives to avoid unnecessary reductions in share value, it undoubtedly contributes to discouraging managers from seeking inefficient rules with respect to insignificantly redistributive issues. This threat, however, does not align the interests of managers and shareholders perfectly. As the market for corporate control operates, any limited reduction in share value increases only to a limited extent the likelihood of ouster in a takeover or a proxy contest. The likelihood is small that the limited reduction in share value would lead to a takeover bid or proxy contest that otherwise would not have occurred.[94] Consequently, the market for corporate control cannot be

---

[91] *See* Easterbrook, *supra* note 12, at 564; Fischel, *supra* note 12, at 919; Winter, *supra* note 4, at 256, 264–66.

[92] *See* Winter, *supra* note 4, at 266.

[93] *See* Easterbrook, *supra* note 12, at 564; Fischel, *supra* note 12, at 919; Winter, *supra* note 4, at 266. The race for the top argument that the market for corporate control induces managers to seek only value-increasing state law rules is a straightforward application of the general argument that the threat of takeovers induces managers to maximize shareholder value. For the original statement of the argument that the market for corporate control aligns managers' and shareholders' interests, see Henry G. Manne, *Mergers and the Market for Corporate Control*, 73 J. POL. ECON. 110, 112–13 (1965). For a more recent discussion of the disciplinary role of tender offers in particular, see Easterbrook & Fischel, *supra* note 46, at 1165–74.

[94] Whether a takeover bid will occur depends on whether the value of the company in the

relied upon to discourage managers from seeking value-decreasing rules with respect to issues that are significantly redistributive. Consider, for example, a value-decreasing state law rule that reduces by $1,000,000 the total value of a large company originally worth $1,000,000,000. This 0.1% reduction in the company's total value is likely to increase only minimally the probability of a takeover bid or proxy contest. Therefore, if the corporate issue governed by this rule is significantly redistributive, and the value-decreasing rule produces a direct benefit to managers worth, for example, $200,000, the very small increase in the probability of ouster resulting from incorporation in a state with this value-decreasing rule will be unlikely to discourage managers from incorporating in such a state.[95]

2. *Managerial Labor Market.* — Like the market for corporate control, the managerial labor market induces managers to take shareholders' interests into account.[96] Managerial compensation schemes constitute one mechanism that provides managers with such incentives.[97] Because managers' compensation is often tied to the firm's performance, it is argued, managers have an incentive to enhance shareholder value.[98] Similarly, managers' compensation often includes shares of the company's stock, thus providing managers with a direct interest in the value of this stock.[99] Furthermore, the market for managerial labor also disciplines managers by virtue of the detrimental effect that reductions in shareholder value have on their employment opportunities.[100] A company's success may well affect the managers'

---

eyes of some potential buyer exceeds the sum of the market price, the expected premium that would be necessary for a takeover, and the expected transaction costs involved in such a takeover. The likelihood that the company's market price is just slightly above this threshold, so that a small reduction in this price would be necessary and sufficient to satisfy the above condition, is generally quite small.

[95] To be precise, the market for corporate control would not discourage managers from seeking a given value-decreasing rule as long as the direct private benefit to the managers from the rule exceeds the increase in the probability of the managers' losing their control as a result of this rule multiplied by the private benefits to managers of being in control.

[96] *See* Easterbrook, *supra* note 12, at 554–55; Fischel, *supra* note 12, at 919.

[97] *See* Easterbrook, *supra* note 12, at 554; Fischel, *supra* note 12, at 919.

[98] *See* Easterbrook, *supra* note 12, at 554; Michael C. Jensen & Jerold L. Zimmerman, *Management Compensation and the Managerial Labor Market*, 7 J. ACCT. & ECON. 3, 4–5 (1985); Artur Raviv, *Management Compensation and the Managerial Labor Market: An Overview*, 7 J. ACCT. & ECON. 239, 240 (1985).

[99] *See* Easterbrook, *supra* note 12, at 554 (noting that managers who are awarded with stock options or phantom stock will tend to exercise their discretion to serve shareholders' interests because doing so increases the value of their stock holdings); Fischel, *supra* note 12, at 919 (arguing that stock option plans provide managers with an incentive to keep stock prices high and thus to maximize shareholders' wealth); Jensen & Zimmerman, *supra* note 98, at 4–5; Raviv, *supra* note 98, at 240.

[100] *See* Fischel, *supra* note 12, at 919 (arguing that managers have strong incentives to maximize the market value of their services). As Fischel further notes, the impact of share price on managers' employment prospects not only encourages them to act in the shareholders'

opportunities for continued employment and promotion at the company as well as their future employment prospects at other firms.[101]

These features of the managerial labor market do serve to align shareholders' and managers' interests. They clearly lead managers to prefer, all else being equal, to avoid a reduction in share value. Thus, the managerial labor market may well induce managers to seek only value-maximizing rules with respect to issues that are not significantly redistributive. However, the operation of this market does not perfectly align the interests of managers and shareholders; it does not induce managers to avoid all reductions in share value regardless of the size of the direct private benefit to them.

Because reductions in share value may have nothing to do with managerial failure, the managerial labor market operates in such a way that managers are penalized only to a limited extent for a reduction in share value.[102] Indeed, empirical evidence indicates that when a company's total stock market value increases, the annual salary and bonus of its CEO increase on average by an amount equal to only 0.002% of the change in the company's total value, and the CEO's total pay-related wealth increases by just 0.075% of the change in the company's total value.[103] The evidence also indicates that 80% of CEOs hold less than 1.38% of their company's stock, and that the median percentage of CEO ownership is 0.25%.[104]

Because the managerial labor market operates in such a way that managers bear only a very limited fraction of any reduction in total share value, managers may well favor corporate law rules that are

---

interests, but also encourages them to monitor other managers' behavior. Because the managerial labor market uses the performance of the firm as a whole to gauge individual managers' abilities, each manager thus has a stake not only in the manager's own performance, but also in the performance of other managers at the firm. *See id.*

[101] *See* Eugene Fama, *Agency Problems and the Theory of the Firm*, 88 J. POL. ECON. 288, 292 (1980).

[102] Even if managerial compensation schemes were set optimally in the shareholders' interests, we would still expect these schemes to impose rather limited penalties on reductions in share value. Reductions in share value need not be the result of managers' actions. Therefore, given that managers are risk-averse, the optimal compensation scheme does not penalize managers drastically for reductions in share value, which may depend in part on factors beyond the control of the managers. *Cf.* Bengt Holmström, *Moral Hazard and Observability*, 10 BELL J. ECON. 74, 74–80 (1979) (analyzing the optimal contract in a principal-agent relationship); Steven Shavell, *Risk Sharing and Incentives in the Principal and Agent Relationship*, 10 BELL J. ECON. 55, 66 (1979) (same). Similarly, because future employers realize that share value is only a "noisy" signal of managers' quality, it is unlikely that any given reduction in share value will result in a drastic reduction in a manager's future employment prospects. *See* Fama, *supra* note 101, at 304–06.

[103] *See* Michael C. Jensen & Kevin J. Murphy, *Performance Pay and Top Management Incentives*, 98 J. POL. ECON. 225, 260 (1990). "Total pay-related wealth" includes not only the increase in the compensation in the year in which the change in value takes place, but also the estimated positive effect on compensation in future years.

[104] *See id.* at 237.

significantly redistributive in management's favor, in spite of any adverse effect that such rules may have on the value of managers' compensation and stock holdings. Consider a rule that would produce a loss of $10,000,000 in total stock market value and a gain of $3,000,000 to the managers. It seems likely that the managers would prefer this rule to its value-maximizing alternative because the $3,000,000 direct benefit is likely to exceed substantially the rule's adverse effect on the managers' compensation and stock holdings.

Similarly, the effects of a reduction in share value on future employment and promotion are unlikely to be substantial enough to discourage top managers from seeking value-decreasing rules that are significantly redistributive in their favor. Although poor company performance does somewhat increase the risk of dismissal of top managers, the evidence suggests that even managers of poorly performing firms face a very small chance of dismissal.[105] And the effect of company performance on future employment is not of significant concern to most top managers, because such managers are likely to remain at their firms until retirement.[106]

3. Market for Additional Capital. — Race for the top adherents also rely on the market for additional capital as a source of market discipline.[107] When managers make incorporation decisions, they may contemplate the need to return to the equity markets to raise additional capital. To the extent that the company's state of incorporation has value-decreasing rules, so the argument goes, the corporation's effort to raise additional capital will be more difficult.[108] Conse-

---

[105] *See* Jerold B. Warner, Ross L. Watts, & Karen H. Wruck, *Stock Prices and Top Management Changes*, 20 J. FIN. ECON. 461, 487–88 (1988); Michael S. Weisbach, *Outside Directors and CEO Turnover*, 20 J. FIN. ECON. 431, 443 (1988). *But see* Anne T. Coughlan & Ronald M. Schmidt, *Executive Compensation, Management Turnover, and Firm Performance: An Empirical Investigation*, 7 J. ACCT. & ECON. 43, 60–61, 65 (1985) (arguing that the probability of management turnover is inversely related to stock price performance). Because CEOs are rarely fired openly, researchers looked at all cases in which a CEO departed before the normal retirement age and assumed that some of these departures were in fact camouflaged dismissals. Even among firms that performed most poorly, researchers found that the likelihood of a CEO departure before retirement age was small and that the effect of a decrease in performance on the likelihood of departure was also quite small. For example, looking at the difference between the median performing firm and a firm in the bottom 20% in terms of performance, Weisbach found that the likelihood of the CEO's departure increased only from 4.9% to 5.6%, *see* Weisbach, *supra*, at 443; Warner, Watts, and Wruck found that it increased only from 11.6% to 12.4%, *see* Warner, Watts & Wruck, *supra*, at 478; and Coughlan and Schmidt found that it increased only from 7.7% to 10.5%, *see* Coughlan & Schmidt, *supra*, at 64. Note that a decline from median performance to a performance in the bottom 20% is quite substantial (larger than one may think would arise from most value-decreasing corporate law rules).

[106] *See* Jensen & Murphy, *supra* note 103, at 34–35 (finding that most departing CEOs leave their positions only after reaching normal retirement age).

[107] *See* Easterbrook, *supra* note 12, at 543–46; Winter, *supra* note 4, at 256, 275.

[108] *See* Winter, *supra* note 4, at 275 (noting that investors "must be attracted before they can be cheated").

quently, incorporation in a state with value-decreasing rules will be unattractive to managers.

Incorporation in a state that provides certain value-decreasing rules, however, would not generally prevent a company from raising additional equity. To be sure, fully informed investors would be willing to pay less for shares than they otherwise would. But managers would still be able to raise the same amount of capital simply by offering a larger number of shares (thus reducing the remaining stake of the existing shareholders).

Thus, reincorporation in a state with value-decreasing rules will not prevent the raising of additional capital to finance expansion; it will simply increase the cost to existing shareholders of such financing. That this reduction in the value of existing shares is undesirable to the managers is due to the operation of the corporate control market and the managerial labor market. Thus, the market for additional equity does not impose on managers any constraints that are significantly different from those that have already been examined.

Finally, the effect of future capital needs on managers' decisions is even weaker than the above discussion may indicate because extra capital can be obtained in the form of debt rather than equity. As long as the reincorporation in a state with value-decreasing rules does not change the likelihood that the company will default on its debt, which often would be the case, it will not change the cost of debt. Even if the cost of debt were to increase, this increase, again, would not hinder expansion but only reduce the value of the existing shareholders' stake. At most, then, future capital needs create the same type of incentives that the examination above has found insufficient to eliminate managerial opportunism.

4. *Product Market.* — Race for the top adherents view product markets as another source of constraints on managers.[109] According to this argument, if management acts inefficiently, the company's business will contract or fail, and the managers will find themselves with a shrunken empire or indeed no empire at all.[110] This prospect is thought to discourage managers from seeking incorporation in states with value-decreasing rules.

Although product market competition does provide managers with some valuable incentives, it cannot discourage managers from seeking value-decreasing rules that are significantly redistributive in their favor. For one thing, most rules of this kind would not affect the operational efficiency of the company. That is, such rules generally

---

[109] *See* Easterbrook, *supra* note 12, at 557; Winter, *supra* note 4, at 264. For a statement of the general argument that product market competition constrains the behavior of managers, see Oliver D. Hart, *The Market Mechanism as an Incentive Scheme*, 14 BELL J. ECON. 366, 367 (1983).

[110] *See* Easterbrook, *supra* note 12, at 553–54; Winter, *supra* note 4, at 264.

would not alter the cost and quality of the company's products but rather the manner in which the value produced by the company is divided between managers and shareholders. Accordingly, such rules would not adversely affect the company's ability to compete in product markets. For example, a rule that permitted the managers of Hewlett-Packard to make certain insider trading profits at the expense of shareholders would likely have little effect on the prices at which Hewlett-Packard can sell its printers.

Furthermore, even if a certain value-decreasing rule does affect a company's operational efficiency, the disciplinary force of product markets is quite limited. Product markets are often not perfectly competitive; large companies generally operate in markets characterized by oligopolistic or monopolistic competition.[111] Because the survival of firms in such markets is hardly threatened by the existence of some operating inefficiencies, managers may well be willing to sacrifice some operating efficiencies for the direct and substantial benefits provided to them by rules that are significantly redistributive in their favor.

5. Conclusion. — The markets for corporate control, managerial labor, additional capital, and company products discipline managers' decisions to some extent. The operation of these markets may well ensure that managers will seek (and states in turn will provide) only value-increasing rules with respect to issues that are not significantly redistributive. However, as the analysis of this section has shown, the various market forces invoked by race for the top adherents do not ensure that managers will not seek value-decreasing rules with respect to other types of issues. In particular, market discipline notwithstanding, managers may seek such rules with respect to issues that are significantly redistributive.

C. Issues that Directly Affect the Strength of Market Discipline

While redistributive issues involve the private interests of managers, they need not directly implicate the strength of market discipline. Therefore, the above analysis took as a given the strength of the disciplinary force exerted by the markets for corporate control, managerial labor, capital, and the company's products. In the case of certain corporate law issues, however, the choice of a legal rule directly affects the strength of these market forces.

The best and most important illustrations of this point are rules that affect the disciplinary force exerted by the market for corporate control. For any given company, the likelihood that it will receive a takeover bid depends not only on the market price of its stock but also on the set of rules governing such bids — both the rules governing

[111] *See* JEAN TIROLE, THE THEORY OF INDUSTRIAL ORGANIZATION 277–303 (1988).

the behavior of bidders and the rules governing the use of defensive tactics by targets. Similarly, the likelihood that a proxy contest will be initiated with respect to a company may well depend not only on the company's stock price, but also on the rules governing the various aspects of proxy contests, including the disclosure required of challengers, the challengers' access to the proxy machinery, and the potential reimbursement from the corporation. Therefore, rules that make it more difficult or less profitable to make a takeover bid or launch a proxy contest weaken the disciplinary force of the market for corporate control.

Similarly, the disciplinary force of the managerial labor market may well depend on the legal rules governing certain corporate law issues. A good example is the extent to which courts scrutinize the process by which managers' compensation is set. Rules that make it easier for managers to secure generous compensation regardless of their company's performance clearly weaken the disciplinary force of the market for managerial labor.

It is worth noting that although issues that directly affect the strength of market discipline are generally redistributive, they need not be *significantly* redistributive. For example, consider a rule that makes a takeover virtually impossible. Such a rule may reduce the value of a large company by two billion dollars while providing the managers with extra security worth only twenty million dollars.

With respect to all issues that directly implicate the strength of market discipline, managers making incorporation decisions may well seek rules that weaken this discipline even if these rules are value-decreasing. Consider, for example, whether managers would find attractive a state with a value-decreasing rule that impedes takeover bids and proxy contests. Even if managers recognized that this rule reduces share value, they may well prefer it. Recall that a major reason that managers care about share value is the market for corporate control; all other things being equal, any reduction in share value increases the probability of ouster in a takeover or proxy contest. But in the case of a rule that makes bids and contests more difficult, all other things are not equal. The direct effect of the rule in reducing the likelihood of ouster at any given stock price may be sufficiently significant so that, despite the accompanying reduction in share value, the probability of ouster with the rule will be substantially smaller than without it. To take an extreme case, consider a state law rule that completely insulates managers from tender offers and thereby reduces shareholder value. In considering the appeal of this rule, managers are unlikely to be deterred by the threat of a takeover. The rule will completely eliminate this very threat, and thus the likelihood of a takeover will be smaller with this value-decreasing rule than without it.

In fact, state law rules that make it more difficult for challengers to mount takeover bids and proxy contests are very common. States have both enacted powerful antitakeover statutes[112] and permitted managers to employ a wide range of defensive tactics to fend off control challenges.[113] Indeed, the widespread adoption of antitakeover measures by states has been puzzling for race for the top adherents, who believe that charter competition produces efficient state rules and also typically view impediments to takeovers as inefficient.[114] In *Amanda Acquisition Corp. v. Universal Foods Corp.*,[115] a case involving the constitutionality of the Wisconsin antitakeover statute, Judge Easterbrook acknowledged the tension between his two strongly held views — that state competition generally drives states to adopt value-increasing rules and that antitakeover measures are value-decreasing.[116]

The analysis of this section, however, suggests that there is no reason to be surprised by the states' adoption of antitakeover rules. Indeed, such rules are to be expected, regardless of whether one views

---

[112] *See, e.g.*, Roberta Romano, *The Political Economy of Takeover Statutes*, 73 VA. L. REV. 111, 113–14 (1987).

[113] *See, e.g.*, Paramount Communications, Inc. v. Time Inc., 571 A.2d 1140, 1152–54 (Del. 1990).

[114] *See, e.g.*, Easterbrook & Fischel, *supra* note 46, at 1164; Winter, *supra* note 4, at 288–89.

[115] 877 F.2d 496 (7th Cir.), *cert. denied*, 493 U.S. 955 (1989).

[116] Since then, Judge Easterbrook and Professor Fischel have accepted that antitakeover rules present one instance in which state competition has failed. *See* FRANK H. EASTERBROOK & DANIEL R. FISCHEL, THE ECONOMIC STRUCTURE OF CORPORATE LAW 221–22 (1991). But they view this failure as an isolated phenomenon rather than, as the analysis of this Article suggests, a manifestation of a more general problem.

Ralph Winter also struggled with the tension between the race for the top logic and the view that state antitakeover laws are detrimental to the interests of shareholders. *See* Winter, *supra* note 4, at 288. Winter sought to explain the existence of the then-existing state antitakeover statutes — which, unlike today's statutes, were not limited in their application to corporations chartered in-state — on the ground that these statutes were motivated by considerations other than the desire to attract incorporations. In particular, he argued that because the statutes had an extraterritorial effect, states' interest in attracting incorporations was not a significant factor in states' decisions to adopt such a statute. Indeed, in his view, "takeover statutes are a chartering issue in only a peripheral sense." *See id.* at 288–89.

In 1982, however, the Supreme Court declared unconstitutional extraterritorial state antitakeover statutes. *See* Edgar v. MITE Corp., 457 U.S. 624, 643–46 (1982). Antitakeover statutes since that time have been limited in their application to corporations chartered in-state, *see* Romano, *supra* note 2, at 726 n.48, and statutes limited in this way have been upheld against constitutional challenge, *see* CTS Corp. v. Dynamics Corp. of America, 481 U.S. 69, 93–94 (1987) (rejecting a Commerce Clause challenge to an Indiana antitakeover statute). The development of state antitakeover laws since the publication of Winter's article therefore undercuts his attempt to square the prevalence of state antitakeover laws with the race for the top logic. *See* Romano, *supra* note 2, at 726 & n.48.

them as beneficial or detrimental to shareholders.[117] Antitakeover rules provide managers with direct benefits. And, as this section has shown, because such rules weaken the disciplinary force of the market for corporate control, market discipline can hardly be relied on to discourage managers from seeking these rules.

D. The Need for Shareholder Vote to Reincorporate

The analysis in sections B and C demonstrated that, despite the operation of market forces, managers may well prefer that their company be governed by certain value-decreasing rules. This conclusion by itself indicates that states, at least those states that are already successful in the charter competition, may well elect to provide these rules. For a state as successful in the charter competition as Delaware, retaining the companies it already has is of great importance. As explained earlier, a reincorporation requires a board decision, and managers thus have a veto power over their company's departure from its present state of incorporation. Thus, as long as the managers of Delaware companies are pleased with Delaware's corporate law, these companies will not migrate. Therefore, if the managers of Delaware companies prefer, despite the operation of market forces, a certain value-decreasing rule, Delaware will have an incentive to provide this rule.

In addition to retaining the companies a state already has, however, a state may be also interested in attracting more companies. In considering how to attract out-of-state companies, a state will know that making its law attractive to the managers of these companies may not be sufficient to bring in these companies. A reincorporation requires not only a board decision but also an approving vote by the company's shareholders.[118] It may be argued that this need for shareholder approval can discourage states seeking to attract reincorporations of out-of-state companies from providing value-decreasing rules.

---

117 My personal view is that some common state law rules governing takeovers — in particular, those enabling certain defensive tactics — are harmful. I do believe, however, that control share acquisition statutes can be beneficial. My overall view with respect to state law rules governing takeovers is that they discourage takeovers more than is desirable for target shareholders. *See* Lucian A. Bebchuk, *Toward Undistorted Choice and Equal Treatment in Corporate Takeovers*, 98 HARV. L. REV. 1693, 1771–74 (1985); Lucian A. Bebchuk, *The Sole Owner Standard for Takeover Policy*, 17 J. LEGAL STUD. 197, 197–99 (1988).

118 Reincorporation requires shareholder approval because the usual reincorporation mechanism is a merger with a newly formed company incorporated in the destination state, *see* source cited *supra* note 87, and mergers must be approved by shareholders, *see* CLARK, *supra* note 3, § 10.2.4, at 416–17; *see also* 8 DEL. CODE ANN. § 251 (1991) (requiring shareholder approval for mergers).

To examine this argument, suppose that Delaware's corporate law includes certain value-decreasing rules. As the analysis below will show, the shareholders of a given company may well approve a proposed move to Delaware despite the presence of these rules. First, the proposed move to Delaware may on the whole increase shareholder value. Second, even if the proposed move were harmful to shareholder value, shareholders may still approve it because they may have imperfect information about the consequences of the move. Third, even if shareholders were aware that the proposed move would decrease shareholder value, they may still vote for the move if the managers tied the move to another measure or course of action desired by shareholders.

1. The Move May Increase Shareholder Value Overall. — Suppose that Delaware's rule for the governance of a certain corporate law issue, *X*, is value-decreasing. Even assuming that shareholders are aware of the expected consequences of Delaware's rule with respect to *X*, the shareholders may prefer, and vote in favor of, a move to Delaware. For the shareholders may judge the effects of the move to be positive overall.

First, although Delaware's rule for the governance of *X* is value-decreasing, the rules Delaware offers with respect to some issues, which are insignificantly redistributive or non-redistributive, may well be superior to the rules offered by the company's current home state. As discussed above, state charter competition works well with respect to certain issues.[119] The benefit to shareholders from Delaware's rules for the governance of these issues may outweigh the costs to shareholders of Delaware's rule for the governance of *X*.

In addition, as Roberta Romano's analysis has pointed out, Delaware's long domination of the state charter competition provides its corporate law with some attractive features that are independent of the substantive content of its corporate law rules.[120] These advantages include the availability of a large body of precedent as well as a specialized and experienced judiciary.[121] Shareholders may rationally attach a value to these features, and this value may also contribute to a conclusion that, notwithstanding Delaware's value-decreasing rule with respect to *X*, the move to Delaware would be value-increasing on the whole.

Finally, it is important to note that Delaware's value-decreasing rule for the governance of *X* may be no different than the rule governing *X* in the company's home state. Indeed, because Delaware's dominant position in the state charter competition has produced wide-

---

[119] *See supra* p. 1457.

[120] *See supra* pp. 1446–47.

[121] *See* Romano, *supra* note 25, at 277–78; Romano, *supra* note 2, at 722.

spread diffusion of its corporate law rules,[122] it is likely (though by no means certain) that competing states have the same value-decreasing rule with respect to *X*. That is, state competition may well have produced an equilibrium in which not only Delaware but also the company's current home state, and possibly other states, all provide value-decreasing rules for the governance of *X*. In such an equilibrium, of course, shareholders' evaluation of a proposed move to Delaware would disregard Delaware's rule with respect to *X*.

It is important to emphasize that the shareholders' *overall* preference for Delaware, despite its value-decreasing treatment of *X*, does not imply that state charter competition produces generally optimal results. Consider first the case in which shareholders prefer the legal treatment of *X* in their company's home state to the value-decreasing treatment of *X* in Delaware but nevertheless approve a move to Delaware because Delaware's legal regime as a whole better serves their interests.[123] If state competition did not lead to Delaware's value-decreasing treatment of *X*, the shareholders would find reincorporation in Delaware even more attractive. Thus, if federal law governed *X* and applied a value-maximizing rule with respect to it, shareholders would be better off. For such a federal rule would in no way eliminate the benefits that make incorporation in Delaware attractive to shareholders in the first place.

Consider now the case in which the legal treatment of *X* in Delaware is identical to the legal treatment of *X* in the company's home state and in which shareholders prefer Delaware on independent grounds. Again, shareholders would find Delaware even more attractive if the legal treatment of *X* were not determined by a race for the bottom with respect to *X*. Governance of *X* by federal law would eliminate the adverse consequences of the race for the bottom forces and permit a movement away from the undesirable equilibrium in which many or all states have value-decreasing legal rules governing *X*.

2. *Shareholders May Be Imperfectly Informed.* — Even if a move to Delaware would, on the whole, reduce a given company's value, the company's shareholders may well vote to approve such a reincorporation. The shareholders are likely to vote in this way because, in contrast to the assumptions made thus far with respect to the shareholder approval process, shareholders may well be imperfectly informed about the consequences of reincorporation in Delaware.[124]

---

[122] *See supra* notes 32–33 and accompanying text.

[123] Delaware's legal regime as a whole may better serve the shareholders' interests either by virtue of its substantive provisions governing issues other than *X* or by virtue of Delaware's unique institutional features.

[124] For a discussion of the general problem of imperfect information in corporate voting, see CLARK, *supra* note 3, § 9.5, at 389–96; *see also* Bebchuk, *Limiting Contractual Freedom*, *supra*

Facing a vote on a proposed move to Delaware, the great majority of shareholders would rationally elect to remain ignorant about the expected consequences of the move. For any shareholder who holds a small stake in the company, the expected benefit of acquiring and processing information about the move is very small; the shareholder's own vote is highly unlikely to be pivotal to the vote's outcome and thus is highly unlikely to affect the shareholder's interests.[125] Because the expected benefit to individual shareholders of casting an educated vote is so small, shareholders lack sufficient incentives to acquire information about the effects of the proposed reincorporation.[126] Indeed, given the extremely small likelihood of casting a decisive vote, small shareholders will rationally decline to inform themselves even if they can do so at fairly minimal cost — say, by spending three hours reading proxy materials.[127]

Indeed, small shareholders will likely remain uninformed even if, at the time of the vote on the proposed move, the company happens to have one or more large shareholders who do have a good assessment of the move's consequences. To start with, such large shareholders

---

note 17, at 1836–40 (discussing imperfect information as a problem for shareholder approval requirements).

[125] An individual shareholder's chance of casting the deciding vote is small even in the case of shareholders with such significant blocks as one or two percent of the company's stock. The probability of casting the deciding vote is obviously even smaller in the more common case of shareholders with insignificant holdings. *See* Gary Chamberlain & Michael Rothschild, *A Note on the Probability of Casting a Decisive Vote*, 25 J. ECON. THEORY 152, 152–53 (1981).

[126] The rational ignorance dimension of the voting mechanism may be described as a collective action problem. If an individual shareholder votes in an informed manner, then the expected outcome of the vote will be closer to the outcome that would have been obtained in the presence of perfect information. The benefits associated with a better outcome of the vote are enjoyed not only by the individual shareholder in question, but also by all other shareholders, yet the costs of acquiring and processing information are borne by the shareholder alone. Accordingly, the individual shareholder will underinvest in the acquisition and processing of information. For general discussions of the collective action problem that afflicts the voting mechanism, see ANTHONY DOWNS, AN ECONOMIC THEORY OF DEMOCRACY 208–16 (1957); ALBERT O. HIRSCHMAN, EXIT, VOICE, AND LOYALTY (1970); and MANCUR OLSON, THE LOGIC OF COLLECTIVE ACTION 60–65 (2d ed. 1971). In the context of corporate voting, a shareholder's acquisition and processing of information is a public good and, like public goods generally, will be produced by private parties at a suboptimal level.

[127] It is worthwhile to note that the situation of a shareholder confronted with a corporate vote differs significantly from the situation of a shareholder considering an initial purchase of shares. While, as explained in the text, an individual shareholder's decision about how to vote is unlikely to affect the outcome of the vote and, accordingly, unlikely to affect the purchaser's interests, a potential purchaser's decision whether to buy shares is certain to affect the decision-maker's interests. Therefore, a potential purchaser has a much greater incentive to make an informed decision than a shareholder facing a corporate vote. In light of the distinction between a shareholder's decision about how to vote and a potential purchaser's decision whether to buy shares, even those who believe that shareholders will fully inform themselves before committing their money must still recognize the likelihood that shareholders may *vote* on the basis of imperfect information.

may well lack sufficient incentive to disseminate their information to other shareholders; they would bear all the costs of the dissemination even though its benefits would be shared by all shareholders. In addition, even if the large shareholders attempted to disseminate information to other shareholders, the dissemination would likely be ineffective. As explained above, small shareholders may well lack sufficient incentives even to read materials sent to them. Moreover, the anticipation that attempted dissemination would be ineffective would discourage the large shareholders from attempting it in the first place.[128]

The informational problems discussed in the preceding paragraphs afflict not just votes on reincorporation proposals but shareholder voting generally.[129] The magnitude of these problems, however, appears to be especially large in the reincorporation context because of the substantial amount of information necessary to evaluate fully the complex consequences of reincorporation in a new state. The only cases in which shareholders become sufficiently informed to oppose management involve votes on proposals whose main consequences are fairly apparent, such as proposals to adopt antitakeover provisions. By contrast, assessing the merits of reincorporation in Delaware (or any other state) requires that shareholders consider a great variety of

---

[128] It may be argued that shareholders can inform themselves cheaply about the merits of a proposed reincorporation by observing the stock market reaction to the reincorporation proposal. This argument, however, is not valid. To start with, shareholders typically would have difficulty discerning the market's reaction to the proposed reincorporation. Movements in the market price of the company's stock in the wake of the proposal reflect not only the market's reaction to the proposal, but also the market's reaction to other information about the company, the industry, and the economy that becomes available at the time. Indeed, the proposal itself may well convey to the market important information about other developments concerning the company (such as future acquisitions) that are more significant than its proposed reincorporation. *See* Coffee, *supra* note 25, at 767–68; Romano, *supra* note 25, at 267 & n.58. *See generally supra* notes 59–60 and accompanying text (explaining the problems with inferring from stock market reactions the desirability to shareholders of reincorporation as distinguished from other events signalled by reincorporation). Thus, because movements in stock price reflect reactions to different types of information, shareholders may well be unable to draw reliable inferences from such movements about the merits of a proposed reincorporation.

Furthermore, the argument considered — that shareholders can rely on stock market reactions to inform themselves about the merits of a reincorporation proposal — is logically inconsistent. If proposals of value-decreasing reincorporations were generally accompanied by price drops and such price drops induced shareholders to reject reincorporation, then there would be no reason for price drops in the first place. That is, in a rational market, a price drop could accompany the proposal of a value-decreasing reincorporation only if shareholder approval of the reincorporation proposal were possible. In economic terminology, the case in which a proposal of a value-decreasing reincorporation is accompanied by a price drop and is subsequently rejected by shareholders (either as a result of the market decline or for other reasons) is not an equilibrium: price drops can occur in an equilibrium only if there is a positive probability that the proposal will receive shareholder approval.

[129] *See* Bebchuk, *Limiting Contractual Freedom*, *supra* note 17, at 1836–40.

issues, spanning all areas of the company's affairs. This complexity exacerbates the informational problems that are commonly present in shareholder voting.

3. The Move May Be Tied to Another Measure. — Finally, even if a proposed reincorporation would, on the whole, decrease a corporation's value and shareholders are aware of this consequence of the move, shareholders may nonetheless vote in favor of reincorporation. To obtain such approval, managers may use their control over the corporate agenda and the company's policy. In particular, managers may tie the reincorporation issue to some other matter, thus distorting shareholders' votes on the proposed reincorporation.[130]

For example, management may couple the proposal, either explicitly or implicitly, with another measure or course of action that shareholders desire independently. Management also might threaten, explicitly or implicitly, to follow a course of action less desirable to shareholders if the proposed reincorporation is not approved. As long as such a tie or threat is credible and the overall package is more desirable to shareholders than the alternative, shareholders will rationally elect to vote in favor of the proposed reincorporation even if they know that the reincorporation by itself will be value-decreasing.[131]

4. Conclusion. — The preceding analysis shows that the requirement of shareholder approval for reincorporation proposals cannot be relied on to discourage managers from seeking — and states in turn from providing — value-decreasing rules with respect to certain corporate law issues. This conclusion, however, does not imply that the shareholder approval requirement serves no purpose. To the contrary, the requirement may establish some boundaries on how far Delaware (and other states) will go (and how far managers will want them to go) in providing value-decreasing rules. For our purposes, however, the important point is that, notwithstanding the requirement of shareholder approval, Delaware and other states have significant room (and incentives) to adopt value-decreasing rules for the governance of certain corporate law issues.[132]

---

130 The problem of distorted shareholder voting (in the context of approving dual class recapitalizations) has been analyzed in detail by Professor Gordon. *See* Jeffrey N. Gordon, *Ties that Bond: Dual Class Common Stock and the Problem of Shareholder Choice*, 76 CAL. L. REV. 1, 39–60 (1988).

131 Market discipline cannot be relied upon to discourage managers from using their control over the corporate agenda and company policy to distort shareholders' votes on a proposed reincorporation that decreases shareholder value. The very fact that the reincorporation is formally proposed to shareholders despite its adverse effect on shareholder value indicates the existence of some shortcoming in market discipline. And the same factors that are behind this shortcoming are likely to impede the effectiveness of market discipline in inducing managers not to abuse their power in order to extract approval from shareholders.

132 Even after concluding that the approval requirement does not at present provide an

E. Companies with a Dominant Shareholder

This Part has focused until now on companies that do not have a dominant shareholder at the time an (explicit or implicit) reincorpor-

---

effective check on managers, it may be argued that the approval process is not inherently imperfect. In particular, it may be argued, the imperfections of the approval process could be remedied by adopting, possibly by federal law, regulations aimed at improving this process. An analysis of possible such regulations, however, indicates that it is very difficult to design regulations that would turn the approval requirement into an effective constraint. To illustrate this point, I discuss below two possible reform strategies.

Consider first the possibility of adopting disclosure requirements that would require managers to provide shareholders voting on a reincorporation with a great deal of information. To start with, recall that the analysis of this section identified three reasons why shareholders may approve a move to Delaware even if Delaware provides a value-decreasing rule with respect to a given issue. The considered disclosure requirements would have no effect with respect to two of these reasons — the possibility that the move is positive on the whole despite the value-decreasing rule, and the possibility that the managers will tie the reincorporation, at least implicitly, to another measure or policy. Thus, the disclosure requirements would aim only at one problem discussed in this section — the possibility of shareholders' being imperfectly informed about the consequences of the move to Delaware — and it is far from clear that the disclosures that regulations can mandate would do much to remedy this problem.

Indeed, following the existing general proxy rules, managers already provide shareholders voting on a reincorporation proposal with a great deal of "raw" information about the proposed move and the differences between the two states' corporate law systems. But providing shareholders with all the relevant raw facts can do little to solve the problem of imperfect information. Even with all these facts, a shareholder would not be able to form a judgment on whether the move is desirable on the whole without making a significant investment in evaluating and aggregating this information. And, for the reasons explained above, most shareholders would not have an incentive to do so. Finally, one may consider requiring managers to reveal to shareholders not all the relevant raw facts, but rather the conclusion that can be derived from them regarding whether the reincorporation would be desirable. But because there is generally no objective, indisputable answer to this question, such a requirement would be practically meaningless.

Consider next the possibility of imposing a supermajority requirement for a reincorporation. Again, such a regulation would have no effect with respect to two of the three reasons identified in this section regarding why shareholders may approve a reincorporation in Delaware even if Delaware has certain value-decreasing rules; such a regulation would, again, aim only at addressing the problem of shareholders' imperfect information. Some of the shareholders may have accurate information about the consequences of a proposed reincorporation, it may be argued, and a supermajority requirement would have the desirable effect of making the reincorporation depend on the approval of these informed shareholders.

Now a supermajority requirement can clearly make it more difficult to obtain shareholder approval of a reincorporation. But an effective approval requirement is not simply one that makes reincorporations in general more difficult. Reincorporations may be value-increasing (that is, "good") as well as value-decreasing (that is, "bad"). An effective approval process is one that screens incorporation proposals well, distinguishing good reincorporations from bad, and enabling the former while preventing the latter. Unfortunately, designing a supermajority requirement that would effectively serve such a screening function does not seem feasible.

To see this point, observe first that the presence of good reincorporations implies the clear undesirability of any supermajority requirement that is close to unanimity. Because many shareholders, aware of the very small effect of their vote, are unlikely to bother to participate in any corporate vote, a demanding supermajority requirement, say one of ninety percent, would make it quite difficult to have even a very desirable reincorporation. Moreover, such a deation decision is made. I now turn to the case in which a dominant shareholder is present. As explained below, when a company with a dominant shareholder makes a reincorporation decision, its managers may well seek, and states wishing to attract such a corporation will in turn provide, rules that transfer wealth from public shareholders to the controlling shareholder — even if these rules are value-decreasing.[133] Examples of rules that potentially involve such transfers are those rules that govern the allocation of opportunities between a parent and its subsidiary, and those rules that govern fiduciary duties and appraisal rights in going-private and parent-subsidiary freezeouts.

In a company with a dominant shareholder, that shareholder generally controls the selection of managers. Thus, in such a case managers have a strong incentive to make incorporation decisions that serve the interests of that shareholder. Neither market forces nor the requirement of shareholder approval will discourage the managers from serving the interests of the dominant shareholder. To start with, the presence of a dominant shareholder makes the shareholder approval requirement even less effective than in the case of a company without a dominant shareholder.[134] Often the controlling shareholder will be able to gain the necessary approval simply by voting its own shares. And even if the controller's own shares are insufficient in

---

manding supermajority requirement may put some shareholders in a position to block a reincorporation and thus give them an undesirable hold-up power.

Thus, what remains to be considered is the possibility of raising the decisive fraction of approving shareholders to some high level that is still reasonably below unanimity, for example, two-thirds or three-quarters. Such a requirement, however, would not effectively screen reincorporation proposals. Although such a requirement would probably enable the great majority of good reincorporations to take place, it could not be relied upon to prevent all bad reincorporations. As the analysis of this section has demonstrated, the great majority of shareholders, including institutional investors, do not have sufficient incentive to become well informed about the consequences of a proposed reincorporation. Thus, it may well be that not even as much as one-third or one-quarter of the shareholders of a company will become well informed about these consequences. The problem, in essence, is that there is no supermajority level that would be not so high as to make difficult the adoption of many good reincorporations yet at the same time high enough to ensure that the fraction of informed shareholders would be sufficient to prevent bad reincorporations. For the fraction of shareholders that would be well informed in a given reincorporation vote depends on various features of the company and the situation, and, accordingly, it cannot be specified in general or in advance.

In an earlier article, I analyzed in detail the difficulties in designing rules to improve the effectiveness of shareholder approval requirements. *See* Bebchuk, *Limiting Contractual Freedom, supra* note 17, at 1852–58. In addition to supermajority requirements, that analysis also demonstrated the ineffectiveness of appraisal rights. Although that analysis was explicitly concerned with shareholders' approval of charter amendments, the arguments it made largely apply also to the context of shareholders' approval of reincorporations.

133 A rule that transfers wealth from public shareholders to the controller will reduce total shareholder value if the loss suffered by public shareholders exceeds the gain enjoyed by the controller.

134 *See* Victor Brudney & Marvin A. Chirelstein, *Fair Shares in Corporate Mergers and Takeovers*, 88 HARV. L. REV. 297, 299–307 (1974).

number, the controller's hold over the proxy machinery will usually enable it to gain easily the extra votes necessary to ensure approval.

Similarly, market forces can do very little to discourage the managers of a company with a controlling shareholder from seeking value-decreasing rules that transfer value to a controller. The market for corporate control exerts no disciplinary force because, with a dominant shareholder in place, takeover bids and proxy contests are not possible. Similarly, the managerial labor market will not discourage the managers from seeking such rules; in fact, the managers may well expect increased compensation and higher chances of being retained if they act in ways that serve the controller's interests. In sum, notwithstanding market forces and the shareholder approval requirement, managers of companies with a dominant shareholder may well seek, and states in turn may well provide, rules that transfer wealth from public shareholders to the controlling shareholder.

F. Initial Incorporation Decisions

Thus far, this Part has assumed that states focus solely on (explicit and implicit) incorporation decisions made subsequent to initial incorporation. I now introduce initial incorporation decisions into the analysis. By "initial incorporation decision" I mean the choice of the company's state of incorporation at the time the company first goes public.[135]

I consider below whether the presence of initial incorporation decisions affects the validity of the preceding sections' conclusions. It is useful to proceed with this examination in two stages: first, to consider how state competition would work in a hypothetical world in which companies make only initial incorporation decisions; and second, to consider the case of a world such as ours, in which companies make both initial incorporation decisions and reincorporation decisions. The analysis shows that introducing initial incorporations does not change the basic conclusion that state competition works poorly with respect to certain corporate law issues.

1. A World with Only Initial Incorporations. — Consider a hypothetical world in which, because of legal or practical impediments to reincorporation, public companies make only initial incorporation decisions. In such a world, buyers of stock in a company's initial public offering can expect that the corporate law rules of the state in which the company is incorporated at present will govern the company forever.

[135] The company, of course, may have moved from state to state prior to going public. But incorporation decisions of close companies differ from those of public companies. *See supra* p. 1442.

In a world with only initial incorporations, a state seeking to maximize local incorporations must make its corporate law attractive to those parties who control companies at the time that the companies first go public. Suppose that an entrepreneur has set up a company, wishes to sell the company's shares to public investors in a public offering, and now must choose the state in which the company will be incorporated at the time it goes public (and forever thereafter). What corporate law rules would such an entrepreneur seek and states thus have an incentive to provide? The answer depends upon the extent to which the price that the entrepreneur expects to obtain in the public offering of the company's shares accurately reflects the consequences of the corporate law rules governing the company.

To understand this point, suppose that the entrepreneur expects buyers of stock to be perfectly informed about all the consequences of the incorporation state's law. In this case, the entrepreneur will not wish to have any rule that is inefficient — even if the rule seems to provide the entrepreneur with some direct benefit. Suppose, for example, that the entrepreneur expects to manage the company after it goes public and that a certain rule concerning self-dealing would produce (relative to an alternative rule) a direct benefit of $10 to the first manager but a reduction of $20 in the company's value. Given that buyers of stock are aware of the consequences of the self-dealing rule, the entrepreneur can expect to obtain $20 less for the company's shares than if the company were governed by the alternative rule. The entrepreneur's interest, therefore, would not be served by the self-dealing rule. Thus, as long as the price of shares sold in initial public offerings accurately reflects the consequences of any given corporate law rule, entrepreneurs will seek, and states will have incentives to offer, only value-increasing rules.[136]

The logic of the above analysis also indicates, however, that if buyers of stock are imperfectly informed about the consequences of corporate law rules, the entrepreneur's interests may be best served by a rule that provides the entrepreneur with some direct benefit even if the rule is value-decreasing. Consider again the above example of a rule that produces a direct benefit of $10 for the entrepreneur and imposes a loss of $20 on the shareholders, and suppose now that potential buyers of stock are imperfectly informed and will assess the rule's cost to them at only $5. In this case, the entrepreneur will

---

[136] Another way to see why entrepreneurs will seek efficient corporate law rules when pricing is accurate is to view the shares sold by the entrepreneur as a product, and to view each of the corporate law rules governing the company as a feature of this product. When the potential buyers of a product have complete information about each feature of the product, it will be in the producer's interest to make an efficient choice with respect to all of the product's features. Analogously, it will be in the entrepreneur's interest to seek efficient corporate law rules when potential purchasers are fully informed.

prefer the self-dealing rule to its value-maximizing alternative; for the rule will reduce by only $5 the amount obtained for the shares sold in the public offering while yielding a direct benefit of $10.

Thus, one's conclusions about the merits of state competition in a hypothetical world with only initial incorporations depend on one's view about whether the price at which shares are sold in a public offering accurately reflects the consequences of all the corporate law rules governing the company going public. This question is one on which commentators have different views. In the view of some commentators, stock prices reflect the consequences of all relevant corporate law rules.[137] To be sure, these commentators recognize that many buyers of stock rationally may elect not to study the various corporate law rules governing a company. But they believe that certain sophisticated players do engage in such activity and that various market mechanisms incorporate these players' information into prices. Thus, when examining the case of a world with only initial incorporations, commentators who hold this view would conclude that there is no basis for concern that opportunism on the part of those taking companies public would prevent state competition from working well.

Other commentators, however, believe that the price of stock in initial public offerings may well fail to reflect accurately the consequences of all the corporate law rules governing a company.[138] Although these commentators agree that market mechanisms improve the accuracy of prices, they believe that such mechanisms are not sufficiently effective to ensure the accurate pricing of every corporate law rule. Consequently, even when considering a hypothetical world with only initial incorporations, these commentators still would find a basis for concern about the consequences of state competition. In particular, they would be concerned that opportunism on the part of those parties that take companies public would lead states to adopt rules that favor these parties even when such rules are value-decreasing.

---

[137] *See, e.g.*, Frank H. Easterbrook & Daniel R. Fischel, *The Corporate Contract*, 89 COLUM. L. REV. 1416, 1430–32.

[138] *See, e.g.*, LUCIAN A. BEBCHUK, FREEDOM OF CONTRACT AND THE CORPORATION: AN ESSAY ON THE MANDATORY ROLE OF CORPORATE LAW 50–62 (Harvard Program in Law and Economics Discussion Paper No. 46, 1988); Victor Brudney, *Corporate Governance, Agency Costs, and the Rhetoric of Contract*, 85 COLUM. L. REV. 1403, 1411–27 (1985); Robert C. Clark, *Contracts, Elites, and Traditions in the Making of Corporate Law*, 89 COLUM. L. REV. 1703, 1718–19, 1730–31 (1989); John C. Coffee, Jr., *The Mandatory/Enabling Balance in Corporate Law: An Essay on the Judicial Role*, 89 COLUM. L. REV. 1618, 1676–77 (1989); Melvin A. Eisenberg, *The Structure of Corporation Law*, 89 COLUM. L. REV. 1461, 1516–18 (1989); Jeffrey N. Gordon, *The Mandatory Structure of Corporate Law*, 89 COLUM. L. REV. 1549, 1569–73 (1989).

Thus, even if all incorporation decisions were made before public companies first went public, state competition may well produce undesirable results with respect to some corporate law issues. But this is not the argument that I wish to stress. Instead, I turn now to show that, because companies in the real world also make reincorporation decisions, state competition works poorly in certain contexts regardless of the accuracy of stock prices in initial public offerings.

2. *A World with Both Initial Incorporations and Reincorporations.* — Consider now a world such as ours, in which companies make both initial incorporation decisions and reincorporation decisions. As the analysis of the preceding sections has shown, states that seek to attract reincorporations may well adopt value-decreasing rules with respect to a certain set of issues. Let us call this set *X*. As explained below, introducing initial incorporations into the analysis does not change the basic conclusion that state competition is likely to produce undesirable results with respect to the set *X* of issues.

Consider first the incentives of states, such as Delaware, that have enjoyed considerable success in the competition for corporate charters and that serve as domicile for many companies. As explained in the preliminary discussion of the centrality of reincorporations,[139] states such as Delaware are likely to focus on ensuring that their corporate law rules are attractive to those who make (explicit or implicit) reincorporation decisions. By focusing on such decisions, these states can hope not only to attract companies currently incorporated elsewhere, but also, perhaps more importantly, to retain the many companies currently incorporated in-state. The interest of these states in making their corporate law attractive to those making reincorporation decisions seems likely to outweigh their interest in making their law attractive to those making initial incorporation decisions. Thus, with respect to any issue, if such a state is forced to choose between a rule that would be attractive to those making reincorporation decisions and a rule that would be attractive to those making initial incorporation decisions, it would likely adopt the former rule.

It remains to consider, however, the incentives of those states that do not presently serve as domicile for many public companies. These states may of course focus on attracting reincorporating companies. But states that initially have very few in-state incorporations also may seek to increase the number of such incorporations by adopting a strategy of offering corporate law rules designed to attract initial incorporations. In particular, such a state, say Kansas, may seek to attract initial incorporations by adopting efficient rules with respect to the set of issues *X*. In this way, so the argument goes, Kansas

---

139 *See supra* subsection II.A.1.

would be able to attract a significant fraction of the initial incorporations taking place. Over time, Kansas would become home to many public companies, and these companies would be governed by efficient rules with respect to the set of issues *X*.

It should be pointed out at the outset that, for such a strategy to have a chance of succeeding, the price in initial public offerings of Kansas companies must reflect the value of the efficient rules offered by Kansas. Now note that the Kansas rules are likely to be "innovative" by virtue of their departure from the familiar rules that Delaware and other states with many in-state incorporations offer. And there are reasons to believe that the pricing of "innovative" rules is especially likely to be inaccurate.[140] But in any event, let us grant that buyers of stock would be perfectly informed about the rules offered by Kansas. As explained below, even under this strong assumption, it is far from clear that the considered strategy would work.

To start with, even if Kansas offers efficient rules with respect to the set of issues *X*, Delaware law may still, on the whole, be better for shareholders and thus more attractive to initial incorporators. First, as discussed earlier, Delaware is likely to offer efficient rules with respect to issues that do not belong to the set *X*.[141] Furthermore, even if Kansas imitates all of the rules provided by Delaware with respect to issues that do not belong to the set *X*, Delaware still offers certain significant advantages such as a substantial body of precedents and an experienced judiciary.[142]

More importantly, buyers of stock in the initial public offering of a Kansas company will not expect the company to be governed forever by the efficient rules that Kansas now offers with respect to the set of issues *X*. Accordingly, they will substantially discount the value that they attach to the fact that these efficient rules now govern the company. The buyers will have such expectations for two reasons. First, although the company is now incorporated in Kansas, it later may reincorporate in some other state, such as Delaware.[143] Second, Kansas may, at some later point in time, replace its current value-maximizing rules for the governance of *X* with the rules in force in

[140] *See* Gordon, *supra* note 138, at 1569–73. Gordon argues that investors will view innovations with suspicion and therefore tend to draw negative inferences from departures from prevailing corporate law rules. Consequently, investors will pay less for the stock of companies governed by innovative arrangements. *See id.*

[141] *See supra* subsection II.D.1.

[142] *See supra* subsection I.B.3.

[143] The fact that a reincorporation would require a vote of shareholder approval does not eliminate this possibility. Managers may be able to obtain the required approval even if the move to Delaware would be value-decreasing. This may result from the problem of uninformed voting, *see supra* subsection II.D.2, or from the problem of distorted voting (as a result of the managers' coupling the reincorporation proposal with some other measure), *see supra* subsection II.D.3.

Delaware. Indeed, if the strategy of Kansas is successful and attracts many initial incorporations, a later shift to Delaware-like rules is precisely what is likely to occur. Once Kansas has chartered many corporations, it will have an incentive to focus on — or at least pay significant attention to — ensuring that these corporations remain chartered in Kansas.[144]

The above discussion assumes that companies initially incorporated in Kansas would have the option of reincorporating elsewhere later on. Without such an option, buyers of stock in a Kansas company would expect the company to be governed forever by efficient rules with respect to the set of issues X; they would neither expect that the company might later migrate nor fear that Kansas, wary of such potential migration, might abandon its value-maximizing rules. Thus, what remains to be considered is the possibility that Kansas, as part of its strategy, would adopt rules that eliminate companies initially incorporated in Kansas from reincorporating elsewhere. But while the adoption of a rule that prohibits migration would eliminate certain problems, it would create others. Most importantly, under such a rule companies would not be able to migrate to other states for "good" reasons as well as "bad." In particular, initial incorporators thus will have reason to fear that, once enough companies are incorporated in Kansas with no way out, Kansas may take advantage of them, say by greatly increasing franchise taxes. Therefore, the adoption by Kansas of a rule that prohibits reincorporation elsewhere would not accomplish the goal of attracting initial incorporations.[145]

Thus, whether or not the prices obtained in public offerings accurately reflect the consequences of the governing corporate law rules, the introduction of initial incorporations into the analysis does not change the basic conclusions of the preceding sections. As a result of the possible divergence between shareholders' interests and the interests of those making incorporation decisions, state competition is likely to produce undesirable results with respect to a significant set of issues.

G. Conclusion: Managers' Opportunism and the Shortcomings of State Competition

This Part has identified several types of issues with respect to which state competition is likely to produce value-decreasing rules.

---

[144] Only a strategy that is not expected to attract many public companies to Kansas could allay the rational fear that, once successful, Kansas would have an interest in changing course. But a strategy that is not expected to attract many companies would not be worth undertaking.

[145] Moreover, for a rule that prohibits migration to be effective, it must be accompanied by substantial limits on the freedom of Kansas companies to merge with out-of-state companies. Otherwise, the prohibition on reincorporation could be easily circumvented by a Kansas company merging into, say, a much smaller Delaware corporation. The necessary limits on the freedom to merge may well involve significant costs.

First, state competition is likely to work poorly with respect to issues that are significantly redistributive, including self-dealing, taking of corporate opportunities, and insider trading. Second, state competition may well produce undesirable results with respect to issues that directly implicate the strength of market discipline, including the regulation of corporate takeovers and proxy contests. Third, state competition is likely to produce value-decreasing rules for the governance of issues that involve potential transfers between public shareholders and a dominant shareholder, including going-private freezeouts, parent-subsidiary mergers, and the allocation of opportunities between parent companies and subsidiaries.

With respect to all of these issues, state competition can be expected systematically to produce rules that favor managers and dominant shareholders more than would the value-maximizing rules. This conclusion in no way depends on a direct assessment of the merits of Delaware's or other states' law governing these issues. It simply follows from a recognition of the structural forces at work in the state charter competition.[146]

The identified shortcomings of state competition suggest that it may be desirable to constrain this competition with respect to the issues identified above. That is, it may be desirable to subject these issues to federal rules or at least to federal minimum standards. For the identified structural distortions would not be in play in the federal lawmaking process.

Federal law already governs some of the identified issues. In particular, federal law currently regulates insider trading and aspects of takeover bids and proxy contests. But some of the identified issues are not governed by federal law. Consequently, the analysis of this Part suggests that we should consider the possibility of a significant expansion of federal law. Most importantly, we should consider expanding federal law to govern — or at least set minimum standards for — managers' fiduciary duties, the fiduciary duties of controlling shareholders in freezeouts and allocation of opportunities, and the various aspects of takeover bids and proxy contests now governed by state law.[147]

---

[146] Note that the conclusion is not that, in the identified contexts, state competition necessarily produces rules that sacrifice to the greatest conceivable extent the interests of public shareholders in favor of the interests of managers and dominant shareholders. Some state law rules may be so value-decreasing that market constraints or the need for shareholder approval would effectively prevent their adoption. Alternatively, fear of federal intervention may dissuade states from adopting extremely value-decreasing corporate law rules. *See supra* notes 75–77 and accompanying text. My conclusion is simply that, in certain contexts, state competition likely produces legal rules that sacrifice maximization of shareholder value for wealth transfers to managers and dominant shareholders.

[147] While the federal law process would not suffer from the identified distortions, it may have other shortcomings. Thus, even after recognizing that state competition is likely to perform

III. State Competition and Externalities

This Part describes the ways in which — and the issues with respect to which — state charter competition leads to socially undesirable results in the presence of externalities. To focus on the problems resulting from the presence of externalities, it will be useful to ignore in this Part the agency problems on which Part II focused. To this end, I assume that companies' managers have only the shareholders' interests in mind. In this case, managers making incorporation decisions will seek corporate law rules that maximize shareholder value, and states seeking to attract incorporations will provide such rules. When externalities are present, however, rules that maximize shareholder value may well diverge from the socially desirable ones.

A. The Externality Problem

Consider a given corporate law issue that implicates not only the interests of shareholders, but also those of third parties.[148] From the perspective of efficiency, the socially desirable rule is the one that maximizes the aggregate wealth of society's members.[149] Accordingly, because interests other than those of shareholders are involved in the choice of the legal rule governing the considered issue, these interests must be taken into account in arriving at the socially optimal rule. But shareholders, managers, and entrepreneurs who seek to maximize shareholder value will ignore these interests in evaluating corporate law rules. Consequently, if states seek to attract incorporations by offering rules that enhance shareholder value, the offered rules may well differ from the socially desirable ones. In particular, the rules produced by state competition will be systematically less favorable to non-shareholder parties than the socially desirable ones.

Note the difference in this regard between federal and state law. If a rule is designed at the federal level, it is possible that officials shaping this rule will take into account the interests of parties other than shareholders. But if the rule is designed by the states, then the competition among them will lead state law officials to exclude consideration of such interests. This powerful, structural bias against the

---

poorly with respect to the identified issues, one might oppose federal intervention if one believed that these other shortcomings would be so severe that the federal law process would perform even worse than state competition. Section V.A therefore discusses the possible imperfections of the federal law process, and explains the reasons for my view that, with respect to the identified issues, the federal process would perform better than state competition.

[148] For a discussion of the general problem of externalities in corporate law, see Bebchuk, *Foreword*, *supra* note 17, at 1405–06.

[149] This definition of efficiency is standard in economic analysis of law. *See, e.g.*, A. Mitchell Polinsky, An Introduction to Law and Economics 7–10 (1983). For discussions of the normative premises and problems with this definition, see, for example, *Symposium on Efficiency as a Legal Concern*, 8 Hofstra L. Rev. 485 (1980).

consideration of such interests is absent from the federal lawmaking process.

The difference between federal and state law follows from the fact that state corporate law, unlike federal law, does not govern a company unless the company chooses to incorporate in-state. Suppose that a state considers shaping a corporate law rule to take into account the interests of parties other than shareholders. Such a strategy may lead companies to migrate to other, more shareholder-friendly domiciles. In the end, the state may both lose its incorporations and fail to achieve any protection of third parties' interests. The fundamental difference between federal and state law is this: if the former provides protection to parties other than shareholders, shareholders cannot easily avoid its reach, whereas if the latter does so, they can.

It is worth emphasizing that the claim here is not that state law is designed in general without attention to externalities, only that state corporate law is designed in this way. While a state's corporate law applies only to those companies that elect to be incorporated in the state, other bodies of state law may well apply to all business operations that take place in the state and that impose externalities on the state's citizens. When a state designs consumer law, tort law, or employment law to govern operations conducted within the state, it will likely pay attention to the effects of the adopted rules on the state's consumers, potential tort victims, and employees. But the state in these cases can do so without fear that companies will be able to avoid the adopted rules while continuing their operations within the state. By contrast, companies can — simply by reincorporating elsewhere, without any change in their operations — completely avoid their state's corporate law rules.

Thus, there can be no question that, in the presence of externalities, state competition may produce undesirable results. The important question, however, is whether this problem is significant in a practical sense. The problem's significance depends on the pervasiveness and severity of externalities in corporate law. Some may question whether corporate law issues involve significant externalities; in particular, they may argue that non-shareholder parties are well protected by bodies of law other than corporate law or by privately adopted contractual rules. As explained in the following section, however, certain important areas of corporate law do implicate significant externalities.

B. Corporate Law Issues that Involve Significant Externalities

1. Regulation of Takeover Bids and Proxy Contests. — The legal rules governing takeover bids and proxy contests are an important element of corporate law. As explained below, the success of a takeover bid or a proxy contest not only affects the interests of the target's shareholders, but also confers benefits on those seeking to acquire control. If rules governing takeovers and contests are designed solely to serve shareholders' interests, however, potential benefits to bidders and challengers will not be taken into account.[150]

The externality associated with takeover bids was first analyzed by Sanford Grossman and Oliver Hart.[151] The success of a takeover bid generally provides some gains to the bidder. Thus, because rules governing takeover bids influence the likelihood that a given bid will succeed, the design of these rules clearly affects not only the interests of target shareholders, but also the interests of bidders. When states design takeover rules, they will tend to disregard the externality identified by Grossman and Hart. Accordingly, such state corporate law will tend systematically to facilitate bids to a lesser degree than is socially desirable.[152]

Turning now to proxy contests, Marcel Kahan and I have pointed out the externality implicated by such contests: success in a proxy

---

[150] To be sure, certain effects on bidders and challengers may be desirable to shareholders and, accordingly, may be reflected in legal rules designed to serve shareholders' interests. For example, rules that benefit bidders and challengers may help shareholders by inducing bidders and challengers to perform monitoring roles that are valuable to shareholders. The point, however, is that the effects of legal rules on bidders and challengers get no independent weight in a calculus aimed solely at serving shareholders' interests, but would receive independent weight in a calculus aimed at maximizing aggregate social wealth.

[151] *See* Sanford J. Grossman & Oliver D. Hart, *Takeover Bids, the Free-Rider Problem, and the Theory of the Corporation*, 11 BELL J. ECON. 42, 42–43 (1980).

[152] While Grossman and Hart's article analyzes third-party benefits to bidders from legal rules that facilitate takeover bids, Frank Easterbrook and Daniel Fischel argue that such rules confer third-party benefits also on others. *See* Easterbrook & Fischel, *supra* note 137, at 1438; Easterbrook & Fischel, *supra* note 46, at 1176–77. They argue that rules that facilitate takeovers of certain companies benefit other potential targets because such rules encourage search activity by potential bidders. Increased search activity benefits all companies that may be subject to this search both because its presence disciplines managers and because it may lead to a premium offer by a bidder.

I do not find Easterbrook and Fischel's argument persuasive. A state law arrangement that facilitates takeovers of certain companies (or, indeed, a charter provision providing for such an arrangement) will increase search activity by potential bidders only with respect to the group of companies governed by the arrangement. Easterbrook and Fischel's argument appears to assume that potential bidders cannot tell prior to studying a target whether the target is governed by the takeover-facilitating arrangement and that bidders will thus devote equal attention to companies governed by the arrangement and companies not governed by the arrangement. But if the takeover-facilitating arrangement is adopted by state law (or by a charter provision), potential bidders should be able to identify in advance and at minimal cost the companies governed by the arrangement. In particular, if the arrangement is adopted by state law, the bidder would need only to determine the state of incorporation of any company that it considers studying. Thus, a potential bidder would engage in significant search activity only if a company were in fact governed by the takeover-facilitating arrangement. It follows that the fact that a given company is governed by such an arrangement would not confer a positive externality on companies not governed by the arrangement.

battle confers benefits on the challenger.[153] Again, state law rules designed to serve shareholders' interests will not take these benefits into account. Accordingly, the rules provided by states with respect to proxy contests will tend systematically to favor incumbents and discourage control challenges relative to the socially desirable rules.

Thus, this Article's analysis has identified two distinct reasons for why, to the extent that takeover bids and proxy challenges are governed by state corporate law, state rules will tend to facilitate such bids and challenges less than is socially desirable. First, as Part II demonstrated, because managers have substantial influence on incorporation decisions and because takeovers and proxy contests affect managers' private interests, states have incentives to provide rules that facilitate takeover bids and proxy contests less than is desirable to target shareholders. Second, as this section has pointed out, the rules that are desirable to target shareholders are themselves ones that facilitate takeover bids and proxy contests less than is socially desirable. Therefore, both the manager-shareholder agency problem and the externality problem push in the same direction, driving states to provide rules that discourage bids and contests more than is socially desirable. Thus, the case for federal regulation of all aspects of takeover bids and proxy contests appears to be very strong.[154]

---

[153] *See* Lucian A. Bebchuk & Marcel Kahan, *A Framework for Analyzing Legal Policy Toward Proxy Contests*, 78 CAL. L. REV. 1073, 1089–95 (1990).

[154] Some may argue that the impediments erected by state corporate law to transfers of control (by takeovers or by proxy contests) are desirable because of the negative externalities imposed by transfers of control. While the discussion above has focused on the positive externalities that control transfers confer on those who obtain control, it may be argued that such transfers may also involve negative externalities. In particular, it may be argued that some transfers of control may impose externalities on consumers (for example, when a takeover creates increased market power), on workers (for example, when a takeover results in dismissals), on communities (for example, when a takeover leads to relocation of headquarters) and so on. Because transfers of control create such externalities, so the argument goes, they might be undesirable even if they benefitted the shareholders of the target and the acquirer. Therefore, the state corporate law rules that impede takeovers and proxy contest would be desirable.

Note that this argument does not assume that, in adopting rules that discourage takeovers (and proxy contests), state law officials are motivated by the negative externalities created by takeovers. Indeed, as we have seen, state law officials are unlikely to take externalities into account when designing corporate law rules. Rather, granting that state law officials adopt rules discouraging takeovers in order to protect managers, the argument is that the adopted rules are nonetheless desirable because they reduce the negative externalities produced by transfers of control.

I find this argument in favor of state corporate law impediments to takeovers and proxy contests unconvincing. State competition leads state law officials to adopt rules that impede takeovers in general or either those takeovers resisted by incumbent managers. These rules are a very poor means of addressing the negative externalities produced by control transfers. Negative externalities do not arise in the case of all takeovers, and whether or not they arise is not correlated with whether or not the takeover is resisted by incumbent managers. Thus, the state corporate law rules may prevent beneficial takeovers that do not impose any negative externalities (but nonetheless are resisted by managers for some self-serving reason), and they

2. *Protection of Creditors.* — Let us now turn to corporate law rules governing the relationship between a company and its creditors. Clearly, if a corporate law rule can be designed to transfer value from creditors to shareholders, then shareholders may well find the rule attractive even if it is inefficient (that is, produces a gain to the shareholders that is smaller than the creditors' loss). Therefore, to the extent that rules affecting creditors are left to state law, the concern arises that state competition will produce inefficient rules that diverge systematically from the socially desirable ones in ways that are unfavorable to creditors.

To be sure, it may be argued that state corporate law will not provide rules that are harmful to creditors — that is, rules that transfer value from creditors to shareholders — because creditors are able to protect themselves contractually. Lenders, so the argument goes, will anticipate the effects of state law rules and will charge an appropriate interest rate. Thus, such rules cannot be used by shareholders to transfer value from creditors. And since any efficiency costs associated with such rules will ultimately be borne by shareholders, shareholders will never want to have inefficient rules even if the rules seem to (but actually do not) benefit them at the expense of creditors.

Not all creditors, however, can protect themselves contractually against the adverse consequences of state law rules.[155] For one thing, there are involuntary creditors such as tort victims. Because these creditors do not become creditors as a result of voluntary decisions to enter into contracts with the company, they cannot protect themselves by adjusting the interest rate or some other contractual term. In addition, there are some voluntary, contractual creditors that cannot protect themselves against the adverse consequences of corporate law rules. The transactions of these creditors with a company may be

---

may not prevent some takeovers that would impose substantial negative externalities (but are not resisted by incumbent managers).

If one considers the negative externalities created by control transfers to be a serious problem, then one should seek legal rules that discourage takeovers that create such externalities (rather than rules that discourage takeovers resisted by incumbent managers). While an examination of how such rules may be designed is beyond the scope of this Article, it should be clear that states generally have no incentive to develop and adopt such rules as part of their state corporate law. If one were to believe that such rules are indeed desirable, then one's only hope would be that such rules would be provided by federal law or by bodies of state law other than state corporate law (that is, by bodies of state law that apply not to companies incorporated in the state but to companies operating within the state).

[155] *See* Henry B. Hansmann & Reinier Kraakman, *Toward Unlimited Shareholder Liability for Corporate Torts*, 100 YALE L.J. 1879, 1920 (1991) (noting that some classes of creditors cannot arrange for ex ante compensation for bearing the risks associated with the limited liability of corporations).

sufficiently small in value to make it difficult, given the informational and transactional costs involved, to adjust the terms of trade to counteract the state law rules governing the company. Because these two groups of creditors are unable to protect themselves contractually, it is possible to design corporate law rules that transfer value from these creditors to shareholders. And states would have an incentive to offer precisely such rules.

To illustrate this general point, consider the rules that govern the amount of dividends that companies may pay out to shareholders. When a company does not have "enough" capital, a payment of dividends may transfer to the shareholders some of the capital that would be otherwise used to pay debtholders. Regulation of corporate dividend policy is an important corporate law issue and traditionally has been accomplished by state law.[156] As is well recognized, the limits on dividends established by state law are generally so weak and ineffectual as to have virtually no practical significance.[157] To be sure, companies often agree to much stricter limitations on their dividend policy as part of their contracts with banks and bondholders.[158] But why does state law not go somewhat in that direction and establish some basic meaningful limits on dividend payments? This Article suggests a simple answer: because companies are free to choose their states of incorporation (and thus the state corporate law that governs them), states have an incentive to offer shareholders rules that impose practically no significant restrictions on the payment of dividends.

3. Regulation of Corporate Disclosure. — Disclosure of information by a given public company may well confer significant benefits on other companies. Consequently, if the regulation of such disclosure were left to the states, states would likely adopt rules that produce substantially less disclosure than is socially desirable.

Easterbrook and Fischel have identified the externality effects associated with corporate disclosure.[159] To start with, a company's revelation of information may confer benefits not only on the company itself (by enabling it to attract investors), but also on competitors.[160]

---

[156] *See* CLARK, *supra* note 3, § 2.5, at 86 (describing state corporate law dividend statutes); *id.* § 14.3, at 610–24 (same).

[157] *See, e.g., id.* § 2.5, at 87–88.

[158] *See id.* § 2.5, at 88; Clifford W. Smith, Jr. & Jerold B. Warner, *On Financial Contracting: An Analysis of Bond Covenants*, 7 J. FIN. ECON. 117, 131–136 (1979) (discussing the nature and frequency of contractual restrictions on dividend payments).

[159] *See* Frank H. Easterbrook & Daniel R. Fischel, *Mandatory Disclosure and the Protection of Investors*, 70 VA. L. REV. 669, 669–87 (1984).

[160] *See id.* at 685; *see also* CLARK, *supra* note 3, § 17.5, at 758–59 (discussing third-party effects of disclosure on a company's competitors). A company's disclosure of information helps its rivals whenever the disclosure reveals something about the company's ability to compete or about the industry in which it operates, because such information is useful to rivals in planning their own operations. *See* Easterbrook & Fischel, *supra* note 159, at 685. Disclosure may also

Furthermore, a company's disclosure may benefit other companies with overlapping lines of business by facilitating comparison across firms.[161] Finally, investment by a disclosing company in the development and use of an optimal disclosure format has a positive externality effect on companies generally, because it enables these companies to communicate information more effectively to their own investors.[162]

A system of state law regulation of corporate disclosure cannot achieve optimal disclosure rules because states competing to attract incorporations have no reason to take into account the externality effects of the disclosure rules they adopt. The existence of positive externalities associated with disclosure implies that state law governance of disclosure would tend systematically to result in suboptimal disclosure levels and formats.

4. Protection of Constituencies Other than Providers of Capital. — A classic question in the theory of corporate law is whether a corporation's managers should ever exercise their discretion to further the interests of constituencies other than providers of capital. This question has often been debated under the rubric of corporate social responsibility.[163] Corporate social responsibility may include attention to constituencies such as workers, communities, and consumers, and to goals such as preservation of the environment.[164] Indeed, the corporate law of some countries provides workers with certain formal

---

enable rival companies to attract investors without having to bear all the costs of providing information to such investors. *See* CLARK, *supra* note 3, § 17.5, at 759; Easterbrook & Fischel, *supra* note 159, at 685, 686.

[161] *See* Easterbrook & Fischel, *supra* note 159, at 686. The argument is that, to the extent that the company reveals comparative information, it confers third-party benefits on companies in the same line of business by enabling them to free-ride on their competitor's disclosure of this information to investors. *See id*; *see also* CLARK, *supra* note 3, § 17.5, at 759 (arguing that the production of comparative information about firms implicates positive externality effects).

In both the case in which companies benefit from a given company's provision of comparative information and the case in which firms benefit from a given company's provision of information generally, the less companies in the industry differ, the greater the positive spillover associated with the company's disclosure. *See* Easterbrook & Fischel, *supra* note 159, at 686. Of course, the greater the spillover associated with the above disclosure, the greater the externality effects implicated by disclosure regulation.

[162] *See* Easterbrook & Fischel, *supra* note 159, at 686–87; *see also* Michael J. Fishman & Kathleen M. Hagerty, *The Optimal Amount of Discretion to Allow in Disclosure*, 105 Q.J. ECON. 427, 439–40 (1990) (concluding that their formal model of information disclosure provides support for the proposition that the specification of disclosure formats benefits companies generally).

[163] *See, e.g.*, CLARK, *supra* note 3, § 16.1–.4, at 675–703; David L. Engel, *An Approach to Corporate Social Responsibility*, 32 STAN. L. REV. 1, 5–11 (1979).

[164] *See generally* RALPH NADER, MARK GREEN & JOEL SELIGMAN, TAMING THE GIANT CORPORATION (1976) (arguing that corporations should be made more responsive to society's needs).

rights to participate in corporate governance and thus ensures that managerial decisions will be attentive to at least one constituency other than providers of capital.[165]

State corporate law in this country, however, has traditionally taken the position that the managers' duty is to serve shareholders' interests — specifically, the maximization of long-run profits. The classic statement of this position is *Dodge v. Ford Motor Co.*,[166] which held that a business corporation is organized and carried on primarily for the profit of the stockholders and that managers cannot devote themselves to "a general purpose and plan to benefit mankind."[167]

In this Article, I do not wish to examine or take a position on the substantive merits of the question whether managers should serve constituencies other than providers of capital. I grant that the most efficient legal rule may be one that requires managers to serve only shareholders' interests and leaves the protection of other constituencies to non-corporate bodies of law such as antitrust law, consumer protection law, and employment law. The resolution of this question requires a full-fledged analysis of managerial monitoring and incentives under alternative regimes and is therefore beyond the scope of this Article.[168] What I wish to stress, however, is that the decision about the appropriate goal of managers should be made at the federal level rather than at the state level. For even if the socially desirable rule were one that required managers to take into account the interests of constituencies other than providers of capital, state law would be unlikely to provide such a rule. Those that make incorporation decisions would not want to have such a rule, and states competing to attract incorporations would thus have an incentive not to provide such a rule, even if it were socially desirable.[169]

To be sure, several states have in recent years passed constituency statutes that enable the consideration of the interests of non-share-

---

[165] For example, under Germany's codetermination system, workers in large firms participate equally with providers of capital in electing representatives to the firm's board of directors. *See* Henry Hansmann, *When Does Worker Ownership Work? ESOPs, Law Firms, Codetermination, and Economic Democracy*, 99 YALE L.J. 1749, 1803 (1990).

[166] 170 N.W. 668 (Mich. 1919).

[167] *See id.* at 684. Indeed, several states have even limited the purpose for which shareholders may review corporate records to the long-run maximization of share value. *See* CLARK, *supra* note 3, § 3.1, at 100, 102–104.

[168] For an analysis of the implications for managerial monitoring and incentives of managers' responsibility to groups other than providers of capital, see Henry Hansmann, *Ownership of the Firm*, 4 J.L. ECON. & ORG. 267, 281–301 (1988).

[169] *See* REPORT OF THE CORPORATION LAW REVISION COMMISSION OF NEW JERSEY, N.J. STAT. ANN. § 14A, at x–xi (1969), *reprinted in* Cary, *supra* note 10, at 666 (stating that any attempt to provide protection to employees, customers, and the general public through state incorporation acts would "drive corporations to more hospitable jurisdictions").

holder constituencies.[170] These statutes, however, are largely directed at managers considering the use of defensive tactics in the face of hostile takeover bids,[171] and they generally permit managers (rather than require them) to take various constituencies' interests into account.[172] Because meaningful judicial review of managerial decisionmaking is virtually impossible when the spectrum of permissible decision factors includes interests that are not easily verifiable or quantifiable, the primary effect of these constituency statutes is simply to enhance managers' discretion in responding to hostile takeover bids. Accordingly, the constituency statutes should be understood not as measures to safeguard these constituencies' interests but rather as instruments by which managers can block hostile takeovers. Thus, the adoption of the statutes is best explained on the grounds that Part II described — the managerial role in incorporation decisionmaking leads states to provide rules that unduly discourage takeovers.

5. Positive Externalities from Standardization? — Up to this point, this Part has focused on externalities that arise in connection with specific areas of corporate law. This section now considers a general externality argument that may be made for having any given corporate law issue governed at the federal level. A regime in which all companies are subject to the same standard rules may be thought preferable to one in which they are subject to a multitude of different rules. Making a given company subject to a standard rule may confer benefits on other companies subject to that rule. For parties that deal with the former company may become familiar with the rule and thus face lower information costs when dealing with such other companies. Furthermore, parties dealing with these other companies will have more precedents on which to rely. Thus, it may be argued, there is a benefit from having federal law govern all corporate law issues, not only those issues that present special reason to suspect that state competition fails with respect to them.[173]

This general externality argument, however, does not appear to be sufficiently weighty to justify an expansion of federal law beyond the specific corporate law areas in which state competition is likely to

---

[170] *See, e.g.*, ILL. REV. STAT. ch. 32, para. 8.85 (1989); IND. CODE § 23-1-35-1(d) (1988); OHIO REV. CODE ANN. § 1701.59(E) (Baldwin 1991).

[171] For example, although the Indiana constituency statute on its face applies to managers' decisionmaking generally, the language of the statute makes clear that its purpose is to allow managers to defend against hostile takeovers. *See* IND. CODE § 23-1-35-1(f) (1988).

[172] *See, e.g.*, IND. CODE § 23-1-35-1(d) (1988).

[173] The positive externality produced by the adoption of "standard" rules is noted by Gordon. *See* Gordon, *supra* note 138, at 1567–69. Charny systematically analyzes this externality and views it as a consideration that should be given significant weight in delineating the limits on state competition. *See* Charny, *supra* note 16, at 442–445. My judgment on the weight that should be accorded to this consideration differs from Charny's for the reasons described below.

produce inefficient rules. To start with, although positive externalities from standardization do undoubtedly exist in theory, their size is likely to be quite limited. For those issues with respect to which structural problems of managerial opportunism and externalities do not exist, the positive externalities of standardization seem smaller than the benefits of having states compete to supply the best rules.[174]

Furthermore, and more importantly, state law governance of a given issue does not imply foregoing the benefits of standardized corporate law rules. For the way in which state competition works — and has worked — is not that American companies are governed by fifty totally different sets of corporate law rules. Rather, a substantial fraction of these companies is subject to the rules established by the most successful state, Delaware. Moreover, with respect to most corporate law issues, companies incorporated outside of Delaware are likely to be subject to the same or similar rules; for other states often move in the same direction as Delaware, either responding to the same structural incentives or simply following Delaware's lead.[175] Thus, state competition, as it has thus far operated, is consistent with realizing most of the benefits of standardization.[176] As Dean Bayless Manning put it, "[W]e now have a national corporate law — Delaware law."[177]

C. Conclusion: Externalities and the Shortcomings of State Competition

This Part has shown that state competition may well produce socially undesirable results whenever a corporate law issue involves significant externalities. Furthermore, the analysis has identified several areas of corporate law that involve such significant externalities — the regulation of takeovers and proxy contests, the protection of creditors, disclosure regulation, and the protection of constituencies other than providers of capital. Because of the presence of significant externality effects, it may well be desirable to have federal decisionmaking about the legal rules governing these areas. For the identified

---

[174] Indeed, the benefits from standardization seem to be much larger with respect to the construction of many technical products, such as VCRs and certain types of communication and computer systems, than with respect to the construction of corporate law rules. Nevertheless, the magnitude of the benefits from standardization in the case of these technical products has not been thought to be substantial enough to warrant limiting competition between suppliers of these products.

[175] *See supra* notes 32–33 and accompanying text.

[176] To stress again a point made earlier, the problem with state competition is not the lack of a standard rule but the likelihood that the standard rule will differ — with respect to certain corporate issues — from the rule that is socially desirable.

[177] Bayless Manning, *State Competition: Panel Response*, 8 CARDOZO L. REV. 779, 783 (1987).

structural distortion, which leads states to disregard the third-party effects of their corporate law rules, would not be present in the federal lawmaking process.

This general conclusion can be used to evaluate the existing balance between state and federal corporate law. Federal involvement is at present greatest in the area of disclosure. Federal law largely governs the disclosure of information by and with respect to public companies.[178] The analysis of this Part suggests that the substantial role federal law plays in disclosure regulation may well be warranted.

Takeovers, proxy contests, and creditor protection are now governed by a combination of federal and state law. The federal involvement is significant. In particular, the Williams Act regulates the behavior of bidders,[179] the Securities and Exchange Act of 1934 regulates proxy contests,[180] and the Bankruptcy Act provides rules that protect the interests of creditors in corporate bankruptcy.[181] Major aspects of these areas, however, are governed by state corporate law. In particular, state law governs the fiduciary duties of managers in the face of a takeover bid; it also governs important aspects of proxy contests, such as the reimbursement of campaign expenses and the access by challengers to the list of shareholders. Similarly, state corporate law governs significant aspects of the relationship between a company and its creditors, such as limitations on dividend payments. The analysis of this Part suggests that it may well be desirable to adopt federal law rules — or at least federal minimum standards — with respect to all of these issues.

Finally, state law now decides (and gives a negative answer to) the question whether corporate managers have a fiduciary duty toward, and must take into account the interests of, constituencies other than providers of capital. The analysis of this Part suggests that it may well be desirable for this question to be answered at the federal rather than the state level. To be sure, requiring managers to focus on shareholders' interests may be the socially desirable rule and the one that federal law officials would adopt. But it may well be desirable for the governing rule to be determined by a federal lawmaking process — which would potentially take into account the full social consequences of alternative rules — rather than by a state lawmaking process which is structurally biased in favor of shareholders' and managers' interests.[182]

---

178 *See, e.g.*, Easterbrook & Fischel, *supra* note 159, at 669–70.

179 *See* CLARK, *supra* note 3, § 13.3–.4, at 546–68.

180 *See id.* § 9.2, at 366–74.

181 *See* 11 U.S.C.A. §§ 101–1330 (West 1979 & Supp. 1992) (codifying the Bankruptcy Reform Act of 1978, Pub. L. No. 95-598, 92 Stat. 2549, as amended).

182 Again, even after recognizing that state competition may well produce socially undesirable rules with respect to the identified issues, one might oppose federal intervention if one believed

IV. STATE COMPETITION AND CONTRACTUAL FREEDOM: CONNECTING THE DEBATES

Alongside the state competition question, another basic question in corporate law is that of contractual freedom: to what extent should companies be allowed to opt out of corporate law rules (established either by state or federal law) by adopting charter provisions to that effect? This longstanding question has in recent years been the subject of lively debate,[183] culminating in a symposium issue of the *Columbia Law Review*.[184] The aim of this Part is to show how the state competition and contractual freedom questions are logically interconnected.[185] In particular, I suggest that those who support mandatory rules with respect to some corporate law issues, as most scholars of corporate law do,[186] cannot consistently support state regulation of these issues.

In the contractual freedom debate, two main arguments have been advanced in support of placing limits on opting out by companies. The first argument is that, if opting out is permitted, managers may propose, and shareholders approve, certain midstream charter amendments that will reduce shareholder value but serve managers' private interests. In particular, I have argued that market forces are insuffi-

---

that the federal process would perform even worse as a result of some other shortcomings. For the reasons discussed in section V.A below, my own view is that the federal process would perform better than state competition with respect to the identified issues.

183 *See, e.g.*, RICHARD A. POSNER, ECONOMIC ANALYSIS OF LAW 372 (3d ed. 1986); Bebchuk, *Limiting Contractual Freedom*, *supra* note 17, at 1820–25; Victor Brudney, *Corporate Governance, Agency Costs, and the Rhetoric of Contract*, 85 COLUM. L. REV. 1403, 1443–44 (1985); Dennis W. Carlton & Daniel R. Fischel, *The Regulation of Insider Trading*, 35 STAN. L. REV. 857, 861–66 (1983); Robert C. Clark, *Agency Costs Versus Fiduciary Duties*, *in* PRINCIPALS AND AGENTS: THE STRUCTURE OF BUSINESS 55 (John W. Pratt & Richard J. Zeckhauser eds., 1985); John C. Coffee, Jr., *No Exit?: Opting Out, the Contractual Theory of the Corporation, and the Special Case of Remedies*, 53 BROOK. L. REV. 919, 923–25 (1988); Easterbrook & Fischel, *supra* note 12, at 401–02; Frank H. Easterbrook & Daniel R. Fischel, *Corporate Control Transactions*, 91 YALE L.J. 698, 698 (1982); Daniel R. Fischel, *The Corporate Governance Movement*, 35 VAND. L. REV. 1259, 1261–65 (1982); Jonathan R. Macey, *From Fairness to Contract: The New Direction of the Rules Against Insider Trading*, 13 HOFSTRA L. REV. 9, 39–47 (1984).

184 *See* Symposium, *Contractual Freedom in Corporate Law*, 89 COLUM. L. REV. 1395 (1989). The symposium contains articles both in support of contractual freedom, *see* Easterbrook & Fischel, *supra* note 137, and in opposition to the view that companies should be generally free to opt out of corporate law rules, *see* Robert C. Clark, *Contracts, Elites, and Traditions in the Making of Corporate Law*, 89 COLUM. L. REV. 1703 (1989); Coffee, *supra* note 138; Eisenberg, *supra* note 138; Gordon, *supra* note 138. For an overview of the debate over the desirability of contractual freedom, see Bebchuk, *Foreword*, *supra* note 17.

185 The value of connecting the state competition and contractual freedom debates is also discussed in Charny, *supra* note 16, at 425–26, 437–38.

186 Even Easterbrook and Fischel, the leading proponents of contractual freedom, support mandatory rules prohibiting defensive tactics designed to ward off hostile takeovers. *See* Easterbrook & Fischel, *supra* note 137, at 1436–42.

cient to check such managerial behavior with respect to certain corporate law issues.[187] The second argument in support of mandatory rules is based on the presence of externalities. In particular, it has been argued that mandatory rules are necessary to prevent companies from adopting opt-out provisions that impose negative externalities on other parties and that are consequently socially undesirable.[188]

These arguments roughly parallel the arguments that this Article has developed in favor of limiting state competition. The parallelism is no mere coincidence. Rather, it follows from the logical connection between the state competition and contractual freedom questions. Both questions turn on whether, in the presence of agency relationships and externalities, companies[189] should be able to choose among different legal rules for the governance of their affairs.[190]

When an issue is subjected to state law, with states free to offer different rules, the issue essentially is not subject to mandatory legal treatment — even if states do not allow companies incorporated in-state to opt out of the state law rule governing this issue. Consider an issue governed by state law, and suppose that each of the fifty states imposes a mandatory legal rule with respect to the issue. In an important sense, companies do have an ability to opt out. By reincorporating, companies can opt out of the rule in their home state and replace it with any one of the rules offered by the other states. To be sure, companies do not have the unlimited choice they would have if they were allowed to adopt opt-out charter provisions. But companies may still have some choice. And, more importantly, the existing choices offered by states would probably include the very rules that companies would wish to have. Because states compete to attract incorporations, some state would likely provide (as a mandatory rule for companies incorporated in-state) the very rule that companies would tend to adopt if they were free to make their own rules; for this would make the state more attractive to those making incorporation decisions.

Thus, logical consistency requires that one's view on the desirability of contractual freedom with respect to a given issue inform one's view on the merits of having state corporate law govern this issue. Suppose one holds the view that companies should not be allowed to

---

[187] *See* Bebchuk, *Limiting Contractual Freedom*, *supra* note 17, at 1835–47.

[188] For an overview and evaluation of this argument, see Bebchuk, *Foreword*, *supra* note 17, at 1405–06.

[189] Throughout this Part, the term "companies" refers to the parties — shareholders or managers — that effectively control corporate decisions in a given context.

[190] The contractual freedom question turns on whether companies should be able to choose between the (default) rule of their home state and alternative arrangements, and the state charter competition question turns on whether companies should be able to choose among the laws of different states.

opt out of the legal rule governing a certain issue. Then one must believe that, due to the presence of managerial opportunism or externalities, contractual freedom with respect to this issue would produce value-decreasing rules. But then one would also have a strong reason to be concerned about having the issue governed by state law. For, by the analysis of Parts II and III, the problems of managerial opportunism and externalities imply that state competition, like contractual freedom, will produce socially undesirable rules.

The interconnection of the state competition and contractual freedom questions can perhaps be best expressed by stating that there is an inherent tension, or even contradiction, in any view that supports a mandatory state rule. By and large, issues should be governed either by a state rule from which companies are free to opt out or by a mandatory federal rule. This choice is the one that must be addressed squarely with respect to any corporate law issue.

The connection between the state competition and contractual freedom questions can be illustrated further by considering what may be termed the enforcement dimension of mandatory state rules. As already pointed out, the presence of state competition reduces the effectiveness of a mandatory state rule. Indeed, skepticism may be expressed about the value of mandatory state corporate law rules on the grounds that state competition presents an insurmountable enforcement problem for such rules. But this skepticism assumes that we are wedded to a regime in which state law governs the issues with respect to which mandatory rules are thought to be appropriate. The concern about the enforceability of mandatory state rules poses no problem for the view put forward in this Article — that it is desirable, and perfectly consistent, to impose limits on both contractual freedom and state competition.

The logical connection between questions of state competition and contractual freedom requires many commentators to reconsider their previously expressed views of state competition. While most commentators endorse mandatory rules for the governance of some corporate law issues, there is widespread support for the dominant role of states in the governance of corporate affairs. The analysis of this Part, however, suggests that commentators who support mandatory rules with respect to certain issues must reexamine whether they wish to support (as many of them have done in the past) governance of these issues by state rather than federal law.

Consider first commentators with free-market views, such as Frank Easterbrook and Daniel Fischel. While Easterbrook and Fischel view contractual freedom as generally desirable,[191] they do believe that corporate law rules should be mandatory with respect to certain issues;

---

[191] *See* Easterbrook & Fischel, *supra* note 137, at 1446.

in particular, they endorse mandatory rules with respect to the important case of takeover bid regulation because takeover bids have externality effects.[192] Easterbrook and Fischel, however, have expressed broad support for state charter competition and the corporate law rules that it produces.[193] But, for the reasons explained above, if mandatory rules for the governance of takeover defensive tactics are desirable because of the externality effects associated with takeover bids, then state competition is also likely to produce undesirable rules with respect to these issues. Accordingly, Easterbrook and Fischel should support, as they have not done, governance by federal law of managerial fiduciary duties in the face of takeover bids.[194]

Consider now those commentators who, unlike their free-market counterparts, do support mandatory rules for a wide range of corporate issues, including many of the most important ones.[195] Most of these commentators still seem to accept the current dominance of state law in the governance of corporate affairs.[196] The analysis of this Part suggests, however, that these commentators should reconsider their views on the desirable balance between state and federal corporate law.

V. Some Notes on Federal Intervention

This Part discusses issues that arise when one considers the possibility of expanding the federal role in corporate law to address the identified shortcomings of state competition. Section V.A considers the possible imperfections of the federal law process and explains the reasons for my belief that this process would perform better than the state law regime with respect to the issues identified by the analysis. Section V.B discusses the implications of international charter competition for a program of federal regulation.

---

[192] *See id.* at 1437–39 (noting that mandatory rules may be justified in the presence of externalities and that the regulation of takeover bids implicates externality effects); *see also* Easterbrook & Fischel, *supra* note 46, at 1176–77 (describing the negative externality effect of managerial resistance to takeover bids).

[193] *See* Easterbrook & Fischel, *supra* note 12, at 398, 427; Fischel, *supra* note 12, at 919–20.

[194] Indeed, had Easterbrook carried his recognition that the regulation of takeovers implicates externality effects to its logical conclusion, he would not have been as puzzled by states' adoption of antitakeover rules as he was in Amanda Acquisition Corp. v. Universal Foods Corp., 877 F.2d 496 (7th Cir.), *cert. denied*, 493 U.S. 955 (1989). *See supra* notes 115–116 and accompanying text. For if one believes that takeovers create positive externalities, then one should expect states to provide rules that discourage takeovers to a greater degree than is socially desirable.

[195] *See, e.g.*, Coffee, *supra* note 138, at 1690; Eisenberg, *supra* note 138, at 1524; Gordon, *supra* note 138, at 1597–98.

[196] *See, e.g.*, Gordon, *supra* note 138, at 1552.

A. Would Federal Law Do Even Worse?

Most of this Article is devoted to analyzing the shortcomings of state competition, and the main contribution that this Article seeks to make is the identification of the areas in which state competition is likely to work poorly. Gaining such an understanding of the shortcomings of state competition is valuable regardless of the normative implications, if any, that one draws from the analysis. Regardless of how flawed state competition is with respect to the identified issues, some may believe that federal law would perform even worse with respect to these issues and that state competition should therefore be left unconstrained. But even those holding this view should know the ways in which state competition fails. An understanding of the shortcomings of state competition is necessary for the formation of an accurate picture of the performance of our corporate law system, and scholars of corporate law should have such a picture.

For one thing, the race for the top view implies that state corporate law rules should be considered as presumptively efficient,[197] and scholars subscribing to this view have applied such a presumption in evaluating the desirability of various existing and alternative rules.[198] As the analysis of this Article has demonstrated, however, a presumption of efficiency is quite inappropriate for the rules produced by state competition with respect to many issues. Indeed, with respect to the issues identified by the analysis, one should treat the rules produced by state competition not with deference but rather, on the contrary, with caution and with alertness to the possibility that the rules are distorted by the structural biases resulting from managerial opportunism and externalities.

My own view, however, is that the conclusions reached regarding the shortcomings of state competition do have normative implications. In particular, I believe that we would be better off having federal law govern the identified issues and that federal law, though imperfect, would likely perform better than state competition with respect to these issues. While a full analysis of the possible imperfections of the federal process is beyond the scope of this Article, I wish to explain briefly the basis for my view that the federal law process would likely perform better.

In evaluating the relative performance of the federal law process, the best starting point is the observation that this process does not

---

[197] *See* sources cited *supra* note 45.

[198] *See, e.g.*, Dennis W. Carlton & Daniel R. Fischel, *The Regulation of Insider Trading*, 35 STAN. L. REV. 857, 860 (1983) (arguing that the fact that states did not prohibit insider trading prior to the enactment of the federal securities laws is evidence of the efficiency of allowing insider trading); Easterbrook & Fischel, *supra* note 12, at 397–98 (using the presumption that state competition yields efficient corporate law rules in analyzing corporate voting rules).

suffer from the structural biases that afflict the performance of state competition with respect to the identified issues. As we have seen, states have an interest in making their laws attractive to those making incorporation decisions, and this interest introduces two structural biases. First, with respect to issues that involve managerial opportunism, states have an incentive to make themselves attractive to managers and dominant shareholders, and states therefore may well provide rules that benefit managers and dominant shareholders even if the rules are value-decreasing. Second, with respect to issues that involve externalities, states have an incentive to disregard the interests of parties other than managers and shareholders, and this disregard may well lead states to adopt value-decreasing rules that systematically disfavor the third parties upon whom externalities are imposed. Because federal law officials would not be affected by incorporation decisions in the same way that state law officials are, the federal law process would not suffer from the above two structural biases.

Thus, for one still to oppose federal rules with respect to the identified issues, one must believe that the federal law process would suffer from some other shortcomings, and, moreover, that these shortcomings would be so severe that they would outweigh the advantage of eliminating the two significant biases that afflict state competition. Below, I briefly discuss and evaluate the two main imperfections that may be involved in the federal law process.

1. Errors Due to Lack of Information or Effort. — Suppose initially that federal law officials would all be well-meaning in that they would prefer to adopt the socially desirable rules over some other rules. It may still be argued that the federal law process would fail because federal law officials would generally err in identifying the socially desirable rules. As noted earlier, in a state law regime, the incorporation decisions of companies provide state law officials with information, whereas, under a federal law system, officials would not be able to get information from this mechanism.[199] Also, in a state law regime, the fear of visible failure in the form of corporate migration may discipline officials, whereas federal law officials may lack such a competitive pressure to do their best.[200] Therefore, so the argument goes, because federal officials would lack information and incentives to exert effort, they would frequently err in identifying the socially desirable rules — and consequently would perform poorly — even if they were all well-meaning and wanted to adopt only socially desirable rules.

But, supposing federal law officials would generally be well-meaning and would want to adopt only socially desirable rules, the prob-

---

199 *See supra* p. 1457.

200 *See id.*

lems of information and effort hardly imply that federal law officials would perform worse with respect to the identified issues than state law officials. Even if federal law officials had less information overall and exerted less effort, the critical point is that, unlike state law officials, they would not be putting whatever information and willingness to work they would have in the service of the wrong objective. With respect to the identified issues, the rules desired by those who make incorporation decisions — and the rules that state law officials therefore seek to provide — may well differ from the socially desirable rules. As far as getting close to the set of socially desirable rules is concerned, we may well be better off with officials who would shoot relatively inaccurately at the right target than with officials who would shoot with somewhat greater accuracy but at another, wrong target.[201]

To be sure, if federal law officials were to shoot totally in the dark — if they had no clue about what the socially desirable rules are — then their interest in hitting the right target would provide us with little cause for celebration. But if one is not so pessimistic about the information that federal law officials would have and the effort that they would exert — and I am not — then the possibility that these officials may make some errors should not lead one to conclude that they would perform worse than state law officials with respect to the identified issues.[202]

2. *Lobbying by Interest Groups.* — The above discussion — regarding the possibility that federal law officials may err in identifying the socially desirable rules — assumed that these officials would be well-meaning and would want to adopt only socially desirable, value-

[201] Alternatively stated, the point is that, with respect to the identified issues, the fact that incorporation decisions provide state law officials with information and pressure to make an effort hardly provides a reason for preferring that these officials — rather than federal law officials — make the choice. The information provided by incorporation decisions merely helps state law officials identify the rules that are desired by those who make incorporation decisions. Similarly, the competitive pressure exerted by incorporation decisions merely induces state law officials to make a greater effort to identify the rules desired by those who make incorporation decisions. Thus, both factors make state law officials more likely to provide the rules that are desired by those who make incorporation decisions. But this conclusion provides little reason to prefer that state law officials choose rules with respect to the identified issues. For the identified issues are exactly those with respect to which those who make incorporation decisions may well prefer rules that differ from the socially desirable ones.

[202] It is worth noting that our past experience with the SEC does not provide us with a basis for a pessimistic belief that federal law officials would lack information and the willingness to exert effort. Although observers may differ in their views about the rules that the SEC has produced over the years, I believe that few would claim that SEC officials have generally acted with little information and with a lack of zeal. Indeed, the possibility of having federal rules produced by a specialized and active federal agency may lead some to believe that, in fact, federal law officials can draw on more overall information and deploy more human resources than state law officials. *Cf.* Romano, *supra* note 47, at 133 & n.57 (suggesting that because state law officials have limited resources and limited staffs to devote to information gathering and processing, they are especially susceptible to lobbying).

maximizing rules. But it may be argued that federal law officials sometimes may instead seek rules serving some special interest groups. To be sure, federal law officials would not be concerned about incorporation decisions and thus would not be affected by the distorting biases that afflict state competition. But it may be claimed that the decisions of such officials would be subject to some other distorting biases and, in particular, to those resulting from the pressures and efforts of interest groups. The critical question, then, is whether the influence of interest groups is likely to distort the federal law process so much that it would perform even worse than state competition with respect to the identified issues. In examining this question, it is useful to discuss separately those corporate law issues that involve managerial opportunism and those that involve externalities.

(a) Issues Involving Managerial Opportunism. — As we have seen, with respect to issues involving a sufficiently severe problem of managerial opportunism, state competition may well produce inefficient rules that favor managers (and dominant shareholders). The argument that needs to be examined is that, because of lobbying by managers' interest groups (as well as those of dominant shareholders), the federal law process would produce rules that are even worse.[203]

I do not find this argument convincing. To start with, managers (and dominant shareholders) can also lobby state law officials. Indeed, there are some reasons to believe that the lobbying power of manager interest groups relative to that of public shareholder interest groups is stronger on the state level than on the federal level.[204] And, even if this is not the case, it is hard to see why this relative power would be weaker on the state level than on the federal level.[205]

More important, in a state competition regime, even if managers (and dominant shareholders) engage in no lobbying, they will still

[203] In theory, it is also possible to raise the argument that interest groups of public shareholders would seek to get from federal law officials some value-decreasing rules that would nonetheless benefit public shareholders at the expense of managers and dominant shareholders. But public shareholders would generally be quite unlikely to benefit from value-decreasing rules and thus would generally not have any interest in pushing to have such rules adopted.

[204] *See* Romano, *supra* note 47, at 133, 145. Romano argues that lobbyists can have greater influence on legislators when resource and staffing constraints make it difficult for legislators to gather information independently. *See id.* at 133. Romano concludes that both her study of the experience of one state (Connecticut) and a regression analysis of states' experience in the aggregate provide support for the proposition that lobbying by manager interest groups can be most effective in small states with part-time legislatures. *See id.* at 133–34, 145.

[205] In evaluating the lobbying power of managers' interest groups on the state level, one should be careful not to draw inferences from the amount of existing lobbying. Given that the dynamics of state competition already provide states with powerful incentives to adopt rules favorable to managers, there is commonly little reason or need for managers to lobby state decisionmakers. In those instances in which managers want a state to adopt a rule that it has not yet provided, they may well have ample ability to lobby for it. *See* Romano, *supra* note 47, at 123–24.

benefit from the substantial, structural bias in their favor introduced by the dynamics of state competition. Given Delaware's interest in making its law attractive to managers and dominant shareholders, officials of Delaware who are well-meaning — that is, ones who seek only to advance Delaware's interests and who pay no attention to the activities of interest groups — would still give great weight to the interests of managers; for state competition already builds the interests of these parties and dominant shareholders into Delaware's interest. It is for this reason that manager interest groups do not engage in frequent, active lobbying activity in Delaware;[206] while they do not lack the ability to do so, the dynamics of state competition make it unnecessary for them to do so.

By contrast, on the federal level, the lobbying efforts of managers (and dominant shareholders) would not be made against the background of such a distorted baseline. Federal law officials who are well-meaning — that is, ones who only seek to do their job right and pay no attention to the efforts of interest groups — would not aim at an objective with a built-in focus on the interests of managers and dominant shareholders. Thus, whereas managers and dominant shareholders do not need to lobby at all to have state law officials focus on their interests, they would need to engage in significant lobbying efforts to distort the federal process in their favor. At most, if the power of managers' interest groups on the federal level would be overwhelming relative to that of public shareholders' interest groups, the former would do as well under the federal process as under the state competition regime. Otherwise, managers' interests (and dominant shareholders' interests) are likely to have weaker influence overall on the federal law process than on the state law process.[207]

---

[206] *See* Alva, *supra* note 4, at 917–18. According to Alva, the only time that significant lobbying took place with respect to Delaware corporate law legislation was in connection with the enactment of Delaware's antitakeover statute. *See id.* at 904.

[207] In examining the issue just discussed, it may also be useful to compare how federal and state law have performed with respect to takeover regulation in the last two decades. Although various groups have pushed for federal regulation that would discourage takeovers, Congress has not gone beyond the Williams Act. Thus, federal law officials have not provided the significant impediments to takeovers that incumbent managers would have liked. But states have gone beyond the Williams Act and have adopted several generations of antitakeover statutes. *See* Romano, *supra* note 47, at 113–14. And state fiduciary duty law has enabled incumbent managers to use powerful defensive tactics. *See, e.g.*, Paramount Communications, Inc. v. Time Inc., 571 A.2d 1140, 1154–55 (Del. 1990).

Some of the impediments to takeovers erected by states have been the result of active lobbying by incumbent managers and those acting on their behalf. *See* Romano, *supra* note 47, at 133–34, 136–37 (describing how management interest groups engaged in lobbying to get antitakeover statutes enacted); *see also* Letter from Marty Lipton, Partner, Wachtell, Lipton, Rosen & Katz, to Clients (November 3, 1988) (on file at the Harvard Law School Library) (suggesting that if the *Interco* decision of the Delaware Chancery court, *see* City Capital Assoc.

(b) Issues Involving Externalities. — Some of the issues now governed by state corporate law affect not only the shareholders and managers of the governed company, but also other parties, such as creditors, potential acquirers of control, rival companies, workers, and so forth. As we have seen, with respect to issues involving such externalities, states have an incentive to disregard the interests of third parties and to provide protection to such interests only if such protection happens to be in the interest of shareholders and managers. While federal law officials would not face such an incentive to disregard the interests of third parties, the question is whether such officials may nonetheless perform even worse than their state law counterparts because of the influence of various interest groups.

A worse performance of the federal law process with respect to issues involving externalities cannot result from lobbying by manager and shareholder interest groups. Because states already have an incentive to give weight only to the interests of shareholders and managers, lobbying by shareholders and managers by definition cannot lead the federal law process to give even more weight to these interests. Thus, the only possibility that needs to be considered is that the worse performance of the federal law process would result from lobbying by the non-shareholder groups affected by the relevant issues. To the extent that the lobbying power of such groups is not too strong relative to that of shareholders and managers, their lobbying would do no more than ensure that federal law officials would take into account the interests of these groups, which would likely be desirable. Thus, to oppose federal rules for issues affecting non-shareholder groups, one would have to believe that the lobbying power of such groups would be so strong relative to that of shareholders and managers that federal law officials would distort their rules in favor of these non-shareholder groups. Moreover, one would also have to believe that this distortion would be so severe that it would be worse than the existing distortion of state corporate law against these non-shareholder groups.

I have identified in Part III four corporate law areas that involve significant externalities — the protection accorded to creditors, disclosure regulation, the regulation of control contests, and corporate social responsibility. I doubt that critics of federal law would make the

---

Ltd. Partnership v. Interco Inc., 551 A.2d 787 (Del. Ch. 1988), was not reversed — which it subsequently was by the Delaware Supreme Court, *see* Paramount Communications, Inc. v. Time Inc., 571 A.2d 1140 (Del. 1990) — it may be in the interests of clients to migrate out of Delaware). Other impediments to takeovers may have resulted not from any active lobbying, but rather from the general distortion of state corporate law in favor of managers. In any event, although the development of takeover regulation in the last two decades does not provide a decisive proof, it does seem to support the hypothesis that managers' interests are likely to have a weaker influence on the federal law process than on the state law process.

above argument with respect to the first three areas. We already have federal regulation of some aspects of these three areas, and whether or not one believes that the federal rules are desirable, I doubt that critics would claim that the rules are severely distorted in favor of the affected non-shareholder groups (say, creditors in the area of protection accorded to creditors) and against shareholders and managers.

But my guess is that some may well raise the considered argument in opposing federal regulation of the question of corporate social responsibility — that is, whether managers should use their discretion to advance the interests of constituencies other than shareholders. Critics may well oppose resolution of this issue by federal law on grounds that lobbying by groups of workers, consumers, environmentalists, and so forth would lead to the adoption of rules that would produce an inefficient scheme of corporate governance.

It seems to me that such an objection to federal resolution of the corporate social responsibility issue would be based largely on a strongly held view with respect to what the best substantive rule for this issue is. In other words, the opposition to federal resolution would not be based on a judgment that, because the power of non-shareholder groups would be so much greater than that of shareholders and managers, the federal law process would be more distorted than the existing state process. Rather, the opposition would likely be based on an a priori view that the optimal rule is one that directs managers to focus generally on shareholders' interests (leaving the protection of other constituencies to bodies of law other than corporate law). If one believes this to be the desirable rule, then one will surely support state resolution of this issue, for state competition can be relied on to produce this rule, and thus there is only something to lose and nothing to gain from a federal law resolution. The fact that state competition would likely produce this rule even if it were not socially desirable would not bother someone who is confident that this rule is in fact the socially desirable one.[208]

The above point can be stated in a more general form. If one is confident that a certain rule is desirable for a given issue, and if state competition provides this rule with respect to this issue, then by definition one will have no reason to want federal regulation of this issue, no matter how flawed the state process is.[209] Thus, whenever

---

[208] My own view is that the rule directing managers to focus on shareholders' interests is likely to be the optimal rule. But I do not have sufficient confidence in this judgment to oppose resolution of this issue by the federal law process.

[209] For example, suppose that one believes that (i) state competition is distorted in favor of managers, and (ii) the optimal rule with respect to a certain issue involving managerial opportunism is a lax rule currently provided by state competition. Then one would have no reason to support federal regulation of this issue, despite one's view that the state law process is distorted in favor of managers. The fact that state competition would produce this lax rule

we attach significance to the question whether a state or a federal process is better for regulating a given issue, we presumably lack confidence or agreement concerning what constitutes the best rule. When we lack confidence or agreement about the identity of the socially desirable rule, we seek to choose that process which would be most likely to produce this rule. It is precisely this kind of inquiry that the analysis of this Article seeks to inform.[210]

B. *International Charter Competition*

Thus far I have limited my discussion to charter competition among states within the United States (or some other federal system). But companies raising capital or operating in the United States may also have the option of incorporating (or reincorporating) in another country. Thus, even if state competition in the United States is constrained, some international charter competition will remain. The effectiveness of this competition will depend on the extent to which companies incorporated outside of the United States will face an economic disadvantage (relative to companies incorporated within the United States) when raising capital or operating in the United States.[211]

---

with respect to the issue anyway — even if such a rule were not desirable — would not be bothersome to someone who believed that such a rule is indeed desirable.

[210] Finally, it is worth considering another fault that critics of federal law may put forward — the possibility of a "disaster." Above, I considered the two main imperfections of the federal law process — errors in identifying the socially desirable rules and distortions resulting from the influence of interest groups — and I explained why in my view these imperfections are unlikely to lead to worse results with respect to the identified issues than the state process. But it may be argued that, even assuming that these imperfections are smaller in magnitude than those of the state law process on an *expected value basis*, the worst case scenario under the federal law regime is more worrisome. With a state law regime, so the argument goes, there is a certain lower bound on how bad state corporate law can become; if for some reason Delaware law became quite bad, companies would have a way out. But with respect to federal law, it may be asserted, there would be the possibility of a disastrous state of the law with companies having nowhere to go.

I do not find this disaster scenario sufficiently real to undermine my support for federal rules with respect to the identified issues. As should be clear, the problem of potential disaster is not an independent problem, but rather one that depends on one's evaluation of the problems of errors and interest groups. In particular, the disaster scenario should affect one's position only if one is sufficiently pessimistic about the potential severity of these two problems, and for the reasons explained in this section, I am not.

In deciding whether to be pessimistic about the possibility of a disaster, one may wish to consider the experience we have had with federal corporate law rules thus far. We have had a substantial body of federal corporate law for sixty years. Although opinions may differ on the overall quality of this body of law, in my view it is very hard to see anything in this experience that reinforces the plausibility of the disaster scenario.

[211] The international charter competition is not as effective as the state charter competition because, whereas companies incorporated in one state can operate in any other state without any significant disadvantage, companies incorporated abroad may face such a disadvantage

While an examination of the complex problems introduced by international charter competition is outside the scope of this Article, I wish to note briefly the implications of the presence of such competition for federal intervention.[212] The presence of international charter competition implies that, even when an issue is governed by a federal rule, companies may still have some ability to opt out of this rule by incorporating abroad. Thus, a federal rule would not completely eliminate the ability of those who make incorporation decisions to seek a different rule.

A main corollary of this observation is that if we decide that a given corporate law issue warrants federal regulation, then we should also consider limiting the ability of the relevant companies to escape the federal rule by incorporating abroad. This is because the dynamics of international charter competition are similar to those of state competition. Therefore, if we conclude that companies should not be provided with unconstrained freedom to choose through their state incorporation decision the rule governing them with respect to a given issue, this conclusion should carry over to the international context. That is, if state competition is likely to produce undesirable results with respect to a given corporate law issue, then unconstrained international charter competition is likely to have undesirable consequences as well.

Therefore, if we conclude that a given issue should be governed by a federal rule because of problems of managerial opportunism, we should consider applying this rule not only to companies incorporated in the United States but to all companies, regardless of their place of incorporation, that have a sufficiently substantial fraction of their shareholders in the United States. Similarly, if we decide that a federal rule should govern a given corporate law issue because of the presence of significant externalities, we should consider applying this rule not only to companies incorporated in the United States, but to all companies that have a sufficiently substantial fraction of their operations within the United States.[213]

---

when operating in the United States. For one thing, foreign companies face prohibitions and restrictions on their participation in certain United States sectors, including domestic air transport, nuclear energy, broadcasting, telecommunications, and insurance. *See* EDWARD M. GRAHAM & PAUL R. KRUGMAN, FOREIGN DIRECT INVESTMENT IN THE UNITED STATES 96 (1989); SARKIS J. KHOURY, TRANSNATIONAL MERGERS AND ACQUISITIONS IN THE UNITED STATES 93–100 (1980).

[212] The state competition literature has thus far largely disregarded the possibility of international charter competition. *See, e.g.*, Romano, *supra* note 2, at 712 ("Practically speaking, there would be no competing sovereigns [under a federal corporation law system] to attract disaffected corporations.").

[213] Applying federal rules to companies incorporated outside the United States obviously involves a host of enforcement problems as well as other problems. For this reason, alternative strategies for addressing the problem of international charter competition may be explored —

VI. Conclusion

This Article has developed an analytical framework for identifying the corporate law issues with respect to which state charter competition is likely to work poorly. One major source of the shortcomings of state competition is the possible divergence between the interests of managers and controlling shareholders and the interests of public shareholders. Notwithstanding market forces and the need for shareholder approval to reincorporate, there are many issues with respect to which managers may well seek, and states in turn may well provide, rules that do not maximize shareholder value but rather serve the private interests of managers and controlling shareholders. In particular, the analysis has shown that state competition is likely to produce undesirable results with respect to issues that are significantly redistributive, issues that directly affect the strength of market discipline, and issues that involve potential transfers from public shareholders to a controlling shareholder.

The second major source of the shortcomings of state competition is the presence of externalities. Because states seeking to attract incorporations have an incentive to focus on the interests of shareholders and managers, they will tend to ignore the interests of other parties. As a result, state competition may well produce undesirable rules whenever significant externalities are present. Because of this externality problem, state competition cannot be relied upon to produce socially desirable rules with respect to the regulation of takeovers, proxy contests, and disclosure; it also cannot be relied upon to provide socially desirable rules with respect to the protection accorded to creditors and other non-shareholder constituencies.

Based on this analysis of the shortcomings of state charter competition, this Article has put forward a set of recommendations concerning the desirable balance between state and federal corporate law.

---

for example, harmonizing, and obtaining mutual recognition of, the rules of the major economies. For a discussion of the problems involved in the application of United States rules to foreign companies and the alternative strategies that may be adopted in response, see generally U.S. SECURITIES AND EXCHANGE COMMISSION, INTERNATIONALIZATION OF THE SECURITIES MARKETS (1987).

Finally, it should be noted that, to the extent that international charter competition is not completely eliminated, then, even if we were to adopt federal rules for given issues, we would still have some competition, and those who make incorporation decisions would still have some ability to choose among different sets of rules. This would mean that federal involvement would not completely eliminate the identified shortcomings of state competition. But it would also mean that federal involvement would not imply foregoing all the alleged virtues of state competition. For example, federal law officials would be able to draw from incorporation decisions some information about the rules desired by those making incorporation decisions. And, to the extent that one worries about a disaster scenario, *see supra* note 210, the ability of companies to incorporate abroad would provide a check as well as an advanced warning mechanism.

My analysis largely endorses federal intervention with respect to those corporate law areas currently governed by federal law, including insider trading, corporate disclosure, certain aspects of takeover bids and proxy contests, and creditor protection in bankruptcy. Moreover, the analysis suggests that the federal role should be expanded significantly to cover important areas currently governed by state law. In particular, federal rules, or at least federal minimum standards, are warranted with respect to self-dealing transactions, taking of corporate opportunities, freezeout mergers, all aspects of takeover bids and proxy contests, and limitations on dividends.

Finally, this Article has identified the connection between the state competition debate and the debate on contractual freedom in corporate law. The two questions turn out to be very much related. In particular, whenever concerns exist that justify limiting the ability of companies to opt out of the rule that governs a given corporate law issue, the same concerns also likely justify limiting state competition with respect to this issue. Therefore, those who endorse mandatory rules for certain issues cannot consistently support, as many of them have in the past, state law governance of these issues.

[8]

NEW WAYS IN CORPORATE GOVERNANCE: EUROPEAN EXPERIMENTS WITH LABOR REPRESENTATION ON CORPORATE BOARDS

Klaus J. Hopt *

TABLE OF CONTENTS

I. CORPORATE GOVERNANCE IN EUROPE AND THE EUROPEAN COMMUNITIES IN THE 1980'S

A. *The Problem*

Corporate governance has been discussed in Europe for over 150 years.[1]

---

* Professor of Law, Tuebingen University, and Judge at the Court of Appeals, Stuttgart, Germany. M.C.J. 1966, New York University; Dr. jur. 1967, Munich University; Dr. phil. 1968, Tuebingen University. — Ed.

1. On developments during the first half of the nineteenth century, see Hopt, *Ideelle und wirtschaftliche Grundlagen der Aktien-, Bank- und Börsenrechtsentwicklung im 19. Jahrhundert,*

Indeed, in the 1840's, when the first Corporation Act was enacted in Prussia, three troubling features of the corporate organization form had already been discerned: (1) the vulnerability of small investors who lacked the influence and sophistication to control the corporation; (2) the risk to creditors and the public created by the limited liability of the corporation, especially when combined with inadequate funds and poorly controlled management; and (3) the power that big corporations could amass economically, by monopolizing markets, and politically, by exerting influence on public opinion and government.[2]

Today these features of the "modern" corporation — separation of ownership and control; the lack of "personal" responsibility vis-à-vis creditors and the public, who bear the consequences of corporate decisions and corporate failure; and the ubiquitous presence of corporate power in what has been called a "corporate society" — have been examined from both a theoretical and an empirical viewpoint in the United States as well as in Europe.[3] Yet, in spite of an endless number of reform proposals and a good number of actual corporate law reforms,[4] the problem of corporate governance remains acute. Indeed, the development of more complex corporate structures, such as groups of companies,[5] and the appearance of transnational enterprises[6] has exacerbated the problem. Legislators and courts in

in 5 WISSENSCHAFT UND KODIFIKATION DES PRIVATRECHTS IM 19. JAHRHUNDERT: GELD UND BANKEN 128 (H. Coing & W. Wilhelm eds. 1980). On the period between 1860 and 1920, see Horn, *Aktienrechtliche Unternehmensorganisation in der Hochindustrialisierung (1860-1920). Deutschland, England, Frankreich und die USA im Vergleich*, in RECHT UND ENTWICKLUNG DER GROSSUNTERNEHMEN IM 19. UND FRÜHEN 20. JAHRHUNDERT 123 (N. Horn & J. Kocka eds. 1979) [hereinafter cited as N. Horn & J. Kocka] (German with English summary).

2. *See Instruktion, die Grundsätze in Ansehung der Konzessionierung von Aktiengesellschaften betreffend, vom 22.4.1845*, 1845 MINISTERIAL-BLATT FÜR DIE GESAMTE INNERE VERWALTUNG IN DEN KÖNIGLICH PREUSSISCHEN STAATEN 121 (concerning the practice under the Prussian Corporation Act of 1843); R. von Mohl, *Die Aktiengesellschaften, volkswirtschaftlich und politisch betrachtet*, 1856 DEUTSCHE VIERTELJAHRS-SCHRIFT pt. 4, at 1, 38, 52.

3. *See, e.g.*, A. BERLE, JR. & G. MEANS, THE MODERN CORPORATION AND PRIVATE PROPERTY (1932); L. GOWER, J. CRONIN, A. EASON & LORD WEDDERBURN OF CHARLTON, PRINCIPLES OF MODERN COMPANY LAW 49-57, 494-95 (4th ed. 1979) [hereinafter cited as L. GOWER]; E. HERMAN, CORPORATE CONTROL, CORPORATE POWER (1981); E. MESTMÄCKER, VERWALTUNG, KONZERNGEWALT UND RECHTE DER AKTIONÄRE 78-89 (1958); R. WIETHÖLTER, INTERESSEN UND ORGANISATION DER AKTIENGESELLSCHAFT IM AMERIKANISCHEN UND DEUTSCHEN RECHT 270-338 (1961).

4. *See* L. GOWER, *supra* note 3, at 28-30, 39-57 (discussing English reforms); 2 J. HAMEL, G. LAGARDE & A. JAUFFRET, DROIT COMMERCIAL 1-16 (G. Lagarde 2d ed. 1980) (French); 1 H. WIEDEMANN, GESELLSCHAFTSRECHT: GRUNDLAGEN 24-34 (1980) (German).

5. *See, e.g.*, M. EISENBERG, THE STRUCTURE OF THE CORPORATION: A LEGAL ANALYSIS 213-315 (1976) (as to the U.S.); 2 LEGAL AND ECONOMIC ANALYSES ON MULTINATIONAL ENTERPRISES: GROUPS OF COMPANIES IN EUROPEAN LAWS (K. Hopt ed. 1982) [hereinafter cited as Hopt] (as to Germany, England, France, Belgium, Switzerland, Sweden, and the European Communities); F. WOOLDRIDGE, GROUPS OF COMPANIES (1981) (as to Britain, France, and Germany).

6. On the historical development of the transnational enterprise, see the series of contributions in *Multinational Enterprises*, 48 BUS. HIST. REV. 277-446 (1974); *see also* Hawrylyshyn, *The Internationalization of Firms*, 5 J.W.T.L. 72 (1971). On the legal policy problems, see B. GROSSFELD, PRAXIS DES INTERNATIONALEN PRIVAT- UND WIRTSCHAFTSRECHTS: RECHTSPROBLEME MULTINATIONALER UNTERNEHMEN (1975); Tunc, *Multi-national Companies in French Law*, in LAW AND INTERNATIONAL TRADE: FESTSCHRIFT FÜR SCHMITTHOFF 375

several European states are very conscious of the corporate governance problem, but their responses to it have been dissimilar.

B. *The Different Reform Strategies in European States*

European states appear disillusioned with attempts at achieving better corporate governance through increased shareholder democracy.[7] This is hardly surprising, since, apart from the problem of the lack of sophistication exhibited by a broad stratum of the shareholding public, the cost-benefit balance for small shareholders of investing more effort in participation and control is clearly negative.

Furthermore, although several European states have posited the need for fundamental corporate law reform,[8] the likelihood of achieving anything more than piecemeal reform remains speculative. Although an exception is found in Switzerland, where revision of the corporation law is going on slowly but steadily,[9] Switzerland's unique tradition in the area of corporate governance explains this departure from the norm.[10] Thus, in the absence of convincing designs for new corporation law, most European states experiment with rather concrete reform strategies, and in the process exhibit their different theoretical views of the corporate governance problem.

When grouped according to the control mechanisms chosen, the most common of these reform strategies is to enhance use of the liability device. The immediate targets of this device are management and the board of directors. In most European countries, the duties and liabilities of manage-

(Fabricius ed. 1973); Vagts, *The Multinational Enterprise: A New Challenge for Transnational Law*, 83 HARV. L. REV. 739 (1969).

7. *See, e.g.*, H. WIEDEMANN, *supra* note 4, at 352-53; *see also* M. EISENBERG, *supra* note 5, at 19, 56-63 (as to the U.S.).

8. As to Great Britain, see L. GOWER, REVIEW OF INVESTOR PROTECTION (1982) (The Gower Report was produced by a commission set up under the Secretary of State for Trade to advise on the need for new legislation.). As to Germany, see the report of the Enterprise Law Commission, a group set up by the Federal Ministry of Justice: BUNDESMINISTERIUM DER JUSTIZ, BERICHT ÜBER DIE VERHANDLUNGEN DER UNTERNEHMENSRECHTSKOMMISSION (1980) [hereinafter cited as the Enterprise Law Commission Report]. The Enterprise Law Commission worked from 1972 until 1979, producing a report of over 1000 pages. However, because it was composed of members of various factions and interest groups, it has remained divided over nearly every major problem. For a critical evaluation of its work, see Kübler, *Unternehmensorganisation zwischen Sachverstand und Interessenpolitik*, 10 ZGR 377-92 (1981). Total revisions of the corporate law have been enacted in Germany in 1965, in France in 1966, and in the Netherlands in 1970-1971.

9. Botschaft über die Revision des Aktienrechts vom 23. Feb. 1983, No. 83.015. This draft law on the corporation (26th title of the Swiss Code on Obligations dating from 1936) contains only those proposals that are considered indispensable, other proposals being postponed. Some of the major targets of the draft law include investor protection, better disclosure, clearer delineation of the competences and tasks of corporate organs, especially the board and auditors (Revisionsstelle), and corporate capital requirements.

In Belgium, a draft law on commercial companies was presented to the Parliament on December 5, 1979, and is still under consideration by that body. *See* Lempereur, *The Belgian Bill to Amend the Corporation Law — New Perspectives for Belgian Securities Regulation*, 5 J. COMP. BUS. & CAP. MKT. L. 195 (1983).

10. In the context of merger control, see Schluep, *The Swiss Act on Cartels and The Practice of the Swiss Cartel Commission Concerning Economic Concentration*, in 1 LEGAL AND ECONOMIC ANALYSES ON MULTINATIONAL ENTERPRISES: EUROPEAN MERGER CONTROL 123 (K. Hopt. ed. 1982) [hereinafter cited as 1 EUROPEAN MERGER CONTROL].

ment and the board are continuously refined by courts through legal doctrine. France and Belgium, however, have developed the "action en comblement du passif,"[11] which can be brought against directors of a bankrupt corporation who, if found to have acted negligently, may be held personally liable not only for specific damages, but for all or part of the corporate deficit. The philosophy behind this action is that the privilege of incorporation with limited liability is not without bounds, and that the real corporate actors should be required under certain conditions to back up their actions with their personal wealth.[12]

A more general reform strategy may be discerned in the new and intense focus on the functions of the corporate board.[13] It is well known in Europe that the corporate board does not live up to the legislature's expectations with respect to the board's supervision and control of the corporation's management.[14] Thus, the attempt is being made to activate this controlling function by giving boards greater rights to information from management,[15] by discarding or mitigating the temptations of self-interest[16] and by imposing legal liability on directors.[17]

Not only is the corporate board's controlling function being revitalized but attention has turned as well to those "who control the controllers." This attention has led to the imposition of liability on auditors and banks. In

11. *See* Art. 99 of the French Act No. 67-563 of July 13, 1967 J.O. 7059, 7065, 1982 D.S.L. 269, 275; *see also* B. MERCADAL & P. JANIN, SOCIÉTÉS COMMERCIALES (MÉMENTO PRATIQUE FRANCIS LEFÈBVRE), 1981-1982, at 928-31 (12th ed. 1981) (Nos. 3848-55: obligations des dirigeants au paiement du passif social) (French case law). For Belgium, see van Ommeslaghe, *Les groupes de sociétés et l'expérience du droit belge*, in Hopt, *supra* note 5, at 59, 92-94.

12. For the historical developments concerning this philosophy, see L. GOWER, *supra* note 3, at 43-57 (England). For an analysis of the outer bounds of limited liability in modern corporation law, see H. WIEDEMANN, *supra* note 4, at 217-36.

13. *See* CORPORATE GOVERNANCE — DIRECTORS' DUTIES AND LIABILITIES 15-18, 29-30, 113-16, 166-73, 429, 449 (K. Hopt & G. Teubner eds. 1984) (papers to the International Colloquium in Florence, Apr. 13-16, 1983) [hereinafter cited as CORPORATE GOVERNANCE]; Papers to the Congress on Corporate Governance, Paris, Mar. 9-11, 1983 (forthcoming).

14. In Germany, with its obligatory division between management board and supervisory board, this had already been discussed extensively by the turn of the century. *See* A. CAHN, DER AUFSICHTSRAT DER AKTIENGESELLSCHAFT 249-64 (1907). The development of the supervisory board in the nineteenth and early twentieth centuries is treated by Hopt, *Zur Funktion des Aufsichtsrats im Verhältnis von Industrie und Bankensystem*, in N. Horn & J. Kocka, *supra* note 1, at 227. For Great Britain, see Wedderburn, *The Legal Development of Corporate Responsibility*, in CORPORATE GOVERNANCE, *supra* note 13, at 20-32. *Cf.* A. CHANDLER, JR., THE VISIBLE HAND: THE MANAGERIAL REVOLUTION IN AMERICAN BUSINESS (1977); M. MACE, DIRECTORS: MYTH AND REALITY (1971) (for the United States).

15. *See, e.g.*, M. LUTTER, INFORMATION UND VERTRAULICHKEIT IM AUFSICHTSRAT (Abhandlungen zum deutschen und europäischen Handels- und Wirtschaftsrecht No. 25, 1979); Mertens, *Zur Berichtspflicht des Vorstands gegenüber dem Aufsichtsrat*, 25 AG 67 (1980). As regards the flow of information to the board and the role of the accountant, see M. EISENBERG, *supra* note 5, at 186-211.

16. *See* K. Hopt, *Self-Dealing and the Use of Corporate Opportunity and Information: Regulating Directors' Conflicts of Interest*, in CORPORATE GOVERNANCE, *supra* note 13, at 285-326 (Europe); Brudney & Clark, *A New Look at Corporate Opportunities*, 94 HARV. L. REV. 998 (1981).

17. In this regard, see the *Schaffgotsch* decision of the German Federal Court Judgment of December 21, 1979. Bundesgerichtshof, W. Ger., 33 NJW (Vol. 2) 1629 (1980); *cf.* Ulmer, *Aufsichtsratsmandat und Interessenkollision*, 33 NJW (Vol. 2) 1603 (1980).

Switzerland, a new body of case law holds corporate auditors liable in cases of malfeasance.[18] And in Germany, where banks traditionally play a key role in the corporate proxy machinery and on corporate boards, this role is being bolstered by the imposition of legal duties and liabilities on banks and bank representatives in various corporate contexts.[19] This is quite unlike what the United States attempted to do with the Glass-Steagall Act, which was designed to negate the role of banks on corporate boards.[20] For Germany, it is safe to say that traditional corporate law and governance cannot be understood without knowledge of the developments in banking law. On the whole, however, none of these measures solve the problem of corporate governance.

Taking into consideration the phenomenon of director ineffectiveness, which in part seems but an outgrowth of the broader phenomena of organizational slack and bureaucratic inefficiency,[21] some European countries have turned to the market to find a control mechanism. The market for corporate control, which provides such a check,[22] has thus become the object of regulatory concern in Great Britain, France, and Belgium. These countries have delineated the rights and duties of the participants in corporate takeovers, which are now supervised by state or self-regulatory bodies.[23] Germany, however, has not witnessed such a development: in Germany, takeovers in general, let alone unfriendly ones, do not play a

18. In particular, see the decision of the Swiss Federal Court. Judgment of Sept. 23, 1980, 106 BG II 232, *summarized in* 70 DIE PRAXIS DES BUNDESGERICHTS 68 (1981); *see also* Forstmoser, *The Duties and Liabilities of Auditors under Swiss Law,* 5 J. COMP. BUS. & CAP. MKT. L. 305 (1983). For Germany, see W. EBKE, WIRTSCHAFTSPRÜFER UND DRITTHAFTUNG (Schriften zum Deutschen und Europäischen Zivil-, Handels- und Prozessrecht No. 95, 1983). For the United States, see Pitt & Williams, *The Convergence of Commercial and Investment Banking: New Directions in the Financial Services Industry,* 5 J. COMP. BUS. & CAP. MKT. L. 137 (1983). The system of all-purpose banking that is practiced in Germany, Switzerland, and other countries has been the object of scrutiny as to its economic and legal implications. The results of this scrutiny favor such a system so long as legal safeguards are maintained. GERMAN FEDERAL MINISTRY OF FINANCE, BERICHT DER STUDIENKOMMISSION "GRUNDSATZFRAGEN DER KREDITWIRTSCHAFT" (1979) (Banking Law Study Commission).

19. Examples of such contexts include use of the banks' depository vote; conflicts of interest of bank representatives on corporate boards; prospectus liability of banks; piercing the corporate veil in the event of bank participation; fiduciary duties of banks to shareholder-clients; and the duties and liabilities of banks involved with failing companies. *See, e.g., Zeitschrift für das gesamte Handelsrecht und Wirtschaftsrecht,* 147 ZHR 165-222 (1983); 145 ZHR 177-272 (1981); 143 ZHR 113-226 (1979) (contributions to three Banking Law Symposia).

20. Banking Act of 1933 (Glass-Steagall Act), ch. 89, 48 Stat. 162, 184 (codified at various sections of 12 U.S.C., including 12 U.S.C. §§ 24, 78, 335, 377 & 378) (1982).

21. *See* J. MARCH & H. SIMON, ORGANIZATIONS 36-82 (1958); H. MINTZBERG, THE STRUCTURING OF ORGANIZATIONS 372-79 (1979) (discussing problems of coordination, discretion, and innovation, and the danger of dysfunctional responses).

22. To what degree it does so in reality is open to question. Available evidence shows that quite often financially healthy enterprises are the target of tender offers. Furthermore, all real markets are imperfect, and these imperfections are especially marked for capital markets in Europe. *See* EEC COMMISSION, DER AUFBAU EINES EUROPÄISCHEN KAPITALMARKTS (1966) (Segré report).

23. *See* C. SCHMITTHOFF, F. GORÉ & T. HEINSIUS, ÜBERNAHMEANGEBOTE IM AKTIENRECHT (Arbeiten zur Rechtsvergleichung No. 77, 1976) (takeover bids); Immenga, *Öffentliche Übernahmeangebote (Take over Bids),* 47 Schw. AG 89 (1975); *cf.* Behrens, *Rechtspolitische Grundsatzfragen zu einer Europäischen Regelung für Übernahmeangebote,* 4 ZGR 433 (1975) (European harmonization).

major role.[24]

More generally, since capital markets can also act as a check against inefficient corporate management by, for example, making corporate and credit relations with banks more difficult, these markets have become the object of regulation by laws and ongoing scrutiny by capital market commissions. Again, this is the case in France, Belgium, and, in a more complicated and self-regulatory fashion, Great Britain. In Germany, capital market law is less developed and there is no body other than the stock exchanges in charge of supervising the capital markets.[25] However, Germany has been the first to realize the significance of the relationship between corporate power and antitrust law, particularly merger control, by using antitrust law to control transnational enterprises.[26]

Improving corporate governance through market forces is, of course, problematic. Unresolved questions include how to develop such market forces if they do not yet exist or work satisfactorily;[27] what is the right mix between state regulation and self-regulation for these markets;[28] and how state-controlled corporations, groups of companies, and transnational enterprises can be effectively exposed to such market forces.[29]

At any rate, there is widespread conviction in Europe that these and other means of controlling the performance of corporate managers and board members — such as the use of contingent salary mechanisms, premiums, and stock bonuses — do not solve the problem, even though they may be steps in the right direction.[30] This conviction has contributed to the willingness of various European states to experiment with labor representation on corporate boards. Indeed, the idea of worker co-determination on the board is widespread and has even reached a stage in which the European Communities are considering making such co-determination obligatory in one way or another for all member states. This movement finds its rough

24. In Germany, there are only nonbinding guidelines, which were recommended by the Stock Exchange Experts Commission in January 1979. For the text and (short) commentary, see BAUMBACH, DUDEN, & HOPT, HANDELSGESETZBUCH MIT NEBENGESETZEN (OHNE SEERECHT) 1059-63 (25th ed. 1983).

25. *See* F. KÜBLER, GESELLSCHAFTSRECHT 365-75 (1981); Hopt, *Vom Aktien- und Börsenrecht zum Kapitalmarktrecht?,* 141 ZHR 389 (1977); Kohl & Walz, *Kapitalmarktrecht als Aufgabe,* 22 AG 29 (1977).

26. *See* Hopt, *Merger Control in Germany,* in 1 EUROPEAN MERGER CONTROL, *supra* note 10, at 71.

27. *See* Kübler, *Unternehmensstruktur und Kapitalmarktfunktion — Überlegungen zur Krise der Aktiengesellschaft,* 26 AG 5 (1981).

28. *See* L. GOWER, *supra* note 8, ¶¶ 8.10-8.27 (self-regulatory agencies). In continental European countries, especially Germany, the attitude towards complete self-regulation is basically negative, such as in the context of insider regulation.

29. Each of these organizations exhibits a strong tendency to insulate itself from outside control, whether by markets or by law. In state-controlled corporations, this insulation stems from the lack of responsiveness to financial pressures. In groups of companies, the specific corporate structure facilitates insulation, while in transnational enterprises, the territoriality principle and the differentials of nation-state regulation contribute to insulation from outside control.

30. *See* Baellwieser & Schmidt, *Unternehmensverfassung, Unternehmensziele und Finanztheorie,* in UNTERNEHMENSVERFASSUNG ALS PROBLEM DER BETRIEBSWIRTSCHAFTSLEHRE 645, 662-77 (K. Bohr, J. Drukarczyk, H.-J. Drumm & G. Scherrer eds. 1981) [hereinafter cited as K. Bohr].

equivalent in the trend in the United States toward the appointment of outside directors.[31] Both movements are characterized by high hopes, contrasted with an overall evaluation so far that may dampen these hopes. Before turning to such an evaluation of the European movement, however, this Article shall outline the most recent developments in corporate governance in the European Communities.

C. *Harmonizing Corporate Governance Rules in the European Communities: The 1983 Draft of the Fifth Directive*

After a sluggish fifteen-year period, the harmonization movement in European company law gained momentum in the late 1970's. Already, six company law directives based on article 54(3)(g) of the European Economic Community (EEC) Treaty have been enacted by the Council and are binding on Member States. The core of the harmonization work concerning company structure is contained in the draft Fifth Directive. The original version of the draft presented by the European Commission in 1972[32] led to great controversy in the European Parliament and in the Member States because of its proposals on an obligatory two-tiered board, labor co-determination, and other issues. After ten years of deliberation, however, the European Parliament gave its opinion[33] and the European Commission responded quickly by presenting an extensively revised draft Fifth Directive in 1983.[34]

The 1983 draft focuses only on stock corporations, where transnational activities are predominant. For Member States like Germany, where other company forms compete very successfully with the stock corporation,[35] this

31. *See* M. EISENBERG, *supra* note 5, at 144-46, 174-77; E. HERMAN, *supra* note 3, at 30-48, 281-83; Brudney, *The Independent Director — Heavenly City or Potemkin Village?*, 95 HARV. L. REV. 597 (1981).

32. Commission Directive, Proposition d'une cinquième directive tendant à coordonner les garanties qui sont exigées dans les États membres, des sociétés, au sens de l'article 58 paragraphe 2 du traité, pour protéger les intérêts, tant des associés que des tiers en ce qui concerne la structure des sociétés anonymes ainsi que les pouvoirs et obligations de leurs organes, art. 58, 15 J. O. COMM. EUR. (No. C 131) 49 (Dec. 13, 1972). For reviews in English, see Lang, *The Fifth EEC Directive on the Harmonization of Company Law* (pts. 1-2), 12 COM. MKT. L. REV. 155, 345 (1975); Conlon, *Industrial Democracy and EEC Company Law: A Review of the Draft Fifth Directive*, 24 INTL. & COMP. L.Q. 348 (1975).

33. European Parliament Minutes of Proceedings of May 11, 1982, 25 O.J. EUR. COMM. (No. C 149) 12, 20-43 (June 14, 1982) [hereinafter cited as European Parliament].

34. Commission Preparatory Act, Amended proposal for a Fifth Directive founded on Article 54(3)(g) of the EEC Treaty concerning the structure of public limited companies and the powers and obligations of their organs, 26 O.J. EUR. COMM. (No. C 240) 2 (Sept. 9, 1983) [hereinafter referred to as draft Fifth Directive]. For a first comment in German, see Kolvenbach, *Die Fünfte EG-Richtlinie über die Struktur der Aktiengesellschaft (Strukturrichtlinie)*, 36 DER BETRIEB 2235-41 (1983).

35. In Germany, there are 2140 stock corporations, of which some 450 have their shares quoted at the stock exchange, while there are 300,000 limited liability companies (GmbH, as of 1984). *See Der Aktienmarkt in der Bundesrepubik Deutschland und Seine Entwicklungs Möglichkeiten*, MONATSBERICHTE DER DEUTSCHEN BUNDESBANK, Apr. 1984, at 12-21.

The number of partnerships with a limited liability company as the only fully liable partner (GmbH & Co) is not recorded. On the resulting regulatory problems, compare Kübler, *supra* note 27, with Schmidt, *Mehr Unternehmen an die Börse durch differenzierte Marktorganisation* in 1981 HANSEATISCHE WERTPAPIERBÖRSE HAMBURG 4 (Annual Report of the Hamburg Stock Exchange).

restriction tends to widen the regulatory gap that exists between the different company forms and to intensify the movement away from the stock corporation. Thus, the danger exists that the harmonization envisaged by the draft Fifth Directive, which applies only to segments of the real enterprise world, may give rise to complacency.[36] After all, regulatory goals such as investor and creditor protection and management responsibility do not lose their importance when an enterprise leaves the corporate form or chooses another form from the start. In terms of the European theoretical discussion, the slogan "from corporate law to enterprise law"[37] reflects this concern.

The European Commission has exhibited a clear preference for the German two-tier board system, not only because it appears to bolster the supervisory function in general, but also because the two-tier board is a much easier target for the varying co-determination formulas.[38] Yet the Commission understood that it could not successfully promote its 1972 proposal of an obligatory separation between a management board and a supervisory board. Thus, the 1983 draft contains a compromise. The dual system is introduced as a general rule, but each Member State may opt for a unitary board system. This arrangement lasts for only five years, at which time the Commission is to evaluate the system and decide whether further harmonization will be necessary. Given the realities of the present decisionmaking process in the Commission, however, such a possible revision may be little more than a face-saving provision for the Commission.

As a result, the draft contains elements of separation even for the optional unitary board system. Managing and nonmanaging members of the unitary board must be distinguished. Managing members are to be appointed by nonmanaging members, and the number of nonmanaging members must be higher than that of managing members. All this is designed to prepare the way for labor co-determination. Even the obligatory nomination of a member of the management board as the member who is primarily responsible for labor relations is maintained under the unitary board system: this so-called labor director (Arbeitsdirektor) must be a managing member of the unitary board. Member States that currently use a unitary board system will undoubtedly realize that under these circumstances their option to continue such a system under the Fifth Directive is little more than nominal, and will react accordingly. In practice, however, the acceptance of the proposed reforms would result in less radical change than one watching this harmonization struggle might expect, since in many large corporations the unitary board acts much like a supervisory board vis-à-vis management.[39]

---

36. This danger has become real with the Fourth Directive Concerning Disclosure and Balance Sheets, which does not reach the German GmbH & Co., *see* note 35 *supra*, even though GmbH and GmbH & Co. are company forms that are in many ways equivalent alternatives for business. The German legislature does not intend to apply the Fourth Directive to GmbH & Co., even though the resulting discrepancies are quite arbitrary.

37. *Cf.* Enterprise Law Commission Report, *supra* note 8.

38. Co-determination can be confined to the supervisory board, the functions of which are undetermined, *see* note 14 *supra*, but which in any case do not include the whole range of entrepreneurial decisionmaking in the corporation.

39. *See* L. GOWER, *supra* note 3, at 71 (England); E. HERMAN, *supra* note 3, at 30-48, 52.

The other main controversy under the 1972 draft was labor co-determination.[40] In this battlefield the Commission was forced to acknowledge the political realities confronting its Member States and sound the retreat. Thus, the draft provides for labor co-determination on the following terms: The threshold for obligatory labor co-determination is a work force of 1000 or more employed within the same group of companies. Member States may provide that the majority of the workers of the corporation can vote against co-determination. This option is modeled after similar solutions in Scandinavia and Great Britain and has been on the list of requests by the European Parliament. If such a veto of the workers is not expressed, four possible models of co-determination may be prescribed by the Member States:

(1) Selection of at least one-third, but no more than one-half, of the members of the supervisory board by labor. In the latter case ultimate decisionmaking power must lie with the representatives chosen by the general assembly. This is necessary to make this model compatible with the German Constitution.[41] Member States may also provide that no more than one-third of the board members can be elected other than by the general assembly or the workers, leaving open the possibility of a third group of public-interest directors or state representatives, like that which exists in certain French state enterprises, most recently in those enterprises nationalized in 1982.[42]

(2) Co-optation of new members by the supervisory board itself. In this case, the general assembly and the work council have the right to appeal to an independent state-appointed body. This model is a near total imitation of the Dutch co-determination system.[43]

(3) Informing and deliberating with a separate labor representation body within the corporation. This model has received attention in the British reform debate[44] and has parallels in Norwegian corporation

40. For a comparative law inventory as well as a critical appreciation of the different co-determination models and their difficulties, see Hopt, *Grundprobleme der Mitbestimmung in Europa*, 13 ZFA 207 (1982); Westermann, *Tendenzen der gegenwärtigen Mitbestimmungsdiskussion in der Europäischen Gemeinschaft*, 48 RABELSZ 123 (1984)

41. *See* Judgment of Mar. 1, 1979, Bundesverfassungsgericht, 50 BVerfG 290, *reprinted in* 32 NJW 699 (1979). For a summary of this decision, see 28 AM. J. COMP. L. 88 (1980) and the critical comment by Wiedemann, *Codetermination by Workers in German Enterprises*, 28 AM. J. COMP. L. 79 (1980). For a much more positive view, see Simitis, *Workers' Participation in the Enterprise — Transcending Company Law?*, 38 MOD. L. REV. 1 (1975). Most observers today would say that one can live with the German Codetermination Act of 1976 and with the Court's decision upholding it. *See* Part III *infra*.

42. Blanc-Jouvan, *La participation des travailleurs à la gestion des entreprises en droit français*, in MITBESTIMMUNG DER ARBEITNEHMER IN FRANKREICH, GROSSBRITANNIEN, SCHWEDEN, ITALIEN, DEN U.S.A. UND DER BUNDESREPUBLIK DEUTSCHLAND 33, 54 (Arbeiten zur Rechtsvergleichung No. 92, 1978); Loi de nationalisation (no. 82-155 du 11 février 1982), art. 7, 1982 J.O. 566, 567, 1982 D.S.L. 92, 92.

43. As to the Dutch Codetermination Act of 1971, see Sanders, *Employee Participation in the Netherlands*, 1977 J. BUS. L. 209. As to experiences with the Act, see Honée & De Groot, *The Appointment of Supervisory Directors in Major Companies* (Report in Dutch) (1979) (Summary in English) (Social and Economic Council, 's-Gravenhage 1979); Honée, *Erfahrungen mit der Kooptation von Aufsichtsratsmitgliedern in den Niederlanden*, 11 ZGR 87 (1982).

44. *See* INQUIRY ON INDUSTRIAL DEMOCRACY COMMITTEE, FIRST REPORT, CMD. 6706 (1977) (Bullock Report); Kahn-Freund, *Industrial Democracy*, 6 INDUS. L.J. 65 (1977); Davies,

law.[45]

(4) Introduction of co-determination either within or outside of the board under terms that are the result of collective bargaining. Such a system is in force in Sweden[46] and has had a strong appeal to the partisans of labor co-determination in England.

From the compromises reached regarding two main areas of contention, to wit, the propriety of a two-board system and of labor co-determination, one might conclude that even if the draft is adopted by the Council, which is hard to predict, the ambitious goal of European harmonization of company structure will be reached only to a modest degree. Yet such a conclusion is superficial for several reasons.

First, there exist many areas, such as the ambit of the general assembly and the rights of shareholders, on which harmonization without hedging will be reached. It is true that most of these areas are less conspicuous and of a more technical nature than the propriety of a two-board system or of co-determination, but corporate governance is reached only by a full configuration of many protective devices.

Second, one can hardly expect harmonization to be reached in a single leap. Not surprisingly, company law harmonization shares the fate of European integration in general.[47] The European Commission has favored the only sensible route, taking the European bull by the horns and narrowing the options as far as possible: politics, after all, is the art of the possible.

Third, and most important, even a full harmonization of company law and labor co-determination on the board would not ensure harmonization of behavior, decisionmaking processes, and the locus of responsibility within the corporation. Transplanting legal devices and institutions from one country to another and from one socioeconomic context to another is social experimentation with all its attendant uncertainties. This general observation applies with great force in the field of labor relations and co-determination.[48] Indeed, full harmonization as planned in 1972 might lead to less *real* homogeneity than that proposed in 1983, since in some countries trade unions that are oriented towards conflict and class struggle in the Marxian tradition may use co-determination in quite a different spirit than,

---

The Bullock Report and Employee Participation in Corporate Planning in the U.K., 1 J. COMP. CORP. L. & SEC. REG. 245 (1978).

45. *See* Kolvenbach, *supra* note 34, at 2239.

46. *See* F. SCHMIDT, LAW AND INDUSTRIAL RELATIONS IN SWEDEN (1977). For a rather critical opinion, see Victorin, *Co-determination in Sweden: the Union Way*, 2 J. COMP. CORP. L. & SEC. REG. 111 (1979). The most recent study is by economists E. Gerum & H. Steinmann, Unternehmensordnung und tarifvertragliche Mitbestimmung in Schweden — Ein Beitrag zur vergleichenden Unternehmensverfassungsforschung aus sozioökonomischer Sicht, 2 vols. (text and materials) (DFG-Abschlussbericht Ste 97/9, Mar. 1983) (report available from the German Science Foundation).

47. *See generally* R. BUXBAUM & K. HOPT, EUROPEAN INTEGRATION IN THE LIGHT OF THE AMERICAN FEDERAL EXPERIENCE (forthcoming) (contribution to the Florence Project on European Integration in the light of the "American Federal Experience") (directed by M. Cappelletti) (discussing the harmonization of company and capital market law).

48. *See* Summers, *Worker Participation in the U.S. and West Germany: A Comparative Study from an American Perspective*, 28 AM. J. COMP. L. 367, 367-68, 391-92 (1980).

for example, the German trade unions, which have been very successful with co-determination.

II. The Many Roads to "Industrial Democracy": Political Crossroads to Worker Co-determination

A. *Basic Strategies of Enhancing Labor's Influence on the Corporation*

In European countries labor's influence on corporations has grown steadily since World War I. This growth has not followed any logical sequence, since the development of labor representation on corporate boards has not occurred as a result of rational decision, but rather through a process of political assertion and compromise. One must take into account the institutional framework within which such boardroom co-determination has developed.[49]

The main source of labor influence on the corporation has been collective bargaining. The preeminence of this mechanism remains unquestioned even when other devices such as boardroom co-determination are requested or obtained by labor. This does not, however, preclude conflicts between collective bargaining and boardroom co-determination.[50] Indeed, the former is basically an adversarial strategy which includes such tools as strikes and lockouts, while the latter can succeed only if practiced with a sense of cooperation. It is precisely because of this conflict that boardroom co-determination has been denounced by some as the last trick of capitalism. On the other hand, the scope of collective bargaining — the main, but by no means exclusive, object of which is to fix wages — may expand if, as in Sweden, it extends to various forms of co-determination within the enterprise and within the board.[51]

More important than the body of law in this area are the traditions, behavior, and goals of the trade unions in a particular European country. Just as European and American trade unions are purported to be completely different, trade unions within the European Community vary widely in character.[52]

Work councils are found in most European countries. These councils

49. For the historical development of co-determination in Germany from the early nineteenth century until today, see MITBESTIMMUNG: URSPRÜNGE UND ENTWICKLUNG (Zeitschrift für Unternehmensgeschichte Beiheft No. 19) (H. Pohl ed. 1981). For the socioeconomic background in England, see Wedderburn, *supra* note 14. For a very sharp comparative study of the institutional framework of worker participation in the United States and West Germany, see Summers, *supra* note 48. For Sweden, see F. SCHMIDT, *supra* note 46. *Cf.* INDUSTRIAL DEMOCRACY IN EUROPE (IDE), INTERNATIONAL RESEARCH GROUP, INDUSTRIAL DEMOCRACY IN EUROPE (1981) (comparing the worker participation schemes in twelve countries); INDUSTRIAL DEMOCRACY IN EUROPE (IDE) INTERNATIONAL RESEARCH GROUP, EUROPEAN INDUSTRIAL RELATIONS (1981) (describing the various legal and socioeconomic factors relevant to a comparison of the twelve countries studied).

50. *See* Summers, *Codetermination in the United States: A Projection of Problems and Potentials,* 4 J. COMP. CORP. L. & SEC. REG. 155, 163-67 (1982).

51. For the ensuing, highly difficult problem of reconciling corporation law and these collective agreements, see Victorin, *supra* note 46, at 130-33.

52. *See* Wedderburn, *supra* note 14, at 19.

are usually imposed by law, but may also be formed voluntarily.[53] They are geared towards increasing the participation of workers at the *plant level* in shaping the workplace environment. Accordingly, participation is organized from the bottom up, that is, at the shop-floor level. The participatory rights of these work councils vary greatly. Depending on the country, work councils range from the merely informational, to councils with obligatory consultation and co-deliberation rights, and finally, to councils with full participation rights and a veto in decisionmaking. Again, conflicts between collective bargaining and work council participation exist, but they are usually mitigated by the legal priority of the former.[54]

Labor participation from below implies at least indirect influence on the level above, and decisions at the plant level ultimately affect the social and economic policy of the enterprise as such. This observation, and the thrust of the participation movement in the last decade, justify the conclusion that participation necessarily transcends the plant level and plays a role in co-determining enterprise policy.[55] Short of outright board room co-determination, such participation at the enterprise level may be practiced within a system that fosters strategic informational exchange and consultation with labor.

The organization and extent of this participation differ widely. In Germany, the economic committee of the workers must be informed in a timely and thorough manner about a wide range of economic matters, such as the economic and financial situation of the enterprise, the production and investments program, changes in the organization, and other plans that could vitally affect the employees' interests.[56] In Sweden, similar rights are given to the trade unions in order to promote "informed bargaining."[57] In France, the "comité d'entreprise" has recently obtained not only the right to full information about the enterprise and its economic prospects but also the right to present requests to and consult with the board.[58] Also, European countries are presently engaged in heated discussion concerning the far-reaching information rights to be granted to the workers in transnational enterprises, particularly those working in subsidiaries with foreign parents.[59]

---

53. Examples are given by Kübler, *Dual Loyalty of Labor Representatives*, in CORPORATE GOVERNANCE, *supra* note 13, at 431; Simitis, *supra* note 41, at 3-4.

54. For comprehensive legal information on many countries, see W. KOLVENBACH, EMPLOYEE COUNCILS IN EUROPEAN COMPANIES (1978). For an empirical study on the practice under the German work council system, see H.U. NIEDENHOFF, PRAXIS DER BETRIEBLICHEN MITBESTIMMUNG (1979).

55. *See* Simitis, *supra* note 41, at 7.

56. *See* Betriebsverfassungsgesetz arts. 106-111, 1972 BGBl I, pt. 1, at 13, 34-36 (W. Ger.). For an English translation and commentary, see M. PELTZER & R. BOER, BETRIEBSVERFASSUNGSGESETZ/LABOR MANAGEMENT RELATIONS ACT 240-59 (2d. ed. 1977).

57. *See* E. GERUM & H. STEINMANN, *supra* note 46, at 54-56; *cf.* L. GOWER, *supra* note 3, at 68-69 (England).

58. *See* Loi no. 82-915 du 28 octobre 1982 relative au développement des institutions représentatives du personnel, art. 29, 1982 J.O. 3255, 3263, 1982 D.S.L. 456, 463 (inserted into the labor code art. 432-5 (new)); *cf.* Viandier, *La loi no. 82-915 du 28 octobre 1982 et le droit des sociétés*, 1983 J.C.P. I No. 25, at 3116 (éd. générale).

59. This is the so-called Vredeling-Proposal of the European Commission. *See* Commission Proposal for a Council Directive on procedures for informing and consulting the employ-

These strategies combine with and culminate in labor representation on the corporate board. Sometimes such labor representation on the board is characterized as a German experiment. Yet, while it is true that this system is most entrenched in Germany, various degrees of and formulas for worker representation on corporate boards have been instituted in the Netherlands, Denmark, Luxembourg, Norway, Sweden, and Ireland.[60] In 1982, France took a step in the same direction.[61] Thus, labor representation on the corporate board can be fairly described as a European movement. Of course, all these systems are instituted or at least supported by appropriate legislation, in stark contrast to the American case where Chrysler and the United Automobile Workers (UAW) simply appointed UAW President Douglas Fraser to the Chrysler board.[62]

B. *Trade Union Representation on Corporate Boards*

One of the major problems of co-determination stems from the natural antagonism between the trade unions, on the one hand, and the workers and their bodies, on the other hand, that exists in the single enterprise or plant. The development of work councils illustrates this phenomenon.[63] Employers have not always resisted the temptation to play work councils off against trade unions. And trade unions themselves have often opposed the development of a work council system, or at least a system that did not incorporate their interests. For example, English trade unions were clearly opposed to any kind of work council outside the trade union machinery, while in Germany the work council system could be built up only after the unions decided to use the work councils as their outposts in the plant. In fact, in Germany eighty percent of council members and nearly all work council chairmen today are union members.

The process of instituting boardroom co-determination has displayed this very same tension.[64] In Germany, boardroom co-determination was

---

ees of undertakings with complex structures, in particular transnational undertakings, 23 O.J. EUR. COMM. (No. C 297) 3 (Nov. 15, 1980). *See also* Birk, *Unterrichtung und Anhörung der Arbeitnehmer in transnationalen Unternehmen*, in RECHTSVERGLEICHUNG, EUROPARECHT UND STAATENINTEGRATION: GEDÄCHTNISSCHRIFT FÜR LÉONTIN-JEAN CONSTANTINESCO 33 (G. Lüke, G. Ress & M. Will eds. 1983); Vandamme, *L'information et la consultation des travailleurs dans la proposition de directive sur les entreprises à structure complexe, en particulier transnationale*, 24 REV. MARCHÉ COMM. 368 (1981).

The European Parliament has recommended extensive modifications to this draft directive. The European Commission has responded with a modified draft. *See* Commission Amendment to the proposal for a Council Directive on procedures for informing and consulting employees, 26 O.J. EUR. COMM. (No. C 217) 3 (Aug. 12, 1983) [hereinafter referred to as *European Commission*]. This new draft is commented upon by Westermann, *supra* note 40, at 169-79. For a complete documentation, see R. BLANPAIN, F. BLANQUET, F. HERMAN & A. MOUTY, THE VREDELING PROPOSAL (1983); *Cf.* the critique in L'INFORMATION ET LA CONSULTATION DES TRAVAILLEURS DANS LES ENTREPRISES MULTINATIONALES (J. Vandamme ed. 1984).

60. *See* Hopt, *supra* note 40; *see also Symposium: Worker Participation in Management*, 4 COMP. L. Y.B. 3-163 (1981) (information on nine countries).

61. *See* notes 42 and 58 *supra*.

62. *See* Summers, *supra* note 50, at 155-56.

63. *See* L. GOWER, *supra* note 3, at 68-69 (England); H. WIEDEMANN, *supra* note 4, at 587-88 (Germany).

64. The development of German legislation in the area of union representation is briefly

possible only because union representatives obtained up to one-third of the workers' seats. As a consequence, German labor is represented by at least some professional spokesmen who will look beyond short-term enterprise interests to broader and more long-term work force and union interests. In 1983, for example, seventy-five percent of all labor directors were members of unions belonging to the Deutscher Gewerkschaftsbund, and eight percent belonged to the Deutsche Angestellten-Gewerkschaft. Thus, German unions have assumed a role in the enterprise whereby they take a certain responsibility for the enterprise and its workers.

Direct union representation is difficult, however, if, *unlike* in Germany, a large part of the work force is not unionized or there are many competing unions in a single enterprise.[65] Furthermore, both organization theory and union practices show that the unions themselves do not always have a free and democratic structure.[66] This problem led the European Commission to prescribe certain minimum standards for unions in its draft Fifth Directive.[67] Antagonisms between different layers of the work force, antagonisms between white-collar and blue-collar workers, and antagonisms between executives with managerial tasks and the rest of the work force, illustrate the difficulties here. In Germany, these difficulties have been resolved in the 1976 Co-determination Act by guaranteeing at least one seat on the board to executives, while taking into account the interests of wage-earning and salaried employees through the voting procedure.[68]

C. *The Parity Problem*

Organizing labor representation on corporate boards involves many political decisions, as is illustrated by the options made available to the Member States by the 1983 draft Fifth Directive. It is beyond the scope of this Article to compare in depth the unitary system with the two-tier board system, or the experiences of the German election model with those of the Dutch co-optation model.[69] However, this Article shall address briefly

described in P. HANAU & P. ULMER, MITBESTIMMUNGSGESETZ § 7 No. 32-37 (1981). For English developments, see L. GOWER, *supra* note 3, at 74-75.

65. Direct union representation is still possible in such a situation. *See, e.g.*, Summers, *supra* note 50, at 160-63 (United States).

66. For Germany, see R. MICHELS, ZUR SOZIOLOGIE DES PARTEIWESENS IN DER MODERNEN DEMOKRATIE (Kröners Taschenausgabe No. 250, 2d ed. 1970); H. STINDT, VERFASSUNGSGEBOT UND WIRKLICHKEIT DEMOKRATISCHER ORGANISATION DER GEWERKSCHAFTEN (1976); *see generally* BEITRÄGE ZUR SOZIOLOGIE DER GEWERKSCHAFTEN (1979). For the United States, see Summers, *supra* note 48, at 385-91.

67. Art. 4(i) of the 1983 draft Fifth Directive requires the Member States to respect the following principles: (a) labor representatives must be elected in a proportional representation scheme with specific protection for minorities; (b) all workers must have the chance to participate in the elections; (c) elections must be secret; (d) free expression of one's opinion must be granted. *See* draft Fifth Directive, *supra* note 34, at 10.

68. Mitbestimmungsgesetz [MitbestG] art. 15(2), 1976 BGBl, pt. I, at 1153, 1157 (W. Ger.) (1976 Codetermination Act). The Act was pushed through by the liberal Free Democrats in the face of protest by the trade unions, which perceived the Act as threatening to the homogeneity of labor. The Act has been justified by the idea that all three factors—capital, labor, and disposition—are to be represented. The rule has made it necessary to alleviate the strict incompatibility between management and supervisory board membership.

69. *See* notes 39, 40 & 43 *supra*.

what has been the most controversial policy issue of boardroom co-determination in Germany, to wit, the parity problem.

The parity problem has been approached on three different levels. The first is a philosophical one, and raises questions of what risks workers bear within the corporation and what kind of influence corresponds to such risk-bearing. Two opposing answers have been posited. According to one view, the shareholders bear the entrepreneurial risk and therefore should have the influence. According to another view, since the workers bear the risk of losing their jobs, they are members of the company to a far greater extent than the shareholders and deserve the lion's share of influence within the corporation.[70]

A second level of the parity problem is legal-political. This level involves questions of what degree of influence in the corporation can be achieved in the political arena, how the resulting compromise may be codified, and whether such law is compatible with the country's constitution.[71]

A third level of the parity problem involves issues such as how shareholders, management, and workers behave under a parity model; what economic and societal effects various models of underparity, parity, and overparity may have; and whether the uncertainties involved in answering such questions favor boardroom co-determination. The first attempts to address this level were made in Germany in 1970 by the Biedenkopf Commission; this attempt was based on the Commission's extensive use of questionnaires and hearings concerning experiences with the full-parity German coal and steel co-determination.[72] Since the late 1970's, a growing body of experiences with the quasi-parity co-determination under the 1976 Act has become available.[73] Some of the most recent contributions are made either by economists or by those writing with a socioeconomic perspective on the law.[74]

70. The first view is the conventional one. For the second view, see, e.g., L. GOWER, *supra* note 3, at 10-11; Jonsson, *Labour as Risk Bearer*, 2 CAMBRIDGE J. ECON. 373 (1978); Summers, *supra* note 50, at 170.

71. This corresponds to most of the discussion led in Germany before the 1976 Codetermination Act and until the decision of the Federal Constitutional Court in 1979. *See* note 41 *supra*. In the meantime (1984) German unions continue to ask for full parity and in some socialist-governed German states, as for example Hamburg, they will get it on a voluntary basis in all state companies.

72. *See* Mitbestimmungskommission, Mitbestimmung im Unternehmen: Bericht der Sachverständigenkommission zur Auswertung der bisherigen Erfahrungen bei der Mitbestimmung (1970) [hereinafter "The Biedenkopf Report"].

73. *See, e.g.*, MITBESTIMMUNG UND EFFIZIENZ (F. J. Säcker & E. Zander eds. 1981).

74. *See generally* K. Bohr, *supra* note 30; R. WICKENKAMP, UNTERNEHMENSMITBESTIMMUNG UND VERFÜGUNGSRECHTE (1983); Gäfgen, *Zur volkswirtschaftlichen Beurteilung der Entscheidungsteilnahme in Unternehmungen: Die deutsche Mitbestimmungsregelung als Beispiel*, in H. STEINMANN, G. GÄFGEN & W. BLOMEYER, DIE KOSTEN DER MITBESTIMMUNG 9 (Gesellschaft, Recht, Wirtschaft No. 5, 1981); EIGENTUMSRECHTE UND PARTIZIPATION (J. Backhaus & H.G. Nutzinger eds.) (Frankfurter Abhandlungen zu den gesamten Staatswissenschaften No. 2, 1982).

III. The Economic and Societal Impact of Labor Representation on the Board: Myth, Hope or Reality?

A. *Intra-Enterprise Effects*

Labor representation on corporate boards that is mandated by law involves a choice of governance. Judging the impact of this choice is an uncertain and inexact "science." Thus, although lately implementation research has become a major interdisciplinary effort, it has taught us to be aware of methodological pitfalls and to dampen our expectations.[75] Still, legislators and lawyers must act in the face of uncertainty, while welcoming whatever certainty may be gleaned from experience. In this field direct causal relationships seldom exist, and the evaluation of specific decisions is difficult. But it seems that, at least, impact tendencies are recognizable and, even under the line of extreme retreat marked by von Hayek, that pattern predictions are possible. Thus, it makes sense to discuss what players should participate, and how to set the game or the market.[76] This also applies to the task completion ability of alternative corporate governance structures[77] and to labor co-determination through which new actors are introduced into the corporate board.[78]

Within the corporation, a first and rather obvious impact of labor representation on the board is the creation of an additional layer of control both on the supervisory board and on management. In contrast to outside directors in the United States, who characteristically play a passive role as invited guests "tied to the inside hosts by some sort of personal or business relationship,"[79] the worker-directors belong to different social strata and have experienced a different socialization process than their co-directors. In addition, worker-directors are on the board by their own right, as representatives of the work force, and through the union, to which they feel loyalty and by which they are controlled.[80] Union representatives are usually professionals like the other members on the board, while nonunion labor

75. *See generally* 1 IMPLEMENTATION POLITISCHER PROGRAMME, (R. Mayntz ed. 1980) (Empirische Forschungsberichte); 2 IMPLEMENTATION POLITISCHER PROGRAMME (R. Mayntz ed. 1983) (Ansätze zur Theoriebildung). For a recent survey of German contributions, see Reese, *Implementationsforschung*, 1982 SOZIOLOGISCHE REVUE 4, 37-44.

For labor co-determination, see especially Gäfgen, *supra* note 74, at 9-11, 14-19; Steinmann, *Kosten-Nutzen-Analyse der Mitbestimmung?*, in H. STEINMANN, G. GÄFGEN & W. BLOMEYER, *supra* note 74, at 39.

76. *See* F. VON HAYEK, DIE THEORIE KOMPLEXER PHÄNOMENE (Vorträge und Aufsätze No. 36, 1972); F. VON HAYEK, *Die Anmassung von Wissen*, 26 ORDO 12-21 (1975).

77. *See* Williamson, *The Modern Corporation: Origins, Evolution, Attributes*, 19 J. ECON. LITERATURE 1537 (1981); *see also* Comment, *An Economic and Legal Analysis of Union Representation on Corporate Boards of Directors*, 130 U. PA. L. REV. 919 (1982) (attempting to apply Williamson's approach to labor co-determination).

78. The following observations relate primarily to the large modern corporation under the system of full parity (with a neutral eleventh board member) in the German coal and steel industry, and under the general system of quasi-parity (i.e., representatives of the shareholders having the last say by means of a double vote of the chairman of the board) under the 1976 Co-determination Act. A complex institutional framework is thereby assumed as a given. *See* Part II *supra*.

79. E. HERMAN, *supra* note 3, at 48.

80. There are instances in which a labor representative on the board has been considered a renegade and has been harassed by the unions and the press as a result of this branding.

representatives typically are not, compensating for their lack of professional training with full-time devotion, training provided by the unions, and the experience they have garnered at the grassroots level of the enterprise. Additional compensation is not an important motivating force for these worker-directors, mainly because the unions have persuaded their members to keep only a basic amount of their compensation and turn the excess over to a union foundation. Status, influence, and career chances within the labor movement are more powerful incentives for serving as a worker-director.

The worker-directors' monitoring function is facilitated by information flows to which nonworker directors are not privy. This information emanates from the work councils, to which many worker-directors belong, and from the unions, to which most worker-directors belong even if they were not elected as union representatives. Of course, even if obstructionary tactics such as denying full and equal access to committee work are blocked, as was recently done by the German courts,[81] this merely means an improved *possibility* of monitoring by worker-directors.

Co-determination has clearly had an impact on board decisionmaking, transforming and slowing down the whole process. A substantial number of shareholders and board members asked by the Biedenkopf Commission deemed this to be a significant disadvantage of co-determination.[82] While these complaints were made in the context of the full-parity coal and steel co-determination approach, the impact under the quasi-parity system is no different since, much to the chagrin of the nonworker board members, the worker representatives have overwhelmingly chosen to act as a clique under this system. Thus, even under the quasi-parity system, the decision-making process is complicated by the need for counter-fractionalizing, prior arrangements, separate meetings, adjournments, and group bargaining. And although most decisions made by the supervisory board require careful deliberation, co-determination has contributed to the growing bureaucratization of the whole decision-making process, with its well-known spillover effects.[83] This slowdown and bureaucratization of the board's decision-making process is thus one negative effect of co-determination to be weighed against the possible informational and motivational gains achieved through worker representation on the board.[84]

The effect of co-determination on the substantive decisions made by the board is less clear, but certain tendencies can be observed. Co-determination has led to greater consideration of the societal impact of enterprise decisions. Decisions concerning new investments, cutbacks or shutdowns of works, geographical transfer of works, and other changes in the organiza-

81. Judgment of Feb. 25, 1982, Bundesgerichtshof, 83 BGHZ 106; Judgment of Feb. 25, 1982, Bundesgerichtshof, 83 BGHZ 144; Judgment of Feb. 25, 1982, Bundesgerichtshof, 83 BGHZ 151 (all W. Ger.).

82. *See* The Biedenkopf Report, *supra* note 72, at pt. III, No. 32. In the Netherlands, a work council's complaint against a specific co-optation to the board was most often based on not having been left enough time to deliberate. *See* Honée, *supra* note 43, at 99.

83. *See* Zander, *Personalwirtschaftliche Konsequenzen der unternehmensverfassungsrechtlichen Mitbestimmung*, in K. Bohr, *supra* note 30, at 309, 326-28; *see also* note 21 *supra*.

84. *See* Gäfgen, *supra* note 74, at 24.

tion are acceptable for the labor representatives only if the social impact of these changes is taken into account.[85] Thus, when Volkswagen planned to open a subsidiary in the United States, labor feared that this would foreclose the creation of new jobs in Germany, or even lead to layoffs. As a result, the final decision was blocked for two years, and consent was finally given only in part and under the condition that there would be no layoffs in Germany for a certain period of time and that further investment in the United States would be subject to the prior consent of the board. Similar effects have been noted in the area of dividend distributions. The worker representatives on the board favor the retention of earnings rather than distribution to the shareholders, a position in which management concurs. This effect of co-determination reinforces the tendency of German enterprises to keep dividends at a fixed and relatively low level, instead of giving out varying dividends according to the year's business. Labor's concern with the societal impact of enterprise decisions should not be construed as a rejection of the profit motive, however. In fact, the Biedenkopf Report could point to no case in which the profit motive was abandoned by a board under the co-determination system.[86] And although cutbacks and shutdowns were delayed considerably, they were never finally blocked.

Finally, co-determination has exhibited effects on management, which is nominated by the supervisory board. The shareholders' side rarely uses its second vote to get its candidate nominated, since this would lead to a deterioration of the cooperative climate within the enterprise and would make it difficult for the manager to fulfill his tasks. Instead, prior agreement is nearly always sought and reached between capital and labor about new appointments. Sometimes the shareholders' side gets the representative of the executives with managerial tasks to favor their candidate, as in the recent appointment of the president of Daimler Benz, but even in such a case a formal split of the labor faction hardly ever occurs. As a matter of fact, the representatives of the executives with managerial tasks vote regularly with the other worker-directors, with occasional exceptions when the above-mentioned *Arbeitsdirektor* is to be nominated. Such agreements between capital and labor have their price. In a number of cases, the candidate favored by labor is nominated. More significantly, the profile of management changes.[87] New appointees must be acceptable to labor, who will examine their attitudes and their prior record toward labor. This implies that top managers must attempt to establish and maintain good relations with labor if they want to be reelected in the same enterprise or to have a chance to be elected in another enterprise that is subject to union co-determination. This effect of labor is even stronger on the member of the managing board who is in charge of social matters and labor relations (the *Arbeitsdirektor*), especially if the unions obtain veto power over this post.[88]

Whether the increased influence of labor under a system of co-determi-

85. *See* The Biedenkopf Report, *supra* note 72, at pt. III, Nos. 33-53.

86. *Id.* at pt. III, No. 36. *See generally* D. Brinkmann-Herz, Entscheidungsprozesse in den Aufsichtsräten der Montanindustrie (1972); W. Tegtmeier, Wirkungen der Mitbestimmung der Arbeitnehmer (Wirtschaftspolitische Studien No. 30, 1973).

87. For the Netherlands, see Honée, *supra* note 43, at 98-106, 107.

88. *See* Zander, *supra* note 83, at 313-17.

nation results in a greater acceptance of board decisions by workers, and thereby has the effect of promoting intra-enterprise efficiency,[89] is not fully clear. While there is empirical evidence of a correlation between participation and worker motivation, this evidence relates to the more direct participation of the single worker at his particular work place or, at the most, in his plant.[90]

B. *Effects on Markets and the Economy*

Effects on markets and the economy from a system of co-determination are probable, but somewhat difficult to confirm and describe. Some conclusions follow from observations of the intra-enterprise effects of labor co-determination, while others are more speculative.

To begin, however, the notion that co-determination mandated by law rather than by market forces is inefficient[91] must be discarded. This notion not only ignores important legal goals, but it fails to consider that although individual actors in the market may be efficient in minimizing their own transaction costs, they may also neglect externalities and the overall economic consequences of their behavior.[92]

The clearest effects of co-determination are on the capital markets. As previously noted, labor representatives on the board tend to reduce dividend payments to shareholders and, insofar as they have any influence, favor higher salaries and social benefits for the workers. Furthermore, labor representatives tend to slow down and weaken management decisions that may affect jobs and other labor interests. These effects are not without consequences on the valuation of the shares of the co-determined corporation, even though these consequences may be difficult to prove empirically. Even more important, however, shareholders will be reluctant to extend more capital to corporations with a co-determination system and will instead look for other investments.[93] Proposals to make the burden even for all companies within a state are of doubtful merit, since there is always the possibility of exporting one's capital abroad to a less regulated area.

89. *See* Gäfgen, *supra* note 74, at 12, 19-20, 23; Steinmann, *supra* note 75, at 59-60; *cf.* Cable & FitzRoy, *Productive Efficiency, Incentives and Employee Participation: Some Preliminary Results for West Germany,* 33 KYKLOS 100 (1980) (discussing voluntary participation below the board level).

90. *See* G. Teubner, Co-Determination Through Law: Social Functions of Law in Institutional Innovations 9-11 (European University Institute Paper, Florence 1982) (unpublished) ("somewhat depressing findings").

91. *See* Furubotn, *Codetermination and the Efficient Partitioning of Ownership Rights in the Firm,* 137 ZEITSCHRIFT FÜR DIE GESAMTE STAATSWISSENSCHAFT 702, 705 (1981); Jensen & Meckling, *Rights and Production Functions: An Application to Labor-managed Firms and Codetermination,* 52 J. BUS. 469, 473 (1979); Pejovich, *Codetermination: A New Perspective for the West,* in THE CODETERMINATION MOVEMENT IN THE WEST 3, 16-20 (S. Pejovich ed. 1978).

92. *See* Brinkmann & Kübler, *Überlegungen zur ökonomischen Analyse von Unternehmensrecht,* 137 ZEITSCHRIFT FÜR DIE GESAMTE STAATSWISSENSCHAFT 681, 683 (1981); Picot, *Der Beitrag der Theorie der Verfügungsrechte zur ökonomischen Analyse von Unternehmungsverfassungen,* in K. Bohr, *supra* note 30, at 153, 168-69. Principal objections to the transaction cost approach in this context are voiced in 1 E. GERUM & H. STEINMANN, *supra* note 46, at 108-12 ("costs follow the constitution").

93. *See, e.g.,* Engels, *Arbeitsorientierte Unternehmensverfassung und Risikenmechanik,* in K. Bohr, *supra* note 30, at 199, 212-18; Gäfgen, *supra* note 74, at 28-30.

It has been alleged that co-determination will increase costs for labor (salary, social benefits, job security) that cannot be sufficiently offset by improved efficiency, and that co-determination will thereby lead to competitive disadvantages vis-à-vis foreign firms. It has also been claimed that necessary changes may be delayed, potential innovations reduced, and the dynamics of the economy affected.[94] However, these dire prognoses lose some of their theoretical force when one considers that real markets are imperfect and leave management with considerable room for decisionmaking. Profit maximization has long since given way to a full range of goals pursued by the management of the large corporation, profit being a general guideline only except in specific difficult situations when it becomes pivotal again.

Furthermore, co-determination may have a number of positive effects on the economy. It may lead to decisionmaking, both inside the board and in the collective bargaining context, based on more information, which results in better decisions. Efficiency of production and economic allocation may thereby be enhanced. More important, however, co-determination is expected to reduce the level of conflict between capital and labor, to make unions more cooperative and responsive, and to reduce the economic losses that are caused by strikes and lockouts.[95] The traditionally excellent German record in avoiding strikes is sometimes cited to support this last expectation. The German record, however, is due to many institutional and other factors, and cannot be used to prove the above hypotheses. Specifically, two factors are crucial to the German success story, to wit, the character of the German trade union movement and the overall economic position of Germany. If these factors were to change — if, for example, German co-determination were exported to a country with trade unions hostile to the system, or if co-determination were practiced during a serious and long-lasting recession — the record might very well be quite different.

C. *Societal Effects*

Most difficult of all to ascertain are the societal effects that may be expected from co-determination. Differences in political and economic theory influence any evaluation of such societal effects. This problem in evaluation is aptly illustrated by examining the antitrust concerns that co-determination has spawned. Thus, American observers of co-determination have voiced reservations about such a system because they fear its potential for anticompetitive effects through the presence of union members on many boards.[96] Viewed from the German experience, which relies heavily on the

---

94. *See* G. Prosi, Volkswirtschaftliche Auswirkungen des Mitbestimmungsgesetzes 1976 (1978) (This was an opinion mandated by the shareholder side in the proceedings before the Federal Constitution Court. *See* note 41 *supra*.); Prosi, *Mitbestimmung und Innovationen*, in Innovationsprobleme in Ost und West 115-21 (A. Schüller, H. Leipold & H. Hamel eds. 1983) (Schriften zum Vergleich von Wirtschaftsordnungen No. 33).

95. *See* Gäfgen, *supra* note 74, at 18-19, 22-23; Summers, *supra* note 50, at 167, 168, 184; *see also* Picot, *supra* note 92, at 169 (at least in the short term no impairment of efficiency by co-determination, but this could possibly be due to extraneous factors).

96. *See* Steuer, *Employee Representation on the Board: Industrial Democracy or Interlocking Directorate?*, 16 Colum. J. Transnatl. L. 255, 270-74 (1977); Summers, *supra* note 50, at 179-83.

societal and libertarian aspects of antitrust policy, this concern is overstated. While some scenarios of co-determination may imply such dangers, for example, a scenario in which unions constructed information systems about enterprises and used them on the boards of different enterprises in a collusive way,[97] no such fears have been realized. Thus, at least at the moment, it is fair to say that the relationship between co-determination and antitrust does not present problems in Germany.[98]

Other expectations of the societal effects of co-determination are connected with two schools of thought that have been influential in postwar German legal theory and for which Habermas and Luhmann are the main proponents. The concept of industrial democracy, and labor's request that it be given representation and voting power on corporate boards, may be characterized as examples of the free dialogue ("herrschaftsfreier rationaler Diskurs"). According to Habermas and the Francfort and Erlangen school of thought, this free dialogue, if led by equal partners in a constructive spirit, may be the only way to modern problem-solving in philosophy, as well as in government and in society.[99] It would be too easy to dismiss this — as has been done in the philosophical debate — by merely pointing to the real world difficulties in creating the structural and motivational preconditions for such a dialogue on free and equal terms. Some of these difficulties have already been mentioned, and include questions as to the professional competence of both partners, the willingness to cooperate, the internal democracy of the employers' associations and trade unions, whether labor has enough financial support to qualify as an equal partner, and whether a hospitable economic and political situation exists for such a dialogue. Yet the idea that in modern society the need for consensus is growing, that conflicts between blocks of interests are best solved by dialogue and bargaining, has its appeal. Such problem solving may also ultimately produce better overall economic effects.

Clues as to the societal effects of co-determination are also provided by social systems theory. The economy and single large corporations are conceived of as (sub)systems with a relatively large degree of independence. Systems theory as applied to the enterprise sector can draw upon the fact that markets, as well as state intervention, fail to fulfill the governing and steering functions that are conventionally attributed to them. One way out of this dilemma may be to make the systems themselves responsive to other and more general needs than their own, by organizing them in a way that makes the pursuit of outside interests possible and even probable. In this sense, co-determination is an instrument of societal steering by decentralized systems organization.[100] Again, it would be easy to dismiss this ap-

97. *See* Hopt, *supra* note 40, at 229.

98. *See* P. HANAU & P. ULMER, *supra* note 64, at Einleitung no. 7.

99. *See especially* Steinmann, *supra* note 75, at 46-48 (discussing the philosophical sources of co-determination); Steinmann, *The Enterprise as Political System*, in CORPORATE GOVERNANCE, *supra* note 13, at 402-05; Gäfgen, *supra* note 74, at 34-35; *see also* H. STEINMANN & E. GERUM, REFORM DER UNTERNEHMENSVERFASSUNG: METHODISCHE UND ÖKONOMISCHE GRUNDÜBERLEGUNGEN (Abhandlungen zum deutschen und europäischen Handels- und Wirtschaftsrecht No. 33, 1978) (addressing the philosophical sources of enterprise law in general).

100. *See* G. Teubner, *infra* note 105, at 160-64 (specific reference to Luhmann). *See gener-*

proach philosophically, as well as in its application to co-determination. Indeed, the theory may be formulated in such generic terms as to make it meaningless for practical problems, or even worse, so as to hide choices and value judgments in seemingly neutral language. Yet the concept of decentralized steering, that is, setting up a framework for corporate organization and decisionmaking such as co-determination, cannot be easily dismissed. The challenge to such decentralized steering lies less in the many problems with all alternative steering instruments, but rather in such a system's reliance on structural and procedural control mechanisms[101] and in its potential for delegalization.[102] The crucial question remains, of course, whether performances that in classical theory have been attributed only to markets can also be claimed for forms of enterprise organization. The evolution of the modern corporation seems to give an affirmative answer, if one agrees that leaving certain economic activities to the market place or internalizing them in an intra-enterprise or intra-group structure has not been the result of historical coincidence, but rather of economic choice and performance.[103]

IV. Conflicts of Interest, Board Secrecy, and Other Legal Problems

A. *Recognizing Conflicting Loyalties*

Through the political and socioeconomic decision to mandate labor representation on corporate boards, national legislatures install the players and set up the game. Writing the rules of the game in detail, and rendering them compatible with other fields, is left to the lawyers and the courts. The body of such rules is growing fast, and is the focus of attention of both enterprises and of that part of the legal and academic profession addressing co-determination issues.[104] The overwhelming impression garnered from the German and other European experiences is that, contrary to what is sometimes believed in the United States, problems arising from labor representation on corporate boards, such as conflicts of interest and threats to board secrecy, are difficult but resolvable.

---

ally Teubner, *Substantive and Reflexive Elements in Modern Law*, 17 Law & Soc'y. Rev. 239 (1983).

101. On this point, many participants of the Florence colloquium on corporate governance, *see* note 13 *supra*, seem to agree. *See* Wedderburn, *supra* note 14, at 44; G. Teubner, *supra* note 90, at 166-72; Hopt, *supra* note 13, at 315-20; Kübler, *supra* note 53, at 439-41; and Steinmann, *supra* note 99, at 422-25; *see generally* Simon, *From Substantive to Procedural Rationality*, in Method and Appraisal in Economics 129 (S. Latsis ed. 1976); Ballwieser & Schmidt, *supra* note 30, at 677.

102. *See generally* Galanter, *Legality and its Discontents: A Preliminary Assessment of Current Theories of Legalization and Delegalization*, in Alternative Rechtsformen und Alternativen zum Recht 11 (6 Jahrbuch für Rechtssoziologie und Rechtstheorie 11 (1980)); *see also* H. Zacher, S. Simitis, F. Kübler, K. Hopt & G. Teubner, Verrechtlichung von Wirtschaft, Arbeit und Sozialer Solidarität (1984) (symposium, Bonn, Sept. 21-24, 1983).

103. *See, e.g.*, Williamson, *supra* note 77.

104. For information about the struggle between German enterprise and unions over these rules even after the affirmative decisions of the Federal Constitution Court, see sources cited in note 41 *supra; see also* Hopt, *supra* note 40, at 224-26. For details about the state of the law, see P. Hanau & P. Ulmer, *supra* note 64.

The most obvious legal problem arising from co-determination is the conflict of interest that it creates for labor directors. The conventional wisdom of traditional corporate law was that board members owed loyalty only to the corporation and, directly or indirectly, to the shareholders. This conventional wisdom never reflected the reality of large corporations, however. Indeed, there is a long history in Germany of the broadening of this traditional concept to include other corporate goals and beneficiaries of corporate fiduciary duties.[105] Under co-determination the standard formula used to prescribe the object of the board member's duty of loyalty is the interest of the enterprise, whatever that may be. Opinions of what is encompassed by the interest of the enterprise range from strict profit maximization, to long-term profit optimization with wide discretion in the board, and finally, to the explicit inclusion of external goals and interests. The same controversies that were observed with respect to the effects of co-determination on markets and the economy apply as well to the duty of loyalty. Thus, while there are those who want to subject management and the board to the strict control of profit and market forces, the reality of imperfect markets and undisputed discretion in corporate decisionmaking seems to argue against this position.

Although much of the discussion of the conflicting loyalties of worker board members lies within the realm of legal theory, practical answers are needed to some important questions. For example, may a labor director participate in decisions of the board relating to wage policy, social matters, and industrial relations and conflicts? Or may the union member who sits on the board actively join or even organize strikes and other measures against the enterprise? In some jurisdictions, such as Denmark and Ireland, legislation provides that they may do neither. In others, the delineation between the permissible and the impermissible is extremely controversial.[106] Compromise solutions, such as allowing labor directors to deliberate but not to participate in a final vote, or limiting union members to passive participation in strikes, have been offered. If expectations of the economic and societal benefits of co-determination are translated into legal rules, these solutions are hardly convincing. The conflicting loyalties of the

105. For a short survey in English, see Vagts, *Reforming the "Modern" Corporation: Perspectives from the German*, 80 HARV. L. REV. 23, 38-43 (1966) (changing the corporate purpose). For a procedural approach, see sources cited in note 101 *supra; see also* A. GROSSMANN, UNTERNEHMENSZIELE IM AKTIENRECHT (Abhandlungen zum deutschen und europäischen Handels- und Wirtschaftsrecht No. 29, 1980); Laske, *Interrehmensinteresse und Mitbestimmung*, 8 ZGR 173, 196-200 (1979); G. Teubner, *Corporate Fiduciary Duties and Their Beneficiaries: A Functional Approach to the Legal Institutionalization of Corporate Responsibility*, in CORPORATE GOVERNANCE, *supra* note 13, at 154-55.

106. *See* P. HANAU & P. ULMER, *supra* note 64, at § 25, Nos. 27-28, 96-98; § 26, Nos. 19-25 (containing different answers and further references); Kübler, *supra* note 53, at 432-38. For England, see the discussion between Kahn-Freund, *supra* note 44, at 76-77, and Davies & Wedderburn, *The Land of Industrial Democracy*, 6 INDUS. L.J. 197, 200-02 (1977); *see also* L. GOWER, *supra* note 3, at 580. For the United States, see Note, *Serving Two Masters: Union Representation on Corporate Boards of Directors*, 81 COLUM. L. REV. 639, 656-60 (1981); Summers, *supra* note 50, at 165, 169-71; Comment, *supra* note 77, at 954. Whether the worker-director *himself* prefers to abstain or even suspend his participation in such matters is an altogether different question. UAW President Fraser did just that while on the Chrylser board, as did the worker-directors in the German Arbed Saarstahl GmbH when drastic reorganization measures were required.

labor director have to be respected by *not* depriving him of his vote and by *not* forcing him to desert his fellow union members. Otherwise the factionalization of the board members is reinforced, and the functions of the union representative both on the board and in the union are impaired.

B. *Board Secrecy: Different Standards for Shareholders' and Workers' Representatives?*

Even more controversial than the conflicting loyalties of labor members of corporate boards is the issue of whether the traditional obligation of maintaining board secrecy applies equally to worker-directors. In Germany, it is generally held that there cannot be different standards for shareholders' and workers' representatives to the board. This is also the express position of the 1983 draft Fifth Directive.[107] But while board secrecy is not much of a burden for the shareholders' representatives,[108] this is not true for worker representatives.

Workers' representatives are expected by the work councils, the unions, and the work force of the enterprise to report on their participation on the board and the current problems facing the enterprise. These constituencies expect workers' representatives to express their interest in the board and to show that they are performing competently in their role. Even if such expectations are contrary to German law, where board secrecy is strictly upheld and informing the work force may be exclusively a decision for the management board,[109] reality does not always correspond to this legal picture. There have been clear cases in which even highly sensitive information, such as the planned sale of an unprofitable subsidiary to another group of companies, or plans and decisions as to cutbacks, shutdowns, and reorganization measures, has been released prematurely.

Whether this gap between law and reality can be left open indefinitely is questionable. Approaches to a somewhat more flexible attitude can be discerned, however. In Germany, for example, important information interests of the work force have been characterized as part of the enterprise interest and therefore properly taken into account. This might lead to the conclusion that such information cannot be treated as secret, so that the information would thereby become disclosable without imposing different standards on shareholders' and workers' directors. Furthermore, a board member must be allowed to get expert advice if this is necessary to fulfill his function;[110] but if the expert is not bound by professional secrecy, the board

107. *See* draft Fifth Directive, *supra* note 34, at 12.

108. This does not mean that there are no conflicts of interest, but simply that the expectations of those who send the representative to the board, like banks, major business partners, lawyers, and other professionals, are usually different from labor. As to the difficult questions regarding the conflict of interest of the former, see Lutter, *Bankenvertreter im Aufsichtsrat*, 145 ZHR 224 (1981) (Germany). For a comparative analysis, see note 1 *supra*. For the United States, see E. HERMAN, *supra* note 3, at 129-37, 283-89.

109. As to the latter, see M. LUTTER, *supra* note 15, at 136. *But see* F.J. SÄCKER, INFORMATIONSRECHTE DER BETRIEBS- UND AUFSICHTSRATSMITGLIEDER UND GEHEIMSPHÄRE DES UNTERNEHMENS 82 (Schriften des Betriebs-Beraters No. 60, 1979). *See generally* P. HANAU & P. ULMER, *supra* note 64, at § 25, No. 99-115.

110. *See* Judgment of June 5, 1975, Bundesgerichtshof, 64 BGHZ 325, 331-32 (W. Ger.). But the individual labor representative does not have the right to take an outside expert with

member has the duty to oblige him contractually to keep the secret. These rules are important and should not be construed too narrowly, for if co-determination is expected to have a positive economic impact by better informing the unions and the work force, it would hardly make sense to impede such an information flow with legal rules.

The difficult task is, as always, the delineation of what is secret, because even though the need for secrecy is often exaggerated, every enterprise needs some inner secrecy beyond the mere withholding of industrial secrets to maintain strategic maneuverability. Sweden has come up with one interesting alternative to legal rule making in this area. There, collective bargaining may also extend to the question of what board matters shall be kept secret.[111] Under the German model, an equivalent procedural approach would be to leave the issue of confidentiality to the shareholders' and workers' representatives on the board to discuss and decide, but then to make this board decision binding on all individual members. This approach seems to have been taken in doubtful cases by the co-determined boards in the coal and steel industry.[112]

C. *Co-determination in Groups and Transnational Enterprises: Towards the Limits of Law*

Together, groups of corporations and transnational enterprises define modern corporate reality. Regulatory ideas and corporate governance concepts meet their ultimate test with these entities. Corporate law has not yet come to grips with groups, and is even further away with transnational enterprises.[113] This is the case for Germany, with its first codified law of groups, and for the United States, where the phenomenon of transnational enterprises was first observed and analyzed. Co-determination is plagued by this same inability of the law to keep pace with modern corporate reality. Problems posed by this inability in the field of co-determination are quite challenging, but the scope of this Article permits only two final observations on the European scene.[114]

First, the difficulty of installing co-determination in company groups[115] consists in finding a solution that on the one hand gives the workers, including those in the subsidiaries, effective influence on the parent corporation

him when inspecting the auditors' report of which no personal copies are given out. *See* Judgment of Nov. 15, 1982, Bundesgerichtshof, 85 BGHZ 293 (W. Ger.).

111. *See* 1 E. Gerum & H. Steinmann, *supra* note 46, at 146-48.

112. *See* Enterprise Law Commission Report, *supra* note 8, at No. 477. There was complete disagreement about the best solution to the board secrecy problem. *Id.* at Nos. 461-85.

113. *See* sources cited in note 5 *supra.*

114. For details, see the abundant German literature on art. 5 of the 1976 Co-determination Act (co-determination within the group of companies) and on the territorial reach of the Act. Some of it is recorded in P. Hanau & P. Ulmer, *supra* note 64, vor § 5, vor § 1. For some empirical data, see Gerum, Richter & Steinmann, *Unternehmenspolitik im mitbestimmten Konzern*, 41 Die Betriebswirtschaft 345-60 (1981) (condensed version in; K. Bohr, *supra* note 30, at 293-308).

115. That is, parents with control over subsidiaries. Mere financial participation and ties do not suffice. Whether such control exists in the case of partially owned subsidiaries is as unclear here as elsewhere in corporate law. The difference is that here a complex co-determination structure depends on an answer to this question.

where the real decisions are made, and on the other hand does not impair the control of the parent over the subsidiaries. The German solution, giving all workers of the group a vote for co-determination on the board of the parent and at the same time co-determination in their subsidiary, has met with criticism. The difficulties are increased if the parent is not subject to co-determination, for example, because it is organized as a partnership with the personal liability of a natural person, or because it is a foreign corporation. The German rule of treating the next highest-ranking subsidiary as a fictitious parent for the purposes of co-determination (so-called Teilkonzern) has also been criticized by most commentators. Similar difficulties have arisen in other European countries.[116] These problems have been considered so thorny that the European parliament has requested that most of the Fifth Directive should not be applied to groups. Moreover, the European Commission, while rightly refusing to dilute the directive in this way, has included in its 1983 draft an option for the Member States to postpone applying parts of the directive until the planned Ninth Directive on Harmonization of the Law of Groups is enacted.[117]

Installing effective co-determination in transnational enterprises is even more problematic than is the case with company groups. There are two sets of problems, one legal and one economic. The legal set is an outgrowth of the territoriality principle, and is a well-known problem facing other national regulatory strategies such as antitrust, securities regulation, and banking law. Beyond the usual conflicts of law rules, strategies to deal with this problem are the above-mentioned Teilkonzern in German law or the European Vredeling proposal.[118] Quite apart from these legal problems is the question whether national legislatures are ready to assume the risk of the possible economic consequences of a co-determination decision, to wit, the possible exodus of transnational enterprises from the country, or at least the strategic allocation of new foreign capital and new subsidiaries of the transnational enterprises to competing third countries. The Dutch legislators, fully resigned to this possibility, have granted transnational enterprises far-reaching exemptions from co-determination.[119] The Germans, on the other hand, have not done so, and thus have taken the risk of moving ahead in the hope that the European Communities will follow.

116. For the Netherlands, see Honée, *supra* note 43, at 93; van Veenroy, *Konzernrecht und Mitbestimmung in den Niederlanden,* 14 ZFA 121-40 (1983). For France, see Viandier, *supra* note 58. For Sweden, see Gerum & Steinmann, *supra* note 46, at 24, 135-43.

117. *See* European Parliament, *supra* note 33, at 43 (art. 63(a)); draft Fifth Directive, *supra* note 34, at 36-37 (art. 63(b) and the reasons given for it).

118. *See European Commission, supra* note 59.

119. *See* Honée, *supra* note 43, at 92; Hopt, *supra* note 40, at 233-34 (perspectives for a European harmonization).

Part IV
The End of Corporate Life

[9]

The Yale Law Journal

Volume 91, Number 5, April 1982

Bankruptcy, Non-Bankruptcy Entitlements, and the Creditors' Bargain

Thomas H. Jackson†

Bankruptcy, at first glance, may be thought of as a procedure geared principally toward relieving an overburdened debtor from "oppressive" debt. Yet this discharge-centered view of bankruptcy is correct neither from an historical perspective nor from a realistic appraisal of the presence and operation of most of the provisions in the federal bankruptcy laws over the years.[1] For although discharge of the debtor (and such related issues as "exemptions" that enable an individual debtor to keep assets out of the bankruptcy pool) may well be the motivating *cause* of a majority of bankruptcy cases,[2] most of the bankruptcy *process* is in fact concerned with creditor-distribution questions. Assets are marshalled so that they can be allocated among those holding claims against the debtor or the debtor's property. Claims are determined so that participants in the allocation process may be assembled. And the rules governing priorities determine who, among the claimants, will get what and in what order.

† Professor of Law, Stanford University.

I received extremely useful comments on an earlier draft of this Article from Douglas Baird, Walter Blum, Theodore Eisenberg, Robert Ellickson, Ronald Gilson, Bonnie Jackson, A. Mitchell Polinsky, Roberta Romano, Myron Scholes, Alan Schwartz, and the participants at the Economic and Legal Organization Workshop at the University of Chicago. Much of the work on this Article was supported by the Stanford Legal Research Fund, made possible by a bequest from the Estate of Ira S. Lillick, and by gifts from Roderick E. and Carla A. Hills and other friends of the Stanford Law School.

1. *See* W. HAWKLAND & P. LOISEAUX, CASES AND MATERIALS ON DEBTOR-CREDITOR RELATIONS 461 (1978) ("Although not clearly recognized by the end of the eighteenth century, the right to be discharged has now been firmly established . . . ."); J. MACLACHLAN, BANKRUPTCY 16-17, 20-21 (1956) (historically, discharge not an important element of bankruptcy policy); *see also* Bankruptcy Act of 1800, ch. 19, § 36, 2 Stat. 19, 31 (repealed 1803); Bankruptcy Act of 1867, ch. 176, § 33, 14 Stat. 517, 533 (repealed 1878); Levinthal, *The Early History of English Bankruptcy*, 67 U. PA. L. REV. 1, 14 (1919); Riesenfeld, *The Evolution of Modern Bankruptcy Law*, 31 MINN. L. REV. 401, 406 (1947).

2. J. MACLACHLAN, *supra* note 1, at 15-17.

Although the Bankruptcy Code[3] specifies some of these priority rules, the claimants who fare best in the bankruptcy process hold special entitlements under applicable non-bankruptcy law.[4] The priorities enunciated in the Bankruptcy Code itself deal largely with the **allocation** of rights among persons not entitled to preferential treatment outside of bankruptcy.[5]

Despite the importance and durability of such distributional rules, no normative theory has been developed against which these inter-creditor bankruptcy rules could be examined.[6] This Article will attempt to supply that theoretical analysis by exploring the role bankruptcy should play in shaping rules for distributions among creditors, and then testing certain existing rules against the resulting model.[7] First, the Article provides a justification for the time-honored proposition that non-bankruptcy entitlements, such as security interests, should be recognized in bankruptcy.[8] This justification is developed by using a hypothetical model that I call the "creditors' bargain" in a simple setting where all debts are assumed to be already due and owing. Second, the Article applies that model by considering the role bankruptcy should play in dealing with debts that are not yet due and owing. I call this the phenomenon of "temporal" concerns in bankruptcy.[9] The Article examines two important distinctions made by

3. The Bankruptcy Reform Act of 1978, 11 U.S.C. §§ 101-15,1326 (Supp. III 1979) [hereinafter cited by Bankruptcy Code § only].

4. *See* 2 G. GILMORE, SECURITY INTERESTS IN PERSONAL PROPERTY § 45.2 (1965) (policy determination that "[t]he Bankruptcy Act itself should provide principally a procedural framework for carrying out the liquidation. The determination of which property interests . . . were to be recognized . . . was to be left to state law."); Hill, *The Erie Doctine in Bankruptcy*, 66 HARV. L. REV. 1013, 1035 (1953) ("apparent purpose" of the bankruptcy laws is to provide a system for the effectuation of state-created rights).

5. *See generally* Bankruptcy Code § 507.

6. Neither REPORT OF THE COMMISSION ON BANKRUPTCY LAWS OF THE UNITED STATES, H.R. DOC. NO. 137, 93rd Cong., 1st Sess. pt. 1, at 61-84 (1973) ("A Philosophical Basis for a Federal Bankruptcy Act") nor Shuchman, *An Attempt at a "Philosophy of Bankruptcy,"* 21 U.C.L.A. L. REV. 403 (1973) provides a cohesive normative approach that can be used with precision to examine the rights of creditors *inter se*.

7. This Article, because it deals integrally with reorganizations, will be limited to an examination of *business* debtors, usually in the corporate form. Many of the conclusions, however, would be applicable as well to individual debtors, who may also use Chapter 11, Bankruptcy Code § 109(d). But because of potential normative differences, this Article should not be understood as dealing, directly, with the situation of individual debtors and their creditors. For example, liquidating corporations do not need the bankruptcy process to get a discharge, since state limited-liability rules for shareholders provide the functional equivalent. *See* Bankruptcy Code § 727(a)(1). But in cases where a corporation continues to operate, state limited-liability rules do not provide an effective substitute to bankruptcy discharge. In those reorganization cases, the Bankruptcy Code provides its own discharge. *See* Bankruptcy Code § 1141(c), (d).

8. The discussion will refer only to consensually negotiated entitlements. Other forms of non-bankruptcy entitlements—such as nonconsensual liens—might raise distinct concerns. Some issues surrounding state-created priorities and statutory liens effective only in bankruptcy are discussed *infra* pp. 901-07.

9. By "temporal" concerns, I mean long-term contractual arrangements. For example, temporal concerns would arise with respect to a loan that, apart from a default (including a "bankruptcy

the Bankruptcy Code: between lenders and executory contract-holders on the one hand,[10] and between liquidation and reorganization on the other hand.[11] Justifications for these distinctions are then examined in light of the creditors' bargain model. Finally, the Article explores why the Bankruptcy Code refuses to recognize state-created priorities and statutory liens effective only in bankruptcy despite the fact that it generally recognizes other non-bankruptcy entitlements.[12]

I. Individual Rights in a Collective Proceeding: An Initial Examination of Bankruptcy as a Creditors' Bargain

A longstanding slogan is often used in discussing the non-discharge-related rules of bankruptcy law:[13] "equality is equity."[14] But this phrase explains little. It fails to deal, even roughly, with the plain fact that all bankruptcy laws to date accord substantial respect to non-bankruptcy entitlements.[15] The slogan "equality is equity" similarly fails to explain sat-

clause" default), would not be due and owing until some point in the future—say, five years from now. A loan that was substantially due and owing today, however, would not give rise to temporal concerns. The issues arising in connection with non-temporal loans are dealt with in the first part of this Article.

10. Holders of executory contracts and unexpired leases face possible "de-acceleration" in both a bankruptcy liquidation and a bankruptcy reorganization. Bankruptcy Code § 365. *See infra* pp. 880-92.

11. This inquiry is invited by the Bankruptcy Code's treatment of lenders. The Bankruptcy Code automatically accelerates the maturities of extensions of credit (whether secured or unsecured) in a Chapter 7 liquidation, yet provides the debtor with an ability to de-accelerate these maturities in a Chapter 11 reorganization. *Compare* H.R. REP. NO. 595, 95th Cong., 1st Sess. 353-54 (1977) (discussing Bankruptcy Code § 502(b) and noting that "bankruptcy operates as the acceleration of the principal amount of all claims against the debtor") *with* Bankruptcy Code § 1124(2) (in Chapter 11, a class of claims is unimpaired if, *inter alia*, the maturity of each such claim is reinstated). *See infra* pp. 881-83.

12. Related questions, such as the justification *vel non* for the various "avoiding powers" of a trustee (or *lack* of avoiding powers, such as the trustee's inability to reinstate contracts following an eve-of-bankruptcy termination, *see In re* Beck, 5 Bankr. 169 (Bankr. D. Hawaii 1980)), will not be analyzed in this Article. For an attempt to justify the preference system using what may be considered a creditors' bargain theory, see Note, *Preferential Transfers and the Value of the Insolvent Firm*, 87 YALE L.J. 1449 (1978); *cf.* 3 W. COLLIER, BANKRUPTCY ¶ 60.01, at 744 (14th ed. 1975) (if creditors and debtors could deal with impunity with debtor's assets up to the date of bankruptcy, only "tag ends" of unencumbered assets would remain). For a recent critical look at preference law as applied, see McCoid, *Bankruptcy, Preferences, and Efficiency: An Expression of Doubt*, 67 VA. L. REV. 249 (1981).

13. If the bankruptcy process was concerned *solely* with discharge and its related issues, bankruptcy law would need to define the effect of discharge and, perhaps, specify which of a debtor's existing assets would be free of the claims of creditors. Beyond that, however, the method of allocating non-exempt assets among claimants would not be relevant to these discharge-centered issues. Bankruptcy's long-standing interest in creditor-oriented distributional questions suggests, however, that the bankruptcy process is in fact motivated by additional concerns. *See* Radin, *The Nature of Bankruptcy*, 89 U. PA. L. REV. 1, 9 (1940) ("Whatever purposes bankruptcy attempts to carry out, it does by working on the creditors primarily . . . .").

14. *See* Canright v. General Finance Corp., 35 F. Supp. 841, 844 (E.D. Ill. 1940); *see also* Simonson v. Granquist, 369 U.S. 38 (1962); Kuehner v. Irving Trust Co., 299 U.S. 445 (1937); Worsley v. Demattos, 96 Eng. Rep. 1160, 1161 (K.B. 1758); McCoid, *supra* note 12, at 260-61.

15. Bankruptcy Code § 725 (prior to general distribution, trustee shall dispose of property "in

isfactorily why bankruptcy would ever be an occasion for altering the non-bankruptcy allocation of assets among creditors.[16] Bankruptcy law's beguiling slogan has been little more than a banal reminder that equals are to be treated equally in bankruptcy: the important determination of who those "equals" are is often not resolved under bankruptcy law.[17]

A more profitable line of pursuit might be to view bankruptcy as a system designed to mirror the agreement one would expect the creditors to form among themselves were they able to negotiate such an agreement from an *ex ante* position.[18] It is this approach that I characterize as the "creditors' bargain." This view provides an illuminating vantage point from which to analyze bankruptcy law's treatment of many non-bankruptcy entitlements, and a focus from which to examine the deviations made in the name of bankruptcy policy.

A. *The Creditors' Bargain and Unsecured Creditors*

First, consider a world in which a debtor could consensually create only one class of claimants, called "unsecured creditors." These unsecured creditors would enjoy typical state-law collection rights of attachment, execution, and so forth, but would not (at least prior to the time such collection rights are pursued) have the sort of property interests in or priority rights to any of their debtor's collateral that are enjoyed by secured creditors. In addition, assume for the moment that all these unsecured claim-

which an entity other than the estate has an interest, such as a lien"); Butner v. United States, 440 U.S. 48, 54 (1979) ("Congress has generally left the determination of property rights in the assets of a bankrupt's estate to state law."); *In re* Telemart Enterprises, 524 F.2d 761, 763 (9th Cir. 1975) (bankruptcy law reflects general policy of recognizing property interests); *cf.* Vanston Bondholders Protective Comm. v. Green, 329 U.S. 156, 161-63 (1946) (validity of claims of creditors generally decided under state law, unless in conflict with federal policy and equitable principles); REPORT OF THE COMMISSION ON THE BANKRUPTCY LAWS OF THE UNITED STATES, *supra* note 6, pt. 1, at 70 ("[F]or the most part, [claims arising in the open credit economy] should be recognized in the bankruptcy process.")

16. For an illuminating discussion of this point, see Eisenberg, *Bankruptcy Law in Perspective*, 28 U.C.L.A. L. REV. 953 (1981). For justification of federal bankruptcy rules as a form of risk-spreading compulsory insurance, see P. COLEMAN, DEBTORS AND CREDITORS IN AMERICA: INSOLVENCY, IMPRISONMENT FOR DEBT, AND BANKRUPTCY 13 (1974) (legislators wanted insolvent's property distributed equitably because spreading losses among all creditors might prevent collapse of any one of them).

17. *See* 2 G. GILMORE, *supra* note 4, § 45.2, at 1286-88.

18. Recent work, although incomplete and tentative, hints at such an approach. *See, e.g.*, Ang & Chua, *Coalitions, the Me-First Rule, and the Liquidation Decision*, 11 BELL J. ECON. 355 (1980); Weistart, *The Costs of Bankruptcy*, 41 LAW & CONTEMP. PROBS. 107 (Autumn 1977); *cf.* Clark, *The Interdisciplinary Study of Legal Evolution*, 90 YALE L.J. 1238, 1250-54 (1981) (discussing development of corporate reorganization laws in terms of developing efficient procedures to aid creditors). *But cf.* Bulow & Shoven, *The Bankruptcy Decision*, 9 BELL J. ECON. 437, 454 (1978) (treating bankruptcy as decision made when "coalition of claimants with negotiating power can gain from immediate liquidation"). The focus on bankruptcy as a law of collection from failing debtors may be viewed as consistent with the general historical development of bankruptcy. *See* J. MACLACHLAN, *supra* note 1, at 15; 2 J. STORY, COMMENTARIES ON THE CONSTITUTION OF THE UNITED STATES § 1113, at 50 n.2 (4th ed. 1873).

ants extend credit on a short-term basis.[19] Are there any reasons to believe that this unitary group of creditors would favor the existence of a government-imposed system providing for the collective treatment of claims against a common debtor?

To examine this, it is worth considering a simple hypothetical. *D* has a small printing business. Potential creditors estimate that there is a twenty percent chance that *D* will become insolvent.[20] At the point of insolvency, the business is expected to be worth $80,000 as an operating entity and $60,000 if sold piecemeal. *D* borrows $50,000 from each of two creditors, *C1* and *C2*. *C1* and *C2* expect to spend $2,000 each in pursuit of individual creditor remedies should *D* become insolvent and fail to repay them. Are there any reasons to believe that under these circumstances *D*, *C1*, and *C2* would jointly agree to contract for a collective liquidation system to deal with the twenty percent chance that *D* will not be able to pay *C1* and *C2* in full? From the creditors' point of view (and ultimately from *D*'s, since inefficiencies in a non-collective system will be charged back to *D*—either wholly or in part—in the form of higher credit costs),[21] three reasons suggest themselves: reduction of strategic costs; increased aggregate pool of assets; and administrative efficiencies.[22]

1. *Reduction of Strategic Costs*

A collective system that treats all claimants standing in the same relationship to the debtor alike has the virtue of substituting a sum "certain"[23] for the uncertain amount that might be realized under an individualistic creditors' remedy system. This has two advantages, even in a case where

19. The complications introduced by consideration of longer term extensions of credit will be discussed in detail after the simple model is established. *See infra* pp. 878-901.

20. For present purposes the model is static. I assume that *D*'s investment decisions will not change, and that *D* will not otherwise misbehave or make the business more risky. *See infra* notes 44 & 52.

21. At a number of points in this Article, I will talk about "advantages" to the creditors. In almost every such case, however, the analysis is not complete without noting how these cost savings may get passed on to the debtor. The extent to which these savings are passed on depends on the elasticities of supply of and demand for credit. *See* Meckling, *Financial Markets, Default, and Bankruptcy: The Role of the State*, 41 LAW & CONTEMP. PROBS. 13 (Autumn 1977); Weston, *Some Economic Fundamentals for an Analysis of Bankruptcy*, 41 LAW & CONTEMP. PROBS. 47 (Autumn 1977).

22. A collective process does not seem to be necessary to protect a debtor's right to a discharge. A system could be designed in which a debtor could do such things as announce that henceforth future assets would be free of prior claims. Then the creditors could fight among themselves over the debtor's "old" assets (however defined) for satisfaction of their claims. The debtor, however, may view a collective process as preferable to numerous lawsuits. To the extent that the creditors enjoy advantages from a collective system, a debtor also benefits through lower credit costs, and favors a collective system for that reason, *see supra* note 21.

23. As the discussion indicates, the advantage of a collective system is not that it provides, *ex ante*, a fully determinable sum, but only that one form of uncertainty (relative entitlements *vis-a-vis* other creditors) is eliminated.

the assets will inevitably be sold on a piecemeal basis. First, it eliminates strategic costs that would otherwise be associated with a race to the courthouse. Second, even if no such race would occur, the collective proceeding reduces variance in recoveries—which is itself a virtue to risk-averse creditors.

Consider, first, the incentives for a race and the associated strategic costs. *C1* and *C2*, in our hypothetical, have each loaned D $50,000. Each of *C1* and *C2* knows, however, that if the other creditor gets to the courthouse first (or to *D* first, to persuade *D* to pay voluntarily), that other creditor will collect $50,000, leaving only $10,000 for the "slower" creditor.[24] Absent a prior agreement, this situation presents a classic example of the game theorists' "prisoner's dilemma."[25] The central feature of a prisoner's dilemma is rational individual behavior that, in the absence of cooperation with other individuals, leads to a sub-optimal decision when viewed collectively.[26] This occurs whenever certain rules are in the interest of an entire class of persons but, because of an inability to reach a collective solution, each class member acts out of immediate self interest in such a way that a less efficient solution results. This is precisely what occurs in our hypothetical. Each creditor, unless assured of the other's cooperation, has an incentive to take advantage of individual collection remedies, and to do so before the other creditor acts. Unless each creditor individually attempts to "beat out" the other, that creditor will fare worse than the other. Yet this race not only creates costs for the individual creditors (such as frequent checking of the courthouse records for evidence of actions against the debtor by other creditors), it is also likely to lead to a premature termination of a debtor's business, because each creditor will consider only that creditor's own advantage from racing, instead of the disadvantages imposed on creditors collectively.[27] Thus, each creditor must participate in collectively non-optimal "advantage-taking" simply to avoid being taken advantage of. This creates a race to use individualistic remedies, even though it is not in the creditors' collective interest to use them at

24. Use of these numbers assumes that the individualistic remedies system would inexorably lead to piecemeal dismemberment of *D* in the absence of some sort of an agreement between *C1* and *C2*. This assumption will be relaxed later. *See infra* pp. 864-65.

25. *See* R. LUCE & H. RAIFFA, GAMES & DECISIONS (1957); A. RAPOPORT & A. CHAMMAH, PRISONER'S DILEMMA (1965). For a reasonably non-technical introduction to game theory, see generally J. WILLIAMS, THE COMPLEAT STRATEGIST (1966).

26. *See, e.g.*, P. SAMUELSON, ECONOMICS 482-83 (8th ed. 1970); Gilson, *A Structural Approach to Corporations: The Case Against Defensive Tactics in Tender Offers*, 33 STAN. L. REV. 819, 859-62 (1981).

27. For these reasons, there are costs to a race system that make it less desirable for the creditors as a group. If the game results are zero sum, then there is no prisoner's dilemma. *See* Gilson, *supra* note 26, at 860-61. Even risk-neutral creditors, however, are likely to find themselves in a form of prisoner's dilemma. *See infra* note 28 & pp. 864-65.

Bankruptcy and the Creditors' Bargain

all.[28]

An assumption of creditor risk-aversion facilitates the exposition of the logic of collective action. If both *C1* and *C2* have a fifty percent chance of winning through the use of individualistic remedies, then each faces a fifty percent chance of being paid in full ($50,000) and a fifty percent chance of being paid only $10,000. But if *C1* and *C2* agree to share equally in the event of *D*'s misfortune, each could be assured of $30,000. If *C1* and *C2* are risk-averse, one would expect them, prior to extending credit to *D*, to agree on a distributional system in the event of *D*'s insolvency in which each would receive this partial, but certain, payment of $30,000. The reduction of uncertainty would itself be viewed as a virtue by *C1* and *C2* and, therefore, by *D* as well, who would get lower aggregate credit costs.

Several of the key assumptions lurking in the above analysis might appear questionable. First, if *C1* and *C2* also have a number of other investments (with borrowers other than *D*), the uncertainty as to who will prevail against *D* may appear diversifiable and thus unimportant.[29] Diversification is generally a response to an unavoidable risk, however, and here the risk can be eliminated *ab initio*. Moreover, diversification is a response to risk-aversion, not to the more general point that use of individualistic remedies leads to a collectively undesirable race. The individual "advantage-taking" behavior described above would lead each creditor to incur the costs associated with participating in the remedies race, whether or not that creditor were diversified.[30] Consequently it would still be in the interest of all creditors to avoid these costs by providing for a procedure to institute a mandatory collective system.[31]

A second troublesome feature of the analysis is that a collective system seems to require a homogeneous pool of creditors. If *C1*, for example, were a more astute observer of *D*'s behavior, or had closer relations with

28. A collective agreement would avoid the costs associated with this race only if individual creditors could not avoid the collective proceeding by precipitous conduct. A damage or a specific performance-type rule could be fashioned to protect the collective proceeding. Bankruptcy law, by enabling the trustee (as representative of the creditors) to undo pre-bankruptcy collections through his "preference" power, effectively creates a specific performance rule that not only makes the collective system mandatory but also acts as a deterrent against the sort of "race" that would otherwise occur. *See* Clark, *supra* note 18, at 1251; Note, *supra* note 12; *see also infra* note 148.

29. *See* J. VAN HORNE, FINANCIAL MANAGEMENT AND POLICY 60-65 (4th ed. 1977).

30. This incentive will be particularly troublesome if we assume that this advantage-taking behavior will result in a smaller pool of assets than would exist if the creditors acted collectively. *See infra* pp. 864-65.

31. Moreover, the diversification challenge is overstated. All that it implies in any event is that *C1* and *C2*, if able to diversify fully, would be indifferent between an individualistic system and a collective system. Some creditors, however, may be unable to achieve, in a cost-effective fashion, the degree of diversification necessary to remove the cost of uncertainty. The amount of diversification required to minimize the uncertainty cost may be quite large. *See* Langbein & Posner, *Market Funds and Trust Investment Law*, 1976 AM. B. FOUND. RESEARCH J. 1. We may expect that *some* creditors (those not sufficiently diversified) would favor a collective system, while diversified (or easily diversifiable) creditors would be indifferent between the two systems.

D, *C1* might know ahead of time that she had a better than even chance of winning any race against *C2*, and hence would be unwilling to enter into a collective proceeding agreement in which she would share equally with *C2*. Homogeneity, however, is not an essential element of a justification for a collective system. First, the prisoner's dilemma analogy suggests that all creditors have some incentive to avail themselves of their individual remedies as soon as possible. Because of the resulting race, many of the special advantages held by *C1* are likely to be worthless. Participation in, or monitoring against, that race, however, will be costly for *C1* as well as for other creditors. Second, limitations on the availability of individual creditor remedies may weaken *C1*'s advantages.[32] Finally, even if *C1* does in fact have "advantages" that give her a greater than fifty percent chance of being the first to be paid, those elements of uncertainty and associated increased costs that remain could be eliminated by a collective proceeding. Their elimination, even when coupled with a pro rata treatment of the entitlements of *C1* and *C2*, would, accordingly, still be advantageous to all concerned.

2. *Increased Aggregate Pool of Assets*

The use of individualistic remedies may lead to a piecemeal dismantling of a debtor's business by the untimely removal of necessary operating assets. To the extent that a non-piecemeal bankruptcy process (whether in the form of liquidation or reorganization) is likely to increase the aggregate pool of assets, its substitution for individualistic remedies may be advantageous to the creditors as a group. In the above hypothetical, for example, keeping *D*'s printing business in one piece increases the pool of assets available to *D*'s creditors by $20,000. Whether or not *D*'s printing business should be sold to a third party as a going concern (*i.e.*, "liquidated" at its highest value use), or "reorganized,"[33] it is obviously to the joint advantage of *C1* and *C2* to keep the entity alive. Again, however, *C1* and *C2* face a classic prisoner's dilemma: they are jointly better off if they act collectively, but if they are unable to act collectively, rational individual behavior will require collectively non-optimal advantage-taking on the part of each.[34] It is true that an agreement to act collectively could theoret-

32. For example, judicial liens may not be available until a debt has matured, and certain types of judicial assistance are sometimes limited to particular claims. These rules may frustrate or delay *C1*'s ability to take advantage of special talents.

33. A reorganization involves more than simply keeping a business alive; it also involves a process whereby the original claim holders and interest holders become "owners" of the business. *See infra* pp. 893-95.

34. This illustrates a species of the "common pool" problem. The problem arises with common pool resources, such as oil. Individual owners of drilling rights tapping into this pool have incentives to remove as much oil as each such owner possibly can even though the value of the pool would be

ically be negotiated after a precipitating event (*i.e.*, after *C1* has taken the steps necessary to acquire a judicial lien). By acquiring a judicial lien, *C1* has assured herself of $50,000 prior to the advent of these negotiations. *C2*, however, is faced with losing the difference between $30,000 and $10,000 if he cannot convince *C1* to keep the entity together. This provides a $20,000 bargaining chip for *C1* and *C2* to allocate among themselves through negotiations carried out after *C1*'s attachment but before the ultimate foreclosure.

The bargaining, however, will be costly.[35] This bargaining with *C1* could be avoided if the remaining creditors were able to act collectively and repurchase the asset at the foreclosure rate of $50,000, or replace it for $50,000. In any case in which there is a large number of such creditors, not only would free-rider problems make any collective agreement after one creditor has attached almost impossible,[36] but subsequent creditors would still have incentives to "beat out" the remaining creditors by using their individual remedies and collecting first on the remaining assets.[37] For these reasons, *ex post* deals capable of preserving the debtor's "going concern" value, while possible, would not be very likely in a large number of cases. Such an agreement would be much more likely *ex ante*. Neither *C1* nor *C2* would know at that time which one will be the first to attach.[38] They do know, however, that the total pool of assets available to satisfy their claims may be increased through collective action. For those reasons, one would expect them to agree to a collective system that deterred the sub-optimal behavior of the prisoner's dilemma, and allowed *C1* and *C2* to capture and share the "going concern" value of *D*'s business—the difference between the worth of *D*'s assets in a piecemeal sale and the worth of those assets as a continuing business.[39]

maximized by a slower withdrawal. The solution to a number of "common pool" problems has been statutory "compulsory unitization"—a result that parallels the compulsory collective proceeding solution to the present problem. *See generally* Sweeney, Tollison, & Willett, *Market Failure, The Common Pool Problem, and Ocean Resource Exploitation*, 17 J.L. & ECON. 179 (1974). As before, the *ex post* incentives to achieve the advantages that come from being first may lead to a more-rapid-than-optimal resort to individual creditor remedies, and a more rapid destruction of the debtor's going concern value than would otherwise be the case. *See supra* pp. 861-63.

35. This is an example of bilateral monopoly. *See* R. POSNER, ECONOMIC ANALYSIS OF LAW 45 (2d ed. 1977); Arrow, *The Organization of Economic Activity: Issues Pertinent to the Choice of Market Versus Nonmarket Allocation*, in 1 THE ANALYSIS AND EVALUATION OF PUBLIC EXPENDITURES: THE PPB SYSTEM, 91st Cong., 1st Sess. 47 (1969).

36. J. HIRSCHLEIFER, PRICE THEORY AND APPLICATIONS 537-38, 561-64 (2d ed. 1980); R. POSNER, *supra* note 35, at 45-46; *see also* Easterbrook & Fischel, *The Proper Role of a Target's Management in Responding to a Tender Offer*, 94 HARV. L. REV. 1161, 1170-72 (1981); Grossman & Hart, *Takeover Bids, the Free-Rider Problem, and the Theory of the Corporation*, 11 BELL J. ECON. 42 (1980).

37. *See supra* pp. 861-64.

38. *See supra* p. 864.

39. This agreement would need to provide not only for a collective proceeding, but also for a deterrent or policing device to keep creditors from attempting to avoid the collective proceeding by

3. *Administrative Efficiencies*

Issues such as the precise amount of the debtor's assets and the nature and extent of secured claims must be resolved in virtually every collection proceeding. We have posited that *C1* and *C2* would each spend $2,000 in an individual collection proceeding. In a number of cases, it is likely that *C1* and *C2* will attempt to collect their claims at roughly the same time. This would happen if, for example, *D* were insolvent and had announced that he was implementing his discharge right. A single inquiry into recurring collection questions is likely to be less expensive than the multiple inquiries necessary in an individualistic remedies system.[40] If a collective proceeding costs *C1* and *C2* a total of $3,000, for example, its use would save *C1* and *C2* $500 each. At the time of negotiating the creditors' bargain, this reduced cost would be viewed as a clear advantage of a collective process.[41] Consequently, in the event of *D*'s insolvency, we would expect to see *D*, *C1*, and *C2* prefer a collective system, and therefore agree to the inclusion of a procedure for implementing such a system in their *ex ante* bargain.

The three considerations I have described above make it likely that a general unsecured creditor will agree to a collective system in lieu of a scheme of individualistic remedies. No single creditor, however, would agree to be bound to this collective system unless it were a compulsory system binding all other creditors: to allow the debtor to contract with other creditors on an opt-out basis would destroy the advantages of a collective proceeding.[42]

Although we would expect to see a mandatory collective proceeding as a standard feature of the creditors' bargain, no *ex ante* meeting of the creditors will, realistically, take place. A debtor's pool of creditors changes over time and even the debtor is unlikely to know who the creditors of the business will be at any point in the future.[43] As a result, the creditors themselves cannot be expected to negotiate this agreement,[44] even though

"gun jumping." *See supra* note 28.

40. *See* Weistart, *supra* note 18, at 109.

41. The single inquiry may also be less expensive for *D*, since it would reduce expenditures associated with creditor collection of claims and increase *pro tanto* the pool of assets available for the creditors.

42. *See supra* notes 28 & 39.

43. This is likely to be true with respect to consensual creditors; it is almost certainly true with respect to non-consensual creditors, such as tort claimants.

44. Nor could we expect the debtor to do it for them, by including a procedure for implementing a collective proceeding as a standard contract feature. First of all, a debtor's incentive to take advantage of creditors would make consistent inclusion of this clause implausible. *See generally* O. WILLIAMSON, MARKETS AND HIERARCHIES 26-28 (1975); Jensen & Meckling, *Theory of the Firm: Managerial Behavior, Agency Costs and Ownership Structure*, 3 J. FIN. ECON. 305 (1976); Smith & Warner, *On Financial Contracting: An Analysis of Bond Covenants*, 7 J. FIN. ECON. 117, 125-31 (1979); White, *Public Policy Toward Bankruptcy: Me-First and Other Priority Rules*, 11 BELL J. ECON. 550, 556-

it would be in their joint interest to do so. A federal bankruptcy rule solves this problem by making available a mandatory collective system after insolvency has occurred.

It is important, however, not to overstate the role of the collective system imposed by the government. The *presence* of a bankruptcy system does not mandate its *use*. The realization that a creditor could always initiate the bankruptcy process[45] would deter attempts in any non-bankruptcy collective proceeding to provide any creditor with less than the minimum obtainable in a bankruptcy proceeding. The availability of a mandatory collective system in which distributions are governed by a set of statutory rules is, therefore, important because it stipulates a minimum set of entitlements for claimants that, in turn, provides a framework for implementing a consensual collective proceeding outside of the bankruptcy process.[46] One would normally expect to see consensual deals among creditors outside of the bankruptcy process attempted first,[47] at least to the extent that there are potential cost savings in remaining outside of the formal bankruptcy process,[48] since those savings could be consensually allocated. The formal bankruptcy process would presumably be used only when individualistic "advantage-taking" in the setting of multi-party negotiations[49] makes a consensual deal too costly to strike[50]—which may occur frequently as the number of creditors increases.

But because the bankruptcy rules set the stage against which consensual collective proceedings will be negotiated outside of bankruptcy, it is important that those rules be drawn in a fashion that is likely to minimize incentives for inefficient recourse to a collective proceeding.[51] These rules

62 (1980). In some respects, the situation is analogous to the public corporation context, where government-imposed general corporation rules regulating the relationship between owners and managers are necessary in view of the inability to achieve optimal results through consensual bargaining, due to the large number of stockholders. *See* Brudney & Clark, *A New Look at Corporate Opportunities*, 94 HARV. L. REV. 997 (1981). Secondly, the debtor does not bargain consensually with a number of his claimants, such as non-consensual tort creditors.

45. This would be subject to rules governing creditor initiation of the bankruptcy process. *See infra* p. 892.

46. *See* Moore, *Foreword*, 41 LAW & CONTEMP. PROBS. 1, 9 (Autumn 1977).

47. Such workouts are, in fact, commonly observed. *See, e.g.*, Coogan, Broude, & Glatt, *Comments on Some Reorganization Provisions of the Pending Bankruptcy Bills*, 30 BUS. LAW. 1149, 1154-60 (1975); Krause, *Insolvent Debtor Adjustments Under Relevant State Court Statutes as Against Proceedings Under the Bankruptcy Act*, 12 BUS. LAW. 184, 185 (1957).

48. The extent of these cost savings would depend not only on the relative costs, in the abstract, of the two proceedings, but also on the extent to which the costs of a formal bankruptcy proceeding could be externalized, because a portion of court costs are picked up by the taxpayers as a group. Most of the costs of the bankruptcy process, however, are borne by the participants themselves. *See* Bankruptcy Code §§ 326-331, 503(b)(1) & (2), 507(a)(1), 726(a)(1).

49. *See supra* p. 865.

50. *See Discussion of the Economics of Bankruptcy Reform*, 41 LAW & CONTEMP. PROBS. 123, 171 (Autumn 1977) (comment of Mr. Coogan).

51. *See* Ang & Chua, *supra* note 18.

should be clear and determinable, so as to be ascertainable at low cost in any negotiated non-bankruptcy collective process. The remaining sections of this Article will consider the form some of these rules should take.

B. *Property Claimants and the Creditors' Bargain*

To this point, we have assumed that all creditors were similarly situated in that they all held unsecured claims. Our scope will now be expanded to include creditors whose contracts afford them superior rights *vis-a-vis* other creditors.[52]

Consider, for purposes of this discussion, the utility of the creditors' bargain model in dealing with consensually secured claimants. In this discussion, it is a key assumption that consensually negotiated security interests have aggregate efficiencies: that a secured party is at least as well off with a security interest (and a concomitantly lower return on the investment) as without; that unsecured creditors are also at least as well off (having a riskier investment but a concomitantly greater return); and that the debtor's total cost of credit has been reduced because of efficiencies in allowing secured credit. Consequently, from an *ex ante* position, the debtor and the creditors would view it as in their joint interest to behave in a fashion that will keep the efficiencies of such consensually negotiated security interests.[53]

Assuming that other creditors would consent to the existence of secured creditors, we can now turn to the question of whether those secured creditors would consent to be bound by a collective proceeding. Fully secured creditors[54] are not direct beneficiaries of either the "reduction of strategic costs" or the "increased aggregate pool of assets" advantages of a collective proceeding previously explored.[55] Moreover, fully secured creditors are less likely to view "administrative efficiencies"[56] as a reason to support a

52. These superior rights may result from a consensual agreement between the creditor and the debtor or may be conferred by state law. The conferral of superior rights by state law is discussed *infra* pp. 901-07. The model being developed will, for the most part, treat a firm as having only secured and unsecured creditors. The possibility of distinct treatment between other classes (for example, creditors and equity-interests) will not be discussed in detail, although an analysis of the issues in these situations would be similar. As holders of the residual, however, equity-holders may have additional incentives to engage in risk-preferring activitites that lead to non-optimal bankruptcy decisions. *Cf.* White, *supra* note 44 (incentive effects on firm's investment decisions whenever creditors are paid ahead of equity-holders).

53. *See* Jackson & Kronman, *Secured Financing and Priorities Among Creditors*, 88 YALE L.J. 1143 (1979); Schwartz, *Security Interests and Bankruptcy Priorities: A Review of Current Theories*, 10 J. LEGAL STUD. 1 (1981). *But see* Schwartz, *supra*, at 30-33 (possible advantage-taking of uninformed unsecured creditors by secured creditors).

54. The discussion assumes that the creditors were assured of being fully secured at all times. This assumption makes the following discussion simpler, as it allows us to deal with polar cases.

55. *See supra* pp. 861-63.

56. *See supra* p. 866. Fully secured creditors would also be able to pass the costs of collection back to the debtor and hence, at least in part, to the unsecured creditors. *See infra* note 58.

collective proceeding because at least some of these administratively difficult issues, such as the availability of assets and the priorities of competing claimants, have previously been negotiated away.

These observations ignore, however, the aggregate advantages that will accrue to the debtor and all the creditors[57] from minimizing the debtor's total credit costs. Unsecured creditors have several reasons for desiring a collective proceeding. Consider first the "increased aggregate pool of assets." If a secured creditor could remove collateral from the debtor's estate and remain outside of any collective proceeding this advantage would be diminished or lost. One would expect, therefore, that the unsecured creditors would be willing to pay a secured creditor at least something to agree to join in the collective proceeding. Moreover, while a secured creditor might otherwise be indifferent to the administrative efficiencies associated with a collective proceeding (because a secured creditor's costs of collection are often contractually allocated to the debtor),[58] the debtor and the creditors as a group will benefit as a result of *ex ante* adjustments for the elimination of such costs. Since costs passed on to the debtor by a secured creditor would increase the secured creditor's claim, they would, *pro tanto*, reduce the pool of assets available for the unsecured creditors and thereby increase their costs of credit. As a result, the unsecured creditors would in fact be sensitive to these costs. The introduction of secured creditors into the model, accordingly, should not make a difference: we would still expect the debtor and the creditors (including secured creditors) to select a system in which the aggregate collection costs would be minimized.[59]

The system in which collection costs are best minimized remains the collective proceeding. Since the advantages of secured credit would be weakened to the point of being lost if a secured creditor could be forced to participate on a *pro rata* basis with unsecured creditors in any bankruptcy proceeding,[60] maintaining these advantages requires respecting a secured creditor's ability to be paid first from the assets constituting the secured creditor's collateral. But this is not inconsistent with a mandatory collec-

57. Who gains the advantages will depend, in part, on the elasticities of the supply of and demand for credit. *See supra* note 21. The secured creditor, however, is not precluded from being such a beneficiary.

58. U.C.C. § 9-504(1)(a) (1972) expressly permits contract provisions that pass on to the debtor a secured party's expenses of collection.

59. There are at least two ways of fashioning the argument. The first is to assume that creditors already know their non-bankruptcy entitlements, and, possessing those entitlements, attempt to agree, consensually, to a collective proceeding. This is the descriptive approach of the text, although it is subject to some limitations. *See infra* note 62. It would be equally possible to invoke the Rawlsian "veil of ignorance" by assuming that the debtor and his creditors are trying to fashion a system that would maximize the group's collective welfare before their entitlements are known. *See* J. RAWLS, A THEORY OF JUSTICE 136-42 (1971) (imposition of "veil of ignorance" on those bargaining). The ultimate resolution, however, seems the same using either approach.

60. *See* Schwartz, *supra* note 53, at 34.

tive system: the unsecured creditors, for the reasons we have just explored, would view a secured creditor's ability to ignore the collective proceeding as a cost of credit. It is, therefore, in the joint interest of the unsecured creditors (and hence in the debtor's interest as well) to have a secured creditor included in the collective proceeding. A secured creditor, on the other hand, would have no reason to object to such an inclusion *if* left as well off as before.[61] Thus, the mandatory inclusion of a secured creditor in the collective asset-disbursement process, even if that creditor's preferential entitlements were respected, would produce a net benefit: the secured creditor would be no worse off than before and the unsecured creditors could be made better off.[62]

Consider the hypothetical examined earlier,[63] except allow *C1* to be a creditor with a security interest in *D*'s printing press, the principal piece of *D*'s business equipment. This press could be sold for $50,000 on the open market. By virtue of this security interest, *C1* is "assured" of receiving $50,000, the amount of *C1*'s loan. If *C1* is able to proceed independently of *C2*, however, thereby forcing a piecemeal liquidation, *C2* will

61. The premise of Kaldor-Hicks efficiency—that a move is desirable if the "winners" *could* compensate the "losers," even if no such compensation occurs—suggests, in the abstract, that the advantages of a collective proceeding might warrant its implementation even if the entitlements of secured creditors were not recognized. *See* Hicks, *Foundations of Welfare Economics*, 49 ECON. J. 696 (1939); Kaldor, *Welfare Propositions of Economics and Interpersonal Comparisons of Utility*, 49 ECON. J. 549 (1939); *see also* Coleman, *Efficiency, Utility and Wealth Maximization*, 8 HOFSTRA L. REV. 509 (1980) (a reasonably accessible discussion of Kaldor-Hicks efficiency in legal context). The effects of a collective system in which the value of secured creditors' non-bankruptcy entitlements was not respected suggests, however, that such a system, in addition to potentially involving inter-personal utility comparisons, would be *less* desirable than a system that respected the value of those entitlements. Reducing the entitlements of secured creditors in bankruptcy will presumably reduce some of the advantages of secured credit in the first place. *See supra* note 60. Thus, a collective system that recognized those entitlements would be superior to one that did not. Secondly, the ability to *threaten* secured creditors with a diminution in their non-bankruptcy entitlements by threatening bankruptcy might lead to strategic behavior and non-optimal bankruptcy decisions. *See, e.g.*, Muris, *Opportunistic Behavior and the Law of Contracts*, 65 MINN. L. REV. 521, 532-52 (1981); Posner, *Gratuitous Promises in Economics and Law*, 6 J. LEGAL STUD. 411, 421-24 (1977).

62. *Cf.* Ang & Chua, *supra* note 18 (inefficient liquidation decisions made when non-bankruptcy rights not respected). A collective proceeding that allocates all of the gains to the unsecured creditors is not, of course, the only system possible. One alternative would be for gains to be allocated equally among all creditors. Indeed, in an actual consensual bargain, it is unlikely that secured creditors would agree to the bargain unless they received *some* of the gains resulting from that bargain. The model used here goes no further than to show that the secured crditor would be *indifferent* between the two systems and hence is, in that respect, a bit at odds with a true creditors' bargain model. But a model where the gains are allocated entirely to the unsecured creditors has certain advantages. First, such a system (as represented by Chapter 7 of the Bankruptcy Code) is easy to operate. Moreover, since many (if not most) secured creditors face at least *some* possibility of being an unsecured creditor, the interests of secured parties are not unidimensional. Finally, state law effectively prohibits secured creditors from ever being paid more than in full. Debtors have non-waivable redemption rights and forced-sale rights, and surplus proceeds on disposition of the collateral must be returned to them. *See, e.g.*, U.C.C. §§ 9-501(3), 9-502(2), 9-505, 9-506 (1972). There is unlikely to be a bankruptcy-related reason to upset that state law determination, which sets a maximum on a secured creditor's entitlement.

63. *See supra* p. 861.

receive only $10,000. If *C1* and *C2* proceed collectively (and sell *D*'s business as a going concern), *C2* would recieve $30,000. Thus, at the time *C1* attempted to collect by foreclosing on *D*'s printing press, we would expect *C1* and *C2* to negotiate an agreement to proceed collectively, with *C2* paying *C1* between $0 and $20,000 to agree to this.[64] Exactly as before, however (when *C1* and *C2* were both unsecured, but *C1* had just attached), the uncertainties of these negotiations, plus the inevitable "free rider" problems that would arise if there were multiple unsecured creditors, make an *ex ante* agreement preferable.[65] Under such an agreement, *C2* would assure *C1* of her ability to get her full $50,000, while *C1* would agree to protect *C2*'s ability to get the $30,000, by agreeing to keep *D*'s assets "together" so that they could be sold for $80,000 (again, through a going concern liquidation or a reorganization).[66]

This suggests that there is nothing "unfair" about recognizing a secured creditor's prior entitlements in bankruptcy.[67] Instead, it is exactly the sort of agreement we would expect to see negotiated voluntarily once the issue of the *existence* of secured credit were decided. To the extent there are advantages to secured financing, respecting the non-bankruptcy priority of secured creditors is a necessary corollary of protecting those advantages. Moreover, a secured creditor has already "paid" for this prior entitlement—really a higher probability of being repaid—through receipt of a lower return. Conversely, the unsecured creditors have already been "paid" for allowing this prior entitlement and they receive a higher rate of return because of their lower priority position.[68] The creditors' bargain model, then, provides a satisfying theoretical explanation of why bankruptcy law should make a fundamental decision to honor negotiated non-bankruptcy entitlements.

II. Non-Temporal Applications: Applying the Model to the Bankruptcy Code

Historically the bankruptcy process has recognized non-bankruptcy en-

64. This bargaining process could be circumvented if the creditors were able to act collectively. *See supra* p. 865. The problems of actually obtaining such consensual agreement remain, however.

65. *See supra* pp. 864-65.

66. *C1*'s "payment" for this agreement may be in the form of a higher interest rate. Conversely, C2 would be expected to "pay" for this collective advantage, perhaps by receiving a lower interest rate. This, of course, is not the only possible agreement. *See supra* note 62.

67. Jackson & Kronman, *supra* note 53, at 1148 ("Since creditors remain free to select their own debtors and to set the terms on which they will lend, there is no compelling argument based on considerations of fairness for adopting one legal rule . . . rather than another . . . ."); *see also* Ang & Chua, *supra* note 18; Meckling, *supra* note 21, at 15-16; *cf.* Eisenberg, *supra* note 16, at 956-59 (justifying adherence to non-bankruptcy rules absent clear evidence that they encroach on some bankruptcy-related policy).

68. *See* Jackson & Kronman, *supra* note 53, at 1147-48, 1153-55; *cf.* Eisenberg, *supra* note 16, at 965 ("both groups know the rules of the game when they extend credit").

titlements, and, to that extent, the law seems generally consistent with the normative theory just developed. It is not necessarily true, however, that bankruptcy law faithfully mirrors the normative theory in all respects. For it remains true that the *nature* of a secured creditor's non-bankruptcy entitlements are changed in bankruptcy.[69] A secured creditor is not necessarily paid upon the institution of a bankruptcy proceeding, nor is a secured creditor necessarily allowed to resort to his back-up right to realize on his collateral.[70] To measure whether, and to what extent, the existing bankruptcy process deviates without adequate justification from a recognition of non-bankruptcy entitlements, even in the case of non-temporal loans, it is necessary to examine in greater detail the actual operation of the provisions of the Bankruptcy Code.[71] Although those provisions protect, in theory, the value of a creditor's non-bankruptcy entitlements, in actual application it appears that this value-equivalence is consistently undermined.

A. *"Indubitable Equivalence" and the Invitation to Fudge*

Consider the following set of facts: *D*'s printing press (in which *C1* has a security interest) can be sold for $50,000.[72] *D*'s other business assets can be sold for $10,000. But the value of keeping all of the assets together is $80,000, $20,000 in excess of their individual values. (Assume also that *D*'s printing press cannot readily be replaced on the open market—that is, *D* cannot buy a new press for $50,000 without substantial delay and, therefore, cannot protect the $80,000 value in that fashion.) In this instance, the creditors' bargain model would suggest that the efficient solution would be to pay *C1* $50,000 in cash, and to have *D* keep the printing press. *D* should keep the collateral because the benefits to *D*'s business, and to *D*'s unsecured creditors, exceed the benefits that *C1* would enjoy exerting her individual default right to receive $50,000 in cash. But the

69. This is also true of unsecured creditors who are precluded from resorting to their individual rights to obtain property upon the institution of the collective bankruptcy system. *See supra* pp. 861-66.

70. *See* Bankruptcy Code § 362(a). In a liquidation proceeding, the "automatic stay" affects a creditor's substantive rights only until the assets are actually disbursed. *See* Bankruptcy Code § 725. In a reorganization proceeding, however, the deferral of substantive rights may last longer. *See* Bankruptcy Code § 1129(b)(2)(A), discussed *infra* pp. 882-86.

71. The creditors' bargain theory suggests only that it may be necessary to keep the collateral, so that the debtor's "going concern" value may be captured (or the other advantages of a collective proceeding may be realized). It does not, itself, explain why a secured creditor is not entitled to be paid, in cash, immediately after the initiation of a bankruptcy proceeding. To explain, as the theory does (and as the Bankruptcy Code itself implies, *see* § 362(d)(2)) that the aggregate maximizing solution is to leave property with the estate when it is "necessary to an effective reorganization," does not answer the question of how a secured creditor's pre-bankruptcy rights are protected.

72. Market value is the proper measure of an asset's value from the point of view of the secured creditor, because a debtor can require the secured creditor to *sell* the asset or the debtor may *redeem* the asset. *See supra* note 62.

collective process may then be viewed as a redemption of *C1*'s property rights in the printing press. This may be done in one of two ways. *D* may do it directly, by putting out bids (including among the unsecured creditors) for someone to lend *D* $50,000 to pay off *C1* in return for a security interest in the printing press, which, freed of *C1*'s interest, would become available for such a secured loan.[73] Alternatively, *C1* could be required to make the loan herself by being given the marketplace rate for such a loan. If *C1* is no longer the more efficient lender, this would induce *C1* to assign the claim and its associated security to the efficient marketplace lender,[74] allowing *C1* to gain her $50,000 that way.

While the Bankruptcy Code does not preclude application of either of the two alternatives, neither is used, except perhaps on rare occasions. In the situation represented by the above hypothetical, the Bankruptcy Code, consistent with the creditors' bargain model, would allow *D* to keep the printing press: it would be "necessary to an effective reorganization"[75] in the sense that *D*'s estate would be worth $20,000 more by virtue of keeping the printing press. *C1*, however, is not *necessarily* paid $50,000 in cash (although in theory *C1* could be); instead, *C1* is entitled only to the "indubitable equivalent"[76] of her right to take the printing press and thereupon realize $50,000.

We still have not strayed very far from the learnings of the creditors' bargain model; indeed, the "indubitable equivalence" standard at least purports to preserve the value of the non-bankruptcy entitlement. The conceptual underpinnings of the principle of indubitable equivalence seem to require that *C1* receive something in the bankruptcy proceeding so as to leave *C1* indifferent as between receiving $50,000 in cash, today, and leaving $50,000 "on loan" to *D*, secured by *D*'s printing press.[77] This

73. *C1* might, of course, be one of those bidders.

74. It would be difficult to choose between these two alternatives. If there is no particular reason to believe that *C1* will again be the efficient lender, it would normally seem better to have *D* negotiate directly with potential new lenders. This is so because, depending on the needs or desires of a particular lender, loan terms may be optimized from *D*'s perspective when *D* does the negotiating himself (there is no reason to assume that *D*'s contract with *C1* necessarily contains an optimum set of terms for a secured loan made by another lender). *Cf.* Jackson & Kronman, *supra* note 53, at 1150-61 (discussing factors leading particular lender to make a secured loan). The phenomenon of repeat lending, however, suggests that it is in fact likely that *C1* and *D* would again be the optimal parties to a loan agreement. *C1* and *D*, for example, may well have informational advantages concerning each other that would lead them to continue to deal on much the same terms as before. In that event, it may be more efficient simply to give *C1* the marketplace rate for such a loan.

75. Bankruptcy Code § 362(d)(2). This should be the case even where the debtor's property is being sold as a "going concern."

76. Bankruptcy Code § 361(3). This rather odd statutory language comes from Judge Learned Hand's opinion in *In re* Murel Holding Corp., 75 F.2d 941, 942 (2d Cir. 1935). *See* S. REP. NO. 989, 95th Cong., 2d Sess 127-28, *reprinted in* 1978 U.S. CODE CONG. & ADMIN. NEWS 5787, 5913.

77. *See* H.R. REP. NO. 595, *supra* note 11, at 339 (purpose of Bankruptcy Code § 361 is to ensure that secured creditor receives essentially what was bargained for); *id.* at 342 (automatic stay does not affect rights of creditors but instead simply stays enforcement of those rights pending orderly

would have to be an amount equal, in *C1*'s eyes, to *C1*'s other investment opportunities for $50,000.[78] To achieve that equivalence, the amount would also have to be sufficient compensation for the risks of having outstanding a loan securing a debt owing from a person in *D*'s position. Included in any calculation of the "correct" level of this compensation should be the recognition that if *C1* is no longer the most efficient lender, *C1* may assign the loan contract and security to the lender who is. In that case, the level of compensation should be calculated on the basis of *C1* receiving $50,000 by such assignment (which *C1* could then invest in some venture in which she was the efficient lender). For that reason, indubitable equivalence ultimately requires only that *C1* be compensated on the basis of the market rate for secured loans to such a debtor.[79]

Despite this theoretical harmony, the indubitable equivalence standard ultimately is the device through which adherence to the creditors' bargain model is systematically ignored. The hypothetical satisfaction of an entitlement through a court-determined indubitable equivalent seldom achieves the results dictated by application of the creditors' bargain model,

examination of debtor's and creditor's rights); *In re* Anchorage Boat Sales, 4 Bankr. 635 (Bankr. E.D.N.Y. 1980) (secured creditor must receive compensation equivalent to having today amount equal to value of the collateral that could be reinvested); *see also In re* Alyucan Interstate Corp., 12 Bankr. 803, 807-09 (Bankr. D. Utah 1981) (adequate protection protects value of bargain); *In re* Graydon, 8 Bankr. 475 (Bankr. S.D. Fla. 1981) (general discussion of adequate protection); *cf. In re* Landmark at Plaza Park, Ltd., 7 Bankr. 653 (Bankr. D.N.J. 1980) (Bankruptcy Code § 1129(b) case discussing providing present value equivalence). *Contra In re* American Mariner Indus., 10 Bankr. 711 (Bankr. C.D. Cal. 1981) (undersecured creditor not entitled to compensation for loss of use of money during stay). The concept of indubitable equivalance described in the text of this Article appears to be consistent with Judge Hand's original use of the phrases "adequate protection" and "indubitable equivalence." He wrote:

> It is plain that "adequate protection" must be completely compensatory; and that payment ten years hence is not generally the equivalent of payment now. Interest is indeed the common measure of the difference, but a creditor who fears the safety of his principal will scarcely be content with that; he wishes to get his money or at least the property. We see no reason to suppose that the statute was intended to deprive him of that in the interest of junior holders, unless by a substitute of the most indubitable equivalence.

In re Murel Holding Corp., 75 F.2d 941, 942 (2d Cir. 1935). *See also In re* New York, New Haven & Hartford R.R., 147 F.2d 40, 48 (2d Cir. 1945) (fair and equitable treatment requires banks to be classified as secured creditors to extent that they would have realized on their collateral had they not been restrained from selling).

78. Payment of interest on the loan up to the value of the collateral, therefore, seems called for as a matter of "indubitable equivalence," even if it were not directly recoverable under Bankruptcy Code § 506(b). *In re* Anchorage Boat Sales, 4 Bankr. 635 (Bankr. E.D.N.Y. 1980). The unsecured creditors are, in effect, "redeeming" from *C1* her right to receive $50,000 today because to do so is *pareto superior*. *See supra* p. 870 & note 61. This reasoning is not limited to the case of secured creditors. If any bankruptcy case involved sufficient assets to pay the unsecured creditors in full and still return something to the equity interests, the unsecured creditors should likewise be paid for the "redemption" of *their* individual rights (of execution and so forth) on the ground that to do so is *pareto superior*. In this situation, interest is expressly allowed, *see* Bankruptcy Code § 726(a)(5), although the "legal rate of interest" is probably inadequate. Absent a case in which there would otherwise be assets available to the equity interests, paying interest on the unsecured creditors' claims would be a gesture without meaning, as it would have no inter-class consequences.

79. Plus the costs associated with assignment. These costs may, of course, be quite high.

principally because the current standard requires no reference to available market-pricing mechanisms.[80] Even cases discussed with approval in congressional reports illustrate the inadequacy, in creditors' bargain terms, of the indubitable equivalence standard as applied.[81]

It is likely, therefore, that the compensation that is deemed to be "adequate protection" will rarely provide the secured creditor with the indubitable equivalent of realizing, at the point of bankruptcy, the market value of the item in which that creditor has a security interest.[82] This has two consequences. First, a secured creditor with knowledge of the increased risk of undercompensation at the time of making a loan will be expected to charge the debtor for this risk. This will lead to an increase in the cost of secured credit.[83] Second, it may lead to a distorted evaluation of the relative merits of reorganization versus piecemeal liquidation. For example, if the "going concern" value of the printing press, when used in conjunction with *D*'s business, is $49,000 (and, hence, the going concern

80. It is possible, of course, to overcompensate the secured creditor as well. But it seems safe to say that secured creditors rarely do better in the bankruptcy process than they do in the marketplace. *See* Blum, *The Law and Language of Corporate Reorganization*, 17 U. CHI. L. REV. 565 (1950); Scott, *Bankruptcy, Secured Debt, and Optimal Capital Structure*, 32 J. FIN. 1, 14 (1977); *see also infra* note 81 (discussing *In re Bermec Corp.* and *In re Yale Express System*); *cf.* Kronman, *Specific Performance*, 45 U. CHI. L. REV. 351 (1978) (in case of "unique" goods, uncertainty may impose "an unacceptably high risk of undercompensation on the injured promisee").

81. The court in *In re* Yale Express System, 384 F.2d 990 (2d Cir. 1967), refused to allow Fruehauf Corporation, a secured creditor, either to take possession of its collateral (trailers and truck bodies) or to collect rental payments during the reorganization of Yale Express System despite the fact that the collateral was depreciating. Instead, Fruehauf was deemed protected since "the trustee has offered to fix the value of the security interest claimed by Fruehauf so that its position in any reorganiztion will be unaffected by possible depreciation." 384 F.2d at 992. This case was cited approvingly by H.R. REP. NO. 595, *supra* note 11, at 338-40. Commentators, however, have pointed out the inadequacy of this solution, because Fruehauf was not compensated for the risk that no viable reorganization would emerge. Murphy, *Restraint and Reimbursement: The Secured Creditor in Reorganization and Arrangement Proceedings*, 30 BUS. LAW. 15, 33-46 (1974); Rosenberg, *Beyond Yale Express: Corporate Reorganization and the Secured Creditor's Rights of Reclamation*, 123 U. PA. L. REV. 509, 528-29 (1975). Nor was Fruehauf to be compensated for the interest that was accruing because of the delay itself. The court in *In re* Bermec Corp., 445 F.2d 367 (2d Cir. 1971), cited approvingly by S. REP. NO. 989, *supra* note 76, at 53-54, granted Pacar Financial Corporation, a secured creditor, payments equal "to the actual current depreciation of the value of the rolling stock" in lieu of a right to repossess or a right to collect rentals during Bermec's reorganization. *In re* Bermec Corp., No. 71-B-291 (Bankr. S.D.N.Y.), *aff'd*, 445 F.2d 367 (2d Cir. 1971). Yet this surely fails to provide the "indubitable equivalent" of an immediate right to foreclose: it gives, for example, no compensation for the lost time value of money. Indeed, at least as a first approximation, the rental amounts were a good surrogate for depreciation plus interest on the loan.

82. *See In re* El Patio, Ltd., 6 Bankr. 518 (Bankr. C.D. Cal. 1980) (applying the adequate protection test of the Bankruptcy Code). The largest problem in *El Patio* is a clear under-estimation of the value of the collateral because of a refusal to consider the possibility (apparently substantial at the time of the decision) that a regulatory approval would markedly increase the value of the collateral. *Id.* at 520-21. The court did, however, properly allow the secured party to collect rentals on the property. *Id.* at 522. *Cf.* Butner v. United States, 440 U.S. 48 (1979) (entitlements to rentals decided under state law).

83. While there will also be a decrease in the cost of unsecured credit, as those creditors also adjust for their decreased risk, presumably some of the advantages of secured credit would be lost in the process. *See* Schwartz, *supra* note 53, at 34.

value of *D's* business is $59,000), it would be sensible to sell the printing press for $50,000. This move would increase the value of *D's* estate by $1,000. But if the unsecured creditors[84] are able, by keeping the printing press and giving *C1* "inadequate protection," to reduce the expected value of *C1*'s claim to $48,500, they have an incentive to keep the printing press and try to reorganize *D*'s business, even though the creditors as a whole would be better off by selling the printing press and going ahead with a piecemeal liquidation.[85] The threat of giving *C1* such inadequate protection, in reality, becomes a "bargaining chip" in the unsecured creditors' hands—they can attempt to use it to extract from *C1* some of the $1,500 in benefits that she would get from a piecemeal liquidation by having *C1* "bribe" them to agree to such a liquidation. This scenario involves complex, costly, and potentially intractable negotiations in order to decide which form of collective proceeding to use.[86] A secured creditor, moreover, to avoid being forced to bribe the unsecured creditors, may also engage in strategic behavior by, for example, realizing on the collateral earlier than would be collectively optimal, so as to "beat out" the unsecured creditors and foil their ability to do this.[87]

Avoidance of these "eve-of-bankruptcy" negotiations resulting from attempted advantage-taking and concomitant threats of inefficient uses of the bankruptcy process, or strategic behavior to avoid such advantage-taking would, therefore, appear preferable. This could be accomplished by the creditors agreeing, *ex ante*, among themselves, to respect the value of *C1*'s non-bankruptcy entitlements by means of true "adequate protection" (probably by resort to a market-pricing mechanism). But, for practical reasons,[88] it will be virtually impossible to have all of a debtor's creditors who are in existence at the time of these "eve-of-bankruptcy" negotiations actually reach this result by prior consensual agreement. Consequently, the failure of bankruptcy law itself to provide, as an "off the rack" rule,[89] the sort of agreement that one would predict would be reached if such an

84. The unsecured creditors in a Chapter 7 proceeding may be represented by a trustee elected by unsecured creditors (excluding creditors with interests "materially adverse" to other unsecured creditors). Bankruptcy Code § 702.

85. *See* Posner, *supra* note 61, at 421-24; *see also* Ang & Chua, *supra* note 18; White, *supra* note 44, at 563-64 (management, equity holders, and large lenders may keep failing firm operating because of possibilities for redistribution away from long-term creditors and towards themselves, rather than because continued operation is best use of firm's assets).

86. *See supra* p. 865. Some of these difficulties may be alleviated if the trustee is the sole negotiator for the unsecured creditors.

87. *See supra* pp. 862-65 (discussing the problems inherent in a "race").

88. *See supra* p. 866.

89. The term "off the rack" rule comes from Goetz & Scott, *Liquidated Damages, Penalties, and the Just Compensation Principle: Some Notes on an Enforcement Model and a Theory of Efficient Breach*, 77 COLUM. L. REV. 554, 588 n.87 (1977); *see also* Easterbrook & Fischel, *Corporate Control Transactions*, 91 YALE L.J. 698 (1982).

ex ante agreement were possible, leads to an inefficient system. The point is not so much that secured creditors are unable to adjust for the bankruptcy result but that this adjustment process may lead to a sub-optimal amount of secured credit, with correspondingly greater credit costs for the debtor.[90]

It is particularly puzzling that bankruptcy law not only does not postulate a reason for straying from the creditors' bargain model with respect to this *ex post* reallocation, but does not even appear to sanction the reallocation at all, except in an under-the-table fashion. In retrospect, the related concepts of "adequate protection" and "indubitable equivalence" suffer not so much from theoretical disharmony with the creditors' bargain model, as from inadequate statutory firmness that permits—perhaps nurtures—the belief among bankruptcy judges that adequate protection can be granted without reliance on market-pricing mechanisms. In this respect, it tracks the theoretical consistency but practical disharmony of the absolute priority rule.[91] In both instances the gulf between theory and practice seems to stem principally from the under-utilization of available market devices for providing realistic adequate protection.

B. *Concluding Comments on Non-Temporal Bankruptcy Entitlements*

The indubitable equivalence standard provides protection for holders of secured claims that in theory is entirely consistent with the creditors' bargain model. And insofar as non-temporal questions are concerned, the Bankruptcy Code remains faithful to this theoretical protection for a secured creditor.[92] The Bankruptcy Code starts with a mandate that a secured creditor be granted "adequate protection" from the effects of the automatic stay during the time that the property is held by the bankruptcy estate.[93] At any sale of property pursuant to Bankruptcy Code section 363, a secured creditor's lien will follow the collateral that secures the loan unless "the price at which such property is to be sold is greater than the aggregate value" of the lien, or unless the secured creditor can "bid in"

90. *See supra* note 85; *see also supra* p. 876 (discussing inefficient bankruptcy decisions that may result from "eve of bankruptcy" negotiations).

91. For a discussion of the gap between the absolute priority rule as articulated and as applied, see Blum, *supra* note 80; Brudney, *The Investment Value Doctrine and Corporate Readjustments*, 72 HARV. L. REV. 645, 679 (1959); Friendly & Tondel, *The Relative Treatment of Securities in Railroad Reorganizations Under Section 77*, 7 LAW & CONTEMP. PROBS. 420 (1940); Note, *Absolute Priority Under Chapter X—A Rule of Law or a Familiar Quotation?*, 52 COLUM. L. REV. 900 (1952).

92. The protection provided by the indubitable equivalence standard may be inconsistent with the Bankruptcy Code's treatment of other state-created entitlements, as well as of temporal extensions of credit. *See infra* Parts III and IV.

93. Bankruptcy Code §§ 361, 362(c)-(d); *see supra* note 77.

the lien at the sale.[94] If there has not been such a sale during the course of the proceeding, Bankruptcy Code section 725 requires the trustee to dispose of secured property (and hence of secured claimants) before any distribution to priority claimants and other unsecured creditors.[95] Finally, in reorganizations, Chapter 11 bases payments, in present value terms, on a minimum of Chapter 7 liquidation entitlements.[96] Nothing in these rules is theoretically inconsistent with the basic creditors' bargain model previously sketched.

III. The Complexity of Long-Term Contractual Arrangements

Thus far, in examining the applicability of our normative model to the bankruptcy process, we have been dealing with a hypothetical world in which all credit was "due and owing" as of the date of bankruptcy.[97] One of the most perplexing questions posed by the use of the bankruptcy process, however, is how to deal with an extension of credit (or any other contractual arrangement) in which the principal is still outstanding at the time of bankruptcy.[98]

In applying the creditors' bargain model to these temporal arrangements, it seems most appropriate to examine the framework that the Bankruptcy Code adopts. This framework differentiates along two different planes. First, it distinguishes between lenders (and other holders of non-executory contracts)[99] and persons in long-term executory contractual

94. *See* Bankruptcy Code § 363(f)(3), (k).

95. Bankruptcy Code § 725. If the loan is currently due and owing, these provisions will supply (in value-equivalent terms) the level of protection for such creditors in Chapter 11 as well. Bankruptcy Code § 1129(a)(7)(A)(ii). We will shortly have to deal with divergent treatment of creditors in Chapter 7 and Chapter 11, but this divergence only occurs when temporal (*i.e.*, non-currently due) extensions of credit are involved.

96. Bankruptcy Code § 1129(a)(7)(A)(ii).

97. Either it was already due and owing or it was callable at any time.

98. The "macro" question of whether indebtedness should be treated as matured for purposes of corporate reorganization has received a longstanding examination in the literature, principally focusing on the relative merits of the "absolute priority rule," the "relative priority rule," and the "investment value doctrine." For some of the debate, see, e.g., Billyou, *Priority Rights of Security Holders in Bankruptcy Reorganization: New Directions*, 67 HARV. L. REV. 553 (1954); Blum & Kaplan, *The Absolute Priority Doctrine in Corporate Reorganizations*, 41 U. CHI. L. REV. 651 (1974); Blum, *The "New Directions" for Priority Rights in Bankruptcy Reorganizations*, 67 HARV. L. REV. 1367 (1954); Bonbright & Bergerman, *Two Rival Theories of Priority Rights of Security Holders in a Corporate Reorganization*, 28 COLUM. L. REV. 127 (1928); Clark, *Fair and Equitable Reorganization of Investment Companies*, 53 B.U. L. REV. 1 (1973); Frye, *The "Fair and Equitable" Doctrine: Are Liquidation Rights a Realistic Standard During Corporate Reorganization?* 20 CATH. U.L. REV. 394 (1971).

Recently, economists have begun to focus their attentions on at least some of these rules (although rarely focusing expressly on temporal concerns). *See, e.g.*, Kim, McConnell, & Greenwood, *Capital Structure, Rearrangements and Me-First Rules in an Efficient Capital Market*, 32 J. FIN. 261 (1977); Warner, *Bankruptcy, Absolute Priority, and the Pricing of Risky Debt Claims*, 4 J. FIN. ECON. 239 (1979); White, *supra* note 44. The analysis here focuses not only on "micro" issues—individual debts—it focuses also on liquidation as well as on reorganization.

99. Bankruptcy law uses the concept of an "executory" contract in a special way. "Executory"

relationships with a debtor, such as a lessor under a long-term lease. Second, the Bankruptcy Code distinguishes between liquidation proceedings and reorganization proceedings.

With respect to lenders in long-term arrangements with a debtor, the Bankruptcy Code treats a right of acceleration of principal fundamentally differently in a Chapter 7 liquidation proceeding (whether piecemeal or going concern) than in a Chapter 11 reorganization proceeding. The right of acceleration enjoyed by contract holders in long-term contractual arrangements with a debtor, on the other hand, is treated the same by the Bankruptcy Code in both a liquidation proceeding and a reorganization proceeding. Is there a satisfactory explanation for this different treatment of long-term lenders and other contract-holders? Can bankruptcy law's occasional refusal to recognize non-bankruptcy entitlements in any general category of cases involving either lenders or executory contract-holders be squared with bankruptcy law's general recognition of non-bankruptcy rights?[100] It is these questions that this section addresses, first by focusing on the executory contract versus non-executory contract plane and then by focusing on the liquidation versus reorganization plane.

A. *Lenders and Executory Contract-Holders: The Role of Acceleration*

"De-acceleration" reflects a principle embraced by the Bankruptcy Code in a number of instances, both in its liquidation and in its reorganization provisions. This principle is that the advent of the bankruptcy process is not a proper occasion for the assertion of greater (or different) rights than existed against the debtor, under applicable non-bankruptcy law, the moment before bankruptcy.[101] This may be seen implemented in at least two disparate areas. First of all, it determines, to a significant extent, the treatment of persons holding executory contracts and unexpired leases in bankruptcy.[102] Second, it deals with attempts by a state to prefer certain claimants inside of the bankruptcy process through

generally refers to a contract in which performance remains due, to some material extent, on *both* sides. *See, e.g,* Jenson v. Continental Finance Corp., 591 F.2d 477, 481 (8th Cir. 1979); Countryman, *Executory Contracts in Bankruptcy* (pt. 1), 57 MINN. L. REV. 439, 460 (1973). A loan, accordingly, is not an executory contract once the credit has been extended. *Accord* H.R. REP. NO. 595, *supra* note 11, at 347. What is an executory contract, however, may turn, in part, on a judge's perceptions of bankruptcy goals. *See In re* Jolly, 574 F.2d 349, 351 (6th Cir. 1978); *In re* Booth, 19 Bankr. 53 (Bankr. D. Utah 1982).

100. *See supra* pp. 858, 859-60. In the non-temporal context, this general recognition of non-bankruptcy rights is theoretically consistent with the creditors' bargain model treatment of non-discharge-related issues in bankruptcy. *See supra* pp. 861-78.

101. The de-acceleration principle clearly is at odds with the general recognition of non-bankruptcy entitlements in bankruptcy. *See In re* Telemart Enterprises, 524 F.2d 761 (9th Cir. 1975).

102. *See* Bankruptcy Code § 365; Countryman, *Executory Contracts in Bankruptcy* (pts. 1 & 2), 57 MINN. L. REV. 439 (1973), 58 MINN. L. REV. 479 (1974); Fogel, *Executory Contracts and Unexpired Leases in the Bankruptcy Code*, 64 MINN. L. REV. 341 (1980).

the device of a state-created priority or a statutory lien effective only in bankruptcy.[103]

Holders of executory contracts or unexpired leases with a debtor, even if they have negotiated for the right to terminate their contractual relationships in bankruptcy (or to have those relationships terminate automatically), are faced with the fact that the debtor can "deem" these contracts "unimpaired" by reinstating the original terms of the contract or lease.[104] But unlike the case with lenders,[105] this power is exercisable in both liquidation and reorganization proceedings.[106] Even if a particular contract or lease is not useful to the continued operation of a bankrupt enterprise, the bankrupt estate is still permitted to capture the benefits of the difference between the contract rate and the market price by assigning that contract or lease to a third party.[107]

Whether or not this principle has a persuasive normative justification is an important, but largely unexplored, question. The strength of its justification implicates the wisdom not only of the rules governing executory contracts, but also the separate rules governing lenders. For the acceleration right of lenders *is* respected in bankruptcy liquidations, a result that may find itself under attack by advocates of the de-acceleration principle. The Bankruptcy Code provides no explanation for this distinction between lenders and other contract holders,[108] and the commentators have

103. *See* Bankruptcy Code § 545 (statutory liens); Elliott v. Bumb, 356 F.2d 749 (9th Cir. 1966) (discussion of state-created priorities); Countryman, *The Use of State Law in Bankruptcy* (pts. 1 & 2), 47 N.Y.U. L. REV. 407, 631 (1972). State-created priorities and statutory liens effective only in bankruptcy are discussed *infra* pp. 901-07.

104. An executory contract or unexpired lease "may not be terminated or modified, and any right or obligation under such contract or lease may not be terminated or modified, at any time after the commencement of the case solely because of a provision in such contract or lease that is conditioned on" insolvency, the commencement of bankruptcy, or other related contingencies. Bankruptcy Code § 365(e)(1). Bankruptcy Code §§ 365(a) & (b) permit (in cases not covered by Bankruptcy Code § 365(c)) the trustee to assume such contracts or leases (with "adequate assurance of future performance" protection if there has been a default). Bankruptcy Code § 365(f) permits (in cases not covered by Bankruptcy Code § 365(c)) the trustee to assign such contracts or leases, after assumption, "notwithstanding a provision . . . that prohibits, restricts, or conditions the assignment of such contract or . . . lease." *See also* Bankruptcy Code § 365(e)(1).

105. *See infra* pp. 881-83

106. Bankruptcy Code § 365 serves two disparate functions. First, it performs the same role as the automatic stay of Bankruptcy Code § 362 with respect to executory contracts and unexpired leases. In that role, by refusing to recognize the effect of ipso facto clauses, the section assists in keeping the estate together and in preserving the other benefits gained by a collective proceeding. *See supra* pp. 861-67. In this respect, it is similar to the restrictions imposed on secured creditors in both liquidation cases and reorganization cases. This "automatic stay" function may be justifiable for the reasons already explored with respect to creditors. Second, however, Bankruptcy Code § 365 acts in a *value*-allocating role. It is this function that I wish to examine. For, even assuming that the justifications for the "automatic stay" are valid, the question of respecting the *value* of the non-bankruptcy entitlements still remains. *See supra* pp. 872-77.

107. *See* Scott, *supra* note 80, at 14-15 (examining distinctions in the bankruptcy treatment of lessors and secured lenders and noting alternative means of achieving identical financial result).

108. The Bankruptcy Act of 1898 did not so differentiate. It validated the use of ipso facto clauses in executory contracts and unexpired leases. 11 U.S.C. § 110(d) (1975) (repealed prospectively, effec-

ignored the problem. Is there, however, a coherent justification for this distinct treatment of lenders, whose claims are accelerated in a Chapter 7 liquidation proceeding but whose claims may be de-accelerated by choice of the debtor in a Chapter 11 reorganization proceeding, and of contract holders, whose contracts may be de-accelerated (again by choice of the debtor) in both liquidation proceedings and reorganization proceedings?[109] Insights previously gained from the creditors' bargain model may be used in approaching this question. The first step is to consider whether there is any reason to differentiate, in a general fashion, between the treatment of lenders and other contract holders. The second step is to determine whether there is any reason to differentiate between a liquidation proceeding and a reorganization proceeding. It is these issues that I address in this section of the Article.

1. *Lenders: The Reorganization De-Acceleration Option*

Consider first the treatment of lenders in bankruptcy. A bankruptcy liquidation proceeding under Chapter 7 works an acceleration of the principal of outstanding credit, whether secured or unsecured, and bankruptcy claims are measured on the basis of that accelerated principal.[110] Moreover, as we have already explored, the "adequate protection" standard for secured creditors is apparently based on this accelerated-principal basis.

In moving from a Chapter 7 liquidation to a Chapter 11 reorganization proceeding, however, the Bankruptcy Code shifts focus rather dramatically. Prior to consummation of a plan of reorganization, the basic "adequate protection" standard applies.[111] Even at the time of the confirmation and consummation of the plan, the reorganization provisions provide, consistently enough, a liquidation-based level of entitlements:[112] each creditor must do as well in a Chapter 11 as in a Chapter 7 proceeding.[113]

tive Oct. 1, 1979). This protection, however, was in the process of being watered down by case law before the present Bankruptcy Code was enacted. *See* Queens Blvd. Wine & Liquor Store v. Blum, 503 F.2d 202 (2d Cir. 1974).

109. This is not exactly true. To the extent that the debtor is now a greater risk than before, Bankruptcy Code § 365(b) requires adequate assurance of future performance (in cases where there has been a prior default). A de-accelerated creditor, however, does not receive any direct compensation for the increased risk. The assurance is, instead, indirect: under Bankruptcy Code § 1129(a)(11) the plan must be deemed "feasible."

110. Bankruptcy Code §§ 502(b), 725, 726; H.R. REP. NO. 595, *supra* note 11, at 353.

111. At least nothing seems to call off Bankruptcy Code §§ 361 and 362, nor is there any indication that the "non-impairment" standard of Bankruptcy Code § 1124 permits "adequate protection" *prior* to the confirmation of the plan to be based on anything other than the accelerated principal—the portion of the "allowed claim" under Bankruptcy Code § 502 that is secured under Bankruptcy Code § 506. *See In re* Silverman, 13 Bankr. 72, 74 (Bankr. D. Mass. 1981).

112. Bankruptcy Code § 1129(a)(7)(A) requires that each holder of a claim either accept the plan or "receive or retain under the plan . . . property of a value . . . that is not less than the amount that such holder would so receive if the debtor were liquidated under chapter 7 . . . ."

113. H.R. REP. NO. 595, *supra* note 11, at 412, notes:

The implication that a reorganization under Chapter 11 must leave everyone as well off as in a liquidation under Chapter 7 is, however, quite misleading. For the Bankruptcy Code seems to allow the debtor or the trustee to choose—when it is in the interest of the estate to do so—a non-acceleration-based compensation standard for reorganizations.[114] Bankruptcy Code section 1124(2) deems a class of claimholders "not impaired" if, in addition to curing outstanding defaults, the original maturities of such claimholders' contracts are reinstated. The consequence of a class of claims being considered unimpaired is dramatic—the class is "deemed to have accepted the plan."[115] The Bankruptcy Code provision linking reorganization payments to the liquidation-based level of compensation states that a plan cannot be confirmed unless, with respect to each class, each claimholder has either accepted the plan or will receive, under the plan, payments whose present value equals the amount the claimholder would receive under Chapter 7.[116] The section thus suggests[117] that claimholders in an unimpaired class do not receive the liquidation-based compensation level of protection, and, because Bankruptcy Code section 1129(a)(8) is automatically satisfied,[118] are not entitled to the protections of the absolute priority rule.[119]

> Paragraph (7) [of Bankruptcy Code § 1129] incorporates the former "best interest of creditors" test found in chapter 11 [sic XI], but spells out precisely what is intended. With respect to each class, the holders of claims or interests of that class must receive or retain under the plan on account of those claims or interest property of a value, as of the effective date of the plan, that is not less than the amount that they would so receive or retain if the debtor were liquidated under chapter 7 on the effective date of the plan.

114. It should be obvious that the debtor's option to de-accelerate a lender will be used whenever the contractual rate of interest on a loan is less than the market rate of interest. Conversely, if the contractual rate of interest is greater than the market rate of interest, the loan will be paid off on an accelerated principal basis. This ability to *select* when to "de-accelerate" may skew non-bankruptcy entitlements. (Often, however, loans will be pre-payable under applicable non-bankruptcy law, which would remove this problem.) Any proponent of a plan of reorganization may select de-acceleration as a feature of his plan. But because the debtor typically has an exclusive period in which to propose a plan it seems substantially accurate to refer to the choice as "the debtor's." *See* Bankruptcy Code § 1121(c).

115. Bankruptcy Code § 1126(f).

116. Bankruptcy Code § 1129(a)(7).

117. The import of the section is not certain, as the drafting leaves open a contrary possibility. Bankruptcy Code § 1126(f) deems an unimpaired *class* to "have accepted the plan." Bankruptcy Code § 1129(a)(7)(A) refers to *individual* claimholders. Bankruptcy Code § 1126(f) does not say that each claimholder has accepted the plan, only that the *class* has. Therefore, it is open for an individual claimant in any unimpaired class to argue that he is, nonetheless, entitled to the protection of Bankruptcy Code § 1129(a)(7)(A). *See also infra* note 119. This argument becomes difficult (albeit conceptually still possible) when the class consists of only one creditor, as is normally the case with respect to security interests. *See In re* Palisades-on-the-Desplaines, 89 F.2d 214, 217-18 (7th Cir. 1937); Trost, *Business Reorganizations Under Chapter 11 of the New Bankruptcy Code*, 34 BUS. LAW. 1309, 1327 (1979).

118. Bankruptcy Code § 1129(a)(8) requires, with respect to each class, that "(A) such class has accepted the plan; or (B) such class is not impaired under the plan."

119. The "fair and equitable" standard of Bankruptcy Code § 1129(b) applies when "all of the applicable requirements of subsection (a) of this section other than paragraph (8) are met with respect to a plan . . . ." Moreover, the section only imposes the "fair and equitable" requirement on "each

For example, assume that *SC* loaned *D* $100,000 in 1975, with an annual interest rate of eight percent (payable monthly) and with an original maturity of 1990. The loan is secured by a mortgage on *D*'s equipment, which at all times is worth in excess of $100,000. *D* files for bankruptcy in 1982. If the property were sold (in a liquidation or otherwise), *SC* would be entitled to realize $100,000, which *SC* would then be free to reinvest by, for example, loaning the money out to a new borrower at the then-current (1982) interest rate of sixteen percent. Yet application of Bankruptcy Code section 1124(2) to reinstate *SC*'s loan, with its eight percent interest rate and 1990 maturity, will mean that the expected value of *SC*'s claim in *D*'s reorganization is substantially less than $100,000. To that extent, *D*'s estate benefits at *SC*'s expense and *SC* does not do as well in a Chapter 11 reorganization as in a Chapter 7 liquidation.[120]

2. *Lenders vs. Executory Contract-Holders*

This de-acceleration treatment of lenders in Chapter 11 is consistent with the treatment of executory contract-holders. Executory contract-holders, however, face de-acceleration in both a Chapter 7 liquidation and a Chapter 11 reorganization. To explore this different treatment, compare the status of a contract-holder with the status of a lender. Say that *D* has two principal assets (called "Asset 1" and "Asset 2"), each with a fair market value (and a "going concern" value) of $100,000. *D* also has two major lenders (*C1* and *C2*), each of whom has an outstanding loan to *D* of $100,000, at ten percent interest, maturing in 1990. At the time the loans were made, the prime rate of interest on loans of a similar duration

class of claims or interests that is impaired under, and has not accepted, the plan." Since a de-accelerated class is, by definition, not impaired, the "fair and equitable" test would not apply to it. *See* Orr & Klee, *Secured Creditors Under the New Bankruptcy Code*, 11 U.C.C. L.J. 312, 318 (1979). One court, however, has refused to hold that a creditor who already held a judgment of foreclosure was not impaired when it was de-accelerated, on the express ground that it was thereby "forced to . . . make a forced investment in a risky enterprise under a management demonstrated to the lien holder to be unreliable." *In re* Antilles Yachting, 4 Bankr. 470, 474 (Bankr. D. V.I. 1980). There were particular facts, however, which suggested that the creditor would have sold the property before bankruptcy but for an agreement with the debtor to delay. The treatment of accelerated loans in Chapter 13 may be different, since Bankruptcy Code § 1322(b)(5) makes no reference to reinstating the maturity in addition to curing defaults. *See In re* La Paglia, 8 Bankr. 937 (Bankr. E.D.N.Y. 1981). *But see* DePierro v. Taddeo, No. 81-5053 (2d Cir. July 20, 1982) (can de-accelerate a pre-petition acceleration in Chapter 13); *In re* Davis, 15 Bankr. 22 (Bankr. D. Kan. 1981) (same). This reasoning might be applicable to Bankruptcy Code § 365(b), since that section does not discuss reinstating the original maturity. Several courts, relying on Chapter 13 cases, have held that de-acceleration is not possible under Bankruptcy Code § 1124(2) if a judgment of foreclosure was entered prior to bankruptcy. *See In re* Monroe Park, 18 Bankr. 790 (Bankr. D. Del. 1982); *In re* Saint Peter's School, 16 Bankr. 404, 409-10 (Bankr. S.D.N.Y. 1982). *But see In re* Hewitt, 16 Bankr. 973, 977 (Bankr. D. Alaska 1982).

120. If the converse were true and the loan was made at 16 percent while the present interest rate was only 8 percent, the trustee would not exercise his de-acceleration option. *See supra* note 114. This may not be very significant if the debtor could prepay the debt under applicable non-bankruptcy law. In that case, one would often expect the debtor to have re-financed at the lower rate.

was seven percent; that rate is now seventeen percent. *D* also has various trade creditors (collectively "*TC*"), with currently-due claims amounting to $100,000.

In a Chapter 7 liquidation proceeding, *D*'s trustee would sell Asset 1 and Asset 2 for an aggregate of $200,000. This $200,000 would then be distributed among *C1*, *C2*, and *TC* (each the holder of a $100,000 claim)[121] *pro rata*, with the result that each of *C1*, *C2*, and *TC* would receive $66,667.[122]

In Chapter 11, however, as we have observed, *D*'s trustee could de-accelerate *C1*'s and *C2*'s loans.[123] If the present value of their de-accelerated right of payment was $50,000 each, then, in reorganization, *C1* and *C2* would each receive payments with a present value of $50,000, and TC would receive payments with a present value of $100,000.[124]

What would the result be if *D*'s trustee could de-accelerate *C1*'s and *C2*'s loans in a Chapter 7 liquidation proceeding as well?[125] As we have seen, absent de-acceleration, *D*'s trustee would realize $200,000 by liquidating Asset 1 and Asset 2. *C1*, *C2*, and *TC* would each receive $66,667. But, with an ability to de-accelerate and assign the loans, *D*'s trustee could now offer potential purchasers a financing package. By way of example, the trustee could sell the two assets for $150,000—$50,000 in cash, and the remainder in the form of an obligation to pay *C1* or *C2* $100,000, in 1990, at ten percent interest. If this ten percent interest rate were sufficiently below the market rate of interest for such obligations, so that the present value of the $100,000 obligation maturing in 1990 were $50,000, the cash sales price of $100,000 and the financed sales price of $150,000 would be the same, in present value terms. Assuming both assets were sold using this financing package, *D* would be rid of the obligations to both *C1* and *C2*. *C1* and *C2* would each receive the right to a payment stream worth $50,000. *D*, moreover, would receive $50,000 in cash from each of Asset 1 and Asset 2, and could use that $100,000 to pay *TC* (*D*'s only remaining creditor) in full. In this way, the liquidation result would be harmonious with the reorganization result considered in the previous

121. *C1*'s and *C2*'s principal would be accelerated for purposes of the claim. Bankruptcy Code § 502; H.R. REP. NO. 595, *supra* note 11, at 353.

122. Bankruptcy Code § 726(b).

123. Bankruptcy Code § 1124(2).

124. This conclusion must be qualified. *See supra* note 104. There is also a question of whether Chapter 11's classification requirement would allow this. *See* Bankruptcy Code § 1122. In any event, this would hold true if *C1* and *C2* were secured creditors and could be separately classified as such.

125. Since this example involves a liquidation proceeding, to effectuate this de-acceleration, the trustee would also need to have the right to assign the de-accelerated loans. *See* Bankruptcy Code § 365(f). Assignment of executory contracts and unexpired leases is discussed later. *See infra* pp. 896-201.

paragraph.[126]

Assume now that Asset 1 and Asset 2 are held by *D* under long-term leases, and *C1* and *C2* are the lessors. The rental rate for these leases is below market, so that the difference, in present value terms, between the value of each leasehold at the current market rate ($150,000) and the cost of that leasehold at the contract rate ($100,000) is $50,000. If *C1* and *C2* have the right to terminate the leases upon *D*'s bankruptcy,[127] *C1* and *C2* can either remove Asset 1 and Asset 2 from *D*'s estate, and negotiate a new lease with a third party for $150,000 each, or negotiate another lease with *D* for $150,000. In either case, *C1* and *C2* receive $50,000 that they would not have received but for bankruptcy and TC gets (out of these assets at least) nothing. If, however, *D* has the right to de-accelerate and assign *C1*'s and *C2*'s leases in bankruptcy, *D* will be able to sell each lease (of Asset 1 and Asset 2) for the lease rate/market rate differential of $50,000. By de-acceleration, therefore, *D* will be able to garner $100,000 for *TC* (and concomitantly reduce the value of what both *C1* and *C2* would receive, if able to accelerate, by $50,000).[128]

So viewed, the consequence of de-acceleration, in either a liquidation or a reorganization, is a reallocation of asset values from *C1* and *C2* (whether secured lenders, unsecured lenders, or contract-holders) to *TC* in equal and opposite amounts. Is there anything that justifies this *ex post* reallocation? And, even if there is, is there any reason for according different treatment to contract holders than to lenders?

In discussing de-acceleration of lenders, the Senate Report explains that this process of unimpairment should cause no consternation: "The holder of a claim or interest who under the plan is restored to his original position, when others receive less or get nothing at all, is fortunate indeed and has no cause to complain."[129] This comment is apparently premised on the unstated view that bankruptcy is a fortuitous event allowing the lender to achieve a "windfall" by accelerating a debt that has a below-market interest rate.[130] Presumably, this is also the unarticulated rationale behind

126. If *C1* and *C2* were made secured lenders, a similar result would follow. Absent de-acceleration and assignment (the situation in liquidation) *C1* and *C2* would each receive $100,000 and *TC* would receive nothing. But de-accelerating *C1*'s and *C2*'s loans would result in each of them receiving $50,000 (the present value of the de-accelerated loan contracts) and in *TC* receiving $100,000.

127. *See infra* pp. 887-892.

128. The same result would occur in a reorganization if *D* kept the leases after de-acceleration, instead of assigning them to a third party. In that event, *D* would "save," in present value terms, $50,000 per lease over current market rentals for comparable assets. This savings would enable *D* to pay *TC*, in present value terms, $100,000 more than otherwise.

129. *See* S. REP. NO. 989, *supra* note 76. The ability to de-accelerate applies to unsecured creditors as well as to secured creditors. An unsecured creditor, however, would generally be de-accelerated only when unsecured creditors were being paid in full. It seems plausible to treat such unsecured creditors as sharing many of the same attributes as secured creditors.

130. This "windfall" rationale appears to apply both to liquidation proceedings under Chapter 7

Bankruptcy Code section 365's de-acceleration of executory contracts and unexpired leases.[131]

But this justification is unsatisfying. It suggests, first of all, that a de-acceleration option should be available in a Chapter 7 liquidation as well as in a Chapter 11 reorganization proceeding, allowing the trustee to treat a below market loan as an asset of the estate, thereby entitling him to "assign" the loan with collateral (if a secured loan) or otherwise (if an unsecured loan).[132] More importantly, it is inaccurate to say that reinstatement of contract terms is all that *C1* or *C2* is "entitled to" since it was but a "fortuity" (for *C1* and *C2*) that *D* went into bankruptcy. For this is a "fortuitous event" that *C1* and *C2* have bargained for: in essence, *C1* and *C2* have received an option to call in their respective loan (or contract) and to reloan or release it at the then-market rate for such a loan or contract.[133] The lender or contract-holder has already paid for this option (just as a secured lender, for example, has paid for other entitlements that are recognized in bankruptcy). It is difficult, as a consequence, to view the below-market loan or contract somehow as an "asset" of the debtor that the debtor (or other creditors) is entitled to on the ground of preventing windfalls. Moreover, neither section 365 nor section 1124 of the Bankruptcy Code is evenhanded in its treatment of the event. To the extent that there has been an exogenous change in the world, such a change may be viewed as random from the point of view of the contracting parties. But de-acceleration is left to the discretion of the trustee, who will presumably choose to exercise his right of de-acceleration only when the loan rate or contract rate is below market.[134]

Dismissing the potential rights of *C1* and *C2* by referring to them as "windfalls," then, obscures analysis. The relevant question is whether *C1* and *C2*, on the one hand, or *TC* (*D*'s other creditors), on the other hand, should be "benefited," *ex post*, by the value of *C1*'s and *C2*'s below-

and to reorganization proceedings under Chapter 11. Bankruptcy Code § 1124(2), however, is applicable only in a Chapter 11 reorganization proceeding.

131. Fogel, *supra* note 102, at 349 ("The fact that section 365(e) invalidates bankruptcy clauses in liquidation cases as well as rehabilitation cases indicates that Congress intended to deny the nonbankrupt party to an executory contract or unexpired lease any windfall from the fortuity of the debtor's bankruptcy. . . .")

132. As already noted, this option is available in liquidation as well as in reorganization against the holders of executory contracts, but not against creditors holdings loans. The operation of this de-acceleration principle (whether in or out of reorganization) may have consequences apparently not imagined by the draftsmen of the Bankruptcy Code. Since executory contracts to make loans are not enforceable by the trustee, Bankruptcy Code § 365(c)(2), *see supra* note 99, holders of such contracts avoid de-acceleration completely. Bankruptcy Code § 1124(2), therefore, may lead to long-term loans being divided into shorter segments, in an attempt to preserve future segments as "executory" within Bankruptcy Code § 365(c)(2).

133. For an accessible introduction to options and their uses, see Black, *Fact and Fantasy in the Use of Options*, 31 FIN. ANALYSTS J. 36 (July-Aug. 1975).

134. This is, at best, a skewing of expectations. *See supra* note 114.

market loans or leases. Assuming acceleration was provided for in the contract, both *C1* and *C2* have effectively bargained for an "option": the right to call in the loan (or contract). Once *ex ante* adjustments are considered, nothing we have yet seen supports the conclusion that application of the de-acceleration principle produces a compelling reason for interfering with negotiated non-bankruptcy entitlements.

It is not, however, just that the case for interference has not been made. Even though creditors can adjust for a bankruptcy de-acceleration rule, there may be reasons to think that this interference imposes an undesirable cost on the debtor and the creditors considered as a group. To examine this, we need to start more broadly with the question of the purposes served by the variety of clauses that allow one party to pull out of a contractual relationship with another party.

3. *The Role of "Ipso Facto" Clauses in Bankruptcy*

"Bankruptcy" or "ipso facto" clauses typically declare that a loan or contract is either terminated or accelerated automatically upon the filing of a petition in bankruptcy, or that bankruptcy constitutes an event of default, entitling the lender or contract-holder to terminate or accelerate the terms of the contract or lease.[135] These clauses are the direct target of de-acceleration. Yet, presumptively, such clauses are to the mutual benefit of the debtor and the contract-holder. Ipso facto clauses are candidates for override only if their presence is evidence either of a systematic breakdown in contractual bargaining between the debtor and the contract-holder, or of unaccounted-for third-party effects.

First consider an ipso facto clause from the perspective of the debtor and the contract-holder. One might imagine that an ipso facto clause is designed either to provide a creditor with some measure of protection against a debtor's non-systematic, non-misbehavior-induced risk,[136] or to provide a creditor with an opportunity to re-evaluate a contract to account for systematic market changes.[137] Neither of these reasons, however, seems

135. These clauses are effectively the ones discussed *infra* p. 888. Normally, these clauses will also cover collective proceedings *outside* of bankruptcy, for the reason that such expansion reduces negotiations over the level of entitlements owing to such a party in a non-bankruptcy collective proceeding. *See* Bankruptcy Code § 365(e)(1); *see also infra* pp. 901-06.

136. An ipso facto clause, in other words, might be perceived as designed to protect *C1* from a substantially increased chance of nonpayment, with the attendant inconveniences, delays, and uncertainties, upon certain unfortunate changes in *D*'s position, as measured externally, by the occurrence of an event such as bankruptcy. As such, it may provide the contracting party with the opportunity to reassess the credit-worthiness of the assignee or the risks of continuing with the original party after a clear signal has been given that the risk level has changed. *See infra* pp. 896-901.

137. Systematic changes in market conditions may have nothing at all to do with the likelihood of repayment by a particular debtor. An ipso facto clause could be perceived as serving this role by providing for the ability to accelerate upon the occurrence of a specified event such as bankruptcy.

convincing in light of other available means for achieving the same goal that will not cause the "bankruptcy incentive" disadvantages of an ipso facto clause.[138] Non-systematic risks (other than of the misbehavior sort) can be handled through diversification[139] and an *ex ante* cost adjustment while systematic risks can be dealt with equivalently by a shortening of the term of the contract.[140]

Although the presence of ipso facto clauses is not necessarily motivated solely by monitoring concerns,[141] it seems promising to view ipso facto clauses as serving a role akin to a range of other contractual covenants. The utility of such covenants (often called "financial covenant" or "restrictive covenant" clauses) in loan or other contracts is commonly perceived as one of policing.[142] After entering into a loan or a contract at a defined interest (or contract) rate, a debtor has an incentive to engage in activities that unilaterally increase the riskiness of the loan or contract—by, for example, changing investment decisions to include riskier choices.[143] Financial covenant clauses may be designed to allow a creditor to police this species of misbehavior by giving the lender the option of calling in the loan upon the occurrence of such opportunistic behavior.[144]

138. *See infra* pp. 891-892.

139. Considered *ex ante*, however, the non-systematic risk (described *supra* note 136) represents the overall chance that a debtor of a certain class will use bankruptcy. In the event of bankruptcy, acceleration will entitle the lender (or other contract-holder) to receive payment today (or to get the property back). This increased riskiness can presumably be contractually adjusted for *ex ante*. In that event, the presence of the clause is not required for reasons of efficiency. Langbein and Posner note that there is "no sound economic reason" for screening out of portfolios firms that are "in danger of going bankrupt." Langbein & Posner, *Social Investing and the Law of Trusts*, 79 MICH. L. REV. 72, 93 (1980).

140. Since the initiation of bankruptcy is a matter of statistical probability, the inclusion of an ipso facto clause has the same effect as shortening the term of the loan. A shortening of the term of the loan permits more frequent adjustments to systematic market changes, which, in turn, reduce the uncertainty associated with lengthier contract terms. Again, there is no particular reason to view a "bankruptcy termination" clause as serving any different function, in this respect, than a shorter term loan. Hence systematic risk provides no particular reason to believe the disappearance of such clauses would be missed.

141. Ipso facto clauses may serve other beneficial roles as well. A debtor may believe that it is very unlikely that he will go into bankruptcy yet have no effective way to convince a creditor of that so as to be placed in a lower risk class. *Cf.* A. KRONMAN & R. POSNER, THE ECONOMICS OF CONTRACT LAW 224 (1979) (discussing signalling function of penalty clauses). *See also infra* note 150 & p. 898 (discussing use of ipso facto clauses to provide contract-holder with ability to assess whether bankruptcy operates as delegation of debtor's duties).

142. *See, e.g.*, R. BREALEY & S. MYERS, PRINCIPLES OF CORPORATE FINANCE 389-93 (1981); Smith & Warner, *supra* note 44. *But cf.* Van Horne, *Optimal Initiation of Bankruptcy Proceedings by Debt Holders*, 31 J. FIN. 897, 908 (1976) ("The obvious advantage to the lender of protective covenants is the additional ability it affords him to force bankruptcy . . . .")

143. *See, e.g.*, R. POSNER, *supra* note 35, at 293-94; Jensen & Meckling, *supra* note 44, at 334-37; Muris, *supra* note 61.

144. Miller, *The Wealth Transfers of Bankruptcy: Some Illustrative Examples*, 41 LAW & CONTEMP. PROBS. 39, 43 (Autumn 1977). This is not to say that such financial covenant clauses necessarily reduce the *costs* of policing. Rather, they have some *in terrorem* effect by saying that *if* a debtor is caught misbehaving there will be certain costly consequences. The possibility of such occurrence raises the costs of misbehavior and should, therefore, lower its incidence.

The ability of a debtor, by resorting to bankruptcy, to defuse these clauses by means of "de-acceleration" would weaken the valuable misbehavior-monitoring function of financial covenant clauses.[145] In such cases, application of the de-acceleration principle would not simply be a "wash" (by virtue of *ex ante* adjustments for *ex post* events), but would result in a less efficient system, considered in the aggregate.

An ipso facto clause might be present in a given contract precisely because it serves such a policing role. To be sure, it does not allow a creditor to say "because you have misbehaved, I am terminating the loan," for it identifies no misbehavior. The contract or loan may be terminated only *after* the debtor has gone into bankruptcy (or a similar collective proceeding outside of bankruptcy). As such, it may serve as a broad-brush *in terrorem* clause designed to deter misbehavior in general[146] by imposing a cost on the debtor who resorts to bankruptcy, and hence imposing a cost on engaging in activities that increase the likelihood of bankruptcy.[147] Thus, an ipso facto clause may serve much the same function as a general legal rule ("one shall drive at a reasonable speed") or presumption ("anyone who drives off the roadway shall be presumed to be driving negligently") as opposed to the function of a specific legal rule ("speed limit 55 MPH").[148] Unlike most other financial covenant clauses, which identify defined quantums of increased riskiness, an ipso facto clause relies on a rough, but easily determined, surrogate for increased riskiness. As such, an ipso facto clause performs a general function that could not be done as

145. Miller, *supra* note 144, at 43. Financial covenant clauses may allow a lender to call in a loan when there have been systematic market shifts even where these shifts are unrelated to debtor misbehavior. To the extent this is true, however, it is a problem not related to bankruptcy and one that presumably has been effectively priced out. There seems to be little reason to have a bankruptcy rule here that attempts to "cure" this inefficiency.

146. Bernanke, *Bankruptcy, Liquidity, and Recession*, 71 AM. ECON. REV. 155, 155 (1981); Goetz & Scott, *supra* note 89.

147. This explanation for the presence of ipso facto clauses presupposes that they are an effective deterrent. If the debtor (the equity owners) would receive nothing in bankruptcy anyway, ipso facto clauses would not seem to deter misbehavior. *See also infra* note 158. Yet ipso facto clauses may inspire deterrence from other quarters. For one thing, *ex ante*, a debtor will not know whether the institution of bankruptcy will leave him with nothing. Futhermore, misbehavior of the sort we are concerned with involves the debtor engaging in risk-increasing activities that effectively lower the interest rate he is paying on previously-incurred contracts. *See* Jackson & Kronman, *supra* note 53, at 1149; *supra* note 143. Ipso facto clauses effectively allow the contract-holder to adjust the interest rate in response to such opportunistic behavior. Even if the debtor is indifferent to such adjustments *ex post*, as long as the debtor needs the participation of subsequent creditors in his opportunistic behavior schemes, the result may well be the same because of *ex ante* adjustments. Subsequent creditors will view potential de-acceleration by earlier contract-holders as a cost to them, which may deter acquiring subsequent credit because it will limit the debtor's ability to "get something for nothing." Ipso facto clauses, finally, may also increase the monitoring incentives of short-term trade creditors, who may be the most efficient monitors. *See* Jackson & Kronman, *supra* note 53, at 1160-61.

148. For a discussion of the utility of both sets of rules from an economic standpoint, see Ehrlich & Posner, *An Economic Analysis of Legal Rulemaking*, 3 J. LEGAL STUD. 257 (1974); *see also* Easterbrook & Fischel, *supra* note 89 (discussing fiduciary duty rules in corporate context as alternative to direct monitoring by replacing prior supervision with deterrence).

well by another, more specific, contract term.[149] Viewed this way, application of the de-acceleration principle to ipso facto clauses appears unwise. Such application would eliminate the deterrence function of such clauses, which would in turn increase aggregate credit costs.[150]

Even if justified as between debtor and contract-holder, there may be externalities associated with the use of ipso-facto clauses.[151] Whatever the justification for the existence of ipso facto clauses, their presence introduces an inevitable problem.[152] If ipso facto clauses are enforceable in bankruptcy, *C1* may, under certain circumstances, have an incentive to see *D* file for bankruptcy.[153] Under the facts of our hypothetical, for example, *C1*, by possessing the rights an "ipso facto" clause would give her, is $100,000 better off the moment *D* goes into bankruptcy. *C1*, therefore, will have an incentive to have *D* put into bankruptcy whenever the market rate exceeds the contract price, even if this is not to the creditors' collective advantage. In those circumstances, *D*'s other creditors are at least $100,000 better off if *D* does not go into bankruptcy.[154] *C1* could, of course, bargain with the other creditors (directly or through a re-negotiation of the contract with *D*) for some of the advantages they would realize (over and above $100,000—which would be *C1*'s minimum demand) for

149. Use of an ipso facto clause in this manner is most striking when dealing with unsecured loans. Secured lenders, as well as many holders of contracts and leases, may be better insulated against the effects of misbehavior, and therefore have less need for a general rule policing against such misbehavior. *See* Jackson & Kronman, *supra* note 53, at 1149-58. If this were entirely true, ipso facto clauses would not be needed for misbehavior-deterrence. One might then construct a bankruptcy process that would recognize ipso facto clauses in the case of unsecured loans but would not recognize such clauses in the case of secured loans, temporal contracts or leases. Justifying the establishment of this hypothetical system would depend on establishing that ipso facto clauses were inefficient in cases of secured loans and temporal contracts and leases. *See infra* note 158 (discussing some of the fallacies inherent in such a position). Interestingly, even if the net inefficiency of ipso facto clauses in the case of secured loans and temporal contracts and leases were established, de-acceleration would be inappropriate in liquidation cases, because of the independent justifications for general non-delegation rules. *See infra* pp. 896-901.

150. Ipso facto clauses may exist because of their unique ability to serve as a form of non-delegation clause. Non-bankruptcy law generally prohibits delegation of contractual duties when the delegating party is divested of continuing responsibilities for performance under the contract. *See infra* pp. 897-901. Determining when the composition of the "owners" of the debtor has changed sufficiently so as to prohibit delegation under those general rules may be difficult in bankruptcy. *See infra* notes 182 & 186. An ipso facto clause may permit the contract-holder to make those determinations alone.

151. If accounted for, a cost could not technically be an "externality." *See* J. DUKEMINIER & J. KRIER, PROPERTY 56 (1981); *see also* Demsetz, *Toward a Theory of Property Rights*, 57 AM. ECON. REV. 347 (1967).

152. *See* Hirschleifer & Riley, *The Analytics of Uncertainty and Information—An Expository Survey*, 17 J. ECON. LIT. 1375, 1390-91 (1979); Pauly, *The Economics of Moral Hazard: Comment*, 58 AM. ECON. REV. 531 (1968).

153. *See* Van Horne, *supra* note 142, at 908. Thus, use of an ipso facto clause effectively introduces an element of moral hazard. Even if the ipso facto clause covered non-bankruptcy collective proceedings, the discussion in text would still apply because *C1* would have an incentive to force *D* to undergo one of these non-bankruptcy proceedings.

154. The debtor often has the power to "avoid" unfavorable loans or contracts by invoking the bankruptcy process. *Cf.* White, *supra* note 44, at 552-56 (noting other incentives debtors have to go into bankruptcy).

not having D put into bankruptcy. This result would, however, be predictably costly to negotiate, as there may be multiple parties in *C1*'s position, as well as a number of other creditors.

But to say that there exists an inevitable moral hazard problem arising from the presence of an ipso facto clause does not itself say that an unaccounted-for externality has been demonstrated that would justify a rule barring the effectiveness of such clauses in bankruptcy.[155] For, if the costs of an ipso facto clause outweighed its benefits, we would expect to see the clause excluded *ab initio*.[156] The costs introduced by the presence of the clause presumptively have been "priced out" because a debtor will be affected directly by the costs the clause imposes on his other creditors in the form of higher credit charges by them.[157] In that event, the externality problem effectively disappears, because its costs, having been accounted for by third parties, are internalized.[158]

The presence of an ipso facto clause, therefore, suggests its net utility.[159]

155. *See* Goetz & Scott, *supra* note 89, at 584-85.

156. Historically, ipso facto clauses served a useful role in allowing a creditor with an otherwise non-provable claim to participate in the bankruptcy distribution. Use of ipso facto clauses for such purposes is traced in Kuehner v. Irving Trust Co., 299 U.S. 445 (1937), and Oldden v. Tonto Realty Corp., 143 F.2d. 916 (2d Cir. 1944). Discarding the concept of provability in the Bankruptcy Code removes this function of ipso facto clauses. *See* Bankruptcy Code §§ 101(4), 502(a)-(c).

157. *See* Jackson & Kronman, *supra* note 53, at 1147-43; *supra* p. 871. These conclusions would be upset if one believed that the debtor and a contract-holder could impose these costs on the other creditors because of ignorance, unsophistication, or other reasons. *See* Schwartz, *supra* note 53, at 30-31. But establishing such advantage-taking may depend on showing widespread ignorance. *See generally* Schwartz & Wilde, *Intervening in Markets on the Basis of Imperfect Information: A Legal and Economic Analysis*, 127 U. PA. L. REV. 630 (1979). To effect nonrecognition of ipso facto clauses in bankruptcy, while other clauses are presumptively legitimated, would also require showing that such ignorance particularly affected this type of clause.

158. *See supra* note 151. Because of the difficulties of policing a debtor, it is possible that the presence of an ipso facto clause may not indicate its net efficiency. *See supra* note 44. Creditors may have difficulty ensuring that D does not enter into contracts and leases that grant the bankruptcy-inducing ipso facto clauses to future creditors. It might be the case that creditors will charge D on the assumption that such clauses will in fact be granted in the future. The individual "wasteful" costs of such a clause in a given contract may be too small to warrant the necessary monitoring expenses by any one creditor. Under those circumstances, the efficient solution may be for the creditor to charge for that risk, since it is too difficult to police. *D*, accordingly, might not appear to have the proper incentives to resist inclusion of such clauses. This, however, does not satisfactorily explain the presence of most ipso facto clauses. Equity-holders will have a strong incentive to have the clause excluded because it reduces the value of their residual. The interests of equity-holders are congruent with those of management with regard to senior classes of creditors such as debt-holders. *See* Jensen & Meckling, *supra* note 44. There are ample incentives to ensure that ipso facto clauses will be included only if their presence is advantageous to the debtor and the creditors, considered as a group.

159. *See also supra* note 141. The advantage-taking opportunities afforded lenders or creditors by virtue of an ipso facto clause may be no greater than those provided by the acceleration right given debtors upon the occurrence of bankruptcy. "Financial covenant" clauses, since they are unrelated to the occurrence of bankruptcy, do not suffer from the "bankruptcy incentive" problem of pure ipso facto clauses. Even if ipso facto clauses were suspect, financial covenant clauses should not be. The distinction between these two types of clauses mirrors the de-acceleration principle itself. If the loan could be accelerated outside of the bankruptcy context, there is no particular *bankruptcy-related* reason to refuse to recognize the existing right of acceleration. *See also infra* pp. 901-907 (discussing another application of de-acceleration principle).

The more appropriate inquiry would be to see if a more finely-tuned approach could be pursued that would recognize ipso facto clauses in bankruptcy, and attempt to control misbehavior by a lender or contract-holder in other ways. Rules regulating creditor-initiated implementation of the bankruptcy process may provide a set of rules that promote efficient asset-disbursement decisions. Such rules will, therefore, protect against pure "advantage-taking" action by creditors without detracting unduly from the utility of bankruptcy laws. The Bankruptcy Code has such rules. For example, the Bankruptcy Code limits the ability of creditors to initiate bankruptcy proceedings by requiring a minimum of three or more creditors with unsecured claims.[160] The Bankruptcy Code also limits creditor-initiated bankruptcies to situations in which the debtor is generally not paying debts as they become due.[161] These particular bankruptcy initiation rules may not be optimal,[162] but a system that incorporates these sorts of rules as a means of deterring individualistic advantage-taking may be preferable to a system that contains a blanket prohibition on the effectiveness of ipso facto clauses, because such a blanket prohibition would completely eliminate the general- or presumption-type rule deterrence function of such clauses.

B. *Liquidation and Reorganization: Is There a Difference?*

The general recognition of ipso facto clauses in bankruptcy, such as existed under the Bankruptcy Act of 1898,[163] is preferable to a general bar

160. An involuntary bankruptcy requires:

> three or more entities, each of which is . . . a holder of a claim against [the debtor] that is not contingent as to liability . . . if such claims aggregate at least $5,000 more than the value of any lien on property of the debtor securing such claims held by the holders of such claims. . . .

Bankruptcy Code § 303(b)(1). Only one claim-holder is required if there are fewer than 12 claim-holders (not counting employees, insiders, and holders of certain voidable transfers). Bankruptcy Code § 303(b)(2). These rules may involve complicated factual determinations. *See In re* Covey, 650 F.2d 877 (7th Cir. 1981).

161. Bankruptcy Code § 303(h)(1). This limitation is ignored if other creditors have initiated a non-bankruptcy collective process. Bankruptcy Code § 303(h)(2). In that event all creditors presumably need the threat of a resort to the bankruptcy process in order to protect their minimum entitlements. *See supra* p. 867. It is not certain that this modified "cash-flow" insolvency test is preferable to other tests such as the "balance sheet" insolvency test in Bankruptcy Code § 101(26) and used elsewhere in the bankruptcy process. *See* Bankruptcy Code §§ 547(b)(3), 548(a)(1), (a)(2)(b). The Bankruptcy Act of 1898 relied on a form of balance sheet insolvency to define when involuntary petitions in bankruptcy could be filed. *See* 11 U.S.C. § 21 (1975) (repealed prospectively effective Oct. 1, 1979); *see generally* Rostow & Cutler, *Competing Systems of Corporate Reorganization: Chapters X and XI of the Bankruptcy Act*, 48 YALE L.J. 1334, 1374 (1939). *See also* Bankruptcy Code § 305(a)(1) (permitting dismissal of case when interests of parties would be better served by such dismissal).

162. A rule specifying a minimum number of creditors can be circumvented by paying other creditors to file. *See In re* Win-Sum Sports, 14 Bankr. 389 (Bankr. D. Conn. 1981) (filed on behalf of three creditors who had received a written indemnity from manager against costs in connection with the petition).

163. 11 U.S.C. § 110(d) (1975) (repealed prospectively effective Oct. 1, 1979); see *supra* notes 108 & 156.

on the effectiveness of such clauses. We have not, however, focused on how the Bankruptcy Code should treat contracts that do not contain ipso facto clauses. Bankruptcy law does not distinguish between contractual acceleration rights and acceleration rights in the absence of a contractual provision. Yet, it does distinguish between lenders and executory contract-holders: lenders are subject to a general de-acceleration right in the debtor's control only in a Chapter 11 reorganization proceeding.[164]

1. *A Theory of Reorganization and Liquidation*

Before this inconsistent treatment accorded general rights of acceleration can be satisfactorily explored,[165] we must have a conceptual understanding of what a "reorganization" is. A reorganization, at least as a start, may be viewed as a *form* of liquidation. The business entity, however, is sold to the creditors themselves rather than to third parties.[166] The drafters of the Bankruptcy Code and almost all commentators have ignored the fact that the Bankruptcy Code's separate system of reorganization is not the only alternative to a piecemeal liquidation of assets. A business may be disposed of ("liquidated") as a *unit*[167] and, if its highest and best use is as a "going concern," it would seem that a properly conceived-of Chapter 7 proceeding would require the entity to be sold (*i.e.*, liquidated) as a unit rather than piecemeal whenever its going concern value exceeds its piecemeal liquidation value.[168]

164. *See supra* pp. 882-883. Although the examination was only in the context of *secured* creditors, the discussion should not be limited to them. *See supra* note 129.

165. De-acceleration is available generally in the case of executory contracts. *See supra* p. 880. Furthermore, de-acceleration seems to be available, regardless of the reasons for the acceleration. *But see In re* La Paglia, 8 Bankr. 937 (Bankr. E.D.N.Y. 1981) (discussed *supra* note 119). Having already concluded that there does not seem to be a reason for disparate treatment of lenders and executory contract-holders, one ought not reject the Bankruptcy Code's treatment of lenders without exploring the concepts of liquidation and reorganization.

166. *See* Clark, *supra* note 18, at 1252-54.

167. This could be done, for example, by hiring an investment company to find a private buyer or by imposing a new capital structure and selling the entity to the public as is done in a public offering. That the Bankruptcy Code ignores this alternative is yet another example of the under-utilization of available market mechanisms.

168. *See supra* pp. 864-865. *Cf.* Bulow & Shoven, *supra* note 18 (discussion of merger as alternative to bankruptcy); Weston, *supra* note 21, at 65. This view exposes two likely fallacies in the distinct treatment of the best interest of creditors test in Bankruptcy Code § 1129(a)(7) and the "absolute priority rule" in Bankruptcy Code § 1129(b). First of all, the best interest of creditors test, which provides a "not less than liquidation" protection for impaired individual creditors, should not be as distinct from the absolute priority rule protection afforded *classes* of creditors as the drafters apparently believed. The difference between the two is perceived by the drafters of the Bankruptcy Code as a question of class-wide allocation of the "going concern surplus." *See* J. TROST, G. TREISTER, L. FORMAN, K. KLEE, & R. LEVIN, RESOURCE MATERIALS: THE NEW FEDERAL BANKRUPTCY CODE 335-39 (1979) [hereinafter cited as J. TROST, RESOURCE MATERIALS]. This perception ignores the fact that an enterprise can be liquidated as a going concern. There is no reason why Chapter 7 would not be an appropriate mechanism for a "going concern" cash sale to third parties—or, indeed, why such a sale should not be *mandatory* if it would maximize distributions to creditors. But then, the "not less than liquidation" test of Bankruptcy Code § 1129(a)(7)(A) would compare a going concern sale

Reorganization proceedings provide nothing more than a method by which the sale of an enterprise as a going concern may be made to the creditors themselves. This process, like any liquidation procedure, involves two steps. First, the assets of the enterprise are sold. Second, the claims against the debtor are paid out of the proceeds of this sale.[169]

What differs in the situation in which the enterprise is sold to its own claimants is that the valuation of the proceeds out of which the claims against the debtor are to be paid is more difficult. In a straight piecemeal liquidation, either the assets are distributed in kind to secured claimants (thus mimicking their non-bankruptcy rights) or the assets are sold (usually for cash) and the cash is distributed to the parties, principally in the order of their non-bankruptcy entitlements. In a going concern liquidation, the business is sold to a third party, usually for cash and/or marketable securities. In many instances, therefore, the liquidation process will involve simply paying off the claims, in the order of their non-bankruptcy entitlements. The value of the payment for these claims will be easily determinable.[170] In a reorganization, however, the proceeds from the "sale" out of which claims against the debtor will be paid will consist principally of new claims against the same enterprise. This makes the valuation of the payment to the claimants substantially more difficult. It is principally these valuation issues that provide the core of the reorganiza-

to third parties in Chapter 7 to a Chapter 11 reorganization. To the extent there is an "extra" going concern surplus in Chapter 11, it consists of the surplus that results where the going concern value of a sale to the *creditors themselves* exceeds the going concern sale value of a sale to some third party. *See* Clark, *supra* note 18, at 1252. But this is almost certain to be a smaller differential than would exist in comparing a going concern reorganization to a piecemeal liquidation. Further, there is a general assumption that the cumbersome absolute priority rule procedures of Bankruptcy Code § 1129(b) can often be avoided, because classes of creditors will want to avoid the incremental procedural costs of a full valuation hearing. *See* J. TROST, RESOURCE MATERIALS, *supra*, at 337 (Bankruptcy Code § 1129(b) valuation will be sufficiently time-consuming so as "to stimulate senior classes to permit juniors to receive a portion of the going concern bonus in return for elimination of the full valuation hearing"); *cf.* H.R. REP. NO. 595, *supra* note 11, at 414 ("While section 1129(a) does not contemplate a valuation of the debtor's business, such valuation will almost always be required under section 1129(b) to determine the value of the consideration to be distributed.") This assumption ignores that determining whether a dissenter has received as much as he would have received in Chapter 7 requires a determination of what the value of the business would have been if liquidated. *See* Bankruptcy Code § 1129(a)(7). If the concept of a Chapter 7 liquidation includes, as it should, going concern sales to third parties, the valuation of the debtor's business for purposes of Bankruptcy Code § 1129(a)(7) will be as difficult as is § 1129(b)'s absolute priority rule valuation. Moreover, it will be impossible to determine how well a dissenter has done in Chapter 11 without valuing the consideration to be received by that creditor. When the consideration consists of claims against the debtor, valuing this consideration necessarily involves valuing this debtor's enterprise. *See* Blum, *Corporate Reorganization Doctrine as Recently Applied by the Securities and Exchange Commission*, 40 U. CHI. L. REV. 96, 110 (1972).

169. *See* Note, *Giving Substance to the Bonus Rule in Corporate Reorganizations: The Investment Value Doctrine Analogy*, 84 YALE L.J. 932, 943-46 (1975).

170. Clark, *supra* note 18, at 1252 (payment-type valuation problems do not exist when liquidation or receivership results in sale to outsiders for cash). The more difficult it is to value the consideration, the more this third-party sale will involve the problems inherent in a "pure" reorganization.

tion chapter's provisions.[171]

The point, however, is that the difficulties associated with a reorganization proceeding are in the valuation of the proceeds received upon the sale of the enterprise. Whether the process be a piecemeal liquidation, a going concern liquidation (*i.e.*, a sale of the entity to a third party), or a reorganization liquidation (*i.e.*, a sale of the entity to the creditors), nothing in the form of the process seems to call for a different standard of *allocation among claims* (the second step) in one type of proceeding than in another.[172]

This suggests that the relevant inquiry in choosing a Chapter 7 liquidation (piecemeal or going concern) or a Chapter 11 reorganization should be at the first step when the decision is made as to which of the three conceptual processes to use. As the creditors' bargain model would suggest, this decision should be made on the basis of which form provides the greatest aggregate dollar-equivalent return from the assets[173]—a determination that should be made without considering the claims outstanding against those assets (this consideration becomes relevant at the payout, but not at the sale, stage).[174]

2. *Of Bankruptcy Incentives and Property Rules (Herein of the Law of Assignments)*

In one respect, this account of the similarities between liquidation and

171. Bankruptcy Code §§ 1111(b), 1121-29. These provisions state the basis for determining who formulates a "plan" and what sorts of constraints exist on the terms of a plan, and they provide a set of procedures for approving the plan. These provisions also demonstrate that the universe of potential arrangements (*e.g.*, whether bondholders get debentures or common stock) is expanded greatly when the consideration used to "pay off" claims is other than cash or market-tested equivalents. Their absence in Chapter 7 reflects the substantially easier valuation and payment questions that confront a sale of assets for cash or market-equivalents.

172. Brudney, *supra* note 91, at 677; *see also* Note, *supra* note 169, at 944-46 (discussion of the two stages of a reorganization); *cf.* Public Utilities Holding Company Act of 1935, 15 U.S.C. § 79k (1976) (mandating capitalization of public utilities to simplify their extremely complex capital structures). (While liquidation values were *not* used in the Public Utility Holding Company Act (on the ground that this statutory recapitalization should not mature rights that were created "without regard to the possibility of simplification" of this sort, Otis & Co. v. SEC, 323 U.S. 624, 638 (1945)), courts insisted that *shifting* of going concern values from one class to another not occur. The question of whether this standard was appropriate in bankruptcy reorganization has been argued in detail. *See supra* note 98.)

173. This is not only the socially efficient way to decide on how to use the debtor's resources, it is also a result wholly consistent with the creditors' bargain model. By using the optimal form of "liquidation" or "reorganization" under such a selection standard, each creditor can be left at least as well off as under the selection of some other form, and some creditors can be made better off. *See* White, *supra* note 44; *see also supra* notes 61 & 62.

174. The choice of the type of bankruptcy proceeding is *already* a selection that works in the favor of the "lower entitlement classes" by maximizing aggregate returns and by providing that no class should be paid more than in full. *See supra* p. 870 & note 62. There is no normative reason that suggests further redistribution, depending on the type of bankruptcy proceeding, of non-bankruptcy entitlements from one class to some other class.

reorganization obscures an important difference between them. Normally, in a liquidation under Chapter 7, the assets are sold off and the "debtor" is, effectively, removed from the picture. Third parties are almost certainly involved, as "owners" if not as managers. The essence of a reorganization, however, is that third parties are *not* involved: the debtor is "continued," albeit the "owners" of the debtor may be replaced to some extent. Although it is possible to overstate this distinction, it is plausible to view a reorganized enterprise as a "continuation" of the web of relationships between the debtor and its former owners and creditors[175] while a liquidation, almost by necessity, involves a disruption of those relationships. Liquidations, therefore, may differ from reorganizations in this respect. Is there, however, any analytical relevance to this difference?

At this point, we need to examine non-bankruptcy law and the possible substantive distinction, in that law, between contracting parties and third parties. The law of assignments places two general obstacles in the way of an attempted delegation of duties without prior consent: it prohibits the delegation of certain duties entirely, and it does not allow the divesting of responsibility by a party. Consider, first, the general question of delegation. Contract law generally distinguishes the delegation of "fungible" duties from the delegation of "non-fungible" duties.[176] Certain kinds of contracts, often called "personal service contracts," are deemed by the common law to be non-delegable because they are based on particular skills or other unique features of the contracting party.[177] In essence, holders of these contracts are protected by a property rule: they do not have to deal with any assignees of their contracting counterpart unless permission for such assignment is obtained. This protects the expectations of a party that has contracted with a particular entity in much the same way the specific performance rule does in other circumstances.[178]

175. A reorganization procedure "made economic sense whenever there were no or few potential outside buyers with accurate and timely information about the true state of affairs and the future prospects of the business." Clark, *supra* note 18, at 1252. The end result of the process is a system "that would primarily involve a reshuffling of the paper claims against the business assets." *Id.* at 1253.

176. 4 A. CORBIN, CORBIN ON CONTRACTS 865 (1951); *see* Taylor v. Palmer, 31 Cal. 240 (1866).

177. "Delegation of performance is a normal and permissible incident of many types of contract. . . . The principal exceptions relate to contracts for personal services and to contracts for the exercise of personal skill or discretion." RESTATEMENT (SECOND) OF CONTRACTS § 318 comment c (1981); *see also* Munchak Corp. v. Cunningham, 457 F.2d 721 (4th Cir. 1972); Evening News Ass'n v. Peterson, 477 F. Supp. 77 (D.D.C. 1979); U.C.C. § 9-318(c) (1972); J. CALAMARI & J. PERILLO, THE LAW OF CONTRACTS 662-65 (2d ed. 1977). With regard to executory contracts and unexpired leases, these rules are generally respected by Bankruptcy Code § 365(c).

178. The analogy of the concept of non-delegable duties to contract law's concept of specific performance should be obvious. For a discussion of the rule of specific performance in terms of property rules, see Kronman, *supra* note 80; *see also* Schwartz, *The Case for Specific Performance*, 89 YALE L.J. 271 (1979). Even in cases in which the general rules of contract law would not call a duty non-delegable, however, the parties are free to draft their own anti-delegation clause. In this respect, parties are free to contract into their own creation of a property rule. *See, e.g.*, Eastern Advertising

Even when duties may be delegated without prior consent, the original contracting party remains ultimately responsible for the performance of his contractual obligations.[179] That is to say, even in the case of delegable duties, a person subject to a contractually-created obligation does not ordinarily have the right or power to divest himself of liability by substituting another in his place without the consent of the person to whom the duty is owed. While the delegatee may be entitled to perform for the original obligor if the duty is of the delegable sort, nonetheless, the original obligor remains ultimately liable until discharged by performance (or otherwise).[180]

This learning may be applied to our discussion of bankruptcy liquidation and reorganization proceedings. From the perspective of contract law, an attempt to continue a contractual obligation of a debtor past a piecemeal liquidation proceeding involving that debtor would almost certainly be viewed as a "delegation" of that obligation to a new entity, coupled with a divesting of duties by the debtor.[181] At the opposite end, many bankruptcy reorganizations would not be viewed as involving a delegation at all, much less a divesting of duties, under applicable non-bankruptcy law, especially where management remained in place and the old owners retained some substantial ownership position. It may be more difficult to make a general rule about "going concern" liquidations, which exhibit some of the features of a piecemeal liquidation and some of the features of a "pure" reorganization.[182] If we are trying to locate general presumptions for the purpose of fashioning off the rack rules, however, it seems plausi-

Co. v. McGaw, 89 Md. 72, 42 A. 923 (1899); RESTATEMENT (SECOND) OF CONTRACTS § 318(2) (1981). This could be done either directly as a matter of assignment ("*A* cannot assign his obligation to deliver wheat to me"), or indirectly, as a term of the contract ("*A* must deliver to me wheat grown on *A*'s farm, located at Blackacre, Kansas"). Games such as this may be played under the Bankruptcy Code, which, while striking down anti-assignment clauses, requires the assignee to give adequate assurances of performing the terms of the contract. Bankruptcy Code § 365(f)(2).

179. The general rule governing delegation of duties absent express agreement is that "delegation of performance . . . [does not] discharge any duty or liability of the delegating obligor." RESTATEMENT (SECOND) OF CONTRACTS § 318(3) (1981). *See also* J. CALAMARI & J. PERILLO, *supra* note 177, at 644 (assignor cannot divest himself of his duties; may sometimes delegate them, but remains liable for their due performance); U.C.C. § 2-210(1) (1972); Wetherall Bros. Co. v. United States Steel Co., 200 F.2d 761 (1st Cir. 1952); Smith v. Wrehe, 199 Neb. 753, 261 N.W.2d 620 (1978); Western Oil Sales Corp. v. Bliss & Wetherbee, 299 S.W. 637 (Tex. Comm. App. 1927); New York Bond Note Co. v. Hamilton Bank Note Engraving & Printing Co., 180 N.Y. 280, 293, 73 N.E. 48, 52 (1905).

180. *See* RESTATEMENT (SECOND) OF CONTRACTS § 316 comment c (1981).

181. *See, e.g.*, Western Oil Sales Corp. v. Bliss & Wetherbee, 299 S.W. 637 (Tex. Comm. App. 1927); Boston Ice Co. v. Potter, 123 Mass. 28 (1877); *cf.* The British Waggon Co. v. Lea & Co., 5 Q.B.D. 149 (1880) (assignment of duties by company in process of winding up permissible "so long as [that company] continues to exist"). *But cf.* Macke Co. v. Pizza of Gaithersburg, 259 Md. 479, 370 A.2d 645 (1970) (allowing purchaser of obligor to assume contract); Evening News Ass'n v. Peterson, 477 F. Supp. 77 (D.D.C. 1979) (assignment permitted upon merger because assuming corporation substantially similar to original corporation).

182. For example, management may remain the same while the owners are changed.

ble to treat bankruptcy liquidations (whether piecemeal or going concern) under Chapter 7 as the equivalent of cases involving both delegation and divesting of duties under applicable non-bankruptcy law, and to treat bankruptcy reorganizations under Chapter 11 as involving neither such delegation nor divesting.[183] Parties that felt uncomfortable with these off the rack rules could, of course, contract around them. Indeed, it seems likely that ipso facto clauses may on occasion serve as contractual clauses allowing the contract-holder to make his own determination about whether a particular bankruptcy proceeding implicated the concerns underlying non-bankruptcy law's delegation rules.[184] But whether or not such contractual clauses are allowed,[185] a general de-acceleration rule, such as exists in the case of executory contracts and unexpired leases under the Bankruptcy Code, sweeps too broadly. The distinction between reorganization and liquidation proceedings that applies to lenders appears normatively preferable.

For a reorganization proceeding, then, a general de-acceleration rule that is applicable in the absense of a contrary clause may be viewed as reflecting, in rough fashion, the non-bankruptcy rules underlying its treatment of non-delegable duties.[186] A liquidation proceeding, however—which centers around the sale of assets and (if permitted by bankruptcy law) the delegation of duties to third parties—does run up against, in a direct way, the justifications underlying both the general rule allowing contractual non-delegation clauses and the non-bankruptcy prohibition against non-consensual divesting of duties by a contracting party.[187] For the ability to de-accelerate in a liquidation proceeding would be meaningless without the concomitant right of assignment to a third-party and, almost inherent in the concept of a liquidation, release of the debtor from further obligation.[188] A bankruptcy rule that provided gener-

183. In this examination, I am not dealing with a situation in which a trustee (as distinguished from the debtor, the debtor-in-possession, or possibly even the debtor with new trustee management) will be performing the duty. These cases (which would largely be *individual* debtor cases) obviously raise distinct issues. For example, nothing I am saying here attempts to justify the trusteee of a famous opera singer assuming his obligation to sing the lead tenor role in *Aida*. *See In re* Taylor Mfg., 6 Bankr. 370 (Bankr. N.D. Ga. 1980).

184. *See supra* note 150.

185. *See supra* p. 890 & note 158. There are substantial reasons for allowing such clauses. *See supra* pp. 888-892.

186. This is so because the entity is emerging with essentially the same owners, and hence would not generally be considered to be a "delegation." *In re* Milton L. Ehrlich, Inc., 5 N.Y.2d 275, 157 N.E.2d 495 (1959). *See* RESTATEMENT (SECOND) OF CONTRACTS § 318 illustration 8 (1981). This, of course, assumes that there is no assignment to an entity other than the reorganized debtor, under Bankruptcy Code § 365(f), which would involve not only a de-acceleration but also an assignment.

187. *See* Arkansas Valley Smelting Co. v. Belden Mining Co., 127 U.S. 379 (1888); Crane Ice Cream Co. v. Terminal Freezing & Heating Co., 147 Md. 588, 128 A. 280 (1925).

188. While a corporation does not receive a discharge in a bankruptcy liquidation, Bankruptcy Code § 727(a)(1), the corporation almost certainly will thereupon dissolve under applicable state corporation law.

ally—even in the absence of a specific clause—for the acceleration of rights in a liquidation proceeding would, therefore, respect the non-bankruptcy rules on delegation in that it would protect not only the property rule established to deal with the special category of non-delegable duties[189] but also the "secondary" property rule that, in all cases, disallows discharge of the delegating party without express consent of the other party to the contract.[190]

The reasons for respecting this property rule in the bankruptcy context seem sensible.[191] Consider, first, the situation of unsecured lenders. The general common-law rule is that loan contracts are non-delegable.[192] Why is this so? Consider the long-term unsecured creditor—the creditor "disembodied" from any particular asset. For such a creditor, the question of who the debtor is may be of paramount importance. The decision whether or not to loan is based on such factors as knowledge of and confidence in the debtor, the ability to monitor the debtor, and so forth.[193] A liquidating debtor's assignment of an existing obligation to repay a loan would raise the same issues as underlie the common law's treatment of the assignment of a contract to make a loan.[194] In both cases, allowing the transaction has the effect of "discharging" the original debtor from any obligation and substituting a new party without the lender's consent.

Secured creditors and "property-specific" contract-holders (such as lessors) may seem to be in a different situation since they have identified property to look to in the event of non-performance. While this attachment to specific items of property may reduce the need to monitor, it is not likely to weaken substantially the interest in who the particular debtor

189. These represent *both* cases in which duties are generally non-delegable under applicable law and cases in which a contractual provision has made them non-delegable. *See supra* notes 177 & 179.

190. *See* Smith v. Wrehe, 199 Neb. 753, 261 N.W.2d 620 (1978); Western Oil Sales Corp. v. Bliss & Wetherbee, 299 S.W. 637 (Tex. Comm. App. 1927); RESTATEMENT (SECOND) OF CONTRACTS § 318(3) (1981).

191. All contracts with the federal government may be non-assignable for purposes of Bankruptcy Code § 365(c)(1), (e), & (f). *See* 41 U.S.C. § 15 (Supp. IV 1980); *In re* Adana Mortgage Bankers, 12 Bankr. 977 (Bankr. N.D. Ga. 1980). The justification for this rule is that the prohibition on assignment is designed " 'to secure to the United States the personal attention and services of the contractor,' . . . and to assure that the government 'might also know with whom it was dealing until the contract was completed and settlement made.' " *Id.* at 984 (citation omitted).

192. *See* Arkansas Valley Smelting Co. v. Belden Mining Co., 127 U.S. 379 (1888); Texas & N.O.R. Co. v. Phillips, 196 F.2d 692 (5th Cir. 1952); *In re* Adana Mortgage Bankers, 12 Bankr. 977 (Bankr. N.D. Ga. 1980); Frissell v. Nichols, 94 Fla. 403, 114 So. 431 (1927); Menger v. Ward, 87 Tex. 622, 30 S.W. 853 (1895); Rice v. Gibbs, 40 Neb. 264, 58 N.W. 724 (1894). The actual rule is a bit more limited: the non-delegation rule applies where "one of the duties sought to be delegated is the execution of a promissory note or other instrument of credit . . . ." J. CALAMARI & J. PERILLO, *supra* note 177, at 664; *see, e.g.*, E.M. Loew's v. Deutschmann, 344 Mass. 765, 184 N.E.2d 55 (1962); Lojo Realty Co. v. Estate of Isaac G. Johnson, 253 N.Y. 579, 171 N.E. 791 (1930). *See also* Bankruptcy Code § 365(c)(2).

193. Crane Ice Cream Co. v. Terminal Freezing & Heating Co., 147 Md. 588, 128 A. 280 (1925); *see infra* note 196.

194. *See supra* note 192.

is. For example, a secured party with inventory as collateral may care very much who the debtor is, because of concerns over property maintenance, levels of misbehavior, and so forth, even though the secured party may not monitor the debtor carefully (for precisely the reason that the decision as to the level of monitoring required is based, in the first instance, on an evaluation of the characteristics of the debtor).[195] Thus, it seems entirely correct that non-bankruptcy law also protects these people with a property rule by prohibiting non-consensual discharge of the original contracting party from underlying liability.[196]

This suggests that, even if one were suspicious of contractually created ipso facto clauses in general, a rule providing for the override of ipso facto clauses by an ability to de-accelerate in a reorganization proceeding,[197] but generally allowing acceleration in a liquidation proceeding, when coupled with a general rule prohibiting the non-consensual delegation of contractual duties, would be the preferred solution. Such a rule would respect the well-settled property rights that support the non-delegation rules of contract law.[198] General hostility to contractually created ipso facto clauses (which in itself seems unjustified)[199] should not obscure the fact that contract law's usual refusal to allow a delegation of duties without the consent of the other party to the contract, unless the delegator remains contractually responsible for performance, is not such an ipso facto clause, and should not be condemned along with them.

195. The pervasive inclusion of anti-assignment clauses in leases may suggest the desire to protect, through use of a "property rule," the intangibles that underlie the general non-delegation rule. Moreover, a number of executory contracts (such as for the delivery of "requirements" in the future) leave a seller in essentially the position of an unsecured creditor following each delivery. Arkansas Valley Smelting Co. v. Belden Mining Co., 127 U.S. 379 (1888). The Uniform Commercial Code gives a seller a limited right to reclaim goods delivered while the buyer was insolvent, although this right may be subject to competing claimants. U.C.C. § 2-702 (1972). *See In re* Samuels & Co., 526 F.2d 1238 (5th Cir.) (en banc), *cert. denied*, 429 U.S. 834 (1976). (This right has been given substantial recognition in bankruptcy. *See* Bankruptcy Code § 546(c); *In re* A.G.S. Food Systems, 14 Bankr. 27 (Bankr. D.S.C. 1980). Apart from this limited right, a seller who has a long-term contractual commitment but no security interest will find himself, after each delivery, to be an unsecured creditor.

196. *See supra* note 179; U.C.C. § 2-210 comment 6 (1972) (noting that non-assigning party has stake in reliability of person with whom he has contracted); Funk v. Baird, 70 N.D. 396, 295 N.W. 87 (1940) ("The personal convenants of the heirs may be better than those of the vendor, but the defendants are not bound to accept them . . . .")

197. Such an override would be accomplished by giving the debtor the ability to de-accelerate in a reorganization. Presumably this ability would apply to both lenders and other contract-holders, as the reasons underlying the rule for executory lenders of Bankruptcy Code § 365(c)(2) would be reflected in the more general rule. Again, there seems to be no persuasive reason to treat lenders of money separately from other extenders of credit (or supplies). *See supra* note 132.

198. It is likely that most "forced" bankruptcies will result in a reorganization rather than a liquidation or, alternatively, in dismissal of the petition. *See* Bankruptcy Code §§ 305, 706, 707; *In re* Luftek, Inc., 6 Bankr. 539 (Bankr. E.D.N.Y. 1980). As a consequence, protecting the property rights underlying general contract law's non-delegation rules, by generally allowing acceleration in liquidation proceedings, would not seem to trench unduly on a solution to any perceived "bankruptcy incentive" problem.

199. *See supra* pp. 888-892.

This suggests a fundamental flaw in the reasoning underlying the general ability to assign executory contracts and unexpired leases in Bankruptcy Code section 365. While Bankruptcy Code section 365(c) mirrors the "personal service" rules of non-delegation, it ignores the second property rule underlying the treatment of delegable duties under non-bankruptcy law. For that second rule only permits delegation of duties if the original obligor remains liable.[200] The override of that non-bankruptcy rule seems to be without normative justification.[201]

IV. The De-acceleration Principle, State-Created Priorities, and Bankruptcy Statutory Liens

We have explored the uncertain justifications underlying the application of bankruptcy's de-acceleration principle[202] to consensually-created arrangements. The de-acceleration principle, however, has another, quite separate, role to play in the bankruptcy process. Beginning in the late 1930's, changes made to the Bankruptcy Act of 1898[203] have consistently moved in the direction of refusing to recognize attempts by a state to elevate the claims of any one type of claimant in bankruptcy through the device of either a state-created priority[204] or a statutory lien effective only in bankruptcy (or a similar non-bankruptcy occurrence).[205] These at-

200. *See supra* notes 179 & 196.

201. The Bankruptcy Code is quite insistent on overriding this property rule. *See* Bankruptcy Code §§ 365(k), 727(b), 1141(c), (d). While Bankruptcy Code § 365(f)(2)(B) does require that adequate assurance of future performance by the assignee be provided prior to any assignment, this is not a substitute for the property rule. Rather, it reflects a general rule of contract law regarding delegation. Under this general rule, such assurances must be provided even where the original obligor remains ultimately liable. *See* U.C.C. § 2-210(1), (5) (1972); Funk v. Baird, 70 N.D. 396, 295 N.W. 87 (1940).

202. *See supra* pp. 879-881.

203. Chandler Act, ch. 575, 52 Stat. 840-940 (1938). *See* S. REP. NO. 1159, 89th Cong., 2d Sess. (1966); *In re* Federal's, 553 F.2d 509 (6th Cir. 1977); *In re* Telemart Enterprises, 524 F.2d 761 (9th Cir. 1975).

204. "Priorities are to be distinguished from property rights. . . . The priority creditor . . . has no property right, merely a statutory advantage to be given effect on distribution." J. MACLACHLAN, *supra* note 1, at 145. A brief history of the demise of state-created priorities is contained in *Analysis of H.R. 12889*, 74th Cong., 2d Sess. 201 (1936); 3A W. COLLIER, *supra* note 12, at 2053-54.

205. The 1938 legislation, which dropped the bankruptcy priority for state-created priorities, also expressly validated state-created statutory liens, but declared that they would be paid after administration and wage priorities. Chandler Act, ch. 575, § 67c, 52 Stat. 877 (1938). In 1952, an amendment struck down all statutory liens that attached to personal property and were not accompanied by "possession, levy, sequestration or distraint." Act of July 7, 1952, ch. 579, 66 Stat. 420. When this test proved unsatisfactory, Congress amended § 67c of the Bankruptcy Act of 1898 to strike down statutory liens that became "effective upon the insolvency of the debtor, or upon distribution or liquidation of his property, or upon execution against his property levied at the instance of one other than the lienor" or were not "perfected or enforceable at the date of bankruptcy against one acquiring the rights of a bona fide purchaser from the debtor on that date . . . ." 11 U.S.C. § 107c(1)(B) (1975) (repealed prospectively, effective October 1, 1979); *see* Kennedy, *Statutory Liens in Bankruptcy*, 39 MINN. L. REV. 697, 703-22 (1955). *See generally* Marsh, *Triumph or Tragedy? The Bankruptcy Act Amendments of 1966*, 42 WASH. L. REV. 681, 713-27 (1967).

tempts by a state were felt to contradict, in a fundamental way, the notion that "equality is equity." Initiation of a bankruptcy proceeding is not, under this view, a reason for calling forth a different set of allocative entitlements by any creditor or class of creditors than existed outside of bankruptcy. The refusal to recognize a state's attempt to influence directly bankruptcy's allocation rules has raised few, if any, eyebrows. Indeed, the opposite has occurred: the purported application of the de-acceleration principle has sometimes struck down state-created entitlements that, instead of suffering from the "bankruptcy only" problems of state-created priorities or bankruptcy statutory liens,[206] appeared to be all but indistinguishable from ordinary non-bankruptcy entitlements.[207]

What, if anything, is wrong with state-created priorities and bankruptcy statutory liens?[208] Surprisingly little critical attention has been directed to this inquiry.[209] Two questions, however, seem to be raised. First, is there any justification at all for a state's attempt to prefer a given type of creditor in bankruptcy? Second, if there is a justification for such an attempt, is there any reason to believe that the use of state-created priorities and bankruptcy statutory liens is not a proper way to implement those desired preferences?

Several reasons, other than simply political expedience or special interest group pressure, may explain a state's desire to provide a level of protection to certain types of claimants, instead of leaving the issue to the area of consensual security interests. First, non-consensual claimants, such

206. Hereinafter, statutory liens effective only in bankruptcy will be referred to as "bankruptcy statutory liens," to distinguish them from statutory liens of a normal sort, which have a recognized existence and validity in and out of bankruptcy.

207. *See infra* note 228; *see also* MacLachlan, *Improving the Law of Federal Liens and Priorities*, 1 B.C. IND. & COM. L. REV. 73 (1959). Since the date of these enactments, few statutes involving true state-created priorities or bankruptcy statutory liens have been tested. A possible example of such a statute was MASS. GEN. LAWS ANN. ch. 254, § 31 (West 1961). The statute "causes a lien to arise in favor of materialmen upon the adjudication in bankruptcy of certain contractors." N.W. Day Supply Co. v. Valenti, 343 F.2d 756 (1st Cir. 1965) (declaring the statute invalid in bankruptcy); *see also* Strom v. Peikes, 123 F.2d 1003 (2d Cir. 1941).

There has also been a lengthy debate over the validity of U.C.C. § 9-306(4) (1972) under these provisions. *See* Countryman, *Code Security Interests in Bankruptcy*, 4 U.C.C. L.J. 35, 45-49 (1971); Henson, *"Proceeds" Under the Uniform Commercial Code*, 65 COLUM. L. REV. 232 (1965).

208. With respect to ipso facto clauses, which are also directed specifically at the bankruptcy process, we were able to rely on a contractual model to tentatively justify their existence. *See supra* pp. 887-892. Such an explanation is obviously not available with respect to state-created liens and priorities.

209. Most commentators note, approvingly, that the refusal to recognize state-created priorities or bankruptcy statutory liens promotes national uniformity and furthers the goal of creditor equality by striking down state interference directed at the bankruptcy process. *See, e.g.*, *Analysis of H R. 12889*, *supra* note 204, at 201; 3A W. COLLIER, *supra* note 12, at 2053-54; Kennedy, *supra* note 205, at 699-70; Comment, *Statutory Liens Under Section 67c of the Bankruptcy Act: Some Problems of Definition*, 43 TUL. L. REV. 305 (1969); Note, *Statutory Liens Under Section 67c of the Bankruptcy Act*, 62 YALE L.J. 1131 (1953). These reasons are unsatisfying in light of the numerous instances of deference to non-bankruptcy entitlements. *See In re* Telemart Enterprises, 524 F.2d 761 (9th Cir. 1975).

as tort creditors, pose special problems to which application of a consensual model seems largely inapplicable. Should a state believe that a certain level of deterrence is desirable to protect against certain behavior, a system of priority entitlements to "victims" of that behavior may help the state achieve that goal, at least with respect to some types of torts.[210] By giving non-consensual tort claimants priority over general unsecured creditors, those general creditors (whose chance of repayment has been made more risky than under a proportional payment scheme) will have an increased incentive to monitor the debtor to reduce the likelihood of such torts occurring in the first place.[211] Second, a state may have reason to believe that, with respect to a particular class of claimants, there is systematic advantage-taking of them by other creditors, because of an informational disparity or other reasons.[212] Intervention by a state, in giving this class of claimants priority entitlements, may be a way of addressing a form of market inefficiency.[213] Finally, the state is itself likely to be a claimant (oftentimes, as in its taxing capacity, a non-consensual one), in which case the level of priority it provides is a part of the cost calculus it has decided on in setting its rates (whether tax rates or otherwise).

There may be inefficient interferences by a state as well, due to politically-motivated causes.[214] But the relevant point is that state interventions may sometimes be efficient or otherwise justified and, in any event, are generally recognized in bankruptcy. The bankruptcy law upholds state-created entitlements unless the entitlement is directed specifically at the bankruptcy process.[215] Unless there is some reason to believe that inefficiently motivated instances of state interference are more common with

210. *Cf.* Posner, *The Rights of Creditors of Affiliated Corporations*, 43 U. CHI. L. REV. 499, 506 (1976) (discussing involuntary extensions of credit in negotiation-based model). To be sure, insurance may also serve some of these goals. But it is unlikely that insurance will be able to curb that behavior as well as a priority rule. Therefore, even if one were to have an insurance scheme, one might nonetheless want to have a priority scheme as well.

211. The issue of priority among creditors that is raised by a state-created priority or bankruptcy statutory lien does not deal directly with incentives to have the debtor behave in a socially desirable fashion. Equity-holders come after creditors, whether or not a state-created priority is created or recognized. (Indirectly, of course, there are incentives arising from monitoring and the cost of credit.) Direct incentives are created by such things as removing the discharge right with respect to certain debts. *See* Bankruptcy Code § 523(a)(6) (non-discharge of debts resulting from intentional torts); *In re* Shawsheen Dairy, 47 F. Supp. 494, 498 (D. Mass. 1942); Note, *Tort Claims and the Bankrupt Corporation*, 78 YALE L.J. 475, 479-80 (1969).

212. *See* Schwartz, *supra* note 53, at 30-33.

213. The case for this form of intervention may be difficult to make. But once a state has made such a determination, the justifications for second-guessing by a federal bankruptcy rule may likewise be slender. *See* Eisenberg, *supra* note 16, at 957-58; Schwartz, *supra* note 53, at 36.

214. *See, e.g.*, R. POSNER, *supra* note 35, at 404-07; Peltzman, *Towards a More General Theory of Regulation*, 19 J.L. & ECON. 211 (1976); Posner, *Theories of Economic Regulation*, 5 BELL J. ECON. 335 (1974).

215. *See* Bankruptcy Code § 545 (distinguishing between valid and invalid statutory liens); 124 CONG. REC. H11,114 (Sept. 28, 1978).

respect to state-created priorities or bankruptcy statutory liens than with respect to other forms of state-created entitlements, inquiry into the validity of an entitlement should first be directed at the *form* of the intervention. The relevant inquiry is whether there is anything particularly undesirable about state-created priorities or bankruptcy statutory liens that justifies the blanket prohibition against them in the bankruptcy process and that distinguishes them from other forms of non-bankruptcy entitlements.

State-created priorities and bankruptcy statutory liens attempt to direct allocative entitlements in bankruptcy, but in this respect they are indistinguishable from other types of non-bankruptcy entitlements routinely recognized in bankruptcy.[216] The difficulty with state-created priorities and bankruptcy statutory liens is that they suffer from the same "bankruptcy incentive" problems previously discussed in connection with ipso facto clauses.[217] Since the rules of the bankruptcy process set the minimum level of entitlements against which non-bankruptcy "workouts" must be evaluated,[218] a creditor enjoying a state-created priority effective only in bankruptcy will demand to be treated similarly outside of bankruptcy as well.[219] A creditor with such a priority might push for initiation of the bankruptcy process when it is not in the aggregate interests of the creditors to do so.[220] But because a creditor with a state-created priority does not necessarily have that priority right outside of the bankruptcy process, he must negotiate with the other creditors in order to receive that preferential treatment. These negotiations, because they are likely to involve a number of unsecured creditors, may involve free-rider problems that will not only make negotiations costly but also may lead ultimately to an inefficient use of the bankruptcy process.[221] Moreover, unlike the case of consensually negotiated agreements, there is no persuasive reason to believe that this state of affairs involves policing or other sorts of efficiencies that may justify retention of the system.[222] Therefore, at our creditors' bargain

216. Occasionally, a state-created priority will be distinguished from a lien on the ground that its holder is paid only after all "true" lienholders have been paid, and therefore is somewhat suspicious. *See* Comment, *supra* note 209. From the perspective of general creditors, however, the effect is the same: the person with the entitlement must be paid in full first. *See* Strom v. Peikes, 123 F.2d 1003, 1006 (2d Cir. 1941).

217. *See supra* pp. 890-892.

218. *See supra* p. 867.

219. Pre-bankruptcy payments to the holder of a state-created priority would have added protection against attack by the trustee. Bankruptcy Code § 547(b)(5) provides that a trustee may not avoid such a transfer unless it "enables such creditor to receive more than such creditor would recieve if (A) the case were a case under chapter 7 of this title; (B) the transfer had not been made; and (C) such creditor received payment of such debt to the extent provided by the provisions of this title." *Id.*

220. *See supra* p. 876.

221. An inefficient use of the bankruptcy process will occur if the negotiations break down. *See supra* pp. 890-891.

222. *See supra* pp. 887-892. Since the priority rights of these people are not fixed until bank-

meeting, if it were clear that a particular creditor was going to receive a state-created priority or bankruptcy statutory lien, we would expect the creditors as a group to view it as in their interest to give that creditor a lien that is valid both in and out of bankruptcy. Refusing to recognize state-created priorities and bankruptcy statutory liens simply requires a state that wishes to give someone a "priority" to do so by means of an entitlement that is good in and out of bankruptcy.

The puzzle with respect to state-created priorities and bankruptcy statutory liens is why a state would ever enact an entitlement that is good only in bankruptcy.[223] Part of the answer is that, at least based on reported cases from the last twenty-five years or so, few such statutes have been passed.[224] Ironically, bankruptcy law's failure to recognize entitlements only good in bankruptcy may be viewed as justified, not on the ground that it is protective of something fundamental to the bankruptcy process itself, or even of general unsecured creditors, but rather on the ground that it protects claimants in the aggregate (and ultimately the debtor) against presumptively illogical actions by state governments, which accrue to no one's advantage.[225]

From another perspective, however, the greater irony may be that bankruptcy law's obsession with formulating a rule on the subject may have done more harm than good. For while the prohibition on state-created entitlements good only in bankruptcy may occasionally strike down an aberrant state statute designed to create an irrational form of entitlement, the presence of the federal rule has, meanwhile, led to substantial confusion in its application.[226] For if an entitlement is enforceable both in

ruptcy (or similar event) they do not enjoy the protections of a first-in-time rule such as exists in Article 9 of the U.C.C. and which is a necessary part of the efficiencies (if any) of that system. *See* Jackson & Kronman, *supra* note 53, at 1161-64.

223. Even assuming that the legislative process results in inefficient decisions some of the time, it is not clear what group would lobby for a state-created priority instead of, say, a full status lien or what group would oppose full status lien treatment (if the choice were solely between that and a state-created priority). Prior to 1938, when the bankruptcy laws contained an open invitation to create state-created priorities, it is conceivable that this was viewed as a safe way to proceed.

224. *See supra* note 207. While there have been several cases striking down state-created priorities and bankruptcy statutory liens, these cases have normally not involved "bankruptcy incentive"-type statutes, *see infra* note 228. Even a statute such as U.C.C. § 9-306(4) (1972) would not create a "bankruptcy incentive" on the part of a secured creditor, as that section usually gives such a secured creditor less than he would get outside of bankruptcy. 2 G. GILMORE, *supra* note 4, at 1337-38 ("§ 9-306(4) is the reverse of . . . [a state-created priority or bankruptcy statutory lien], since it sharply cuts back the secured party's rights when insolvency proceedings are instituted"). Ironically, U.C.C. § 9-306(4) may be a statute that gives a "bankruptcy incentive" to unsecured creditors in the event of insolvency. This result might seem to be equally undesirable.

225. The creditors as a whole are not benefited because the costs of such a system are greater than the costs associated with a full-status lien system, nor does any discernable group appear to be benefitted. *See supra* note 223.

226. Indeed, the pre-1938 explicit recognition of state-created priorities by the Bankruptcy Act of 1898 may itself be the root of the evil. *See supra* note 223.

and out of bankruptcy, there is no reason, stemming from the justifications underlying condemnation of state-created priorities or bankruptcy statutory liens, to refuse recognition of the entitlement.[227] The failure to recognize this simple point has led to a variety of confusing and ill-considered decisions by appellate courts.[228] The rule against state-created priorities and bankruptcy statutory liens, if correctly understood, may be harmless and even occasionally beneficial. But since the reasons for the rule are misperceived, the resulting misapplications may engender more uncertainty than continuation of the rule is worth.[229]

227. There would be an independent reason to refuse recognition of the entitlement if it was decided that the state intervention was otherwise inefficient. *See* Schwartz, *supra* note 53, at 33-37. Few, if any, judicial decisions even reach this question, much less have adequate data on which to base a reasoned decision to strike down the state entitlement.

228.

The Ninth Circuit, for example, has had an extremely difficult time distinguishing between legitimate state preferences and invalid state-created priorities and bankruptcy statutory liens. This difficulty is likely to increase credit costs because it creates uncertainty. A California statute provided that all the assets of an agent selling checks and money orders would be impressed with a trust in favor of the principal and the trust would remain until the amount due to the principal was paid. The Ninth Circuit, after noting that this would "relieve check and money order principals from the burden of tracing commingled funds," concluded that:

> Giving effect to the provisions of [the California statute] . . . would open the door to state creation of priorities in favor of various classes of creditors by labeling such priorities as "trusts." This would tend to thwart or obstruct the scheme of federal bankruptcy.

Elliott v. Bumb, 356 F.2d 749, 759-55 (9th Cir.), *cert. denied*, 385 U.S. 829 (1966). The holding misperceives the nature of the inquiry. All state-created entitlements act in favor of some group of creditors, but bankruptcy law generally recongizes them nonetheless The inquiry, which *Elliott v. Bumb* ignored, is whether the statute applied only in bankruptcy. Without further inquiry into the efficiencies of a *particular* application of statutory trust doctrine there is nothing to suggest that these impressed trusts should be considered contrary to bankruptcy policy. The legislative history of the Bankruptcy Code recognizes, in discussing "tax trusts," that there is little difference between a "trust" and a "lien." 124 CONG. REC. H11,114 (Sept. 28, 1978). Similarly, in *In re* Leslie, 520 F.2d 761 (9th Cir. 1975), the Ninth Circuit stopped at an examination of a label, although the state statute in question is of doubtful utility given that it used a priority scheme that seems flawed. *See supra* pp. 904-05. The efficient solution—although not one open to the Ninth Circuit—would have been to strike the statute down *in toto*. *See* Eisenberg, *supra* note 16. In *Leslie*, California law had established a system of priorities for payment of creditors of a liquor dealer upon transfer of a liquor license. Citing Grover Escrow Corp. v. Gole, 71 Cal. 2d 61, 65, 453 P.2d 461, 463, 77 Cal. Rptr. 21, 23 (1969), the Ninth Circuit stated that the statute established "statutory priorities, not statutory liens," and struck the scheme down as inconsistent with the Bankruptcy Act of 1898. It is true that *Grover Escrow Corp.* invoked the word "priority," but it is also clear that it meant "lien":

> The precise issue is whether that section precludes a creditor from establishing priority over the escrowed proceeds of such a transaction by attachment or garnishment. We conclude that section 24074 represents a mandatory and exclusive scheme for payment of creditors of liquor license transferors, giving creditors who comply with that section priority over those who employ any form of levy on the proceeds.

71 Cal. 2d at 62, 453 P.2d at 461, 77 Cal. Rptr. at 21. Again, why is *this* state-created entitlement bad, when others are upheld? Since this statute was applicable both in and out of bankruptcy, nothing in the Bankruptcy Act of 1898 condemned its use.

229. *See* 2 G. GILMORE, *supra* note 4, at 1287 ("As appellate judicial review becomes more sporadic, it also becomes more unpredictable. . . . If [a federal judge] exercises his own judgment in a bankruptcy case, the result may well be aberrational.") (footnote omitted).

Conclusion

The bankruptcy rules governing state-created priorities and bankruptcy statutory liens reflect a normative view of the world that is consistent with the creditors' bargain model presented in this Article. But the application of those rules to particular facts seems haphazard, as the application is usually uninformed by any consistent normative model. At other places the Bankruptcy Code itself seems to deviate, without explanation, from a model that seems to illuminate and justify much of the bankruptcy process.

Bankruptcy law has, for too long, been molded and interpreted without any systematic questioning or understanding of its normative role in a larger legal, economic, and social world. This Article asserts that not only is there a coherent normative theory justifying a bankruptcy system that deals with inter-creditor questions, but also that we would be better able to formulate and apply principled bankruptcy rules if we would give systematic and critical attention to the impact of those rules on non-bankruptcy entitlements. That the answers to creditor-allocation questions posed by the bankruptcy process will often be difficult does not excuse the failure of the statutory drafters, bankruptcy judges, and the bankruptcy bar from even identifying the questions they purport to be answering.[230] Greater attention to the relevance of the creditors' bargain model in formulating the non-discharge related rules of the bankruptcy process appears to be a promising, and necessary, beginning to a principled development of our bankruptcy laws.

230. *See* Eisenberg, *supra* note 16, at 998:

> Although a Congress fully cognizant of the issues addressed here might nevertheless adhere to its existing reform decisions, it ought to do so knowing the costs of poor coordination with nonbankruptcy law. Unfortunately, the new act not only reflects these costs, but to some degree reinforces bankruptcy law's isolation, a development that can be expected to generate future discontinuities between bankruptcy and nonbankruptcy law.

Id.

[10]

The University of Chicago Law Review

VOLUME 54 NUMBER 3 SUMMER 1987

Bankruptcy Policy

Elizabeth Warren†

Bankruptcy is a booming business—in practice and in theory. From headlines about LTV's 10,000-page filing to feature stories about bankrupt consumers (usually Joe-and-Ethel-whose-names-have-been-changed-to-protect-their-privacy), bankruptcy has become an increasingly popular news item in the past few years. Both organized labor and the consumer credit industry made concerted efforts to put bankruptcy issues before the public in their recent pushes to amend the new Bankruptcy Code. Lawyers have been drawn to the bright lights. Firms that did not have a single bankruptcy practitioner five years ago now field large bankruptcy sections. Bankruptcy seminars have been sellouts. And—perhaps the most reliable indicator of increased attention and activity—bankruptcy jokes have begun to make the rounds.

As bankruptcy has flourished in the popular press and in law practice, it enjoys what may be looked back on as a golden age in academe. Law review articles on bankruptcy abound, and enrollments in bankruptcy and related commercial law classes are reported to be on the rise across the country. Uncertainty about how

† Professor of Law and Jay H. Brown Centennial Faculty Fellow in Law, The University of Texas School of Law. I am grateful to Julius Getman, Douglas Laycock, Lynn LoPucki, Richard Markovits, Jay Lawrence Westbrook, and Kimberly Winick. They have taken time to read and argue, and they have caused me to write a better article than I would have written without them.

the new Bankruptcy Code will be interpreted and dramatic shifts in the strategic use of bankruptcy have prompted reporters to call law professors for in-depth interviews or quotable statements for the evening news. Rumor has it that requests for expert help are on the increase and consultation fees are up for more than a few academics specializing in bankruptcy. All in all, it's not a bad time to know something about bankruptcy.

In the midst of this attention and noise and clamor, however, there is a quiet but persistent question: what function does bankruptcy serve? After the statutory arguments have been exhausted and the cases have been explored, most academic discussions of bankruptcy can be distilled to this question. Currently, the policies endorsed to support bankruptcy pronouncements are wide-ranging and, at the extremes, very much in opposition. Despite the critical importance of different policy presumptions, the policy elements underlying most discourses are asserted only obliquely, and they are rarely challenged directly.[1]

Professor Douglas Baird and I have undertaken to debate in writing the basis of bankruptcy policy.[2] We offer this paired set of essays in the spirit of the old "Point-Counterpoint" segment of television's "Sixty Minutes." While we cannot promise the dripping invective and snarling satire that made that old feature so delightful, we can try to push forward the debate by making direct challenges and responses. In the belief that a good fight is far more interesting than a host of polite compliments and careful hedgings, Professor Baird and I undertake an aggressive and irreverent debate.

In order to join issue more clearly and to narrow the focus of the debate somewhat, Professor Baird and I have agreed to debate

---

[1] A recent exception to the practice of ignoring disagreeable policy differences was the debate between Professor Kripke and Professors Jackson and Schwartz. See Homer Kripke, Law and Economics: Measuring the Economic Efficiency of Commercial Law in a Vacuum of Fact, 133 U. Pa. L. Rev. 929 (1985); Thomas H. Jackson and Alan Schwartz, Vacuum of Fact or Vacuous Theory: A Reply to Professor Kripke, 133 U. Pa. L. Rev. 987 (1985).

[2] Professor Baird has coauthored much of his work with Professor Thomas H. Jackson. Although Baird has written the other article in this exchange without Professor Jackson, it seems fairly clear from their jointly authored works as well as from their individual pieces that they are in substantial agreement on the basic policy premise of bankruptcy and the implications of that policy in state-federal conflicts. On the other hand, it seems equally clear that since Professor Baird is the only one participating directly in this exchange, it would be most unfair to refer constantly to Professor Jackson's views as well. Therefore, I refer in this article to Professor Baird as the proponent of the points with which I disagree, without absolving his absent coauthor one whit, and I refer to the opinions expressed in their joint pieces as those of Professor Baird. I expect that my frequent coauthor, Professor Westbrook, may suffer the same fate.

the basis of bankruptcy policy in the context of business bankruptcies. While we both believe that the principles we discuss have significance in a consumer setting as well, we recognize that additional issues should be a part of a discussion about consumer bankruptcy policy and that those issues would make the discussion even more complex.

Professor Baird and I hold very different views of the purpose bankruptcy law serves. I see bankruptcy as an attempt to reckon with a debtor's multiple defaults and to distribute the consequences among a number of different actors.[3] Bankruptcy encompasses a number of competing—and sometimes conflicting—values in this distribution. As I see it, no one value dominates, so that bankruptcy policy becomes a composite of factors that bear on a better answer to the question, "How shall the losses be distributed?"

By contrast, Baird has developed a coherent, unified view of bankruptcy that revolves around a single economic construct. According to Baird, the only goal of bankruptcy is to enhance the collection efforts of creditors with state-defined property rights.[4] He explains that all bankruptcy laws are to be tested by a single measure: whether they enhance or diminish the creditors' collective benefits.[5] With that construct, Baird purports to answer a host of wide-ranging questions and translate his policy into specific statutory recommendations.[6]

As Baird and I begin this debate, I am acutely aware that we disagree not only about what bankruptcy policy should be, but also about how that policy should be derived. Baird begins with hypothetical behavior and ends with firmly fixed answers. I begin with a historical observation about legal structures, I surmise the concerns of the drafters, and I end only with tentative conclusions and

---

[3] Readers interested in futher exposition of these views should see, e.g., Elizabeth Warren and Jay Lawrence Westbrook, The Law of Debtors and Creditors: Text, Cases, and Problems 3-7 (discussing the concept of leveraging and how various elements of the collection system interrelate), 219-26 (discussing claims and distribution) (1986) ("Debtors and Creditors").

[4] See, e.g., Douglas G. Baird and Thomas H. Jackson, Corporate Reorganizations and the Treatment of Diverse Ownership Interests: A Comment on Adequate Protection of Secured Creditors in Bankruptcy, 51 U. Chi. L. Rev. 97, 103 (1984) ("Corporate Reorganizations") (bankruptcy law should focus only on the interest of those "who, outside of bankruptcy, have property rights in the assets of the firm").

[5] Id. at 103-04; Douglas G. Baird and Thomas H. Jackson, Cases, Problems and Materials on Bankruptcy 31 (1985) ("Baird and Jackson Casebook").

[6] Corporate Reorganizations at 110 (cited in note 4) (once the idea of collectivism is accepted, "analysis of adequate protection of secured creditors in bankruptcy is straightforward").

more complex questions. Baird presumes that there can be a simple answer to explain all of bankruptcy, and that the relationship between statutory law and modification of the behavior of debtors and creditors is known and can be predicted in new circumstances. I see bankruptcy as a more complex and ultimately less confined process than does Baird.

In this paper I discuss our differing views, explaining first the central policy justification of bankruptcy as I see it. In the second section, I contrast my conception of bankruptcy with Baird's view, and I take up his application of theory to the difficult problem of undersecured creditors. In the spirit of forthright debate, I try to expose my ideas enough to provide a target for Baird, and I take direct and specific aim at his work.

I. The Central Policy Justification of Bankruptcy: Coping with Default in an Integrated System

Discussing the debtor-creditor system is much like focusing a camera. Different elements of the system are always in view, but depending on where the focus is directed, different features of the system take on greater importance. I want to begin the discussion of bankruptcy by looking briefly at the role the debtor-creditor system plays in a much broader pattern of promise enforcement.

A. Default and Contract Enforcement

The debtor-creditor system is itself part of a larger, integrated order of public enforcement of promises between individuals. An analysis of promise enforcement should begin with contract law—the laws enforcing private promises—and come full circle with bankruptcy law—the laws sanctioning default on private promises.[7] Each element of this system balances against the other.

A contract is not a legally enforceable obligation to do a promised thing. Holmes observed that the understanding of contract should always be modified by the statement that the law requires only that the promise be performed or that the money equivalent be paid.[8] A bankruptcy scholar would point out that Holmes's focus is still too narrow: a contract requires a party to do the thing

[7] Obligations to pay money arise from several sources, including, of course, tort law and property law. Even criminal actions can create payment obligations. When regarded as a separate legal specialty, however, rules about repayment can best be studied in the context of the contract—the prototype for most debtor-creditor relations. For ease of discussion, I use that single example here.

[8] Oliver Wendell Holmes, The Common Law 236 (Mark DeWolfe Howe ed. 1967).

promised or to pay the money equivalent *or* to discharge the promise through the bankruptcy system. That is a positive description—a statement of the law as it is, with contract enforcement and bankruptcy default. I am willing to argue that it is also a normative description—a statement of precisely what the law should be to create a coherent system of promise enforcement.

Default is a distasteful idea, one to which we give as little attention as possible in discussing legal theory and in training young lawyers. One of my dyspeptic joys in introductory commercial law classes is to point out how lofty we contract scholars are (and I am always careful to mention my hope to be counted among the chosen): once we have cleverly proven that a promise is legally enforceable and have even gone so far as to detail the appropriate remedy, we contract scholars strike our colors and retire from the field, satisfied we have completed the serious labor. In our view, there can be little more work requiring the talents of a thoughtful and expensive scholar. Getting the money paid is a matter of course, or of honor, or—if it should come to that—of grubby technical steps.

Notwithstanding these prejudices, it is useful to pause occasionally to reflect that a system of enforceable promises necessarily involves an escape valve—a way to avoid the enforcement of those promises when sufficiently compelling circumstances arise. Contract law today can be relatively coherent as an intellectual scheme in part because of debtor-creditor law.

The enforcement scheme in debtor-creditor law acknowledges values different from those central to contract law. Idiosyncratic factors involved in the changed circumstances of debtors in extreme financial distress become important. Debtors may not be able to meet their obligations for a host of different reasons. Their stupidity, greed, misfortune, bad judgment, or inadequate foresight may leave them unable to pay. They may not be able to pay over the short term or the long term. They may be victims of their own mistakes or of unforeseeable circumstances. Contract law need not take account of the values relevant to sanctioning debtor default, because these values are accounted for in the debtor-creditor collection scheme. Without the refined and balanced system of debtor-creditor law—which includes a well-developed concept of bankruptcy—contract law itself would look very different, and its enforcement would be considerably more constrained.

The definition of an enforceable contract allows some leeway to consider social concerns. Contract principles such as impossibility, mutual mistake, and more recently, duress and unconscionability undercut any naive view of "strict" enforcement. But for the point of this paper, it is sufficient to note that once an agreement has been struck, the subsequent inability of a party to pay or the high cost of payment is rarely an overt feature of contract doctrine. Relatively strict enforceability of contract can prevail precisely because the debtor-creditor system instills a measure of temperance, an ability to respond to changed circumstances, a notion that enforcement should not offend deeply held social norms.[9]

Default—or nonpayment—of debt has long been an essential feature of a system of promise enforcement. Centuries before bankruptcy law became an integrated part of the collection scheme, default existed. Biblical jubilees, medieval English debtor sanctuaries, and poorhouses are evidence of society's past attempts to balance rightful demands for payment with some possibility of escape.[10] When organized forgiveness has been unavailing, debtors have devised their own nonpayment plans. Debtors have been known to flee the jurisdiction, to threaten their creditors, or—as an extreme measure—to die.[11] Even today, with corporate debtors and risk-spreading creditors, a significant feature of the debt collection system is the possibility of escape from payment through a variety of maneuvers, both legal and extralegal. Anyone who ever extends credit faces the possibility that repayment will not be forthcoming. Interest is structured, among other things, to pay the creditor for assuming the risk of nonpayment.

B. Default and the Collection System

The current debt collection system has two primary responses

---

[9] For a fuller discussion of bankruptcy as an exercise in moral ambiguity, in which policymakers hold conflicting and vaguely articulated views of appropriate bankruptcy policy, see Teresa A. Sullivan, Elizabeth Warren, and Jay Lawrence Westbrook, As We Forgive Our Debtors (forthcoming 1987); Teresa A. Sullivan, Elizabeth Warren, and Jay Lawrence Westbrook, The Use of Empirical Data in Formulating Bankruptcy Policy, 50 L. & Contemp. Prob. 195, 198, 235 (1987) ("Use of Empirical Data"); Teresa A. Sullivan, Elizabeth Warren, and Jay Lawrence Westbrook, Folklore and Facts: A Preliminary Report From the Consumer Bankruptcy Project, 60 Amer. Bankr. L. J. 293, 312 (1986).

[10] See, e.g., The Bible, Deuteronomy ch. 15, verses 1-18 (on jubilees); W. S. Holdsworth, 3 A History of English Law 303-07 (3d ed. 1923) (on sanctuaries); Peter J. Coleman, Debtors and Creditors in America: Insolvency, Imprisonment for Debt, and Bankruptcy, 1607-1900 at 4-5 n.1 (1974) (on poorhouses).

[11] See, e.g., Joseph W. McKnight, Protection of the Family Home from Seizure by Creditors: The Sources and Evolution of a Legal Principle, 86 S.W. Hist. Quart. 369, 393 (1983); Man Killed While Trying to Collect Debt, St. Louis Post-Dispatch 4A, col. 4 (Oct. 24, 1984); Barry Siegel, A Tragic Dilemma: Woman's Stand, Death Sparks Debate Over Lien Laws, Dallas Times Herald 2A, col. 2 (Nov. 18, 1984); Charlotte Grimes, Cheated by Life, Lien Victim Found Revenge in Death, St. Louis Post-Dispatch 1A, col. 1 (Aug. 26, 1984).

to a debtor's default: state collection law and federal bankruptcy law. When discussing the two collection schemes, it is important to bear in mind that property and contract rights are not synonymous with collection rights. Bankruptcy is only a collection scheme; it necessarily depends on other legal rules for the determination of substantive rights underlying bankruptcy claims.[12] Whether a contract is enforceable, a tort has been committed, or an owner has clear title to a piece of land are issues of substantive state or federal law. Similarly, state collection law is different from the underlying substantive law. State collection law presupposes the enforceability of an underlying claim (as does bankruptcy) and focuses on the rights of a creditor to extract the payment owed (as does bankruptcy). State collection law is about judgments, statutory liens, voluntary security interests, exemptions, garnishment, prejudgment remedies, and so on. The state system and the bankruptcy system are both only collection systems.

Although this distinction between substantive rights and collection rules might seem obvious, it is important to the policy debate, which often centers on the degree to which bankruptcy law should "rely" on underlying state law. The answer depends on which underlying state law is under discussion. The real issue is not whether bankruptcy law—or state collection law, for that matter—relies on state law for the definition of substantive rights. The issue is whether the state collection and distribution scheme presumptively should be the federal scheme. That bankruptcy builds on state substantive law does not require it to build on state collection law.

It would, of course, be possible to create a single, fully integrated debt collection scheme rather than the separate state and federal schemes now in effect. But even a unified scheme would have to consider two prototypes of default: first, the single default where only one creditor complains about repayment and the remaining creditors are evidently (even if only temporarily) content with their repayment prospects; and second, the debtor's widespread default and collapse in which every creditor's prospects for repayment are sharply diminished. These two kinds of default involve some overlapping issues about appropriate collection rights, and a factual continuum from a single default to complete collapse better describes the world that includes the two extremes. None-

[12] There are, of course, substantive rights created by federal law as well. The language is less burdensome if "state law rights" is read to encompass all substantive rights other than those created in federal bankruptcy.

theless, the policy issues involved in the two exemplary circumstances differ importantly, and they must be addressed separately whether they are part of one collection system or two.

The current debt collection system treats these issues in different fora: state collection laws cope with a wide spectrum of limited defaults, while the bankruptcy scheme concentrates on default in the context of the debtor's imminent collapse. The state collection scheme occasionally deals with complete collapse, but overall it is rationalized in order to serve a wide variety of collection needs. The federal bankruptcy scheme, by contrast, reckons with a much more limited factual context, and with very different legal devices such as discharge of debt and distribution of unavoidable losses. The different factual contexts change the focus of the policymaking decisions of state collection law and bankruptcy.

C. Default and State Collection Law

A central purpose of state debt collection law is to provide a means for collection of a single unpaid debt. State collection law swings into action on the complaint of a single creditor, and it provides that creditor an avenue to pursue payment of the obligation owed to it. In enforcing the rights of one creditor, state collection law does not address the possible consequence that the collection will render the debtor unable to pay its remaining creditors.

Notwithstanding how much law professors and newspapers focus on complete collapse, a state system that specializes in the collection of single debts makes a great deal of sense. When one creditor demands payment through the state law system, other creditors are not necessarily affected. Many collection lawsuits are brought because a debtor denies liability on a debt or because the debtor has other disputes with the creditor. Sometimes the debtor is simply slow to pay, or irrationally stubborn, or downright vindictive. State collection law is a system in which one creditor can isolate the debtor's default and enforce repayment. A complex factual inquiry into the consequences for others of the collection of the single debt need not be a part of every collection lawsuit.

Of course, paying one creditor may affect the debtor's ability to repay other creditors. In the race of the diligent, the slower creditor always runs the risk that by the time it arrives, the assets will be depleted. Moreover, the state law system permits enhanced collection rights for certain creditors, which increases the likelihood that the unfavored creditors will find the debtor's bones bare. Article 9 of the Uniform Commercial Code (UCC) and the state law of liens create priority arrangements that permit a creditor to isolate certain property and to ensure that it will be used to pay that creditor before it is sold or seized to profit anyone else. These state law priority systems create what sometimes turn out to be effective rank-orderings of collection rights.

In some cases, then, state collection laws will resolve the relative collection rights of parties when a debtor collapses. But it does not follow that the state system is well-suited to the circumstances of debtor collapse. I submit that the state law system is *not* well-suited to those circumstances precisely because it necessarily must consider too broad a range of possible debtor-creditor relationships and follow collection principles inconsistent with those raised in the circumstances of complete collapse.

State collection laws are many and varied. To pick a single example from UCC Article 9, the consequences of delay in filing a security interest involve very different considerations depending on whether the delay takes place in the context of single-debt collection or complete collapse. In Article 9, only a purchase money creditor attempting to beat a previously perfected security interest needs to worry about the time elapsed between the debtor's receipt of the property and the time the creditor files its notice. All other creditors can delay as they wish, risking only that another creditor will file on the same property ahead of them. Public notice is an option creditors can exercise at any time, but their security interests are enforceable against debtors and others who are aware of the security interest even if the creditor avoids the public notice system.[13] In the context of bankruptcy, however, a creditor who delays during the 90 days preceding bankruptcy will find that its security interest is invalid.[14] The Article 9 provisions are drafted with a concern for the creditor's costs and inefficiencies, and for the possibility that the debtor and creditor may wish to keep their deal private. In the context of complete collapse, however, the policy interests shift: the risk of collusion between the debtor and a favored creditor and the possibility that fraudulent schemes may be imposed on the remaining creditors outweigh the advantages of letting the parties keep the security interest secret.

There are many other examples of policy differences between

---

[13] UCC § 9-312(3), (4) (purchase money security interest, if filed within specified time limits, has priority over previously perfected security interest in same collateral); id. § 9-312(5) (if no exception applies, the first creditor to file wins); id. § 9-501(2) (creditor with security interest has rights and remedies outlined in Article 9; no reference to any need for the creditor to file to make these rights enforceable against the debtor).

[14] 11 U.S.C. § 547(b) (1982).

state law debt collection and bankruptcy. In Article 9 alone, there are special repossession rights that vary from one set of circumstances to another, different perfection rules depending on the type of collateral, and priority schemes that depend on who is demanding what interest in the collateral. All these options give secured creditors different bundles of rights if the debtor defaults, and all wrestle with a wide variety of possible circumstances of the debtor, the creditor, the property, and parties ancillary to the transaction.

This is not the place for an extended discussion of the balancing of numerous interests behind various state collection law rules. My point is simply that it is naive to think that these interests, and the appropriate balance among them when a single creditor is asserting a claim against a debtor, are also optimal legal rules when a debtor faces collapse. The impact of repossession rights when a debtor faces collapse requires specialized analysis—best undertaken in the context of a comprehensive system designed to deal with just that circumstance. But, because state collection law must balance debtor and creditor rights in a variety of factual circumstances, state priority systems do not automatically fit the bill.[15]

State collection law and bankruptcy law also differ in their central policy considerations because they rest on fundamentally different collective premises. The two systems make very different adjustments for the survival of creditors' unpaid claims. Although it is an obvious point, it is worth noting that the premise of state law rank-ordering is that no claim is extinguished. Nothing in state law discharges the lawful claim of a creditor who is unable to collect. A creditor seeking collection may face a debtor with insufficient assets to pay a debt, but the state system merely streamlines the collection operation to ensure that the creditor can be the first to collect if the debtor's circumstances improve. Similarly, a creditor may face a debtor whose assets are tied up by Article 9 security interests, but just as the state system puts the Article 9 creditor at the head of the collection line, state law finds a place in line for every other creditor.[16] And state law carefully establishes proce-

[15] There are, of course, some state law actions designed specifically to deal with collapse and the multiple creditors who may be affected. Receiverships and assignments for the benefit of creditors are collective actions. They are, however, often little more than burdensome state law versions of bankruptcy that have become outmoded and are seldom used if federal bankruptcy is available.

[16] UCC § 9-301(4) develops the process by which lien creditors can secure their next-in-line position, limiting the first creditor's future advances under the original security agreement.

dures by which the diligent creditor can make a judgment survive in perpetuity.[17] State law promises that if the creditor is persistent, the corporate debtor can escape payment only through death: the corporation must cease operations and return its charter to the state. Nothing in state law allows a corporation to continue to operate while denying the enforceability of a lawful debt.[18]

To structure collection rules and priorities in the context of inextinguishable claims is to create one kind of system. To graft that set of collection rules and priorities onto a system that discharges debt is to create a very different collection system—one that should be evaluated separately and not accepted simply because some of the rules make sense in a different, state law scheme.

D. Default and Bankruptcy

By contrast with state law, which sees only one default, bankruptcy begins with a presumption of default on every obligation the debtor owes.[19] Although some debtors are able to repay all their debts in bankruptcy, the statutory scheme presumes that some creditors will not enjoy repayment in full. Bankruptcy law aims first to conserve and divide an estate that cannot meet all its obligations, and second to terminate the rights of unpaid creditors. Unlike state law, which considers innumerable circumstances of default, bankruptcy law is sharply focused on the consequences of a debtor's imminent collapse.

The difference from state collection law is fundamental. Bankruptcy disputes do not share the debtor-versus-creditor orientation of state collection law. In bankruptcy, with an inadequate pie to divide and the looming discharge of unpaid debts, the disputes center on who is entitled to shares of the debtor's assets and how these shares are to be divided. Distribution among creditors is not incidental to other concerns; it is the center of the bankruptcy scheme. Accordingly, bankruptcy disputes are better characterized as creditor-versus-creditor, with competing creditors struggling to push the losses of default onto others. The Bankruptcy Code reflects this orientation: a significant part of its distributional

[17] See Debtors and Creditors at 43-44 (cited in note 3) for a discussion of dormancy and revivor actions.

[18] This rule is of particular significance in the case of corporations, since they have no exempt assets with which to continue operations. If a creditor is sufficiently motivated to pursue its claims, a corporation cannot escape payment and survive.

[19] See, e.g., In re Hoffman, 51 Bankr. 42, 46 (W.D. Ark. 1985) ("the filing of a bankruptcy acts to accelerate the maturity of all debts"); In re Manville Forest Products Corp., 43 Bankr. 293, 297 (S.D.N.Y. 1984) (bankruptcy accelerates all claims).

scheme is oriented toward establishing priorities among creditors.

The battle between secured and unsecured creditors has commanded much interest, but the Bankruptcy Code tackles a wide variety of other distributional issues as well. Some rights are destroyed in bankruptcy, and some are preserved. Priority distributions reorder the competing interests of employees, taxing authorities, fishermen, and farmers. Landlords and business partners receive special treatment. Parties to executory contracts hold an identified place in the bankruptcy pecking order. The beneficiaries of state statutory liens find their rights reordered in bankruptcy. Ordinary course creditors and creditors making contemporaneous exchanges discover that their positions differ from other unsecured creditors. Creditors lending to consumers are distinguished from creditors lending to businesses. Banks with setoff rights are treated differently from banks not in a setoff position. This list is suggestive rather than definitive, but it serves to show that the Bankruptcy Code is concerned with making hard choices about which creditors belong where in a financial hierarchy.[20] These are choices about distribution and redistribution, and they are not controlled by state law.

The distributional design of the Code is even more thorough than the straightforward state law's rank-ordering of easily identified creditors such as fishermen and farmers. The bankruptcy system goes so far as to anticipate the consequences of default on a host of potential creditors, including, for example, future tort claimants who have not yet discovered their injuries or their legal rights and a government agency that might uncover toxic wastes and demand that a debtor clean them up. Bankruptcy law recognizes these rights even though they may not be mature under state law at the time of the bankruptcy filing. In the state law system, these creditors would simply wait until they discovered the injuries and then would sue one at a time for the appropriate remedy.[21] They would take their debtors—tortfeasors or toxic polluters—as they found them when their claims matured, whether the debtors were fat with profits or stripped to a hollow shell after earlier creditors had concluded other disputes.

---

[20] These various provisions of the Bankruptcy Code can be found at 11 U.S.C. §§ 507, 365(d)(3)-(4), 303(d), 365(a)-(c), 545, 547(c)(1), (2), (7), 553 (1982 & 1985 Supp.).

[21] Of course, some claimants join class action suits, but even these suits have a one-at-a-time quality: the class sues on behalf of all the victims of a particular wrong, but the class still lines up with other creditors trying to reach the debtor for payment of other obligations.

But because bankruptcy recognizes that the pre-bankrupt debtor will not survive to be sued another day, its distributional scheme necessarily focuses on how to deal with future claimants. Several alternatives are possible. Bankruptcy's distributional scheme could leave future claimants to bear their losses in full, refusing to compensate them at all and effectively barring their future claims. If, instead, their rights to compensation continue notwithstanding the bankruptcy, the distributional consequences of bankruptcy will depend on whether the debtor succeeds or fails in any reorganization attempt. Still a third distributional scheme is created if the future claimants are participants in a distribution plan and provisions are made for their eventual—if limited—recovery.

The Bankruptcy Code clearly rejects the alternative of leaving future claimants uncompensated. It defines "claim" broadly to pull future creditors into the debtor's distribution plan and to require participation by anticipated claimants.[32] The Code does not specifically address how to establish funds to pay future claimants and determine appropriate payout priorities, and as a result, the courts must take on the difficult task of devising workable plans.[33] Nonetheless, it is clear that dealing with the effects of default on future claimants was intended to be a significant feature of bankruptcy's distributional scheme.

The Bankruptcy Code accomplishes other distributional ends less directly. By providing for impairment of state law collection rights in a court-supervised reorganization, Chapter 11 of the Bankruptcy Code gives bankrupt businesses another opportunity to succeed. The opportunity may not often result in genuine success, but the reports of Toys-Я-Us, Wickes, Continental Airlines, Evans Home Products, and a host of other bankruptcy success stories serve as a reminder that at least some Chapter 11 reorganizations conserve and maximize the wealth of the debtor's estate for the benefit of all claimants—an important objective of bankruptcy.

But the revival of an otherwise failing business also serves the distributional interests of many who are not technically "creditors" but who have an interest in a business's continued existence. Older employees who could not have retrained for other jobs, customers

---

[32] 11 U.S.C. § 101(4) (1982).

[33] See, e.g., In re Johns-Manville Corp., 36 Bankr. 743, rearg. denied, 39 Bankr. 234 (S.D.N.Y. 1984). Professor Roe wrestles with the problem at a more conceptual level than have the courts, and suggests creative approaches to compensating mass torts victims. See Mark J. Roe, Bankruptcy and Mass Tort, 84 Colum. L. Rev. 846 (1984).

who would have to resort to less attractive, alternative suppliers of goods and services, suppliers who would have lost current customers, nearby property owners who would have suffered declining property values, and states or municipalities that would have faced shrinking tax bases benefit from the reorganization's success. By giving the debtor business an opportunity to reorganize, the bankruptcy scheme acknowledges the losses of those who have depended on the business and redistributes some of the risk of loss from the default. Even if dissolution is inevitable, the bankruptcy process allows for delay, which in turn gives time for all those relying on a business to accommodate the coming change.

Congressional comments on the Bankruptcy Code are liberally sprinkled with discussions of policies to "protect the investing public, protect jobs, and help save troubled businesses,"[24] of concern about the community impact of bankruptcy,[25] and of "the public interest" beyond the interests of the disputing parties.[26] These comments serve as reminders that Congress intended bankruptcy law to address concerns broader than the immediate problems of debtors and their identified creditors; they indicate clear recognition of the larger implications of a debtor's widespread default and the consequences of permitting a few creditors to force a business to close.

These comments are also a reminder that, while the broader effects of business failure can be elusive to measure, they are nonetheless very real. Congress—whether out of a crass concern about reelection or a superior view of the deeper social implications of business failure in a highly integrated society—accepted the idea that bankruptcy serves to protect interests that have no other protection. The older employee, the regular customer, the dependent supplier, and the local community are important; and bankruptcy attends to many of their concerns, regardless of whether they have rights recognized at state law.

Bankruptcy does not, of course, offer complete protection to all those who might be affected by the outcome of a bankruptcy

---

[24] 124 Cong. Rec. 32392 (Sept. 28, 1978) (statement of Rep. Edwards).

[25] Bankruptcy Reform Act of 1978, Report of the Committee on the Judiciary, H.R. Rep. No. 95-595, 95th Cong., 1st Sess. 53-62 (Sept. 8, 1977), reprinted in 1978 U.S. Code, Cong. & Admin. News 6014-23 (letter from Judge Conrad Cyr responding to congressional request for information about cases with special community impact). See also, e.g., Report of the Commission on the Bankruptcy Laws of the United States, Part I, H.R. Doc. No. 93-197, 93rd Cong., 1st Sess. 72 (Sept. 6, 1973) (discussion of the "overriding community goals and values" in bankruptcy).

[26] 124 Cong. Rec. 33990 (Oct. 5, 1978) (statement of Sen. DeConcini).

dispute. Businesses can still sell off their assets, dismantle their corporations, and flee the state or even the country, leaving a wake of disappointed expectations. For those decisions, the businesses are left largely to their own self-interested decisions. To recast it in economic lingo, the *debtor* is always free to redeploy the firm's assets. But the creditors in a bankruptcy proceeding are not.

Chapter 11 offers only limited protection against the *creditors'* making the decision to dissolve the business.[27] The creditors must defer some collection rights in Chapter 11 in order to give the debtor an opportunity to continue as a viable business. But Chapter 11 is not a license for the old management to continue the same old business; in order to get a second chance, the debtor business may have to be restructured and slimmed down to become newly competitive. And even with radical changes, the business may fail. Chapter 11 bankruptcy is only a chance, available in limited circumstances and offering limited help. But it is a valuable, deliberately created chance nonetheless.

E. Distributive Rationales in Bankruptcy

By definition, the distributional issues arising in bankruptcy involve costs to some and benefits to others. Enforcing the state law collection rights of secured creditors often comes at the cost of defeating the state law collection rights of unsecured creditors whose claims are discharged without payment. A priority payment to one unsecured creditor necessarily leaves less for the remaining creditors. The debtor's estate—and thus its creditors—profits from assigning a favorable lease, but this costs the landlord whose lease specifically provided for no assignments. The benefits reaped by the employees or suppliers relying on the continuation of a business are purchased at the expense of every creditor who gives up valuable state collection rights as part of the plan to allow the debtor business a second chance at success.

It might be reasonable to ask about the legitimacy of forcing losses on those with lawful expectations of repayment. The difficulty with this question, however, is that it posits that bankruptcy is the "cause" of the cost. Bankruptcy is not the cause of the

[27] The debtor is left with decisions such as whether to move or terminate the business, but the creditors, with less information and less at stake, are restricted in their ability to force a dissolution that the debtor does not want. If one were so inclined, one could restate this argument in the terms of economic analysis, noting that the law permits the entity with superior information and a greater stake in the business to make these critical decisions regarding deployment of the business's assets.

cost—it is merely the distributor of the cost. The cost of default is occasioned by the debtor's inability to repay.

Without a bankruptcy system, someone would still bear the costs of default. Perhaps, under the state law collection system, those costs would be borne entirely by unsecured creditors or employees or suppliers or landlords or creditors with loans secured by inventory that is difficult to monitor. But speculation on what would happen at state law is nothing more than the substitution of a different distributional scheme—one created indirectly by focus on the collection of a single debt rather than one created deliberately with an overriding attention to widespread default.

Even if there were no legal scheme to distribute the costs of default, the losses would be distributed by some method. The distribution of losses might be determined by creditor speed (who first backs up to the warehouse with big trucks) or strength (who can carry away the most while others look on) or by debtor favoritism (who gets the first call when the debtor decides to give up). Indeed, outside bankruptcy, it is not clear as an empirical matter whether losses are distributed according to the state law scheme or according to creditor strength, debtor favoritism, or some other factor. But the point is that the costs must be distributed in some manner. Bankruptcy is simply a federal scheme designed to distribute the costs among those at risk.

On what basis does bankruptcy law distribute these costs? Below are some of the important features for ordering distributional priorities. The list is only partial, but it identifies some of the key issues.

1. *Relative ability to bear the costs of default.* Some creditors are not likely to have anticipated the risks of termination of the business, and others may face especially acute difficulties in absorbing the costs of a debtor's default. For example, a debtor's employees may be particularly ill-suited to bear the costs of default. Employees are among the creditors least likely to have spread the risks of default. They seldom are able to contract with several different employers, and losing a paycheck will quickly deplete modest savings. The Bankruptcy Code reflects a concern for these creditors, granting a priority to limited employee wage and retirement fund payments.[28]

2. *Incentive effects on pre-bankruptcy transactions.* The Bankruptcy Code also requires creditors to disgorge payments re-

[28] 11 U.S.C. § 507(a)(3)-(4) (1982). Code provisions regarding consumers' deposits with businesses also reflect these principles. Id. § 507(a)(6).

ceived from the debtor in the days preceding bankruptcy.[29] Protecting these payments would encourage aggressive collection efforts when debtors' financial positions are obviously deteriorating—perhaps rewarding those whose demands needlessly forced into bankruptcy a debtor who otherwise could have escaped complete collapse. This rule has exceptions for creditors whose transactions do not immediately worsen the debtor's pre-bankruptcy position. For instance, the Code exempts the contemporaneous exchange creditor, the secured purchase money lender, and the ordinary course creditor from having their pre-bankruptcy transactions unraveled.[30] Such transactions facilitate continued operation of a tottering business, and they are essential if the business is to have a chance to avoid bankruptcy.[31]

3. *Similarities among creditors.* The Code's treatment of the debtor's executory contracts illustrates another distributional objective of bankruptcy: treating like creditors alike. Before the bankruptcy filing, the debtor may abrogate a contract at the cost of incurring damage liability to the aggrieved party. A subsequent bankruptcy filing gives the party an unsecured damage claim. The debtor in bankruptcy also may abrogate an executory contract, giving the aggrieved party a similar unsecured damage claim.[32] Were the debtor in bankruptcy unable to abrogate its contracts, some contract creditors might be able to jump the priority queue and extract payments in excess of their unsecured claims by forcing performance on economically infeasible obligations.[33] Instead, all contract partners face the same bankruptcy risk. The requirement that unsecured creditors be classified together and receive pro rata distributions is another attempt to treat creditors with similar

[29] Id. § 547(b)(4).

[30] Id. § 547(c)(1)-(3).

[31] Secured credit may also be essential to weak businesses and, accordingly, the effects of bankruptcy laws on the role secured credit plays in nonbankruptcy transactions is another important distributional concern. To the extent that pre-bankruptcy security interests are enforced in the bankruptcy scheme, the Code encourages their nonbankruptcy use. But to the extent that security interests do not give unfettered collection rights in bankruptcy, secured creditors are discouraged from relying solely on their security interests for complete protection. The "unreliability" of a security interest in a bankruptcy creates pressure on secured creditors to minimize the likelihood that the debtor is driven to complete collapse and a bankruptcy filing.

[32] 11 U.S.C. § 365(a) (1982 & 1985 Supp.).

[33] Sometimes, however, a technical distinction can make an enormous difference in abrogating executory contracts. For instance, the landlord who declares a default before the debtor files bankruptcy will find herself in a very different position from the landlord who attempts to declare a default just minutes after the filing. See id. § 365(c)(3).

characteristics alike.[34]

4. *Owners bear the loss when a business fails.* An almost axiomatic principle of business law is that, because equity owners stand to gain the most when a business succeeds, they should absorb the costs of the business's collapse—up to the full amount of their investment. The Code provides that the equity owners participate in distributions or maintain ownership interests following reorganization only if the creditors have been paid in full or if the creditors consent to their continued ownership.[35] Moreover, by incorporating equitable subordination principles into bankruptcy, the bankruptcy scheme forces the same last-place distribution on those who are nominally listed as creditors but who nonetheless exercise ownership control.[36]

5. *Benefit to the bankruptcy estate.* In some cases, a creditor's nonbankruptcy rights can be impaired, forcing it to share in the losses of bankruptcy, in order to give the failing business a chance to survive. For example, the Bankruptcy Code refuses to honor a landlord's "default on bankruptcy clause."[37] This benefits the bankruptcy estate if the lease is profitable for the debtor. If the lease is unprofitable, the debtor can choose instead to reject the lease and to limit the resulting damages according to bankruptcy rules rather than the terms of the agreement. The Code's treatment of labor contracts even more acutely highlights the concern for maximizing the bankrupt debtor's estate. By requiring that a "balance of the equities" dictate the status of a labor contract, the Code suggests that the distributional aim of bankruptcy should be tailored to the facts of the case—permitting impairment of labor contracts if it is essential for a successful reorganization and rejecting it if it is not.[38] Thus, even though Congress is other-

---

[34] Id. § 544(a).

[35] Notwithstanding this statement, I have no illusions about the absolute priority rule as it has worked its way through the courts. The courts have attempted to fashion a workable principle out of an unflinching rule; they must face the reality that the current owner is essential to the success of the reformed business and his continuing participation in the business may come at the price of equity participation. See, e.g., In re Ahlers, 794 F.2d 388, 402-03 (8th Cir. 1986) (farmer's contribution of labor sufficient to permit continuing equity ownership); In re Star City Rebuilders, 62 Bankr. 983, 988-89 (W.D. Va. 1986) (stockholder-president of debtor corporation could keep "worthless" stock even over objections of impaired creditors).

[36] Equitable subordination has been developed by the courts and incorporated by reference into 11 U.S.C. § 510(c) (1982). See, e.g., Matter of Pancho's Intern., Inc., 26 Bankr. 5, 8 (M.D. Fla. 1982).

[37] 11 U.S.C. § 365(b)(2)(A)-(C) (1982 & 1985 Supp.).

[38] Id. § 1113(c)(3). Just how seriously the courts take that balancing is indicated by Wheeling-Pittsburgh Steel v. United Steelworkers, 791 F.2d 1074, 1085 (3d Cir. 1986), where

wise solicitous of the peculiarly vulnerable position of employees, some losses may be thrust upon them in order to permit the business to survive.

The list offered here is preliminary at best, and any example given undoubtedly could be explained by several distributional rationales. The point of this paper, however, is not to explore every value weighed in bankruptcy's distributional scheme, but to establish that such values exist, that Congress gives them credence, and that collectively they have a significant impact on the bankruptcy process.

F. Sorting Cases in a Dual System

A process such as bankruptcy, designed to consider the rights of more than two parties and to distribute the losses occasioned by the debtor's failure, is necessarily expensive. It requires more detailed factual inquiries into both the circumstances of the debtor and the conflicting claims of many creditors than does state collection law. The expense of this process is justified by a normative conclusion that spreading the losses of default by an organized scheme, developed by Congress and supervised by the courts, is superior to an unmonitored distribution by powerful creditors or self-interested debtors.

No law requires that firms defaulting on all their obligations do so only in bankruptcy. Instead, the scheme permits an efficient self-selection by the affected parties. The cheaper,[39] less comprehensive state law system operates until a party can show that the bankruptcy system is required.[40] The collecting creditor can select the appropriate enforcement device, or—more often—the debtor can decide that state collection law no longer provides an adequate framework to resolve the debtor's increasing financial problems. But once a party appropriately petitions for bankruptcy, the reso-

---

the court required that the debtor show that it could not succeed in reorganization without impairing the rights of the employees.

[39] The state law system is a less expensive way to resolve a *single* dispute than is bankruptcy. If all the outstanding obligations against the debtor are at issue, however, the scale economies in resolving the various claims in a single forum probably make bankruptcy the "cheaper" system.

[40] The debtor, of course, can call for the bankruptcy system by a voluntary filing. 11 U.S.C. § 301 (1982). If the debtor is in widespread default, some creditors can force an involuntary bankruptcy. Section 303(b) specifies that only creditors with claims that are not contingent and that total in excess of $5,000 in unsecured debt can force an involuntary bankruptcy. Typically, to demonstrate widespread default, three creditors must sign the petition. Only if the debtor has fewer than twelve total creditors will one petitioning creditor suffice. See id. §§ 303(b)(1)-(2).

lution is in bankruptcy without further dispute.[41]

Of course, not all businesses that terminate do so in bankruptcy. Any debtor may expire without bankruptcy by simply relinquishing its corporate charter. This observation does not, however, indicate that state law and bankruptcy serve the same functions. There are a host of reasons why a debtor might expire outside bankruptcy. Undoubtedly, some debtors dissolve without bankruptcy because they have paid their creditors and no losses need be distributed. In some small businesses, the owner is personally liable for the loans, so that dissolution of the corporate shell is of little interest to the creditors.[42] Still other businesses collapse without formal bankruptcy proceedings when the distribution they settle upon meets creditors' expectations of what they would have received in bankruptcy. This latter alternative is especially likely when a single secured creditor will clean out the business in or out of bankruptcy; the distribution of losses will be clear to all concerned.

Nonetheless, a very real issue—and one often ignored—is whether the barriers to involuntary filings discourage too many creditors who should force a defaulting creditor into the bankruptcy process. Some businesses collapse outside bankruptcy because information or transaction costs preclude any interested party from filing. Creditors with small claims may reasonably conclude that the costs of an involuntary filing are too great to make bankruptcy an attractive alternative. In effect, these creditors often depend either on the debtor or on creditors with larger claims to make filing decisions—even when the small-claim creditors would gain from a bankruptcy resolution. Some other creditors may have enough at stake to make it worthwhile for them to institute an involuntary filing, but they will not file if they lack the information to make a rational decision. They too may rely on the filing either of the debtor or of other creditors with superior information. The rub, of course, is that small or uninformed creditors must rely on parties who may be able to profit more (legally or otherwise) outside bankruptcy and who are disinclined to lead the debtor into bankruptcy.

Thus, practical economics effectively ensures that deserving parties sometimes will be denied the protections of bankruptcy. To

---

[41] The bankruptcy court can refuse the case if it believes the filing is not in the best interests of both the debtor and its creditors. Id. § 305.

[42] See Sullivan, Warren, and Westbrook, As We Forgive Our Debtors (cited in note 9) for a discussion of the number of entrepreneurs who have guaranteed their business's loans.

the extent that Chapter 11 offers the debtor a chance to reorganize, it may mitigate this effect by enticing the debtor to file. But the Code also exacerbates the inaccessibility of bankruptcy by imposing stiff penalties for wrongful involuntary filings, thus discouraging creditors from filing unless they are very certain that their choice to file will be upheld in court.

Because the bankruptcy system relies on private parties to initiate proceedings, it necessarily presumes information and transaction costs are sufficiently small to permit rational choices. If this empirical assumption is unfounded, the bankruptcy system cannot operate effectively and its distributional objectives will not be accomplished. To give statutory protections that the beneficiaries reasonably cannot use is to fail to implement stated bankruptcy policies.

But to paper over the differences between debt collection decisions in the context of a single troublesome debt and complete debtor collapse, by pretending that the same rules must be applied all the time, will not make either the differences or the costs go away. Two different kinds of problems must be resolved: extracting repayment from the debtor who fails to repay a single debt and redistributing the losses from a debtor's imminent failure. Even when these two problems are meshed into a single collection system, bringing each into play at the appropriate time involves costs of selection. Selection costs can be avoided only if the law is designed to respond inadequately to the problems it is charged with resolving. To force the detailed examination now required only in bankruptcy every time a debtor defaults or to resolve all debtor defaults in the one-at-a-time, first-come-first-served pattern of state law would avoid selection costs, but only at the greatly increased costs of inapt solutions and less than optimal results. Some choices about applicable law must be made within the debt collection system. The costs of resolving collection problems stem from the different kinds of problems to be resolved—not from the creation of a system designed to resolve them.

G. Preliminary Conclusions: A Premise That Raises More Questions

While I hope that it is useful to have distinguished the policymaking thrust of state collection law from that of bankruptcy and to have identified the distributional rationale of bankruptcy, it may be more valuable to examine what I have not done. I have not offered a single-rationale policy that compels solutions in particular cases. I have not given any answers to specific statutory issues.

I have only identified normative considerations that may drive legislative and judicial decisions.

For a hard-nosed commercial lawyer (once again, I aspire to be among the chosen), the obvious question is: what good is it to identify the premises of bankruptcy law if they won't yield any specific answers? Aside from the fact that debating these issues is good, clean fun, what does it accomplish?

Even if it does not compel specific answers to hard questions, identifying the premise of bankruptcy has a very real impact on how those questions are answered. If the central policy justification is nothing more than a single economic construct, specific conclusions with systemwide impact follow neatly from an abstract principle.[43] But if the justification for bankruptcy is also distributional, the relevánt inquiry is necessarily larger: what are the values to be protected in the distributional scheme, and is the implementation scheme effective? The questions become more difficult, and the answers, while less certain, take into account many more of the considerations important to a reasonable decision.

A policy that focuses on the values to be protected in a bankruptcy distribution scheme and on the effective implementation of these values assists the decision-making process even if it does not dictate specific answers. This approach illuminates the critical questions. The distributional objectives of bankruptcy cannot be considered without inquiries into many issues, including who may be hurt by a business failure, how they may be hurt, whether the hurt can be avoided, at what cost it can be avoided, who is helped by the business failure, whether aid to those helped offsets the injury to those hurt, who can efficiently evaluate the risks of business failure, who may have contributed to the business failure, how they may have contributed, whether the contribution to failure serves other useful goals, who can best bear the costs of business failure, and who expected to bear the costs of business failure—just to name a few. These questions are normative, and each contains essential empirical questions as well.[44]

Bankruptcy policy has always rested on an unarticulated

---

[43] Baird describes as "straightforward" the process by which he reasons from collectivism to how undersecured creditors should be able to collect for pendency interest. Corporate Reorganizations at 110 (cited in note 4).

[44] The implementation issues in bankruptcy also put a premium on trying to identify the likely effects of a particular proposal. Any inquiry into whether distributional objectives can be met through the current bankruptcy scheme necessarily requires a pause to consider the empirical elements of the inquiry. See Use of Empirical Data at 196-202 (cited in note 9).

blend of empirical assumptions and normative conclusions.[45] The approach I describe denies that the uncomfortable normative issues can be avoided by playing a narrow game of logic. My approach also exposes and highlights the empirical assumptions underlying specific bankruptcy policy decisions. Even if few academics are moved to explore more empirical bankruptcy questions,[46] the inquiry at least suggests caution as to decisions that depend critically on empirical considerations when the decision maker is unarmed with facts.[47]

My approach does not assume that current bankruptcy policy is unfailingly rational, either normatively or empirically. In the current distributional scheme, some creditors may enjoy preferences over others who, according to the distributional values articulated earlier, are more deserving. Or, the current scheme may thwart well-considered distributional objectives because the implementation is faulty and too few interested parties are able to invoke the bankruptcy process. The current system may be flawed, but the point of this analysis is to highlight the questions appropriate to exploring bankruptcy's functions, and to caution that normative considerations and empirical evidence are critical to evaluating any bankruptcy rule.

The difficulty of the process does not mean that the considerations amount to fuzzy "do equity" preachments of the hopelessly confused, who leave good results to good people and assume that ideas and analysis have no content. Instead, the questions are tough and specific. The distributional premise of bankruptcy is implemented through a difficult and complex tapestry of empirical presumptions interwoven with normative concerns, some of which I have tried to identify here. The process yields better, but never complete, answers to specific bankruptcy questions. There are easier solutions and easier solutions are seductive. A focus on the difficulty of the appropriate questions helps stiffen the spine against easy answers and makes the task of imperfect search for the illusive answer a little more tolerable.

II. Baird's Approach: Collectivism Alone

Professor Baird's view of the bankruptcy world is much neater than mine. He explains that there is a single justification for bank-

---

[45] Id. at 198-99.

[46] My pessimism is explained in id. at 217-22.

[47] See id. at 233-35.

ruptcy: enhancing the collective return to the creditors. He also explains that there is only one interest to be protected: the interest of those "who, outside of bankruptcy, have property rights in the assets of the firm filing a petition."[48] Baird has rejected the notion that any values other than collectivism may be important in fashioning bankruptcy policy. As the following passage indicates, he at times recognizes the questions that lead eventually to a complex, multifactored analysis:

> Consider the "rehabilitation" goal of a Chapter 11 proceeding. No one, to our knowledge, argues that keeping a firm intact is *always* a good thing. Yet as soon as one concedes that a reorganization may not always be desirable, one is faced with the problem of understanding and articulating *why* reorganizations are favored in the first place and *how much* should be given up to facilitate them.[49]

Yet Baird evidently sees the questions he poses as either unanswerable or too silly to answer, for, having identified them, he says no more. He simply observes:

> The economy of an entire town can be disrupted when a large factory closes. Many employees may be put out of work. The failure of one firm may lead to the failure of those who supplied it with raw materials and those who acquired its finished products. Some believe that preventing such consequences is worth the costs of trying to keep the firm running and justifies placing burdens on a firm's secured creditors.
>
> We think that this view is, as a matter of bankruptcy policy, fundamentally wrong.[50]

Without further discussion, Baird concludes that such attempts are "beyond the competence of a bankruptcy court."[51]

Baird makes a point he can defeat by making it too big. Because bankruptcy will not *always* save a company, and because *sometimes* the cost of saving the company is too high, this must *never* be a goal of any bankruptcy policy. Baird refuses to acknowledge the possibility that bankruptcy might give a corporation a limited opportunity to succeed—an opportunity that balances the cost of trying to the creditors against the likelihood of eventual

---

[48] Corporate Reorganizations at 103 (cited in note 4).

[49] Id. at 99-100 (original emphasis, footnote omitted).

[50] Id. at 101-02 (footnote omitted).

[51] Id. at 102.

success. He acknowledges neither the potential benefit of a second chance nor the possibility that bankruptcy policy might aim toward a broad balance between the competing interests of the debtor, the creditors, and the many others who may be injured by the debtor's collapse.

Baird also considers the role of other distributional issues in bankruptcy and concludes that they should play none. He explains, for example, that the question of whether secured creditors should be paid ahead of anyone else "is not one peculiar to bankruptcy law" and then does little more than assert that the arguments for or against favoring the payment rights of secured creditors

> would apply with equal force to any group given favored treatment under nonbankruptcy law. The desirability of secured credit—or other nonbankruptcy property rights—is ultimately not a bankruptcy question and attempting to transform it into one creates incentives that are perverse and counterproductive.[52]

Thus, the distributional issues involved in determining the creditors' legal pecking order are, according to Baird, the same whether the debtor is in default on a single obligation or in a state of complete collapse.

Having dispensed with any other policy considerations, Baird is ready to turn to his single justification for bankruptcy: enhancing the collective return for creditors who have identified property rights.[53] Here Baird purports to use only careful logic to answer some of the most intractable bankruptcy problems, all the while avoiding any discussion of the distributional consequences of his work. The difficulty with Baird's approach is that collectivism alone won't get him where he is going. He necessarily uses—even if he does not discuss—distributional principles. Moreover, Baird endorses the wholesale use of the state law distributional scheme, but he does not defend the distributional rationale of that scheme, nor does he address the possibility that the state scheme was designed

---

[52] Id. at 129, 130.

[53] Baird describes collectivism as the "unique function of bankruptcy" and explains that "at its core" bankruptcy is designed only to further collectivism. Id. at 105, 100. Equally important, in his articles on corporate reorganization and on toxic wastes in bankruptcy, Baird nowhere suggests that any other value or rationale might be a part of the bankruptcy system. See, e.g., Douglas G. Baird, The Uneasy Case for Corporate Reorganizations, 15 J. Legal Stud. 127 (1986); Douglas G. Baird and Thomas H. Jackson, *Kovacs* and Toxic Wastes in Bankruptcy, 36 Stan. L. Rev. 1199 (1984).

to resolve questions significantly different from those to which he applies it.

Baird is engaged in a game of pulling rabbits from other hats. He may actually have a distributional principle to defend; he could argue that state law better distributes risks between secured and unsecured creditors than does current bankruptcy law. We could debate that conclusion, but even that debate would accept the premise that bankruptcy is designed to resolve difficult distributional choices. Instead, Baird purports to avoid distributional concerns—and the attendant normative and empirical issues—by discussing only the "neutral" principle of collectivism. I believe Baird only diverts the debate from the central issues.

A. Collectivism: The Test that Isn't

Collectivism provides a useful way to examine some bankruptcy problems. Baird shows how the need for collectivism can explain why the bankruptcy system substitutes a single, lower-cost action for expensive, multiple individual actions.[54] His analogy between state collection law and the wild car races of "It's a Mad, Mad, Mad, Mad World"[55] makes a delightful story that helps explain a very important function of bankruptcy: bankruptcy calls a halt to the superaggressive, wasteful, and potentially damaging creditor activity permitted by state law.

My dispute with Baird centers instead upon his attempts to use collectivism not only to explain significant features of the bankruptcy system, but also to justify the entire system and to provide answers to specific, complex questions. Baird sees collectivism as something of an intellectual yardstick, a tool that he can use to determine whether a particular bankruptcy proposal is good or bad—solely by measuring whether it promotes or impairs collectivism.[56] Yet Baird ultimately uses collectivism, once a useful theme in a more complex bankruptcy system, to obscure a very different analysis.

Baird chooses to test his collectivist principle in an *American*

---

[54] Baird and Jackson Casebook at 33-34 (cited in note 5).

[55] Douglas G. Baird and Thomas H. Jackson, Teacher's Manual: Cases, Problems and Materials on Bankruptcy 12-13 (1985).

[56] Baird describes as follows the process for justifying any deviation from state law:

> [W]e examine the protection afforded to secured creditors in bankruptcy, asking, first, what exactly the secured creditors' nonbankruptcy rights are and, second, whether any modification of those rights is necessary in order to preserve or enhance the firm's assets for the general benefit of the investor group.

Corporate Reorganizations at 101 (cited in note 4).

Mariner situation where he wrestles with the very difficult question of how to determine appropriate rights for the undersecured creditor during a pending bankruptcy proceeding.[57] Baird observes that creditors often have interests hostile to each other in the resolution of a bankruptcy case. The secured creditor is often interested in immediate liquidation, repossession, and repayment from the sale of the repossessed collateral. By contrast, the unsecured creditors—who are likely to receive little or nothing in a liquidation—are interested in allowing the company to retain the collateral and to make one more try at reorganization. Secured creditors claim that unsecured creditors are trying to deny them access to their collateral and to risk its eventual loss, while unsecured creditors claim that secured creditors are destroying the reorganization before it can begin. Baird resolves this impasse with the measuring stick of collectivism: collectivist goals will be met only if the bankruptcy estate (effectively, in Baird's example, the debtor and the unsecured creditors) bears the interest costs of using the secured creditor's collateral during the period of the reorganization and repayment plan.[58] According to Baird, only if all secured creditors—including the undersecured—receive post-petition interest will collectivism be served.

Baird illustrates his thesis with a hypothetical debtor who has only one asset worth $10,000, and one secured creditor owed at least $10,000. Baird observes that if the property would bring $10,000 now and the creditor could invest the $10,000 at 6 percent in treasury bills, in a year the creditor could have $10,600 from a

---

[57] Id. at 114-16. The reference is to In re American Mariner Industries, Inc., 734 F.2d 426 (9th Cir. 1984). The *American Mariner* problem—that Baird proposes to answer using the "straightforward" analysis of collectivism—has proven to be one of the most intractable for the courts, with at least three different circuit opinions emerging as the dispute grows. Compare American Mariner, 734 F.2d at 429-35 (pendency interest required for undersecured creditors), and In re Alhers, 794 F.2d 388, 395 (8th Cir. 1986) (pendency interest for undersecured creditors required in some circumstances), with In re Timbers of Inwood Forest, 793 F.2d 1380, 1384-1416 (5th Cir. 1986) (barring pendency interest for undersecured creditors).

Baird does not give separate treatment to the case of the undersecured creditor. Instead, he regards it as indistinguishable from the case of the oversecured creditor. The undersecured creditor presents the far more interesting question, and I use it here to highlight our differences.

[58] Corporate Reorganizations at 121 (cited in note 4). Baird explains his interpretation:

> A rule that forces general creditors and shareholders to give secured creditors the full value of their claims (including compensation for the time value of money) puts the cost of a decision to reorganize the firm entirely on the junior classes, who already stand to benefit if the firm succeeds.

Baird then concludes that secured creditors should be paid interest from the time of filing. Id. at 124.

liquidation for virtually no risk. If the property had a fifty percent chance of being sold in one year for $11,000 and a fifty percent chance of being sold in one year for $10,000, the value of holding the property on speculation of resale is $10,500. Baird sees this average value of the two possibilities as the sole value of a successful Chapter 11 reorganization in his example. He points out that an economically rational sole owner would sell the property now and take $10,600 rather than wait for the reinvestment opportunity that is correctly valued now at $10,500.[59] Although one might question whether a court could know with sufficient certainty the numbers needed to make such a proposition work for any given debtor, the principle certainly makes sense.

Baird argues that in bankruptcy, however, a different result will follow unless the secured creditor is granted interest.[60] If the estate can speculate without paying interest, the estate (representing the debtor and the unsecured creditors) has nothing to lose and everything to gain from trying the reorganization. If it need not pay interest, the estate will always speculate—in effect, choosing the $10,500 deal (attempting reorganization) over the $10,600 deal (liquidating).[61] A collectivist decision as Baird explains it would mean that the property should be liquidated at a value of $10,600 rather than retained at an expected value of only $10,500. Baird argues that the only way to accomplish this in bankruptcy is to make the estate pay the undersecured creditor the use-value of the collateral ($600 in interest), thus permitting a reorganization only if the present value of the venture exceeds the interest costs of retaining the collateral.[62]

Ultimately Baird's argument is not one of collectivism so much as one of economic rationality: the aim of bankruptcy policy is to make certain that assets go to their highest-valued use.[63] Baird is at pains to avoid the economic lingo,[64] but he cannot es-

[59] Id. at 122-23. In order to simplify the example, Baird has discounted all values to current dollars.

[60] Id. at 122.

[61] Baird refers to this as a "perverse incentive." Id.

[62] Id. at 122, 124-25.

[63] See, e.g., id. at 109, 120, 121.

[64] Baird does not refer to "economic rationality" or use the other jargon of economic analysis. Indeed, when he steps too close to economic terminology, he is quick to back away. For example, after endorsing the claim that "those with rights in a debtor's assets are moved, for the most part, by the course of action than brings them the highest return under existing legal rules" and citing financial and economic policy works, Baird concludes that the "basic point, however, does not depend on this assumption." Id. at 109 (footnote omitted).

cape the conclusion that the only value he protects is economic wealth maximization for the bankrupt estate. As Baird has used it in the *American Mariner* debate, collectivism is nothing but a veil to conceal his relentless push for single-value economic rationality, an excuse to impose a distributional scheme without justifying it, and, incidentally, a way to work in a damn good deal for secured creditors. By focusing on an economic rationale—without defending this exclusive focus—Baird eliminates without discussion or proof any other values that may be served by bankruptcy.

Even if that single value were accepted, Baird isn't home free. He quietly works distributional elements into his economic example, all the while denying a distributional consequence. For example, by arguing that the only way to ensure that reorganization values exceed liquidation values is to give all secured creditors interest on their claims, Baird makes a distributional decision as well.[65] Indeed, it is simply not possible to avoid a distributional decision. To destroy the special, pre-bankruptcy rights of some creditors is to make a distributional decision. To enforce those rights is to make a different distributional decision. Baird does not want to discuss distributional objectives, but he cannot avoid them by pretending they are not there.[66]

---

[65] Id. at, e.g., 101. Baird comes dangerously close to recognizing the distributional aspects of his analysis when he asserts that he will demand interest for secured creditors but that he will force them to give up their repossession rights. He explains that secured creditors cannot be allowed to retain repossession rights in bankruptcy because "to permit a secured creditor the full exercise of his rights may hinder efforts to preserve the going-concern value of the business." Id. at 117 (footnote omitted). This argument is overtly distributional. If the estate cannot pay enough to delay repossession through a voluntary transaction, in light of the full risks at issue, why should the secured creditor be forced to accept a judicially determined interest that is unlikely to reflect the market rate for the kind of transaction involved? Baird could explain that the secured creditor is a monopolist with power to extort excessive payments. This is a conventional economic argument, but it is also a distributional argument. Baird ultimately argues that the secured creditor has too much power, and the Bankruptcy Code should diminish that power in order to accomplish other objectives—which, in fact, are distributional.

[66] Baird evidently has mixed feelings about the distributional issues in bankruptcy. On the one hand he explains that "someone must decide not only how best to deploy the assets, but also how to split up the returns from those assets." Id. at 105 (footnote omitted). On the other hand, he resists the notion that he is making a distributional argument when he gives undersecured creditors their interest claims. He explains that bankruptcy law "should aim to keep the asset-deployment question separate from the distributional question, and to have the deployment question answered as a single owner would answer it"—that is, according to collectivist principles. Id. at 108 (footnote omitted). He then treats the payments to undersecured creditors as "asset-deployment" issues, not distributional issues. But "asset deployment" need only involve ensuring that the estate makes the economically rational choice between liquidation and reorganization—not ensuring that any particular creditor receive any particular distribution.

Baird's distributional consequence is not compelled, as he asserts, by collectivism alone. The interest payments he requires in the name of efficiency could, for example, be paid into a fund for *all* creditors—secured and unsecured. If all the creditors—not just the secured creditors—shared the assets of the estate, their incentives to maximize the return on the estate would converge. But Baird doesn't bother to consider this or any other alternative to paying the secured creditors.

In fact, Baird ignores the most effective way to make certain that the structure of bankruptcy promotes collectivism: recognize no security interests in bankruptcy. If no class of creditors were superior to any other class of creditors and all creditors in bankruptcy stood to lose or gain on a pro rata basis, then the issue of what to do with the collateral would be simple. The creditors, collectively, would either keep the collateral or sell it, whichever brought the most money. No one would have any interest except maximizing the return to the estate, because no one would profit except by such maximization.

To obliterate all creditor differences in bankruptcy would, of course, impose costs elsewhere in the debtor-creditor system. The values encompassed in bankruptcy's current distributional scheme—such as permitting enhanced collection opportunities for employees, consumers, and a host of others—would be destroyed. The ramifications for the nonbankruptcy behavior of different parties would likely be profound and, at our current understanding of the credit system, unpredictable. In sum, were we to adopt Baird's collectivism truly untempered by any other values, it would threaten significant disruption to the debtor-creditor system.

Ultimately, Baird rounds out collectivism with additional objectives. His earlier work does not illuminate those objectives, but in his response to this article he asserts that he is concerned about the pre-bankruptcy maneuverings of creditors about to go into bankruptcy that would result if bankruptcy and nonbankruptcy fora gave creditors different rights. Baird argues that a single state law scheme is needed to preclude such presumptively evil maneuvers. The implications of strategic planning pose yet another debate Baird and I might have, but my point here is made: collectivism alone doesn't go so far as Baird always claims. He needs to incorporate other values into his tight, "neutral" scheme in order to justify adoption of a specific plan.

B. Collectivism and Bankruptcy Judges

The coincidence that Baird's solution to the economic disincentives caused by conflicts between the secured and unsecured creditors works a significant redistribution in wealth is not accidental. If Baird only wants efficient collectivism, he needs only to support rules that require disposition of the property in a way that maximizes the value of the bankruptcy estate. The problem Baird poses arises only when one of a competing group of creditors—in his case, the unsecured creditors—controls the liquidation decision. To avoid Baird's problem, it should suffice to have a decision-making mechanism that balances the competing interests of creditors and prevents one creditor from dominating.[67]

I would have supposed that the appropriate decision-making mechanism would be a bankruptcy judge armed with a Code that reflects the distributional aims Baird implicitly proposes. Bankruptcy judges are impartial decision makers. They balance the competing interests of the parties according to statutory guidelines. Their meat-and-potatoes job is to make decisions about lifting stays, approving plans of reorganization, and the like—decisions requiring an understanding of the interests of the debtor and all the creditors and a willingness to search the statute to follow its distributional scheme.

The Bankruptcy Code already does much to serve Baird's economic values. Section 1129(a)(7) requires that the creditors receive in reorganization at least as much as they would have gotten in liquidation,[68] and section 1129(a)(11) and the case law it has spawned require that the plan be confirmed only if success is feasible.[69] If Baird's overriding concern is to maximize the assets of the

---

[67] The balance must be genuinely evenhanded: neither secured nor unsecured creditor interests should dominate. The thrust of Baird's argument for collectivism is that we should avoid letting unsecured creditors dominate decisions about disposition of the assets, but he also recognizes that secured creditors could attempt to dominate. Id. at 112. Baird is nevertheless content to trust the bankruptcy courts to curtail secured creditors' anticollectivist impulses, even while he argues that unsecured creditors must be curtailed by a specific rule that demands payments to the secured creditors.

[68] 11 U.S.C. § 1129(a)(7) (1982 & 1985 Supp.) explains that unless an impaired creditor has accepted a plan, the creditor "will receive or retain under the plan on account of such claim or interest property of a value, as of the effective date of the plan, that is not less than the amount that such holder would so receive or retain if the debtor were liquidated under chapter 7 of this title on such date." This would seem to suggest that if liquidation values exceed reorganization values, including the time value of the money, the liquidation should be preferred. Of course, this decision does not arise until it is time to confirm a plan, but it does relate to Baird's concern. Perhaps Baird would need to move this decision back in time to accomplish his collectivist goals, but he seems to prefer a more aggressive stand—one that immediately transfers cash to undersecured creditors.

[69] For a summary of the effects of section 1129(a)(11), see Debtors and Creditors at 574 (cited in note 3).

estate, that end would seem to be accomplished by reminding bankruptcy judges that the Code does not permit approval of plans where the going-concern value to the estate does not exceed the liquidation value of the assets.[70]

But Baird is not interested in exhortations to courts or stronger statutory language to further maximization of the wealth of the estate. Instead, he insists that the *only* way to accomplish his collectivist ends is to pay interest to undersecured creditors. No balancing, no discussion—just give the secured creditors the money. Baird does not want the courts to make a better decision; he wants to give them no opportunity to make any decision at all.

Why should this be? Here Baird makes an astonishing assertion: bankruptcy judges cannot be trusted to make decisions to protect the collective value of the estate or to balance the competing interests of the parties, because bankruptcy judges are lousy decision makers. Baird notes: "The record of bankruptcy courts [in implementing the Bankruptcy Code] has been mixed at best."[71] He continues:

> A few [bankruptcy judges] seem to show either an inability or an unwillingness to comprehend the possibility that secured credit may be something more than a perverse and unfair creature of state law that should be thwarted at every turn. Even more remarkable is their wonderful capacity for hope, their unshakable faith that, given time, the firm's ship will come in.[72]

Baird says that there is a "tendency of bankruptcy judges to undercompensate the secured creditor" and that the only right-thinking judges are "those who are not immersed on a daily basis in bankruptcy law, and who therefore have some perspective." Baird expresses his ultimate contempt for bankruptcy judges by concluding that an "inability to persuade anyone—other than a bankruptcy judge—that the firm should stay alive seems good evidence that it should not."[73]

I have several difficulties with Baird's attack on bankruptcy

---

[70] If these statutory provisions have too much slippage to guarantee sufficient attention to economic analysis, then Baird could reasonably support stiffening the standards—and then we could debate that proposal. That debate would focus on whether the distributional objectives that can be accomplished by attempting a reorganization are worth the cost imposed on the secured creditors.

[71] Corporate Reorganizations at 125 (cited in note 4).

[72] Id. at 126 (footnote omitted).

[73] Id. at 128, 97 n.1, 128.

judges. Thus far, he has offered no evidence to support his empirical conclusion that courts undercompensate secured creditors and overestimate debtors' chances of future business success. My own experience in interviewing judges for an empirical study of bankruptcy has been that bankruptcy judges are much like other judges—some seem to have fairly strong pro-plaintiff views, a few seem to have fairly strong pro-defendant views, and the great majority are somewhere in the middle trying conscientiously to work through a balanced, well-reasoned position that is faithful to the statute. Before Baird can convince me to pay interest to all secured creditors just to prevent the bankruptcy judges from giving them a raw deal, he must offer something more than the naked assertion that the judges are all hopelessly pro-debtor.[74]

Another difficulty with Baird's attack on the bankruptcy judges is that the argument is too large. After all, the interest payment to be granted under Baird's proposal will be set by the same "uncomprehending" judges he decries. Moreover, if bankruptcy courts cannot properly ascertain the liquidation or reorganization values of businesses in bankruptcy, then interest payments to undersecured creditors are among the least of our problems. The interplay between automatic stay and adequate protection, or the cramdown and plan confirmation requirements,[75] (to name just two examples) rest on a court's fair determination of values. The court's alleged inability to compare the value of liquidation and reorganization affects all of the court's other valuation decisions, but Baird makes no proposals to wrench any other decisions from the courts. Why judges should be unfair on the single issue of when to permit reorganization, and not in every other case, is something Baird never explains.

Baird's attack on the courts is central to his argument for guaranteed interest payments to undersecured creditors. Without it, the economic rationality he supports can be met with court-imposed policies—but that sort of evenhandedness and attention to the attempt by any one party to dominate bankruptcy decisions would not necessarily put money in the hands of undersecured creditors. The thrust of Baird's goal is normative: secured creditors

[74] Baird concludes his plea for the secured creditors with the unsupported claim that they have been "undercompensate[d] . . . both in theory and practice." Id. at 129.

[75] The valuation issues and strategic interaction between the § 362(a) automatic stay provisions and the § 362(d) adequate protection requirement are discussed generally in Debtors and Creditors at 403-29 (cited in note 3). The implications of valuation for § 1129(b) cramdown and § 1129(a) plan confirmation are discussed in id. at 596-97, 608, 625-27.

should get no less inside bankruptcy than they would get outside of it. But he fails to supply the policy analysis necessary to support a normative claim. Even if the courts undercompensate secured creditors, Baird must explain why full compensation of these and only these creditors is essential. But that debate is one that will focus squarely on the distributional objectives of bankruptcy. Baird cannot avoid that debate by invoking "neutral" collectivist principles and then requiring payments to undersecured creditors because judges are too dumb to make reasonable economic decisions.

C. Collectivism and State Law

In discussing bankruptcy policy, Baird assumes away the very thing I think we should discuss: how to distribute the losses occasioned by the debtor's widespread default. It is important to understand exactly how he avoids this central issue. To Baird, distributional issues are the same in and out of bankruptcy.[76] Baird seems to believe that this presumption not only permits him to support a single-issue bankruptcy policy, but that it also permits him to ignore any distributional consequences of the policies he embraces. By announcing that he is merely enforcing nonbankruptcy rights, and declaring, in effect, that he is changing nothing, Baird seeks to build a presumption into bankruptcy—a presumption that it will always follow the state-determined collection scheme—without ever defending that scheme. State law, as Baird explains it, is merely "our baseline," from which any bankruptcy "modification" must be justified.[77]

Baird cannot assert that he is offering *no* distributional scheme simply because he accepts the scheme that exists in state collection law. Any scheme distributes, whether Baird chooses to discuss it or not. If he proposes to adopt state collection law as the baseline for federal bankruptcy, he is obligated to offer some rationale for this choice and to make some examination of the consequences of using state distribution within the very specialized context of bankruptcy.

Baird ignores the fact that the way state collection law operates outside of bankruptcy is fundamentally different from the way it operates when grafted onto a bankruptcy system. There is in this respect a delicious irony in Baird's relentless defense of the se-

[76] Corporate Reorganizations at 129-30 (cited in note 4).

[77] Id. at 103, 101.

cured creditor's demand for its "nonbankruptcy rights." At state law, the secured creditor was promised repossession rights if the debtor defaulted on its loan obligations. But, as anyone who has practiced a little collections law will readily acknowledge, there is many a slip twixt default and cash from the sale of collateral. The collateral may be hard to find. Some of it may be in another jurisdiction. The debtor may resist the creditor's self-help repossession, requiring the creditor to file a lawsuit. Some debtors seek restraining orders to prevent court-ordered repossession. State courts can be quick to restrain repossession and excruciatingly slow to give final effect to repo orders. As a strategic move to hold off creditor foreclosure, some debtors have turned to lender liability suits.[78] Notwithstanding any contractual agreements, the debtor may sell the collateral or give it to another creditor to satisfy loan obligations. The list goes on, and, to the frustrated creditor, it may seem endless.

Life is no bed of roses for the secured creditor drawn into a bankruptcy: the bankrupt debtor may still resist payment, and for some creditors the delays of bankruptcy simply follow the delays of the state court process. But a few things may improve in bankruptcy. In one stroke, all the lawsuits are in a single forum.[79] The bankruptcy court, unlike many state courts, recognizes the importance of time and the likelihood that the debtor will use court processes for delay. Several critical bankruptcy rules require that the court act quickly, often within thirty days. The debtor cannot seek temporary restraining orders to avoid enforcement of court orders or file harassing lawsuits in other courts. The creditor gets nationwide service of process regardless of where the collateral is located. The court monitors the debtor's behavior, restricting the debtor's control over the disposition of assets. No other creditor

[78] Suits against the lender have become a newly popular device to stave off state foreclosure attempts. The Hunts put themselves back in the news again recently—in typically grand style—with a $14 billion suit against twenty-three banks. A Fort Worth lawyer explained that such suits are an attempt to "buy time" to forestall foreclosure. Kenn McGill, Hunts File an Appeal Over Order, Fort Worth Star-Telegram, business sec. 1, col. 5 (Sept. 9, 1986). See also Suit Against Lenders Seen As Possible Landmark Case, Wall St. J. 35, col. 3 (Sept. 15, 1986).

[79] I could make that statement with more confidence before the 1984 amendments to the Code. Today, some cases can go back to state court, but the run-of-the-mill collection cases seem to stay in bankruptcy court. See 28 U.S.C. § 157 (1982 & 1985 Supp.). See also Debtors and Creditors at 709-11, 714-15 (cited in note 3) (discussing the effect of the 1984 amendments); Elizabeth S. Gibson, Removal of Claims Related to Bankruptcy Cases: What is a "Claim or Cause of Action"?, 34 U.C.L.A. L. Rev. 1 (1987) (arguing for a narrow view of when bankruptcy claims can be removed to federal district court for adjudication).

may slip away with the debtor's assets. The bankruptcy court uses its contempt power to back up its rules for monitoring and conserving the property. And, perhaps most importantly for the secured creditor, the debtor in bankruptcy is the one that didn't close up in the middle of the night, shipping out its assets in a rented truck.

Without giving up any of these benefits, the creditor whose debtor has filed bankruptcy pleads unblushingly that it "just wants what was promised at state law." The secured creditors want all the court supervision and control, national jurisdiction, protection against other creditors, and speedy trials of bankruptcy. Then they want the foreclosure rights (or the equivalent interest value) of state law. Baird may find that cry moving; I find it disingenuous.

In short, once the debtor is in bankruptcy, no one gets "just what was promised at state law"—neither secured nor unsecured creditors. The sort of "forum shopping" Baird claims he wants to avoid may lead secured creditors as well as unsecured creditors to conclude that bankruptcy is a better deal than state collection proceedings. With its debtor in bankruptcy, every creditor gets something more by way of control over the debtor and the competing creditors, and something less by way of curtailed collection rights. The secured creditor can claim it has given up too much, and we can debate that issue. But the simple claim that the secured creditor wants only what it had at state law adds nothing to the debate. Once the debtor is in bankruptcy, it is no longer possible to give any party to the dispute its state law rights.

Whether the "baseline" for creditor rights in bankruptcy is state collection law or some other collection scheme, once the dispute enters the federal bankruptcy forum changes are made and a new collection system is created. The starting points have little to do with whether the system, in the end, accomplishes reasonable distributional objectives. Those objectives cannot be ignored, and the special consequences of how they will play out in the context of widespread default in bankruptcy cannot be wished away. The distributional issues of bankruptcy must be resolved at every step in determining bankruptcy policy. There is no way to escape them.

My view is that the central job of bankruptcy is to apportion the losses of the debtor's default, and that a variety of factors impinge on the difficult policy decision of where to let those losses fall. It may be ironic, but I am willing to concede that Baird's concern for secured creditors may be well-founded. If his charge against the current system is proper, and the balance in apportioning bankruptcy losses does favor debtors and some creditors too greatly, then let that round of debates begin. But let's not hammer out the appropriate system balances in a debate by proxy over collectivism.

My disagreement with Baird might come down to a question of who bears which burdens. Baird simply starts with a state law "baseline," offering not a single insight into why any particular policy has been adopted or should be followed. Baird takes the position that if it exists in the state law scheme, it should be followed. If he wants to defend the state law collection system—or any other system—then he needs to come up with something more. Otherwise, he offers nothing.

Conclusion

I have offered a dirty, complex, elastic, interconnected view of bankruptcy from which I can neither predict outcomes nor even necessarily fully articulate all the factors relevant to a policy decision. Baird has offered a rational, clean approach in which he claims few factors are relevant and solitary conclusions are always compelled. Baird's view of bankruptcy is more chic than mine, but I believe my view is more realistic and more likely to yield useful analysis.

Baird and I disagree about the fundamental purpose of bankruptcy law. But the differences Baird and I nurture run deeper. Baird believes in a method of policymaking that will ineluctably yield a single right answer. I believe in an approach that only asks better questions, focuses on better evidence, yields closer approximations, and offers increasingly better, but still tentative, answers.

Professor Robert Scott has declared that Professor Baird and his coauthor Professor Jackson have, with their single-issue economic analysis of bankruptcy, "set the terms of the scholarly debate for the next decade."[80] The economic analysis of bankruptcy has enjoyed a central position in the discussion of bankruptcy policy, and according to Professor Scott, it will grow in intellectual dominion. The increasing number of scholarly articles that wrestle with difficult bankruptcy problems and eventually bring them to

[80] Robert E. Scott, Through Bankruptcy with the Creditors' Bargain Heuristic, 53 U. Chi. L. Rev. 690, 692 (1986), reviewing Baird and Jackson Casebook. To be fair to Professor Scott, I should note that what he endorses is the heuristic device of asking a single question over and over throughout a casebook. Even Scott expresses hesitation about the accuracy of Baird and Jackson's analysis, but he nonetheless approves what amounts to teaching students everything about bankruptcy through a narrow question that hammers home an unrelenting economic analysis.

heel with a single, deft stab of economic analysis gives credence to Scott's point.

The attractions of an abstract economic analysis such as Baird's are many. A simple economic analysis of bankruptcy is clear, straightforward, and always promises to yield firm answers to hard questions.[81] The fact that the economic analysis is utterly self-referential also spares the proponent from nasty hours searching out empirical evidence or trying to learn about what happens in real borrowing and lending decisions. The business of writing articles and advising courts about the proper path of bankruptcy policy can proceed apace when all conclusions flow from just one or two easily identified assumptions. And the assumptions themselves are garbed in neutral terms, lending an aura of fairness to the development of policy. The economic analysis Baird practices is seductive.

Mine is not an entertaining (or, I suspect, popular) position for an academic. I cannot claim that bankruptcy, at its heart, is an intellectual construct or that I can reason to a meaningful conclusion by doing nothing more than thinking hard about logical consequences derived from a handful of untested assumptions. I would like to endorse something that requires only library time and yellow legal pads to uncover ideal solutions to legal problems. The trouble is that I can't do it.

But I do not think Baird can do it either. The certainty of Baird's position is a fiction. Although he purports to avoid difficult normative questions and he ignores empirical issues, Baird's conclusions are nonetheless driven by normative values and empirical assumptions. By hiding these values and assumptions, Baird simply makes the debate a shadow game that offers little real illumination.

Ultimately, I disagree not so much with what Baird argues as with how he argues. Baird makes an excellent point about the competition between unsecured and secured creditors. He may be right that unsecured creditors will push for any wild scheme that risks assets of the estate in order to get some shot at repayment. The factors Baird identifies are important, and his economic analysis of pressures that might influence the behavior of debtors and credi-

[81] The emphasis of my protest is on the "simple" in "simple economic analysis." There are economic models that are not easy and that do not pretend to yield ineluctable answers. There are those that clearly expose their empirical and normative presumptions. Economic analysis is a powerful tool with a great deal to offer. I complain when models become too simple and the assumptions are concealed, so that the tool is used perversely.

tors is insightful. The economic analysis Baird offers could rightly enrich the inquiry about the effective implementation of a distributional scheme. But Baird uses his economic analysis to limit the inquiry—and there is the final rub.

Economic analysis can be used to further the inquiry into what happens in bankruptcy, or it can be used to close it off. Baird begins with an artificial construct of behavior, applies a few immutable principles, and jumps directly to specific statutory recommendations. Nowhere is there room to consider other factors that should be part of the decision-making process, or to make empirical observations that will indicate whether the model conforms sufficiently to reality to be useful. If Baird wants to add his questions to all the others that should be considered in making distributional decisions, then I will readily endorse his work. But so long as he explains his analysis in terms of the *sole* issue involved, the *single* question to be answered, and the *only* parties to be protected, I contend that his approach gives answers that are both illusory and dangerous.

I readily admit that I do not offer a single rule that will resolve all disputes. Instead, I call attention to the difficult distributional issues in bankruptcy, and I identify factors that influence how those distributional issues are resolved. Perhaps more importantly, I advocate a process of framing and refining questions, considering both their normative and empirical elements, to give content to the bankruptcy debate. Slick economic analyses give quick answers, but only by sliding past the troublesome issues that pervade the resolution of real problems.

Baird's single, unified theory of bankruptcy is more fun for academic games than is a complex view of bankruptcy that constantly reminds the player how little she knows about the empirical assumptions that underlie the game or whether other elusive values influence the balance among competing interests. His theory also runs an extraordinary risk of providing answers that are quite sensible within a confined, abstract scheme but that will not work in a complex reality. If the only test for acceptance of a specific statutory rule of law is whether the rule conforms to a logical—but possibly incomplete—concept, then grievous mistakes will go unchecked.

I undoubtedly overstate the risk that any abstract analysis could become the basis for an overhaul of the bankruptcy system and that significant changes could be made with little consideration of any implications other than a select few. Academics do not make these decisions anyway. Final decisions are in the hands of politicians and judges, who may be much better at remembering to weigh the consequences of any rule than are the scholars who are tied to a single talisman. But if we academics take ourselves seriously, we should put single-issue theories into a somewhat less exalted position in order to minimize the harm we can do. And we should get about the business of asking harder questions, looking for better evidence, and approximating better answers.

Name Index

www.ingramcontent.com/pod-product-compliance
Lightning Source LLC
LaVergne TN
LVHW081342011026
849161LV00013BB/2989
* 9 7 8 0 8 1 4 7 9 2 7 4 2 *